FROMMER'S
DOLLARWISE
CALIFORNIA AND LAS VEGAS
MARY RAKAUSKAS

1989

Published by Prentice Hall Trade Division
A Division of Simon & Schuster, Inc.
Gulf + Western Building
One Gulf + Western Plaza
New York, NY 10023

ISBN 0-13-217811-7
ISSN 0899-3319

Manufactured in the United States of America

*Although every effort was made to ensure the accuracy
of price information appearing in this book,
it should be kept in mind that prices
can and do fluctuate in the course of time*

CONTENTS

MAPS

INFLATION ALERT: It is hardly a secret that costs will rise regardless of the level of inflation. The author of this book has spent laborious hours attempting to ensure the accuracy of prices appearing in this guide. As we go to press, I believe we have obtained the most reliable data possible. Nonetheless, in the lifetime of this edition—particularly its second year (1990)—the wise traveler will add 15% to 20% to the prices quoted throughout these pages.

DOLLARWISE
CALIFORNIA

□ □ □

Eureka! (I have found it!) is the motto of the State of California—and people have been echoing that sentiment since 1542, when navigator Juan Rodriguez Cabrillo in fact did find it. The first permanent settlers were the Franciscan fathers who came from Spain to convert the heathen as part of Spain's plan to colonize California. They persevered, taming the vast and savage land as well, and erecting a chain of 21 missions extending almost 600 miles from San Diego to Sonoma. The famous Mission Trail, begun in 1769 with the San Diego Mission, grew into El Camino Real (The Royal Road), which can be followed to this day.

It was almost a century later that the next wave of immigrants found their way to California—half a million Forty-Niners from clear around the world lured by the cry of "Gold!" Many of those who came for gold stayed to find their fortunes farming the millions of acres of virgin soil.

With the planting of orchards and vineyards—first sown by the mission padres—came great numbers of Mexican, Chinese, and Japanese laborers to tend them. Still more immigrants arrived from distant shores with the discovery of oil in the 1890s. And in the 1930s it was dreams of a land of milk and honey that prompted "Okies" by the thousands to leave their dust-storm-ravaged lands behind and head for California.

By this time, of course, the movie industry (itself a New York emigrant) was firmly rooted on West Coast soil, and Hollywood hopefuls were flocking to California to pursue glittering stardom.

Of course, not everyone who came to California found the rainbow's end. Very few of the prospectors of 1849 unearthed a gold mine (the daily profit of the average speculator was about $1). Only a relatively small number of aspirants ever struck oil, achieved stardom, or found the Promised Land. But that reality has not daunted California's incredible growth. One out of every 11 Americans lives here, making it the nation's most populous state. Following a deep-rooted American tradition, people are still heading west to the Golden State—tourists and settlers, dreamers and speculators, spiritual seekers and political idealists— all lured by the sunshine, the wide-open spaces, the laid-back, free-and-easy lifestyle, and most of all, by California's magical ability to assume the shape of any dream.

FROM THE REDWOOD FORESTS TO THE L.A. FREEWAYS: Pack up your own dreams, and I can guarantee you'll run no risk of disappointment. California is a tourist mecca overflowing with attractions sufficient to satisfy and surprise the most jaded of visitors.

A land of almost excessive natural beauty, it contains Mount Whitney, at 14,500 feet the tallest mountain in the contiguous United States. Death Valley, not far away in the Mojave Desert, is the lowest point in the entire Western Hemisphere—almost 300 feet below sea level. Some 400 miles of towering trees make up the majestic "Redwood Empire." Visitors can marvel at the picturesque vineyard regions of the Napa Valley and Sonoma, explore quaint, historic towns like Monterey and Carmel, discover delightful beach resorts from Santa Cruz to Santa Barbara—and still not have seen the greater part of California.

There are more miles of coastline—1,264 to be exact—than in any other state except Alaska. Perhaps the most breathtakingly beautiful vista in the world is from the road that winds along the Big Sur Coast—yet it's only one of many awe-inspiring California sights.

The results of human effort in California are equally impressive—and as diverse. Los Angeles and San Francisco are both "typical" of California, yet they share no apparent similarities—nor do they wish to.

Los Angeles presents a glamorous, often ostentatious face. Crisscrossed by an astonishing number of freeways, it sprawls on seemingly forever. It's the home of the stars, stomping grounds of wealthy jet-setters, right-wingers, and every faction of the lunatic fringe—a colossal, Technicolor ode to modernity, chic, sophistication, and success.

About 400 miles up the coast and a world away is mist-enshrouded San Francisco, draped delicately over steep hillsides—small, enchanting, elegant, yet still a trifle zany. It's almost a conglomerate of tiny self-contained cities squeezed into a small area superficially shaped like a compressed accordion.

San Diego, the second most populous city in California, has an ideal climate, a marvelous zoo, and less air pollution than Los Angeles (as of this writing). It also has more Navy personnel, more golf courses, and possibly more retirees than either Los Angeles or San Francisco, but it does not appear to be seeking increases in any of these categories, with the possible exception of the golfing facilities.

Sporting enthusiasts in particular will find there's too much to do in just one trip to California. Facilities abound for everything from skiing to hang-gliding, the wide spectrum encompassing fishing, boating, golf, tennis, surfing, hiking, scuba-diving, snorkeling, horseback riding, mountain climbing, even skateboarding.

Then, of course, there are the "special" attractions of California. They range from Disneyland (one of scores of amusement-park extravaganzas) to Hearst Castle, to across-the-Nevada-border gambling centers at Lake Tahoe and Las Vegas (both of which are included in this book).

All of this, along with much, much more, is why so many tourists come to California and why so many never leave.

ABOUT THIS BOOK: In brief, this is a guidebook giving specific, practical details (including prices) about hotels, restaurants, nightlife, sightseeing attractions, and other tourist-related activities throughout California and Las Vegas. I've tried to open up some new realms for you to explore, to give you the data you need to make a vacation into an adventure. Establishments in all price ranges have been described, from the luxurious Beverly Hills Hotel in L.A. to a little bath-in-the-hall budget hostelry in San Francisco. No restaurant, hotel, or other establishment has paid to be included in this book. What you read are entirely personal recommendations, carefully checked out and judged by the strict yardstick of value. If they measured up—gave good value for your money—they were included, regardless of price range.

You'll find that the majority of listings are geared neither to the super-rich nor to the best-things-in-life-are-free contingent. Rather, the book is aimed at the dollarwise, middle-income traveler who wants occasionally to splurge and occasionally to save, but always to get maximum value for his or her dollar.

CALIFORNIA HOTELS: As a state that yearly receives millions of visitors, California is well prepared for the onslaught with the best accommodations situation I've ever seen. In just about every city, I found a good selection of hotels, motels, and inns in every price range and category.

For the Frugal

I've covered all kinds of hotels, but I want to make a special recommendation here for the traveler who is on a particularly tight budget. The no-frills **Motel 6** chain, charging $17.95 to $31.95 for a single room, $23.95 to $37.95 for a double, depending on locale, has motels in over 90 key California locations, including Anaheim, South Lake Tahoe, Monterey, Napa, Palo Alto, San Diego, San Jose, San Luis Obispo, Santa Barbara—even posh Palm Springs. All units have air conditioning and bath, most have a swimming pool, and they're almost all centrally located, frequently near some luxury hotel in whose plush coffeeshop you can enjoy your morning bacon and eggs. Rooms now have free TV and phones in the rooms with free local calls. For a listing of all Motel 6 locations, write to Motel 6, Inc., 14651 Dallas Pkwy., Dallas, TX 75240. It's best to make reservations as far in advance as possible.

Another excellent budget-saving choice is **Allstar Inns,** of which there are over 50 in convenient California locations including Fullerton (near Disneyland), La Mesa (San Diego), Long Beach, Rancho Mirage (Palm Springs), Carpinteria (Santa Barbara), and Vallejo (near Marine World Africa USA). All units are air-conditioned, have a full tub and shower, free color TV, and free local phone calls. Most locations have a pool. For a listing of Allstar Inn locations, write to Allstar Inns, Inc., P.O. Box 3070, Santa Barbara, CA 93130.

First Come Is NOT First Served

To reiterate, tourists flock like lemmings to California shores. I've seen enormous conventions of Shriners, Rosicrucians, and once even (shudder!) I.R.S. employees fill an entire city of hotel rooms. You're taking a big chance, and certainly lessening your options, if you don't book ahead, particularly in summer. Don't waste hours of precious vacation time hunting down hotel rooms when a simple call or two in advance will take care of business. Be a smart lemming and you won't drown in a sea of tourists and conventioneers.

CALIFORNIA CAMPING: If you prefer roughing it, California has a terrific state park system. For a guide to California's parks, you can write to the California Department of Parks and Recreation, Publications Unit, P.O. Box 942896, Sacramento, CA 94296. Enclose $2 for the guide, postage, and handling. For more information, telephone 916/445-6477.

CALIFORNIA CLIMATE: The two words "California climate" create a phrase about as meaningless as any I've ever heard. Climate here varies from the sizzling Palm Springs desert to the cool mountain regions, and factors like the cold Humboldt current and the warm Japanese current swirling about don't make things any easier. Regional generalizations follow.

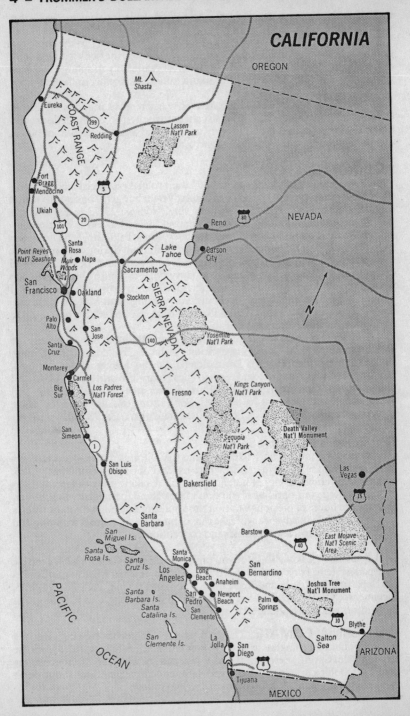

CALIFORNIA

OREGON

Mt.
Shasta

Eureka

COAST RANGE

299
Redding

Lassen
Nat'l Park

NEVADA

Fort
Bragg
Mendocino

5

Ukiah

80

Reno

101   20

Santa
Rosa

Lake
Tahoe

Carson
City

Point Reyes
Nat'l Seashore

Muir
Woods   Napa

Sacramento

San
Francisco

Oakland

Stockton

SIERRA NEVADA

Palo
Alto

San
Jose

Santa
Cruz

140

Yosemite
Nat'l Park

Monterey

Carmel

Big
Sur

Los Padres
Nat'l Forest

Fresno

Kings Canyon
Nat'l Park

Death Valley
Nat'l Monument

San
Simeon

1

Sequoia
Nat'l Park

San Luis
Obispo

Bakersfield

Las
Vegas

15

Santa
Barbara

San
Miguel Is.

Santa
Rosa Is.

Santa
Cruz Is.

Barstow

East Mojave
Nat'l Scenic
Area

40

Santa
Monica

Long
Beach

Los
Angeles

Anaheim

San
Bernardino

Joshua Tree
Nat'l Monument

Santa
Barbara Is.

Santa
Catalina Is.

San
Pedro

Newport
Beach

San
Clemente

Palm
Springs

10

Blythe

San
Clemente Is.

La
Jolla

San
Diego

Salton
Sea

ARIZONA

PACIFIC

OCEAN

Tijuana

MEXICO

AVERAGE MONTHLY TEMPERATURES (°F)

Los Angeles		San Francisco	
January	55.8	January	50.7
February	57.1	February	53.0
March	59.4	March	54.7
April	61.8	April	55.7
May	64.8	May	57.4
June	68.0	June	59.1
July	73.0	July	58.8
August	73.1	August	59.4
September	71.9	September	62.0
October	67.4	October	61.4
November	62.7	November	57.4
December	58.2	December	52.5

As far as weather is concerned, Southern California (an area encompassing San Luis Obispo to San Diego) has no one particular tourist season. The climate doesn't vary too much, although the summer months are the warmest and there is a rainy season (excepting San Diego) from January to May. After that don't even bother packing your umbrella. When it rains in summer, Southern Californians go outside to look at the novelty. Be warned that when the sun goes down the air is cooler, so pack some warmer apparel for nocturnal adventures. The Los Angeles monthly temperature chart in the box will give you a fair indication for the entire region.

Up north, the climate is even trickier. In San Francisco, for instance, the mercury rarely dips below 40° or rises above 70°. When the latter occurs Bay Area residents go into a tropical stupor and mutter darkly about a "heat wave," while astonished New York tourists consider the weather balmy. Anyway, San Francisco seldom gets more than a few hottish days every summer, and a warm jacket or coat is a *must*—much more important than your bathing suit. Coastal regions north as far as Mendocino and south to about Santa Cruz are fairly close to San Francisco in climate, give or take a few degrees. Once again, check the average monthly temperature chart for San Francisco in the box.

Areas farther east of the coast get progressively warmer, unless they're in the mountains—like South Lake Tahoe, where, for instance, April temperatures will be anywhere between 1° and 74°!

In the coastal area between San Luis Obispo and Santa Cruz things might vary in either direction.

In summation: When you go to sunny California, take some warm clothes along.

CALIFORNIA LANGUAGE: It is now law in the State of California that English (or for those who are sticklers, American) is the official language of the State, though it may not always seem so.

AN INVITATION TO READERS: Like all the Dollarwise Guides, *Frommer's Dollarwise California and Las Vegas* hopes to maintain a continuing dialogue between its writers and its readers. All of us share a common aim to travel as widely and as well as possible, at the best value for our money. And in achieving that goal, your comments and suggestions can be of tremendous help. Therefore, if you come across a particularly appealing hotel, restaurant, store, even sightseeing attraction, please don't keep it to yourself. And the solicitation for letters applies not only to new establishments, but to hotels or restaurants already recommended in this guide. The fact that a listing appears in this edition doesn't give it squatter's rights in future publications. If its services have deteriorated, its chef grown stale, its prices risen unfairly, whatever, these failings should be known. Even if you enjoyed every place and found every description accurate—that, too, is good to know. Send your comments to Frommer Books, Prentice Hall Press, One Gulf + Western Plaza, New York, NY 10023.

FROMMER'S™ DOLLARWISE® TRAVEL CLUB—HOW TO SAVE MONEY ON ALL YOUR TRAVELS

In this book we'll be looking at how to get your money's worth in California, but there is a "device" for saving money and determining value on *all* your trips. It's the popular, international Frommer's Dollarwise Travel Club, now in its 27th successful year of operation. The club was formed at the urging of numerous readers of the $-A-Day and Dollarwise Guides, who felt that such an organization could provide continuing travel information and a sense of community to value-minded travelers in all parts of the world. And so it does!

In keeping with the budget concept, the annual membership fee is low and is immediately exceeded by the value of your benefits. Upon receipt of $18 (U.S. residents), or $20 U.S. by check drawn on a U.S. bank or via international postal money order in U.S. funds (Canadian, Mexican, and other foreign residents) to cover one year's membership, we will send all new members the following items:

(1) Any *two* of the following books
Please designate in your letter which two you wish to receive:

Frommer's™ $-A-Day® Guides
Europe on $30 a Day
Australia on $30 a Day
Eastern Europe on $25 a Day
England on $40 a Day
Greece (including Istanbul and Turkey's Aegean Coast) on $30 a Day
Hawaii on $50 a Day
India on $25 a Day
Ireland on $30 a Day
Israel on $30 & $35 a Day
Mexico (plus Belize and Guatemala) on $25 a Day
New York on $50 a Day
New Zealand on $40 a Day
Scandinavia on $60 a Day
Scotland and Wales on $40 a Day
South America on $30 a Day
Spain and Morocco (plus the Canary Is.) on $40 a Day
Turkey on $25 a Day
Washington, D.C., & Historic Virginia on $40 a Day

Frommer's™ Dollarwise® Guides
Austria and Hungary
Belgium, Holland, & Luxembourg

Bermuda and The Bahamas
Brazil
Canada
Caribbean
Egypt
England and Scotland
France
Germany
Italy
Japan and Hong Kong
Portugal, Madeira, and the Azores
South Pacific
Switzerland and Liechtenstein
Alaska
California and Las Vegas
Florida
Mid-Atlantic States
New England
New York State
Northwest
Skiing USA—East
Skiing USA—West
Southeast and New Orleans
Southwest
Texas
USA (avail. Feb. 1989)

(Dollarwise Guides discuss accommodations and facilities in all price ranges, with emphasis on the medium-priced.)

Frommer's™ Touring Guides

Australia
Egypt
Florence
London
Paris
Thailand
Venice

(These new, color illustrated guides include walking tours, cultural and historic sites, and other vital travel information.)

Gault Millau

Chicago (avail. April 1989)
France (avail. July 1989)
Italy (avail. July 1989)
Los Angeles
New England (avail. April 1989)
New York
San Francisco
Washington, D.C.

(Irreverent, savvy, and comprehensive, each of these renowned guides candidly reviews over 1,000 restaurants, hotels, shops, nightspots, museums, and sights.)

Serious Shopper's Guides

Italy

London
Los Angeles
Paris
(Practical and comprehensive, each of these handsomely illustrated guides lists hundreds of stores, selling everything from antiques to wine, conveniently organized alphabetically by category.)

A Shopper's Guide to the Caribbean
(Two experienced Caribbean hands guide you through this shopper's paradise, offering witty insights and helpful tips on the wares and emporia of more than 25 islands.)

Beat the High Cost of Travel
(This practical guide details how to save money on absolutely all travel items—accommodations, transportation, dining, sightseeing, shopping, taxes, and more. Includes special budget information for seniors, students, singles, and families.)

Bed & Breakfast—North America
(This guide contains a directory of over 150 organizations that offer bed & breakfast referrals and reservations throughout North America. The scenic attractions, and major schools and universities near the homes of each are also listed.)

Dollarwise Cruises
(This complete guide covers all the basics of cruising—ports of call, costs, fly-cruise package bargains, cabin selection booking, embarkation and debarkation and describes in detail over 60 or so ships cruising the waters of Alaska, the Caribbean, Mexico, Hawaii, Panama, Canada, and the United States.)

Dollarwise Skiing Europe
(Describes top ski resorts in Austria, France, Italy, and Switzerland. Illustrated with maps of each resort area. Includes supplement on Argentinian resorts.)

Guide to Honeymoon Destinations
(A special guide for that most romantic trip of your life, with full details on planning and choosing the destination that will be just right in the U.S. [California, New England, Hawaii, Florida, New York, South Carolina, etc.], Canada, Mexico, and the Caribbean.)

Marilyn Wood's Wonderful Weekends
(This very selective guide covers the best mini-vacation destinations within a 200-mile radius of New York City. It describes special country inns and other accommodations, restaurants, picnic spots, sights, and activities—all the information needed for a two- or three-day stay.)

Manhattan's Outdoor Sculpture
(A total guide, fully illustrated with black and white photos, to more than 300 sculptures and monuments that grace Manhattan's plazas, parks, and other public spaces.)

Motorist's Phrase Book
(A practical phrase book in French, German, and Spanish designed specifically for the English-speaking motorist touring abroad.)

Paris Rendez-Vous
(An amusing and *au courant* guide to the best meeting places in Paris, organized for hour-to-hour use: from power breakfasts and fun brunches, through tea at four or cocktails at five, to romantic dinners and dancing 'til dawn.)

Swap and Go—Home Exchanging Made Easy
(Two veteran home exchangers explain in detail all the money-saving benefits of a home exchange, and then describe precisely how to do it. Also includes information on home rentals and many tips on low-cost travel.)

The Candy Apple: New York for Kids
(A spirited guide to the wonders of the Big Apple by a savvy New York grandmother with a kid's-eye view to fun. Indispensable for visitors and residents alike.)

The New World of Travel
(From America's #1 travel expert, Arthur Frommer, an annual sourcebook with the hottest news and latest trends that's guaranteed to change the way you travel —and save you hundreds of dollars. Jam-packed with alternative new modes of travel that will lead you to vacations that cater to the mind, the spirit, and a sense of thrift.)

Travel Diary and Record Book
(A 96-page diary for personal travel notes plus a section for such vital data as passport and traveler's check numbers, itinerary, postcard list, special people and places to visit, and a reference section with temperature and conversion charts, and world maps with distance zones.)

Where to Stay USA
(By the Council on International Educational Exchange, this extraordinary guide is the first to list accommodations in all 50 states that cost anywhere from $3 to $30 per night.)

(2) Any one of Frommer's™ City Guides
Amsterdam
Athens
Atlantic City and Cape May
Boston
Cancún, Cozumel, and Yucatán
Dublin and Ireland
Hawaii
Las Vegas
Lisbon, Madrid, and Costa del Sol
London
Los Angeles
Mexico City and Acapulco
Minneapolis and St. Paul
Montréal and Québec City
New Orleans
New York
Orlando, Disney World, and EPCOT
Paris
Philadelphia
Rio

Rome
San Francisco
Santa Fe and Taos (avail. March 1989)
Sydney
Washington, D.C.

(Pocket-size guides to hotels, restaurants, nightspots, and sightseeing attractions covering all price ranges.)

(3) A one-year subscription to *The Dollarwise® Traveler*

This quarterly eight-page tabloid newspaper keeps you up to date on fastbreaking developments in low-cost travel in all parts of the world bringing you the latest money-saving information—the kind of information you'd have to pay $35 a year to obtain elsewhere. This consumer-conscious publication also features columns of special interest to readers: **Hospitality Exchange** (members all over the world who are willing to provide hospitality to other members as they pass through their home cities); **Share-a-Trip** (offers and requests from members for travel companions who can share costs and help avoid the burdensome single supplement); and **Readers Ask . . . Readers Reply** (travel questions from members to which other members reply with authentic firsthand information).

(4) Your personal membership card

Membership entitles you to purchase through the club all Frommer publications for a third to a half off their regular retail prices during the term of your membership.

So why not join this hardy band of international budgeteers and participate in its exchange of travel information and hospitality? Simply send your name and address, together with your annual membership fee of $18 (U.S. residents) or $20 U.S. (Canadian, Mexican, and other foreign residents), by check drawn on a U.S. bank or via international postal money order in U.S. funds to: Frommer's Dollarwise Travel Club, Inc., Gulf + Western Building, One Gulf + Western Plaza, New York, NY 10023. And please remember to specify which *two* of the books in section (1) and which *one* in section (2) you wish to receive in your initial package of members' benefits. Or, if you prefer, use the order form at the end of the book and enclose $18 or $20 in U.S. currency.

Once you are a member, there is no obligation to buy additional books. No books will be mailed to you without your specific order.

CHAPTER I

GETTING THERE

□ □ □

1. TRAVELING TO CALIFORNIA
2. TRAVELING WITHIN CALIFORNIA
3. THE ABC'S OF CALIFORNIA

How you get to the Golden State, and how you get around it, obviously depends on where you're coming from, how much you want to spend, how much time you have, and similar considerations. What follows is information on the various options.

1. TRAVELING TO CALIFORNIA

BY AIR: TWA, United, Eastern, Pan Am, and American Airlines connect most major American cities with San Francisco and Los Angeles.

Best bet is to consult a travel agent (it's free) who can tell you the latest developments and newest fares. Make your arrangements as soon as you know your departure date, since some budget fares depend on advance purchase and can be substantially lower than regular coach fares.

Packages
All of the above-mentioned airlines, and many others, offer packages that include land arrangements—car rental, tours, hotel, etc.—along with air fare. If you're interested in a package, it's once again advisable to discuss the many options with a travel agent, who can find the plan that most perfectly fits your needs.

BY BUS: The **Trailways/Greyhound** system encompasses every major American city and many less-than-major cities in their vast transportation networks. The line offers excellent excursion sales. For instance, the regular New York to Los Angeles or San Francisco round-trip fare is $250, or $150 if you pay 30 days in advance of departure.

Depending on how you take to bus travel, and how many places you want to visit, Greyhound/Trailways **Ameripass** can provide terrific savings. These passes offer unlimited travel between *all* route cities for a fixed price during a given time period. Prices are $189 for 7 days, $249 for 15 days, and $349 for 30 days. It's also a good idea to ask if any special rates are in effect.

BY TRAIN: Amtrak, the nation's most complete long-distance passenger railroad network, connects about 500 American cities, over 30 of them in California.

By train, in coach, round trip between New York and San Francisco, and New York and Los Angeles, is $300. However, as with bus travel, special rates may be available, so be sure to ask. This is a 45-day excursion rate allowing two stopovers.

Amtrak also has family plans, tours, and other money-saving fares. And often they offer good value to and from cities other than New York. Call them for details and further information.

2. TRAVELING WITHIN CALIFORNIA

BY CAR: In every chapter of this book, easy-to-follow driving instructions have been provided. Within this chapter as well those on San Francisco, Los Angeles, and Las Vegas, there are data on car rentals. Of course you'll want to pick up a good map of the state before you start your trip and keep it handy in the glove compartment. In addition, a glance at the boxed mileage chart will give you a quick idea of distances between various California cities.

DISTANCES (IN MILES) BY CAR FROM SAN FRANCISCO TO:

Oakland	13	Avenue of the Giants	240
Muir Woods	17	Yosemite	193
Tiburon	18	South Lake Tahoe	209
Napa Valley	46	Monterey	130
Sonoma	45	Big Sur	156
Marriott's Great America	45	San Simeon	224
San Jose	48	San Luis Obispo	266
Santa Cruz	74	Santa Barbara	332
Mendocino	125	Los Angeles	460
Fort Bragg	166	Palm Springs	565

FROM LOS ANGELES TO:

San Diego	125	Las Vegas	298

My first two words of advice on car rentals are *plan ahead*. If you intend to rent a car during your vacation, check your policy and call your insurance agent to determine the limits of your coverage before you leave home. Does your insurance cover collision damage to the rented car? If not, you may want to pay the added cost for the collision- or loss-damage waiver. As of this writing, most rental firms make customers liable for damage up to the total value of the car. The waiver currently averages $10 to $12 per day.

It's becoming increasingly difficult to keep up with the changes many car-rental companies are making. One such change is the shift of responsibility for theft of vehicles or damage caused by vandalism (previously covered by the company) to renters. To avoid liability for damage or theft, as well as collision damage, renters must buy what is now called the loss-damage waiver (formerly the collision-damage waiver).

First, let's say that if you rent from one of the well-established companies, large or small, the odds are that the car won't be a clunker. You're obviously going to check the cost (daily or weekly) and the charge for mileage, as well as optional insurance and taxes. And since not all rental companies are located at the airport, ask about pick-up and delivery—you may need a taxi (heaven forbid) or shuttle ride to or from the terminal. Those are the basics.

If you plan to pick up the car at one location and return it to another, ask about the drop-off charge, if any. And if you rent the car at a weekly rate and decide to return it early, you may be charged at the much higher daily rate. *Ask!*

Then before you drive away, check the registration—make certain it's still in effect. Finally, find out if the company has its own emergency phone number and one for emergency road service.

BY AIR: National airlines, as well as local airlines, provide service to San Francisco, Los Angeles, San Diego, and Las Vegas. The airlines serving these points are listed under the "ABC'S" in the chapters covering each of these cities.

BUS AND TRAIN: Once again, Greyhound/Trailways can provide bus service to just about anywhere you want to go in California plus Las Vegas, and Amtrak has trains serving over 30 California cities.

3. THE ABC'S OF CALIFORNIA

The information contained below is intended to arm you with facts suitable for coping with assorted general needs and contingencies. You'll find more detailed basic information (ABC'S) for the larger cities at the beginning of the chapters on San Francisco, Los Angeles, San Diego, and Las Vegas.

AIRLINES: Every major domestic carrier and most international carriers serve California; international flights arrive and depart via San Francisco International Airport (SFO) and Los Angeles International Airport (LAX), the two most heavily trafficked airports in the State.

AIRPORTS: See the "ABC'S" section of the individual cities.

AREA CODES: See chart, below.

CALIFORNIA TELEPHONE AREA CODES

Anaheim	714	Palm Springs	619
Berkeley	415	San Diego	619
Big Sur	408	San Fernando Valley	818
Buena Park	714	San Francisco	415
Burbank	818	San Jose	408
Carmel	408	San Luis Obispo	805
Fort Bragg	707	San Simeon	805
La Jolla	619	Santa Barbara	805
Los Angeles	213 or 818	Santa Cruz	408
Monterey	408	Sausalito	415
Napa Valley	707	Sonoma	707
Newport Beach	714	South Lake Tahoe	916
Oakland	415	Yosemite	209

Telephone numbers with 800 as the area code may be dialed toll free from anywhere in the U.S., unless otherwise indicated.

BANKS: As with most states, banks are generally open from 10 a.m. to 3 p.m. Monday through Friday, some later. However, if you need to cash a check, your hotel may be your best resource, depending on the amount involved.

BUSES: The merger of Greyhound and Trailways has resulted in the elimination of some of their former terminals. In some cities, as in San Francisco, the name Greyhound is still the only designation for the merged bus system and its terminal at 50 Seventh Street. The main Greyhound/Trailways terminal in Los Angeles is downtown at 208 E. Sixth Street; in San Diego, the terminal is at 120 W. Broadway.

CHARGE CARDS: Please note that not all restaurants, stores, or shops in California accept all major credit cards, and some accept none. Therefore, do check first if you expect to use plastic for a large expenditure—it can save annoyance and possible embarrassment. If you're visiting from another state, you may not know that in California you can charge package liquor purchases—quite handy if you decide on a purchase of a case or two of vintage wines.

CLIMATE: See the "California Climate" section in the Introduction.

CRIME: As in all states with a considerable influx of tourists from within the U.S. and abroad, crime is always a problem in the larger cities. To avoid an unpleasant incident or an end to a pleasurable trip, use common sense. One practical option is to leave valuables in the hotel safe.

CURRENCY EXCHANGE: Foreign currency exchange services are provided by the **Bank of America** in San Francisco and Los Angeles at both international airports; for other locations, it's best to check with the bank. A branch of **Deak International** also serves San Diego, San Francisco, and Los Angeles.

DENTISTS: Hotels usually have a list of dentists, should you need one, but they are always listed in the *Yellow Pages* as well. Or contact the local Dental Society for referrals.

DOCTORS: Here again, hotels usually have a list of doctors on call. For referrals, contact the local Medical Association.

DRIVING: For a start, California law requires buckling up seat belts; this applies to both driver and passenger. Then be sure to carry registration and proof of insurance in the car, whether you're driving your own vehicle or a rented one. Pay attention to signs and arrows on the streets and roadways or you may find yourself in a lane that requires exiting or turning when you wanted to go straight on. You can turn right at a red light, unless otherwise indicated— but be sure to come to a stop first. Pedestrians always have the right of way. And whatever your destination, if you are unfamiliar with the area, get a map and orient yourself before you're on the freeway. For some reason I've yet to determine, freeway signs frequently indicate direction by the name of a town (one you may never have heard of) rather than north, south, east, or west.

  As for individual cities, driving in San Francisco is relatively easy if you have no hang-ups about stopping at the top of a hill and waiting for the light to change or negotiating your way through snug traffic. On-the-street parking is tough to find there, and garage parking is relatively expensive, especially if you expect to park for only an hour or two. And remember, cable cars—like pedestrians—always have the right of way; on wet days it's a good idea to avoid their slippery tracks.

Driving in Los Angeles is a cross between an art form and a competitive sport. It poses few problems once you get the hang of the freeway system—where the freeways are and where they go. A good map, courage, and much patience, especially during the drive-to-and-from-work hours, will help. In fact, to save yourself much aggravation, it would be best to avoid driving during the usual commuting hours.

Driving in San Diego is a cinch compared to driving in Los Angeles, but here, too, a good map will help to work out the freeway system. And don't forget what I've said about getting the lay of the land before you plunge onto the freeways.

EARTHQUAKES: There will always be earthquakes in California—most of which you will never notice. However, in case of a significant earthquake, there are a few precautionary measures to take, whether you're inside a high-rise hotel, out driving, or just walking.

When you are inside a building, seek cover; do not run outside. Move away from windows in the direction of what would be the center of the building. Get under a large, sturdy piece of furniture (e.g., a desk in an office, a bed in a hotel) or stand against a wall or under a doorway. When exiting the building, use stairwells, NOT elevators.

If you are in your car, pull over to the side of the road and stop, but not until you are away from bridges or overpasses, and telephone or power poles and lines. Stay in your car.

If you are out walking, stay outside and away from trees or power lines or the *sides* of buildings. If you are in an area with tall buildings, find a doorway to stand in.

EMERGENCIES: For police, fire, highway patrol, or medical emergencies, dial 911.

EVENTS AND FESTIVALS: See the "ABC'S" section of the individual cities.

FOOD: San Francisco and Los Angeles are cities with restaurants for everyone. There are over 100 Chinese restaurants and more Italian restaurants than you would believe could prosper just in San Francisco alone. Both cities also have Indian, American, Japanese, Moroccan, French, Greek, Basque, Czech, Jewish, Tuscan, Vietnamese, Lithuanian, Mexican, Salvadorean, old nouvelle, new nouvelle, and cuisines that combine several into one. Some of the most creative chefs in the country work in one or the other of these two cities. And the food ranges from good to superb. San Diego is working toward this stature.

LIQUOR LAWS: In California, liquor and grocery stores, as well as some drug stores, can sell packaged alcoholic beverages between 6 a.m. and 2 a.m. Most restaurants, night clubs, and bars are licensed to serve alcoholic beverages during the same hours. The legal age for purchase and consumption is 21 and proof of age is required.

MEDICAL SERVICES: See "Doctors and Dentists," above.

PETS: Hotels and motels generally will not accept pets. If you're traveling with Rover or Katie the Cat, ask before making the reservations. Motel 6 will accept a pet (of a size within reason) in the room, but will not permit the animal to be left unattended.

POLICE: For emergency help dial 911. I stress the word "emergency"—this does not include misplaced objects, flat tires, etc. However, theft, burglary, and other crimes should be reported immediately.

SPORTS (SPECTATOR): The three major cities in California all have baseball and football teams of note, though of varying degrees of proficiency. Two have top-notch basketball teams. You'll find more details on all of the teams and where you can view the action (or inaction, in some instances) under the "ABCs" for each city.

STORE HOURS: Stores are usually open from 10 a.m. to 6 p.m. Monday to Saturday, closed Sunday.

TAXES: California state sales tax is 6%.

TIPPING: In most California restaurants, just follow the usual U.S. tipping practices: standard 15%, 20% if the service was excellent. However, in some California restaurants, 15% will automatically be added to the cost of the meal, in which case you will see it listed above the total.

If you're checking into a hotel with several bags, a tip of $5 is par for the course.

Valet parking is a great convenience at many state hotels. A tip of $1 is appropriate for the service, over and above the charge for parking.

When you're leaving the hotel, a tip of $1 per day for the period of your stay, left in your room, will be appreciated.

TRAINS: **Amtrak** service to Los Angeles and Seattle operates out of Oakland. Regularly scheduled connecting buses leave San Francisco from Transbay Terminal. From Los Angeles, Amtrak has service south to San Diego and north to Oakland, Seattle, and points in-between. Amtrak also has daily service between Los Angeles and Las Vegas. **Southern Pacific** has train service from San Francisco to the towns of the Peninsula.

CHAPTER II

SAN FRANCISCO

□ □ □

1. GETTING AROUND

2. THE ABC'S OF SAN FRANCISCO

3. HOTELS

4. RESTAURANTS

5. SIGHTS

6. AFTER DARK

What is the secret of San Francisco's continuing attraction? Ask anyone who has fallen in love—it's romantic, breathtaking, classy, bohemian, frequently unpredictable, a bit eccentric, exciting, gutsy, stunning, and very much a survivor. The appeal of this collection of intriguing attributes exists even for those who have never seen Nob Hill or eaten sourdough bread.

There are thousands of quotable quotes about San Francisco, from Georges Pompidou's approbatory tribute—"Your city is remarkable not only for its beauty. It is also, of all the cities in the United States, the one whose name, the world over, conjures up the most visions and more than any other incites one to dream"—to the pithy praise of Francis Ford Coppola: "I kinda like this place."

Most people do. The only negative sentiment I've ever heard uttered about San Francisco dates back to the 16th century, when the English navigator Sir Francis Drake wrote in his ship's diary: "Anchored here in a stynkinge fogge."

"Fogge" notwithstanding, this 47-square-mile peninsular city exerts a compelling charm, composed of open-air fish markets at the Wharf, Victorian houses, exotic ethnic districts (from whence springs a lauded international cuisine), quaint, bell-clanking cable cars, and sudden, breathtaking glimpses of the ocean and Golden Gate Bridge from atop steep hills.

The hills at first seem of an impossible steepness (bring comfortable shoes), but you'll soon find yourself enjoying the exercise, the views, and the camaraderie of fellow mountaineers. And as someone once said, "When you get tired of walking around San Francisco, you can always lean against it."

GETTING YOUR BEARINGS: San Francisco is a town to walk in. The hub of the city is **Union Square,** flanked by Geary, Post, Powell, and Stockton Streets. Named for a series of violent pro-Union demonstrations staged here in Civil War days, today it is an impeccably manicured 2.6-acre park, planted with palms, yews, boxwood, and flowers. You'd never know you were sitting on top of a huge underground garage capable of housing over 1,000 automobiles.

This compact area is the logical setting for many of San Francisco's hotels.

From Union Square it's an easy walk to the gateway to **Chinatown** at Bush Street and Grant Avenue.

Adjoining Chinatown is **North Beach** (where Columbus crosses Grant), home of San Francisco's Italian community and a slightly passé bohemian outpost similar to New York's Greenwich Village; the scene has moved elsewhere, but the atmosphere lingers on.

Keep going in the same direction and you come to the **Embarcadero,** one of the world's largest and busiest ports. Slightly to the west lie **Fisherman's Wharf** and **Aquatic Park.**

Union Square is equally convenient to the **Financial District,** to the northeast; and a few blocks south of Union Square is **Market Street,** the city's seemingly endless main artery.

Golden Gate Bridge

No description of San Francisco would be near complete without mention of the Golden Gate Bridge, the most beautiful bridge in the world—a 1.7 mile-long span of spidery bracing cables and lofty red-orange towers—50 years old in 1987. As beautiful to look at as to look out from, the Golden Gate can be enjoyed from many vantage points of the city, and can be crossed by bus, car, foot, or bicycle. Every year an average of 28 million vehicles cross it, and millions of pedestrians enjoy the terrific views.

Bridge-bound Golden Gate Transit buses depart every half hour during the day for **Marin County,** starting from the Transbay Terminal at Mission and 1st Streets and making convenient stops at Market and 7th Streets, at the Civic Center, and along Van Ness and Lombard Street. Call 332-6600 for schedule information.

San Francisco–Oakland Bay Bridge

Less celebrated, but nonetheless important, this 8¼-mile silvery giant links San Francisco with **Oakland,** her neighbor across the bay. You can drive across the bridge (toll is 75¢ coming into the city, nothing going out). Or you can catch an AC Transit bus at Transbay Terminal (Mission at 1st Street) and ride to downtown Oakland.

1. GETTING AROUND

San Francisco is easier to get around than most large American cities. For one thing, most attractions are in walking distance of your hotel and of each other. And the public transportation is excellent, varied, and efficient.

Most of San Francisco's public transport is operated by the Municipal Railway, always referred to as the **MUNI.** For detailed information, call 673-MUNI or 391-2000, or consult the bus map and routings at the front of the *Yellow Pages* in the San Francisco telephone book.

Its streetcars and buses service an area of about 700 square miles. Fares are an extremely reasonable 80¢ on all buses and streetcars, $1.50 on cable cars (exact change only). Express buses, which stop at major intersections only, also charge 80¢. Transfers are free on all rides and are good in any direction for 1½ hours.

San Francisco bus and streetcar drivers are usually cheerful, courteous, and helpful, but they're not equipped to make change—so have correct fare ready when you board.

STREETCARS: There are five lines, lettered **J, K, L, M,** and **N,** and they all run up and down Market Street past the Civic Center, from whence they proceed in different directions. Streetcars are gradually being replaced by the MUNI metro, a subway that will run alongside of and under BART in the downtown area.

BUSES: Some 70 different bus lines go to virtually every point on the San Francisco map, as well as to Marin County and Oakland. For information on city bus routes, call **MUNI** at 673-MUNI or 391-2000. Other bus information is available from **Golden Gate Transit** (tel. 332-6600) and **AC Transit** (tel. 653-3535).

CABLE CARS: Ever ride a national landmark? A century-old San Francisco tradition, cable cars were named a national historic landmark in 1964.

With no engines, cable cars are hoisted along by means of a steel cable permanently moving at a speed of 9½ miles an hour; it feels considerably faster, though, when you're slamming around curves on San Francisco terrain that turn this ride into a veritable roller coaster. About half the passengers at any given time are tourists aboard for the ride itself, which further enhances the amusement-park atmosphere.

A typical San Francisco sight is the crew manually reversing the cars on a turntable at Powell and Market Streets—always with a crowd of willing helpers. And the cars' clanging bells are an essential part of the San Francisco experience.

The two types of cable cars in use hold a maximum of 90 to 100 passengers, in theory—in practice, it's as many as can grab on somewhere.

There are three lines in all.

The **Powell-Mason line** leads from the corner of Powell and Market Streets in the center of the shopping district up over Nob Hill and down again into the lively hubbub of Fisherman's Wharf.

The **Powell-Hyde line** follows a scenic and exciting vertical and lateral zigzag course from the corner of Powell and Market Streets over both Nob Hill and Russian Hill to a turntable at gaslit Victorian Square in front of Aquatic Park. Ghirardelli Square is less than a block away.

And the **California Street line,** stretching from the foot of California Street in the financial district, cuts through Chinatown and crests Nob Hill to Van Ness Avenue.

The cable-car fare is $1.50 for adults, but it's only 75¢ for students (ages 5 to 17) and 15¢ for seniors. A 40¢ transfer lets you switch to a non-cable-car line.

Cable cars operate from about 6:30 a.m. to 12:30 a.m. Call 673-MUNI for more information.

TAXIS: As everywhere else, this is an expensive way to get about: $2.90 when the meter drops and $1.50 for each mile thereafter. It's about $28 from the airport to downtown.

If you need one, though, it's not too hard to find a cab here. And if you call one, you pay no extra charge. Herewith, a few sample numbers:

Yellow Cab:　626-2345
Veteran's Cab:　552-1300
De Soto Cab:　673-1414
Luxor Cabs:　282-4141
Allied Taxi:　826-9494
City:　468-7200
Pacific:　986-7220

BART: I love to travel on BART (it stands for Bay Area Rapid Transit)—a supermodern, high-speed rapid-transit rail network that connects San Francisco with Oakland, Richmond, Concord, Daly City, and Fremont. Run by a system computerized right down to the ticket gate, BART offers a ride with the feel of a sci-fi adventure.

Its air-conditioned coaches are 70 feet long and come complete with such luxurious trappings as carpeted floors, tinted picture windows, and recessed lighting. They hit a top speed of 80 mph (average, including stops, is 42 mph), and the aforementioned computer system monitors and adjusts speeds and maintains safe spacing.

Minimum fare is 80¢ and extra costs depend on distance ($3.50 from Fremont to Daly City is the highest BART fare). Information boards at all stations show the fares to all other stations. And large maps in the stations and trains make this simple system extra-easy to use.

BART tickets can be purchased in any amount from 80¢ to $20 (it's a $21 value) at the station or at local banks; your ticket is good indefinitely, until its value is used up.

If you're continuing your journey by local bus in the East Bay, get one free transfer to the AC Transit or MUNI bus system from the white machine in the station. Bus route and schedule information can be found in free "BART and Buses" folders in the stations.

BART operates Monday through Saturday from 6 a.m. to midnight (on Sunday from 9 a.m. to midnight). Children under 5 ride free; children 5 through 12 and handicapped persons can purchase a red ticket worth $16 for $1.60; at banks only, senior citizens can purchase a green ticket also worth $16 for $1.20. For information about BART routes and connections with other public transport, call 788-BART. You can pick up a copy of the "Fun Goes Farther on BART" brochure at any station. Or you can pick up the excellent *Regional Transit Guide,* which is sold in many bookstores throughout the city.

Even if you have no real reason to ride BART you might want to try this computerized subway for the experience. It's like jumping into the 21st century.

DRIVING IN SAN FRANCISCO: Chapter I (see "Driving") provides you with an introduction to the fundamentals of getting around California and, to some extent, around the major cities. If you're a newcomer to driving in this state, read it—it can save a lot of wear and tear on all concerned.

As to San Francisco, first let's say that it's a profusion of one-way streets which can create a few small problems in going around the block or in getting from point A to point B; however, most maps of the city indicate which way traffic flows. At the expense of repeating myself, do remember that cable cars are like sailing ships—they *always* have right-of-way. You may notice that they cannot change course. So don't argue with them; they're sturdy vehicles. On wet days their tracks tend to be slippery and are best avoided.

When parking on a grade, engage the hand brake, put the car in gear, and *always* turn your wheels toward the curb when facing downhill; turn them away from the curb when facing uphill. In either case you'll be using the curb as a block. This practice is law in San Francisco. Otherwise, your car may join the hundreds of yearly runaways, or, at the least, you'll get a parking ticket. And when driving downhill, always use low gear.

Street parking is a tough business (the local cops are the quickest tow-away lot I've even seen). Parking lots abound in all the difficult-to-find-a-spot areas, but they're quite expensive. Where street parking is not metered, signs will tell you when you can park and for how long. Curb colors indicate reserved parking zones—red means don't stop, don't park—and they mean it. Blue is for the disabled with California-issued disabled plates or a placard. White is a five-minute limit. Yellow and yellow/black are for commercial vehicles. Once again, the San Francisco Police Department does not regard parking regulations lightly. Violate the law and you may be towed away and that won't be cheap. In total, the tab to retrieve your car may be as much as $90 plus daily storage fees. So resist temptation and don't park at the bus stop or at the fire hydrant and watch for street-cleaning signs. No matter how flush you are, parking in a garage almost always is cheaper and less stressful.

As long as we've brought up the topic of garages—short-term parking is expensive. It can run from $3.75 to as much as $5.25 ($1.75 for 20 minutes) for the first hour. For 24 hours, prices are more reasonable and usually range from $12 to $15. There are some exceptions, however, to the high cost of short-term garage parking. In **Chinatown,** the best (and cheapest) place to park is the Portsmouth Square Garage at 733 Kearny (enter between Clay and Washington). Between 10:30 a.m. and 2:30 p.m. you may wait in line to enter. The price is 50¢ for the first hour, 75¢ for the second hour, $1.75 for the third hour and each hour thereafter for a maximum of $12 for 24 hours. At the **Civic Center** try for the Civic Center Plaza at Taylor and O'Farrell where parking is 50¢ per hour, $15 for 24 hours. **Downtown** head for the Sutter-Stockton Garage at 330 Sutter where it's 50¢ for the first hour, $1 for the second hour and each thereafter, $14 for 24 hours. At **Fisherman's Wharf/Ghirardelli Square,** try the North Point Shopping Garage at 350 Bay where the tab is $1 per half hour, $8.50 maximum; or the Ghirardelli Square Garage at 900 North Point where they charge $1 per half hour, $6 maximum. On **Nob Hill,** the least costly I've found is Park & Lock at 877 California where the fee is $1.50 per hour, $5.75 maximum. On Union Street, in the area of high-traffic shopping, try for the Cow Hollow at 3060 Fillmore for $2 per hour, $7 maximum.

Car Rentals

If you ordinarily rent a car for business, and the company pays for it, you may not need to know much about the subject. However, for those who are personally footing the bill, I've discussed the topic of car rentals in Chapter I under "Traveling Within California."

You don't need a car to explore most of San Francisco, and in crowded areas like Chinatown it's a handicap. But if you're going farther afield, you may want to utilize one of the many car-rental firms in the area.

Rentals of specific size vehicles, including vans, are almost always easier to obtain from the big rental-car companies. Each of the companies I've mentioned below has an airport office at San Francisco International and at Oakland International, as well as more than one office in town. **Avis** is at 675 Post St. (tel. 415/885-5011, or toll free 800/331-1212); at the San Francisco Airport (tel. 415/877-6780); and at the Oakland Airport (tel. 415/562-9000). **Budget Rent-A-Car** is at 321 Mason (Union Square) (tel. 415/775-5800, or toll free 800/527-0700); at the San Francisco Airport (tel. 415/875-6850); and at the Oakland Airport (tel. 415/568-4770). **Hertz** is at 433 Mason (tel. 415/771-2200, or toll free 800/654-3131); at the San Francisco Airport (tel. 415/877-1600); and at the Oakland Airport (tel. 415/568-1177). **National Car Rental,** at 531 Sutter (tel. 415/788-4941, or toll free 800/328-4567), is at the San Francisco Airport (tel. 415/877-4745) and at the Oakland Airport (tel. 415/632-2225). Whichever rental company you use, once again it is always a good idea to check out the car before you leave.

ARRIVING BY AIR: The **San Francisco International Airport** has recently
undergone massive rebuilding to accommodate the increased air traffic of the '80s. Located on the bay, 15 miles south of the city, the airport is served by almost every major domestic and international air carrier. It's the eighth-busiest airport in the world. Travelers should allow at least 40 minutes of travel time from the city. Airporter coaches ($5 for adults, $2.50 for children under 17 ac-

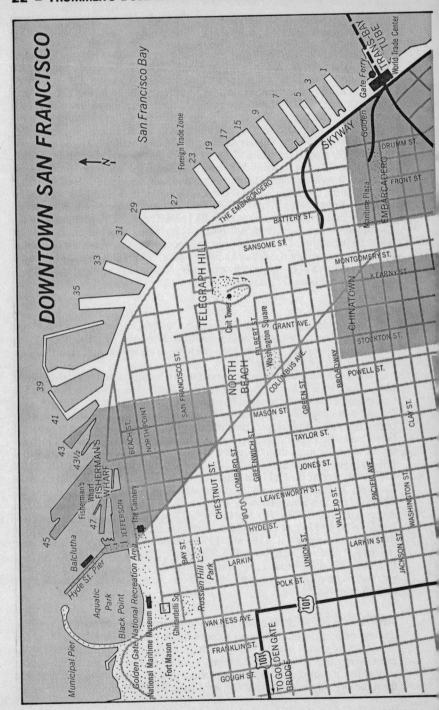

DOWNTOWN SAN FRANCISCO

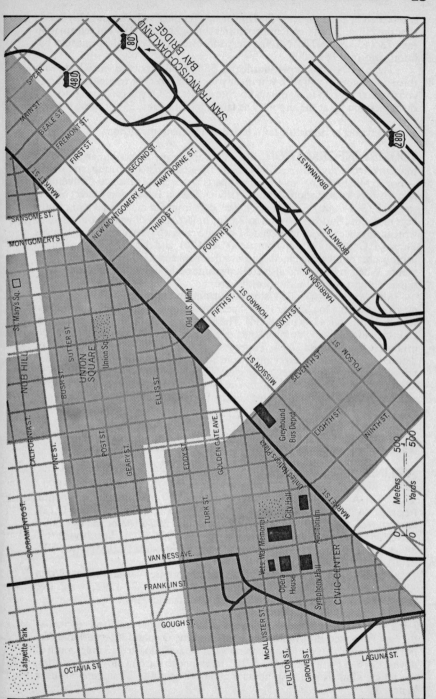

companied by an adult) serve the Downtown Terminal at Taylor and Ellis Streets near the Hilton, with frequent departures throughout the day. For information call 673-2433. SAM-TRANS buses serve downtown as well as the peninsula. For information call 761-7000.

There's a 24-hour Super Shuttle (tel. 558-8500) airport service which, with three-hours notice, will pick you up at your door (hotel or residence) and take you to the airport 45 to 60 minutes before departure. Or you can arrange to have them pick you up at the airport. The fare is $9 for adults, $4 for those under 5 years.

No airport or departure tax is levied on international visitors.

TOURIST INFORMATION: Questions about any aspect of San Francisco tourism can be fully answered in German, Japanese, French, Spanish, and Italian —not to mention English—by the experts at the **San Francisco Convention and Visitors Information Center,** Hallidie Plaza at Powell and Market Streets (tel. 415/391-2000). They're open weekdays from 9 a.m. to 5:30 p.m., Saturdays to 3 p.m., Sundays 10 a.m. to 2 p.m. In fact, it's well worth your while to write in advance of your trip: send $1 to San Francisco Convention and Visitors Bureau, P.O. Box 6977, San Francisco, CA 94101, and they'll send you an invaluable packet of literature, including a tourist map and a four-month calendar of events. When in town, dial 391-2001 any time of the day for a recorded description of current cultural and sporting events.

Also worth a visit is the **Visitors Information Center** of the Redwood Empire Association, One Market Plaza, Spear Street Tower, Suite 1001, San Francisco, CA 94105 (tel. 415/543-8334). The walls are lined with racks of brochures, and the staff will help you plan tours of San Francisco and points north. Their invaluable free *Redwood Empire Visitor's Guide,* updated annually, is chock-full of detailed information on everything from Sonoma County farm trails to favored fishing areas in the entire northern region. There's also a guide to over 100 wineries north of San Francisco. (If you write for either guide, enclose $1 for postage and handling.) It's open Monday to Friday from 9 a.m. to 4:30 p.m.

2. THE ABC'S OF SAN FRANCISCO

This section organizes, in alphabetical order, some basic information intended to help make your trip as enjoyable and frustration-free as possible.

AIRLINES: Domestic carriers serving the San Francisco International Airport, include **Air Cal** (tel. 433-2660), **Alaska Airlines** (tel. 931-8888 or toll free 800/426-0333), **American** (tel. 398-4434 or toll free 800/433-7300), **Continental** (tel. toll free 800/258-1212), **Delta** (tel. 552-5700 or toll free 800/221-1212), **Eastern** (tel. 474-5858), **Northwest Airlines** (tel. 392-2163 or toll free 800/225-2525), **Piedmont Airlines** (tel. toll free 800/251-5720), **Southwest** (tel. 885-1221 or toll free 800/531-5601), **TWA** (tel. 864-5731), **United** (tel. 397-2100), and **USAir** (tel. toll free 800/428-4322).

Domestic carriers serving the Oakland Airport are **Alaska Airlines, Alpha Air** (tel. toll free 800/421-9353), **America West** (tel. 839-1292, or toll free 800/247-5692), **American, Continental, United,** and **USAir.**

AIRPORTS: There are two airports within striking distance of San Francisco— the **San Francisco International Airport** and the **Oakland International Airport.** The former has the higher volume of traffic and is located 15 miles south of downtown San Francisco on U.S. 101. Travel time to the downtown area during morning and afternoon rush hours is about 40 minutes, 25 minutes at other hours.

The Oakland International Airport is about five miles south of downtown Oakland on Calif. 17 (I-880) at the Hegenberger Road exit. It primarily serves East Bay communities, though some San Francisco travelers do use it. There's lots of parking space and bus service is available from various Bay Area locations. Shuttle buses from the Oakland Airport connect with BART trains. The SFO helicopter operates between Oakland and San Francisco Airports.

If you need to know the location of the terminal at the airport from which you will be departing, the *Smart Yellow Pages* of the San Francisco telephone directory gives a handy illustration at the front of the book under the "Airports" heading.

AREA CODE: The telephone area code for San Francisco is **415.**

BABYSITTERS: If you're staying at one of the larger hotels, the concierge can usually recommend organizations to call. Be sure to check on the hourly cost (which may vary by day and time) as well as any additional expenses such as transportation and meals for the sitter. One such service is **Temporary Tot Tending** (tel. 355-7377, 871-5790 after 6 p.m.), which offers childcare by licensed teachers, by the hour or day, for children from infants on up. Open 6 a.m. to 9 p.m. Monday through Friday, except for conventions.

BANKS: As with most cities, banks are generally open from 10 a.m. to 3 p.m. Monday through Friday. However, if you need to cash a check, your hotel may be your best resource, depending on the amount involved.

BUSES: Greyhound Bus Lines serves San Francisco from most cities in California. Greyhound is located at (you guessed it) the Greyhound Depot, 50 Seventh St. (tel. 433-1500). For general information and schedules, call your nearest ticket office.

CHARGE CARDS: Please note that not all restaurants, stores, or shops in California accept all major credit cards, and some accept none. Therefore, do check first if you expect to use plastic for a large expenditure—it can save annoyance and possibly some embarrassment. Purchases of package liquor can be charged in California.

CLIMATE: One major point to remember is that San Francisco has a cool marine climate year-round. There usually is morning and evening fog in the summer, a good deal of rain in the winter, and sun much of the remainder of the year. Women should take a light jacket or warm sweater, or wear a suit. Men should wear light- to medium-weight suits or sports clothes. Bringing an all-weather coat is a good idea for both sexes. Lightweight summer clothes are rarely, if ever, useful.

CRIME: As in all cities with a considerable influx of tourists from within the U.S. and abroad, crime is always a problem. San Francisco is no exception. To avoid an unhappy incident or an end to what might have been a pleasurable trip, use discretion and common sense. One sensible option is leaving valuables in the hotel safe, if you are staying at one of the larger hotels.

CURRENCY EXCHANGE: Foreign currency exchange services are provided by the **Bank of America** and **Deak International,** among others. Bank of America has offices at 345 Montgomery St. in the Financial District (tel. 622-2451), open from 9 a.m. to 3 p.m. Monday through Thursday, till 5 p.m. on Friday; and at the Central Terminal International Building, San Francisco International Airport for the convenience of incoming and outbound passengers, open from 7 a.m. to 11 p.m. daily. Deak International is at 100 Grant Ave., downtown (tel. 362-3452), open Monday through Friday from 9 a.m. to 5 p.m. for foreign currency exchange.

DENTISTS: Hotels usually have a list of dentists should you need one, but they are also listed in the *Yellow Pages*. The **San Francisco Dental Society** can be reached at 421-1435.

DOCTORS: Here again, hotels usually have a list of doctors on call. The **San Francisco Medical Society** number is 567-6234.

DRIVING: Driving in San Francisco is relatively easy if you have no hang-ups about stopping at the top of a hill and waiting for the light to change or negotiating your way through snug traffic. As I've pointed out, on-the-street parking is tough to find, and garage parking is relatively expensive, especially if you expect to park for only an hour or two.

If you plan to drive very far outside of the city, you might want to call about California road conditions (tel. 557-3755) or weather (tel. 936-1212).

EARTHQUAKES: See the "ABC'S of California" section of Chapter I.

EMERGENCIES: For police, fire, highway patrol, or medical emergencies, dial 911. Otherwise, you can reach ambulance service at 931-3900; the nonemergency police number is 553-0123. To reach the Poison Control Center, call 476-6600.

EVENTS AND FESTIVALS: For a listing of annual events in advance of your trip, write to the San Francisco Convention and Visitors Bureau, P.O. Box 6977, San Francisco, CA, 94101, and enclose a self-addressed stamped envelope. During your stay, you can pick up a copy of *Key* or the *San Francisco Guide*—two excellent free weekly publications, both found at most hotels. A third alternative for what's going on in a given week is the pink "Date Book" section of the Sunday edition of the *San Francisco Examiner and Chronicle*.

FOOD: There are lots of places to eat in this city for less than $4; on the other hand, you can spend as much as $75 for a meal, per person, without wine. This is a city with a restaurant for everyone—there are over 100 Chinese restaurants, more Italian restaurants than you could believe would prosper, plus Indian, American, Japanese, Moroccan, French, Greek, Basque, Czech, Jewish, Tuscan, Vietnamese, Lithuanian, Mexican, Salvadorean, etc. And the food ranges from good to superb. Those restaurants located in hotels are described in Section 3; the majority are listed in Section 4. I've tried to select some of the best in all price categories.

If you're planning to charge a meal, you might call ahead to see if the restaurant takes plastic. Not all of the better restaurants do and not all of them take every major credit card.

HAIR SALONS: If your hotel does not have a hair salon on the premises, they're usually glad to make a recommendation.

HOLIDAYS: Obvious holiday occasions and dates of major conventions are not the times to try for reservations on short notice. While the city's many hotels can accommodate conventions of almost any size and scope, bear in mind that San Francisco hosts over 8,000,000 tourists, conventioneers and travelers each year. So if you're not certain what events are in the offing, and you have specific vacation dates in mind, send for the annual list—see "Events and Festivals" above.

HOSPITALS: CliniCARE at St. Francis Memorial Hospital, 900 Hyde St., on Nob Hill (tel. 775-4321) provides drop-in outpatient services from 8 a.m. to 5 p.m. Monday through Friday. No appointment is necessary. The hospital also has 24-hour emergency service.

INFORMATION: The **San Francisco Visitor Information Center,** 900 Market St. (tel. 391-2000), is on the lower level of Hallidie Plaza at Market and Powell Streets. Their multilingual staff is there to answer your questions weekdays from 9 a.m. to 5:30 p.m., Saturday till 3 p.m., and Sunday from 10 a.m. to 2 p.m. A 24-hour recorded message (tel. 391-2001) lists daily events and activities. Similar recorded information is available in French (tel. 391-2003), in German (tel. 391-2004), in Spanish (tel. 391-2122), and in Japanese (tel. 391-2101).

LIQUOR LAWS: Liquor and grocery stores, as well as some drug stores, can sell packaged alcoholic beverages between 6 a.m. and 2 a.m. Most restaurants, night clubs, and bars are licensed to serve alcoholic beverages during the same hours. The legal age for purchase and consumption is 21 and proof of age is required.

If you are in the wine country and decide to make some larger-than-usual purchases of a vintage or two, unlike many other states, California permits you to purchase package liquor with a credit card. The store may also handle the shipment of wine and relieve you of what might otherwise be a weighty problem.

NEWSPAPERS: The *San Francisco Chronicle* and the *San Francisco Examiner* are widely distributed throughout the Bay Area. The Sunday edition of the *San Francisco Examiner and Chronicle* will fill you in on happenings in the upcoming week.

RELIGIOUS SERVICES: San Francisco has hundreds of churches and synagogues, and about 100 denominations. Your hotel desk can help direct you to the nearest church of almost any given denomination. If not, the *Yellow Pages* can be helpful for the location and, frequently, the times of the services.

SPORTS (SPECTATOR): As of this writing, the Bay Area has two major league baseball teams—the **San Francisco Giants** (tel. 392-7469, 467-8000) and the **Oakland Athletics,** or "A's" (tel. 638-0500, 638-4900); an NFL football team—the **San Francisco 49ers,** locally known simply as the "Niners" (tel. 468-2249, 467-8000); and an NBA basketball team—the **Golden State Warriors** (tel. 638-6000). Both the Giants and the 49ers roost at Candlestick Park (where no one can hold a candle to the wind), located on Giants Drive at Gilman Avenue. The Warriors reside at the Oakland Coliseum Arena at the 66th Avenue or Hegenberger Road exit from Interstate 880. You'll find a complete schedule of games at home and away under "Sports Schedules" at the front of the *Yellow Pages*.

And, finally, there's the Sport of Kings. Bay Meadows Thoroughbred Racing season runs from August through the latter part of January. Quarter horse racing is February through April. The track is located at the intersection of Hillsdale Blvd. at Bayshore Freeway 101 (San Mateo) (tel. 574-7223).

STORE HOURS: Stores are usually open from 10 a.m. to 6 p.m. Monday to Saturday, closed Sunday. Stores in Chinatown are generally open from 10 a.m. to 10 p.m. daily.

TRAINS: Amtrak service to Los Angeles and Seattle operates out of Oakland. Regularly scheduled connecting buses leave San Francisco from the Transbay Terminal (tel. 982-8512).

Southern Pacific has train service from San Francisco to the towns of the Peninsula. The depot is at 700 Fourth St., at Townsend (tel. 541-1000).

USEFUL TELEPHONE NUMBERS: You can obtain **weather information** for San Francisco at 936-1212, **time** at 767-8900, information on **highway conditions** at tel. 557-3755, and of course **directory assistance** at 411.

3. HOTELS

One of the world's great hotel cities, San Francisco has over 45,000 rooms for visitors, and is constantly adding more. The wide variety of high-quality facilities, however, is matched by the large volume of tourist and convention traffic (about 3,000,000 visitors per year accommodated). Especially in peak season—from late May to late September—it's foolish not to make prior reservations.

San Francisco boasts over a dozen hotels in the international luxury class. A cross section of these, from the old-world traditional to the supermodern, comprises the first two categories in this book—deluxe and upper bracket—the latter a shade less expensive and luxurious than the former. The bulk of the selections fall in the moderately priced range, and the hotel section concludes with budget listings for those traveling on limited funds.

But all these hotels have one thing in common. They come up to an exacting standard of comfort, hospitality, and cleanliness. Most (although not all) are in the downtown area. There's something to suit just about every taste and pocketbook—read carefully and you'll find what you're looking for.

Remember: There is an 11% tax on all hotel bills in San Francisco, which must be added to the price.

THE DELUXE HOTELS: The **Four Seasons Clift Hotel,** Geary and Taylor Streets, San Francisco, CA 94102 (tel. 415/775-4700, or toll free 800/332-3342), is a 329-room hotel emphasizing excellence of service, quiet but unimpeachable style, and total comfort. There is a gaggle of pricey hotels in San Francisco—huge, with every type of shop, cities within a city—but few of them have the warm elegance, finesse, and sophistication of an era associated with tuxedos, pearls, polo—in summary, "class." The Four Seasons Clift is the familiar haunt of discreet and knowledgeable travelers who care more about quality than the number of celebs in residence. It's the kind of place where the staff remains unchanged year after year and guests' names and preferences are remembered.

Spacious accommodations are among the most elegant in town. Color schemes are exquisite. A typical room might have peach rugs, bedspreads, and drapes, with pale-green and plum velvet furnishings. Beautiful artwork adorns the walls. All rooms have oversize beds and pillows, color TVs, clock radios, extension phones in the bath, and a bathrobe in your dressing room. Fine grades of linen and toweling are used. At night your bed is turned down, a mint and a rose placed on your pillow. Free newspapers and another rose come with your morning breakfast tray. Room service is available around the clock, and a traditional

English tea is served in the lobby every afternoon. For families, the Four Seasons Clift also has prepared a folder listing the many items the hotel can provide for children, from baby blankets to teddy bears, baseball cards, and coloring books. Room service stands ready with a supply of Oreo cookies and milk, popcorn, and a long list of other goodies.

There are two restaurants: in the prestigious French Room you dine beneath ornate 18th-century crystal chandeliers. The adjoining Redwood Room, designed by architect Albert Lansburgh in 1934 (he also did the San Francisco Opera House), is paneled in 2,000-year-old redwood burl. Art deco in style, its furnishings are plush forest-green velvet. Both rooms serve breakfast, lunch, and dinner. You start your day with fresh-baked croissants or eggs Benedict. Dinner might begin with a mousse of scallops flavored with truffles. Dinner entrees cost $25 to $35; house specialties include roast prime rib au jus with Yorkshire pudding and creamed horseradish and oven-roasted Cornish hen seasoned with oregano and basil butter. For dessert there are strawberry-filled crêpes flamed in brandy and Grand Marnier for two. The wine list is extensive and well chosen.

To live in quiet comfort away from the parvenus and the convention trade will cost you $165 to $235 single, $165 to $255 double; suites begin at $525.

The newest of San Francisco's luxury high-rise hostelries, the **Ramada Renaissance Hotel,** 55 Cyril Magnin St. (at Market and North 5th), San Francisco, CA 94102 (tel. 415/392-8000, or toll free 800/228-9898), is ideally situated in the heart of the city—two blocks from Union Square and a half-block from the Powell Street cable car. Built at a cost of $130 million, the hotel is palatial in scope and appearance. It occupies an entire city block and has 1,005 rooms and all the extra services and conveniences even the most sophisticated traveler might expect.

As you enter the hotel, there is an imposing seven-panel bas-relief mural of the history of San Francisco by Ruth Asawa. Two stone lions hold court in the travertine marble lobby. Ahead is the main staircase covered in a rich beige-pink-blue Tai Ping sculpted carpet woven in China. Above this is an oil by Tony Chimento depicting the Renaissance woman.

The second-floor lobby looks upward into a three-story atrium. Here you can enjoy a leisurely drink at the Piazza while listening to contemporary and classical music played on a grand piano, somehow fitting in a room this size. Mushroom-colored velvet sofas and beech chairs done in seafoam green are interspersed throughout. Two eight-foot-high gray marble statues of a Roman couple accent the height of the atrium, as do the huge vases of fresh flowers.

Throughout the hotel, guest rooms reflect the same subdued elegance, from the beige carpeting and furnishings of bleached ash to the floral and city prints of the area. Each room has the conveniences and attention to detail that make a stay pleasurable: king-size beds, bathroom phone, well-lit makeup mirror, shower massage, even French-milled hand soap on the marble vanity, and window vents that open if you want fresh air! The ultimate in security is provided by a computer-coded guest-room key card, which is changed at the end of each stay. And there are rooms with special facilities for handicapped persons.

Should you need special cosseting, check into the Renaissance Club, which occupies the top four floors and features the amenities one might expect of a private club. Personal check-in and concierge service, a continental breakfast and afternoon hors d'oeuvres, and access to the health club are included in the basic charge. Guest rooms are supplied with terrycloth robes, hair dryers, the daily newspaper, and evening turndown service. Seven suites contain private whirlpool baths.

You will be pleased by the Ramada Renaissance's helpful staff and the number of services provided. You'd expect a concierge and bell captain, but there is also a foreign-language information desk, currency exchange, a tour desk, and on request, acoustic couplers linking personal computers to off-site computers. And all guests are offered complimentary morning limousine service to the financial district.

As one might expect, the hotel has not stinted in its restaurant facilities. There are two areas for dining, both on the second floor—the Corintia Ristorante and the Veranda. The Corintia specializes in northern Italian cuisine, and what cuisine! (I've covered the restaurant in more detail in Section 4.) It's worth your review. The Veranda's menu features both traditional favorites and some innovative specialties for breakfast, lunch, and dinner. If you yearn for salsa piquante at breakfast, the guacamole omelet will satisfy your innermost craving.

For Mexican-food urges at lunch, the tostada grande with chicken, avocado, tomato, cheese, and refried beans is delicious. For dinner, sautéed pork medallions with chanterelles are excellent; barbecued veal short ribs are always reliable too. Luncheon entrees range from $8 to $14; at dinner they run $10 to $19 (lobster, $30).

Single rooms at the Ramada Renaissance range from $135 to $195, the higher price for a junior suite; doubles run $160 to $220; suites, from $240 to $380. Rates for the Renaissance Club range from $185 for a single and $210 for a double; suites are $400 and $950. Children 18 or under stay for free in the same room with their parents.

If you're in town for a grand evening of theater or a personal celebration, the hotel has special packages you might want to check into. Some include complimentary champagne, continental breakfast, even limousine service.

The **Stanford Court,** 905 California St. (at Powell Street), San Francisco, CA 94108 (tel. 415/989-3500, or toll free 800/227-4736). Housed on the site of the former Nob Hill mansion of multimillionaire Leland Stanford, this gracious establishment has made few concessions to the modern world. The *porte cochère* entrance is under a lofty stained-glass dome. The distinguished interior speaks of old elegance. Japanese Imari bowls and jardinières from the lobby of the Grand Hôtel in Paris overflow with fresh-cut flowers, and throughout are French provincial and Empire antiques and reproductions.

In each of the 402 guest rooms, a reproduction of a classic French armoire serves as a desk and a discreet hideaway for the color TV (there's a second TV and an additional phone in the bath/dressing-room area). The rooms feature handcrafted bamboo furnishings, AM/FM clock radios, marble bedside tables, and original wall lithographs of early San Francisco scenes; some even have canopied beds. Rates range from $175 to $235 single, $205 to $265 double, $425 and up for suites.

The Café Potpourri, a delightful dining area encompassing three intimate cafés, serves breakfast and lunch.

The hotel also houses a fine gourmet restaurant—Fournou's Ovens. Open for dinner nightly, Fournou's offers a warm French provincial ambience in which succulent specialties like roast rack of lamb emerge from massive tiled oak-burning, open-hearth ovens. Fournou's features traditional and nouvelle French cuisine. You might begin your meal here with bay shrimp in sour cream with mushrooms or with a bowl of cream of artichoke soup with hazelnut. Oven-roast potatoes and fresh vegetable du jour are served with all entrees, which run $20 to $35. Dacquoise is a memorable Fournou's dessert.

The antiques that decorate the restaurant walls and grilled balcony levels—including authentic 18th-century French armoires and chests—were collected from five continents. The floors are terracotta tile, the beamed ceilings of substantial mahogany. And the series of conservatories with curved floor-to-ceiling windows providing views of the city's skyline and the bay beyond are very beautiful. They're modeled after the glass-enclosed winter gardens popular in European architecture during the early 19th century. One of them contains Fournou's Bar, featuring piano music nightly.

Another Nob Hill hostelry is the elegant **Mark Hopkins Inter-Continental,** No. 1 Nob Hill, San Francisco, CA 94108 (tel. 415/392-3434, or toll free 800/ 332-4246). It also occupies the site of one of the most ornate and extravagant homes built by railroad tycoons in the 1870s, the gabled and turreted Mark Hopkins mansion. In its over half a century of operation the Mark has been headquarters for distinguished visitors and celebrities ranging from Prince Philip, King Hussein, and Eleanor Roosevelt to Frank Sinatra and Michael Jackson.

When the hotel opened its doors it was (with 20 stories) the highest point in San Francisco, and each room was designed to offer an expansive view. All guest rooms, recently renovated at a cost of $9 million, are beautifully furnished and have sumptuous baths and huge closets. Thoughtful extras include hair dryers, bathrobes, makeup lights on bathroom mirrors, and proper hangers for all types of clothing. Seventeen of the suites offer the ultimate in luxury and comfort, as does the Jacuzzi Suite which affords a spectacular view of the Golden Gate Bridge.

The hotel's warm, oak-paneled Nob Hill Restaurant serves breakfast, lunch, and dinner daily. The restaurant specializes in French and California cuisine, using the finest and freshest of ingredients. The end result is an exceptionally fine meal. Dinner here might begin with an appetizer of sautéed escalope of goose foie gras with lentils, apple purée and olive oil, continue with roast loin of lamb in a fresh herb coulis with garlic sauce and braised red cabbage, and conclude with a delectable crème brûlée. Entrees cost $20 to $35. If you're going to be in town for more than a day, there are some dishes the restaurant prepares specially for two persons minimum and must be ordered one day in advance. One of these is a lobster bouillabaisse with fennel and orange, traditional rouille, and garlic croutons ($50 for two)—truly worth writing home about.

Afternoon or evening, there's a visual feast to be had at the Top of the Mark, a glass-walled room offering a panoramic 360° view of the city with your cocktails.

Rates at the Mark Hopkins are $175 to $235 single, $205 to $265 for doubles and twins. Suites cost $350 to $1,100.

Just across the street is the magnificent stone and marble carriage entrance to the **Fairmont,** at California and Mason Streets, San Francisco, CA 94106 (tel. 415/772-5000, or toll free 800/527-4727), a third Nob Hill hostelry where old-world luxury and graciousness are still alive and well. The historic main building with its opulent marble-walled and colonnaded lobby contains 340 rooms and 40 distinctive suites. The adjoining tower has 200 more rooms and 20 suites, all with bay views.

There are five restaurants to choose from: the Tonga, offering dancing on a boat deck along with Chinese and island specialties; the Crown Room—29 stories high and reached by an outdoor glass elevator—wherein lavish buffet luncheons, dinners, and Sunday brunches are this establishment's counterpart to the Top of the Mark; the award-winning Canlis, where international fare is served; the dome-ceilinged Squire Room, serving gourmet continental cuisine; and the Venetian Room, an elegant supperclub featuring top-name entertainment (see "After Dark"). In addition, there's live music nightly in the New Orleans Room, afternoon tea, cocktails, and piano music in the newly redecorated Cirque. The Brasserie is the Fairmont's informal 24-hour restaurant.

Guests are pampered with nightly turndown service; extra pillows, electric shoe polishers, AM/FM clock radios, bathroom scales, makeup mirrors, oversize towels, and custom-made soap are among the other little conveniences. Room decor is richly traditional.

Rates in the Fairmont's main building are $140 to $180 single, $170 to $210 double or twin, suites from $400. In the Tower, singles go for $180 to $200; doubles or twins cost $210 to $255; and suites are $500 and up.

Another distinguished hostelry in the Nob Hill section, is the **Huntington Hotel,** 1075 California St. (between Mason and Taylor), San Francisco, CA 94108 (tel. 415/474-5400, or toll free 800/227-4683). Lee Radziwill designed some of the 145 luxurious rooms, and room service is provided by the prestigious L'Étoile, which is on the premises. Each of the rooms is uniquely furnished with exquisite antiques and custom-made pieces to create the atmosphere of an elegant private residence. All are extremely comfortable and equipped with every amenity—color TV, radio, direct-dial phone, etc. Some rooms have refrigerators and wet bars, and many look out over Huntington Park. Baths are fitted out with Irish linen hand towels with the Huntington crest. Personal service is highly stressed: the Huntington takes no convention trade, records guests' preferences for future visits, offers nightly turndown service, and pampers guests in every possible way.

Lunch and dinner are served in the Big Four, named for the railroad tycoons C. P. Huntington, Charles Crocker, Mark Hopkins, and Leland Stanford. Photographs of their mansions adorn the walls of this plush walnut-paneled restaurant. Substantial and clubby in decor, with green-leather furnishings and white-clothed candlelit tables, it is a place where you can imagine the big four dining comfortably. Dinner entrees are in the $22.50 to $35 range.

L'Étoile offers a different brand of elegance with crystal chandeliers, Louis XIV–style furnishings, gilt-framed French oil paintings, enormous urns of fresh flowers, and potted ferns on marble pedestals. Both service and fare are impeccable. Entrees at L'Étoile range from $27 to $35. It's open for dinner only.

Rates at the Huntington are $155 to $210 single, $175 to $235 double; suites run $250 to $700.

On opening night there was a spectacular star-studded party. An Indian guru blessed the place, and a ritual Victorian-style murder in the best Agatha Christie tradition was enacted with "the body" tumbling down the grand staircase. The scene of these happenings: Bob Pritikin's poshly located **Mansion Hotel,** a sprawling, twin-turreted Queen Anne house—yes, it *is* a mansion—at 2220 Sacramento St. (between Laguna and Buchanan Streets), San Francisco, CA 94115 (tel. 415/929-9444).

It's where hip young couples up for the weekend from L.A., the requisite sprinkling of celebs—like Barbra Streisand, Robin Williams, and Joan Baez—and in-the-know New Yorkers stay. And even locals check in occasionally just for the fun of it. You arrive at a magnificent edifice, set high on a terraced garden knoll, enhanced by no fewer than five Bufano sculptures. You're received in the Grand Foyer by a host or hostess in Victorian attire who offers you a glass of sherry (note the strains of baroque music wafting from the music room), then conducts you up the exquisitely paneled grand staircase, its walls adorned—like those in most of the public areas—with murals of turn-of-the-century San Francisco.

But before I get to the rooms, just a note that in addition to the Victorian Cabaret Theater (wherein a live parrot, not to mention an ostensible ghost, resides, and concerts/magic shows take place several times weekly), the main floor also contains a game room. Also notable as you walk are the original set from Edward Albee's *Tiny Alice,* and the largest number of Beniamino Bufano's works on display anywhere.

As for the 20 rooms: Each is dedicated to a historic San Francisco personality, and a mural on the wall tells his or her story. There is, of course, a Bufano Room, plus a Coit Room, a Huntington Room, etc.—even a Pritikin Room, which salutes the Mansion's eccentric owner (no doubt he will go down in San Francisco history). Most rooms look out over the rose garden or sculpture garden; from some, in season, you can reach out your window and pick a plum off a tree. Each is different, but all have antique furnishings, velvet drapes, Victorian memorabilia, and brass beds with handmade quilts. There's nothing as vulgar as a TV, but you do get a direct-dial phone. Baths are in the rooms or a step away; towels are thick and luxurious. All rooms are abundantly charming, one with an antique sink, another with a marble fireplace, etc. The ultimate indulgence is the very French Empress Josephine Room, furnished in priceless antiques and renting at $200 a night.

Dinner is available to everyone. The Mansion Hotel has one of San Francisco's fine restaurants.

The price for returning to a bygone era: $75 to $150 for single occupancy, $90 to $200 for double occupancy. And these rates include a full breakfast, fresh flowers in your room, concerts, and the opportunity to experience whatever else is happening at the time. It's not just a place to stay, it's theater, and Pritikin's motto is, "The Mansion is only as good as its last performance."

The **Hyatt Regency,** 5 Embarcadero Center, San Francisco, CA 94111 (tel. 415/788-1234, or toll free 800/228-9000), takes us not only to another section of town from the above-mentioned listings, but also to another century—the ultra-modern 20th. Even if you don't stay here, you might want to come by to ogle this amazing seven-sided pyramid hotel and its spectacular atrium lobby—the setting for events from big-band ballroom dancing to a high-wire circus act. A babbling brook meanders through the vast central court. Longer than a football field, it's lined with 150 live trees, and 15,000 potted ivy plants hang from the lofty balconies that ascend 17 stories. Daylight filters down from the skylight roof, casting a rosy glow. The centerpiece is an enormous aluminum sculpture—*Eclipse,* by Charles Perry—rising four stories over a huge reflecting waterfall pond. Arrangements of flowers, live birds in cages, eating areas here and there, and strolling musicians complete the picture.

Off the lobby are five glass-cylinder elevators, each highlighted by 500 tiny lights. One of these will whisk you, at a speed of 500 feet per minute, to the Equinox, a revolving rooftop restaurant that provides a complete sweep of San Francisco scenery every 45 minutes. There are several other restaurants as well—most of them located off the lobby—plus a nightclub and several cocktail lounges.

The hotel's 16th floor houses the Regency Club, with 52 deluxe guest rooms, private bar and game room lounges, complimentary continental breakfast, after-dinner cordials, and private concierge.

As for the rooms on all other floors, over two-thirds offer bay views. They're done in tranquil earth tones set off by splashes of royal burgundy. Custom-designed modern furnishings are softened by elm burl and cane accents, brushed-bronze hardware, and sheer draperies. Above the beds are abstract paintings. Each room has a dressing area with makeup and full-length mirrors, and there's a choice of six first-run movies on your color TV. Room service is available 24 hours.

Singles range from $189 to $240, and doubles run $215 to $260; add $25 for each additional person. Rooms on the Regency Club floor cost $210 for singles, $240 for doubles. Parking in the plaza is $18 for 24 hours, with in-and-out privileges.

Hyatt on Union Square, 345 Stockton St. (between Post and Sutter Streets), San Francisco, CA 94108 (tel. 415/398-1234, or toll free 800/

228-9000), is another member of the Hyatt chain, and although it's less Space Age spectacular than the Regency, it is quite handsome and exceedingly well located.

Champagne draperies and awninged windows give the hotel an inviting regal appearance when viewed from the street. Inside, the ultramodern decor has an almost theatrical quality of hushed elegance. The 693 rooms, restaurants, many shops, and facilities are housed in a three-story forebuilding and a 40-story tower fronted by a lovely brick courtyard. Bedecked with potted trees and flowers, the old-world courtyard is the setting for Ruth Asawa's bronze fountain sculpture, the design of which imaginatively depicts the city's familiar landmarks.

Your room at the Hyatt will be spacious and contemporary, with subtle earth tones predominating in the decor. Sliding doors open onto a railed parapet. The carpeted baths have marble sinks. And, once again, there are first-run movies available on your color TV.

Business people will appreciate the free limousine service to the financial district weekday mornings, but you can also avail yourself of the early-morning chauffeured limo to travel to the jogging course at the Embarcadero Center.

A good inexpensive restaurant, Napper's, Too, is on the ground floor. It's a most pleasant place to partake of the daily "country buffet" lunch. The Plaza Restaurant, also overlooking the courtyard, and featuring a stained-glass skylight dome overhead, is another Hyatt dining choice. With floor-to-ceiling windows, bamboo furnishings, an abundance of potted palms—even a fountain—it's like dining in a delightful garden, and the continental fare is quite good. You can also watch the sunset, enjoy cocktails, take lunch, dinner, or Sunday brunch comfortably ensconced in a plush and private tufted-leather and velvet banquette at One-Up, 36 stories skyward. The One-Up Lounge is open daily for cocktails, served with piano music until 2 a.m. Great view, very romantic.

Rates at the Hyatt are $165 to $220 single, $190 to $245 double, the higher rates, generally, for rooms on upper floors. Suites cost from $500.

Since 1904, the centrally located **Westin St. Francis,** 335 Powell St. (at Union Square), San Francisco, CA 94102 (tel. 415/397-7000, or toll free 800/228-3000), has welcomed thousands of prominent guests, from royalty to theatrical luminaries. Rebuilt after massive damage from the 1906 earthquake, this ever-changing hotel's expansion—the addition of the 32-story Tower—brought room capacity to 1,200. Sporting five glass-enclosed elevators that run along the outside of the building (the view is spectacular!), the Tower is topped by a fine rooftop restaurant, Victor's, offering first-rate nouvelle cuisine and an extensive wine selection in posh surroundings. Oz, a leading San Francisco disco, also occupies the 32nd floor. The oak-paneled English Grill, featuring fresh seafood, is another dining option, as are the Dutch Kitchen, a coffeeshop, and Dewey's Union Square Bar and Monument Saloon. Compass Rose, just off the lobby, serves a weekday lunch but is most popular with locals for cocktails.

Rooms throughout are quietly elegant, with cream-colored walls, very attractive furnishings, and all modern appurtenances. Those in the original building have unusually high ceilings.

And although to the best of my knowledge Howard Hughes never owned this hotel, he no doubt would have approved their practice of washing all the coins in the cashier's office every day.

The St. Francis has its own garage, charging $18 for 24 hours with in-and-out privileges.

Rates are $140 to $230 single, $170 to $270 double, $350 to $1,500 for suites.

One of the most conveniently situated of San Francisco's deluxe hostelries—and with 1,900 rooms among the largest hotels on the West Coast—is the

San Francisco Hilton (on Hilton Square) 333 O'Farrell St. (at Mason Street), San Francisco, CA 94102 (tel. 415/771-1400, or toll free 800/445-8667). It is the complete luxury hotel, a city within a city, composed of three connecting buildings. Hilton Square includes the original 19-story main building with 955 rooms, a 46-story 569-room tower topped by a panoramic restaurant, and a new 23-story landmark with an additional 386 rooms.

The Hilton is ideally located across the street from the air terminal where you arrive by bus or shuttle from the airport. As a matter of fact, the entire Bay Area is easily reached from the Hilton since the hotel is within easy walking distance to the cable cars, buses, and the city's MUNI and BART transportation systems.

There's a beautiful, sweeping grand entrance to the lobby on imported custom carpet. Inlaid marble defines the 16-bay registration area with a separate concierge desk. An elegant sidewalk cafe, Cafe on the Square, provides a lovely spot for spectators to eye the passing parade and the promenade of hotel shops.

One of the Hilton's unique features is its internal parking system. Notify the hotel that you are bringing a car and it will book you into a room that is directly accessible to the parking levels. (There's a daily parking charge.) And at the 16th-floor level of the original tower, an inner courtyard is outfitted with a heated swimming pool and cabaña/garden rooms.

Hilton Square offers several characteristically San Francisco restaurants to choose from. Henri's, on the 46th floor, serves classic California cuisine in a breathtaking setting I promise you won't forget for as long as you remember San Francisco. The magnificent 360° view displays the Golden Gate Bridge and the Bay Bridge, Sausalito, Telegraph Hill, and the East Bay. And the retractable skylight exposes the night sky in all its grandeur. Kiku of Tokyo, an intimate corner of Japan itself, presents authentic Japanese cuisine. And Phil Lehr's Steakery, a restaurant that has been a unique San Francisco tradition for over 40 years, offers prime cuts by the pound.

All guest rooms are spacious and modern in typical Hilton style. Memorable floor-to-ceiling views are available from many of these spacious and grandly appointed rooms, as well as color TVs with first-run movies, mini-bars, radios, marble bathrooms, and 24-hour room service to pamper each guest during her or his stay.

Room rates range from $150 to $215 single, $170 to $235 double; suites are $365 to $640.

The **Meridien San Francisco,** 50 3rd St. (at Market), San Francisco, CA 94103 (tel. 415/974-6400, or toll free 800/543-4300), came into national prominence shortly after its 1983 opening when it first played host to French President François Mitterrand and then served as headquarters for Democratic nominee Walter Mondale during the convention. Located near Union Square and the Moscone Convention Center, the Meridien attracts both business people and tourists. There are 700 beautifully appointed rooms here and 26 suites on 32 floors. All are elegantly decorated in pastels, and there are luxuries galore— remote-control color TVs with in-house movies, mini-bars, nightly turndown service, direct-dial phones, air conditioning, expansive floor-to-ceiling windows, AM/FM clock radios, 24-hour room service, and—from the upper floors— breathtaking views of the city and bay.

The Meridien boasts two excellent restaurants: Café Justin, an informal dining room that serves three meals a day (open from 6 a.m. to 11 p.m.); and Pierre at the Meridien, an elegant, intimate French restaurant open for dinner Monday through Saturday from 6:30 to 10:30 p.m.

Rooms at the Meridien cost $155 to $200 single, $180 to $225 double.

The smallest luxury hotel in town (126 rooms) is the **Campton Place Ho-**

tel, 340 Stockton St. (between Post and Sutter), San Francisco, CA 94108 (tel. 415/781-5555, or toll free 800/647-4007, 800/235-4300 in California). But smaller is better, according to the management; it allows the staff to offer better and more personal service. The hotel's buildings—formerly occupied by the Drake-Wiltshire—were renovated to the tune of $25 million, and the results are spectacular. From the small, cozy lobby to the luxurious rooms, it's obvious that no expense was spared to make this one of San Francisco's jewels.

Guest rooms are beautifully appointed, with king-size or double-double beds, concealed color TVs with remote control, AM/FM clock radios, direct-dial phones, air conditioning, and luxurious bathrooms with marble floors, vanity and tub, and luxurious bathrooms with marble floors, vanity and tub, brass fixtures, bathrobes, telephone, special soaps, shampoos, and bath gels.

The Campton Place pampers its guests: there's a concierge to arrange for theater tickets, restaurant reservations, and travel plans; and there are maids and butlers available to pack and unpack your luggage for you.

On the premises is the Campton Place Restaurant, one of the "in" spots for breakfast, lunch, and dinner.

Rooms at the Campton Place rent for $200 to $260, single or double; suites begin at $550. Overnight parking is available for guests at $20.

Another luxury hotel in San Francisco is the **Donatello** (formerly the Pacific Plaza), 501 Post St. (at Mason Street), San Francisco, CA 94102 (tel. 415/441-7100, or toll free 800/227-3184, 800/792-9837 in California). The marble lobby is small but elegant, containing many antiques and a massive tapestry on one wall.

Many of the rooms also have walls adorned with tapestries. They're very large and are decorated in subdued colors, live plants adding a homey touch. Amenities include extra-length beds, remote-control TVs, clock radios, robes for each guest, and free local phone calls. With some hotels in town charging a dollar a call, this is a welcome bonus.

Donatello, the hotel restaurant, has gained a good reputation in the city; local patrons fill the place at breakfast and dinner. The menu is à la carte and features classic northern Italian cuisine. Pasta is excellent here and can be enjoyed as an appetizer preceding entrees like quail and boneless squab. Entrees range from $20 to $28. Cocktails are served in the lounge daily from 11 a.m. to 1 a.m.

Single rates range from $175 to $250, and doubles run $195 to $250. Suites range from $345 to $550. Parking is available for $17 a day, with in-and-out privileges.

THE UPPER BRACKET: The **Inn at the Opera,** 333 Fulton St. (near Franklin), San Francisco, CA 94102 (tel. 415/863-8400, or toll free 800/325-2708, 800/423-9610 in California), is a unique part of San Francisco's cultural heritage. Originally built over 50 years ago to cater to visiting opera stars, the Inn recently was transformed into a small (48 rooms) luxury hotel situated at the heart of San Francisco's creative center—only steps from the Opera House and Davies Hall. The Inn still caters to many performing artists.

Approaching the Inn is like stepping into another, more gracious age, with its portico, the flower boxes, polished brass, curtained windows, and carpet to the door. The interior of this jewel is every bit as handsome as the entry implies. The reception area is light and airy with European furnishings, soft pastel colors, and a floral French area rug in warm, delicate browns, pinks, and greens. At the desk you'll find apples, along with the fresh flowers and old brass inkwells. There's an elegance, classic beauty, and intimacy difficult to find in the best of the luxury hotels, and concerned attention to needs.

Each room in the Inn reflects the same feeling of warmth. Subtle tones of green and beige complement finely checked drapes and huge stuffed pillows in floral prints, some edged with the drapery design. But the comfort of the room is only the beginning. There's a well-stocked refrigerator with wines, patés, soda, and other gourmet items, and there are wine glasses on the wet bar. Other pleasant amenities are the terrycloth robes you'll find in the armoire and the chocolates placed on your pillow before you turn in.

One of the true joys of the Inn at the Opera is the Act IV Lounge, whether you're dining or lounging. The broad, deep-brown, teal, and green Rousseau-like floral wall tapestry enhances the warm woods and green velvet and leather chairs. And the plump throw cushions can induce you to spend the evening in total comfort on overstuffed sofas. Sitting at the handsome mahogany bar is a pleasure. The bar chairs are both good-looking and comfortable. In the evening, the fireplace and the music of the pianist at the grand piano give the lounge a quiet intimacy. Act IV is open daily for dining from 6:30 to 11 a.m. and dinner from 5:30 to 10 p.m. An après-theater menu is served until 1 a.m.—a flawless last act after the ballet, opera, or the theater. Sunday brunch is served from 10:30 a.m. to 3:30 p.m. The continental menu is excellent, offering a good range of entrees, moderately priced. Quite simply, it's a delight you'll savor at all times.

Whether you're a romantic or one who simply enjoys the attention, charm, luxury, and quiet of an elegant, small hotel, the Inn at the Opera is highly recommended. Guest rooms range from $105 to $135 for single or double occupancy; suites are $145 to $195. The Inn will obtain tickets to the opera, symphony, or ballet.

A handsome four-story hotel, reminiscent of an English garden inn, the **White Swan Inn,** 845 Bush St. (between Taylor and Mason), San Francisco, CA 94108 (tel. 415/775-1755), has charm, serenity, and style, and it's geared to fill the needs of the most sophisticated traveler. It's an enchanting discovery in an era of cost efficiencies.

The hotel was originally constructed in the early 1900s and recently renovated by Four Sisters Inc. A handsome reception area boasts a cheery fireplace, a carousel horse (Sir Winston) with a handsome but nameless teddy bear astride, an antique oak breakfront, plants, soft chairs—all surrounded by rich warm woods.

There are 27 rather spacious rooms in all, each with its own teddy bear companion. Softly colored English wallpaper and floral-print bedspreads add to the feeling of warmth and comfort. As for the more utilitarian details, each room has a wet bar with a refrigerator, a working fireplace (especially welcome on crisp San Francisco days), private bath with fluffy oversize towels, color TV, and bedside telephone. There is turndown service in the evening, a morning newspaper at your door when you arise, and if you put your shoes outside the door at night, you will wake to find them polished.

Each morning a generous breakfast is served in a lovely common room just off a tiny garden. High tea is also served, and includes hors d'oeuvres, sherry, wine, and home-baked pastries. You can have your sherry in front of the fireplace while you browse through the books in the library.

The White Swan Inn will also arrange reservations for restaurants, theaters, sports, and special events, and for limousine service, if needed.

Just 2½ blocks from Union Square, 2 blocks from Nob Hill, and 1½ blocks from the Powell Street cable car, the inn is excellently located. Rooms are $150 to $165, double occupancy; $15 for an extra person. The Ashleigh suite is $260 and offers a large separate sitting room in addition to the sleeping quarters. Valet parking can be arranged at $15 per day.

On the scene for over half a century, the superbly located **Sir Francis Drake,** right on Union Square at Sutter and Powell Streets, San Francisco, CA 94101 (tel. 415/392-7755, or toll free 800/227-5480, 800/652-1668 in California), offers quality service and tasteful surroundings. The lobby sets the elegant tone, with richly carpeted marble floors, marble and mirrored walls, 30-foot-high vaulted ceilings with gold-leaf trim, and crystal chandeliers.

Crusty's Café offers reasonably priced full dinners nightly. And there's dancing nightly, as well as cocktails and complimentary hors d'oeuvres served from 4 p.m. on the Starlite Roof, 21 stories up.

The 415 rooms are handsomely furnished. You get an AM/FM clock radio, and first-run movies are available on the color TV. Single rooms are $110 to $180; doubles and twins are $130 to $200, suites $280 to $550.

Just across from the Drake is the excellent **Holiday Inn Union Square,** 480 Sutter St. (at Powell), San Francisco, CA 94108 (tel. 415/398-8900, or toll free 800/464-4329). The 400 rooms (mostly double-doubles or king-size) are attractively decorated in muted earth tones and have large bay windows. Of course, all the expected conveniences are on tap, right down to an AM/FM clock radio and first-run movies on your color TV.

A rooftop cocktail lounge is seemingly a San Francisco hotel prerequisite; this one's on the 30th floor and is called S. Holmes Esquire. It features a private collection of Holmes memorabilia and a posh decor with backgammon tables, velvet furnishings, and wood-burning fireplaces. There's a pubby eatery on the premises too, the White Elephant, complete with framed foxhunting prints on the walls and items like prime rib on the menu.

Rates are $130 to $140 single, $145 to $160 double; children 12 and under stay free in their parents' room.

A unique kind of luxury accommodation is offered at the **Miyako Hotel,** 1625 Post St. (at Laguna, in Japan Center), San Francisco, CA 94115 (tel. 415/922-3200, or toll free 800/533-4567)—a first-class Japanese hotel just a mile from the heart of downtown. Here your room, decorated in shades of gold and subtle autumn hues, will feature shoji screens, wood paneling, delicate watercolors or scrolls, and a *tokonoma*—an alcove for flowers, a bowl, or perhaps a statue of the Buddha. Rooms also have direct-dial phones, clocks, AM/FM radios, color TVs, and whatever other accoutrements of modern living you might expect.

Most of the bathrooms have Japanese sunken tubs, wherein you'll find instructions on how to take a Japanese bath; a packet of Beta bath powder, which turns the water a tranquil green, adds refreshing fragrance, and softens the skin. There are showers too, for those not in the mood for a ritual bath. Some accommodations also have built-in saunas, and most have balconies.

Four rooms and two suites are entirely Japanese in decor. Here you sleep on the floor on Japanese beds called *futons*—downy quilts laid out on tatami mats. In the suites there's even a bamboo and rock garden in your room. Ceilings are wood paneled and there are fusuma screens and shoji panels. Most Japanese prefer the hotel's American-style accommodations, but I think the Japanese rooms are exquisite and romantic, as do many Westerners; if you want them, reserve far in advance.

A brand-new elegant lobby restaurant serves a combination Continental-Japanese cuisine. The waitresses dress in kimonos, and service is swift and smiling.

Single rooms here are $100 to $150; doubles and twins run $130 to $170. Japanese suites are $215 to $350 a night for one or two persons.

Although I've stressed the downtown area, many tourists prefer to stay near Fisherman's Wharf, a part of San Francisco chock-full of visitor attractions, because of which prices tend to be higher than those elsewhere. The upper-bracket hotel of choice in this part of town is the **Sheraton At Fisherman's Wharf,** 2500

Mason St. (at Beech Street), San Francisco, CA 94133 (tel. 415/362-5500, or toll free 800/325-3535), a modernistic stucco hostelry with tree-lined court-yards that looks ever so much like a Vail ski condominium.

The interior, also ski-lodgey, sports a good deal of raw redwood paneling. Facilities include a glass-enclosed sidewalk café called Chanen's Windowbox; one lounge, Chanen's (a Victorian-style piano lounge with entertainment); the Mason Beach Grill restaurant specializing in beef; shops; and an outdoor heated swimming pool with sundeck for the polar-bear set.

The 525 rooms are attractively done in soft pastel color schemes. All have every accoutrement right down to in-room movies on the television and AM/FM clock radio; in the bathroom you'll find extra-thick towels and 24-hour room service.

The rates: $110 to $160 single, $120 to $200 double.

Every year in San Francisco a growing number of elegant old apartment buildings and Victorian dwellings are converted into inns, bed-and-breakfast hostelries, and small but luxurious hotels. Most are in the deluxe or upper-bracket categories, and are immensely popular. It's a trend I heartily commend, because it offers visitors an ever-increasing choice of accommodations.

One such enterprise is Bob and Marily Kavanaughs' **Bed & Breakfast Inn, 4** Charlton Court (off Union Street, between Buchanan and Laguna), San Francisco, CA 94123 (tel. 415/921-9784). Their charming Victorian house is a European-style luxury pensione with a country-inn feel. Each of the ten rooms is charmingly decorated—perhaps in *Casablanca* motif with rattan furnishings and an overhead ceiling fan, perhaps with cherished family antiques. Each is provided with fresh flowers and fruit, live plants, books and magazines, down pillows, a clock, and a Thermos of ice water. Rooms with bath have color TV and plug-in phones if desired, and the bathless accommodations open onto a lovely enclosed garden with Cinzano umbrella tables. The Kavanaughs are a friendly couple who delight in offering gracious service to their guests. Breakfast (fresh-baked croissants, orange juice, and coffee, fancy teas, or cocoa) is served in a sunny flower-bedecked dining room decorated with framed English prints; you can also have it brought to your room with the morning paper. Sherry is available at all times. There's also a library for guests, with a backgammon table and a writing desk.

Rooms with shared bath cost $73 to $90 a night, single or double, the higher prices for larger, more luxurious accommodations. Rooms with private bath are priced at $123 to $194, the latter for an entire flat with a complete kitchen, a private plant-filled latticed terrace, a bedroom up a spiral staircase, and a double-tub bath. Rates include breakfast.

San Francisco has some of the finest hotels in the United States, in all categories, but it excels when it comes to small inns. The **Petite Auberge,** 863 Bush St. (between Mason and Taylor), San Francisco, CA 94108 (tel. 415/928-6000), is the *crème de la crème.* It's a small place, with only 26 rooms of varying sizes, all decorated in French country style with floral wallpapers, antiques, quilts, and lacy throw pillows. Eighteen rooms have fireplaces and bathrooms with tubs; one of these is a suite with Jacuzzi tub, wet bar, private entry, and private deck. The other eight rooms (some of them quite small) have shower bathrooms. All rooms have direct-dial phones, and cable color TVs concealed in armoires. Other amenities include a selection of shampoos, conditioners, and bath gels, a daily newspaper, shoeshining service, afternoon sherry and hors d'oeuvres, and a hearty morning breakfast consisting of eggs, cereals, muffins, croissants, breads, yogurts, fresh fruits and juices, coffee and tea. Coffee, tea, and soda are also available around the clock.

The Petite Auberge staff is friendly and always willing to help with reservations, plans, and even valet parking, available at a nearby security garage (for $17 a night).

Rooms at the Petite Auberge cost $110 to $170, single or double; the suite rents for $205. An extra person pays $15.

The **Queen Anne Hotel,** just a mile from Union Square at 1590 Sutter (at Octavia), San Francisco, CA 94109 (tel. 415/441-2828, or toll free 800/227-3970, 800/262-2663 in California), looks exactly like what it is—a handsomely restored Victorian mansion. At the turn of the century, in its first life, the building was Miss Mary Lake's School for Girls; later it became a private gentlemen's club, then returned to its original gender as the Girl's Friendly Society Lodge. After a complete renovation and restoration, it opened as the Queen Anne in 1981.

The English-oak-panelled lobby is furnished in antiques; inside, 49 unique rooms manage to preserve a turn-of-the-century atmosphere while providing all modern conveniences. Each room has been individually decorated: some have corner turret bay windows that look out on tree-lined streets, as well as separate parlor areas and wet bars; others have cozy reading nooks and fireplaces. All rooms have telephones with extensions in the bathroom and remote-control color TV. The Queen Anne provides complimentary continental breakfast, brought to your room along with the morning's newspaper. Complimentary afternoon tea and sherry are served in the parlor from 4 to 6 p.m.

Rates range from $95 to $150, and weekly rates are available.

A converted 19th-century Edwardian home is the setting for Helen Stewart's **Union St. Inn,** 2229 Union St. (between Fillmore and Steiner), San Francisco, CA 94123 (tel. 415/346-0424). Ms. Stewart, a gracious hostess (one journalist described her as looking "as if she spent her life sipping tea in a velvet-walled drawing room"), treats guests as she might in her own home. The parlor here actually is velvet walled (it also has a fireplace), and guests wandering into it are likely to be offered wine, hors d'oeuvres, even homemade pâté. Breakfast is served in the parlor, although you can also have it served in your room or out on a terrace overlooking a rustic garden of lemon and plum trees. The six exquisitely furnished rooms have brass or canopied beds, tasteful art and antiques, live plants, and fresh flowers. All have sinks, and two have private baths. The newest room, the Carriage House, has a private bathroom with a Jacuzzi. Some have multipaned bay windows overlooking the garden. There are no TVs, but phones are available upon request.

Rates, including breakfast (fresh-baked croissants, fresh-squeezed orange juice, homemade kiwi or plum jam, and coffee), are $85 to $185, single or double.

MODERATELY PRICED ACCOMMODATIONS: If the feeling of an English country inn, or breakfast with scones and crumpets is your style, the small (62-room) **Abigail Hotel,** at 246 McAllister St. (near Larkin), San Francisco, CA 94102 (tel. 415/861-9728, or toll free 800/243-6510, 800/553-5575 in California), British owned, may be your pot of tea. What the Abigail lacks in luxury it more than makes up for in charm. The hotel's handsome white exterior, with its canopy and polished brass, seems to have been plucked from London and set down two blocks from the San Francisco Opera. Enter and you'll find a small desk, Oriental area rugs, polished woods, ceiling-to-floor white drapes, and wicker straight-back chairs at red-clothed tables in the breakfast area, all reflecting a very English aura. However, don't be astounded at the hunting trophies in the lobby—they're less from India than from auction.

The guest rooms carry out the English tone with blue floral drapes, white curtains, old prints, and an occasional antique table or lamp. Most rooms are quite light and quiet, though you might inquire when making your reservations. All have the usual amenities of a Touch-Tone telephone, color television, and private bath. Valet service is available. J. A. Melon's Restaurant and Bar adjoins the hotel.

Single rooms are $57 to $67; doubles, $68 to $73; and suites, $160. There is an additional charge of $8 for an extra person.

Hotel Vintage Court, 650 Bush St. (between Powell and Stockton), San Francisco, CA 94108 (tel. 415/392-4666, or toll free 800/654-1100, 800/654-7266 in California), is a handsome European-style hotel conveniently situated one block from Union Square and the cable car. It's a relatively small establishment (106 rooms), which allows for the personal touch in service.

As you enter the hotel, the classically comfortable armchairs, fireplace, flowers, and warm brown tones of the furnishings create an intimate, cozy feeling. The decor of the rooms has the same character. Floral prints on the bedspreads and drapes are complemented by white furnishings and framed floral prints. Each room has a private refrigerator and mini-bar stocked daily, as well as the usual color television and Touch-Tone phones. Complimentary tea and coffee are served in the morning, and wine in the evening. For a day in the country to write home about, the hotel can arrange to introduce you to the nearby wine country.

The charm and popularity of this hotel require that reservations be made at least two to three weeks in advance. Rates are $94 for all rooms—single, double, and twin.

The famous Masa's restaurant adjoins the hotel, but each is a separate operation.

It would be hard to find a more convenient place to stay than the **Villa Florence,** 225 Powell St. (near Geary), San Francisco, CA 94102 (tel. 415/397-7700, or toll free 800/553-4411, 800/243-5700 in California, 800/345-8455 in Canada). It's ideal for anyone who wants to be in beautifully appointed surroundings in the center of the downtown area, near Union Square.

On the Powell Street cable car line with easy access to Fisherman's Wharf, the hotel lies two blocks in any direction from the heart of the financial district, the Moscone Convention Center, or the BART and MUNI stations. It's adjacent to Saks Fifth Avenue, Macy's, Neiman Marcus, and enough specialty shops to satisfy the heart of the most dedicated shopper.

The Villa Florence, opened in May 1986, is the superb result of a $6.5-million renovation of what once was the turn-of-the-century Manx Hotel. As soon as you enter the hotel, you'll have an idea of the magnificent refurbishing job done throughout: the arched entryway, graceful palms, marble columns, murals of Florence, huge marble fireplace, rich maroon upholstered chairs, Etruscan-style table lamps, giant urns on pedestals, fresh flowers, and maroon-and-tan floral carpet all reflect an aura of Italian grandeur.

The beautiful, elegant bedrooms feature pink-and-blue floral chintz drapes and matching spreads, as well as white furnishings including very comfortable chairs. Though the rooms are a bit smaller than most, the décor and the high ceilings afford a feeling of airiness. All modern amenities grace the rooms—color TVs and pull-out writing tables concealed in the chest of drawers, direct-dial phones, and well-stocked honor-bar/refrigerators. The bath has makeup mirror lighting, overhead heat lamps, hand-milled soap—some of life's little pleasures for your convenience and comfort.

There are 177 rooms in all, including junior and deluxe suites. Rooms are $97, single or double occupancy, Junior suites are $114; deluxe suites, $154.

If there were nothing more to be said about the Villa Florence, its price and location would be enough to consider it an exceptional buy. However, as you enter the hotel, you'll notice a dining area to your left separated from the main body of the hotel by glass walls elegantly etched with simple shell designs. Beyond the dining area is Kuleto's, the northern Italian restaurant with specialties from Tuscany. See the "Restaurant" section of this chapter for details of this gem.

I suspect that Thomas Jefferson would have been pleased with the **Monticello Inn**, 127 Ellis St. (between Cyril Magnin and Powell), San Francisco, CA 94102 (tel. 415/392-8800, or toll free 800/669-7777). Opened in September 1987—a renovation of a 1906 building—it's a first-rate addition to the neighborhood. Certainly the only early-American influence near Union Square, it's attractive, beautifully decorated, and exceptionally reasonable.

The Monticello Inn recreates colonial American charm at the San Francisco frontier. The spacious lobby is replete with Early American reproductions hanging on Williamsburg blue walls, a Federal-period desk, a stately grandfather clock, fresh floral displays, and, to the rear, a charming parlor where you can enjoy a late afternoon glass of sherry by the fireplace.

Each of the 91 rooms features the country colonial luxury and elegance of canopied beds, with spreads in light blue, pale-yellow, and peach floral prints, and upholstered chairs to match. Baths are spacious and afford all the amenities one expects in a fine hotel. And for the peace and quiet of a superb night's rest, the rooms are thoroughly soundproofed. There's also a stocked honor-bar and refrigerator in each room, color TV with remote control, and digital clock/radio. In-room videos are available.

The inn provides complimentary continental breakfast and evening wine service at the cozy fireplace in the parlor, as well as complimentary limousine service to the financial district. Same-day laundry and valet service are available. For those with cars, the in-house parking is a real blessing in this part of town. Nondrivers will find the inn quite conveniently located—it's two blocks from Union Square and a half-block from the Powell Street cable car.

Guest rates are $94, single or double occupancy; suites are $114 to $123. Should you need information of any sort, the young, friendly staff is very helpful.

The Corona Bar & Grill, adjacent to the hotel and at the corner of Ellis and Cyril Magnin, opened in November 1987. You will find this extraordinary restaurant discussed in the next section of this chapter; don't miss it.

Right in the center of everything, just one block from Union Square, cable cars, and shops, the **King George Hotel**, 334 Mason St. (near Geary), San Francisco, CA 94102 (tel. 415/781-5050, or toll free 800/227-4240, 800/556-4545 in California), is another European-style renovation. Across from the stage door of the Geary Theater, the hotel is entered via a pleasant lobby with an air of country charm with its green and white decor and collection of European period prints.

On the mezzanine above the lobby, the Bread & Honey Tearoom serves a bountiful light breakfast. Every afternoon, except Sundays, a piano recital accompanies a proper high tea complete with scones, trifle, tea sandwiches, and assorted pastries.

Remarkable as it may seem, there's a Japanese restaurant, Ichirin, adjacent to the premises; you'll find a detailed discussion of this excellent eatery in the "Restaurant" section of this chapter.

The hotel also has a most comfortable cocktail lounge and nightly piano bar.

The 143 rooms have all been redone in cheery colors and equipped with color TVs, direct-dial phones, and private baths. Laundry, valet, and room service are available. Parking is conveniently located directly across the street.

Rooms range from $79 to $85.

The **Commodore International**, 825 Sutter St. (at Jones), San Francisco,

CA 94109 (tel. 415/923-6800, or toll free 800/327-9157), built in 1920, welcomes guests in a warmly old-fashioned lobby, replete with a ticking grandfather clock.

The 113 rooms have all been redecorated and provided with full baths and large wardrobes, as well as direct dial phones and color TVs.

Just off the lobby is a pleasant coffeeshop-restaurant-cocktail lounge, open daily for breakfast and lunch. Some of the city's most famous restaurants are less than two blocks away.

The hotel is centrally located, four blocks from Union Square and five blocks from Chinatown.

Rates are $45 to $65 single; doubles and twins run $50 to $90.

Billing itself as San Francisco's "little elegant hotel," the **Raphael**, 386 Geary St. (at Mason, one block from Union Square), San Francisco, CA 94102 (tel. 415/986-2000, or toll free 800/821-5343), provides quite luxurious accommodations at moderate prices. Its 155 rooms occupy 12 stories, and the door to each is individually hand-painted, making for very cheerful hallways. Each interior is uniquely attractive. All rooms have two phones, color TV with HBO, AM/FM radio, individually controlled air conditioning/heating, clock, makeup mirror, and 21-hour room service. Mama's restaurant and cocktail lounge adjoins. Of course, there are also hundreds of eateries within walking distance. Singles are $77 to $98, doubles $90 to $111.

I was attracted to the **Lombard Hotel**, 1015 Geary St. (at Polk Street), San Francisco, CA 94109 (tel. 415/673-5232). From the outside, it resembles the kind of hostelry you might expect to find on a fashionable London street. The lobby houses a small restaurant, the Gray Derby, where delectable continental meals (daily at breakfast and lunch; dinner on Thursday, Friday, and Saturday; and weekend champagne brunch) are served by waiters in formal attire. The other part of the marble-floored lobby, boasting a grand piano and fireplace, is the perfect setting for an afternoon drink.

The 100 rooms are all newly decorated in terracotta or brown shades, and most feature king- or queen-size beds. All have color TVs, phones, and private baths with tubs and/or showers. The hotel is located about six blocks from Union Square and three blocks from the Civic Center.

The Lombard's rates are $76 to $80, single or double.

The **Andrews Hotel**, 624 Post St. (near Taylor), San Francisco, CA 94109 (tel. 415/563-6877, or toll free 800/227-4742, 800/622-0557 within California), has 48 charming rooms and evokes the casual atmosphere of a country inn, yet is just two blocks west of Union Square. Rooms are furnished with California gypsy willow chairs and tables and oak-framed mirrors, beds are covered with European spreads, and lace curtains grace the bay windows. Amenities include fresh flowers, private baths with tubs and/or showers, phones, and color TVs. Kimberly Higgins is a warm and friendly host, and the rest of the staff emulates her courtesy. One of the nicest things about the Andrews is the adjoining Post Street Bar and Café (see the "Restaurant" section of this chapter for details).

Rates at the Andrews are $71 to $81 for a single or double, and $97 to $101 for the petite suites. All include complimentary continental breakfast and a glass of wine in the evening.

An attractive establishment on the "motel strip" that stretches from the Golden Gate Bridge to Van Ness Avenue is the **Chelsea Motor Inn**, 2095 Lombard St. (at Fillmore), San Francisco, CA 94123 (tel. 415/563-5600). Opened in May 1982, this 60-room motor inn is perfectly located for a stroll along Union Street, and there are restaurants at almost every turn.

Rooms are very comfortable and pleasantly decorated in shades of rust, blue, or brown. Each is equipped with a color TV, tub/shower combination bath, and phone. Parking is free, and buses run regularly to almost every part of the city.

Rates are $70 to $85 single, $75 to $95 double.

Under the same ownership are the **Cow Hollow Motor Inn,** 2190 Lombard St. (at Steiner), San Francisco, CA 94123 (tel. 415/921-5800), and the **Coventry Motor Inn,** 1901 Lombard St. (at Buchanan), San Francisco, CA 94123 (tel. 415/567-1200). Accommodations and prices are similar to those at the Chelsea.

Among the more reasonable establishments near Union Square the **Handlery Union Square Hotel,** 351 Geary St. (between Mason and Powell), San Francisco, CA 94102 (tel. 415/781-7800, or toll free 800/223-0888, 800/522-5455 in New York) is the product of a merger of two names (Hotel Stewart and Handlery Motor Inn) and the completion of a $3 million renovation in 1988. All the guest rooms at the Hotel Stewart, now simply called the hotel section, were totally renovated and refurbished.

What had been The Handlery Motor Inn is now The Handlery Club—the concierge section of the new hotel which has managed to maintain reasonable rates, although it now offers services one usually expects from a larger hotel. Rooms in the club are truly large and luxurious. They include such frills as bedside remote-control color TV (with movies available), electric shoe polishers, coffee makers, in-room safes, dressing rooms with makeup mirrors, Vidal Sassoon bathroom amenities, and balconies. The merged facilities still include a large, heated outdoor swimming pool and sauna. The shopping, theater, and financial districts are easily accessible from this location, which is half a block from Union Square. The hotel offers overnight valet parking, truly a bargain at $8.

Rates in the hotel section are $75 to $90 single, $84 to $99 double. Rates in the Handlery Club are $120 single, $135 double.

Built in 1924, the 17-story **Hotel Californian,** 405 Taylor St. (at O'Farrell), San Francisco, CA 94102 (tel. 415/885-2500, or toll free 800/227-3346, 800/622-0961 within California), offers an ideal location two blocks from Union Square, a block from the airline bus terminal, and accommodations that have been carefully maintained and frequently refurbished. The gracious lobby has a beamed and stenciled ceiling, ornate columns, elegant draperies, and a charming brick fireplace. The rooms have white walls and furniture with colorful drapes and bedspreads. All have color TVs, direct-dial phones, and tub/shower combination baths.

A tour desk, car-rental office, and barbershop are on the premises, and so is Dudley's Bar and Grill, open for breakfast, lunch, and dinner; and Mrs. Edwards famous coffeeshop, open for breakfast and lunch.

The staff here can manage eight languages, and hotel services/tourist information are described in English, Spanish, French, and Japanese.

Room rates at the Californian are $66 to $75 single, $75 to $85 double or twin.

Conveniently located in San Francisco's tiny theater district, the **Bellevue,** 505 Geary St., at Taylor Street, San Francisco, CA 94102 (tel. 415/474-3600, or toll free 800/421-8851, 800/532-8800 within California), is a popular and well-maintained establishment. Off the elegant lobby—replete with gold and crystal chandeliers—a magnificent carpeted staircase simply begs for a dramatic descent. Rooms are attractively furnished and have shag carpeting, tile baths with tub and shower, direct-dial phones, color TVs, and radios. The Yum Yum Coffee Shop, open from 6 a.m. to 10 p.m., and the Belle Tavern cocktail lounge are on the premises, as are men's and women's hair salons, and a car-rental service.

Rates are $59 to $98 single, $68 to $104 double and twin and $95 to $165 for suites.

Ironically, since it's located at the gateway to Chinatown, the **Beverly Plaza Hotel,** 342 Grant Avenue at Bush Street, San Francisco, CA 94108 (tel. 415/781-3566, or toll free 800/227-3818, 800/652-1535 in California), has made considerable effort to court Japanese visitors. Brochures and guidebooks in Japanese can be obtained in the lobby, and the Midori Restaurant has a Japanese menu, decor, and staff.

Rooms are decorated in shades of blue and green, with matching floral-print drapes and spreads, color TVs with movies available, and direct-dial phones color coordinated to your room decor. Other facilities include a handy electric map in the lobby (like the ones in the Paris Métro).

The friendly staff and concerned management here are noteworthy. Room rates—very good value for the money—are $60 to $65 single, $68 to $72 double and twin. Suites are $105 to $160.

Under the same ownership, but exhibiting no pull to the East, is the **Hotel Cecil,** 545 Post St. (between Mason and Taylor), San Francisco, CA 94102 (tel. 415/673-3733, or toll free 800/227-3818, 800/652-1535 within California), offering a superb location, comfortable accommodations, and a friendly staff. Furnished in French provincial style, the newly decorated rooms are pretty and clean. They have cheerful tile baths, Touch-Tone phones, and color TVs with available in-room movies.

If you feel like a little sun, there's a sundeck and cabaña on the seventh floor. For refreshments there's a comfortable cocktail lounge on the premises. Parking in a nearby garage is $13 a night with in-and-out privileges.

Note: As we go to press, the Cecil is closed for complete renovations and will re-open in early summer 1989.

Single rooms are $58 to $75; doubles and twins, $70 to $80; triples, $90 to $100.

As of this writing, there are plans for renowned chef and entrepreneur Wolfgang Puck to open a restaurant (as yet unnamed) at the hotel. Puck will own a one-third interest in the restaurant and will be supervising the kitchen and doing the menu. Noted restaurant designer Pat Kuleto (of Kuleto's in the Villa Florence, the Fog City Diner, and Corona Bar & Grill, to name a few) will be responsible for the interior. Puck's intent is to create a contemporary San Franciscan style based on the city's culinary heritage. Look for it (though if prior experience is any indication, the crowds will lead you there).

Step into the lobby of the **Hotel Beresford,** 635 Sutter St. (at Mason), San Francisco, CA 94102 (tel. 415/673-9900), and you'll find yourself in a Victorian drawing room with gaslight lamps, flocked wallpaper, and a gilt-framed portrait of Lord Beresford overlooking the scene. This delightful European-style hostelry is the homiest in town, from the flowerboxes adorning the street windows to the friendly staff offering good old-fashioned service. There's a writing parlor off the lobby with wicker furniture, desks, and a color TV.

Rooms have white drapes, white Valley Forge bedspreads, stippled shag rugs, baths with tubs and/or showers, color TVs, and direct-dial phones.

The White Horse Taverne, here, reputedly an authentic replica of an old English Pub, contains an antique bedwarmer and an ancient crossbow hung over the fireplace. A congenial pub, the White Horse also offers home-cooked breakfasts and lunches; they use only fresh produce and fresh-caught fish.

If you like European charm—and who doesn't?—this well-located hotel is a good choice. Rates are $60 single, $65 double; family doubles accommodating three are $70, or $75 for four.

No room at the Beresford? Try the nearby **Beresford Arms,** 701 Post St. (at Jones), San Francisco, CA 94109 (tel. 415/673-2600), equally European in ambience and run in the same friendly way by the same owners. Many of the 87 rooms here have fully equipped kitchens; all are immaculate and homey, equipped with color TVs, direct-dial phones, and tub/shower baths. A recent renovation has produced several Jacuzzi suites featuring queen-size beds, baths with brass fixtures, and antique furnishings from the 18th and 19th centuries. Rates are the same as at the Beresford, except for the Jacuzzi suites which also have kitchen units or wet bars and rent for $80. Parlor suites are $105.

Similarly charming and well situated is the **Cartwright Hotel,** 524 Sutter St. (at Powell Street), San Francisco, CA 94102 (tel. 415/421-2865, or toll free 800/227-3844), a cozy little place where the owners and management take pride in its reputation for comfort and efficiency—a pride that is reflected in every nook and cranny. Rooms sparkle with cleanliness; each is unique in size, shape, decor, and antique furnishings. All are brightened with fresh flowers and have pretty matching spreads and drapes, private bathrooms, with shower massage and thick fluffy towels, direct-dial phones, color TVs, and little extra touches that add to guests' comfort—a third sheet to insulate skin from the roughness of blankets, turndown service, and the availability of such items as irons, hair dryers, and large reading pillows. Complimentary tea and cakes are served in the lobby from 4 to 6 p.m.

There's a little restaurant at the Cartwright too: the charming French-provincial Teddy's serves delicious breakfasts and light lunches.

Singles at the Cartwright cost $75 to $80, doubles and twins run $81 to $90, and family suites accommodating up to four people cost $135 to $155.

The **Hotel Savoy,** 580 Geary St. (between Taylor and Jones), San Francisco, CA 94102 (tel. 415/441-2700, or toll free 800/227-4223, 800/622-0553 within California), is a delightful little place, just three blocks from Union Square. Rooms here have antique or antique-style furnishings and a variety of pastel color schemes. Corner rooms are especially nice; they have lots of windows, and are light and airy. The little extras are in evidence here—full-length mirrors, triple sheets, turndown service—along with direct-dial phones (there is a charge for local calls), color TVs, and modern bathrooms. The Savoy has no restaurant, but the complimentary continental breakfast can be served in your room or in the Savoy lounge. Other extra touches include complimentary late afternoon tea and sherry, and weekly newspapers. The staff is friendly and helpful, full of smiles for guests and visitors.

Rooms at the Savoy rent for $67 to $80 single, $77 to $90 double or twin. Suites are available from $120.

Another charming hostelry is the **Bedford,** 761 Post St. (between Leavenworth and Jones), San Francisco, CA 94109 (tel. 415/673-6040, or toll free 800/227-5642, 800/652-1889 within California). The hotel is three blocks from Union Square on the southwest slope of Nob Hill. Each of its 144 redecorated rooms is brightly painted in shades of yellow, gray, and white, with color-coordinated drapes and skirted beds. All have color TVs, a video tape player, fully stocked refrigerator/honor-bar, and direct-dial phones, and there are good views of the bay or the San Francisco skyline from the upper floors. In the white marble-floored lobby, the beautiful chandeliers of the past remain. Café Bedford, the elegant award-winning gourmet restaurant that serves breakfast and dinner, has open skylights, and six large ficus trees thrive in the sunlight that streams in. A multilingual staff, among them proficient in at least ten languages, is on hand to serve you. Room service is available, as is valet parking for overnight guests.

Rooms at the Bedford cost $95 for a single or double; suites begin at $150.

Under the same management is the **Galleria Park Hotel,** 191 Sutter St. (at Kearny), San Francisco, CA 94104 (tel. 415/781-3060, or toll free 800/792-9639, 800/792-9855 within California). From its lobby, complete with fireplace, to its beautifully appointed 177 rooms and 15 suites, the Galleria Park has been totally restored in the art nouveau style of the time of its original construction. The hotel features a full-time concierge, room service, a bar, and a sundries shop. And the Galleria is the only hotel in San Francisco to have an outdoor running track and park. The hotel also features Bentley's Oyster Bar & Restaurant (under separate management) offering fresh seafood specialties, oysters at a grand-scale bar, and a diversity of other dishes.

Rooms at the Galleria Park let for $99 to $115, single or double. Suites begin at $140.

The **Hotel Union Square,** 114 Powell St. (at Ellis), San Francisco, CA 94102 (tel. 415/397-3000, or toll free 800/553-1900), located just a couple of blocks south of Union Square itself, dates from the early 20th century, when it was known as the Golden West. It's been renamed and renovated. There are 131 guest rooms with art deco decor and soft floral-print bedspreads and curtains. Shampoos, conditioners, bath gels, and soaps are supplied in the bathrooms. Each morning complimentary croissants and coffee are served in a small hall lounge on each floor and each evening there is turndown service.

The Union Square has no restaurant of its own, but two neighboring establishments, Tad's and Les Joulins, offer room service from 7 a.m. to 11 p.m. daily. And of course there are dozens of restaurants in the area. There's parking for guests' cars on the hotel property, at $12 a day.

Rates are $75 to $105, single or double. Penthouse suites with redwood decks and garden patio begin at $175.

A delightful example of the bed-and-breakfast inn in San Francisco is the **Albion House,** 135 Gough St. (at Lily), San Francisco, CA 94102 (tel. 415/621-0896). Built as a small hotel in 1907, it was remodeled under the aegis of innkeeper Richard Meyer. There are eight rooms here, including one two-room suite; each is decorated differently. Sonoma, for example, evokes the wine country with a double-size brass bed and floral prints; and Cypress, inspired by the Lone Cypress in Carmel, is decorated in tans and furnished with a queen-size bed. All rooms have telephones and private baths (the Garden Room's is across the hall); some rooms have color TV.

The heart of the Albion House is the common room, a large living room decorated in cool pinks with exposed redwood beams and a fireplace. Breakfast (included in the room prices) is served here every morning; you can feast on fresh-squeezed orange juice, croissants, eggs, and coffee.

Albion House is near the Symphony Hall, Opera House, and Civic Center, and convenient to the entire city via public transportation. If you come by car, there are inexpensive lots and garages nearby, as well as lots of overnight street parking in the area.

Rooms at the Albion House rent for $70 to $100, single or double, and $110 to $120 for suites.

The **El Cortez Hotel,** 550 Geary St. (near Taylor), San Francisco, CA 94102 (tel. 415/775-5000, or toll free 800/821-0493, 800/228-8830 in California), as the name and the arched entranceway indicate, is distinctly Spanish in flavor. The attractive, high-ceilinged lobby has white stucco walls, a ceramic tile floor, and graceful pillars. The 170 rooms are actually apartments, with kitchenettes, dressing rooms, tub/shower baths, and color TVs. They're also Spanish style, as are the stucco-walled hallways.

Surprisingly, the hotel's restaurant is not Spanish but French, and very elegantly French at that. Modeled after the hunting lodge of an actual French country estate, La Mère Duquesne has quaint wallpaper, brass chandeliers, many antiques, and hunting trophies.

The rates: singles are $55 to $57; doubles and twins, $63 to $70; suites, $160.

BUDGET HOTELS: The **Adelaide Inn,** 5 Adelaide Pl. (off Taylor Street), San Francisco, CA 94102 (tel. 415/441-2261), as billed, evokes memories of a European pensione and runs like one. The inn has 18 rooms on two floors above ground level and is situated on a tiny dead-end street conducive to peace and quiet.

There is no emphasis on decor inside the inn, but the travel and art prints make you feel as though you're on holiday in France. You may have to walk up two flights to your room, but rest assured that all rooms are clean, bright, and comfortable. There are no private baths, though all rooms have washing facilities and shared baths are well kept. Sorry, TV is black-and-white, and while there are no phones in the rooms, the inn will take messages.

The Adelaide Inn is a relaxed, pleasant place where guests quickly become friends. The hosts, Serge and Mary, are gracious fonts of information on almost any topic relating to your stay in San Francisco.

If hotel services are what you must have, this is not the place for you. However, if you'll accept simple, clean, and comfortable accommodations, it's hard to beat the price. Singles are $30 to $34 and doubles run $40 to $44, including continental breakfast.

Edward II Inn (read "the Second"), 3155 Scott St. (at Lombard), San Francisco, CA 94123 (tel. 415/922-3000), is among the newest and least expensive of San Francisco's inns. It has recently been transformed into a handsome forest-green and white bed-and-breakfast. Even the fire hydrant out front is a sparkling white.

The decor of the 32 rooms and suites is simple and charming, with quilted bedspreads, antique dressers, and white plantation shutters. There are black-and-white TVs in the rooms (color TV for those with a private bath), and all rooms now have phones.

The inn also has two luxuriously appointed suites and two carriage house suites complete with Jacuzzis and wet bars.

Upstairs, a skylight with a beautiful stained-glass panel offers an aesthetic experience; downstairs, a stained-glass door leads to more down-to-earth delights, connecting the lobby with the Cuneo Italian-French Bakery, where guests can enjoy a complimentary continental breakfast. The bakery also sells an impressive collection of calorie-rich pastries, but if you can't survive on pastry alone, you might try the Marina Cafe and Restaurant next door. The Marina offers a good selection of Italian and seafood specialties. A complimentary glass of wine is offered to the Inn's guests with dinner at the Marina Cafe.

Rooms, either single or double occupancy, are $47 to $52 with shared bath; $65 to $75, with private bath. Light sleepers should request rooms to the rear of the building. Suites are not in the "budget" category. Those with Jacuzzis are $135; carriage house suites are $160 or $210. Limited overnight parking close by is available for $8.

The location of the **Pacific Bay Inn,** 520 Jones St. (between Geary and O'Farrell), San Francisco, CA 94102 (tel. 415/673-0234, or toll free 800/445-2631)—just three blocks west of Union Square and the Powell Street cable car—is good, and so is the price.

This pleasant, recently renovated little place offers what it refers to as "no nonsense service." As you approach the hotel, it's easily identified by its blue-and-gold canopy resting on well-polished brass poles. The lobby is a cheery place with maroon-and-cream upholstered chairs and a small collection of palms, ficus trees, and other greenery.

Singles are $42.50; doubles, $47.50. Rates include a continental breakfast. The rooms are cozy, light (no view, but did you expect one at these prices?), done in an airy peach color with maroon floral-print spreads, and maroon-and-gray carpeting throughout. The rooms have showers only, no tubs. The inn has a 24-hour desk which can arrange services from a tour to a late-night pizza or a limousine. They also provide reduced-rate tickets for parking in the Taylor Street Garage, around the corner.

The Pacific Bay Inn is in what was once a rather frumpy neighborhood. It's still not Nob Hill, but the area is rapidly improving by virtue of the expansion of some of its neighbors—the new San Francisco Hilton Square and the very elegant Nikko Hotel.

If you want a really inexpensive, hearty meal, it's hard to beat the Family Inn across the street, open from 6:30 a.m. to 6 p.m. The menu varies daily, but homemade soups are part of the fare at lunch, and how can you beat pot roast, mashed potatoes, a vegetable, bread, and dessert—all for $3.75? Need I add that it's nothing in the least fancy—just counter seats, crowded, a hard-working kitchen in front of you—but the food is wholesome, good, and the price is right.

As of this writing, the **YWCA** at 620 Sutter St. (between Mason and Taylor), San Francisco, CA 94102 (tel. 415/775-6500), under reconstruction since 1987, has not yet re-opened, but it is expected to shortly. Those thinking about using their facilities should phone ahead. This YWCA is very centrally located, and while it has not had a restaurant, the area is flooded with them.

The downtown area also has a **YMCA Hotel,** at 166 Embarcadero St. (near Mission Street), San Francisco, CA 94105 (tel. 415/392-2191, or toll free 800/622-9622), and it is open to men, women, and families.

The 260 rooms are located on eight residential floors, and as one would expect, they are plainly furnished but provide the basic necessities. Baths are shared, those for women are on a separate floor. This YMCA does offer a somewhat more attractive look on the top floor—color-coordinated rooms with carpeting and solid-oak furniture.

Guests have access to a wide range of facilities, including a laundromat, TV recreation lounge, gymnasium and sauna, racquetball courts, and a swimming pool.

Singles start at $26, and doubles start at $37. The highest rate is for top-floor accommodations.

Unfortunately for those who always look for the economy and convenience of a **Motel 6,** there is not one to be found in San Francisco. However, don't despair: one is located in Palo Alto at 4301 El Camino Real, Palo Alto, CA 94306 (tel. 415/949-0833) near U.S. 101, and one in Oakland (discussed in detail in Chapter III). For the extra $1 in the basic room rate, and about the same drive time to San Francisco, I'd pick Palo Alto. The Motel 6 in Oakland is in an area I'd rather not stay in again.

If you don't mind a dormitory, none of the budget accommodations in San Francisco can beat the **San Francisco International Hostel,** Building 240, Fort Mason, San Francisco, CA 94123 (tel. 415/771-7277)—$9 a night. From Bay and Van Ness Streets, follow the hostel signs to the grounds of Fort Mason. Call for space from 7 a.m. to 2 p.m. and 4:30 p.m. until midnight. Anyone can use the dormitory, regardless of age. The only limitation to your stay is time—at the end of three nights you must move on to new lodgings. For families or compatible couples, there are three rooms with four bunks each, obviously in great demand.

Kitchen facilities are available, as are lockers, laundry facilities, snack-vending machines, and several community rooms with fireplaces, stereo, piano, and a wide selection of books. You'll also find several bulletin boards with information on tours and places to go during your stay.

4. RESTAURANTS

Only New York can surpass the quality, quantity, and ethnic variety of eateries in what Trader Vic (he lives here) once called "the city that knows chow" (a variation on President Taft's tribute to San Francisco—"the city that knows how").

What's your dining pleasure: Indonesian rijsttafel, Filipino chicken in adobo sauce, dim sum, Russian piroshky, or a chopped liver on rye? From acclaimed (and pricey) gourmet French cuisine to budget Basque, San Francisco has a place to please every palate. And the special savor of dining out in San Francisco is enhanced by California wines, which are frequently less costly than imported labels.

In the upcoming section I've selected over 50 of the city's 3,000-or-so restaurants, and ranged them according to price bracket, subdivided by nationality. I could easily add another hundred worthy establishments, but that would fill the whole book. Be sure, too, to consider the hotel restaurants recommended throughout the previous section as well as those discussed here. Particularly worthy choices are **Ristorante Donatello** at the Donatello Hotel (formerly the Pacific Plaza), and the **French Room** at the Clift.

As we go to press, I would be remiss in not mentioning the advent of a new restaurant (as yet unnamed) to be located at the Hotel Cecil (see "Hotel" section). If prior experience is any indication, the creations of the famous chef Wolfgang Puck will provide a new look to San Francisco's already famous cuisine.

LUXURY ESTABLISHMENTS: Splurge at least once during your visit at one of the following venerables. Several are highly acclaimed internationally, and each provides a dining experience par excellence—a romantic and memorable evening made up of sumptuous cuisine, distinguished service, and ambience. If your budget doesn't stretch to dinner, try lunch—at one of those places that serves lunch—same chef, same dishes, lower prices. Also notice that in some spots you can go early and get a full set dinner for the price that one entree might cost on the à la carte menu served later.

A final word about prices. They're in a permanent state of one-way flux— upward. Here as elsewhere. So while you will find most of the listed rates models of accuracy, you may discover unannounced increases by the time you get here. Don't blame me, please. With or without high inflation, prices do rise.

Masa's, 648 Bush St., between Powell and Stockton (tel. 989-7154), was started by Masataha Kobayashi, who left New York City for Auberge du Soleil in the Napa Valley, and ultimately opened Masa's in San Francisco. After his death in 1984 there was some question about the restaurant's survival. There is none now. The cuisine has been polished to a brilliance surpassing even the talents of Masa by chef Julian Serrano. Masa's is now regarded as one of the country's great French restaurants.

As you enter Masa's you can't help but be impressed by its elegant simplicity. There's obviously no need for decor to compete with the food. The chairs and carpeting are a quiet plum; the walls are buff, and small chandeliers are placed at useful and attractive intervals. You expect this to be the setting for great performances to come.

Dinner is prix fixe at $70—unquestionably expensive, but a memorable dining experience. Generally you may choose from among four appetizers, five entrees, and three or four desserts. The menu changes daily. You might begin the evening with the fresh foie gras sautéed with a sauce created from the pan juices, cognac, and black truffles. The entree of medallions of venison, marinated for several days in zinfandel, sautéed and served with a superb rich brown sauce, is a glory and unlike any other you've ever tasted. Should any one of several game birds be available as entrees, take advantage of the occasion to order it. Rarely have game birds been prepared as well by any other hand. I don't know how to extol the beauties of a salade mélange au fromage other than to say don't pass it by. The dessert, whether sorbet, frozen soufflé, or a special combination of sorbets and mousse, will be among the best endings to any meal you've ever had.

As you might expect, Masa's wine list is selective and includes some excellent older French wines as well as an impressive group of California wines. You'll also be pleased to discover that the quality of the service happily matches that of the dinner.

Reservations are taken up to 21 days in advance. It may be difficult to get a weekend reservation if you wait until a day or two ahead of time; if you have your heart set on a Friday or Saturday night dinner, phone ahead from whatever city you're in. If you wonder whether Masa's is worth the price or the advance reservation date, it may be one of the very few restaurants in the country that is.

Masa's is open for dinner only, Tuesday to Saturday from 6 p.m., with last seating at 10 p.m.

Another of San Francisco's prestigious and elegant restaurants, **Ernie's**, 847 Montgomery St., at Pacific (tel. 397-5969), proffers distinguished continental fare in suitably plush surroundings. The decor is ornate Victorian; the intimate parlor and massive mahogany and stained-glass bar so exquisite, it would be a shame not to enjoy a quiet drink before dinner. At any rate, Ernie's is an experience to be slowly savored. Many of the furnishings here originally adorned San Francisco's extravagant turn-of-the-century mansions.

And unlike many restaurants in this category, where the quality of the haute cuisine is only matched by the icy hauteur of the staff, the maître d' and waiters at Ernie's are actually polite and friendly.

The menu is à la carte, and every dish is excellent. I'd suggest a dinner starting with caviar of eggplant, followed by scallops ragoût in cilantro fumet, and then roasted squab and braised cabbage, with raspberry flan for dessert. If your taste is for fish, the turbot filets sautéed and presented with spinach lasagne are touched with brilliance. Or one of Ernie's truly exceptional creations is saddle of lamb en croûte (as with beef Wellington) with a green mustard and honey sauce. Entrees average $22 to $45. Of course, you'll order one of Ernie's fine wines to complement your meal, and who could resist the sumptuous desserts? So expect your total bill to be at least $150 for two—a worthy splurge.

Dinner is served nightly from 6:30 to 10:30 p.m. Coats and ties are required for men; reservations essential.

The lavish decor of the elegant **Fleur de Lys**, 777 Sutter St., between Taylor and Jones (tel. 673-7779) is a superb setting for dinner before an evening on the town. Open for dinner from 6 to 10 p.m.; closed Sunday.

This downtown restaurant is a visual and gastronomic delight. The Fleur de Lys is one of the city's most romantic dining spots: the lovely interior was designed by the late Michael Taylor, who created a feeling of an immense garden tent set in the French countryside. The deep-red fabric, locally hand-printed with an autumnal design, creates a rustic mood enhanced by strategically placed floor-to-ceiling mirrors.

One of the many joys of the Fleur de Lys is that co-owner and host Maurice Rouas has kept a watchful eye on service since 1970, assuring its continuing excellence for each guest. His new partner and executive chef, Hubert Keller, is a master of his trade, having served under such great French chefs as Roger Verge, Paul Haeberlin, and Paul Bocuse.

As for the fare, it is Provençal with appetizers such as a composition of American foie gras, sea scallop mousseline, and thinly sliced salmon; entrees (prices average $22 to $35) such as medallions of veal on a tomato and coriander coulis, green onion compote and pasta crepes; and perhaps a fresh berry sabayon soufflé for dessert. Besides the impressive à la carte menu, a four- and five-course tasting menu is offered ($47 and $52, respectively). The dishes are representative of what is freshest in the market and therefore change daily.

Even the coffee at Fleur de Lys is special; rather than the usual mass-produced brew, you are presented with your own pot of *café filtre* (regular or de-caffeinated). To complement your meal, there's an extensive wine list. Reservations are required. Fleur de Lys gets my highest recommendation.

L'Etoile, 1075 California St., between Mason and Taylor (tel. 771-1529) is open from 6 to 11 p.m., closed Sunday.

Located in the posh Huntington Hotel, L'Etoile offers a romantic setting, with pink-clothed candlelit tables, lots of flower arrangements, copper-colored leather booths and banquettes, crystal chandeliers, oil paintings, and potted ferns on marble pedestals. As you dine in these elegant, social-set surroundings, pianist Peter Mintun entertains with music from the '20s and '30s.

L'Etoile boasts not only a magnificent ambience but also a quality of cuisine that has motivated the famous to wax eloquent over the superb talents of the chef. The dinner menu features entrees such as breast of duckling with pear, blueberries, and orange sauce, or Dover sole in Pinot Noir sauce, in the $27 to $35 range. For dessert, you might choose one of the pâtisseries du chef. Reservations are required, as are jacket and tie.

EXPENSIVE RESTAURANTS: Just a shade less grandiose than the bastions of haute cuisine we've looked at up till now, the following restaurants are nonetheless elegant and delightful in every respect. In general, they offer meals in varying price brackets, and with a careful perusal of the menu you needn't spend a king's ransom. All offer superb cuisine and a suitable atmosphere in which to enjoy it. If your budget doesn't stretch to dinner, try lunch where it's available—same chef, same dishes, lower prices. Also, notice that some spots serve a full dinner early in the evening for the price of an entree later on.

American

Jack's, 615 Sacramento St., at Montgomery (tel. 986-9854), a venerated San Francisco institution, was founded in 1864 and proudly displays its "One Hundred Year Club" certificate awarded by the state. It has been run by the Redinger family (currently Jack Redinger, though the restaurant was not named for him) since 1902. Located deep in the financial district, it has a fanatically faithful following among the financial wizards.

The wooden Thonet chairs, the unpretentious gold-embossed walls adorned with brass coathooks, the old tile floors, and the dignified waiters all look as they might have a century ago. Jack's specializes in rex sole, calves' head, and fowl dishes, but entrees run the gamut from cheese blintzes to roast turkey with dressing and cranberry sauce to a rack of spring lamb with potatoes boulangère. Prices range from $8 to $20. Desserts also cater to a wide variety of moods—anything from apple pie à la mode to zabaglione.

Complete dinners, served from 5 to 9 p.m. only, cost $18.50. Jack's accepts American Express. Reservations are advised, and jackets and ties are required for men.

Jack's is open from 11:30 a.m. to 9:30 p.m. Monday to Friday, from 5 to 9:30 p.m. on Saturday and Sunday.

The **Post Street Bar and Café,** 632 Post St., next to the Andrews Hotel (tel.

928-2080), is a charming little restaurant that is outstanding among a growing number in California beginning to take full advantage of the tremendous quality and variety of foodstuffs grown or raised in the state. The basic philosophy is to serve the best and the freshest available, in a style that is perhaps not just Californian but truly American, and chef Renée Gianettoni at the Post Street Café does it admirably.

It's a small place adjoining the lobby of the Andrews Hotel. As you enter the café from the street, a grand and quite handsome mahogany bar leads you into the main dining area. High ceilings and arched windows of hand-poured glass give the room a light, open, and airy feeling. In season, the brick fireplace gives a cheery touch of warmth. White tablecloths, fresh flowers, and original watercolors add charm and style. And completing the ambience is the jazz played softly in the background.

The Post Street Café's menu is seasonal, but at any time of the year you can expect delectable appetizers. The café also has daily pasta and fresh fish specials to satisfy the pickiest palate. The linguine with pancetta and squash and the sea bass with basil should not be ignored. Meat eaters will wonder how they could have lived this long without tasting home-cured pork loin medallions with hash brown sweet potatoes, or the café's double chicken breast marinated with rosemary and served with a lemon-chive butter.

To accompany your meal, the café has a nice selection of California wines, several of which you can enjoy by the glass. Despite its relative low price, I found a fine choice to be the Spencer California Chardonnay—a lovely product of one of the several boutique wineries featured by the café. Be sure to save room for dessert, if you can; the selections are prepared specially every day. Dinner entrees average $17; with an appetizer, add another $7.

You can also lunch at the Post Street Café: the menu offers a selection of delicious and surprising combinations. You might think a sandwich to be less than inspired until you've had the chicken salad with toasted pecans and pepper-cured bacon, or the thinly sliced leg of lamb sandwich with sweet red onions and horseradish mayonnaise. For the more conservative there's a grilled rib-eye steak open-face sandwich with horseradish butter and grilled onions. Pasta and fresh fish are also available. Luncheon entrees range from $5.50 to $10.

Eating at the Post Street Café is an enjoyable experience you won't want to miss. Be sure to make reservations. It's open for lunch Monday through Friday from 11:30 a.m. to 2:30 p.m., and for dinner Tuesday through Saturday from 6 to 10 p.m.

For Dashiell Hammett and/or Sam Spade fans, **John's Grill,** 63 Ellis St., between Stockton and Powell (tel. 986-DASH), should be at the top of the "don't miss" list. The restaurant has been around since 1908; in the 1920s, it was one of Hammett's hangouts. It's even one of the San Francisco landmarks Hammett used to make *The Maltese Falcon* come to life. (Before setting out on a wild goose chase after the mysterious Brigid O'Shaughnessy, Sam Spade stops by John's Grill for a dinner of chops, baked potato, and sliced tomatoes.)

The restaurant works hard to preserve the Hammett/Spade legend. The main dining room and bar on the ground floor are decorated in wood and leather, with glass chandeliers and white-clothed tables. It looks like it must have in Hammett's day. On the two upper floors are the Dashiell Hammett and Maltese Falcon rooms, used for spillover dining and banquets. John's Grill is headquarters for the Dashiell Hammett Society of San Francisco, which was founded in 1977 by William F. Nolan, who wrote a biographical study of Hammett, and Jack Kaplan, director of Pinkerton's. (Hammett was a Pinkerton detective during his early days in San Francisco.) A coincidence has even added an extra touch:

the restaurant is owned by Gus Konstantinides; Charilaos Konstantinides is named in *The Maltese Falcon* as a Greek dealer who found the bird "in an obscure shop in Paris." (As far as is known, the two are not related.)

You can begin your experience at John's Grill with a Bloody Brigid— named after Spade's Miss O'Shaughnessy—consisting of sweet-and-sour vodka, soda, fresh pineapple, lime, grenadine, and other ingredients. It comes in a souvenir glass, which you can take home with you. (Souvenir glasses, copies of the art deco menu cover, Maltese Falcon ties, and a Dash Hammett mural are also available for purchase.) For dinner, there's "Sam Spade's Chops," a recreation of the detective's *Maltese Falcon* meal. You can also partake of several entrees recommended by *Gourmet* magazine: chicken à la Girard or chicken Jerusalem, with fresh artichokes and mushrooms and marsala or white wine; oysters Wellington; and filet of sole stuffed with crab and shrimp, baked in lemon and butter sauce. And then there's Jack La Lanne's favorite salad of crab, shrimp, avocado, mushrooms, chopped egg, tomato, and a very special dressing for $13.95. Dinner entrees are mostly in the $12 to $20 range. At lunch many of the same dishes are available for $9 to $18. There are also salads, omelets, and sandwiches for $7 to $14.

Reservations are strongly advised for lunch or dinner; the restaurant is popular with local business people and reporters from both city newspapers, as well as mystery buffs and writers. Dining at John's Grill is a real San Francisco experience. It's open Monday through Saturday: lunch is served from 11 a.m. to 4 p.m., and dinner, from 4 to 10 p.m.

Chinese

With over 100 Chinese restaurants in San Francisco, one might wonder why there would be a need for another. **Harbor Village**, 4 Embarcadero Center, on the center lobby (tel. 781-8833), was opened in 1985 to introduce Imperial cuisine—the famous classical Cantonese cuisine of Hong Kong—to this country. It differs from most Chinese food served in American restaurants in its complexity and subtlety. Harbor Village has five chefs, each with a specialty, all of whom came from sister Hong Kong establishments. While most of the dishes are classical Cantonese, spicy Szechuan items and "northern" specialties such as crackling Peking duck are part of the restaurant's repertoire.

Harbor Village is impressive: its atmosphere and decor represent a successful merger of nouveau California and Chinese influences. The attention to elegant detail reflects the belief that only the best will do: crystal chandeliers, place settings of the finest Chinese porcelain, delicate gleaming glassware, engraved chopsticks. Four opulent private dining rooms with Chinese antiquities and teak furnishings serve 9- to 15-course miniature Imperial feasts, and one outdoor area can accommodate parties of 15 to 200.

The "only-the-best-will-do" philosophy applies also to the quality and freshness of the ingredients the Harbor Village uses in preparation of its dishes. Near the kitchen entrance are two large fish tanks filled with what may be your fresh dinner swimming about.

Lunch is an excellent dim sum affair, with an average cost of about $2.20 per dish. The extensive dinner menu offers a remarkable selection of appetizers, from pot stickers through a collection of elegant choices such as shredded spicy chicken, minced squab in lettuce cups, or roast duck. Soups, too, are unusual and exceptional—for example, the julienne duck with fish maw, Empress seafood, mushroom with eggflower soup, or the shark's fin in suprême broth. There are some 30 seafood dishes, including four featuring braised abalone—at least one to please most any palate.

A number of the entrees have a very delicate flavor, while others are more strongly seasoned—say, the fresh prawns stir-fried in garlic and butter, or the sizzling beef in black-bean sauce with vegetables. A very courteous professional staff can guide you through the menu or recommend dishes that do not appear on it.

Dinner entrees average $7 to $14 with some obvious exceptions: abalone dishes are $22 to $24; crackling Peking duck, $26; shark's fin soup, $18. Prices vary for seasonal specialties such as the Dungeness crab or lobster. Appetizers will add another $7 to $12; soups, apart from the exceptional, are $6 to $10. Dinner for two can range from $30 to $85, without wine. The Harbor Village does have a respectable wine list, and the house chardonnay is quite good at $12 a bottle. Harbor Village is open weekdays from 11 a.m. to 2:30 p.m. and 5:30 to 10 p.m., weekends from 10:30 a.m.

Harbor Village has free validated parking at 3 and 4 Embarcadero Center garages, at the foot of Clay Street, after 5 p.m. on weekdays and all day on weekends and holidays.

Located in the Woolen Mill Building, the **Mandarin,** 900 North Point in Ghirardelli Square (tel. 673-8812), is the domain of gracious owner/hostess Madame Cecilia Chiang. Her northern Chinese cuisine is among the best in town, the setting as elegant, I'm told, as her palatial childhood home in Peking. Reminiscent of an ancient Chinese temple, the rich interior is accented by quarry floor tiles, burnt-orange carpeting, and Mandarin furnishings. The focal point of the dining area is the Mongolian fire pit, where guests can barbecue their own dinners or have the chef do it for them. The ceiling is lined with haige twigs and supported by heavy rough-hewn beams. The walls are exposed brick or covered in gold silk; exquisite paintings, priceless antiques, and forbidden-stitch embroideries (using stitches allowed for the court only) from Madame Chiang's home complete the decor. Some tables offer bay views.

A complete dinner for two including three to ten dishes (about $25 to $40 per person) might include hot-and-sour soup, almond chicken, oyster-sauced beef, gourmet vegetables, ham fried rice, jasmine tea, and cookies. For each extra person taking part in the meal another dish is added.

If ordering à la carte, an appetizer of chiao tzu—grilled meat-filled dumplings served with vinegar and hot pepper oil—is heartily recommended, as is a cauldron of sizzling rice soup that serves four. Smoked tea duck, baked to crispness in special ovens over burning tea leaves, and Mongolian beef—slices of lamb or beef grilled quickly over the fire pit, served in hot Mandarin buns—are specialties. Or you might share minced squab or walnut chicken. These entrees and others cost $20 to $30. For a superb finish, try the Mandarin glazed apples or bananas, dipped in batter, glazed with candy syrup, and plunged into ice water at your table to crystallize the coating.

At lunch you can order a very good Mandarin chicken salad or sautéed shrimp with peas for $10 to $15, that price including soup, rice, and tea.

Open daily from noon to 11:30 p.m. Reservations are recommended.

For haute cuisine Cantonese style, the magnificent **Imperial Palace,** 919 Grant Ave., between Washington and Jackson (tel. 982-4440), is as elegant as the name implies. Entered via imposingly tall Chinese red doors, the interior is papered in gold with alternating panels framing ancient Chinese paintings. A velvet-lined showcase displays Ch'ing Dynasty antiques. Large bouquets of flowers are judiciously placed, and red roses enhance the beautifully appointed tables. Soft lighting is provided from candle lamps and gold-and-crystal chandeliers above. Strains of Chinese music can be heard in the background.

As you enter you'll notice a wall lined with photos of prominent clients, of which there are many—John Travolta, Alex Haley, Francis Ford Coppola, Clint Eastwood, Barbra Streisand, James Caan, even Richard Nixon.

Prints of ancient Chinese paintings on rice paper adorn the elaborate menu. You might begin with a crabmeat puff—wrapped fillings of crabmeat and cheese, deep fried. For your entree, which costs $15 to $20, you might choose the squab Macao style (marinated in wine and deep fried), tossed chicken Imperial (shredded fried chicken with onions, parsley, chopped almonds, and spices), or fresh prawns in a crystal glaze sauce. Exotic desserts include flaming black leaf lichee and almond delight pudding. A complete dinner including soup, appetizer, two entrees, rice, tea, and cookies is $20 to $40 per person, and a comprehensive wine list is available. Prices are considerably reduced at lunch.

If you're part of a group, consider the following—for $350 per table you can partake of a banquet. Begin with stuffed clams baked on rock salt, honey-glazed spareribs, and bird's nest soup in fresh coconut (served individually); move on to Peking duck with lotus buns, flaming quails (served individually), fresh Maine lobster with ginger roots and green onions, filet of beef with roasted walnuts, sliced filet of rock cod on peach halves in Chinese fruit sauce, and triple mushrooms with seasonal greens; and finish with honey-glazed apples. Most assuredly it would be something to write home about, on more than a postcard.

Open daily Sunday to Thursday from 11:30 a.m. to 1 a.m., on Friday and Saturday till 2 a.m. Reservations essential.

Indian

Be it in Bombay, New York, Delhi, San Francisco, Palo Alto, or Beverly Hills, **Gaylord's,** here at Ghirardelli Square (tel. 771-8822), is one of my favorite Indian restaurants. The candlelit setting is as exquisite as the authentic and deliciously spiced northern Indian cuisine. Windows all around offer tranquil views of boats on the bay, there are cushiony banquettes covered in paisley cotton and handsome mahogany chairs to sit on, large potted plants here and there, napkins and tablecloths of dusty rose-pink linen, and Indian art on the walls. Ragas play softly in the background; all is lovely and peaceful.

Full dinners are priced from $22 to $28 for everything from an all-vegetarian meal to the maharaja feast: mulligatawny soup or dal, tandoori chicken or fish, two kinds of lamb kebab, chicken tikka, nan (an Indian bread), lamb in mildly spiced cream sauce with nuts, saffron-flavored rice with vegetables, vegetables with farmer's cheese in a spiced gravy, choice of exotic desserts, and tea or coffee. The style of the food is northern Indian, with subtle seasonings. There's a wide selection of à la carte choices ranging from vegetable dishes to tandoori prawns. You can even choose from eight varieties of freshly oven-baked Indian breads. Gaylord's is the kind of place you'll want to visit again and again to try everything offered, then begin all over ordering favorites. Complete lunches are $14 to $18.

Open daily for lunch from noon to 2:30 p.m., and nightly from 5 to 10:45 p.m. for dinner. Reservations suggested. There's another Gaylord's at 1 Embarcadero Center (tel. 397-7775).

Italian

When Lorenzo Petroni and chef Bruno Orsi started the **North Beach Restaurant,** 1512 Stockton St., between Union and Green (tel. 392-1587), they vowed to serve the finest *cucina Toscana* possible. And they do! They prepare their own fresh pasta daily (highest honors to the fettuccine), use only fresh vegetables, hang and cure their own prosciutto hams, and serve fine California wines.

The decor is cheerful and unpretentious, with a certain unmistakable dignity, especially at night when the white-clothed tables are candlelit. Tables downstairs are under Martini & Rossi umbrellas. The ambience is flamboyantly Italian; women can expect frank ogling and admiration.

But it's the food one comes to revel in. The specialty of the house (which should come as no surprise) is pasta. Complete dinners include antipasto, mixed green salad or soup du jour, pasta della casa with prosciutto sauce, fresh vegetable, dessert, and coffee, for $18 to $28, with an entree of rex sole meunière or half a chicken in herbs. Entrees are also available à la carte. For dessert, zabaglione is a supreme joy. The North Beach is less expensive at lunch.

Open daily from 11:30 a.m. to 11:45 p.m.

Moroccan

Marrakech, 419 O'Farrell St., between Taylor and Jones (tel. 776-6717), is a superb place to enjoy an evening of Arabian splendor.

The interior is exotic, with fancy Moorish domes and a splashing marble fountain. The dining areas are carpeted with Berber and Oriental rugs; seating is also covered with rugs and an abundance of plush velvet cushions; the lofty ceiling is blue punctuated by hand-painted beams. Light filters down through cut-brass lamps, creating yet another pattern. Middle Eastern music plays, and a belly dancer weaves between the tables.

The meal is a ritual feast—don't eat all day in preparation—served by waiters in maroon Zouave costumes and fez (they look rather like Shriners) and hostesses in flowing djelabbas. It begins when a hostess brings out a brass pot and basin filled with hot water. She washes and dries your hands, and you keep the towel to use as a napkin. You'll need it, since the entire meal is eaten with your hands—no plates or silverware are supplied!

There are 11 complete dinners to choose from (all under $28 per person), and all begin with a piquant Moroccan salad scooped up with hunks of home-made bread. Then come several entrees, which might include chicken with lemons, lamb with honey and almonds (exquisite), and hare and raisins. It's all twice as tasty and twice the fun pulling off bits of meat with your fingers. The entrees are followed by a delicious couscous with vegetables, easily a meal in itself. Fresh fruits and mint tea (poured from a height of several feet in good Moroccan tradition) are the finale.

As you lounge, satiated, over tea or after-dinner drink (it's perfectly okay to recline on the cushions), the hostess once again washes your hands and sprays you with refreshing rosewater.

Marrakech is open for dinner Monday through Saturday from 6 p.m. to 10 p.m., and reservations are essential.

Natural Foods

A longtime favorite in San Francisco is **Greens at Fort Mason,** Building A, Fort Mason Center (tel. 771-6222), an enterprise of the Tassajara Zen Center. It's located in an old warehouse building, though from the inside you'd never know it. It's open, light and airy, with a huge redwood burl sculpture near the entrance. The food is simple and natural, but it bears little resemblance to what most of us think of as "health food." Dinner on Friday and Saturday is a fixed-price, multicourse meal costing around $30 per person. (Tuesday through Thursday dinner is à la carte.) The menu changes nightly; you might feast on linguine with caramelized onions and walnuts in walnut oil; followed by a tomato and white bean soup; then a cauliflower timbale in curry sauce with broccoli, carrots, mushrooms, and sun-dried tomatoes; and a salad of spinach, butter lettuce, and radicchio in orange vinaigrette. If you still have room, you can choose from desserts like almond and raspberry tart, chocolate and Grand Marnier custard, and lemon mousse. There's an extensive wine list to choose from. Lunch is a simpler affair, with the likes of tofu sandwiches, spinach salad, chili, and soup, as well as specials like spinach fettuccine for $6 to $10.

Greens at Fort Mason is open Tuesday to Saturday for lunch from 11:30 a.m. to 2:30 p.m., Friday and Saturday for the prix-fixe dinner from 6 to 9:30 p.m. by reservation only, two weeks in advance. Dinner Tuesday through Thursday is served from 6 to 9 p.m. The Greens bakery is open Tuesday to Saturday from 9:30 a.m. to 4:30 p.m.

Polynesian

At the San Francisco branch of **Trader Vic's,** 20 Cosmos Pl., off Taylor Street between Post and Sutter (tel. 776-2232), the old trader himself, Victor Jules Bergeron, could sometimes be seen. Some quotes from the great man: "When I started the restaurant business, I did everything to keep customers. I sang and I even let them stick an ice pick in my wooden leg." On the South Seas decor: "It intrigues everyone. You think of beaches and moonlight and pretty girls without any clothes on. It is complete escape, relaxation."

Trader Vic's outdoes all others in creating an ambience of South Seas enchantment—lush jungle foliage, authentic tapa-covered walls, spears, lots of bamboo and rattan, even a palm-frond canoe overhead. It's a great place for people-watching and, strange as it seems, it is *the* society restaurant. Go once just for the experience.

The menu is enormous—order one of the potent rum concoctions to sip while you peruse at leisure (order a second and you won't care if they serve you a Big Mac).

There are lots of hors d'oeuvres, including typically Polynesian caviar with blinis and sour cream. A more "conventional" start would be bongo bongo (cream of puréed oyster) soup. A whole page is devoted just to accompanying vegetables and salads. One hundred entrees, ranging in price from $15 to $35, include Malay peanut chicken, a wide variety of curries served with nine condiments, Trader Vic's special oysters flambé, Szechuan beef, roast Indonesian lamb, and breast of peach blossom duck. Save room for one of the 29 exotic desserts—perhaps rum ice cream with praline sauce. The luncheon menu, although extensive, is simpler and a bit less pricey.

Open for lunch weekdays from 11:30 a.m. to 2:30 p.m., for dinner nightly from 5 to 11 p.m., and for late supper Monday to Saturday till 12:30 a.m. Reservations recommended. Jacket and tie are required for men.

Seafood

Established in 1849—along with the Gold Rush—the **Tadich Grill,** 240 California St., between Battery and Front (tel. 391-2373), is a venerated old California institution. A mahogany bar and counter extends the entire length of the restaurant. On the wall is an old wooden clock with Roman numerals. Tables, draped in no-nonsense white linen and provided with big plates of sourdough bread and lemon wedges, are ranged along the wall, separated from the counter by a mahogany partition. There are also seven enclosed private booths. (I imagine discreet business deals are more frequent than romantic trysts in these compartments, more's the pity.) Lighting is provided by brass wall lamps and art deco fixtures.

The food is just fantastic. Seafood is the specialty. For a light meal you might try one of the delicious seafood salads, like shrimp or prawn Louis, with a glass of wine, fresh sourdough bread, and butter. Hot entrees include baked avocado with shrimp diablo, baked casserole of stuffed turbot with crab and shrimp à la Newburg, and char-broiled lobster tail with butter sauce. The sand dabs, rex sole, and calamari steak are truly exceptional. Entrees cost $14 to $30. A side order of big, tasty french fries is hard to resist, as is the homemade custard pudding for dessert—probably the best ever.

Open Monday to Friday from 11 a.m. to 9 p.m. No credit cards are accepted.

MODERATELY PRICED RESTAURANTS: The following choices are in the moderate price range that most of us prefer when dining out. Yet many offer a great deal of "atmosphere," along with affordable prices and first-rate cuisine.

American

Housed in an old brick building facing Sydney G. Walton Square, **MacArthur Park,** 607 Front St., at Jackson (tel. 398-5700), offers a garden ambience with plants and trees flourishing in the sunlight streaming in from skylights overhead. Long and L-shaped, its exposed brick walls are tastefully adorned with framed *Paris Review* posters. In the back, with a wood-burning fireplace, is the Jimmy Webb Room (he wrote the song). Fresh flowers on pink-clothed tables provide a cheerful note, and there's a long oak marble-topped bar behind which are racks containing some of the Park's extensive wine collection.

This is a good spot for dinner after the theater, or lunch after a morning of exploring Jackson Square. MacArthur Park prides itself on serving great American food. You might wonder how exceptional a club sandwich or Cobb salad can be for lunch. Order either one and you'll know, since both include chicken and bacon smoked to perfection by the restaurant itself. Lunch will cost you $7 to $12. And at any time there are great baby back ribs and at least six kinds of mesquite-broiled fresh fish available. Dinner fare, entrees alone, will cost about $12 to $24. Items for dinner can also be ordered for lunch. For dessert, Judy's mud pie—a blend of coffee and chocolate ice creams in a chocolate cookie crust smothered with hot fudge sauce—is as good as it sounds. Or you can ask for baked-to-order chocolate-chip cookies, served warm from the oven.

A very impressive wine list features many California wines available by the glass. Reservations are essential at this deservedly popular restaurant.

The restaurant schedule seems more like a listing of train times. It is open for breakfast Monday through Friday from 7 to 10 a.m., and for Sunday brunch from 10 a.m. to 2 p.m. Lunch is served Monday through Friday from 11:30 a.m. to 2:30 p.m., and dinner, Sunday through Thursday from 5 to 10:30 p.m., on Friday and Saturday to 11 p.m.

Hard Rock Café, 1699 Van Ness, at Sacramento (tel. 885-1699). If standing in line with 18-year-olds is not your bag, go to the Hard Rock Café for lunch instead of dinner. But regardless of your age, or the time of day, the Hard Rock Café is fun, interesting, and noisy. It's a look back at the '50s and '60s. If you're a traveler, there's an HRC in Los Angeles, New York City, Chicago, Houston, London, Stockholm, and Frankfurt.

This one is rather like a large hall (actually it's a former auto showroom) decorated with a candy-apple caddy hanging from the ceiling; gold records; front pages headlining the deaths of John Kennedy, Elvis, and John Lennon; Elvis Presley's cape, framed; photos of Presley; Beatles memorabilia; a cow at the door (no, not alive); and "Save the Planet" and "All Is One" signs. It's rather like a family convention center with ceiling fans. The hub of activities is an over-size oblong oak bar. Surprisingly, the decibel level of the background music at midday doesn't inhibit conversation or eating, but it's period rock 'n' roll.

If food is one of your objectives, there are booths, tables, and a counter with lots of elbow room. Food is reasonably good and moderately priced. At the high end of the price range is steak for $12.95 and baby back ribs for $10.95. Then you go down to grilled burgers for $4.95 or a bowl of homemade chili for $4.50.

Salads and sandwiches are the usual assortment, and liquid refreshments are soft or hard, as you wish. Desserts range from homemade apple pie or strawberry shortcake to thick shakes or your choice of floats, from $2.50 to $3.25.

It's open weekdays and Sunday from 11:30 a.m. to midnight, on Friday and Saturday to 1 a.m.

Aptly located in the Wells Fargo Building, its decor evocative of Fargo's 19th-century heyday, the **Stagecoach Restaurant,** 44 Montgomery St., at Sutter (tel. 956-4650), is richly appointed, comfortable, and prosperous looking. Seating is in plush tufted-leather booths and banquettes, complemented by white linen tablecloths. Candles, lamps, wall sconces, and wrought-iron chandeliers provide a soft amber light. The walls are adorned with stained-glass panels, framed mirrors, and oil paintings, the most notable of which is the original nude, *Stella,* from the 1893 World's Fair in Chicago.

The menu offers a wide variety of choices, from light foods like sandwiches, salads, and omelets (for $5 to $10) to pastas, fish dishes like scallops or prawns sautéed with white wine and mushrooms, to filet mignon or New York steak (for $11 to $24). It's open for meals Monday through Friday from 11 a.m. to 8 p.m.; the bar serves till 11 p.m. Reservations are essential at lunch.

Basque

Entered via a bar adorned with jai alai baskets, **Des Alpes,** 732 Broadway, between Stockton and Powell (tel. 391-4249, or 788-9900), has a homey Basque decor: brown-and-white-checked plastic cloths and wainscotted cream walls are hung with travel posters and paintings of French, Spanish, Alpine, and Basque countryside; note an early photo of the restaurant, which dates from 1908.

The cuisine is far from "haute"—it offers French family cooking of the kind you might have eaten once in some little "auberge" in the Midi and have been reminiscing about ever since. A single entree is offered each night—perhaps a choice of lamb stew, filet of sole, or roast beef. Your meal includes soup, stringbean salad, potatoes, green salad, coffee, and ice cream. The price: $9 to $12. A bottle of house wine with your dinner is easily affordable.

Des Alpes is open Tuesday to Saturday from 5:30 to 10 p.m., on Sunday from 5 to 9:30 p.m.

Chinese

So popular was the delicious and reasonably priced Mandarin fare at **Yet Wah,** 1829 Clement St., at 19th Avenue (tel. 751-1231), that the restaurant sprouted another Clement Street location at no. 2140 (tel. 387-8040). (The latter is open daily from 4 to 11 p.m.) The 1829 Clement Yet Wah is elegant in decor, with gold bamboo-print wallpaper, Chinese lanterns overhead, and candlelit tables. It's really very pleasant—always lively and buzzing with conversation. The no. 2140 Yet Wah is larger and more luxurious.

A $14 per-person dinner for two includes sizzling rice soup, su mi (deep-fried wonton), Mandarin beef, almond pressed duck in sweet-and-sour sauce, phoenix and dragon (a shrimp and chicken dish with mushrooms and snow peas), rice, tea, and cookies. Ordering à la carte, you might begin your meal with an order of kuo teh (six crispy pot stickers) or su mi. Entrees, averaging $8 to $14, include kubla lamb (lamb slices in spicy Szechuan brown-bean sauce and scallions), princess garden chicken salad (shredded chicken with lettuce, nuts, green onions, and Chinese parsley, served with fun see noodles), or fried duck with mandarin orange sauce. Everything sounds so good that it's difficult to decide what to order; best to go with a bunch of friends and sample a wide choice of entrees. Domestic and Chinese wines and beers are available to complement your meal.

Open daily from 11 a.m. to 11 p.m.

There's a branch of Yet Wah at the Pier 39 complex (tel. 434-4430), open from 11:30 a.m. to 10 p.m. daily.

The **Hunan Restaurant,** 853 Kearny St., off Columbus (tel. 397-8718), is an insignificant-looking place, but it has drawn praise from the likes of Craig Claiborne, food editor of the *New York Times,* who called it the "hottest Hunan restaurant" in the West. The food is hot indeed, and free of MSG. The onion cakes and dim sum (called pot stickers at most other San Francisco Chinese restaurants) are *de rigueur* as appetizers. The hot-and-sour soup and the cold bean sprout and cucumber salad are also great. The special chicken, shrimps, and scallops with hot black-bean sauce is a favorite entree, and there are smoked specialties and vegetarian items to choose from. Some dishes, the menu claims, are "spicy but not hot," like diced chicken with fresh garlic sauce or the sliced beef with green onions. Entrees cost $6 to $10.

The lunch menu is more limited and even less expensive—most items cost less than $6.

The Hunan Restaurant is open daily from 11:30 a.m. to 9:30 p.m. There's a second location, larger and fancier, at 924 Sansome St. near Broadway (tel. 956-7727), with the same hours as above.

Not to be confused with the above is **Hunan Shaolin on Polk,** 1150 Polk St., between Sutter and Post (tel. 771-6888), another Hunan eatery, located a short distance from Chinatown in "Polk Gulch." There's not much decor to speak of, but the food is more than good enough to make up for it. You can begin your meal with the standards—pot stickers (dim sum) and onion cakes—which are terrific here. So is the hot-and-sour soup. There are lots and lots of entrees to choose from; my favorites are the ironplatter specials like sizzling prawns, and a delicious Manchu beef (it's not on the menu, but you can ask for it). Most dishes here are spicy-hot, but you can ask to have them mild if that's your preference. Dinner entrees cost $6 to $8; at lunch you can order any of 20 entrees for about $5.

The food at Hunan Shaolin is wonderful, and the service is friendly and efficient. In the evening there's valet parking, a bonus in this area of scarce parking spaces. Reservations are accepted only on weekends for large parties.

Hunan Shaolin on Polk is open Monday to Saturday from 11:30 a.m. to 10 p.m., on Sunday from 4 to 10 p.m.

I've been advocating the ordering of pot stickers for several paragraphs; this pleasantly modern Mandarin restaurant, actually called the **Pot Sticker,** 150 Waverly Pl., off Washington Street (tel. 397-9985), specializes in them. A pot sticker, as it's no doubt time I explained, is a pan-fried, thin-skinned dumpling stuffed with seasoned meat or vegetables—and it does, yes, tend to stick to the pot. Here you can order several varieties of the dumplings, as well as other delicious Mandarin dishes.

I especially like the decor—unusually spartan for a Chinese restaurant: exposed brick walls hung with attractive Chinese paintings and scrolls, live plants, and globe lights overhead.

The family dinner includes soup of the day, pot stickers, entrees like almond chicken or sweet-and-sour pork, steamed rice, cookies, and tea, for $8 to $11 per person. À la carte, you might order Szechuan prawns or other entrees for $6 to $9. You can also just gorge yourself on a variety of dumplings (about $2 to $3 a plate). Leave some room for yummy green tea ice cream for dessert.

Open daily from 11:30 a.m. to 4 p.m. for lunch, and 4:30 to 9:45 p.m. for dinner.

There's another Pot Sticker a bit below Haight-Ashbury at 335 Noe St., near 16th Street (tel. 861-6868). It's open daily from 11:30 a.m. to 10:30 p.m.

Brandy Ho's Hunan Food, 217 Columbus, at Pacific (tel. 788-7527), sits at the intersection of Italian North Beach, the financial district, and Chinatown. It has little decor to speak of—tables covered with plaid cloths and clear vinyl, a few Chinese lanterns for color. But who needs decor when the food is great? Don't miss the fried dumplings with sweet-and-sour sauce. Several uncommon soups are offered in addition to the traditional (and excellent) hot-and-sour: there's a moo shu soup with eggs, pork, vegetables, and tree-ear mushrooms, and fish ball soup with spinach, bamboo shoots, noodles, and other goodies.

Entrees are varied and tasty. I recommend a dish called "Three Delicacies," a combination of scallops, shrimp, and chicken with onion, bell pepper, and bamboo shoots seasoned with ginger, garlic, and wine and served with black-bean sauce. The moo shu pork is also good. Most dishes here are quite hot and spicy; the kitchen will adjust the level to meet your specifications. Entrees average $8 to $11.

Brandy Ho's has a small selection of wines and beers to accompany your meal, including plum wine and sake. To cool your tongue after your meal, there's also the traditional lichees and ice cream.

Open weekdays and Sunday from 11:30 a.m. to 11 p.m., on Friday and Saturday to midnight.

For Chinese food in a high-tech setting, you might try **Reds,** 1475 Polk St., at California (tel. 441-7337), on the top floor of a futuristic-looking building on the corner of Polk and California Streets. Reds' decor is minimalist and elegant in red, white, and black. The menu is extensive, with over 120 items offered. In addition to appetizers such as crabmeat puff and ginger eggplant, and such soups as bean curd with spinach and dragon and phoenix (chicken and shrimp), there are dozens of entrees—seafood, pork, beef, lamb, fowl, and vegetable. You might try the hot-and-sour clams or the steak kew with three kinds of mushrooms. There's even Peking duck. Most entrees cost $9 to $17. To accompany your meal there's a nice variety of wines available. Or you can enjoy one of Reds' exotic cocktails like a Chi Chi (vodka, coconut, and pineapple juice) or a Fogcutter (rum, gin, brandy, and fruit juices).

At lunch you can partake of specials for $7. There are combination platters like eggrolls, almond chicken, and fried rice, and rice plates of chicken with barbecue sauce or green pepper beef with steamed rice. All special luncheons come with soup.

Reds is open daily from 11:30 a.m. to 2 a.m.

Crêpes and Quiches

Large and airy, with one wall of windows overlooking a garden courtyard, the **Magic Pan** at 341 Sutter St., between Grant and Stockton Streets (tel. 788-7397), is one of the prettiest branches of this well-known chain. Like the others, the decor here is French provincial, with parquet floors, antique cupboards, oak tables, framed French prints on the walls, pots of hanging ferns, and fresh flowers on every table. Up front is a spacious bar with comfortable couches, very popular at cocktail hour when free hors d'oeuvres are served.

The Magic Pan specializes in crêpes stuffed with a variety of delicious fillings: chicken or seafood with ratatouille, shrimp and snow peas; cordon bleu with layers of ham, turkey, Swiss, and herbed cheeses; and mixed vegetables, to name a few. Crêpe dinners ($9 to $11) give you combinations such as the chicken divan crêpe complemented by a European-blend vegetable crêpe. If you're traveling with a nothing-but-steak eater, don't despair. The Magic Pan has all bases covered with filet mignon, New York strip steak, peppercorn steak, and veal in a variety of dishes ($12 to $16). Pasta, chicken, seafood, and several stir-fry dishes ($9 to $14) complete the extensive menu. All dinner entrees are served with salad or soup. Dessert crêpes are tantalizing, including the likes of a Chantilly crêpe with banana slices in apricot sauce, with whipped cream and toasted almond slivers.

The reasonably priced Magic Pan is popular for lunch and Saturday or Sunday brunch; and this Magic Pan branch is the only one open for breakfast daily, serving a variety of quiches, omelets, gourmet egg dishes, etc., from 7:30 to 10:30 a.m. The restaurant is open Monday through Thursday to 10 p.m., on Friday and Saturday to midnight, and on Sunday to 9 p.m.

There's another Magic Pan at 900 North Point (tel. 474-6733) in Ghirardelli Square.

Situated in the heart of the theater district, and flanked by Jewish delis, **Salmagundi**, 442 Geary St., between Mason and Taylor (tel. 441-0894), offers a chic alternative to chopped liver and pastrami. Contemporary/country French in decor, it's furnished with bentwood chairs, matte white tables, an occasional high table with rattan stools, lots of plants, wicker baskets, antiques, and framed woodcuts on the walls. In the back there's a Spanish-tiled fountain, and windows look out on a garden. There's always good background music—light jazz, classical, or whatever. Crowded at lunch and dinner, bustling with excitement after theater, Salmagundi takes on a casual coffeehouse ambience during off-hours— people hang out drinking wine or cappuccino, playing backgammon, writing letters, or perusing scripts.

Every day three different choices of soup and one kind of quiche are offered. Among the soups, the changing daily menu might list Hungarian goulash, Barbary Coast bouillabaisse, Ukrainian beef borscht, or English country cheddar. As for the quiches, you might find a simple quiche Lorraine listed, but more often it's bedecked with shrimp, broccoli and cheddar cheese, or onion and zucchini. Soups, salads, or quiche alone cost $2.50 to $4. Wine and beer are available, as are homemade desserts.

Open daily from 11 a.m. to midnight.

Other branches are at 2 Embarcadero Center (tel. 982-5603), and at 1236 Market St. (tel. 431-7337) in the Civic Center.

There is only one quiche Lorraine, say the owners of **La Quiche**, 550 Taylor St., between Post and Geary (tel. 441-2711), and this pure and classic quiche is the only one they serve. La Quiche is a charming little bistro such as you might find on a Paris side street. The 20 or so tables are draped with pink cloths. Hanging copper pots and a shelf of decorative plates adorn the beamed walls, and there are lace curtains in the windows.

Meals are accompanied by crusty loaves of homemade French bread (the authentic baguette) and fresh butter in little ceramic pots. The quiche (exceptional —the lightest crust ever) with salad, a glass of wine, homemade chocolate mousse with real crème Chantilly, and a pot of espresso makes an excellent lunch or dinner. Ten delicious crêpes with scrumptious fillings, plus eight dessert crêpes, are also available at both meals. Quiche or crêpes cost $7 to $9.50. Dinner entrees, served with soup, salad, and French bread, might feature boeuf bourguignon or chicken sautéed in Riesling wine, for $11 to $16. At lunch, entrees served with soup, salad, and French bread include chicken in cream and mushrooms, and a very tasty salad niçoise for $8 to $11. There are three specials daily for lunch and dinner.

Open for lunch Monday to Saturday from 11:30 a.m. to 2:30 p.m., and for dinner nightly from 5:30 to 10:30 p.m. La Quiche is a must.

Czechoslovakian

Run by Vlasta and Frank Kucera, and their son John, **Vlasta's Czechoslovakian Restaurant**, 2420 Lombard St., between Scott and Divisadero (tel.

931-7533), is a homey establishment, cozy and intimate. Wood-paneled walls are hung with framed oil paintings, tables are covered with starched white linen, a plant-lined divider creates two dining areas, and soft lighting is achieved by chandeliers overhead and wall sconces. The motherly Vlasta presides in the kitchen, and the entire family makes diners feel like welcome guests.

Dinners include soup of the day and salad. The house specialty is herbed roast duck with red cabbage and Bohemian dumplings. Viennese schnitzel is also on the menu, as are chicken paprika, and goulash topped with sour cream and served with dumplings or potatoes. Entrees, which range from $10 to $12.50, change daily; the above were among the choices on my last visit. Try some of Vlasta's homemade apple strudel for dessert.

Open Tuesday to Sunday from 5:30 to 11 p.m. Reservations are essential.

French

Le Central, 453 Bush St., between Kearny and Grant (tel. 391-2233), is San Francisco's version of a classic Parisian bistro, with a truly elegant bar for waiting. It sports a red "tabac" sign, and the rows of banquettes, mirrored walls, racks of Gauloises and Gitanes behind the gleaming copper-topped bar are all perfectly typical of the genre. Ditto the gauzy white curtains in the window, the blackboard menu, and baskets of fruit and flowers. The ambience is convivial, chic, and cosmopolitan, enhanced at night by background music. Herb Caen and various political types are frequent customers. It's a place to see and be seen.

The cassoulet—a stew rich with chunks of lamb, duck, sausage, and pork, clove-studded onions, beans, etc., is a house specialty; they started it cooking when the restaurant opened and have been adding to it ever since. Returned expatriates will be thrilled to find an authentic steak pommes frites or chou-croûte Alsacienne (sauerkraut cooked in white wine, studded wtih juniper berries, and arranged with bacon, pork loin, Viennese sausage, and Dijon mustard). Entrees cost $11 to $17. Appetizer choices are equally apropos: saucisson chaud, escargots de Bourgogne, onion soup gratinée, etc.

Le Central is open weekdays from 11:30 a.m. to 3 p.m. and from 5:30 p.m. to 10:30 p.m. weekdays, on Saturday from 6 to 10:30 p.m.

Hungarian

Paprikás Fono, 900 North Point, at Ghirardelli Square (tel. 441-1223) has a charming country-inn setting with provincial Hungarian antiques and folk art pieces. The hand-painted chairs are copies of those designed for King Ferdinand of Hungary's hunting lodge at the turn of the century. Walls are hung with farm implements, big bunches of dried flowers, baskets, pottery, etc. And in the center of the room is a hearth with a large copper kettle used to cook goulash soup. An especially pleasant dining area is the glassed-in balcony overlooking the bay.

Whatever you order, ask for the fried peasant bread—it's delicious. Among the entree choices are chicken paprikás, veal Tokany, gypsy steaks, fish paprikás, fresh seafood of the day, and pasta specials, for $12 to $20. The dessert strudels and palacsintas are irresistible. Luncheon entrees are mostly in the $7 to $11 range.

Paprikás Fono is open Monday to Saturday from 11:30 a.m. to 11 p.m., on Sunday to 10:30 p.m. Reservations are advised.

Italian

Even with more than 100 Italian restaurants for competition, **Kuleto's,** 221 Powell St., at Geary (tel. 397-7720), is a tough act to follow. It has chefs who create exceptionally delicious, out-of-the-ordinary dishes, in an extraordinary setting, and at moderate prices. The restaurant is open daily from 7 a.m. to 10:30

a.m. for breakfast, from 11:30 a.m. on through to 11 p.m. for lunch and dinner. The same extensive northern Italian menu with Tuscan specialties is offered for lunch and dinner.

Enter through the bar on Powell Street to get the full impact of this delightful and relaxing place: the years-gone-by high ceilings, black-and-white-marble tile floors, strings of dried peppers and garlic hanging over a magnificent long mahogany bar. Kuleto's has the familiar, friendly air of a restaurant you've known for years: small circular tables with tall bar chairs, dark-wood booths with gray-green cushions, a huge open kitchen with black hood and copper trim housing a group of hard-working chefs—all compose a homey picture.

Reviewing the menu from the top, the antipasti are sufficiently varied to satisfy most every taste, from the roasted garlic or the grilled prawns with sweet peppers to the calamari fritti or the steamed mussels. For the traditionalists, there's always the antipasto platter. As for the second course, there's nothing commonplace about the soup or such salads as the salad Caprice, with whole-milk mozzarella, tomato, basil, and extra-virgin olive oil.

Every entree I ordered was excellent, from the least expensive pasta dish on up the list. You can't go wrong with the risotto Zafferano, with saffron risotto, prawns, scallops, and sun-dried tomatoes. The selection of fresh fish, grilled over hardwoods, changes daily. If you have a yen for chicken, consider the spit-roasted half chicken, lightly smoked and served with roasted garlic sauce, or the breast of chicken stuffed with ricotta and herbs, served with a roasted pepper-butter sauce. If veal is your fancy, the veal piccata consists of medallions served with lemon, artichokes, and capers. For beef eaters, there's a New York steak grilled wtih tarragon-shallot butter, or the Panini grilled sirloin sandwich with mozzarella, tomato, onion, and peppers. On this deliciously diverse menu, entree prices range from $7.50 for tasty capellini Pomodoro to $16.50 for a grilled loin chop of veal with sautéed spinach. Desserts, from the peach tart to the chocolate gelato, are just as unforgettable as the rest of your meal.

The wine list does justice to this fine restaurant, ranging from a choice selection of California and imported wines to some fine champagnes. Kuleto's also offers a dozen first-quality beers, domestic and imported.

It's wise to make reservations for lunch and dinner at this deservedly popular place.

Corintia Ristorante, is in the Ramada Renaissance Hotel at 55 Cyril Magnin St., at Market and North Fifth (tel. 392-8000). Dinner is served nightly from 6 to 11:30 p.m.

One of San Francisco's finest restaurants, Corintia offers northern Italian cuisine prepared for the most discriminating palate. Changes have been made to lighten the interior of the Corintia, but the restaurant still maintains its magnificent deep- (almost midnight-) blue setting with brass pedestals, handsome etched-glass panels, and mirrors overhead, which give the room an aura of sumptuous elegance. Attentive and knowledgeable waiters in sparkling white bistro aprons serve you to background music ranging from Sinatra to Pavarotti.

The Corintia menu features a delectable choice of distinctive entrees. You might begin with one of the excellent antipasti such as the baked brie and roasted garlic bulb, or the zucchini stuffed with prawns. Or go directly to one of several salad selections—say, the insalata Ilsa with arugula, spinach, butter lettuce, and wild mushrooms. Then on to the entrees: among the pasta dishes is a superb veal and wild mushroom cannelloni in cream, parmigiana. If you yearn for beef, the Corintia has created exceptional tournedos of beef tenderloin with a sweet roasted garlic sauce. But don't overlook the sautéed veal filet with fresh tarragon sauce or the baked jumbo prawns with shallots. Fresh fish is also available each day, and the specialty changes with market availability.

Some marvelous extra touches make dining at the Corintia very pleasureable. Fresh-baked breads and grissini are presented with virgin olive oil and individual cheese graters. A well-stocked wine cart is brought to each table with a large selection of wines by the glass, and you're given complimentary samples to help you make your choice. The wine list features only Italian wines (ah, but what wines!) that have been carefully selected from the principal regions to complement the menu. For those who prefer California selections or wines from other European regions, the full hotel list is also available.

To conclude your evening, the cordial cart presents a full selection of Italian liqueurs and grappas, as well as the traditional cognacs. For those who prefer more solid finales, look for the pastry cart—you're sure to want one of everything on it. The dessert selections from the menu includes one of my favorites, the chocolate cassata Siciliana with ricotta and fruits.

Entrees range from $12 to $17. Most wines are reasonably priced below $20 a bottle. Reservations are necessary.

Heralded by white awnings and a small red neon sign in the window, **Ciao,** 230 Jackson St., near Front Street (tel. 982-9500), features a functionalist Milano decor: white rubber flooring, gleaming brass railings, white enamel lamps and fans overhead, and creamy white walls hung with Jasper John prints and Wayne Thiebaud posters.

You can watch the chef at work in an exhibition pasta kitchen and peruse Italian charcuterie in glass display cases, behind which are shelves of colorful biscotti tins. Tables, simply adorned with vases of red carnations, are set on a raised platform.

The same menu is in effect at lunch and dinner. An order of Ciao salad—lettuce, mushrooms, tomatoes, cheese, onions, chick peas, and salami—makes a good beginnng to either meal, as do the thin slices of raw steak in mustard sauce and the fisherman's salad. Does it come as a surprise that the specialty here is pasta? Homemade fettuccine is prepared in a variety of ways—with four different cheeses; with seafood, wine, tomatoes, and spice; with cream, butter, and cheese; etc. A char-broiled mixed grill (pork, sausage, beef, chicken, and quail) is served with fresh vegetables, and a brochette can be ordered with shrimp or sea scallops. Entrees cost $10 to $19, with pasta dishes at the lower end of the scale. Toasted garlic bread with parmesan cheese spread is served with all entrees. Desserts include cheesecake, chocolate fudge cake with marzipan filling, and Italian chocolate torte.

Ciao is open Monday to Saturday from 11 a.m. to midnight, on Sunday from 5 p.m. Reservations essential.

Tommaso's, 1042 Kearny St., between Broadway and Pacific (tel. 398-9696), is a boisterous and utterly delightful Italian trattoria. There's a long row of tables down the center with partitioned dining areas on either side; oil murals of Neopolitan scenes decorate the walls. But the center of attention is Mama Crotti, expertly tossing huge hunks of garlic and mozzarella onto the pizzas and sliding them into a brick oak-burning oven with a long wooden spatula. The pizza's great; try the super-deluxe version: mushrooms, anchovies, peppers, ham, cheese, sausage, basil, and garlic. Less jaded palates will be satisfied with any of 18 other varieties. A basket of hot homemade bread accompanies entrees like veal scaloppine marsala and chicken cacciatore—also oven baked. Homemade manicotti with a side order of chilled broccoli salad makes an excellent meal. Entrees average $12 to $17.50. Of course, you need at least a half bottle of soave with such a feast, and you'd do well to order homemade cannoli and a pot of Italian roast coffee for dessert.

Open Tuesday through Saturday from 5 to 10:45 p.m., on Sunday from 4 to 9:45 p.m.

Decorative plates, plants, sausages, trinkets, dolls, flags, mirrors, and other such oddments (many varnished to a high gloss) are hung from the ceiling and glued to the walls to create a decor best described in *New West* magazine as "a masterpiece of contemporary Sicilian rococo." The **Caffè Sport,** 574 Green St., between Grant and Columbus Avenues (tel. 981-1251), is a great favorite of Italians, bohemians, neighborhood folk, visitors, and celebrities who revel in the lusty Sicilian ambience and the hearty free-hand-with-the-garlic cookery. Those with delicate appetites, temperaments, or digestive systems should read no further; the rest may proceed with gusto.

Sauces are laced with raw chunks of garlic, and portions are immense and delicious. When you are seated at your table, you'll be offered the caffè's only menu for perusal. No matter what you order, though, your waiter will undoubtedly suggest some of his own. (Somehow, everyone seems to end up with the same dishes each meal!) Go along with him; you won't be disappointed. Among the more-than-ample dishes you might get are calamari, prawns, and clams sautéed in garlic and olive oil and laced with white wine, or pasta rustica alla Carrettiera—hollow rigatoni noodles al dente, smothered in parmesan cheese, cream, small bay shrimp, and thick red tomato sauce. Fresh crusty bread and butter come with all entrees, which cost $13 to $29. Lunches are lighter and less expensive, at $8 to $12. If you aren't full to bursting, you can finish your meal with a cannoli and perhaps a belch, which would not be inappropriate here.

Open Tuesday through Saturday from noon to 2 p.m. and 6:30 to 10:30 p.m. Caffè Sport is a real experience, and worth the wait to get in (reservations are accepted only for parties of four or more). Bring a huge appetite, but above all, don't be late if you have a reservation.

By now a tradition in the North Beach area is the **Little City Restaurant and Antipasti Bar,** 673 Union St., at Powell (tel. 434-2900). Colorful prints and paintings line the exposed brick walls, and brass fans whirr slowly overhead. Burgundy café curtains frame the windows, white linen covers heavy, dark-wood tables, and there's a huge oak bar up front. Somehow it all adds up to an unmistakably San Francisco decor.

The menu offers a wide and changing selection of excellent appetizers that can be ordered all day. Among these choices are grilled sausage and polenta, baked brie with roasted garlic, Manila clams, and prawns borracho (marinated in tequila, chilis, garlic, and lime), all in the $5 to $7.50 range. Soups and salads are also available.

After 6 p.m., or for lunch, pasta specials include fettuccine with gorgonzola, walnuts, and sun-dried tomatoes, and spaghetti with wild mushrooms. Daily entrees offer a delicious variety of choices—fresh seabass, tuna and sea scallops, pot roast, osso bucco, stuffed chicken breasts, even a New York steak. Entrees run $12 to $15 (the steak is $16). But save room for dessert. The tiramisu is superb—chilled rum-soaked sponge cake topped with marscapone and shaved chocolate ($3.50, and worth every bite)—crème caramel ($2.75), and other daily specials. There is a limited but excellent wine list, and specials offered by the glass, featuring local wines.

Little City is open daily from 11:30 a.m. to midnight, and the bar stays open until 2 a.m.

A light and airy trattoria, **Prego,** 2000 Union St., at Buchanan (tel. 563-3305), is pretty and pleasant with a garden of seasonal flowers in the window. Crisp, crusty pizza emerges from oak-fired ovens, and a variety of antipasti ($5 to $10), as well as marvelous pastas ($10 to $14), are available with a good selection of wines to accompany them. Desserts have always been my downfall, and the semifreddo al caffè—white-chocolate ice cream, espresso, and whipped cream—made me decide to eat now, diet later.

Prego is open daily from 11:30 a.m. to midnight. Reservations are available at lunch, but be prepared to wait during evening hours, as this very popular eatery takes dinner reservations for parties of six or more only.

"Rain or shine there's always a line" is the motto at **Little Joe's** (Baby Joe's on Broadway), 523 Broadway;, near Columbus (tel. 433-4343). It's the truth as well (or very near it)—no reservations are accepted, and the place is popular enough that customers are willing to wait (sometimes as much as an hour) for a table. At Little Joe's, even queuing up is an experience: you can sip a drink, peruse the menu, and work up an appetite watching the cooks whip up the food and the customers devour it.

Specialties here are veal and pasta. For $8 to $13 you can dig into veal piccata, scaloppine, saltimbocca, ravioli, cannelloni, or rigatoni. (At lunch, everything's about $1 less.) Or you can enjoy an omelet or a sandwich on French bread for $5 to $8. There are daily specials as well—beef stew, roast chicken and gnocchi, or roast lamb—for $8 to $10. And of course there are desserts, like flan or spumoni ice cream.

Little Joe's is open Monday to Friday from 11 a.m. to 10 p.m., on Saturday till 11 p.m. No credit cards.

Japanese

There are three great advantages to dining at **Ichirin**, at 330 Mason St. (tel. 956-6085), adjacent to the King George Hotel. First, its location is excellent for a night on the town—just around the corner from "Theatre Row" with its Curran Theater, ACT at the Geary Theater, and across from a large garage with all-night parking. Second, Ichirin has a menu with considerable variety. Third, the food and service are first-rate.

The simplicity of the main dining room, decorated in subtle green, mauve, and beige with relatively plain tables and booths, sets off the beautiful and colorful kimonos worn by the Japanese women who serve and prepare food at the table. Should the size of your party warrant it, or if you simply enjoy the privacy they afford, tatami rooms are available. And on each floor of the restaurant, you can watch sushi chefs preparing delights.

Ichirin has some 28 special appetizers ranging from such standards as pot stickers (gyoza) and deep-fried chicken wings (teba kara-age) to the exotic. Three excellent choices are the deep-fried eggplant served with a special teriyaki-type sauce (nasu shigi age), the fish cakes with Japanese horseradish (itawasa), and the marinated broiled beef wrapped with green onion (beef asatsuki maki).

The sushi bar offers assortments, combination rolls, and chirashi—the chef's choice of fresh fillets of fish served over sushi rice with seaweed. There's also a "beginners' sushi plate" for those who have never tried sushi before: the shrimp, egg cake, barbecued eel, and two pieces of futomaki roll will be certain to make sushi converts.

Then there are the delicious nabe dishes, cooked at the table for two or more: shabu shabu—thinly sliced beef, vegetables, and tofu, cooked in a tasty broth and served with two special sauces; a marvelous ishikari nabe with salmon and vegetables cooked in a soy-bean-based broth; and chanko nabe with fresh seafood, tender chicken, and crisp vegetables in broth (said to be the most popular nabe among the Sumo wrestlers, and you know how large they grow to be). Other entrees include tempuras, teriyaki dishes, a Japanese-style beefsteak dinner, broiled lobster, and a multitude of udon (flour) and soba (buckwheat) noodle dishes. The adventurous can feast on the Ichirin Omakase dinner—for $35 per person, the chef selects a full-course dinner, from appetizer to dessert, in traditional Japanese fashion.

If you have the kiddies in tow, Ichirin serves a complete luncheon plate for them including broiled and deep-fried items, vegetables, plus fruit for dessert. Dinner appetizers cost $2.50 to $8, though most are in the $4 range. Entrees are $10 to $14, the Ichirin dinner box with the chef's choices of the day is $19. At lunch, donburi dishes (served over a bowl of rice) are $6 to $10, and bento (combination lunch box) range from $7 to $14. Dinner plates for the kids are $6; lunch plates, $5.50.

Ichirin ("single flower") is open daily from 7 a.m. to 10 a.m., 11:30 a.m. to 2 p.m., and 5 to 10 p.m. There is a cocktail lounge on the premises.

An unpretentious little restaurant, **Sanppo,** 1702 Post St., near Laguna, across from the Miyako Hotel (tel. 346-3486), is always filled with a friendly mix of Nihonmachi (Japantown) locals, business people, and tourists. The small room has lots of small tables as well as a square counter area in the center of the room. It is rare to have a private table here, but the food is so good I just don't care.

Sashimi, teriyaki, tempura, sushi, and donburi (dinner in a bowl) all sell for about $5 to $12. Two of my favorite meals here are gyoza (seasoned, ground pork wrapped in pastry and fried) and soba (wheat noodles in broth with tanuki, fried dough). Combination meals—tempura, sashimi, and gyoza or tempura and teriyaki—come with rice, miso soup, and pickled vegetables for $9 to $17.

Sanppo is open from 11:45 a.m. to 10 p.m. Tuesday through Saturday and from 3 to 10 p.m. on Sunday.

Jewish

If you're craving an authentic pastrami on rye, you don't have to hop the next plane to New York. Just head on over to **David's,** 474 Geary St., at Taylor (tel. 771-1600), where a lively crowd of theater-goers will be taking apart the evening's performance over the blintzes. The decor? It's not important, although pleasant enough with white brick walls and Formica tables. Here you come for the food.

A complete dinner—including appetizer, soup, entree, dessert, and coffee —is a good buy for the truly hungry at about $16. Such a meal might consist of chopped liver, matzoh-ball soup, chicken paprikás, and a napoleon. A la carte entrees include cheese blintzes smothered in sour cream and laced with jam, and sweet-and-sour stuffed cabbage with potatoes, for $7 to $10. Don't overlook the appetizers: herring in cream sauce, gefilte fish with matzoh or challah, and chicken liver in schmaltz. Sandwiches come on rye or Siberian soldier's bread and include a traditional hot pastrami, for under $8. Desserts are homemade.

There's also a very pleasant dining room upstairs with café-curtained windows overlooking the street.

Open from 8 a.m. to 1 a.m. daily.

Seafood

Pacific Heights Bar & Grill, at the corner of Fillmore and Pine Streets (tel. 567-3337), is the setting for some of the best seafood in the city. It's handsome and spacious, and has a warmth typical of the neighborhood.

As you enter under the burgundy canopy, the look of the long oak bar on your right, the comfortable lounge chairs arranged around cocktail tables, create a feeling of ease—a place to relax, visit a while, and listen to the soft jazz in the background. The high ceilings and cream-colored walls add to the room's airiness. Tables in the dining area and the banquettes are a rich plum color, as is the carpeting. A huge frosted-glass seascape framed in oak separates the entryway from the inner dining area. A broad expanse of window dominates the room—

great for people-watching and viewing the neighborhood activity. Sea-gray prints decorate one wall. Opposite this is a handsome collection of gray frames of assorted designs, but without pictures. Fresh flowers and greenery add pleasant touches of color.

For lunch or dinner, oysters of at least 12 to 16 varieties including Belons, jumbo Blue Points, and Portuguese, are available individually or by the half dozen. Clams, mussels, and scallops can also be had on the half shell. Prices average 90¢ to $1.30 each, or $5.25 to $6.95 for six. Fresh fish, from amberjack to sturgeon, is the specialty of the house, prepared with tomatillo salsa, tapenade, or lemon dill butter. Lunch prices range from $8.50 to $14.25. If fish is not your choice, never fear—you won't be disappointed in either the quality or quantity of their other fare. The mesquite-grilled burger is a meal in itself for $6.75, or the delectable spinach pasta with spicy Italian sausage, fried zucchini, and tomato sauce for $8.50. Dinner at Pacific Heights Bar & Grill will cost $12 to $17 without your favorite oysters. A good selection of California wines is available by the glass.

Open Sunday from 10:30 a.m. to 10 p.m. Monday to Thursday from 11:30 a.m. to 10 p.m., Friday to 11 p.m., Saturday 3 to 11 p.m. Reservations are recommended for dinner.

Very similar in style to the previously described Tadich Grill, **Sam's Grill and Seafood Restaurant,** 374 Bush St., near Kearny (tel. 421-0594), also has an old mahogany bar, intimate booths separated by mahogany partitions (although here there's even a curtain you can draw for greater privacy), schoolroom lights overhead, and big plates of lemon wedges on every table. Maybe they copied the idea; newcomer Sam's came on the scene almost 20 years after Tadich's—in 1867.

Entrees at Sam's (priced at $9 to $27) include fresh salmon Newburg, fried deep-sea scallops with tartar sauce, rex sole, and deviled crab à la Sam—a specialty. There are many nonseafood offerings as well: half a broiled chicken, for example. Accompanying side dishes might include creamed spinach and/or potatoes au gratin. A glass of house wine can be ordered, and there's a considerable choice of desserts. What to choose? A wedge of camembert, French pancakes with lemon and sugar, or perhaps the traditional homemade cheesecake.

Open Monday to Friday from 11 a.m. to 8:30 p.m.

Steak

For over 40 years **Phil Lehr's Steakery,** in the Hilton Hotel, at Taylor and Ellis Streets (tel. 673-6800), has been one of San Francisco's most popular restaurants. Lehr himself is almost always on the scene making sure the food (every recipe is his own creation) is up to standard and the service faultless. There's no stinting on atmosphere either. Candles in amber glass holders create soft lighting, booths and armchairs are plush brown leather and velvet, crystal-dripping wall sconces adorn mirrored walls, and tables are covered with red-and-black Tartan plaid cloths. Note the gilt-trimmed hand-painted vases; they date from the Napoleonic era.

Flambé dishes are a specialty here, and they're cooked on flameless Fasar ranges (a Lehr creation) using magnetic induction to create evenly distributed heat; you don't have to understand it, just enjoy the results. Lehr also pioneered the pay-by-the-ounce concept of steak service so that people needn't order more than they can eat. A 7-ounce serving of New York, top sirloin, rib-eye steak, or filet mignon; 16 ounces of T-bone; or 18 ounces of porterhouse cost $14 to $25. All dinners come with a relish tray, salad, stuffed baked potato with sour cream, chives, butter, and beef bacon (it's delicious), deep-fried onion rings, and sourdough bread and butter. Excellent beef, chicken, salmon, or lamb rack Wellington can also be ordered. Nothing is cooked in advance and everything is fresh. Although flambé desserts are featured, you can also get cheesecake or a hot fudge sundae.

As one writer said, Phil Lehr has "translated America's penchant for 'plain red meat' into an epicurean American cuisine." The Steakery is open nightly from 5 p.m. to midnight. Reservations suggested.

BUDGET MEALS: The following are for those of you who haven't got too many coins jingling in your jeans. Nothing prosaic, these low-cost eateries range from American to Vietnamese, and are worth investigating even by better-heeled travelers.

American

On the outside, **Tommy's Joynt,** at the corner of Van Ness Avenue and Geary Street (tel. 775-4216), is carnivalesque with brightly painted walls depicting oversize edibles, signs proclaiming world-famous sandwiches, and 22 flags that are purely decorative fluttering in the wind. It's like Coney Island. Inside it's funk-and-junk time: old hockey sticks, a statue of a lion guzzling Löwenbräu, stuffed birds, a Santa Claus mask—and a TV going full blast during big games to add lots of noise to the general confusion.

The food is cafeteria-style and high in quality. Buffalo stew, stronger and gamier than beef stew, is a specialty; a platter of barbecued beef with potatoes or a big turkey leg is also served. Entrees like this cost $5 to $9. You can also order from a variety of salads; and cheesecake is available for dessert. Beer comes in 78 varieties, listed alphabetically by national origin—from Australia to Switzerland. Average price is $2.50 a bottle.

Open daily from 11 a.m. to 2 a.m. The bar opens at 10 a.m.

Sears Fine Foods, 439 Powell St., between Sutter and Post (tel. 986-1160), is a San Francisco tradition, this time for breakfast on the way to work, or lunch to sustain a downtown shopping foray. Located across the street from the Sir Francis Drake Hotel, it's famous locally for its luscious dark-brown waffles, light sourdough french toast, and pancakes. It's a constant for good food. Be prepared for a short wait before you get your seat.

The restaurant is a pleasant place, decorated in browns and golds with framed oil paintings on the walls and pillars, and a choice of counter or table seating.

Two specialties I enjoy are the 18 Swedish pancakes (count 'em!) served with whipped butter and warm maple syrup, also available with smoky Canadian bacon or link sausages; and the strawberry waffle with fresh berries and whipped cream. These and other breakfast entrees cost $4 to $8. At lunch you can't beat the turkey with dressing and cranberry sauce, fresh vegetables, potatoes, and roll and butter. Full lunches or lighter meals run $6 to $9.

Sears is open from 7 a.m. to 2:30 p.m. Wednesday to Sunday.

Chinese

Sam Wo, 813 Washington St., off Grant Avenue (tel. 982-0596), is a Chinatown institution and one of the handiest spots to know, since it's open for anything from midnight snacks to predawn repasts.

Whatever you feel about appearances, don't be put off by the look downstairs. The establishment consists of two tiny dining rooms piled on top of each other on the second and third floors—you have to walk past the kitchen on the first floor and up the stairs to reach the dining areas. The rooms are bare and usually packed, and you almost invariably have to share a table.

The specialty of the house is *jook* (known as congee in its native Hong

Kong)—a thick, wonderfully tasty rice gruel flavored with fish, shrimp, chicken, beef, or pork, and costing $3 to $4. Equally famous is the marinated raw fish salad. I guarantee that you've never seen many of these great-tasting dishes on the menu of your local Chinese restaurant—steelhead fish with greens over rice, sweet-and-sour pork rice, wonton soup with duck, or roast pork rice noodle roll. Chinese doughnuts go for 40¢ per hole. Sam's is for mingling almost as much as for eating.

Hours are 11 a.m. to 3 a.m. six days a week; closed Sunday.

CHINESE TEA LUNCH: The Chinese call it dim sum. Liberally translated, dim sum is "a delight of the heart." Gastronomically, it is a delight to the palate. Small, succulent dumplings with skins made of wheat flour or rice dough, dim sum are filled with tasty concoctions of pork, beef, fish, or vegetables. This cuisine is not limited to the dumpling format, however—it also includes dishes such as congees (porridges), stuffed lotus leaves, spareribs, stuffed crab claws, scallion pancakes, shrimp balls, pork buns, egg custard tarts, etc. At a dim sum meal, you either pick these tidbits from a menu or, more often, from a cart wheeled from the kitchen to the customers. It's not necessary to select all the dishes for your meal on the first pass of the cart—carts come by quite regularly. The bill depends on how many dishes you choose, and this, in turn, is usually calculated by the number of serving dishes that have piled up on your table by the end of the meal. The more people in your party, the more fun this ritual is; a large group can go on sharing dim sum for hours. What's more, it's very economical.

Traditionally, dim sum has been served in teahouses—large, good-natured restaurants where families and friends sit around circular tables talking, eating, and drinking pots and pots of steaming Chinese tea. About 15 or so Chinatown restaurants, and some not in Chinatown, serve dim sum from 11 a.m. to 3 p.m.

The atmosphere at **Yank Sing,** 427 Battery St., between Clay and Washington (tel. 362-1640), is always bustling, with waitresses carrying plate after plate of delicious goodies to your table. Don't grab everything that's offered; wait for the ones that appeal. Plum sauce, chili sauce, and mustard enhance the flavor of your dim sum. Most dishes at Yank Sing cost about $2, and you get two or three items to a plate. Among the daily offerings, you might be served shrimp wrapped in dough, pork balls, curried chicken dumplings, paper-wrapped chicken, rice rolls, fried taro-root dumplings, mushrooms wrapped in dough, bean-curd rolls, stuffed beancake, or a mixture of rice, mushrooms, and sausage wrapped in bamboo leaf. Dessert dim sum include puffy doughnuts, coconut with lotus bean, and egg custard. Soft drinks, beer, and wine are available.

Open daily: Monday to Friday from 11 a.m. to 3 p.m., on weekends from 9:30 a.m. to 4 p.m. Yank Sing has another location at 53 Stevenson St., near 1st and Market (tel. 495-4510). It's open Monday to Friday from 11 a.m. to 3 p.m.

Hang Ah Tea Room, 1 Pagoda Pl., off Sacramento near Stockton (tel. 982-5686), is another good spot for dim sum meals as well as Mandarin specialties.

Tucked into a Chinatown alleyway, it's a pleasant, well-lit, and unpretentious little place with linoleum tile floors, tables covered with white plastic, and pale-yellow walls adorned with Chinese embroideries. Some 25 varieties of tea-lunch delicacies are available, among them fried beef or pork wonton, bean-curd rolls, spareribs in black-bean sauce, and a sesame ball filled with sweet bean paste and coconut. Most plates cost $1.50.

Hang Ah is open daily from 10 a.m. to 9 p.m.

Mexican

Some people perpetually research good French restaurants; my passion has been to discover really great Mexican restaurants this side of the border. I didn't expect to find one as far north as San Francisco, but there it was, all new and shiny as of November 1987—the **Corona Bar & Grill,** 88 Cyril Magnin, at the corner of Ellis and Cyril Magnin (tel. 392-5500).

Entrepreneur Bill Kimpton brought together the restaurant-designing talents of Pat Kuleto, the creative California-Mexican cuisine of chef Robert Helstrom, and the management skills of Sarah Graves. The light peach, delicate rose, and blue-green of the beautiful Corona Bar and Grill create the aura of a sunset over the Pacific.

The Corona is situated directly on the corner of Ellis and Cyril Magnin, with lots of windows for people-watching. Handcrafted Mexican masks, some as old as 100 years, and a large mural of a coastal sunset help make this a warm, comfortable place in which to relax and enjoy the superb margaritas and creative food. Part of the Corona's stunning effect lies in the way it incorporates the basic beauty of food and its preparation into the decor. A 90-foot-long cherrywood bar with an open cooking line stretches across much of the restaurant's length. At the end of the open kitchen, in a continuing state of creative activity, a large glass-front fridge contains an attractive display of oysters and clams on ice.

A variety of appetizers are available from the bar, and then a regular menu is divided into Starters, about appetizer size; Small Plates, for those with medium-size appetites or those who would like to try several dishes; and Large Plates, of entree size. My first order was a "Fresh Oyster Shooter," with peppered Cuervo 1800 from the bar appetizers: it came in a small, attractive square glass (about jigger size) with the sauce of Cuervo on top, and it turned out to be tantalizing introduction for the good things to come. Among the Starter highlights are the quesadilla with shiitake mushrooms and roquefort, once-fried oysters, twice-fried beans, and steamed clams with cilantro and lime. Some of the Small Plate treats are the black-bean cake and grilled prawns, the duck tamale with cilantro pesto and red-pepper butter (absolutely delicious) and the shrimp relleno with a mosaic of sweet peppers. As for the Large Plates, the exceptional choices include a superb roasted duck with tamarind glaze and shoestring yams, a fresh green corn tamale with chicken breast or sirloin and black beans, and roast rack of lamb with a piñon-nut crust and light mole sauce. The food presentation is itself a work of art, and the servers are knowledgeable, friendly, and well-turned-out in white shirts, string ties, and black trousers.

The bar appetizer menu ranges from $1.75 for my "Fresh Oyster Shooter" to $8.50 for a grilled chicken salad. Starters are $4 to $7.75; Small Plates, $5.50 to $8.50; and Large Plates, $9 to $14.50, the top price being for a thin-pounded filet marinated with chiles, scallions, and black beans.

There is a good selection of domestic wines by the bottle and premium wines by the glass, as well as eight varieties of cerveza Mexicana, some gringo beers, magnificent margaritas, and even agua—Calistoga and Penafiel.

The Corona Bar & Grill is open daily for lunch and dinner from 11:30 a.m. to midnight. I would suggest that you make a reservation.

La Victoria, 2937 24th St., corner of Alabama (tel. 550-9309), is the most authentic and least costly of San Francisco's Mexican eateries. Entered via an aromatic bakery-cum-grocery where fresh-from-the-oven breads and pastries, plantains, chiles, cactus leaves, chayote, mangoes, hot sauces, and the like are attractively displayed, it consists of two small rooms divided by an open kitchen with hanging plants over the counter. Mexican travel posters and a plaque of the Virgin adorn red walls, the floor is covered in ginger linoleum, and the tables are brown Formica. During the day it's bright and sunny.

The menu is in Spanish only, and entrees are $7 or less. Among the offerings: two burritos, tacos, or enchiladas with rice and frijoles (beans); orden birria (an order of beef with chiles and sauce); and menudo grande (a large serving of hunks of tripe with fresh lemon, chopped onions, fresh oregano, and red chile). Another specialty is fried pork skin with chile verde. Have a bakery-fresh pan dulce with your coffee and homemade flan for dessert.

Open daily from 10 a.m. to 10 p.m.

Salvadorean

La Santaneca, 3781 Mission St., at Richland (tel. 648-1034), is a small storefront place with simple decor—wood-grain paneling, Formica-topped tables, wooden chairs, hanging plants. It's run by a brother and sister, Oscar and Nena Carcamo, who've been at it for over a decade.

If you aren't familiar with Salvadorean food, Nena will graciously help you make your selections. There are soups, like beef tripe or prawn. For $2.50 to $5 you can order any of a number of typical dishes. A plate of papusas (corn tortillas with cheese or pork stuffing) and another of plantains and beans with sour cream make a wonderful light lunch or supper. They can also serve as prelude to an entree like chile relleno, Salvadorean-style chicken, or a combination platter of steak, prawns, rice, french fries, and salad. Such Mexican classics as tostadas, chorizo (sausage), tacos, or burritos are also available. Entrees, which cost $6 to $8, are served with rice, beans, and a spicy-hot Salvadorean "coleslaw" of cabbage, carrots, vinegar, and chilies.

No liquor is served at La Santaneca, but there's coffee and tea as well as tropical fruit juices and a delicious Salvadorean drink made of rice, milk, peanuts, sesame, cinnamon, and other spices, with the consistency and color of light chocolate milk, called horchata.

La Santaneca is open Tuesday to Thursday from 10:30 a.m. to midnight, Friday through Sunday to 3 a.m. It's a bit off the beaten track, but well worth seeking out. It's easy to get to by car, and can also be reached on the no. 14/ Mission bus or by BART (it's a short walk from the Glen Park stop).

Vietnamese

With the proliferation of Vietnamese in San Francisco, there's been a rash of Vietnamese restaurants. The best, in my opinion, is **Mai's,** 1838 Union St., at Laguna (tel. 921-2861). It's a pleasant, intimate place, with only small touches of the Orient: prints on the wall, and soft Vietnamese music playing in the background. While you peruse the menu you can order a drink from the fully stocked bar. Be sure to start with the Imperial or Vietnamese rolls. (The former are like traditional eggrolls, while the latter are made of shredded pork and lettuce wrapped in rice paper; both are delicious.) Don't miss the hot-and-sour soup; it's quite different from the Chinese variety, with a clear broth, crisp vegetables like tomatoes, bean sprouts, celery, and chives, and lots of cilantro. Entrees include lots of pork, chicken, beef, seafood, and vegetarian dishes, priced from $4 to $8. You can also order a complete dinner of soup, appetizer, selected entree, and rice for about $10. Jasmine tea accompanies any meal. And for dessert, you can order flan, lichees, or tropical fruit.

Mai's is open Monday to Thursday from 11 a.m. to 10 p.m., on Friday and Saturday till 11 p.m., on Sunday from 11 a.m. to 5 p.m. There is another Mai's at 316 Clement St., between Fourth and Fifth Avenues (tel. 221-3046), open weekdays from 11 a.m. to 10 p.m. and weekends from 10 a.m. to 11 p.m.

And in Conclusion

The perfect finale for a meal or a restaurant-listings section, **Just Desserts,** 3735 Buchanan St., between Marina Boulevard and Beach Street, across from the

Marina Green (tel. 922-8675), is a delightful place to indulge in rich chocolate cake, banana-walnut cake with buttercream icing laced with raspberry jam, creamy New York–style cheesecake, or chocolate velvet—layers of light-and-dark-chocolate mousse on gâteau au chocolat. All are baked fresh daily from scratch. Prices range from $1 to $4.50. Fresh-ground coffee, espresso, and a large variety of teas are also served. And if you go for breakfast, there are fresh-baked pastries and authentic French croissants.

Just Desserts is light and airy with lots of windows, a garden room, and patio. It's open Sunday to Thursday from 8 a.m. to 11 p.m. (on Tuesday from 2 p.m.), till midnight on Friday and Saturday. There are three other Just Desserts: at 248 Church St., between Market and 15th; at 836 Irving, between 9th and 10th; and at 3 Embarcadero Center. They have slightly different hours.

5. SIGHTS

San Francisco is chockablock with sightseeing adventures, many of which can best be enjoyed on foot—but in very comfortable walking shoes and if you're in good shape. Chinatown, Japantown, Fisherman's Wharf, the Cannery, Ghirardelli Square, Pier 39, and the like make San Francisco a stroller's paradise, and while you're checking out these attractions you can savor the unique and charming atmosphere of the city.

As long as we're on the topic of walking excursions, you should know that volunteers sponsored by the Friends of the San Francisco Public Library (tel. 558-3857) conduct free tours of historic areas within the city's neighborhoods, generally from May through October. Tours usually take about 1½ hours; reservations are not required. There are tours of City Hall, Coit Tower, Gold Rush City, North Beach, Victorian Houses of Pacific Heights, and Cathedral Hill and Japantown.

In the upcoming pages, I've detailed daytime activities, including those mentioned above, as well as parks, museums, and excursions.

Let's begin with an area of major importance in the San Francisco tourism picture:

CHINATOWN: Head for Grant Avenue at Bush Street, where an ornamental green-tiled archway, crowned by a symbolic dragon, marks the entrance to the biggest Chinese stronghold this side of Taiwan. Here begins an eight-block-long, three-block-wide labyrinthine array of pagoda-roofed buildings, dragon-entwined lamp posts, exotic shops and food markets, renowned restaurants, temples, and museums; here Kuangchou dialect is the mother tongue.

The early-comers from Canton reached San Francisco during the Gold Rush in 1849. They called the city Gum Sum Dai Fow—"Great City of the Golden Hill." Today their numbers have swollen to an estimated 80,000, although some local Chinese sources set the figure at more than 100,000.

Banding together in one tiny area of the city was not totally a clannish choice of these immigrants. They were partly forced into it by anti-Oriental prejudice. It became as ghettos will, ridden with vice, and until the earthquake of 1906 Grant Avenue (San Francisco's oldest artery, then Dupont Street) had an unsavory reputation as "the wickedest thoroughfare in the States." Only after devastation swept away the bordellos, gambling dens, and opium parlors was it given a new name—and a new image.

Along with vice, the earthquake swept away another old Chinatown symbol —the Tong hatchet men, so named because they actually dispatched their victims with an ax. Originally formed as protective societies, because "pigtail bait-ing" was a favorite pastime of San Francisco hoodlums, the Tongs evolved into criminal gangs. Today, however, the Tongs are gone, and, in fact, Chinatown is one of the safest neighborhoods in America. It's packed with interesting sights, which I've detailed below. And while you're here, have a meal or a dim sum feast in one of the restaurants suggested in the previous section.

At the corner of Grant Avenue and California Street, having survived the earthquake and fire in 1906, is **Old St. Mary's Church.** The city's first cathedral, it was erected in 1854 of brick brought around Cape Horn and a granite corner-stone cut in China. Above the clock dial, its red-brick façade bears this warning: "Son, Observe the Time and Fly from Evil." Diagonally across is **St. Mary's Square,** a tranquil, flower-filled retreat, over which an imposing, 12-foot statue of Sun Yat-sen, by sculptor Beniamino Bufano, presides.

The tiny **Chinese Historical Society of America,** at 17 Adler Pl., just off Grant Avenue (tel. 391-1188), open from 1 to 5 p.m., houses a collection of reg-ional Chinese artifacts. The society was started in 1962 to record the history of the Chinese in America; in 1963 the first exhibit of historical artifacts was held at the local Chinese YMCA. The contents of the old, often battered trunks Chinese pioneers left for safekeeping but never claimed formed the basis of the exhibit. Later a fire destroyed this priceless collection of Chinatown memorabilia. Cur-rently you'll view scores of sepia-toned photographs of early arrivals, tiny slippers for the bound feet of aristocratic ladies, a Chinese religious altar built in 1880, a wedding headdress, herb store paraphernalia, a shrimp winnower, mining arti-facts, and gadgets and pipes used in opium dens. And, as in the original collec-tion, there is a trunk full of personal effects that was checked but never claimed. What kept the owner from coming back for his trunk?

In 1969, the society's current home was provided by the Shoong Founda-tion. That same year, the society conducted a seminar on the history of the Chi-nese in California. Subsequently a 90-page syllabus was produced (now in its sixth printing) covering the arrival of the Chinese, their culture and language, and their contributions to various industries in California. Admission to the mu-seum is free, but a generous donation is very much in order.

At 838 Grant Ave., you'll come to the **China Trade Center,** an arcade of shops and restaurants, which is fun to visit.

If you've had your fill of bustling crowds, exotic wares, mountains of souve-nirs, etc., you might want to take a break and stop in at a Chinese movie. Most of the theaters are on Mason and Jackson Streets off Grant Avenue, and many have English subtitles. There's usually a double feature—a classical costume drama and a very Hollywood-style epic, or at least some Hong Kong studio's idea of one. Both are highly entertaining.

Chinese New Year

Chinese New Year occurs sometime in February or March, depending on the fullness of the moon. The merry-making lasts a full week, and celebrations spill onto every street in Chinatown, transforming the streets into noisy and ex-citing fairgrounds. There's a "Miss Chinatown USA" pageant parade, as well as marching bands, floats, barrages of fireworks, ten-foot-tall Taoist deities, block-long dragons, and celestial lions. According to the Chinese lunar calendar 1989 (or 4687 in Chinese dating) is the Year of the Serpent, and 1990 is the Year of the Horse.

Guided Tours

There's actually a Chinese-run Chinatown tour operation—**Ding How Tours,** 753½ Clay St. (tel. 415/981-8399). A taxi picks you up from—and delivers you back to—your hotel. On the 3½ hour nighttime tour, you may dine (it's optional) at a Chinese restaurant; explore narrow back alleys; hear about the old and new Chinese culture and developing events in Chinatown; see the sights and activities of Chinatown at night; and learn about the Chinese language, Chinese painting, and the art of Chinese tea drinking. Without dinner the tour is $19; with dinner, $32.

Gray Line (tel. 415/558-9400) also offers a Chinatown by Night tour which takes you first on a bus ride to Ghirardelli Square, the Cannery, and Fisherman's Wharf, and then on a bus tour through Chinatown, followed by a walking tour of the area. The price of this outing is $20.50 (half-price for children 5 to 11). If you sign on for the Chinatown Dinner Tour, a multicourse Oriental dinner is included with the walking tour and ride through the city at night. Prices with dinner are $35 for adults, half-price for children.

JAPANTOWN/JAPAN CENTER: Set in and around Japan Center, a multimillion-dollar showcase completed in 1968, **Nihonmachi** (Japantown) is as slickly modern as Chinatown is ancient and exotic. The focal point of the city's Japanese business and cultural activities, the area abounds in Japanese art galleries, bookstores, restaurants, hotels, and shops displaying a fascinating array of products from Japan. The five-acre complex, designed by one of America's outstanding architects, Minoru Yamasaki, occupies three blocks bounded by Laguna, Fillmore, Geary, and Post Streets. It is one mile west of Union Square.

Many of the shops and facilities here—including an academy that teaches Japanese flower-arranging, a Japanese doll-making school, and a shiatsu school —are housed in three commercial buildings with staircases built around beautifully landscaped gardens. Two of these buildings are linked by the **Webster Street Bridge,** 135 feet long and lined with shops, a restaurant, and art galleries —including one that exhibits works from the Avery Brundage Collection of Asian Art.

The **Miyako Hotel** (see my hotel recommendations, above) offers traditional Japanese accommodations.

Kabuki Hot Spring, 1750 Geary Blvd. (tel. 922-6000), acquaints visitors with the pleasures of the traditional Japanese bath (individual or communal) and shiatsu massage. Facilities include the furo (big tub), saunas, steam cabinets, and showers.

The hub of Japan Center is the 30,000-square-foot **Peace Plaza,** landscaped with Japanese gardens and reflecting pools. A graceful *yagura* (wooden drum tower) spans the entrance to the plaza, and its focal point is the five-tiered, 100-foot-high **Peace Pagoda.** Designed by world-famous Japanese architect Yoshiro Taniguchi, the pagoda was a gift of friendship and goodwill from the children of Japan. Atop the highest tier is the *kurin,* a nine-ringed spire symbolizing great virtue. The pagoda is illuminated at night.

Buchanan Street between Post and Sutter Streets is another mall area. Here shops and flowering plum and cherry trees line a cobblestone walkway designed to resemble a meandering stream. The mall is graced with two fountains by Ruth Asawa.

Nihonmachi is also the scene of numerous Japanese festivals and events. These include: **Sakura Matsuri** (Cherry Blossom Festival), held for about nine days in April; **Aki Matsuri** (Fall Festival), in late September; **Tanabata** (Star Festival), held the weekend closest to July 7; **Bon Festival,** a Buddhist celebration held one or two days in mid-July, its high point being a community dance with hundreds of costumed dancers; and the **Mochi-Pounding Ceremony,** held one Sunday in the latter part of December, an unusual event that culminates in the making of rice cakes. Colorful occasions, these are often beautifully costumed affairs with music, dance, demonstrations of everything from martial arts to doll making and flower arranging, calligraphy, origami, and exhibits ranging from bonsai trees to dog shows.

In addition to festivals, programs featuring traditional Japanese entertainment and activities are held most Saturday afternoons from June through September.

FISHERMAN'S WHARF AND VICINITY: When the cable cars are running you can take the Hyde and Beach cable car from Powell and Market Streets to the end of the line. Disembark at **Victorian Plaza,** a gaslit replica of a turn-of-the-century park that is the center of ocean-oriented activities stretching from the Maritime Museum and Hyde Street Pier at the western edge of Aquatic Park to Pier 43.

You can go out on sports fishing boats from the Wharf. **Captain Ron's Pacific Charters,** 561 Prentiss St. (tel. 415/285-2000), takes out singles or groups and offers special group rates, with or without tackle. Call for information or reservations from 9 a.m. to 9 p.m.

People jam the area, browsing through the street stalls selling handmade jewelry and craft items, and there are any amount of street musicians, puppet shows, magicians, and ventriloquists. There are even bocci ball courts on the west side of the Maritime Museum.

About 6 a.m. every day, and 3 p.m. in the summer, the fishing fleet sails out through the Golden Gate—a picturesque sight that has diminished but is not much changed since the Italian immigrants of 90 years ago earned their livelihood the same way. Even before the turn of the century the Italians had established a "Little Italy" fishing village in San Francisco. From there, the idea of seafood restaurants was an obvious step. At first the restaurants were really just sidewalk kitchens, but word of the delicious meals spread, and over the years the tiny counters evolved into the larger eateries of today's Wharf. On Taylor Street north of Jefferson Street, however, is a long row of seafood grottos still offering paper cups of crab and shrimp cocktails.

But eateries are just part of the Wharf's attractions. Here are some others you won't want to miss:

Ripley's Believe It or Not® Museum

This unlikely compilation of 2,000-or-so exhibits from the Ripley arsenal at 175 Jefferson St. includes the world's smallest violin, among many other miniatures; a shrunken head from Ecuador; a replica of "Man of Chains" (an ascetic who, clothed in 670 pounds of chains, dragged himself through the streets of Lahore, Pakistan, as an act of self-mortification); the Lord's Prayer on a grain of rice; and so on. Open in summer from 9 a.m. to midnight; the rest of the year it's open from 10 a.m. to 10 p.m. Sunday to Thursday, 10 a.m. to midnight on Friday and Saturday. Admission is $6.95 for adults, $5.75 for juniors 13 to 17, $3.75 for children 12 and under.

Guinness Museum of World Records

This Wharf attraction at 235 Jefferson St. (tel. 771-9890) deals in superlatives. You might even get to meet a record-holder like Sandy Allen, at 7 feet 7 inches the world's tallest woman. Otherwise, you can content yourself with trying to put your arms around a replica of the world's fattest (1,069 pounds!) man. There are exhibits, displays, and videotapes of record-breaking events, even a participation area where you can re-create world records.

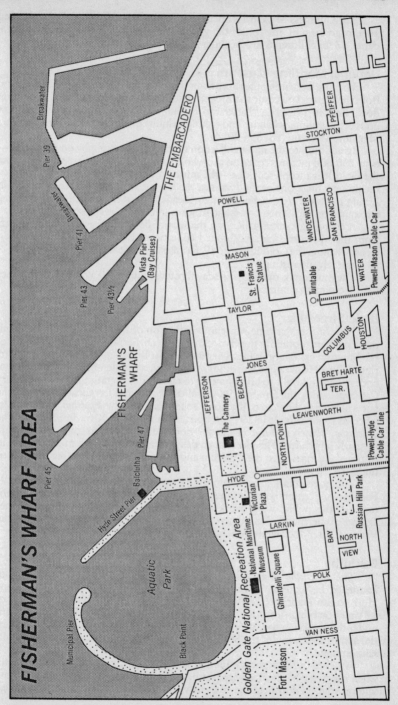

FISHERMAN'S WHARF AREA

The Guinness Museum is open from 10 a.m. to midnight daily in summer, 10 a.m. to 10 p.m. the rest of the year. Admission is $6.50 for adults, $5 students, $3 for children 5 to 12 (under 5, free).

National Maritime Museum

Walking west along the shore from Victorian Park, in the opposite direction from the Wharf, you come to a modernistic building that looks like a huge ship at dock. Built in 1939 as a "Palace for the Public," a huge bathing casino, it now houses the sailing, whaling, and fishing exhibits of the National Park Service's Maritime Museum (tel. 556-2904).

In addition to the finest collection of marine photography on the Pacific— over 250,000 pictures covering the whole subject of West Coast shipping from the Gold Rush to present day—the museum also has wonderful ship models, including a huge one of the *Preussen,* the largest wind-powered ship ever built. Lining the walls are the wooden figureheads favored by the old windjammers, wrought-iron caps, truss bows, and other examples of the shipsmith's craft.

A changing exhibit gallery on the second floor showcases art and artifacts from the Museum's rarely exhibited collections. New exhibits illustrate West Coast whaling, the Gold Rush of '49, ferryboats on the Delta, and much more— all extremely interesting.

The museum is open Wednesday through Sunday, 10 a.m. to 5 p.m., every day till 6 p.m. in summer.

Hyde Street Pier

Four of the Maritime Museum's collection of six National Historic Landmark ships are moored at the Hyde Street Pier (tel. 556-6435), a half block east of the Museum exhibit building. They include the British-built *Balclutha,* a square-rigged Cape Horn sailing ship; the *C. A. Thayer,* a wooden-hulled steam schooner designed and built to bring lumber to rapidly developing turn-of-the-century California cities; the *Eureka,* a 98-year-old paddlewheel ferryboat; the *Alma,* the last sailing San Francisco Bay scow schooner; and the *Eppleton Hall,* a side-wheeled tugboat built in 1914 to operate on the Tyne River in England. The *Balclutha, Thayer,* and *Eureka* can all be boarded. Ranger-led tours and films are regularly scheduled. The pier is open daily from 10 a.m. to 5 p.m., till 6 p.m. in summer. Admission to the Museum and ships is $3 for adults, free to children under 16.

The huge ocean-going steam tug *Hercules,* temporarily moored at Pier 1, Fort Mason Center, is undergoing restoration to steaming condition and is not open to the public while work is underway. The 300-foot steam schooner *Wapama* is berthed in Sausalito at the U.S. Army Corps of Engineers Bay Model Visitor Center dock while undergoing extensive preservation treatment.

Balclutha

The *Balclutha* is a typical merchant ship of the late Victorian period. Launched in Scotland in 1886, *Balclutha's* maiden voyage was around Cape Horn to San Francisco. During her early trading years she rounded Cape Horn 17 times carrying rice, wine, hardware, nitrate, and wool. In 1899 she was put under the Hawaiian flag carrying lumber from Australia and coal from Newcastle, and in 1902, under the Stars and Stripes, began a new career in the Alaska salmon trade.

Wrecked in 1904, she was refitted and renamed the *Star of Alaska.* By 1930, when she made her final voyage north, she was the last square-rigger left in the salmon trade. From here the old girl went Hollywood—renamed the *Pacific*

Queen, and used as a background for motion pictures. But by 1954 she had had it. Plans were afoot to dismantle the old vessel, when she was bought by the San Francisco Maritime Museum Association and restored to her original name and state. As of June 1978 the *Balclutha* and the Maritime Museum became part of the national park system's Golden Gate National Recreation Area.

Today she enjoys yet another incarnation as a playground for nautical-minded youngsters, who can spin her wheel, squint at the compass, and climb into the fo'c'sle.

The Wax Museum

This collection of over 275 wax figures of the famous and infamous is at 145 Jefferson St. (tel. 885-4975). All of the residents were created to look as lifelike as possible. They have real human hair, and the men are given complete beards or, if clean-shaven, a very faint stubble. There is a wax reproduction of just about the entire King Tut show that traveled around the country a few years ago. So if you missed it at the art museums, and can't afford a trip to Egypt, this may be your big chance. Other tableaux deal with royalty (including Prince Charles and Princess Diana), great humanitarians, celebs (Boy George and Michael Jackson), wicked ladies, world religions, and fairytale figures. And, as in every wax museum, there's a chamber of horrors.

Admission is $7.95 for adults, $3.95 for children 4 to 12, $5 for seniors; under 4, free. Summer hours are 9 a.m. to 11 p.m. Sunday to Thursday, to midnight on Friday and Saturday. The rest of the year the museum is open from 10 a.m. to 10 p.m. Sunday to Thursday, till midnight on Friday and Saturday.

The Haunted Gold Mine

The same folks also operate the Haunted Gold Mine at Mason and Jefferson Streets, a haunted funhouse with an abandoned-mine theme. There are mazes, a hall of mirrors, spatial disorientation areas, wind tunnels, and such. It's just the right degree of scary, and kids love it.

Hours during summer are 9 a.m. to 11 p.m. Sunday through Thursday, till midnight on Friday and Saturday; the rest of the year, Sunday to Thursday from 10 a.m. to 10 p.m., till midnight on Friday and Saturday. Admission is $4 for adults, $3 for seniors, $2.25 for children 4 to 12; under 4, free.

Bay Cruises from the Wharf

One of the best ways to see San Francisco is to leave it—just for a while, to enjoy a short cruise around the bay. The following leave from Fisherman's Wharf:

The **Red and White Fleet** (tel. 415/546-2896) runs a 45-minute tour, starting from Pier 41 or 43½, aboard deluxe sightseeing vessels with a passenger capacity of 400 to 500. There are open-air decks and glass-enclosed lower decks, and a snackbar dispenses hot dogs, sandwiches, and coffee. The round trip steers close to Alcatraz and passes under the Golden Gate Bridge.

Frequent departures begin at 10 a.m. year round (weather permitting). Adults pay $11; ages 12 to 17 and 65 or over, $8; children 5 to 11, $6; under 5, free.

Frequent daily departures year round from Pier 39's west marina are offered by the **Blue and Gold Fleet** (tel. 415/781-7877). Their 400-passenger sightseeing boat goes under both bridges, comes within yards of Alcatraz, and sails past Sausalito, Tiburon, Angel Island, and other points of interest. There are food and beverage facilities on board. The 1¼-hour narrated cruise costs $11 for adults, $6 for those 5 to 18, seniors; under 5, free. Departures begin at 10 a.m.

During the winter and spring there are whale-watching cruises on the new catamaran, the *Gold Rush*.

ALCATRAZ ISLAND: A mile and a half out from Fisherman's Wharf, the bay's once-grim bastion, the Rock, has emerged from over a century of isolation. Its history dates from 1775 when the island was discovered by a Spanish explorer who christened the place "Isla de los Alcatraces" (Island of the Pelicans) after its original inhabitants. When the Americans came, they drove off the birds, transformed the rock into a fortress, later an army prison, and finally into the nation's most notorious penitentiary.

The final transformation came in the '30s—America's gangster era—when the likes of John Dillinger and "Pretty Boy" Floyd seemed to bust out of ordinary jails with toothpicks. An alarmed public demanded an escape-proof citadel, and the federal government chose Alcatraz Island on which to erect it.

It seemed an ideal choice. The Rock was surrounded by freezing-cold water, with currents strong enough to defeat even the strongest swimmers. At a cost of $260,000 the old army cages were transformed into tiers of tiny, tool-proof, one-man cells, guarded by machine-gun towers, heavy walls, steel panels, and electronic metal detectors.

Stern prison rules included no talking, no canteen, no playing cards, no privileged trustees or inducements to good behavior. One of the prisoners said it was like living in a tomb. Into that "tomb" went Al Capone, "Machine Gun" Kelly, "Doc" Barker, "Creepy" Karpis, and other big-time criminals. All were broken by Alcatraz, except those who died trying to escape.

But even though Alcatraz was successful in its intended purpose, in many ways it created as many problems as it solved. Its cells were intended to hold 300 convicts, and—happily—there simply weren't that many incorrigible heavies around. So more and more small fry (ordinary car thieves, burglars, forgers, etc.) were sent up just to maintain the population—petty crooks who could just as well have been sent elsewhere at a fraction of the cost. For the expense of maintaining Alcatraz was immense; by the 1950s the money required to keep a single inmate on the Rock could have housed him in a luxury hotel suite.

So when three inmates seemed to stage a successful escape, tunneling out with sharpened spoons (no trace of them was ever found, and likely as not they drowned), the federal government took the opportunity to order the prison "phased out." On March 21, 1963, the Rock's last inmates—27 pale men in wrist and leg shackles—were transferred to other federal penal institutions.

For the next ten years the Rock remained empty, inhabited only by a caretaker, his wife, and an assistant. And for a while, in 1969, a protest group of American Indians took it over with the intention of establishing a Native American cultural center. They left in 1971.

Then in 1973 the National Park Service opened it to the public, running conducted tours from the San Francisco waterfront. Today great numbers of visitors flock to see the island's grim cells and fortifications, to explore the main prison block with its steel bars, the claustrophobic (nine by five feet) cells, mess hall, library, and "dark holes" where recalcitrants languished in inky blackness. If you've ever had an urge to experience instant hysteria, the "deep six" is the place. Just ask the guide to close one of the steel-plated doors behind you. Displays of photographs further enhance the experience.

To take the tour, with the **Red and White Fleet** (tel. 415/546-2896) purchase tickets at Pier 41, or through Ticketron (tel. 415/392-7469) as far in advance as possible. Only 150 people are taken on each tour, and there are always large groups of disconsolate standbys waiting on the windy pier.

The ferry leaves Pier 41 about every hour between 8:45 a.m. and 5 p.m. in summer (to 2:45 p.m. only, the rest of the year), bound for the 1½-hour guided walking tour of the Rock.

Important note: Wear comfortable shoes and a heavy sweater or wind breaker—it can be very cold. And make sure the kids hit the restrooms on the ferry going over. The only restrooms on the island are at the landing, and once you start out on your 1½-hour hike, that's it.

The visit involves a steep rise and some flights of stairs to climb. The National Parks Service advises those with heart or respiratory conditions to reconsider taking the tour if climbing stairs leaves them short of breath. They can either stay at the ranger station and amble through the small museum or, as an alternative, take the trip around Alcatraz described below.

The ranger-guided outdoor walking tour on Alcatraz is free; however, it does not include a look into the cell house, so if you want the details on how unpleasant confinement can be, you'll have to pay $7.50 for the audio tour ($5.25 for children 5 to 11). Round-trip fare is $5 for all over 12, $3 for those 5 to 11, and $4 for seniors; under 5, free.

For those who want to see Alcatraz without all the hiking, the Red and White Fleet also offers a 45-minute boat trip (summer only) around the island, leaving from Pier 41. You don't experience the eeriness firsthand, but you don't exhaust yourself either. The tour is narrated by a former Alcatraz prison guard. There are five departures each Wednesday through Sunday between 11:15 a.m. and 3:45 p.m., from Memorial Day through Labor Day. Tickets cost $7 for adults, $6.50 for seniors, $4.50 for kids 5 to 11.

THE 49-MILE SCENIC DRIVE: If you want a self-guided tour of the scenic and historic spots of San Francisco and have access to a car, there is no better way to see the city than to follow the blue-and-white seagull signs of the beautiful 49-mile (actually more like 51-mile) Scenic Drive. Virtually all the best-known sights are on this tour, as well as some great views of the bay and ocean. The drive covers a majority of the sights listed in this chapter, and more.

In theory, this mini-excursion can be done in half a day, but if you stop to walk across the Golden Gate Bridge or have tea in the Japanese Tea Garden in Golden Gate Park, or enjoy many of the panoramic views, you'll spend the better part of a day. And of course you can break up the drive to extend this interesting trip to more than one day.

The Convention and Visitors Bureau Information Center at Powell and Market Streets can supply you with a map of the route. The blue-and-white seagull signs along the way will direct you counterclockwise, but since a few are missing, the map will be especially useful. It's also a good idea to take someone along to help navigate. And for your sake, as well as the commuters', avoid the downtown area during the weekday rush hours from 7 to 9 a.m. and 4 to 6 p.m.

VICTORIAN HOUSES: San Francisco is a Victorian city (architecturally speaking) as much as it is a modern one. The city has thousands of "painted ladies" dating from the early 20th century, many of them beautifully restored and maintained. The best place to browse for them is in a large area bordered by Baker, Franklin, Union, and Post Streets. Some of the most renowned are: the **Octagon House,** 2645 Gough St., at Union (tel. 441-7512); the **Haas-Lillienthal House,** 2007 Franklin St., at Washington (tel. 441-3004); and the **Whittier Mansion,** 2090 Jackson St., at Laguna (tel. 567-1848). All three are open occasionally for tours; be sure to call ahead for days, times, and admission prices.

The most famous view of San Francisco is to be found at **Alamo Square,** where from the Hayes Street side of the park you can see a row of gorgeous Victorians on Steiner Street with the downtown skyline in the background. It's quite a view, as the proliferation of postcards containing it have proven.

LOMBARD STREET: It's a rare visitor to the City by the Bay who misses the "crookedest street in the world"—Lombard Street. There's one block (between Hyde and Leavenworth) that's so steep that the road curves back and forth like a snake. Needless to say, it's a one-way block—downhill in low gear (be sure your brakes are solid). It's fun to drive it, or just to watch as others do. If you're brave, you can climb the stairs along one side. Lombard is also one of the prettiest streets in the city, with its flowers, cobblestones, and charming homes.

GHIRARDELLI SQUARE: On the north waterfront, between Fisherman's Wharf and the Golden Gate entrance to San Francisco Bay, is Ghirardelli Square—a streamlined architecture-award–winning complex of terraces, shops, theaters, restaurants, cafés, and other diversions.

Originally a chocolate and spice factory built by an Italian immigrant, Domingo Ghirardelli, the property was set on 21.2 acres that included the old Woolen Mill Building (dating back to 1864). When, in the early '60s, the chocolate company decided to sell the plant and relocate, a group of prominent San Franciscans, fearing the site might be acquired for high-rise office buildings, purchased the property with the idea of converting the fine old buildings to a contemporary use. A talented group of architects, landscape artists, and designers was hired to restore and transform the factory to the entertainment center that it is today.

There are nine eateries in the complex (plus another ten spots for noshables), among them an authentic Delhi/Bombay-based Indian establishment **(Gaylord's)**, as well as excellent Chinese **(The Mandarin)**, Hungarian **(Paprikás Fono)**, and seafood **(Pacific Café)** restaurants. A San Francisco branch of New York's once chic (now defunct) **Maxwell's Plum** is also here. Of all the waterfront complexes, Ghirardelli has by far the best restaurants, the above-mentioned all being especially recommendable. If you're exploring the Wharf-Cannery-Pier 39-Ghirardelli area, plan on dining here. At the **Ghirardelli Chocolate Manufactory,** a candy store and soda fountain, you can watch chocolate being made and purchase the rich results. The soda fountain dispenses irresistible and gooey sundaes—like the "Golden Gate Banana Split" that has a base of three flavors of ice cream topped by three syrups and a banana bridge rising above great gobs of whipped cream.

Here, too, there's a cinema, a Japanese art gallery, and over 50 shops where you can buy or browse through Persian rugs, Dutch imports, kites of all nations, handmade Greek pottery, hand-sculptured glass items, music boxes, Japanese cultured pearls, and much more. There's something for everyone. And, as at the Wharf, street entertainers are out in profusion.

Pick up a free copy of the *Don't-Miss-A-Thing Walking Tour of Ghirardelli Square* at the Information Center, in the middle of the central plaza. It's a complete map and guide to all Ghirardelli shops, eateries, and attractions.

During the summer, Ghirardelli Square is open Monday through Saturday from 10 a.m. to 9 p.m., from 11 a.m. to 6 p.m. on Sunday. The rest of the year it's open from 10:30 a.m. to 6:30 p.m. Monday through Thursday, to 9 p.m. on Friday and Saturday, and on Sunday from 11 a.m. to 6 p.m.

Want some more of the same? Proceed to another version of the above formula, known as—

THE CANNERY: The defunct Del Monte produce plant (circa 1894), two blocks to the east of Ghirardelli Square, made an equally dramatic comeback as

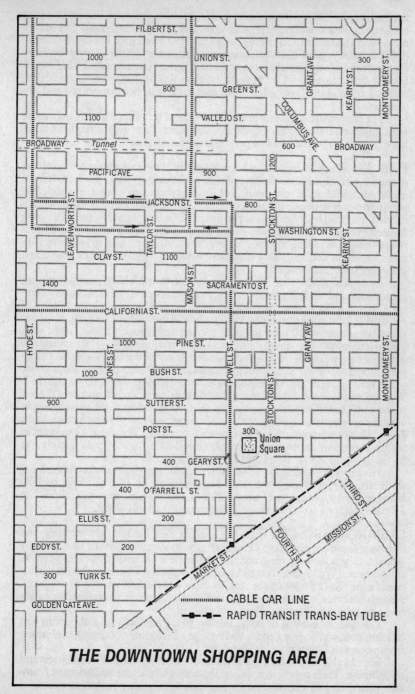

THE DOWNTOWN SHOPPING AREA

the Cannery in 1967. Attorney Leonard V. Martin, obviously inspired by what could be done with a chocolate factory, acquired the pre-earthquake Del Monte cannery at the foot of Columbus Avenue in 1962 and gave it a multi-million-dollar face lift. A great effort was made to preserve the Cannery's early San Francisco exterior of weathered sienna brick with arched entrances and windows. A flower-filled courtyard with gnarled olive trees was landscaped and remodeled, and this became the setting for much entertainment, both organized and impromptu.

The centerpiece of this three-story compound is the open plaza where musicians, jugglers, and magicians entertain. Of course, there are the requisite number of boutiques and restaurants packed into the complex.

PIER 39: This $54-million, 45-acre specialty shopping center and pleasure ground is an ostensible re-creation of turn-of-the-century San Francisco. It has a multitude of shops and restaurants, but if you expect to experience maritime life, you'd do better with one of the ferry trips. There are two marinas which accommodate over 350 boats including the Blue and Gold sightseeing fleet. Ongoing nautical events—boat races, etc.—add a special excitement to the Pier, as does the availability of sailing and sportfishing. The continuing flow of free entertainment alone can keep you busy for hours watching jugglers, mimes, musicians, and other street performers.

As for the shops, Pier 39 has over 100 of them, selling everything from games, toys, and teddy bears to costume and gold jewelry, San Francisco mementos, Christmas decorations year round, everything for left-handers, and kites of the world. After all the to-ing and fro-ing, you'll probably be hungry. To please the palate, there are 10 restaurants of varying ambience and price, some with great views of the bay, and 17 nosheries with everything from hot pretzels to Mexican pastry. Though I still maintain that many of the best waterfront complex eateries are over at Ghirardelli, the ones at Pier 39 offer the best water views.

There's also the **San Francisco Experience** (tel. 982-7394, showtimes 982-7550), a multimedia program that gives you the sights, sounds, and even the feel of the city. The city's history is reviewed, from its founding to the present day, in a rapid-fire presentation using three movie projectors, 32 slide projectors, and a 70- by 35-foot screen (with many surprises thrown in). The show, 27 minutes in length, is presented every half hour daily from 10 a.m. to 9:30 p.m. Tickets cost $5.50 for adults, $4 for those 5 to 18; free for under 5.

The Pier has parking for 1,000 cars, and you can also easily catch a cab out front. Its restaurants are open from 11:30 a.m. to 11:30 p.m. daily; cocktail lounges, until 2 a.m.; shops, from 10:30 a.m. to 8:30 p.m. To inquire about Pier 39 events, marina activities, shops, or restaurants, call 981-PIER.

EMBARCADERO CENTER: Yet another area for leisurely strolling and browsing is the Embarcadero Center, a "total living environment" designed by famed architect John Portman and situated in the financial district on 8½ bayside acres between Wall Street West and the Ferry Building. The hub of activity is just outside the **Hyatt Regency** (be sure to check out the lobby while you're here). Noon is the best time to go—that's when all the street merchants have their stalls set up on the Justin Herman Plaza.

The first three levels of each building (there are four) are a shopping area housing about 175 shops and a wide range of restaurants offering everything from yogurt and sprouts to McDonalds.

You can also stop at the Hyatt's outdoor café (the Market Place) for rest and refreshment. Then continue strolling about and take in the **Vaillancourt Fountain** (made of 100 concrete boxes), as well as the many sculptures scattered throughout the area. These range from a three-foot Bufano bear to works by Louise Nevelson and Willi Gutmann. Many Bufano animals are situated on the open deck of the **Alcoa Building,** from whence you can cross one of the pedestrian bridges to the **Golden Gateway,** a $150-million waterfront renewal program of town houses, apartments, shops, courtyards, and fountains.

GOLDEN GATE PROMENADE: Opened in 1973, this 3½-mile shoreline footpath, providing access to the Presidio and Fort Mason, has been called the most spectacular walk in the United States. Approach is from **Fort Point** (tel. 556-2857)—built in 1863 to protect San Francisco from the Confederate Army (made quite a success of it too!). Now it's a military museum, open from 10 a.m. to 5 p.m. daily, and free guided tours are offered.

From Fort Point you meander along a rocky beach, past the fishermen at Fort Point dock, past the Coast Guard lifesaving station, and on to a sandy beach beside Crissy Field Landing Strip. Farther along are the decorative waterfront plaza of the municipal water treatment plant, the St. Francis Yacht and Marina breakwater—to Fort Mason, and, finally, **Aquatic Park.**

En route you might consider exploring the **Presidio Army Museum** (tel. 921-1403; open from 10 a.m. to 4 p.m. Tuesday through Sunday), established in 1776 as a Spanish garrison. Now the Presidio is a 1,500-acre headquarters for the Sixth U.S. Army. The museum serves as a center of historical research, housing artifacts and memorabilia from the Presidio's past. A second detour might be the **Palace of Fine Arts,** with its Exploratorium (details coming up).

The easiest way to begin this walk is to board a Golden Gate transit bus from Market and 7th Streets or from one of its stops along Van Ness Avenue, and get off at the bridge toll-gate plaza.

GOLDEN GATE PARK: Now the largest man-made park in the world (three miles long by half a mile wide), Golden Gate is a far cry from the windswept wasteland of rolling sand dunes acquired by San Francisco back in 1868. The original plan was for a great public park to compare with the one then being developed in New York by Frederick Law Olmsted. Mr. Olmsted was invited to look at the proposed site and he declared it hopeless. But year after year, park superintendent John McLaren (an indomitable horticulturist and forester whose motto was "trees and more trees") continued planting trees and shrubs, gradually taming the shifting sands. When he died in 1943, after 56 years of service, the park was an unbroken expanse of forest and glen, green lawns, bridle paths, lakes, and flowers.

You reach Golden Gate Park (tel. 558-4268) by taking a no. 38 bus on Geary Street to Tenth Avenue, then changing to a no. 10, which lets you off at the **Music Concourse** where band concerts are held nearly every Sunday and holiday afternoon. Other musical events—Broadway shows, jazz, country music, operas, ballets, etc.—take place on summer Sunday afternoons at 2 p.m. at the **Stern Grove Music Festival** (tel. 398-6551), on Sloat Boulevard near 19th Avenue; admission is free.

Free guided walking tours of the park are offered every weekend from May through October by Friends of Recreation and Parks (tel. 221-1311).

Not far from the Concourse is the **Japanese Tea Garden** (tel. 387-6787), created in 1894 for the California Midwinter International Exposition, and kept on as a permanent attraction. Entered through a hand-carved gateway, it's an enchanting five-acre Oriental garden of bamboo-railed paths, bonsai trees, rock creations, reflecting pools filled with goldfish, pagodas, torii statues, and Oriental art objects including a Japanese bronze Buddha that dates from 1790. The garden is open daily from 8 a.m. to 6:30 p.m., admission 75¢. There's a Japanese tea house where kimono-clad waitresses serve aromatic blended teas. If you come in late March to early April you'll see the cherry blossoms in bloom, not just in the Tea Garden but throughout the park; a few years ago Japan donated 700 cherry trees to the Golden Gate as a Bicentennial gift.

Nearby is **Stow Lake,** where you can rent a rowboat or paddleboat (tel. 752-0347) for a leisurely ride to the island in the center of the lake. The area near the lake is ideal for picnicking.

Other notable park features include:

The **Conservatory of Flowers,** Kennedy Drive near Third Avenue (tel. 558-3973), has tropical plants and a continuous flower show in bloom, open daily from 9 a.m. to 5 p.m. October to April, to 6 p.m. other months. Admission is $1 for adults; 50¢ for children 5 to 12; under 5, free. It's the oldest building in Golden Gate Park.

The **Strybing Arboretum,** South Drive at Ninth Avenue (tel. 558-3622) is open weekdays 8 a.m. to 4:30 p.m., weekends and holidays 10 a.m. to 5 p.m. The arboretum covers almost 70 acres and has in its collection over 6,000 species of plants, trees, and shrubs.

The **M. H. de Young Memorial Museum,** the **California Academy of Sciences,** and **Asian Art Museum** are all detailed below.

The **Golf Course** at 47th Avenue and Fulton Street, next to the archery field (tel. 751-8987), is a nine-hole course with a short and tricky layout.

And then there are football and baseball fields; soccer pitches; bowling greens; tennis, handball, and basketball courts; horseshoe pits; bicycle, equestrian, and hiking trails; track facilities—even a vast enclosed pasture (near John F. Kennedy Drive) where a herd of buffalo roams. What's more, you can picnic anywhere in the park.

The best way to navigate the park is on a bicycle; you can rent one at shops on Stanyan Street. Some of these shops also rent roller skates, as do vans on Fulton Street and Lincoln Way on Sunday.

MISSION DOLORES:
MISSION DOLORES: Founded in 1776, this was the sixth of the original 21 missions established throughout California by Father Junipero Serra. The Mission (believed to be the oldest structure in San Francisco) was erected in what was then wilderness, the city later growing up around it. The name was taken from a nearby lake (Laguna de los Dolores—lake of sorrows), long since filled. The architecture combines Moorish, Mission, and Corinthian styles; the altar and decorations are from Spain and Mexico. Its adobe walls are four feet thick, its hewn roof timbers lashed with rawhide. There's a statue of Father Serra in the Mission garden, where many pioneers and 5,000 Native Americans are buried.

Open from 9 a.m. to 4:30 p.m. daily (till 4 p.m. in the winter). A voluntary donation of $1 is requested. You can reach the Mission by taking the "J" streetcar up Market Street to the corner of Church and 16th Streets, then walking back one block to Dolores Street.

SAN FRANCISCO ZOOLOGICAL GARDENS AND CHILDREN'S ZOO:
SAN FRANCISCO ZOOLOGICAL GARDENS AND CHILDREN'S ZOO: Take the L MUNI Metro from downtown Market Street to the end of the line, and you'll come to one of the great zoos in the United States. Entrances are located on Sloat Boulevard at 45th Avenue and on Herbst Road off Skyline Boulevard.

It all began with a grizzly bear named Monarch, donated in 1889 by the *San Francisco Examiner.* As it evolved at its present site, the San Francisco Zoo was patterned after the pioneering Hagenbeck Zoo near Hamburg, Germany. It now takes up 65 of 125 acres of land. The rest of the park is to be developed in the coming decade under the Zoo 2000 plan.

Most of the animals in the San Francisco Zoo are kept in wonderfully realistic landscaped enclosures guarded by cunningly concealed moats. Construction of Wolf Woods, Gorilla World, and Musk Ox Meadow (described below) began the renaissance of the zoo, replacing small enclosures with open naturalistic habitats. You can see 38 species currently classified as endangered or threatened.

With the record-breaking Giant Panda exhibition and the opening of the Primate Discovery Center and Koala Crossing, the zoo's attendance has grown to over one million visitors per year. The zoo boasts close to 1,000 animals and birds and 6,000 specimens of insects, including a hissing cockroach (those living in New York City haven't evolved to that stage yet) which can be found in the remarkable Insect Zoo, which I'll get to in a minute.

The innovative Primate Discovery Center (we too are primates, though not yet rare) exhibits 16 rare and endangered species in naturalistic settings, from soaring outdoor atriums and meadows to a midnight world for exotic nocturnal primates. This is where you'll find a crab-eating macaque, one of the few primates that can swim; a Senegal bush baby that bounces as it walks, sometimes jumping four feet straight up though it's only six inches tall; and the Patas monkey, one of the fastest primates—it can run up to 35 miles per hour.

Other highlights include the Koala Crossing, patterned after an Australian outback station; Gorilla World, one of the world's largest naturalistic exhibits of these gentle giants; Wolf Woods, offering a chance to learn about the remarkably sophisticated social behavior of the North American timber wolf; Musk Ox Meadow, a 2.5-acre habitat for a herd of rare white-fronted musk oxen brought from Alaska; the Lion House, home to four species of cats, including Prince Charles, a rare white tiger (you can watch them being fed at 2 p.m. daily except Monday); and Penguin Island, with its colony of about 50 Magellanic penguins from Chile.

The Children's Zoo, adjacent to the main zoo, is a special place for everyone to get close to animals and watch zoo babies being tended in the Nursery. You'll have a tough time tearing the children away from the barnyard, alive with strokable, sniffing, cuddlesome baby animals. And there's the fascinating Insect Zoo—the only one in the western U.S. and one of only three such exhibits in the country. You'll see velvet ants, honey bees, scorpions, and the marvelous hissing cockroaches I mentioned earlier. On weekends, there are amazingly popular Tarantula Talks at 2:30 p.m. when visitors can get an intimate look at a live tarantula and learn more about its life style. The Children's Zoo is open daily from 11 a.m. to 4 p.m. Admission is $1 for everyone (kids under 2 are free).

A free informal walking tour of the zoo leaves from Koala Crossing at 12:30 and 2:30 p.m. on weekends. The "Zebra Zephyr" tour train takes visitors on a 20-minute safari tour of the zoo, daily except in winter when it runs only on weekends. The tour is $2 for adults, $1 for children 15 and under.

The main zoo is open daily from 10 a.m. to 5 p.m. Admission is $5 for adults, $2 for a quarterly pass for seniors, free for children 15 and under if accompanied by an adult. For recorded information call 661-4844; otherwise, 661-2023.

WELLS FARGO HISTORY MUSEUM: In a ground-floor area of the bank's headquarters, the History Room houses hundreds of relics and photographs from the Wells Fargo's whip-and-six-shooter days. The centerpiece is the Concord stagecoach, proudly identified as the Wells Fargo Overland Stage—the 2,500-pound buggy that opened the West as surely as did the Winchester rifle and the Iron Horse.

There are samples of the treasure Wells Fargo carried—to wit, gold nuggets from the Sierra Nevada mines—and mementoes of the men who were after it, men like "Black Bart," who single-handedly robbed 28 stagecoaches. There's a gold balance scale so sensitive it could, miners claimed, register the weight of a pencil mark on a piece of paper.

On the mezzanine, you can take an imaginary ride in the replica stagecoach or send off a telegraph message in code, using a telegraph key and the codebooks just the way the Wells Fargo agents did over a century ago.

Those visitors interested in mail of the early days can browse through the Wiltsee Collection of western stamps and postal franks.

The museum is open 9 a.m. to 5 p.m. Monday through Friday. The bank is located at 420 Montgomery St., at California (tel. 396-2619). Free admission.

THE EXPLORATORIUM: This unique do-it-yourself museum is organized around the theme of perception. *Scientific American* has called it the "best science museum in the world."

The Exploratorium is a mind-boggling place. You can't really call it a museum, an exhibit, or a display, because you participate with your senses and stretch them to new dimensions. Plan to spend at least an hour here with the kids.

You'll find this experience in San Francisco's rococo old Palace of Fine Arts, 3601 Lyon St., at Marina Blvd. (tel. 563-7337, or 563-3206 for recorded information); take the no. 30 bus on Stockton Street. This is the only building left standing from the Panama-Pacific Exposition of 1915, which celebrated the opening of the Panama Canal. Almost torn down to make way for real estate developments, it was restored in the mid-1960s because a local millionaire, Walter Johnson, shamed local government by putting up millions of his own money, which the voters supplemented.

There are over 600 exhibits dealing with everything from color theory to Einstein's Theory of Relativity. It's an *Alice in Wonderland* world. Optics are demonstrated in booths where you can see a bust of a statue in three dimensions, but when you try to touch it, it isn't there. The same thing happens with an image of yourself where, as you stretch your hand forward, a hand comes out toward you, and the two hands pass in midair. Every exhibit is designed for participation; "Do Not Touch" signs are nowhere to be seen.

You can talk into a telephone and see a light run a scale like the strength hammer at a carnival; or whisper into a concave reflector and have a friend hear you 60 feet away; or design your own animated abstract art, using sound.

Kids make up their own tours here, and will spend as much time as you allow them without grumbling or asking "What's next?" And if they're surfeited with things scientific, you can take them out to the adjoining lagoon and let them feed the ducks, swans, and seagulls that mooch there.

The Exploratorium is open July 1 through Labor Day on Wednesday from 11 a.m. to 9:30 p.m. and Thursday to Sunday from 11 a.m. to 5 p.m. From Labor Day through June 30 it's open on Wednesday from 1 to 9:30 p.m., on Thursday and Friday to 5 p.m., and on Saturday and Sunday from 10 a.m. to 5 p.m. Admission is free the first Wednesday of each month, and after 6 p.m.; otherwise adults pay $6, seniors pay $3, those 6 to 17 pay $1.50; under 6, it's free.

THE CALIFORNIA ACADEMY OF SCIENCES: At this famous complex of buildings, located on the Music Concourse in Golden Gate Park, you can view a Fijian cannibal fork, weigh yourself on the moon, or join an Arctic Eskimo on a seal hunt. It's actually a cluster of widely differing museums. Taking them one by one, we have first:

The **Steinhart Aquarium,** home to more than 14,500 specimens of fishes from all over the globe, as well as invertebrates, amphibians, reptiles, and aquatic mammals. A big attraction here is the Fish Roundabout, which allows visitors to view—without getting wet—marine life from a ramp *inside* a 100,000-gallon donut-shaped tank; it's like a mid-ocean deep-sea dive. The aquarium also has a "hands-on" area where children can pick up starfish and sea urchins.

Morrison Planetarium, presenting seven different shows a year, explores black holes, neutron stars, quasars, pulsars, UFOs, and other puzzles of the universe. Exhibits in the **Earth and Space Hall** further probe cosmic mysteries.

In the **Wattis Hall of Man** the concept of ecological anthropology—how human societies have related and adapted to their environments—is explored. Exhibits deal with evolutionary history and creative responses of man to each of several environmental situations (arctic, temperate, tropical, and desert), and displays range from gems, insects, birds, and mammals native to North America and Africa, to pre-Columbian art and gastroliths from the stomachs of dinosaurs.

The California Academy of Sciences is open daily from 10 a.m. to 5 p.m. (to 7 p.m. in summer). Admission is $5 for adults ages 18 to 64, $2.50 for senior citizens and those 12 to 17, and $1.25 for those 6 to 11. Everyone gets in free the first Wednesday of every month. Planetarium shows are $2 for adults, $1 for persons under 17. For further information and show times call 750-7145.

M. H. DE YOUNG MEMORIAL MUSEUM: The granddaddy of California museums, the M. H. de Young Memorial had its origin in the California Midwinter International Exposition of 1894. At the end of the exposition, the Fine Arts Building was turned over to de Young, a newspaper publisher who had served as director-general of the fair, for the purpose of establishing a permanent museum.

Located on the Music Concourse of Golden Gate Park, the museum contains 200,000 square feet of exhibit area. Paintings, sculpture, and decorative arts, as well as period rooms, illustrate the cultures of the Western world from the time of ancient Greece and Egypt to the 20th century. Various collections contain works of Fra Angelico, Goya, Rubens, El Greco, Van Dyck, Gainsborough, and Rembrandt, among others. The recently renovated American gallery holds a fine collection of paintings dating from colonial times through the 19th century.

There's a café on the premises with a garden for al fresco dining, open from 10 a.m. to 4 p.m. Wine and beer is served.

The museum is open from 10 a.m. to 5 p.m. Wednesday through Sunday; admission is $5 for adults, $3 for seniors; those 18 and under get in free. The same fee also admits you to the Asian Art Museum and the California Palace of the Legion of Honor. The first Wednesday of the month and every Saturday from 10 a.m. to noon admission is free. For further information call 221-4811.

ASIAN ART MUSEUM OF SAN FRANCISCO: Located in Golden Gate Park adjacent to the Japanese Tea Garden, the Asian Art Museum (tel. 668-8921) houses the world-famous Avery Brundage collection of over 10,000 Oriental art treasures. The scope of the exhibits is dazzling, spanning over 6,000 years of Asian history and prehistory. The entire first floor is devoted to the arts of China, beginning with neolithic ceramics and the earliest Chinese bronzes and surveying all the great ages of Chinese art through the 20th century. A high point is the Chinese jade display. One of the greatest Chinese lacquer collections is now owned by the museum. Arts of India, Central and Southeast Asia, Japan, Korea, the Himalayan region, and Middle East are also well represented on the second floor. Special temporary exhibits are held regularly.

Conducted tours are given daily and provide highly informative background information on the arts of Asia in the museum's collections. Open from 10 a.m. to 5 p.m. Wednesday through Sunday. Entrance is through the de Young Museum. Admission is free on Saturdays 10 a.m. to noon and the first Wednesday of each month. One admission lets you into the Asian Art Museum, the M. H. de Young Museum, and the California Palace of the Legion of Honor.

MUSEUM OF MODERN ART: The San Francisco Museum of Modern Art, 401 Van Ness Ave., at McAllister (tel. 863-8800), opened in 1935 and quickly established itself as an adventurous and dynamic repository of 20th-century art. Through its intensive program of temporary exhibitions and increasingly substantial permanent collection, it retains that position today.

The museum's collection is distinguished by major works from the American abstract expressionist school of painters—Clyfford Still, Jackson Pollock, Mark Rothko, and Willem de Kooning—and by unique holdings in contemporary photography. It also has strengths in German expressionism (Max Beckmann, Max Pechstein), post-impressionism (Henri Matisse), Mexican painting (José de Rivera, José Orozco), and in the art of the San Francisco area.

Half the gallery space displays its permanent collection, but the museum also hosts important traveling exhibitions. Past shows included a Philip Guston retrospective, "Wayne Thiebaud, Robert Hudson: A Survey," and "Photography in California: 1945–1980"—much noted successes.

The museum was one of the first to recognize photography as an art form. Today its collection of 20th-century photography includes holdings of works by Americans such as Alfred Stieglitz, Ansel Adams, and Edward Weston, the German avant-garde artists of the 1920s, and the European Surrealists of the 1930s.

The museum organizes special artistic events, lectures, concerts, dance performances, poetry readings, conceptual-art events, films, and many activities for children. There's a great gift, book, and art shop in the museum, one of the best I've seen outside Manhattan.

Admission is $3.50 for adults, $1.50 for seniors and children under 16; children under 5 are admitted free. Hours are 10 a.m. to 5 p.m. on Tuesday, Wednesday, and Friday, to 9 p.m. on Thursday (admission reduced 5 to 9 p.m.—$2 for adults, $1 for seniors and those under 16); on weekends 11 a.m. to 5 p.m. The museum is closed Monday and holidays.

CALIFORNIA PALACE OF THE LEGION OF HONOR: Intended as a memorial for California's fallen of World War I, this beautiful museum is a replica of the Legion of Honor Palace in Paris, including the inscription "Honneur et Patrie" above the portal. Rising classically white and pillared from a hilltop, the building is neoclassic in architecture, but the collection housed within is French, with special emphasis on the 18th and 19th centuries. Among the artists represented are Corot, Degas, Fragonard, Manet, Monet, and Renoir. There's a comprehensive Rodin sculpture collection, as well as some splendid period rooms, like a Louis XVI salon.

Although the collection is all French, the museum also holds special showings such as "The Vatican Collections"; "Venice: The American View"; "Leonardo da Vinci: Drawings of Horses"; "Maori Art from New Zealand"; and "The Prints of Edvard Münch." And the museum runs a series of auxiliary attractions, such as pipe organ concerts on Saturday and Sunday afternoons.

Location is in Lincoln Park (tel. 221-4811). To get there, take a no. 2 Clement bus from downtown Sutter Street to 33rd and Clement, then transfer to the no. 18 bus into the park. Admission is $5 for adults, $3 for senior citizens, free for those 18 and under. Your ticket is also good for the Asian Art Museum and the M. H. de Young Memorial Museum. Open from 10 a.m. to 5 p.m. Wednesday through Sunday. All three museums are free the first Wednesday of the month.

6. AFTER DARK

The Bay City is a great town for bars—plush bars, laid-back hangout bars, singles bars, Latin bars, gay bars, and neighborhood bars. Discos come in the same categories, and more.

There are enough quality theatrical, concert, ballet, and operatic productions to sustain the most culturally minded visitor. And enough bare pulchritude on one North Beach block to sustain the most salacious. Everything, in fact, for everyone. One special note—don't miss *Beach Blanket Babylon* (about which more later).

The best guide to San Francisco cultural and nightlife is the pink section (called the "Datebook") of the Sunday San Francisco *Examiner and Chronicle.* You can also refer to a small but very handy free publication called *Key,* which appears weekly and can be found in hotel lobbies and at newsstands.

TICKETS: The **San Francisco Ticket Box Office Service (STBS),** patterned after New York's TKTS, provides tickets at half price for day-of-performance sale to all types of performing arts—theaters, concerts, operas, and dance events—in the major theaters and concert halls. In addition, STBS handles advance, full-priced tickets for neighborhood and outlying performing companies, sporting events, concerts, and clubs, as a convenience to the public (tel. 433-STBS). Half-price ticket information is not available by phone.

Things to remember about STBS: Sales of half-price tickets are cash only or traveler's checks; tickets are not available for every attraction, but there will always be something available; no telephone reservations accepted; only in-person sales. A service charge is added to all tickets, ranging from $1 to $3 per ticket, based on the full price of the ticket.

VISA and MasterCard are accepted for full-price tickets. Half-price tickets for Sunday and Monday events, if available, are sold on Saturday. However, STBS cannot predict what tickets will be available at half price on a given day.

STBS is located on Stockton Street between Geary and Post, on the east side of Union Square opposite Maiden Lane. Hours are Tuesday to Thursday from noon to 7:30 p.m. on Friday and Saturday to 8 p.m. (The hours are subject to change.)

THEATER: The **American Conservatory Theater (ACT),** which made its San Francisco debut in 1966, has been heaped with praise, and even compared to the British National Theatre and the Comédie-Française. ACT offers solid, well-staged, and brilliantly acted productions, with some emphasis on the classics, but offering a sufficient number of new and experimental works to keep its repertoire exciting and contemporary. Recent productions, for instance, included *A Christmas Carol, 'night, Mother, Opéra Comique,* Shaw's *You Never Can Tell,* and Sondheim's *Sunday in the Park with George.*

Classic and contemporary plays perform in repertory from October through May at the **Geary Theater,** 415 Geary St. (on San Francisco's little theater row). Reservations can be made by calling 415/673-6440. Tickets range from $11 to $30.

The **Curran Theater,** another theater-row resident at 445 Geary St. (tel. 415/673-4400), features Broadway musicals and comedies coming from or going to New York, usually with major stars—like Judd Hirsch in *I'm Not Rappaport,* James Earl Jones in *Fences,* and Lily Tomlin in *The Search for Signs of Intelligent Life in the Universe.*

Tickets range from $17.50 to $40. Monday is dark.

Under the same auspices as the Curran, and offering an identical Broadway musical format, is the **Golden Gate Theater,** 25 Taylor St., at Market Street and Golden Gate Avenue (tel. 415/775-8800). Built in 1922 and since restored to its original grandeur, the Golden Gate is impressively lavish, with marble floors, rococo ceilings, and gilt trimmings. Since its opening in 1979 with a ten-week run of *A Chorus Line,* it has presented Dick Van Dyke in *The Music Man,* Alexis Smith in *The Best Little Whorehouse in Texas,* Rex Harrison in *My Fair Lady,* and Richard Burton in *Camelot.* Quite a first season! *La Cage aux Folles, Nine, My One and Only,* and *Me and My Girl* were recent offerings. They also stage expansive limited engagements, such as the Ukrainian State Dance Company. There are matinees every Wednesday, Saturday, and Sunday, and evening performances Tuesday to Saturday. Ticket prices are generally in the $20 to $45 range.

Fans would as soon go to India and skip the Taj Mahal as pass up a chance to see a production of *Beach Blanket Babylon* at the **Club Fugazi,** 678 Green St., near Columbus Avenue (tel. 415/421-4222), in San Francisco. This incredible revue is the magical creation of impresario Steve Silver (Cyril Magnin calls him the Flo Ziegfeld of the '80s). It grew out of his Rent-a-Freak service, a group of extraordinary party entertainers who hired themselves out with fabulous gags, props, and costumes. The first production moved to the Savoy-Tivoli in 1974, but the audiences soon grew too large for the facility. A devoted mass following (consisting of almost everyone who has ever seen the show) includes people like Beverly Sills ("I wish I lived in San Francisco so I could see it more"). The first Fugazi production, *Beach Blanket Babylon Goes Bananas* played for three years to an SRO crowd. And the latest evolution, *Beach Blanket Babylon Goes Around the World* has been wildly successful. Skip the trip to Alcatraz, miss Chinatown, but don't miss *Beach Blanket Babylon.* What's all the excitement about? Whimsical costumes and 12-foot high, 40-pound Carmen Miranda hats, dancing palm trees, singing rainbows, and flights of imagination that have to be seen to be believed.

Performances are at 8 p.m. on Wednesday and Thursday, at 8 and 10:30 p.m. on Friday and Saturday, at 3 and 7:30 p.m. on Sunday. Consider that this show has consistently sold out over 5,000 performances since 1974. Minors are welcome at Sunday matinees at 3 p.m. when no alcohol is served. Otherwise, two I.D.s may be required. Prices are $13.50 to $24. If you know what date you're going to be in town, it's wise to write for tickets at least three weeks in advance of that time, or obtain them through Ticketron or STBS.

Note: The club now seats 393. When you purchase tickets they will be within a specific section, depending upon price. However, seating is still first-come, first-seated within that section. Seats in the new balcony are $17 to $21. Royal Box seats are $20 to $24.

The **Orpheum,** 1192 Market St., at Hyde (tel. 415/474-3800), has been the home of the San Francisco Civic Light Opera Association since the spring of 1977. It has been handsomely refurbished, and the shows presented here have been terrific. Recent productions have included *Hair, Nine, Fiddler on the Roof,* and *Sweet Charity.*

There are performances Tuesday through Saturday evenings, and Wednesday, Saturday, and Sunday afternoons. Tickets cost $20 to $45.

The **Eureka Theater,** 2730 Sixteenth St., at Harrison, south of Market (tel. 558-9898), a new 200-seat facility, offers contemporary and classical plays dealing with political and social issues. Eureka has produced a number of outstanding, award-winning plays such as *Top Girls, Cloud Nine,* and *A Bright Room Called Day.* Evening performances begin at 8 p.m. Wednesday through Saturday, 7:30 p.m. on Sunday. Matinees on Sunday begin at 2 p.m. Seats are $14 to $17.

The **Magic Theater,** Building D, Fort Mason, Laguna St. at Marina Blvd. (tel. 441-8822). While somewhat removed from the downtown area, this theater offers interesting and often controversial works of new and established playwrights. Sam Shepard's Pulitzer Prize–winning play *Buried Child* premiered here. More recent productions have included Samuel Beckett's *Happy Days*. Evening performances are at 8:30 p.m. Wednesday through Saturday, 7:30 p.m. on Sunday. Matinees on Sunday are at 2 p.m. Seats are $14 to $18.

OPERA, SYMPHONY, AND BALLET: San Francisco's magnificent **War Memorial Opera House,** built in 1932, is the focal point for most of the city's opera and ballet productions, and the quality of the performances is on a par with the world's greatest companies. The 14-week opera season begins in September. It's a good idea to get your name on the mailing list before your trip and order tickets in advance; they're hard to get. To do this, write to Opera Box Office, War Memorial Opera House, San Francisco, CA 94102. For phone reservations dial 415/864-3330. (There are 300 standee places for opera sold two hours before curtain time.)

The San Francisco Opera Association
Under the direction of impresario Terence A. McEwen, this is actually a multifaceted conglomerate (tel. 415/864-3330), with each branch offering something a little different from the others. They include:

The **San Francisco Opera Company** itself, which features celebrated stars like Kiri Te Kanawa, Marilyn Horne, Placido Domingo, and Luciano Pavarotti. Staging and direction are a wonderful blend of the traditional and the avant-garde. The company has presented 18 U.S. premieres by composers such as Richard Strauss, Britten, and Shostakovich, and provided American opera debuts for the likes of Birgit Nilsson, Leontyne Price, and Renata Tebaldi.

Single (non-subscription) tickets go on sale the first week in August. There are performances each evening (except Monday), with matinees on Saturday and Sunday. Prices range from $15 to $65. Tickets usually are available up to the day of the performance. Standing-room tickets ($7) go on sale two hours prior to the performance. The box office (tel. 864-3330) is open from 10 a.m. to 6 p.m. Monday through Saturday. If you'd like to get on the opera's mailing list, simply write to San Francisco Opera, War Memorial Opera House, 301 Van Ness Ave., San Francisco, CA 94102.

Western Opera Theater offers top-quality opera in English (plus educational programs and workshops) to communities around the country—a feat made possible by the mobility of its specially designed portable stage and lighting equipment.

The **Brown Bag Opera** offers 40-minute noontime productions geared to the typical lunch hour of office and factory workers. Audiences are encouraged to bring a lunch (or purchase one at the auditorium) and eat during the performance. The series is designed to offer opera at a minimal cost. Performances are held in varying locales—sometimes right on the street.

The fifth part of the San Francisco Opera Company is the **Merola Opera Program,** which selects 15 to 20 national audition finalists to participate in a ten-week period of performance and study, including two full-scale performances during the summer.

Finally, there's the **San Francisco Opera Center Showcase** every spring featuring exciting young performers in innovative repertoire.

The San Francisco Pocket Opera
Among the glories of San Francisco's theater and arts season is the unique Pocket Opera, 101 Embarcadero South (tel. 398-2220)—don't miss it if you're in town any time from April through July. Confusing though it may seem at first, the Pocket Opera performs at the Waterfront Theatre (tel. 885-2929) in

Ghirardelli Square, 900 North Point; you'll need to call the administration office above for information.

With just five to ten singers the Pocket Opera treats you to a lively, entertaining, informal operatic work on an intimate, intelligible level—(in English), so no libretto is necessary. There are no costumes or sets to impede your enjoyment or imagination. Translating and rescoring are the products of Donald Pippin, music director and creator of the Pocket Opera. If you've never enjoyed opera before, the Pocket Opera will surely convert you.

Operas adapted in earlier seasons have included *Bluebeard* (1988 premiere), *Martha, Giulio Cesare, Norma,* and (can you believe it) *Yanked from the Harem or Abduction from the Seraglio* by Mozart, as well as *Cosi Fan Tutte, Agrippina,* and *The Beggar's Opera* (1988 premiere). Performances are on Thursday and Saturday evenings at 8 p.m., and on Sunday at 3 p.m. Single performance tickets are $18 and $21.

The San Francisco Ballet

The San Francisco Ballet troupe is the oldest in the United States. Its artistic director is Helgi Tomasson. They perform from January to May at the Opera House, although the season actually begins with the annual December performance of *The Nutcracker Suite.* Call 415/621-3838 for ticket information.

The San Francisco Symphony Orchestra

A cornerstone of the Bay City's cultural life, the San Francisco Symphony Orchestra, led by music director Herbert Blomstedt, is currently in its 78th annual season. The orchestra is headquartered in the Louise M. Davies Symphony Hall, and its season lasts from September to May, featuring many internationally acclaimed guest artists and visiting orchestras. Known the world over by way of its touring and recordings, the orchestra has also built a widespread reputation for its "New and Unusual Music" series. Summer activities for the symphony include a Beethoven Festival, a Summer Pops series, and an annual presentation of the Joffrey Ballet. Tickets can be obtained at Louise M. Davies Symphony Hall, Van Ness and Grove Sts. (tel. 431-5400).

COCKTAILS IN THE SKY: A good place to "get high" prior to an evening on the town, or after one, is at any of the city's plush skyline bars. Most stay open till about 2 a.m.

The loftiest is the **Carnelian Room** (a "must see"), 779 feet up on the 52nd floor of the Bank of America Building, 555 California St. (tel. 433-7500). It's open for a Sunset Dinner from 6 to 7 p.m. (about $26) and cocktails nightly, and neither hills nor high-rises interfere with its glorious outlook. After 7 p.m. there's a prix-fixe dinner for $31. The average drink is $5.25. Dinner reservations are essential. Jacket and tie are required for gentlemen.

The plushest, however, is the Fairmont Hotel's **Crown Room** (tel. 772-5131), on the 24th floor. It's reached by the Skylift, a glass-enclosed elevator that glides up and down the tower's east side. (Acrophobics can avail themselves of an inside lift.) Comfortably seated in tufted gold-leather banquettes you can enjoy the panoramic backdrop. International buffet lunches and dinners and Sunday brunches are served here. Drinks average $6. It's open for cocktails from 11 a.m. to 1 a.m. Sunday through Thursday, Friday and Saturday till 2 a.m.

Originally a private penthouse on the 19th floor of the Hotel Mark Hopkins, the world-famous **Top of the Mark** (tel. 392-3434) is a popular rendezvous spot for San Francisco's well-heeled denizens. It's open daily for cocktails from 4 p.m. to 1:30 a.m. There's brunch on Sunday from 11 a.m. to 3 p.m. Libations average $6.

The **Starlite Roof,** 21 stories skyward, at the Sir Francis Drake Hotel, Powell and Sutter Streets (tel. 392-7755), throws in dancing to a combo along with the view. You can trip the light fantastic from 9 p.m. until 1 a.m. Drinks—even the nonalcoholic ones—cost $5 each. A facelift here a few years back expanded the view by replacing the northwest wall with glass.

Henri's Room-at-the-Top (tel. 771-1400)—the top of the Hilton tower on the 46th floor, that is—has a band and a marble dance floor as well. The dance combo swings into action Tuesday through Saturday at 8 p.m.; a glass roof allows for dancing under the stars. It's very elegant. Drinks average $5 to $6.

Finally, there's **S. Holmes Esquire** (tel. 398-8900) on the 30th floor of the Union Square Holiday Inn, and the revolving **Equinox** (tel. 788-1234) at the Hyatt Regency.

FLOOR SHOWS AND DANCING: The most glamorous club in the city, drawing the biggest names, is without a doubt the Fairmont's **Venetian Room** (tel. 772-5163). This is the kind of place where you might see Joel Grey, Mel Torme, Carol Channing, Tony Bennett, Eartha Kitt, or Ella Fitzgerald. The decor leans to heavy draperies and lots of gold in the color scheme, with scenes of gondoliers around the arches at both ends. The cover charge varies from $25 to $35, depending on the artist appearing. Weeknights are usually less expensive. Drinks go for about $6 to $7.

DANCING TO LIVE MUSIC: For dinner, dancing, and your first tango in San Francisco, head for the Tonga Room in the Fairmont Hotel. Built around what used to be the hotel's swimming pool, the Tonga Room has a South Seas decor complete with thatch-roofed tables and a tropical storm bursting over the pool at random intervals. The band plays in the middle of a lagoon on a roofed barge, and dancing is on what was once the quarter deck of a three-masted schooner. Dinners are Chinese/Polynesian. There's a cover charge of $4 on Friday and Saturday, $3 other nights. Dancing is from 9 p.m. weekends, 8 p.m. weeknights.

DISCO DANCING: They come and go, and the in places certainly change with each edition of this book. San Francisco caught "Saturday Night Fever" with a vengeance a few years ago. As a result the entire Bay Area mushroomed an immense crop of disco spots, ranging from heavenly to hideous, catering to every financial bracket and to a much wider age group than is generally assumed. A handful of the more interesting places are described below.

Considerably more sophisticated than most is **Oz,** on the 32nd floor of the Westin St. Francis Hotel, on Powell Street between Geary and Post Streets (tel. 397-7000). No one is allowed in wearing jeans or casual attire. Disco jockeys are supplied by Juliana's of London, a disco consulting firm with a chic clientele. Reached via a glass elevator, Oz evokes a lush forest glade complete with trees and ferns—a rather unusual forest glade perhaps with Tivoli lights moving to the beat of the music and a superb lighting system. The accoutrements are rather plush—a marble bar, cushioned bamboo armchairs and comfortable sofas, even backgammon and chess tables. The music: disco, new wave, Motown, and oldies, both European and American. Oz is actually a private club, but nonmembers can enter by paying a cover of $8 Sunday through Thursday, $16 on Friday and Saturday. There's disco Sunday through Thursday from 9:30 p.m. to 2 a.m., on Friday and Saturday until 3 a.m. (drinks and hors d'oeuvres are served until 2 a.m.). The average drink is $6.

One of the poshest discos in town is **Alexis,** a basement hideaway at 1001 California St., at Mason (tel. 771-1001), across from the Mark Hopkins Hotel.

The decor is medieval, with Russian tapestries, mounted hunting trophies and zebra skins on the walls, and a large fireplace. This is *not* the kind of place you go in your faded jeans; men must wear ties and jackets, and are expected to keep them on. Surprisingly, for all the plush Le Disque private-club, Nob Hill ambience, there's no cover charge or minimum. The music is pretty-good-quality rock, although they occasionally do a little Frank Sinatra or Tony Bennett. The club caters to an older crowd.

Alexis is open Thursday through Saturday only, from 10 p.m. to 2 a.m. Drinks average $5 to $6.

I-Beam, 1748 Haight St., at Cole (tel. 668-6006 for a recorded message). Large, stylishly done, this is the spot for new rock. Lasers go, and go, and go. It's the home of the floor-quake with a different vibration each night. Monday brings on line the local and national bands; Tuesday to Saturday the I-Beam moves with new rock dancing, video, and laser shows from 9 p.m. to 2 a.m. Weekends attract the Bay Area crowd. Sunday is Gays' Night—there's a tea dance, not like any other you may have attended, which begins at 5 p.m. and goes on to 2 a.m. Video screens feature the latest releases. Admission is $2 to $12 depending on the night and the performers. Drinks are $2 to $4.

Club DV8, 55 Natoma St., between Mission and Howard at First St. (tel. 957-1730), is the town's terribly stylish and posh disco. There's no question that the decor is spectacular—a mix of trompe l'oeil, pop art, candelabras, mirrors, and some extraordinary Dali-esque props. There are two huge dance floors on different levels which separate the members of Club Prive from the plebians. Several rooms have been set apart for just talking over a drink or an espresso. The club is open on Thursday from 10 p.m. to 2 a.m., on Friday and Saturday to 4 a.m. Drinks average $4.

The youth of the city gravitate, in part, to **City Nights,** 715 Harrison St., at Third (tel. 546-7774). The establishment has a DJ, a two-house-size dance floor, large-screen videos, a laser-light show, and mood music from the top 40s. During the day it's part of Little Joe's on Harrison. Life begins Thursday through Saturday at 9 p.m. and goes on through 2 a.m. on Thursday, other nights to 3 a.m. Those 18 to 20 are admitted on Thursday and Friday, but not on Saturdays. Cover charge is $9 on Fridays, $8 Saturdays, drinks average $3.50.

Then there's **Firehouse 7,** 3160 16th St., at Guerrero (tel. 621-1617), once (you guessed it) a firehouse, now a great disco. If you've always known that you were a friendly soul oriented toward the art, music, and film set, Firehouse 7 is your disco destiny. A good local rock or reggae band usually inhabits the premises every Friday, and there's DJ dance music nightly except Monday, which is Film Showcase night when experimental films are screened. And don't miss (as though you could) the display of oversized artworks. Firehouse 7 is open daily from noon to 2 a.m. There's a $6 cover charge on Friday, but drink prices are reasonable—about $2.50.

PUBS AND BARS: To begin with the unusual, there's **Edinburgh Castle,** 950 Geary St., near Polk (tel. 885-4074), a Scottish pub complete with live bagpipe music on Friday and Saturday nights. Scottish coats-of-arms hang from the ceilings, the bartender is from Dundee, and the jukebox is heavy on Scottish airs. Of course there's a dart board, and the fare is the likes of fish and chips with Scottish draft beer to wash it down. You can buy things Scottish at a gift shop on the premises called Highland Faire. It's lots of fun, open till 1 a.m. Sunday to Thursday, till 2 a.m. on Friday and Saturday.

For sardine-packed singles action, there's no place like **Perry's,** 1944 Union St., at Buchanan (tel. 922-9022). The clientele includes many over-30s and tends to the "yuppie" class—successful lawyers, businesspeople, stewardesses—what

New Yorkers would call an Upper East Side crowd. There are several dining areas (the bar action is up front), all very charming with accoutrements like blue-and-white-checked tablecloths, candlelight, ivy climbing the walls, and hanging plants. Posted menus list simple fare like hamburgers (they're good), along with a wide selection of fresh fish, grilled steaks, and salads. On the walls are framed newspaper clippings of events like the moonwalk, movie posters, and other memorabilia. Drinks average $2.50 to $3.50. If you don't meet anyone you can always browse through magazine-rack periodicals like the *Village Voice, New Yorker,* or even the *New York Times.* Open nightly till 2 a.m.

Laid-back, and comfortable, **Specs',** 12 Adler Pl., near the intersection of Broadway and Columbus (tel. 421-4112), is more or less a poets' and acting-types' bar. More or less, because the clientele is diverse, including white-collar conservatives, aging hippies, and seamen, but that's always the case at Village bars. Glass-fronted cupboards are filled with San Francisco memorabilia, scrimshaw, and other items given to Specs (who is usually behind the bar, by the way) by seamen who frequent the place. Entertainment is varied: you might catch a session by a musician from Ireland, Scotland, or Australia, or listen in as a local poet declaims. Unpredictability is the greatest asset of an evening here. Open from 4:30 p.m. weekdays (from 5 p.m. on weekends) to 2 a.m. nightly. Drinks range up from $2.50; beer and wine run $1.50 to $2.50.

In a vaguely similar category is **Vesuvio Café,** 255 Columbus Ave., between Broadway and Pacific (tel. 362-3370), across the alley from that famous haunt of the beat generation, the City Lights Bookstore. A note in Vesuvio's matchbook cover says: "The customers in this bar are entirely fictitious. Any resemblance they may have to actual persons is purely coincidental." But on-the-scene identities make for a great mix of poets, painters, longshoremen, locals, seamen, even a tourist or two. The decor consists largely of paintings and photos of nude women, with stained-glass lights overhead. Drinks are low, at around $2.50; draft beer is $1.50. Open from 6 a.m. to 2 a.m., 365 days a year.

Lord Jim's, at 1500 Broadway, near Polk (tel. 928-3015), owned/hosted by Spiro, is designed for mingling. There are couches, settees, and bar stools, fresh-cut flowers, and the decor is rife with conversation starters. While it is plush prices are reasonable. The crowd is semi-affluent, semi-hip. With the latest expansion, you can dance to live music or enjoy the continental cuisine available from the seafood bar and grill restaurant annex. The annex features a beautiful mahogany back bar and a great oyster depot. All this plus Cecil Wells and the Red Hots, in residence from 9 p.m. to 2 a.m., to sustain those who stay and play all night. Hot hors d'oeuvres are served from 4 to 8 p.m. when standard mixed drinks—premium booze all—are $3 to $4. Lord Jim's is open from 10 a.m. to 2 a.m. daily. Dinner is served until 1 a.m. Most important—there's free parking.

For ambience, you can't beat the **Rusty Scupper,** 1800 Montgomery St. at Francisco, just a few blocks from Fisherman's Wharf (tel. 986-1180). With its raw redwood exterior, raw fir interior, and knotty-pine ceilings, the Scupper looks like a posh ski lodge. Candles glow on tables of ceramic tile or highly polished maple, leafy greenery abounds in the way of hanging and potted plants (there are even trees), and a few very fine rugs and patchwork quilts adorn the walls. The Scupper occupies two floors; upstairs areas are more intimate with banquettes arranged in little alcoves. It's a lovely place for drinking, dining (anything from cheeseburgers to Chinese shrimp scampi on this unique menu), and relaxed hanging out. Open weekdays for lunch, for dinner nightly, and, until the action winds down, for drinks.

MOSTLY FOR MUSIC: Entertainment at the **Last Day Saloon,** 406 Clement St., between Fifth and Sixth Avenues (tel. 387-6343), runs the gamut of rock 'n' roll, country rock, blues, jazz-rock, and Cajun, with dancing nightly. It's a pretty, two-level place with shag-carpeted floors, barnwood walls, large pots of hanging plants, and flowers on the rough wood tables. The cover charge ranges from $4 to $8, and there's always a one-drink minimum. (Drinks average $3 to $4.) There's music Tuesday to Sunday nights from 9 p.m. to 1 a.m.

Sarah Vaughan, Wynton Marsalis, Joan Baez, B. B. King, Maynard Ferguson, and Herbie Mann are just a few of the performers who have played at the **Great American Music Hall,** 859 O'Farrell St., between Polk and Larkin. Other nights you may find new *a capella* groups, satirical comedy, or a folk troubadour. The interior of this turn-of-the-century building is a great open square under carved plaster cupids on the ceiling, with gilded mezzanine boxes supported by huge marble pillars. There also are evenings of music for dancing, usually on weekends, with a wide range of music from the classic '20s and '30s jazz sounds to the '60s rhythym & blues. The cover usually runs between $10 and $22, depending on who's appearing. Snack food is available, and drinks average $3 to $4. The hall is open five to seven nights a week; call 885-0750 to find out who's appearing.

Right across the street from Davies Symphony Hall and the Opera House is **Kimball's,** 300 Grove St., at Franklin (tel. 861-5585 or 861-5555), a handsome old brick building converted to a good-looking, comfortable, two-level restaurant and jazz club. It's a great stop for a nightcap. There's live music featuring some of the top world-class performers on the jazz scene. What's more, the food's good. Kimball's is open Tuesday through Saturday from 4 p.m. to 1 a.m.; however, closing time depends on whether or not there is a show. It's best to call.

Milestones, 376 Fifth St., at Harrison (tel. 777-9997), became part of the San Francisco jazz scene just four years ago. Since that time it has made a name as one of the top jazz clubs in town. It books headliners as well as the best of local talent into its elegant and award-winning listening scene. The tone here is intimate, in contrast to a few of the larger, cooler establishments. If you enjoy soft lights and warm jazz, you'll like Milestones. The club is open Monday through Friday from 4 p.m. to 2 a.m., on Saturday from 6 p.m. to 2 a.m., and on Sunday to 1 a.m.

The **New Orleans Room** is located in the Fairmont Hotel, 950 Mason St., at California (tel. 772-5259). It's the new home of Don Neely's Royal Society Six, playing some of the purest '30s and '40s swing to be heard on the West Coast. The group performs every Tuesday through Saturday from 9:30 p.m. to 1:30 a.m. Jimmy Price and Friends take the stage on Sunday and Monday. The New Orleans Room is open nightly from 6 p.m.

COMEDY: Holy City Zoo, 408 Clement St., between Fifth and Sixth Avenues (tel. 386-4242), is a warm and woody place that offers a comedy format seven nights a week. Local and visiting headliners present a professional showcase Wednesday through Saturday. Sunday and Tuesday are "open-mike" nights when amateurs and professionals drop in to try out new routines on the audience. Monday highlights the All-Pro Comedy Showcase. Usually three professionals entertain on Friday and Saturday nights. An improvisational group called Papaya Juice once played here, and one alumnus of that group made it big playing an alien on television. (You guessed right—it's Robin Williams.)

There's a nightly cover charge ranging from $4 to $10 and a two-drink minimum Wednesday to Sunday. It is best to call ahead because showtimes do vary. Nonetheless, there's usually a 9 p.m. show, plus one at 11 p.m. on Friday and Saturday.

Punch Line, 444 Battery St., between Washington and Clay (tel. 474-3801), is the largest comedy nightclub in the city. The club showcases top national and local talent plus up and coming comedians. Improv night is Tuesday, and there's an open mike on Sunday. Showtimes are 9 p.m. Tuesday through Sunday, plus 11 p.m. on Friday and Saturday. Depending on the night, the cover averages $5 to $9, with a two-drink minimum; drinks start at $2.50. It's advisable to buy tickets in advance if you don't want to wait on line.

Cobb's Comedy Club, The Cannery, 2801 Leavenworth, at Jefferson (tel. 928-4320) gathers an upscale family audience presenting national headliners such as Bob Goldthwait, Paula Poundestone, and Bobby Slayton. There is comedy every night and a seven-comedian Monday Showcase, for $6 to $9. Showtimes are 9 p.m. Tuesday through Sunday; there are 11 p.m. shows on Friday and Saturday. Monday's show at 8 p.m. features talent auditioning for future appearances. Open to minors 18 through 20, and those 16 and 17 accompanied by legal guardian. The club also has an adjoining restaurant and bar, the Café Zero° C.

The **Other Café,** 100 Carl St., at Cole (tel. 681-0748 or 681-7400), is in the Haight-Ashbury section made famous in the '60s. The café is where Robin Williams is said to have gotten his start, and where he sometimes appears, as does Jay Leno, when in San Francisco. Monday and Tuesday night shows feature 15 to 20 auditioning comics—amateur and pro—while Wednesday through Sunday shows present headliners, national and local, like Elayne Boosler and Richard Lewis. There are shows nightly at 9 p.m., with an additional 11 p.m. show on Friday and Saturday. Cover ranges from $4 to $12, with a two-drink minimum. Most drinks are in the $2.50 to $3.50 range.

The Other Café also features a limited menu specializing in homemade soups, sandwiches, and salads. Reservations can be made for priority seating.

POTPOURRI: The following are places where the entertainment is too varied to be categorized elsewhere.

The **Curtain Call Lounge,** 456 Geary St., near Taylor (tel. 474-5918), is just across from the American Conservatory Theatre (ACT). It's a comfortable relaxed place where you expect theater people to walk in after a performance, and they do. There's a great long bar with bentwood chairs and simulated calfskin cushions, lit by overhead lamps with Tiffany-type shades. Reddish-brown walls remind you more of New Mexico than San Francisco, but never mind—they're just about covered with pictures of every movie star you've ever known and some you haven't. Jazz is in front on Saturday and Sunday, variety entertainment is in back, plus an "open mike." Stop by after the theater or after a late dinner. The Curtain Call is open daily from 10 a.m. to 2 a.m. No cover and no minimum.

It's hard to define **Harry's,** 2020 Fillmore St., at California (tel. 921-1000). There's jazz piano nightly in this crowded, friendly saloon where Harry Denton holds sway and mingles with politicians, local hoi polloi—young and well beyond the legal drinking age. If for no other reason than to observe the local fauna, or rich blue walls and the huge antique mahogany bar, or just to sit and listen to the music after the ballet or the opera, Harry's is a fun place to be. There's a small but satisfying menu. Harry's is open nightly from 4 p.m. to 2 a.m.

At the **Cow Palace,** Geneva and Santos Streets, about ten miles from downtown near Daly City (tel. 469-6000), you're likely to catch anything from the San Francisco Sports and Boat Show to the Golden Gate Kennel Club Dog Show, to major rock stars like Kiss, Rod Stewart, Paul McCartney, the Eagles, and Neil Diamond. The Cow Palace has also hosted two Republican National Conventions, presented Russian gymnasts like Olga Korbut, and is used annually for the Grand National Rodeo, Horseshow, and Livestock Exposition each October, not to mention Ringling Bros. & Barnum and Bailey Circus. Check out the goings on at this 14,500-seat facility. Ticket prices for entertainers vary widely. Tickets are available through BASS/Ticketmaster, Ticketron, major ticket outlets, or the Cow Palace Box Office.

PIANO LOUNGES: The Ramada Renaissance Hotel, 55 Cyril Magnin St., at Market and North Fifth Streets (tel. 392-8000), has one of the most comfortable places to relax in handsome plush velvet chairs and listen to old and new melodies played at the **Piazza** on a magnificent grand piano. The three-story atrium surrounding the room provides an elegant background for the music played from noon to 2 a.m.

One of the nicest places in town to listen to piano music is the conservatory-style **Fournou's Bar** at the Stanford Court, 905 California St., at Powell (tel. 989-3500). It's an extremely luxurious, not to say romantic setting, with windows all around providing splendid views in every direction, including the bay.

The Mark Hopkins, just up the street at 1 Nob Hill (tel. 392-3434), also has a pianist entertaining nightly in a delightfully intimate room with handpainted murals—the skylighted **Lower Bar** just off the lobby. It's another very simpatico environment in which to enjoy drinks and music.

And if you're in a quiet, romantic mood, the intimacy of the **Act IV Lounge** at the Inn at the Opera, 333 Fulton St., near Franklin (tel. 863-8400), is a delight. The pianist at the grand plays melodies that soothe the spirit as comfortably as the throw cushions on the handsome green velvet chairs, the fireplace, and overstuffed sofas. The Act IV is open until 1:30 a.m.

CHAPTER III

AROUND SAN FRANCISCO BAY

□ □ □

With San Francisco as your base, you can explore nearby areas that range from the vineyards of Napa Valley to the ancient redwood forests, to sundrenched missions (why does this sound like the lyrics to a song?) and one of America's greatest universities. All these destinations—and many more—can be seen in day trips from San Francisco, and are reached in a few hours, at most, by car or public transport. We'll begin with some fascinating forays in and around San Francisco Bay, traveling counterclockwise. In the next chapter, we'll investigate the Wine Country, and in Chapter V, we'll see what's to the south. First, then, a short and delightful excursion to:

1. ANGEL ISLAND

This 730-acre island is a state park (tel. 415/435-1915), popular for bicycling, hiking, fishing, and picnicking. The park is open from 8 a.m. to sunset. To explore the island, you can bring a bike or just hike along the many trails. There are picnic sites with tables, benches, barbecues, and rest rooms at **Ayala Cove,** where you land, and at **West Garrison.** If you like hiking, 12 miles of trails lead you around the island and to the peak of **Mount Caroline Livermore,** 776 feet above the bay.

One more possible activity: If you feel like digging in the dirt, know that it's rumored pirates and smugglers once hid treasures on the shores of Angel Island.

The Red and White Fleet (tel. 415/546-2896) sails from San Francisco's Pier 43½ to Angel Island. Round-trip fares including admission to the park are $8.20 for adults, $5.15 for children 5 to 11, free for younger ones. For year-round transportation, you can take the **Tiburon–Angel Island Ferry** (tel. 415/435-2131). From June to Labor Day (10 a.m. to 4 p.m., to 6 p.m. weekends) the ferry runs daily; the rest of the year it operates on weekends and holidays only (10 a.m. to 4 p.m.). Round-trip fares cost $5 for adults, $3 for children. There's a $1 charge for bringing a bike.

2. OAKLAND

The name Oakland derives from the oak groves in which the city's first homes were constructed in the mid-19th century. Today a sprawling industrial port town of about 330,000 (the largest East Bay city), Oakland is no longer a few homes in the forest. But what the city lacks in charm is made up for in its several outstanding attractions.

First and most central, in the heart of downtown, is **Lake Merritt,** a 155-acre body of saltwater (the largest natural tidal body of saltwater wholly within an American city) that is Oakland's favorite recreation spot. Part of the lake is a refuge for wild ducks and other waterfowl; in winter the bird count sometimes goes as high as 5,000, and birds banded here have been traced as far away as Siberia.

The lake is encircled by Lakeside Park, which is the setting for **Children's Fairyland** (tel. 452-2259). Entered via the home of the "Old Woman Who Lived in a Shoe," Fairyland features over 60 nursery-rhyme attractions, plus magic shows, live animals, clowns, dancers, musicians, and storytellers. Puppet shows are held at 11 a.m., and 2 and 4 p.m. It's open daily in summer from 10 a.m. to 5:30 p.m.; from 10 a.m. to 4:30 p.m. spring and fall, Wednesday to Sunday; weekends and holidays in winter from 10 a.m. to 4:30 p.m. Admission is $2.50 for adults, $1.75 for children 12 and under.

On the west shore of Lake Merritt you can rent rowboats, sailboats, and canoes.

Adjacent to Lake Merritt, four blocks east of Hwy. 880, is the **Oakland Museum,** 1000 Oak at 10th Street (tel. 273-3401, or 834-2413 for recorded information), which opened in 1969. It documents California's development through art, history, natural sciences, and special exhibitions. The Gallery of California Art includes works ranging from the late 1600s to the most contemporary works of Californians. The Cowell Hall of California History exhibits the artifacts—clothing, tools, furniture, machines, etc.—used to shape the state from the Indian era to the present. Environment and conservation themes are stressed in the Natural Sciences Gallery. The museum is open Wednesday to Saturday from 10 a.m. to 5 p.m., on Sunday from noon to 7 p.m.; closed on official holidays. No admission is charged, though some special exhibits have an entry fee. A snackbar is on the premises. An interesting place to browse (and buy) is the book and gift shop, which specializes in items related to the California theme.

At the end of Oakland's Broadway lies **Jack London Square,** dedicated to the writer, a bust of whom overlooks the scene. At the foot of Webster Street, about a block away, stands the **First and Last Chance Saloon,** 56 Jack London Square, built about a half century ago from the remnants of an old whaling ship. London did some of his writing and much of his drinking here (Robert Louis Stevenson is also supposed to have been a habitué). The corner table London used has remained as it was over 70 years ago, and his photos and other memorabilia abound.

Oakland is also home to hundreds of birds, reptiles, and mammals that roam freely in the 500-acre **Oakland Zoo** in Knowland State Park. For an overall view take the 1,250-foot-long Jungle Lift that takes you high up over the African Veldt where animals graze in a natural setting. A train will take you around the zoo. There's also a **Baby Zoo** where children can feed and pet friendly animals. It's open from 10 a.m. to 4:30 p.m. every day except Christmas. Admission is $4 per car, which includes parking.

For maps and more detailed information on Oakland's attractions, stop in

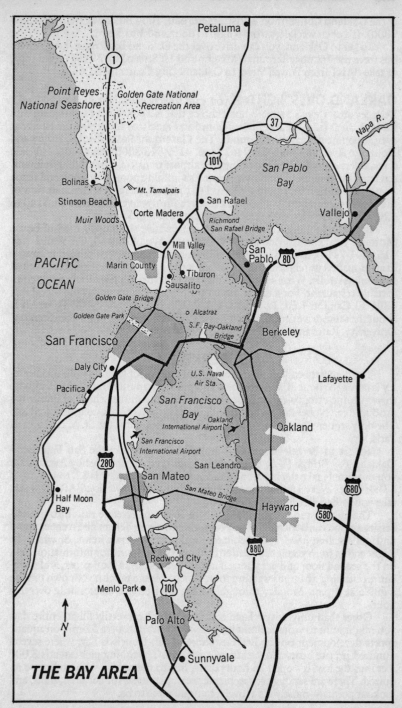

THE BAY AREA

at the **Oakland Convention & Visitors Bureau,** 1000 Broadway (tel. 415/839-9000). It's open weekdays from 9 a.m. to noon and 1 to 5 p.m.

To get to Oakland, you can drive over the Oakland Bay Bridge, take a direct bus from the Transbay Terminal (Mission and 1st Streets) for $2 ($3 round trip), or take BART from Powell Street to Oakland City Center for $1.65.

OAKLAND OVERNIGHT: If you care to stay overnight in the Oakland/Berkeley area, there's a superb hotel choice that is a convenient sightseeing base for both areas (it's just 20 minutes from San Francisco) and a pleasure to stay at even if you never leave the grounds. The **Claremont Resort Hotel,** Ashby and Domingo Ave., Oakland, CA 94623 (tel. 415/843-3000), set amid 22 hillside acres, offers every facility, including free airport transfers, a beautiful restaurant, ten tennis courts, an Olympic-size heated swimming pool, whirlpool, and sauna —not to mention very posh digs. And to top it all, there's a spectacular view of the bay. It's something like being a guest at a European castle. Rates are $140 to $205 single, $160 to $225 double. Suites are $255 to $700.

If you're looking for comfortable, inexpensive shelter, it's hard to beat a **Motel 6.** And there is one at 4919 Coliseum Way, Oakland, CA 94601 (tel. 415/261-7414), located near the I-880 freeway. However, this motel is located in an industrial warehouse district, adjacent to a neighborhood not exactly suited to evening strolls. What's more, you will need to drive a fair distance to a comfortable restaurant. For a dollar more on the basic rate, consider the Motel 6 at 4301 El Camino Real, Palo Alto, CA 94306 (tel. 415/949-0833), which is about the same drive time to the city, just off U.S. 101, and 4 miles from Stanford University. Rates are $30.95 single, $38.95 double.

3. BERKELEY

The complete college town, retirement colony for the under-30 set, Berkeley is home to about 30,000 students and probably an equal number of folk who thrive on the campus energy but are enrolled only in the school of life. It has produced ten Nobel Prize winners and, in the turbulent '60s, countless activists. The only student "town" that matches it in excitement is the St. Michel area of Paris.

To get to Berkeley from San Francisco by car, take the San Francisco–Oakland Bay Bridge (U.S. 80), keep left and turn off onto Ashby Avenue. Or you can simply take the bus from the Transbay Terminal (fare is $2, round trip is $3); it leaves every 15 minutes and goes right to the university. BART will also take you to Berkeley for a fare of $1.50.

The hub of student activities is where Telegraph Avenue runs into the university campus at **Bancroft Way.** Here, and all along Telegraph Avenue, you'll find stalls selling jewelry, felafel, tarot card readings, craft items, or whatever. Right across from you is the **Student Union.** Go to the visitor information desk on the second floor and get yourself a map of Berkeley, a local paper, and a brochure outlining a campus walking tour, which you can take on your own or with a guide at 1 p.m. Monday through Friday; it's free and takes a little over 1½ hours.

Other than university-related activities, which can easily fill an entire day, you might want to visit the **Berkeley Marina Yacht Harbor,** a $2-million aquatic sports development on the Berkeley shore of San Francisco Bay, where several hundred private boats and yachts are anchored. The fishing pier extends 3,000 feet into the bay; it's open 24 hours daily, free to the public, with no license required. There are sandy beaches, picnic areas, play areas for children, trails, and lookout points—mostly it's a lovely, tranquil place to be.

WHERE TO STAY: Near the university, the most pleasant place is **Gramma's,** 2740 Telegraph Ave. (four blocks north of Ashby), Berkeley, CA 94705 (tel. 415/549-2145). These charming restored Victorian houses have 29 rooms altogether, all furnished in period style with antiques, floral-print wallpapers, and pretty patchwork quilts on the beds. All have private baths and phones, some with TVs, and larger rooms have sitting areas. Accommodations out back in the restored carriage house overlook a garden and have fireplaces.

Guests are served a complimentary breakfast in the downstairs dining room or on the deck overlooking the garden. Sunday brunch, not included in rates, is also an option.

Rates: $75 to $140, single or double occupancy. Children under 6 not accepted.

Just one block from the university is the very pleasant **Hotel Durant,** 2600 Durant Ave., near Bowditch, Berkeley, CA 94704 (tel. 415/845-8981). Built in 1928, it's the only full-service hotel this close to the university. New ownership restored it nicely to keep the best of its earlier days while providing conveniences now expected by vacationers and travelers. The rooms are tastefully furnished; most are quite light, done in pastels, and all have cable TV, movies, radio, and phones. Some of the rooms can be connected for family groups. A new restaurant, Henry's Publick House and Grille, is on the premises and serves complimentary breakfast for hotel guests Monday through Saturday from 7 to 9:30 a.m. Henry's is also open for lunch and dinner.

Rates are $70 to $88, single or double occupancy.

WHERE TO EAT: If you really want to get the feel of student life, you can eat on campus in the building directly behind the Student Union Building. There are quite a few choices: on Upper Sproul Plaza the **Terrace** and the **Golden Bear;** on the Lower Sproul Plaza the **Cafeteria,** the adjacent **Bear's Lair Pub and Coffee House,** and a largish establishment that houses the **Deli** and the **Ice Creamery.** You can check them all out and choose your favorite in a matter of minutes; all offer low-priced food and indoor or al fresco dining.

The main drag here is **Telegraph Avenue,** lined with coffeeshops, a wide variety of eateries, bookstores, record stores, head shops, and the like. Currently, the most popular student hangouts (subject to change any minute) are:

Larry Blake's R & B Café, 2367 Telegraph Avenue, off Durant (tel. 848-0886), was a mom-and-pop operation run by Larry and Leona Blake for 45 years. They retired a few years ago, and three young ex-employees took it over; they're doing a great job. Students love the downstairs Blake's Night Club, dark and atmospheric, with a very good jukebox. Live music is presented down there Tuesday through Sunday night (the specialty is blues). Fare ranges from a French dip sandwich to roast prime rib with creamed horseradish, as well as salads, omelets, burgers, and crêpes for $4 to $12. Beer, wine, and liquor are also served. Open weekdays from 11 a.m. to 2 a.m., on Saturday from 10 a.m. to 2 a.m., Sunday to 10 p.m.

Finally, **Spats,** 1974 Shattuck Ave., near University (tel. 841-7225), abounds in Victorian funk and junk—overstuffed couches, antiques, musical instruments, and not just a mounted elk head but a whole stuffed elk. There's a garden room under a skylight ceiling in back, its walls painted with a psychedelic jungle scene. Exotic drinks—such as the Company Z's Mai Tai, described as "a fishbowl full of rums, fruit brandies, and fruit juices, garnished like a Hawaiian wedding"—are featured. You can also dine here on fare ranging from moussaka to veal scallopine to quiche with salad and fruit, for $8 to $14. Open Monday through Saturday from 11:30 a.m. to 2 a.m., on Sunday from 4 p.m. to 2 a.m.

Alice Waters' **Chez Panisse,** 1517 Shattuck Ave., between Cedar and Vine (tel. 548-5525), has been acclaimed as one of the most innovative restaurants in the state. Or to put it another way, if you have never heard of this restaurant and its creator, surely you've been on another planet. California cuisine is so much a product of Waters' genius that all other restaurants, west and east, following in her wake should be dated "A.A.W." (after Alice Waters). A redwood cottage, it's sheltered from the bustle of the street by a lovely garden and patio where guests may sip wine while waiting for tables. Inside there are two separate dining areas. The upstairs café has displays of pastries and fruit and large bouquets of fresh flowers on an oak bar. The café menu is posted daily out front. Offerings might include a delicately smoked gravlax or a roasted eggplant soup with pesto, followed by an entree of lamb ragoût garnished with apricots, onions, and spices served with couscous. Luncheon entrees average $10 to $12. At night there's brick-oven pizza as well as salads and other entrees similar to those offered at lunch. The menu changes daily according to the ingredients that are best and freshest.

There usually is a long wait for the upstairs café since it does not take reservations and the food is superb. The delights include a fabulous calzone, stuffed with mozzarella, goat cheese, and prosciutto. The homemade pastas are just as exceptional. In fact, everything is delicious, and even the ice creams and sherbets are homemade. Take the time, and wait.

In the cozy downstairs room, only one prix-fixe five-course gourmet dinner is served each night. This dining area is redwood paneled and has a working fireplace, art deco lamps, and big bouquets of fresh flowers everywhere. A typical dinner here might include pan-fried oysters with Chino Ranch curly endive, spinach and fennel soup, veal saltimbocca, straw potatoes, salad, and blood orange ice cream in almond cookie cups. The prix-fixe dinner is around $55. The menu is posted each Saturday for the week.

The Café upstairs serves lunch and dinner from 11:30 a.m. to 11:30 p.m. Monday to Saturday. Dinner is served in the downstairs restaurant from 6 to 9:15 p.m. Tuesday to Saturday; there are two sittings—at 6 to 6:30 p.m. and 8:30 to 9:15 p.m. Reservations are advised upstairs and absolutely essential downstairs—up to one month in advance.

Traditional country cooking, Polish style, is the fare at **Warszawa,** 1730 Shattuck Ave., between Virginia and Francisco Streets (tel. 841-5539). Warm and homey, its interior is adorned with Polish posters and folk arts, and the bar actually contains an indoor garden. You might begin with an hors d'oeuvre of Kabanosy flambé, creamed herring, or authentic borscht. Entrees cost $10 to $15 and include roast duckling with apples, prunes, and dumplings; stuffed cabbage; and excellent pirogi (pasta shells stuffed with meat, cheese, and mushrooms, fried in butter, and served with sour cream and a fresh vegetable). It's all pretty rich, and since you've already blown your diet you may as well go all the way and order the homemade rum walnut torte with fresh whipped cream.

Open nightly from 5:30 to 10 p.m., till 11 p.m. on Friday and Saturday, and from 5 p.m. on Sunday. Reservations advised.

For Berkeley breakfasts I like **Smokey Joe's Cafe,** 1620 Shattuck Ave., between Cedar and Lincoln (no phone), a traditional Berkeley hangout with walls plastered with protest posters, leaflets, and messages. It evokes memories of Berkeley's activist past. It's a small place, with pale yellow walls and seating at the counter or tables.

I especially like Smokey's Mexican breakfast with beans and cheese, tortillas, and a garnish of fresh fruit. Other specialties are great pancakes with blueberries or bananas, custom-made omelets, and original creations such as the Holy Mole Frijole Bowl. Prices average about $3 to $5. Open daily from 8 a.m. to 3 p.m.

Should your sweet tooth act up in Berkeley, head for **Cocolat,** a chocoholic's paradise over at 1481 Shattuck, near Vine. You simply can't believe that heaven comes in so many forms of chocolate indulgence. Handmade truffles from an old French recipe are the specialty here, made fresh every day. Then there are chocolates filled with eau de vie (pear, raspberry, quince, kiwi, or Kirsch) which burst as you bite into them, thereby requiring the ultimate joy of plunking the entire bit into your mouth all at once. Each of the shops also offers tortes and cakes. You might indulge in a Tricolor Mousse—three chocolate mousses in one—or Chocolate Decadence, caressed by whipped cream and slices of truffle surrounded by raspberry sauce. Cocolat also has mail order gifts to delight the heart of any chocoholic. Many of their chocolate spectaculars do travel well.

They're open Monday through Saturday from 10 a.m. to 6 p.m., on Sunday from 11 a.m. to 5 p.m. Cocolat now has a second East Bay location at 3945 Piedmont Ave., in Oakland (tel. 653-3676).

Pastries are served at table at four of Cocolat's closest locations—the two East Bay locations noted and in San Francisco at 4106 24th St. (tel. 647-3855), and 2119 Fillmore St. (tel. 567-1223) both open daily.

Just around the corner at 2122 Vine is **Delicktables,** where gelato (Italian ice cream) can be obtained. They also serve soup, sandwiches, cappuccino, espresso, and other desserts. Summer hours are Sunday through Thursday from 10 a.m. to 11 p.m., to midnight on Friday and Saturday. During the winter, the shop closes an hour earlier.

4. MUIR WOODS

One of the best things about San Francisco is that just a half-hour drive away is a 500-acre redwood forest, Muir Woods, one of the most impressive sights in America. It's rumored that even the late Charles de Gaulle was reduced to silence when he viewed these trees.

The redwood trees (or *Sequoia sempervirens*) you'll see here, among the tallest trees on the planet, are also among its longer-lived inhabitants. At the entrance to Muir Woods a cross section of a fallen tree shows growth rings attesting to its birth before the Normans conquered England.

This magnificent forest was almost lost to advancing civilization in the early 1900s when a water company wanted to dam up Redwood Creek, which gives life to the 300-foot spires. But William Kent, a nearby landowner, persuaded President Theodore Roosevelt to proclaim the area a national monument and name it for the great Scottish-American naturalist, John Muir.

There are several trails to follow. A needle-carpeted nature trail will take you to the Cathedral Grove, where a group of redwoods rises skyward as if they were chapel walls. Another highlight is the Family Circle, where you can see how redwoods reproduce, younger trees forming a circle around the fire-scarred stump of a parent. Hikers may also follow a trail up the slopes of 2,600-foot **Mount Tamalpais.** On all the trails, trailside exhibits, signs, and markers will help guide your way, and picnic areas are provided.

But more impressive than the facts and figures as to height, width, age, etc., are the entrancing beauty and tranquility that pervade the forest, the feelings of peace, awe, and reverence that it inspires. One easily understands the sentiment expressed by Joseph B. Strauss, builder of the Golden Gate Bridge, in his poem, "The Redwoods":

> To be like these, straight, true and fine,
> To make our world, like theirs, a shrine;
> Sink down, Oh, traveller, on your knees,
> God stands before you in these trees.

To reach Muir Woods, take U.S. 101 north; signs will tell you where to turn off. Admission is free; the gate opens at 8 a.m. and closes at sunset. Go during the week if you can and avoid the weekend crowds.

There's a visitors center, gift shop, and snack bar; however, I suggest that you have a bite to eat before heading up to Muir Woods.

Be advised that in driving to (and from) Muir Woods the secondary road is a steep series of S curves with very few places to pull over. Be sure to start with ample gas, firm brakes, and good tires. This is not the place to get a flat.

5. TIBURON

This quaint little town grew up around a railroad settlement, wood-burning locomotives pulling the first trains into Point Tiburon in 1884. (If you really want to go back, though, Miwok Indians lived here in 100 B.C.) The depot where passengers waited for trains, as well as the big ferryboats that met the trains, is still here, now the **Peter Donahue Building.** Today the town is a yacht-club suburb—home to several hundred upper-bracket businesspeople who commute daily to San Francisco offices. The bay view is bewitching, the hill setting glorious, and the living expensive. But the view of the San Francisco Skyline and the islands in the bay almost make it worth the price. The pace of this seacoast village is sleepy, with whatever action there is centering on **Main Street,** which is lined with ramshackle old frame buildings that house chic boutiques, expensive antique shops, art galleries, and water-view restaurants.

You can drive the 18 miles from San Francisco via the Golden Gate Bridge and Hwy. 101 (get off at the Tiburon Boulevard exit and take 131), but it's faster and more pleasant to go by boat. **Red and White Fleet** (tel. 415/546-2896) ferries leave from Pier 43½ at Fisherman's Wharf several times a day, and the crossing costs $8 round trip for adults, $4 for children. You can also catch a ferry to Angel Island from here (see Section 1 on Angel Island, above).

WHERE TO EAT: When you're through browsing, cross back over Tiburon Boulevard and begin your exploration of Main Street's shops (or should I say "shoppes") and restaurants. One of the most attractive restaurants is **Christophers** (formerly Sabella's), at 9 Main St. (tel. 435-4600). The elegant interior is carpeted in rich blue and gold, the walls paneled in unfinished redwood. There are many beautiful ship models around, including a large one of the *Flying Cloud,* fastest clipper ship of the 19th century. The upstairs dining room, with window walls overlooking the water and San Francisco skyline, is especially lovely. As you might expect, seafood is the specialty of the house. Dinner entrees, costing $13 to $24, range from a superb calamari steak to a filet-mignon/lobster-tail combination. At lunch, when prices are lower, you might try the seafood crêpe with shrimp, scallops, and mushrooms. Open for dining Monday to Thursday from 11:30 a.m. to 9 p.m., to 10 p.m. Friday to Sunday; bar is open till 1 or 2 a.m., depending on the action.

Tiburon is liveliest on Sunday afternoons, when weekend boatmen tie up at the open docks of the waterside restaurants and there is much singing, laughter, and general conviviality. For over 60 years now, the traditional place to tie up has been **Sam's Anchor Café** at 27 Main St. (tel. 435-4527), a tavern with two 110-foot piers and a large outdoor wooden deck that is filled to overflowing with blithe Sunday spirits from early on; it's laid-back Tiburon's version of the neighborhood bar. Sam's specials are cioppino and fresh seafood items like red snapper piccatta with lemon and capers, for $8 to $13; everything is served with sourdough French bread and butter. Open weekdays from 11 a.m., on Saturday from 10 a.m., and on Sunday from 9:30 a.m., closing nightly about 2 a.m.

At 41 Main St. is **Tiburon Tommie's** (tel. 435-1229), a Polynesian restaurant with the requisite South Seas decor that such establishments generally abound in—South Seas carvings, bamboo, wicker furnishings, a jungle of lush plants, even a waterfall and a rock fountain. Impressively authentic are the Maori Room and adjoining Tapa Room Bar upstairs. Big windows offer bay views. Entrees are $7 to $12 and include dishes like Mandarin duck and cashew chicken. For $9 to $15 per person you can get a complete dinner for two or more, including appetizer, entree, fried rice, cookies, and tea. Food is served till 9 p.m. The bar stays open until midnight to 2 a.m.

Sweden House Bakery-Café, 35 Main St. (tel. 435-9767), has a plant-filled outdoor terrace overlooking the bay for al fresco dining. Inside, the walls are done in yellow-and-white-checked gingham and hung with copper pots and pans, rolling pins, neat little prints, and tapestries. There are fresh flowers on every table and café curtains on the windows. Full breakfasts are served daily, and not just the usual, run-of-the-mill variety. You can have scrambled eggs with a choice of green onions, tomatoes, cheese, mushrooms, shrimp, or slices of smoked salmon. And combination vegetable omelets are offered too. All are served with the restaurant's own toasted Swedish limpa bread. At lunch, there are open-face sandwiches like avocado and bacon with sprouts, or delicious asparagus tips rolled in Danish ham; you can also order such American standards as chicken salad. Garden salads are also an option, and you can have a soup-of-the-day-with-salad combination. Look for the daily luncheon specials too. If you're not up to breakfast or lunch, you can simply sit on the terrace, sip espresso, and enjoy a home-baked Swedish pastry, such as the raspberry-iced, cream-filled napoleon. Everything is very well prepared; prices range from $4 to $7. Sweden House is open Monday through Friday from 8 a.m. to 3 p.m., 8:30 a.m. to 4:30 p.m. on Saturday and Sunday.

FINAL LIBATIONS: After a leisurely browse down Main Street and a relaxed meal at one of the above establishments, head over to the **Tiburon Vintners** (tel. 435-3113), around the corner at 72 Main St. This century-old frame building with its twisting spiral staircase is an outlet for the premium estate-grown wines produced by Rodney Strong and Windsor Vineyards in Sonoma County. Their Victorian tasting room dates to 1888. You may choose from over 40 fine Windsor Vineyards and Rodney Strong wines for complimentary sampling, including many award winners. Windsor has been awarded more than 300 medals at prestigious wine-tasting competitions since 1985—the list is impressive. Tiburon Vintners also carries a good selection of wine accessories and gifts—glasses, cork pullers, gourmet sauces, posters, maps, etc. Carry-packs are available (they hold six bottles); as of now, only California and New York residents can have their wines shipped home for them. Ask about personalized labels for your own selections. The shop is open from 10 a.m. to 6 p.m. daily. If you drive to Tiburon, Vintners will validate your parking ticket from the Main Street parking lot next door.

6. SAUSALITO

Even more "consciously quaint" than Tiburon—and making no attempt to hide it—Sausalito is a picturesque seacoast village just eight miles from downtown San Francisco. Its lovely harbor is filled with vessels of all shapes and sizes, and its streets are lined with restaurants, art galleries, hip boutiques, and shops wherein the arts of candle making, pottery, glassblowing, and scrimshaw are practiced. What other little town can boast eight goldsmiths? But one forgives Sausalito its pretensions. A slightly bohemian, completely nonchalant, and very relaxed adjunct to San Francisco, it has scenery and sunshine and lots of very real charm, both because of, and in spite of, its efforts in that direction.

Sausalito has a fascinating community of houseboats just north of the village (that's where I left my heart). The village can be reached most gloriously by ferry: both the **Red and White Fleet** (tel. 546-2815), for $9 round trip, and **Golden Gate Transit** (tel. 982-8834 or 457-3110), for $8 round trip, offer service to Sausalito. Or you can travel more prosaically by **Golden Gate bus** (tel. 332-6600) for $1.95 one way.

SHOPPING IN SAUSALITO: The town's main street, running along the water, is **Bridgeway;** this, along with one or two side streets, is where most of the action is. What everyone does in Sausalito is shop, stroll, and browse.

The **Village Fair,** 777 Bridgeway, a complex of 40 shops (from a rug-making store to a bath boutique) and restaurants, is a logical place to begin your explorations. Most of the action is on Bridgeway, but Princess Street and Caledonia Street also warrant a look.

DINING AND DRINKING IN SAUSALITO: By now you're no doubt famished and foot-weary, and the shopping bags are getting a little heavy. Sausalito has an abundance of dining choices, from snackbars and coffeeshops to swank gourmet restaurants.

Boasting one of the best "bayscapes" in town is **Ondine,** 558 Bridgeway (tel. 332-0791). Enter via imposing white doors, and then proceed up a gold-carpeted stairway to a dining area with elegantly appointed tables. The expansive and spectacular view provides most of the decor and creates a delightfully tranquil ambience. A specialty here is roast pheasant Vladimir with vodka and sour cream sauce. If you come before 7 p.m. a complete dinner, including potage du jour, salad, dessert, coffee, and an entree like broiled salmon or lobster casserole, costs $18 to $23. Ondine is open daily from 11:30 a.m. to 3 p.m. for lunch, 5 to 11 p.m. for dinner. Reservations are essential and jackets are required for men.

More terrific views from all directions at the **Spinnaker,** 100 Spinnaker Dr. (tel. 332-1500), just off Bridgeway near the ferry landing. Diners sit on comfortable tufted-leather banquettes or chairs facing 14-foot-high picture windows overlooking the bay (the Spinnaker is actually out on the bay). Cork-lined ceilings and fir-trunk columns add a natural note to the elegant decor. Dinner, served from 5 to 10 p.m. daily, on Sunday from 2 p.m., includes soup or salad, ice cream or sherbet, and coffee. Prices vary from $12 to $18 according to the entree you select. Your choice includes the likes of rex sole meunière, New York steak, and scallops sauté. You can also order à la carte from a more extensive menu at lunch or dinner. Open daily from 11 a.m. to 11 p.m.

One of Sausalito's prettiest right-on-the-bay eateries is **Scoma's,** 588 Bridgeway (tel. 332-9551), with boxes of geraniums lining the entranceway, gray wood-paneled walls, and extremely well-selected antique furnishings. A scrumptious cioppino, and linguine and clams in cream sauce, are among the Italian-style seafood entrees at this very charming establishment. All entrees cost $10 to $18 and come with a vegetable and pasta. Open for lunch and dinner Friday through Monday from 11:30 a.m. to 10 p.m., for dinner only Tuesday through Thursday from 5:30 to 10 p.m.

A bit farther out of town (about a mile from the main shopping area) is **Guernica,** 2009 Bridgeway (tel. 332-1512). It's a delightful, homey place, under the aegis of owner Roger Minhondo, a French Basque. The cuisine is—of course —French Basque as well. It's popular with locals and San Franciscans alike, and justifiably so, for both food and ambience. The dining room is small and cozy, with wood and leatherette booths, and white-clothed tables with flowers and candles. A print of *Guernica* (by Pablo Picasso) adorns one wall.

Dinner entrees (costing $12 to $21) come with a soup, salad, and warm crispy rolls. You can choose from delicious dishes like medallions of veal with mustard sauce, chateaubriand for two, and chicken with mushroom stuffing and a port wine sauce. With 24 hours' notice, you can also get beef Wellington or paella Valenciana. Try not to skip dessert; there's chocolate mousse and peach Melba, and (in season) a delicious strawberry tart.

Guernica is open Monday to Thursday from 5 to 10:30 p.m., on Friday and Saturday till 11 p.m., and on Sunday till 9:30 p.m. Reservations are advised.

For a drink and conversation, stop in at the local hangout—the **Bar with no name,** 757 Bridgeway (tel. 332-1392), a combination coffeehouse and tavern easy to overlook, with oak wainscoting, comfortable cushioned wicker and bamboo chairs, and stained-glass panels in the front door. It's owned by a cat named Cinderella. It was originally started by four partners who couldn't agree on a name. It's a very low-key kind of place—reminds you of the White Horse Tavern in New York's Greenwich Village. There's always good taped music playing, a shelf of books to read, and a game of Scrabble or backgammon in progress. In the delightful garden out back you can relax amid vines and plants hanging from a slatted wood arbor above. The bar attracts local artists, yacht skippers, poets, and of course tourists. Drinks start at about $2. A Ramos Fizz is the house specialty.

A HOTEL CHOICE: If you care to spend the night, the best place in town is the **Casa Madrona,** 801 Bridgeway, Sausalito, CA 94965 (tel. 415/332-0502). It's a delightful mix of the old and the new: the original building is an 1885 mansion constructed by a lumber baron (madrona is a type of wood), and there's a large new section connecting the mansion with the lower street. The hotel's 32 rooms, cottages, and suites vary widely. Some rooms in the old house are bathless; others have bathrooms with Jacuzzis. The 16 newest rooms—those that range down the hill—are each decorated by a local designer. Lord Ashley's Lookout is decorated in hunter green, camel, and brass with oak trim, in 19th-century style; Le Petit Boudoir is a Victorian hideaway complete with a rose-colored chandelier. There are cottages as well, including the English Gate House, a four-room English cottage with a harbor view. Amenities in the rooms include quilts, telephones, and baskets of luxury shampoos, bath gels, etc. TVs and radios are available on request. Many rooms have bay views and fireplaces.

On the premises is the excellent Casa Madrona Restaurant (tel. 331-5888), which offers American cuisine for lunch and dinner daily; there's also Sunday brunch. The wine list is excellent, including a very good selection of French wines. The restaurant serves a complimentary breakfast daily for guests only.

Rooms with a shared bath at the Casa Madrona cost $70; other rooms cost $80 to $180. Cottages run $150 to $170, and the Madrona Villa, a three-room suite, rents for $300. All rates are for single or double occupancy; extra persons pay $10. There's a two-night minimum stay on weekends.

7. MARINE WORLD AFRICA USA

About 10 miles south of the Napa wine country, and a bit less than 30 miles northeast of San Francisco off Interstate 80 (exit at Hwy. 37) is the new 160-acre Marine World Africa USA, 1000 Fairgrounds Dr. in Vallejo (tel. 707/643-ORCA for a recorded announcement). It's less than an hour's drive up I-80, or you can have the fun of taking the **Red and White Fleet** high-speed catamaran from Pier 41 (tel. 415/546-2896, or 800/445-8880 in California), at Fisherman's Wharf, pass Alcatraz and the Golden Gate Bridge, and be there in 55 minutes. The round trip, including admission, is $34.95 for adults, $24.95 for seniors over 60, and $24.95 for kids 4 to 12.

Marine World Africa USA features animals of land and air in spectacular shows and innovative habitats; some even stroll the park with their trainers, meeting visitors face to face.

When you plan your visit, count on participation in the shows—it's a big part of your enjoyment and education as a visitor. Throughout the day a variety of events are scheduled. There's a **Killer Whale/Dolphin Show** where seven rows of wet-area seats are saved for guests who want a thorough drenching. In the **Sea Lion Show** you can be a recipient of one of the many kisses handed out by some of the oldest and largest performers in the country.

When you cross the bridge over the waterfalls, through the trees, and past the flamingos, you enter Africa. At the **Elephant and Chimpanzee Show** the young elephants kick beachballs to the spectators. The **Parrot and Predatory Bird Show** is remarkable in its beauty and in the skill of the birds. And the **Wildlife Show** at the **Ecology Theatre** teaches us what a precarious foothold wildlife has on the earth. You'll leave the **Tiger and Lion Show** with a new understanding of what's required to work with 14 lions and tigers as a group. In the **Small Animal Petting Corral,** you can make a friend of a llama for a handful of food you can buy there. Or if the spirit of adventure is in your soul, take a ride on an Asian elephant or a dromedary camel.

You may be sorry you're not a child again when you see the unique playground, the **Gentle Jungle,** that combines education, fun, and adventure. It's one of the most innovative play areas of its type. Among other things, children can crawl through burrows in the prairie dog village and pop up into Plexiglass domes so they learn to see the world through the eyes of these cute little animals. The **Whale-of-a-Time World** combines fun, education, and adventure.

And finally, there's a 55-acre lake (once a golf course) that is the stage for a **Water Ski and Boat Show.** Daredevil athletes jump, spin, and even hang-glide while wearing waterskis.

A wide variety of fast food is available at the restaurant plaza—everything from burgers and pizza to nachos and chicken. Prices are moderate, averaging about $6 to $7 in total. Or you can bring your own food—there are also barbecue facilities on the grounds.

Marine World Africa USA is open daily during the summer (Memorial Day through Labor Day) from 9:30 a.m. to 6 p.m.; it's open Wednesday through Sunday for the balance of the year with hours to 5:30 p.m. during the spring and fall, to 5 p.m. during the winter. Admission is $16.95 for adults, $10.95 for children 4 to 12 and seniors over 60, and free for under-4s. Credit cards are accepted. The price covers all shows: Dromedary camel and elephant rides will add $3. Tickets to Marine World Africa USA are available through Ticketron. All shows and attractions are handicapped-accessible except the elephant and dromedary rides and the Whale-of-a-Time Playground. Some pathways are too steep for easy access, but alternative routes are available.

Note: The best way to cope with the full schedule of shows is to get there early, make up your own itinerary from the leaflet and map given you at the entrance, and then stick to it. Otherwise, you'll find yourself missing parts of each presentation and feeling frustrated.

CHAPTER IV

THE WINE COUNTRY

□ □ □

You're about to enter the wine country, one of the most uniquely lovely and fascinating areas of California. Some of the wineries date back to the days of the Franciscan fathers who planted the first vines as they built their missions. Of course, in those days all the wine was—ostensibly—for sacramental use. Today the many wineries of this picturesque district are giving stiff competition to France. A drive through the wine country, stopping for tours here and there, and a picnic lunch en route, is one of the most delightful outings I can imagine.

A similarly enjoyable day can be spent exploring historic Sonoma, which sprang up around the last of the missions. More wineries here too, if you've not yet quenched your thirst. Then take a slight detour west from Sonoma and visit Fort Ross, founded by the Russians in 1812 (did you know the Russians once occupied parts of California?).

The combination of exquisite scenery and interesting sights throughout the areas coming up make this chapter's offerings especially recommendable for inclusion in your itinerary.

Before you head into the wine country, you may want to visit the **Wine Institute,** 165 Post St., San Francisco, CA 94108 (tel. 415/986-0878), for a free copy of *California Is Wine Country,* which tells about wineries throughout the state. If you write for it, please enclose a stamped, self-addressed no. 10 envelope. Once in the wine country, you can also pick up a free copy of the *Wine Country Review,* a weekly newspaper full of information on every aspect of Napa, Sonoma, and the other wine regions.

There's also a guide to over 100 wineries north of San Francisco available from the **Visitors Information Center of the Redwood Empire Association,** One Market Plaza, Spear Street Tower, Suite 1001, San Francisco, CA 94105 (tel. 415/543-8334); they are open Monday to Friday from 9 a.m. to 4:30 p.m. If you write for the guide, enclose $1 for postage and handling.

1. THE NAPA VALLEY

Nestled in the coastal mountain range some 50 miles north of San Francisco, this fertile valley has close to 25,000 acres of vineyards, and it produces most of California's superior wines. To get there from San Francisco, head north on Rte. 101, turn east at S-37, and proceed to Rte. 29 where the greatest concentration of wineries open to visitors is located. The **Napa Chamber of Commerce,** 1556 First St., downtown Napa (tel. 707/226-7455), will provide you with a list of lodgings, recreational facilities, rides of every kind, antique dealers, picnic facilities, bike routes, etc. They also have maps and brochures for sale. It's open weekdays from 9 a.m. to 5 p.m., weekends from 11 a.m. to 3 p.m.

All over Napa and Sonoma, you can pick up a very informative free weekly publication called the *Wine Country Review*. It will give you the most up-to-date information on wineries and assorted events.

The best and busiest time to visit Napa is during September and October when the grapes are being harvested. But any time of year the very air seems intoxicating in this area of unparalleled scenic beauty. As you drive along Rte. 29, you'll see welcoming signs beckoning you to one winery or another. Almost all offer free tours and samples of their product, most free. Two or three tours are the most you'll want to take, and I've recommended the ones that are more intriguing or picturesque. If you find the lecturers at these a little pedantic, be assured that the situation is much the same or worse at the other vineyards. The tours are nonetheless interesting, and the tasting is lots of fun. There are a number of interesting events that go on each year in the Napa Valley. A small sampling would include the Napa Valley Wine Auction, sponsored by the Napa Valley Vintners Association and usually held in June. This is the most important annual auction, one wine connoisseur would not want to miss. In July, Calistoga holds an old-fashioned Napa County Fair complete with rides, food, etc. At the end of July or the beginning of August, there's a Napa Town & Country Fair at the Napa Fairgrounds. Let's just say that there's always much to see and do in the valley throughout the year. The Napa Chamber of Commerce will be glad to answer any questions you might have or to send you a calendar of events for the month or the year.

Napa Valley now has about 150 wineries and an exceptional selection of fine restaurants and hostelries at all price levels. It's a good idea to plan on spending more than one day if you'd like to tour even a small segment of the valley and its wineries. And if you do spend a weekend, or better yet a week, plan in advance and bear in mind that the summer is quite busy.

For the most part, we'll saunter (by car) north along Calif. 29, though a few of the Napa Valley vineyards I've included are a bit off the main road. But you'll enjoy the diversion—the beauty of the valley is striking whatever the time of year, and especially in the fall season. Throughout Napa, Yountville, St. Helena, and Calistoga, the colors are breathtaking as the leaves on the vines change to gold, rust brown, deep maroon—all in preparation for the next season of grapes.

THE WINERIES: Most of the wineries en route conduct their tours from 10 a.m. to 5 p.m. daily. And there's considerably more to them than merely open vineyards. There are the huge presses and an elaborate system of pipes and vats

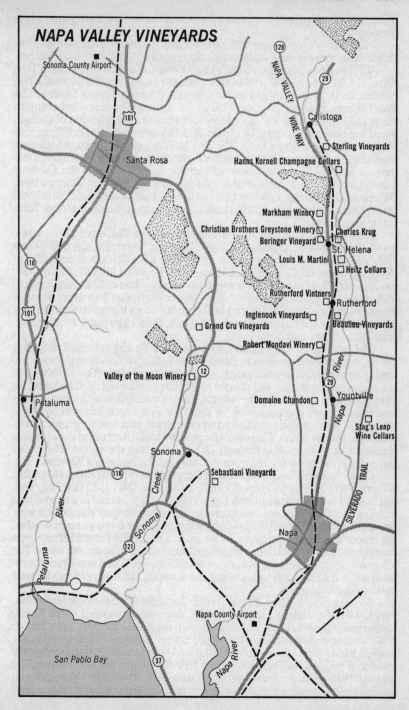

NAPA VALLEY VINEYARDS

Sonoma County Airport

128

NAPA VALLEY WINE WAY

29

Calistoga

□ Sterling Vineyards

101

Santa Rosa

Hanns Kornell Champagne Cellars

□

Markham Winery □

Christian Brothers Greystone Winery □   □ Charles Krug

Beringer Vineyard □   ● St. Helena

Louis M. Martini   □

□ Heitz Cellars

116

Rutherford Vintners

101

Inglenook Vineyards □   ● Rutherford

□ Grand Cru Vineyards   □ Beaulieu Vineyards

Robert Mondavi Winery □

River

Valley of the Moon Winery □   12

29

Domaine Chandon □   ● Yountville

□ Stag's Leap Wine Cellars

Petaluma ●

Napa

SILVERADO TRAIL

Sonoma ●

116

Sebastiani Vineyards □

Creek

Sonoma

Napa

121

Petaluma River

Napa County Airport

N

San Pablo Bay

37

Napa River

through which the wines flow and are blended before mellowing in giant casks in the deep cellars.

Napa Valley's fame began with cabernet sauvignon and, except for the white chardonnay, more acreage is devoted to the growth of this grape than any other.

We'll begin in Napa with **Stag's Leap Wine Cellars,** 5766 Silverado Trail, Napa, CA 94558 (tel. 707/944-2020). For the most part, the Silverado Trail parallels Calif. 29 and you can get there by going east on Trances Street or Oak Knoll Avenue, then north to Stag's Leap Wine Cellars. The man who has guided the destiny of this now famous winery and attracted the attention of France's noted wine experts is Warren Winiarski. A hill hides the group of buildings at its foot that comprise Stag's Leap. The first building of the group, which once housed the entire operation, still offers a summary view of wine making from start to finish. Undoubtedly one of the best-known wines is the Cabernet Sauvignon Cask 23, under Winiarski's distinguished Stag's Leap Vineyard label. (Winiarski also offers good-value wines under the Hawk Crest label.) Sales hours are 10 a.m. to 4 p.m. daily. You can taste selected current releases then too. Tours are by appointment.

Now back to Calif. 29 and its intersection with California Drive, where you'll find **Domaine Chandon,** California Drive, Yountville, CA 94599 (tel. 707/944-2280). The firm produces about 750,000 cases annually of champagne-method California sparkling wines. Founded in 1968, this is a very modern winery. Like its parent company in France, Möet et Chandon, it specializes in sparkling wines. ("Champagne" properly refers only to wines from the province of Champagne in France.) In the winery's cool lobby there's an informative exhibit on the history of sparkling wines, from champagne's "inventor," Friar Dom Pérignon, to the present.

The tour, given from 11 a.m. to 5 p.m., led by very informed and witty guides, goes past sample vines and into the cool, damp cellar where the wines are aged, past the machinery that prepares the wines for market. (On weekdays you can see them in operation.) At the end of the tour you can stop in at Le Salon, for a taste of Domaine Chandon's products. There are no free samples, but you can purchase a glass of sparkling wine for about $3. Free hors d'oeuvres come with your drink. There's also a small shop where you can purchase wines, wine paraphernalia, and souvenirs. The winery is open and lunch is served in the adjoining restaurant daily from May through October. During the winter (November through April) the winery and restaurant are closed Monday and Tuesday.

Continuing on Calif. 29 up to Oakville, you'll arrive at the **Robert Mondavi Winery,** 7801 St. Helena Hwy. (Calif. 29), Oakville, CA 94562 (tel. 707/963-9611). This is the ultimate hi-tech Napa Valley winery, housed in a magnificent mission-style facility. Almost every conceivable processing variable in their wine making is computer-controlled—fascinating, especially if you've never watched the procedure before. Sales hours are 9 a.m. to 5 p.m. After the guided tour, you can taste the results of all this attention to detail with selected current wines. The Vineyard Room usually features an art show, and you'll find some exceptional antiques in the reception hall. During the summer, the winery has some great outdoor jazz concerts.

Farther north on Calif. 29 you'll reach Rutherford and the **Inglenook Vineyards,** 1991 St. Helena Hwy. (Calif. 29, opposite Rutherford Cross Road), Rutherford, CA 94573 (tel. 707/967-3300). Inglenook's history dates back to 1887 when the vineyards were bought by Gustav Niebaum. They stayed in the family's hands until 1964, were sold to Allied Growers, and subsequently were purchased by Heublein, which set about to build the prestige of the wines. The original winery, designed and built by Captain McIntyre, the architect of several neighboring wineries, is now the tasting room and starting point for tours. Sales hours are 10 a.m. to 5 p.m. daily, during which time you can taste current releases. Guided tours are available.

A bit farther on is the **Beaulieu Vineyard,** at 1960 St. Helena Hwy. (Calif. 29), Rutherford, CA (tel. 707/963-2411) founded by a Frenchman named Delatour. During Prohibition, this clever Frenchman built up a nationwide business in altar wines while others were forced to close. When Repeal came he was one of the fortunate few with well-aged wines on hand. In 1938 de Latour brought over a young Russian enologist (wine scientist), who helped him to produce a sensational Cabernet Sauvignon—a wine for which Beaulieu is still famous. This winery offers one of the most comprehensive tours daily from 11 a.m. to 3 p.m. The tour takes about 30 minutes, after which you can sample selected current products in the tasting room and purchase some if you so desire.

Most wineries instruct as to proper tasting procedure: begin with the lightest white wines, go on to the rosés, reds, and finally sherries and dessert wines—sparkling wines come last.

The **Flora Springs Wine Co.** is at the end of West Zinfandel Lane, off Calif. 29 at 1978 W. Zinfandel Lane, St. Helena, CA 94574 (tel. 707/963-5711). While this handsome stone winery dates back to Napa Valley's early days, the Flora Springs label first appeared in 1978. The owners, the Komes family, have vineyards throughout Napa Valley and select choice lots for their own label. They are especially known for their sauvignon blanc and chardonnay, as well as cabernet Sauvignon.

Flora Springs offers an excellent two-hour "familiarization seminar" that almost everyone interested in wines would enjoy. And best of all, it's tailored to all levels of enophiles. Limited to ten participants, the course is held on the second and fourth Saturday of each month at 10 a.m. The program begins in the vineyards where you'll see a good-growing vine and taste the grapes. While the grapes are being crushed, you taste the must (just-pressed juice) and ultimately see how it becomes a beautiful, clear wine. Then you are taught how to evaluate wines; you'll blind-taste different ones and learn to distinguish between them, trying an older and a younger wine, for example, to see what happens with aging. You will also learn to pair wines with different foods. There is a fee of $20 to cover the imported wines that are part of the ten-wine tasting. The two hours will be among the most interesting and enjoyable you'll ever spend. Make reservations by calling Fritz Draeger (tel. 707/963-5711), or by writing to him at the above address.

Be sure to stop at **Beringer Vineyards,** 2000 Main St. (Calif. 29, just north of the business district), St. Helena, CA 94574 (tel. 707/963-7115), if only to look at this remarkable Rhine House and view the hand-dug tunnels carved out of the mountainside, the site of the original winery.

Beringer Vineyards was founded in 1881 by the brothers Jacob and Frederick. The family owned it until 1970 when it was purchased by the Swiss firm of Nestlé, Inc. In true Swiss fashion, the business has prospered. It is the oldest *continuously* operating winery in the Napa Valley. What about Prohibition? you might ask. Beringer made "sacramental" wines during the dry years.

The modern working winery on the opposite side of the road is not open to the public, but you can get a general look at it from the Rhine House. Sales hours are 9 a.m. to 4:30 p.m. Tasting of current products is conducted during sales hours in the manor house. Tours are conducted by very knowledgeable guides.

Just beyond the Beringer Vineyards, still on the same side of the road at the north end of St. Helena, is the showplace of the **Christian Brothers,** P.O. Box 391, St. Helena, CA 94574 (tel. 707/963-0763). In 1987, the Christian Brothers resurrected the body and soul of what has been known as Greystone Cellars

—originally built at the turn of the century to be the largest stone winery in the world. Greystone now has a very detailed and informative visitors' tour through a portion of the first floor of this splendid building; it covers many aspects of wine making, from cooperage to wine aging, discussing the vines at Greystone and pointing out the subtleties of tastings. Sales and tour hours at Greystone are 10 a.m. to 4 p.m. Tasting of selected products is offered after the tour.

Most of the process of wine making goes on at the winery just south of St. Helena, but as it is not designed to accommodate visitors, the winery is not open for tours.

Practically next door is **Charles Krug,** 2800 Main St., St. Helena CA 94574 (tel. 707/963-2761). The winery was founded in 1861—a classic old Napa estate set in a shady grove of oak trees on beautifully landscaped grounds. Krug was one of the first California winegrowers to produce wines by other than the primitive Spanish methods introduced by Father Junipero Serra. Two of his original stone buildings remain the core of the present winery, and the one-time coachhouse holds a small cooperage for aging select wines. Since 1943 the winery has belonged to the Mondavi family. Winemaker Peter Mondavi believes that the human element is as important as modern equipment: "The oldtimers believed the quality of the man's wine depended on his own quality and character. A little bit of himself goes into every bottle. To gain lasting fame a winemaker must be a poet, a philosopher, an honorable man, as well as a master craftsman."

Krug's ably led winery tour shows you the crushers, fermenters, tanks (both redwood and steel), aging cellars, and bottling lines, ending up in the tasting room. Tours are given at regular intervals daily from 10 a.m. to 4 p.m.

Spring Mountain Vineyards, 2805 Spring Mountain Rd. (about 1½ miles west off Calif. 29 via Madrona Avenue and Spring Mountain Road), St. Helena, CA 94574 (tel. 707/963-5233), has probably the most unique claim to fame of any Napa Valley vineyard—it is the setting for the TV program "Falcon Crest." While the grand house was built in the late 19th century, Spring Mountains Vineyards as a working winery is housed in a new structure. The cellars were built in the early 1980s, though the label goes back to 1968. Tours of the winery are free; however, if you're a "Falcon Crest" fan who would like to take a guided tour of the grounds around the house, there is a fee. Sales hours, during which there are tastings, are 10 a.m. to 5 p.m. daily; the last tour of the winery is at 4:30 p.m. Free tours of the grounds are every half hour.

Sterling Vineyards, at 1111 Dunaweal Lane, Calistoga, CA 94515 (tel. 707/942-5151), is just south of the town of Calistoga and approximately half a mile east of Calif. 29. Sterling Vineyards is probably more startling in appearance than any of its neighbors. Perched on top of an island of rock, it looks much more like a Greek or even an Italian mountaintop monastery. Reaching this isolated facility is relatively easy—just take the aerial gondola (there's a $6 per person charge for the ride). However, if you have any infirmity that makes walking or climbing difficult, this is not your cup of tea, or glass of wine. Gravity moves the wine and the visitors. You will go downstairs to fermentors, then down to the aging cellar; you'll climb farther down to the final aging cellar, then up to the reserve cellar, and finally up to the top of the rocky perch where you'll be rewarded in the tasting room. The very informative tour is guided by signs, not humans, so you can set your own pace. (It was kind not to employ a tour guide to make these arduous rounds several times daily.) The winery has changed hands more than once since its founding in 1969; its current owner is the Seagram Classic Wine Company, which produces over 100,000 cases per year. Sales hours and tasting times are 10:30 a.m. to 4:30 p.m. daily; however, the winery is closed to visitors on Monday and Tuesday during the winter.

OTHER THINGS TO DO: While you're in the area, there are a few other activities you can take in while sobering up for the drive back to San Francisco.

You'll find a variety of interesting choices discussed under the town headings. In Yountville, there's the **Vintage 1870 Complex,** originally a brick winery that can keep you occupied for at least a couple of hours. In St. Helena, you'll find the **Hurd Candle Factory,** actually more of a country store and the **Silverado Museum** which is devoted to Robert Louis Stevenson. And Calistoga offers for entertainment **Old Faithful Geyser of California** and the **Petrified Forest,** plus a collection of spas, mud baths, and soaring facilities.

2. NAPA

If you're touring the wine country, you might want to make your base its commercial center, the town of Napa. The gateway to the valley, Napa rose at the juncture of two streams; it was served by ferries and steamboats as early as the mid-1800s, and later by the Napa Valley Railroad. The valley is just 35 miles long, so if you stay in Napa and want to dine, wine, shop, or sightsee in Yountville, Rutherford, or St. Helena, you won't have very far to travel.

WHERE TO STAY AND DINE: To go the way of elegance in Napa is to stay at the **Silverado Country Club & Resort,** 1600 Atlas Peak Rd., Napa, CA 94558 (tel. 707/257-0200, or toll free 800/532-0500). It's north on Calif. 29 to Trancas Street, and east to Atlas Peak Road. Silverado is a 1,200 acre resort lavishly arranged at the foot of the hills. The resort has 280 spacious accommodations ranging from very large studios with a king-size bed, kitchenette, and a roomy, well-appointed bath, to one-, two-, or three-bedroom cottage suites, each with a wood-burning fireplace. Brown carpeting in the rooms sets off the pastel-striped spreads and drapes. The setting is superb: the cottage suites are in private, low-rise groupings, each sharing tucked-away courtyards and peaceful walkways. This arrangement allows for a feeling of privacy and comfort despite the size of the resort.

The main building and center of the resort looks more like an old southern mansion, pillars and all, than a California country resort. Lace curtains, white bentwood chairs, white tables, and gray carpeting complete the picture. Silverado offers exceptional resort services, including eight swimming pools and the largest tennis complex in northern California; 20 superlative Plexi-paved courts with a miniclubhouse, canvas-topped review decks, and sport shop. You say you don't play tennis anymore but have switched to golf? Silverado has two 18-hole courses, occupying some 360 acres, very cleverly designed by Robert Trent Jones, Jr. The South Course is 6,500 yards, with a dozen water crossings (how many balls do you plan to take?); the North Course is 6,700 yards—somewhat longer, but a bit more forgiving. Obviously there is a staff of pros on hand.

Silverado has three restaurants to accommodate your every taste (well, almost). The Royal Oak is the quintessential steak restaurant, with high-back chairs, carved-wood tables, and exposed beams and brickwork. Vintner's Court offers California cuisine in a chandeliered salon with a view of the surrounding eucalyptus and beautifully groomed flower beds. The Silverado Bar & Grill is a large indoor terrace/bar which overlooks the North Course and serves breakfast, lunch, and cocktails.

Rates at Silverado range from $165 for a studio to $190 for a one-bedroom suite, single or double occupancy. Two- to three-bedroom suites are $325 to $365. Special packages are in effect at various times of the year, so be sure to ask.

And now let's look at the other end of the scale—the ever handy low-cost **Motel 6,** at 3380 Solano Ave., Napa, CA 94558 (tel. 707/257-6111). From

Calif. 29, turn west on the Redwood Road turnoff and go one block to Solano Avenue, then half a block south and there you'll find Motel 6. It's location is excellent since you are close to Calif. 29 and just across the street from a pleasant minimall. Rooms are simple, comfortable, and clean. Free TV and feature movies are included in the rate, and now every Motel 6 room has a phone. Local calls are free and there is no motel service charge for long distance calls. Rooms are air-conditioned and there is a small pool. Rates are $29.95 for one person and $6 for each additional adult. One other important feature: the managers of this Motel 6 are pleasant, helpful, and chock-full of useful information (but then I found that to be true of most people in the Napa Valley—it must be the air).

3. YOUNTVILLE

Yountville is casual nouveau posh (and advancing on chi-chi), but undoubtedly the most charming village along Calif. 29. Of less historical interest than St. Helena or Calistoga, it is nonetheless an interesting jumping-off point for a wineries tour or for the simple enjoyment of the beauties of the valley. What's more, it has several lovely places to stay, interesting places to shop, and excellent to superb restaurants at various price levels. And Yountville is walkable—you can easily take a very enjoyable stroll from one end of town to the other.

At the center of the village is **Vintage 1870** (tel. 707/944-2451), once a winery (from 1871 to 1955) and now a gallery with specialty shops featuring art, antiques, wine accessories, country treasures and collectibles, contemporary furnishings, gifts, clothing, music boxes, and chocolates. It is also home to three restaurants and to the Keith Rosenthal Theatre and gallery, where for 15 minutes you can absorb a multi-image film presentation of the valley's four seasons and see the interior of Spring Mountain's famous "Falcon Crest" mansion. The *San Francisco Examiner* has called photographer Keith Rosenthal "the Ansel Adams of the wine country." Admission to see the film is $3 for adults, $2.50 for seniors, and $1 for children under 12. One of the most intriguing shops I found in the complex was the Napa Valley Trading Company, with antique and contemporary furnishings, teddies, weather vanes, pied and silver gray zebra finches (live and absolutely beautiful), stuffed kittens (fabric), and paper hot-air balloons, to name just a few of the many items you'll want to take with you.

And if you've always wanted to try real hot-air ballooning, this may be the place to indulge your airy whim. **Adventures Aloft,** P.O. Box 2500, Vintage 1870, Yountville, CA 94599 (tel. 707/255-8688), is located at Vintage 1870 and is Napa Valley's oldest hot-air balloon company with full-time professional pilots. Groups are small, and the flight will last about an hour. If you're a late sleeper, this may not be your bag since Adventures Aloft flies in the early sunrise hours; it's then that the winds are gentle and the air is cool, which makes for an especially enjoyable trip. If you need reassurance about flying, be advised that modern balloons are operated by licensed pilots under the supervision of the Federal Aviation Administration.

WHERE TO STAY: In Yountville, there are four notable choices. The **Vintage Inn,** 6541 Washington St., Yountville, CA 94599 (tel. 707/944-1112, or toll free 800/982-5539, 800/351-1133 in California), built on an old winery estate in the center of town, is very much the contemporary luxury country inn. The exterior is a brick-and-board construction; the reception lounge has a cathedral ceiling with exposed beams, brick fireplace, deep brown couches, and shuttered windows, giving a sense of the handsome, warm look of the guest rooms. Each room has a fireplace, an armoire concealing the TV, oversize beds, a Jacuzzi, wine bar, refrigerator, and either a patio or veranda. The inn also provides nightly turn-down service. If you insist on exercise other than walking through the lovely village and its shops, the inn has a 60-foot pool heated year round, as well as an exercise room with a sauna, and tennis courts reserved for the use of the guests. A complimentary champagne continental breakfast is served daily in the Vintage Club, as well as afternoon tea.

November through April, rates for singles range from $99 to $119; doubles from $109 to $129; minisuites, from $129 to $139. May through October, singles are $119 to $149; doubles, $129 to $159; minisuites, $159 to $169. The extra-person charge is $12 per night.

The **Burgundy House,** 6711 Washington St., P.O. Box 3274, Yountville CA 94599 (tel. 707/944-2855), offers rooms in a small fieldstone house. Some have private patios or balconies, and five of the rooms share a double bath. There are no TVs or phones—nothing to disturb the blessed peace. All rooms are air-conditioned. Children are not accepted.

Continental breakfast and wine (both complimentary) are served in a breakfast room with a fireplace, or in a pretty little garden. Singles and doubles are $72.50 to $90.

Under the same ownership, and just down the road a bit, is the **Bordeaux House,** 6600 Washington St., Yountville, CA 94599 (tel. 707/944-2855). Accommodations here are surprisingly contemporary (definitely not French wine country) with grasspaper-covered walls, Lucite furnishings, and beds on carpeted platforms. Amenities are also more up-to-date. Your room will have a private bath and a TV; each has a fireplace. There is a complimentary continental breakfast and evening wine over at the Burgundy House. Children are welcome. Rates range from $84 to $135.

And then there's the **Magnolia Hotel,** 6529 Yount St., Yountville, CA 94599 (tel. 707/944-2056), with 12 rooms in a beautifully restored old building (from 1873) as well as in new wing (the latter with fireplaces and sundecks). All rooms are individually decorated in Victorian motif with floral carpeting, and all have private bath but no phone or TV. If you need to compensate for any such perceived disadvantages, a decanter of complimentary port is in each room. On-premises facilities include a large swimming pool, heated from May through October, and a Jacuzzi.

Rates—including a full hot breakfast daily—are $95 to $165, single or double occupancy. A secluded suite overlooking the pool and garden (suitable for four) is $275. No smoking is allowed indoors.

WHERE TO DINE: There are several excellent choices in Yountville. The ambience at **The Diner,** 6476 Washington St. (tel. 707/944-2626), is friendly, warm, and unpretentious. Done in shell pink, with track lighting overhead, the restaurant features a functioning Franklin stove, a collection of vintage diner water pitchers, as well as some interesting photos of what I assume to be local personalities. Seating is at the counter or in wooden booths.

For breakfast and lunch, everything I tried on the extensive menu was delicious and the portions were huge. House specialties range from huevos rancheros served with fried potatoes, a breakfast burrito with eggs scrambled with home-made chorizo, garlic, jalapeños, and cream cheese, to the less exotic, but equally delicious, French toast and a wide range of eggs and pancakes. Fresh fruit with yogurt or cottage cheese is also available. The Diner's selection of natural, baked-on-premises breads usually includes raisin-walnut, whole wheat, cottage dill, and sourdough rye (with a starter descended from San Francisco's famous Larraburu Bakery, circa 1873).

Luncheon specialties include a superior carne asada, as well as several other toothsome Mexican dishes. For more staid tastes, there is quite an assortment of hamburgers, sandwiches, salads, and homemade soups. Sundaes, espresso, cappuccino, and a variety of drinks from fresh-squeezed orange juice and natural-fruit sodas to domestic and imported beer and wine by the glass are all available.

Dinners are exceptional variations on the Mexican theme. Don't pass by the enchiladas with chicken, green chiles, and cream cheese, topped with crème fraîche and jack cheese. And the Tostada Grande—heaped with beans, cheese, lettuce, avocado, turkey breast, tomatoes, sour cream, and salsa—defies any appetite. Burgers, homemade soups, and salads are available at dinner too. If you still have room for dessert, flan, chocolate torte, or New York cheesecake are among the offerings (price range: $2 to $3.25). Service at the Diner is attentive, helpful, and friendly—indeed characteristic of all Napa Valley restaurants and inns.

Breakfast is served from 8 a.m. to 3 p.m.; lunch, from 11 a.m. to 3 p.m.; dinner, from 5:30 to 9 p.m. Prices at breakfast range from $3.50 to $6; lunch, $3.25 to $8; dinner, $5 to $8.50. Open daily except Monday.

Now the setting for the talents of chef Sally Schmitt and her creative American menu, the **French Laundry,** 6640 Washington St., at Creek Street (tel. 707/944-2380), was in truth once a laundry. There is no sign to indicate that this historic old building might be anything but a country home, nor is an address visible, so my advice is to look closely for the very small sign that indicates the cross street.

At the French Laundry, you'll feel as though you are an honored guest in a private home. Infinite care has been taken with every detail of cuisine and decor, from the perfectly arranged flowers, the inviting lovely fabric tablecloths, and still-life paintings and historical prints.

A different five-course prix-fixe dinner (about $42 per person) is offered at the French Laundry each evening. It is difficult to get a reservation, but if you succeed, you're here for a relaxing evening. Your meal begins with a choice of three appetizers—perhaps sautéed sweetbreads and shiitake mushrooms in lemon cream, artichokes with garlic mayonnaise, or smoked trout with red-onion compote. Next comes a soup course, followed by an entree such as suprême of chicken with rosemary and orange, or pork loin with mustard-caper sauce. A simple green salad with a selection of perfectly ripe cheeses at room temperature follows. The meal is capped by a choice of at least three desserts. Sally Schmitt specializes in fruit desserts: a fall favorite of mine is gingered figs with crème à l'anglaise, or the cranberry and apple küchen with hot cream sauce. The coffee is a special house blend, and as you might expect, there's an extensive and well-chosen wine list.

Dinner is served Wednesday through Sunday (there's only one seating, but times of arrival are spread from 7 to 8:30 p.m.). Remember, reservations are essential. A meal at the French Laundry is an experience you'll savor.

A favorite hangout of local winemakers and growers, just north of the village of Yountville, is **Mustards Grill,** 7399 St. Helena Hwy. (tel. 707/944-2424). As a close relative of the Fog City Diner in San Francisco, Tra Vigne in St. Helena, and Rio Grill in Carmel, you might expect the restaurant to be successful—and indeed it has been. Look for the amusing bronze sculpture of a gentleman in bowler on the west side of the road. As you enter a barn-like structure, you'll see beamed cathedral ceilings, a black-and-white tile floor, track lighting, and a small bar. The main dining room is on two levels, and there's an airy glass-enclosed outer dining area for a simulated al fresco experience.

The atmosphere is light, festive, and relaxed, as you might expect it to be in wine country. The blue-jeaned, white-shirted servers are friendly and very knowledgeable. Specials of the day are listed on a blackboard along with featured local wines ranging from $3.50 to $5 by the glass. You can bring your own bottle of wine, as many diners seem to do, but the restaurant does charge a $5 corkage fee. I'd guess that more wine per table is consumed here than in any San Francisco restaurant.

While you review the dining possibilities, half of a sliced, warm, crusty baguette arrives with sweet butter. Among the starters are such gems as a cornmeal pancake with Tobiko caviar and sour cream; warm goat cheese with sun-dried tomatoes and chives; and Chinese chicken salad. Sandwiches, apart from a sizable hamburger or cheeseburger, also include a rib-eye steak with horseradish cream, or smoked ham and Jarlsberg cheese grilled with tomato chutney. Entrees are reasonably priced and range from wood-burning-oven specialties—barbecued baby back ribs, pork chops with Thai marinade, or quail—to such items from the grill as Sonoma rabbit, New York steak with shiitake mushroom ragoût, gulf prawns, lamb chops with braised eggplant, or fresh fish. For dessert, the chocolate-pecan cake with chocolate sauce is a chocoholic's delight. I found the caramel custard with pistachios and cream irresistible. And Mustards has some of the best coffee I've ever tasted.

Back to basics: entree prices range from $9.90 to $17.50; appetizers and sandwiches from $4 to $8. Dessert will add another $3 to $4. Open daily from 11:30 a.m. to 10 p.m.; at lunch, you can dine at the bar. Reservations are necessary for lunch and dinner.

Backtrack a bit on Calif. 29 to California Drive, just south of the Yountville Cross Road, turn west into California Drive, and there you will find **Domaine Chandon** (tel. 707/944-2892), one of California's most exquisite restaurants.

Domaine Chandon forsakes the usual old-fashioned wine-country quaintness for understated modern elegance—the keynote of the decor. It is one of the most dramatic and beautiful settings in the wine country. Multitiered, it has arched fir-paneled ceilings, big picture windows, dark-green chairs at white-clothed tables, and rows of plants and trees at each level. At lunch you can dine outdoors; at dinner, inside by candlelight. The lunch menu varies daily, but might include ahi tuna served in a sauce of butter, fish juices, and Chandon Napa Valley Brut. Luncheon entrees cost $14 to $17. There are lovely pastries and fruit tarts for dessert. At dinner, you might begin with chanterelle soup made with Oregon wild mushrooms, and continue with salmon in champagne and sorrel sauce or sweetbreads with truffle juice and herbs for $22 to $26. Need I add that the wine list is impeccable.

Open for lunch from 11:30 a.m. to 2:30 p.m. and for dinner from 6 to 9 p.m. Wednesday through Saturday from November to April, the same hours daily from May through October. Reservations are essential; you can phone them in daily between 10 a.m. and 5 p.m., no more than two weeks in advance of your visit. The restaurant is closed the last three weeks in January.

4. OAKVILLE

One of the outstanding culinary attractions in Napa Valley is located on St. Helena Highway (Calif. 29) in Oakville, at the Oakville Cross Road. There you will find the **Oakville Grocery Co.,** 7856 St. Helena Hwy., Oakville, CA 94562 (tel. 707/944-8802). Its name, its location, and its exterior disguise one of the finest gourmet food stores this side of Dean and DeLuca in New York City. You'll find the very best of breads, cheeses, pâtés, fresh foie gras (American and French), smoked Norwegian salmon, smoked sturgeon, fresh caviar, smoked pheasant, and an exceptional selection of California wines. (If you find the wine decision difficult, there are sampler sets to help you along.) Special bottles such as the 1983 Stag's Leap Wine Cellars "Cask 23" cabernet or the 1985 Long Vineyards chardonnay are also available in limited quantities. Oakville Grocery can ship wines by the case anywhere in the United States. Remember, you can charge liquor purchases in California; major charge cards are accepted here.

The Oakville Grocery Co. will prepare a picnic basket lunch for you if you give them 24-hour advance notice. Delivery service is available to some areas.

5. RUTHERFORD

WHERE TO STAY AND DINE: For those of you on Calif. 29 (St. Helena Hwy.), take the Oakville Cross Road (at Oakville, of course) east to the Silverado Trail; turn north to Rutherford Hill Road, then east on up the hillside to the French gem of Napa Valley—the **Auberge du Soleil,** at 180 Rutherford Hill Rd., Rutherford, CA 94573 (tel. 707/963-1211). This elegant hideaway with its glorious French country restaurant is nestled in a hillside olive grove overlooking the lovely valley. It's a peaceful spot, air fragrant with eucalyptus, to rest and to eat brilliant classic French and California nouvelle cuisine.

At the auberge's restaurant, a magnificent fireplace (large enough to roast a whole pig), huge wood pillars, banquettes with rainbow-striped cushions, white tablecloths, and fresh flowers combine to create an elegantly rustic—or is that rustically elegant?—ambience. Light opera plays in a room that opens out to a wisteria-decked terrace with white umbrellas, pink-clothed tables, and attractive carved-wood chairs.

At lunch the appetizers include chicken-and-leek sausage with bell-pepper vinaigrette, as well as crab cakes with cucumber-and-mint sauce. Ask about the soup of the day too: I've had a superb and unusual black-bean soup and a pumpkin/sweet potato blend (with a tad of juniper flavor) that I'd love to take home by the gallon. The bread brought to table with sweet butter is deliciously hot. Among the lunch entrees are such excellent seafood dishes as sautéed prawns with tomato-and-dill sauce and grilled salmon with scallions, garlic, and sweet potatoes, as well as a delicious fettuccine with sun-dried tomatoes, porcini mushrooms, and poussin. The desserts are superb: my choice was a delicious puff pastry with fresh fruits and caramel sauce. Luncheon entrees average $13 to $17; appetizers, $5 to $8; desserts, $6.

Dinner at the Auberge du Soleil is a four-course, prix-fixe affair ($52). You might begin with the fish-and-shellfish dumplings (quenelles) with meunière sauce, the wild-mushroom ravioli, the tuna carpaccio, or the pan-fried, hazelnut-coated goat cheese with cassis vinaigrette. The soup of the day is followed by an enticing list of entrees. I find it difficult to pass over the rack of lamb, but the valley squab with truffles and marrow is truly enlightened cuisine. Somewhat more standard tastes might be pleased by the chicken suprême prepared with herbs and wild rice, or grilled New York cut with horseradish sauce, served with grilled eggplant and tomatoes. An extraordinary dark-chocolate sac with tangerine mousse and raspberry sauce, a hot apple tart with apricot sauce, or, in fact, any of the other delights, should satisfy all dessert palates.

Each dish, lunch and dinner, is a work of art. Reservations are necessary, and weekends are often booked a month in advance. The restaurant is open daily for lunch from 11:30 a.m. to 2 p.m., and for dinner from 6 to 9 p.m.

The Auberge du Soleil has 36 rooms, probably the most elegant in the valley, each with fireplace, TV, wet bar, and decks overlooking Napa Valley. One-bedroom rooms and suites range from $205 to $330; two-bedroom suites are $500. Room rates include a continental breakfast and the use of swimming and tennis facilities. Even if you are staying at the inn, it is suggested that lunch and dinner reservations at the auberge restaurant be made in advance of your arrival.

Note: If staying at Auberge du Soleil would strain the budget, do consider at least treating yourself to lunch: it's a modest indulgence and worth every luscious bite.

6. ST. HELENA

Reminiscent in some ways of the south of France, with its tall plane trees arching over the roads, St. Helena also suggests feudal England, with its mansions overseeing the vineyards and valleys from hillside perches. Many of the buildings in the main part of town date back to the 1800s; the modern wares in a variety of shops are also worth a look. It's a friendly place, with some excellent restaurants and inns.

Literary buffs won't want to miss the **Silverado Museum,** 1490 Library Lane in St. Helena (tel. 707/963-3757), devoted to the life and works of Robert Louis Stevenson, author of *Treasure Island, Kidnapped,* etc. It was here that Stevenson honeymooned in 1880, at the abandoned Silverado Mine. Over 8,000 items include original manuscripts, letters, photographs, portraits of the writer, and the desk he used in Samoa. Open daily from noon to 4 p.m., except Monday and holidays. No admission charge.

There's also a small and quite charming complex—the Freemark Abbey where you'll find the **Hurd Beeswax Candle Factory,** at 3020 St. Helena Hwy. (Calif. 29) (tel. 707/963-7211). The candle factory has an open workshop where the public can observe a demonstration hive and the actual handcrafting of beeswax candles into a variety of lovely and intricate shapes. The candles, as well as wine, food items, and books about the area, can also be purchased here—it's sort of a country store.

WHERE TO STAY: The Wine Country Inn, at 1152 Lodi Lane, CA 94574 (tel. 707/963-7077), two miles north of the center of St. Helena, is a handsome hostelry. Set on a hillside overlooking the vineyards, it has 25 rooms decorated in New England inn style. Many have fireplaces (for use mid-October to mid-April), balconies, or patios, and though all have private baths, there are no TVs or phones. The rooms are exquisitely furnished in country antiques. The owner's grandmother made patchwork quilts for the beds and stitchery hangings for the walls. To add to the aura of quiet relaxation, the inn now has an elegant pool and a Jacuzzi. A buffet-style continental breakfast—with homemade breads—is included in the rates. Children under 13 are not accepted. Rates are $96 to $161 for singles, $106 to $171 for doubles.

WHERE TO DINE: Tra Vigne, 1050 Charter Oak Ave., at Main Street (Calif. 29) (tel. 707/963-4444), is one of the most attractive restaurants I've ever seen. Its chic neoclassical Italian look, its innovative, informal Italian-American food, and its attentive, knowledgeable, and friendly service are an unbeatable combination.

You approach the restaurant, which looks like a small Roman forum, from a splendid outdoor patio. To the right, as you enter, is a comfortable bar that extends the entire length of the wall, and to the rear of the dining room is the ultracontemporary pizza oven. An artistic arrangement of dried flowers, salami, bread, garlic, and cheese hangs over the entry to the kitchen.

Whether you go for a drink, an unconventional pizza, lunch, or dinner, Tra Vigne is worth seeing. And the prices are most reasonable. Appetizers go from the hearty homemade minestrone or the pizzetta con aglio (small pizza with garlic) to the smoked prosciutto with persimmons and mascarpone cream. Pasta ranges from a deliciously simple shell-shaped variety with fresh tomato-and-tarragon sauce to delectable ravioli filled with homemade ricotta, spinach, and red chard. Want an adventurous pizza? Consider Pizza Rustica, with pancetta, sautéed red chard, roasted sweet peppers and Parmesan; or Pizza al Gamberi, with prawns, yellow tomatoes, Bel Paese, Parmesan, and pesto. Tra Vigne also has fresh fish daily, braised rabbit with mustard, sage, and juniper (a Tuscan specialty of the house), roasted quail wrapped in pancetta with chervil vinaigrette, and a superb 16-ounce T-bone steak served with fennel roasted potatoes. For dessert, the poached pear in merlot custard with chocolate walnut grissini is above reproach, but you won't go wrong either with the rich coffee caramel custard with Sambuca crème à l'anglaise. Entrees are $6.75 to $11.25 for pasta, and $8.25 to $14.25 for the meat and fish dishes (the T-bone steak is $17.25). Pizza (all are one-person size) is $7.25 to $9.25. Appetizers cost $3.25 to $10.25 for the antipasto misto for two. Desserts average $4.

Tra Vigne has an excellent selection of California and Italian wines, and a choice of several fine grappas in a broad price range.

Tra Vigne is open daily: Sunday through Thursday from noon to 9 p.m., on Friday and Saturday to 10 p.m. Reservations are suggested.

7. CALISTOGA

Sam Brannan became California's first millionaire by building a hotel and spa to take advantage of the area's geothermal springs. His entrepreneurial instincts combined "California" with the name of a popular East Coast resort "Saratoga": Calistoga was born in 1859 and incorporated in 1886, attracting the newly wealthy from San Francisco. Today Calistoga still has a main street about six blocks long, with no building higher than two stories; it looks for all the world like a set for a somewhat updated western. At the northern end of the lush wine country, near the Old Faithful Geyser and the Petrified Forest, the town remains popular. Calistoga is a delightfully simple place in which to relax and indulge in mineral waters, mud baths, sulfur steambaths, Jacuzzis, massages—and, of course, wines.

If you've never had a mud bath before, you might well wonder what it is and how it feels. Although mud baths are not recommended for people with high blood pressure or for pregnant women, all others may enjoy their benefits. The bath is composed of local volcanic ash, imported peat, and naturally boiling mineral hot springs water, all mulled together to produce a thick mud at a temperature of about 90° to 100° F. Once you overcome the hurdle of deciding how best to place your naked body into the stone tub full of mud, the rest is pure relaxation—you are in the mud bath, surprisingly buoyant, for about 10 to 12 minutes. A warm mineral-water shower, a mineral water whirlpool bath, and a mineral-water steamroom visit are followed by a relaxing blanket wrap to cool your delighted body down slowly. All of this takes about 1½ hours; with a massage, add another half hour. The outcome is a rejuvenated, revitalized, squeaky-clean you.

In addition to **Dr. Wilkinson's Hot Springs** (discussed below), other spas providing similar services are the **Lincoln Avenue Spa** at 1339 Lincoln Ave. (tel. 707/942-5296), **Golden Haven Hot Springs Spa** at 1713 Lake St. (tel. 707/942-6793), and the **Calistoga Spa Hot Springs** at 1006 Washington St. (tel. 707/942-6269). All spas offer a variety of other treatments such as hand and foot massage, herbal wraps, acupressure facelift, skin rubs, herbal facials, etc. Appointments are necessary for all of the above services, and you should phone at least a week in advance.

WHERE TO STAY: The **Mount View Hotel**, 1457 Lincoln Ave. (near Fairway), Calistoga CA 94515 (tel. 707/942-6877), offers 25 art deco rooms and nine glamorous suites named after movie idols of the past—like the "Carole Lombard" (it has peach-colored walls and light-green carpeting) and the western-themed "Tom Mix." Amenities include private baths and phones in all rooms; no TV. Facilities also include a heated swimming pool and Jacuzzi.

A continental/nouvelle cuisine restaurant on the premises serves breakfast, lunch, dinner, and Sunday brunch, and the food is excellent. Typical dinner entrees here are rack of lamb with whole-grain mustard, and several fresh fish specials of the day, for $10 to $22. A prix-fixe dinner is $30. There's an extensive California wine list, reasonably priced and well balanced for any menu. A cocktail lounge (the scene of nightly piano music) adjoins.

Rates are $65 to $90 a night, single or double, and $120 to $145 for suites, including a full American breakfast. A special package—"The Suite Life"— includes a suite for two evenings, champagne, and a dinner for two for $205.

Another Calistoga choice, oriented more toward the mud bath/mineral water/massage born-again set, is **Dr. Wilkinson's Hot Springs,** 1507 Lincoln Ave., Calistoga, CA 94515 (tel. 707/942-4102). It's a typical motel with 42 rooms, mostly distinguished by the mud baths on the premises. A mud-bath treatment takes about two hours. This rejuvenating process costs $32, $15 additional if you include a half-hour massage. There's also a hot spring on the premises, and none of these healthful facilities is limited to guests. Be sure to reserve your spa visit four to six weeks in advance. Motel rooms at Dr. Wilkinson's have color TVs, phones, and drip coffee makers. Rates are $48 to $69 single, $52 to $80 double. Lower weekly rates are also available. Facilities include two outdoor and one indoor pool.

WHERE TO DINE: Apart from the fine food at the Mount View Hotel or making the short trip to St. Helena for dining at Tra Vigne, a delightful meal in a combination deli and treasurehouse of wines may be enjoyed at the **All Seasons Market** at 1400 Lincoln Ave. (tel. 707/942-9111). You may choose to eat in or gather provisions for a picnic. However, don't overlook the luncheon and dinner specials here and the fresh desserts. Recent luncheon entrees included a mesquite-grilled chicken sandwich served with homemade bread and salad, and fettuccine with prawns served with cucumber, bell peppers, and tomatoes in virgin olive oil and white wine. Entrees range from $5.50 to $7.50. The menu also includes homemade soup, and an appetizer and salad of the day. The All Seasons Market is open daily; Monday through Thursday from 9 a.m. to 6 p.m., weekends to 10 p.m. The Market serves breakfast, lunch, and dinner on weekends; the balance of the week, lunch is served from noon until 4 p.m., then dinner until closing.

SEEING THE SIGHTS: Before you head off to see the Old Faithful Geyser and Petrified Forest, stop at the **Calistoga Depot,** at 1458 Lincoln Ave. (tel. 707/942-6333), which now houses a variety of shops and the Calistoga Chamber of Commerce. The depot occupies the site of the original railroad station built in 1868; alongside it sit six restored passenger cars dating from 1916 to the 1920s.

If you decided against ballooning in Yountville, Calistoga may have something to lighten your spirits. The **Calistoga Soaring Center** at 1546 Lincoln Ave. (tel. 707/942-5592), is the largest and most active soaring site in the country. You can take a glider ride (they're available for one or two persons) with a federally licensed commercial glider pilot. Sailplanes are built, certified, and maintained to the same standards the government requires of engine-driven aircraft. Twenty minutes of quietly soaring like an eagle above beautiful Napa Valley is $74.50 for one person or $94.50 for two. Trips can be arranged any day of the week from 9 a.m. till sunset.

The **Old Faithful Geyser of California,** 1299 Tubbs Lane (tel. 707/942-6463), has been blowing off steam for as long as anyone can remember. The hot

(350° F) water spews out every 40 minutes, day and night. The performance varies with barometric pressure, the tides, and earth tectonic stress; it lasts about three minutes and you'll learn a lot about the origins of geothermal steam. One of the few geysers in the world that performs at regular intervals, Old Faithful's deviations from the normal pattern generally seem to relate to earthquakes within 500 miles of the area. You can bring a picnic lunch with you and catch the show as many times as you wish. Old Faithful is situated between Calif. 29 and Calif. 128 (there are signs directing you to it from downtown Calistoga). Admission is $2.50 for adults, $1.50 for children under 12, free for those under 6. The geyser area is open year round: from 9 a.m. to 6 p.m. in summer, to 5 p.m. the rest of the year.

Also in Calistoga, off Calif. 128 at 4100 Petrified Forest Rd., is the **Petrified Forest** (tel. 707/942-6667). Don't expect to see thousands of trees turned into stone; however, you can see many interesting specimens of redwoods that have become petrified through the infiltration of silicas and other minerals in the volcanic ash that covered them after the eruption of Washington's Mount St. Helens. Earlier specimens—petrified seashells, clams, and marine life—indicate that water covered the area before the redwood forest. Admission is $3 for adults, free for children under 10. The Petrified Forest is open daily: from 9 a.m. to 6 p.m. in the summer, 10 a.m. to 5 p.m. the rest of the year.

8. SONOMA

Although not far from Napa Valley, Sonoma, 45 miles north of San Francisco, is of sufficient historical interest to warrant a day's sightseeing all its own. To get there, just take Rte. 101 north, make a right at Calif. 37, a left at 121, then head north on Broadway, following the signs.

Centuries before Europeans colonized the area it was inhabited by the Pomo and Miwok peoples. It wasn't until the 19th century that world powers—Spain, Mexico, Russia, and the United States—began to converge in the Sonoma region. During the 1830s and 1840s one man, Gen. Mariano Guadalupe Vallejo—a brilliant Mexican army officer—was given 44,000 acres in nearby Petaluma Valley and charge of the mission of Sonoma. Vallejo's far-reaching civil and military powers brought him immense wealth and undisputed rule of the area as long as California was in Mexican hands. By 1846 he had increased his personal holdings to 175,000 acres; in that same year, however, American frontiersmen under John C. Frémont captured the area and arrested him. He was soon released and he later served as major of Sonoma in 1852 and 1860.

Many aspects of the town, including the approach via a wide boulevard, Broadway, and the central plaza are still here as Vallejo laid them out originally. He left his mark everywhere, as you'll see when you explore Sonoma's major attractions, all of which center around the **plaza**—today a lovely city park, the largest town square in California, and the setting for City Hall. The plaza is also the location of the **Bear Flag Monument,** which stands adjacent to the exact site where a band of adventurers raised the crude Bear Flag. Symbolizing the end of Mexican rule, the Bear Flag was later to become the state standard.

WHAT TO SEE AND DO: Major historical landmarks and attractions are detailed below. For a complete listing, an easy-to-read map, and information on wineries, restaurants, farm trails, and antique shops in the area, make your first stop the **Sonoma Valley Visitors Bureau,** conveniently located at 453 1st St. East, in the Plaza, Sonoma, CA 95476 (tel. 707/996-1090). The bureau is open daily: weekdays from 9 a.m. to 5 p.m., Saturday to 4 p.m., and on Sunday to 3 p.m.

All of the historical landmarks described below, with the exception of the

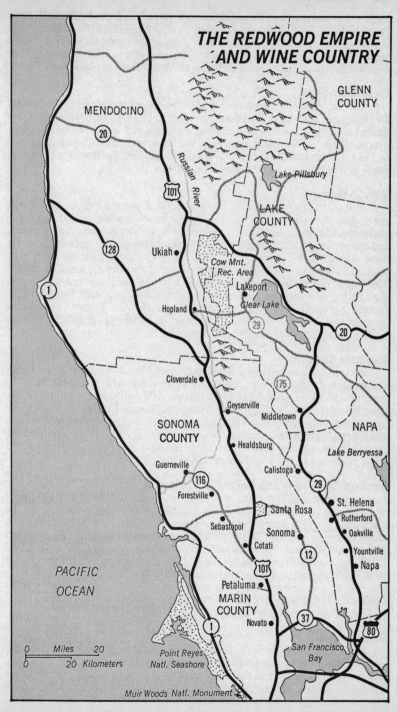

THE REDWOOD EMPIRE AND WINE COUNTRY

Swiss Hotel and the Nash-Patton Adobe, are part of the **Sonoma State Historic Park,** 20 E. Spain St., Sonoma, CA 95476 (tel. 707/938-1519). Tickets to the landmarks can be purchased at any one of them and are good for admission to all on the same day. Fees are $1 per adult, 50¢ per child 6 to 17. All Sonoma State Historic Park landmarks described below are open daily from 10 a.m. to 5 p.m.

Casa Grande

General Vallejo's first home, this Mexican-style adobe was one of the grandest residences in California when it was built in 1836. In its heyday this Spain Street house was the center of social and diplomatic life north of San Francisco. Eleven Vallejo children were born here, and it was here that Vallejo was arrested in 1846. Unfortunately, the main wing of the building was destroyed by fire in 1867, and only the Indian servants' wing remains today.

Vallejo Home

In 1850 Vallejo purchased some additional property about a half mile northwest of the plaza on which to build another estate, called, in Latin, **Lachryma Montis** (mountain tear). Grapevines, a wide assortment of fruit trees, and other foliage and shrubbery were planted, and the quarter-mile driveway was lined with roses and cottonwood trees. An arbor-shaded pathway encircled a pool, and a number of fountains further enhanced the carefully tended grounds. The Victorian-style house went up in 1852, its interior decorated with crystal chandeliers, lace curtains, and elaborate furnishings imported from Europe. General Vallejo and his wife lived here for over 35 years. Today the buildings, grounds, and interior—furnished with many of Vallejo's personal effects—are maintained as closely as possible to the original.

Sonoma Barracks

Erected in 1836 by (you guessed it) General Vallejo, on Spain Street facing the plaza, this wide-balconied, two-story adobe was built to house the Mexican army troops. In the years 1835 to 1846, over 100 military expeditions set out from Sonoma, most with the aim of subduing hostile Indians. Following the military takeover by the Bear Flag party, and the subsequent raising of the Stars and Stripes, Sonoma continued to be an important U.S. Army post. In still later years the building served as a winery, store, law office, and private residence, until it was purchased in 1958 by the state and partially restored.

Mission San Francisco Solano de Sonoma

Founded in 1823, this was the last of the 21 missions founded in California by Father Junipero Serra. It was the only one founded under Mexican rule. The first building was a temporary wooden structure; later a low adobe wing was added for living quarters. This latter building, which stands east of the chapel, is the oldest in Sonoma. The mission reached peak prosperity in 1832 when nearly 1,000 Indian converts were in residence. The present chapel was constructed in 1840 and furnished by Vallejo as a parish church. After later incarnations as a hay barn, winery, and blacksmith shop, the mission became a state monument in 1903 and was restored. It houses many mission artifacts as well as watercolors of mission scenes throughout California by Virgil Jorgensen.

Swiss Hotel

Over at 18 W. Spain St., facing the plaza, this adobe provided yet more living space for Don Salvador Vallejo. Later it was used as a hotel and restaurant, and meals are served here to this day. The furnishings are Eastlake, and the decor is of the ye-olde-inn variety. A menu on the wall from 1936 proffers a full dinner from appetizer to dessert for just $1. Lunches and full-course dinners today are considerably more expensive. Lunch is served Wednesday through Sunday from 11:30 a.m. to 3:30 p.m.; dinner begins at 5 p.m. Closed Monday and Tuesday.

Blue Wing Inn
This 1840 hostelry, at 133 E. Spain St., was erected by General Vallejo to accommodate travelers and emigrants who needed a place to stay while they built their Sonoma homes. It was purchased during Gold Rush days by two retired seafaring men who operated it as a hotel and store. Notable guests included John Frémont, Kit Carson, and Ulysses S. Grant; notorious guests included the bandit Murieta and "Three-fingered Jack." The inn itself is not open to the public. It now houses an antique shop and folk-art shop, which are open Wednesday through Sunday from noon to 5 p.m.

Toscano Hotel
Among the most interesting sights in the plaza area, this wood-frame building next to the barracks looks almost as if the guests and staff just walked out suddenly one day leaving everything behind. In the parlor downstairs a game of cards in progress is laid out on the table. Bedrooms upstairs have period furnishings, rag rugs, lovely quilts, shaving stands, pitcher and bowl for washing up, and antique tortoise-shell dresser sets that include button hooks. On exhibit are some teensy clothes that were traveling salesmen's samples. Free docent-guided tours are given Saturday and Sunday from 11 a.m. to 4 p.m. You'll also get to see the Toscano kitchen, furnished in the same period.

Nash-Patton Adobe
This house, built in 1847, is where one John H. Nash was taken prisoner for refusing to surrender his post as alcade (mayor). The adobe was restored in 1931.

LUNCH BREAK: For gastronomical rather than historical intake, stop in at the **Sonoma Cheese Factory,** 2 Spain St. (tel. 707/996-1000), where a long display case is filled with every variety of Italian meats imaginable, 101 kinds of cheese, plus caviar, gourmet salads, pâté, and the Monterey Jack cheese they make. They'll be happy to put it into a crusty French bread sandwich for you, which, along with a small bottle of wine, will make a great picnic lunch. Picnic tables can be found in the plaza park. The Cheese Factory also has its own outdoor tables. And while you're here you can see a free narrated slide show about cheese making. Open daily from 9:30 a.m. to 5:30 p.m.

WINERIES: Sonoma, like Napa Valley, is wine country. If you're planning a trip to Napa as well, you'll get enough of winery tours without these. Otherwise one you don't want to miss is **Sebastiani,** 389 4th St. East (tel. 707/938-5532), a winery that was founded in 1904 by Samuele Sebastiani. It is the only winery in Sonoma Valley to offer a guided tour and tasting from a full selection of wines which have won 95 awards. The tour through the stone aging cellars containing over 300 carved casks is fascinating and well worth the time. You can see the original crusher and press, as well as the largest collection of oak barrel carvings in the world. One tank here holds 59,666 gallons of wine—if you drank a bottle a day, it would last for 800 years! If you don't want to take the tour you can go straight to the tasting room, where you can sample from an extensive selection of wines. Open from 10 a.m. to 5 p.m. daily. Tours are every 20 minutes until 4:20 p.m.

You can also visit **Buena Vista,** at 18000 Old Winery Rd. (tel. 707/938-1266), slightly northeast of Sonoma. It was founded in 1857 by Count Agoston Haraszthy, the Hungarian emigré who is called the father of the California wine industry. A close friend of General Vallejo, Haraszthy journeyed to Europe at his own expense in 1861 and returned with 100,000 of the finest cuttings from European vineyards, which he made available to all wine growers. An official California landmark, the historic cellars and the original massive stone buildings are open for a self-guided tour. (Winemaking now takes place in an ultramodern facility outside of Sonoma.) Open daily from 10 a.m. to 5 p.m. Tasting takes place in the restored 1862 Press House. The Knights of the Vine wine museum is housed in the 1857 wine cellars. There's also an art gallery and gift shop. Picnic grounds adjoin.

JACK LONDON STATE PARK: A ride to nearby Glen Ellen, about seven miles northwest along Calif. 12, takes you to Jack London State Park (tel. 707/938-5216), where the famed author lived until his death at the age of 40 in 1916. Here you can see the cottage, ranch buildings, and the ruins of **Wolf House,** which London planned but never occupied—a magnificent rustic home of natural wood and stone. On August 22, 1913, a few weeks before the Londons were to move in, the house mysteriously burned down. The house of **Happy Walls,** where London's wife, Charmian, lived for many years after his death, now is a veritable London museum, filled with the author's possessions, mementoes, and artifacts the couple brought back from their travels in the South Seas. A room on the first floor is fitted out as London's office used to be, with his desk, typewriter, and other items. Not far away, under a huge red lava boulder on a wooded knoll, are London's ashes.

The park is open daily from 8 a.m. to sundown or the closing hour posted at the station entrance; the museum, from 10 a.m. to 5 p.m. The park also includes London's ranch buildings, a lake, and hiking trails. There's a $3 per-car entrance fee.

TRAIN TOWN: The **Sonoma Gaslight and Western Railroad,** a meticulous miniature model of a diamond-stack 1875 locomotive, is located a mile south of the town square on Broadway (tel. 707/938-3912). Everything at Train Town is built to the same one-quarter scale, including a depot, freight office, and other business buildings. The train runs a 1½-mile track through a man-made landscape of cedars, hills, and valleys, and around a lake. About midway in the 19-minute trip, a stop is made at a miniature Old West town, Lakeview. Passengers can get off the train and explore, peeking into the windows of a Wells Fargo express office, depot, Victorian bungalow, stores, fire station, and newspaper office. There's even a petting zoo. Trains leave daily every 20 minutes from 11 a.m. to 5 p.m. June 17 through Labor Day; on Saturday, Sunday, and holidays, weather permitting, the rest of the year. Fare is $2.50 for adults, $2 for seniors and those ages 2 to 16; those under age 2 ride free.

9. FORT ROSS

Now a state historic park, Fort Ross, 11 miles north of Jenner on Calif. 1, was once a North American outpost of the Russian empire. It was over 150 years ago, during the "fur rush" days, that Fort Ross was dedicated by the Russian-American Fur Company on the name-day of Czar Alexander I.

The history of Russian imperialistic designs on California (which helped prompt the Monroe Doctrine) actually dates back to 1740, when Russian explorer Vitus Bering brought news that Alaska was teeming with sea otters, for whose pelts the Chinese Mandarins would pay handsomely. Enter the Russian-American Company. By 1799 the Russians had taken possession of Alaska. They soon decimated the other herds of Alaska, and sent ships southward for supplies and to scout out new sources of prey. One of these expeditions, headed by manager Ivan Kuskof, landed at Fort Ross in 1812. In two years they shipped home 200,000 otter skins from the area.

California at the time was more or less administered by Mexico. The Russians conveniently disregarded Mexican rule, trading blankets and beads with the peaceful Pomo coastal tribe in exchange for land.

At first Fort Ross prospered. So highly did the czar value this California outpost that in 1821 he issued an imperial order denying the coast north of San Francisco to all except Russian ships. Mexico rose from apathy and sent one of its officers, Mariano Guadalupe Vallejo, up to the area with a few soldiers and orders to contain the Russians. Two years later President James Monroe promulgated his historic doctrine forbidding the American continent to foreign despots.

But it was neither the Americans nor the Mexicans that caused Alexander's minions to pull back. It was, rather, the work of the otter and the gopher. The limitless herds of otter, indiscriminately slaughtered, were just about extinct by the 1830s. And to make matters worse, gophers (described by the Russians as "hordes of underground rats") began to destroy crops. Fort Ross was fast becoming a liability. That same year Capt. Johann Sutter paid $30,000 for the land and the buildings and the Muscovites sailed home, putting an end to Russia's colonial expansion in the U.S.

In 1906 the State of California acquired the much-crumbled fort and a few acres around it and restorations were performed in the 1910s through the 1920s. Following documents and descriptions, the chapel (since burned down and rebuilt a second time), stockade, commandant's house, and blockhouses were carefully re-created. The park is open daily from 10 a.m. to 4:30 p.m. (except Christmas, New Year's Day, and Thanksgiving); a parking area ($3 per vehicle, $2 if you're 62 or older) and picnic grounds, are on the premises. There's a new **Visitors Center** on the grounds at 19005 Coast Hwy. 1, where you can stop for information, view slide presentations and artifacts; it also houses a gift shop you might want to peruse. Fort Ross' Reef, a campground, has been open about 1½ miles south of the fort. There are 25 sites ($6 per night, $3 per extra vehicle), no hookups, no dogs allowed. For more information call 707/847-3286.

CHAPTER V

DAY TRIPS SOUTH FROM SAN FRANCISCO

□ □ □

1. GREAT AMERICA
2. SAN JOSE
3. SANTA CRUZ

Up to this point we've been heading, roughly, north from San Francisco. Now round up the kids and head south, where an abundance of fun-for-the-family day trips awaits you. A tour of California's myriad amusement and theme parks (of which many, many in Southern California) might begin with the old-fashioned boardwalk amusement park in Santa Cruz, and Great America, a Disneyland-esque 200-acre theme park complete with costumed characters, in Santa Clara. Little-known but eerily intriguing attractions like Winchester House and the Mystery Spot add their own excitement —and that's not the half of it. All this fun is just an hour or two from San Francisco.

1. GREAT AMERICA
South along U.S. 101 (45 miles below San Francisco in Santa Clara—get off at the Great America exit) is a 100-acre theme park with 31 major rides, as well as shows and special attractions, a cinema housing the world's largest motion-picture screen, games, arcades, and plenty more for a full day's entertainment.

Great America has several theme areas: a 1920s rural American town, a replica of the legendary Klondike in the 1890s Gold Rush days, an 18th-century New England seaport, a turn-of-the-century county fair and midway, and a romantic 1850s version of the New Orleans French Quarter.

Attracting great hordes of daredevil San Franciscans, the ride-freak's favorite is the Demon, the only roller coaster in California to turn you upside down four times, speed through steaming tunnels, and plunge into a blood-red waterfall. But for pure hysteria, try the gigantic new wooden roller coaster, the Grizzly. More thrills on the Tidal Wave. This mechanical giant is one of the world's tallest coasters (142½ feet) and has a 76-foot-diameter loop that riders spin through forward and backward. You can get a great view of the proceedings from the top of the Sky Whirl, a triple-armed Ferris wheel, from the cable cars of the Delta Flyer skyride, or from the 20-story Sky Tower. And now there's Rip Roaring

Rapids, a new $5-million white-water-raft ride—you're sure to get wet as you brave the quarter mile of churning water. It's wild and fun, but not scary. For the total coward (I'm one), Great America has just the thing—they've refurbished my favorite ride, the Columbia, the tallest carousel in the world and certainly one of the handsomest. Or you can share the kiddies' Blue Streak roller coaster. Among all Great America's terrific rides, you're sure to find one to match your level of courage.

There are over 100 varied show times daily, with entertainment ranging from dolphin and animal shows to puppet shows, Smurf Woods, to a comical stage show featuring Bugs Bunny and his Looney Tunes buddies live on-stage.

And strolling through the park, you'll see Fred Flintstone, Yogi Bear, Huckleberry Hound, Barney Rubble, and, for the first time, George Jetson and his faithful dog, Astro. In addition to the regularly scheduled acts, there are marching bands, barbershop quartets, parades, concerts, special events in spring and fall, fireworks, and other happenings.

If all the activity doesn't unsettle your tummy, there are 23 low-priced eateries to choose from, serving everything from hamburgers (4,500 are wolfed down every day) to fried chicken. After lunch you can browse through any one of 32 shops and boutiques, watch craftspeople (including totem pole carvers) at work, or test your skill at arcade games.

Guests pay a one-price admission that includes everything except food, games, and gifts. The price is $17.95; seniors over 55 pay $11.50, and kids 3 to 6 pay $8.95; those under 2 get in free. For further information phone 408/988-1800 (recording), or 408/988-1776. Parking is $4 per vehicle.

Great America usually opens about mid-March and closes in October. During the spring and fall it's open only on weekends and holidays from 10 a.m. to about 6 p.m. From May 31 through Labor Day, Great America is open daily from 10 a.m. to about 9 p.m.

2. SAN JOSE

This is the town that Burt Bacharach immortalized some years back with the musical question: "Do you know the way to San Jose?" The answer: Just keep going south for 48 miles on 101, and you'll find yourself in a city that houses seven universities and colleges and an abundance of visitor attractions.

WINCHESTER HOUSE: Most intriguing of all the local sights is the Winchester Mystery House, a 160-room Victorian mansion at 525 S. Winchester Blvd., at the intersection of Hwy. 17 and I-280 (tel. 408/247-2101), built by Sarah L. Winchester, widow of the son of the famous rifle magnate. Convinced by a spiritualist that the lives of her husband and baby daughter had been taken by the spirits of those killed with Winchester repeaters, she was told that she too would share their fate . . . unless, that is, she began to build a mansion on which work could *never* stop. Whether the medium had a strange sense of humor or a husband in the contracting business, no one knows. Maybe she was right—Sarah Winchester followed her instructions and lived to be 82. Starting with an eight-room house, a fortune of $20 million, and an income of $1,000 a day at her disposal, she proceeded to base her life on the medium's advice. At night passersby heard strange ghostly music wafting from the mansion, and a bell in the belfry tolled regularly at midnight to warn off evil spirits and summon good ones to protect her.

Her first move was to hire 22 carpenters and seven Japanese gardeners, the latter to keep the towering hedge thick enough to shut out all view of the premises from the road. None of them ever saw her, nor did the servants, except for the Chinese butler who served her meals on the Winchester $30,000 gold dinner service. All orders were issued by Miss Margaret Merriam, niece, secretary, and finally heiress to the fortune. The work went on seven days a week, 24 hours per day(!), 365 days a year, even on Christmas. (And you thought Howard Hughes was peculiar.)

The rooms are palatially furnished and beautiful to see: there are exquisite gold and silver chandeliers, doors inlaid with German silver and bronze, Tiffany stained-glass windows valued at $10,000 each, beautiful wood paneling, intricate parquet floors, windowpanes of French beveled plate glass, mantels of Japanese tile and hand-picked bamboo—I could fill pages describing the treasures within.

But equally, if not more, interesting are Mrs. Winchester's bizarre constructions to foil the vengeful ghosts—particularly the ghosts of Native Americans, many of whom were dispatched to the Happy Hunting Grounds via Winchester repeaters. Doors lead to nowhere. Some staircases ascend to the ceiling, and others contain steps just two inches high, and go up, down, and up to climb to a height of about seven feet. Such schemes were supposed to confound spirits, particularly those of the "simple redskins" she feared the most. And the number 13 comes up often—13 bathrooms, 13 windows in a room, 13 palms lining the main driveway—and many multiples of 13, such as 52 skylights.

Informative guided tours of this fascinating house take place daily between 9 a.m. and 5:30 p.m. in summer, till 4:30 p.m. in spring and fall, and till 4 p.m. in winter. Admission to the Winchester estate is $9.95 for adults, $8.45 for seniors 60 and older, $5.95 for children 6 to 12, and free for those under 6. Included in the price is admission to the garden and outlying buildings, plus the Winchester Rifle and Antique Products Museums. The Winchester Rifle museum obviously has a large collection of Winchesters, but, as its name suggests, it also displays many rifles, some dating back to the 1800s. A number of these are from other countries, including some beautiful pieces with exquisitely designed stocks from the Middle East. The Antique Products Museum has on display many items made by the Winchester company in the early 1900s—knives, roller skates, fishing tackle, tools, flashlights—products not commonly associated with the name of Winchester. Allow at least 1½ to 2 hours for your visit.

ROSICRUCIAN PARK AND OTHER SIGHTS: Almost as unusual as Winchester House is Rosicrucian Park and the various museums on its grounds. Inside the imposing **Administration Building,** which copies the design of the Great Temple of Rameses III, members of the ancient order, with titles like "Grand Master" and "Supreme Secretary," are doing the organization's work. In the **Egyptian Museum,** thousands of original and rare Egyptian, Assyrian, and Babylonian antiquities are on display: statuary, textiles, jewelry, and paintings; mummified high priests, animals, and birds; toys entombed with a child 5,000 years ago; a full-size reproduction of an Egyptian limestone tomb, sarcophagi, etc.

The **Art Gallery** exhibits an eclectic variety of works of famous local, national, and international artists.

The Egyptian Museum and Art Gallery are open on Saturday, Sunday, and Monday from noon to 5 p.m., Tuesday through Friday from 9 a.m. to 5 p.m. Admission is $3 for adults, $1 for those under 18.

The **Science Museum and Planetarium** deal with subjects ranging from seismography to space travel, demonstrating how fundamental laws of the physical sciences elucidate nature's mysteries. And if you should be interested in the Rosicrucian Order, there's much literature about, as well as people who can answer your questions. Admission to the Science Museum is free.

The Planetarium is open daily from 1 to 4:45 p.m. Shows are presented on weekdays at 2 p.m., on weekends at 2 and 3:30 p.m. It's closed on August 2 and Thanksgiving, Christmas, and New Year's Days. Seven different shows are presented yearly. Adults pay $3; those under 18 pay $2; and there's no charge to see the science exhibits.

San Jose visitors can also take a stroll around **Kelley Park,** one of San Jose's most unique and popular attractions. At the northern end of the park complex is the *Happy Hollow Park and Zoo.* It's a creative children's park with play areas and rides and a domestic animal petting zoo. In the center of the park is the **Japanese Friendship Garden,** 1300 Senter Rd. (tel. 408/295-8383), modeled after the beautiful Korakuen Garden, a serene symbol of goodwill between the sister cities of San Jose and Okayama, Japan. At the southern end of the park is the **San Jose Historical Museum,** Senter Road at Phelan Ave., with exhibits on local history, restored homes, stables, a firehouse, the Bank of Italy, a print shop, and a trolley barn. The museum is open daily: weekdays from 10 a.m. to 4:30 p.m., weekends from noon. Admission is $1 for adults, 50¢ for children 2 to 18 and senior citizens. There are food concessions throughout the park.

DINING IN SAN JOSE: A convenient place for lunch following your exploration of Winchester House is the **Magic Pan,** 335 S. Winchester Blvd. (tel. 408/247-9970). Like the rest of the chain, this restaurant serves a variety of reasonably priced crêpe specialties as well as steaks, seafood, and pasta dishes in a country French setting. It's open daily for lunch and dinner, and Sunday brunch.

3. SANTA CRUZ

When San Franciscans feel like a day at the beach, they willingly drive the 74 miles south along Calif. 1 to Santa Cruz, one of the few northern coastal locations where the water is actually warm enough to swim in—at any rate Northern Californians think it's warm. Whether you do or not, you'll find plenty of ways to amuse yourself.

THE BOARDWALK: The hub of beach activities from May through mid-September and weekends the rest of the year is the old-fashioned Boardwalk. You can spend the morning digging your toes into the sand, surfing, sunbathing, and swimming; later take a walk on the Boardwalk, as the card says. There are over 20 rides, including a roller coaster, log flume, haunted castle, bumper cars, and a hand-carved merry-go-round (just about my speed). There's miniature golf, two big penny arcades, and, of course, food concessions where you can buy hot dogs, corn on the cob, cotton candy, and other classic Boardwalk edibles, so to speak. If you continue your ramble west along the Boardwalk you'll get to—

MUNICIPAL WHARF: And a very nice fisherman's wharf it is, with picturesque shops, fish markets, and seafood restaurants. You can bring or rent tackle, buy bait, and fish off the wharf or in a rented boat. Deep-sea fishing trips depart daily from about February 1 to November 15, and on weekends during December and January, weather permitting.

Among the seafood restaurants is **Malio's** (tel. 408/423-5200), overlooking the water and serving seasonally fresh seafood dinners daily. It's a pretty place, with plank wood walls and ceilings, cream-colored walls, and blue-and-white-checked tablecloths set with royal-blue napkins to add a splash of color. A bit pricey, but the food is good and the service is friendly. Malio's is also open for lunch on weekends only, from noon to 3:30 p.m.

Farther along the wharf is **Miramar** (tel. 408/423-4441), a little fancier than Malio's, recently remodeled with green wallpaper and paint, new carpeting, and large windows overlooking the water. Luncheons here are a good buy: priced at $7 to $12 according to entree, they include soup or salad and rice or french fries. Sample entrees include poached salmon, sole amandine, and scallops. At dinner, similar meals average $12 to $20. Open daily for lunch and dinner.

No need for fancy dining, however; you can stop in any of numerous shops and snackbars and get shrimp cups and other tasty edibles—seating and view are free on the wharf. By the way, there's lots of metered parking at the wharf.

SHOPPING AND BROWSING: Going north from the beach or wharf along Pacific Avenue, you'll come to the **Pacific Garden Mall** (a free shuttle operates from the beach to the mall and back daily in summer every 20 minutes). Scene of frequent craft fairs and festivities, the mall has a wide variety of shops to explore, including the **Cooper House,** a restaurant-shopping complex that was formerly the County Courthouse. Short rambles up side streets from the mall will reveal Victorian and Edwardian mansions, as well as other architectural landmarks, including the **Mission Santa Cruz,** 126 High St. A brochure detailing four historic walking tours will greatly enhance such an architecture stroll—pick one up at the **Conference and Visitors Council,** Cooper and Front Streets (tel. 408/423-1111).

MYSTERY SPOT: Situated in a redwood forest, 2½ miles north of Santa Cruz at 1953 Branciforte Dr. (tel. 408/423-8897; just follow the signs—getting there is no mystery), the "spot" is a section of woodlands, 150 feet in diameter, where the laws of gravity seem to have gone haywire. Wildlife avoids the area and birds will not nest here; instruments on planes flying overhead go dead; even the trees grow aslant. It's all due, we are told, to some mysterious, unexplainable, eerie "force."

There are some theories about what happens here: perhaps there's a trace gas seeping from the earth that disorients visitors; maybe a meteor, minerals, or a magnet are buried deep underground, exerting a magnetic force or distorting the sun's rays. But such explanations don't satisfy scientists or sufficiently explain the phenomenon. The owners of the land have done a fine job of protecting the woodland setting and arranging excellent guided tours for visitors. A series of demonstrations allows you to experience the force for yourself: a ball set down on a slanted plank rolls uphill (skeptics can place the ball themselves or try another object like a lipstick). As you climb the hillside, you'll find you're walking as straight-legged as you would on level ground. A tilted wooden house, used for demonstration purposes, makes the change in perspective most obvious. Ever walk up a wall? You can here, and it's easy. For one of the most amazing demonstrations the guide places two people on either side of a level block (tested with a carpenter's level) and one seems to shrink while the other grows. It's an interesting diversion, even for skeptics. The Mystery Spot is open daily from 9:30 a.m. to 4:30 p.m. Adults pay $4, kids 5 to 11 pay $2. Youngsters adore the Mystery Spot.

RC&BTNGRR: That mess of letters stands for **Roaring Camp and Big Trees Narrow-Gauge Railroad,** a major Santa Cruz area attraction nestled in the Santa Cruz mountains near Felton (off Rte. 9) on Graham Hill Road. America's last steam-powered passenger railroad offering daily scheduled runs, the RC& BTNGRR is a colorful reminder of Gold Rush days, operating authentic 1880 and 1890 equipment on a 6½ mile, 75-minute round trip through magnificent redwood forests. Passengers board trains from the old-fashioned depot at Roaring Camp. The train chugs through forests of trees towering hundreds of feet overhead, past such quaint station points as Big Trees, Indian Creek, Grizzly Flats, and Deer Valley en route to the summit of Bear Mountain. Passengers may detrain here for hiking or picnicking to return on a later train. On spring, summer, and fall weekends there's live country music. You can take this delightful ride any day during summer, on weekends and holidays the rest of the year. Departures are daily every hour and a quarter from 11 a.m. to 4 p.m. in summer; from the end of October to the third week of March trains depart on Saturday, Sunday, and holidays at noon, 1:30 p.m., and 3 p.m. (at noon only on weekdays); from late March until early June departures take place weekends and holidays every hour and a quarter from 11 a.m. to 4 p.m. and weekdays at noon. Regular fare is $11.25 round trip, $8.25 for ages 3 to 15; under 3, free. For further information call 408/335-4484.

CHAPTER VI

HIGHLIGHTS OF NORTHERN CALIFORNIA

□ □ □

The previous two chapters dealt with areas that could be easily explored in day trips from San Francisco. The following are a bit farther along; you might still use San Francisco as a base, but plan to spend at least a night or two away. We'll begin by heading north to—

1. LITTLE RIVER

Take a leisurely drive up the coast, maybe stopping at historic Fort Ross along the way, where for 40 years Russians dominated Northern California (see Chapter IV). When you've traveled 123 miles north along Calif. 1, you'll come to Little River (in the vicinity of Mendocino), where the mountainous seascape has the look of a Renaissance painting backdrop, and quaint old inns welcome north coast travelers. Advance reservations are a must at any of these accommodations.

Such a one is **Heritage House,** Little River, CA 95456 (tel. 707/937-5885), an ivy-covered New England-style inn on the sea side of the road (most rooms have ocean views, with perhaps the best views on the northern coastline). Its main building used to be a farmhouse, built in 1877 by forebears of the present owners. The play *Same Time Next Year* was inspired by this idyllic retreat, and in less tranquil days, "Baby Face" Nelson used the then-abandoned farmhouse as a hideout. Cottages, inspired by old-fashioned institutions and buildings, have names like Scott's Opera House, Country Store, Bonnet Shop, and Ice Cream Parlor. Many antiques from old houses in the area have been used in furnishing rooms here. Heritage House operates on the Modified American Plan (rooms with breakfast and dinner) and rates are $105 to $260 single and $125 to $280 double, with those meals included. Rooms have baths but no phones or TVs.

Even if you don't stay at Heritage House, you must stop by for a leisurely dinner; the dining room here is the long-sought country restaurant of everyone's dreams. Windows overlook the ocean or lush greenery, the interior decor achieves perfect elegance, and there are even outdoor tables (for cocktails) on a terrace bordered by pots of geraniums. Dinner is prix-fixe and ranges from $22 to $24. On a recent visit it included clam chowder, salad, roast chicken with plum glaze, two vegetables, homemade biscuits, cream puffs with hot fudge, fruit, cheese, and coffee. There's an outstanding wine list. Men are requested to wear jackets and reservations are essential.

Little River's other famed accommodation, the **Little River Inn,** Little River, CA 95456 (tel. 707/937-5942), is a rambling mansion, also built in New England style by a lumber pioneer, Silas Coombs, in 1853. And like Heritage House it is maintained by his descendants, a great-grandson and his wife. Eucalyptus trees, planted as a windbreak for the Coombses' orchard, now shelter a nine-hole golf course. Homemade meals (including fresh-baked bread and desserts) are served daily in a dining room on the premises. All rooms offer sweeping sea views, and are equipped with baths. Three types of accommodations are offered at costs ranging from $56 double for Early California attic rooms at the old inn (I prefer these, with their grandmother rockers and dome windows looking out to sea), $85 for cottage units, and $72 for rooms in the contemporary Hilltop Annex.

The old farmhouse, its parlors, public areas, and grounds are picture-postcard pretty. The rooms, other than the attic accommodations, are indifferently furnished; however, several of the Annex rooms have been remodeled and refurnished. Winter rates (midweek from November 15 to April 15) are 20% less, excluding weekends and holidays. Modern amenities at the inn include a dining room (entrees run from $14 to $20) with a bar, and a nine-hole regulation golf course (no pitch and putt, this), and two night-lit championship-caliber tennis courts.

2. MENDOCINO

A few miles farther along is Mendocino, its mixture of 19th-century charm and beauty, weathered barns, old mansions, deep-green forests, blue sea, and white surf providing the backdrop for a major center for the arts on California's northern coast.

Originally known as Meiggsville, the town was so named for one Harry Meiggs, who came to Big River in search of a wrecked cargo of Chinese silk. He didn't find the silk, but he did find another treasure in giant redwoods. He built the area's first sawmill and began shipping cargoes of lumber back to fast-growing San Francisco. He later went to South America where he built the first railroad across the Andes, but his legacy in California was a lumber boom that lasted over 50 years in Mendocino.

The New England woodsmen who followed him to California built a New England–style town at Big River, thus accounting for the misplaced architecture still seen today. Steeply pitched roofs are slanted to shed snow—which, of course, never falls in Mendocino—and many old houses even have widow's walks.

As the port grew in importance, coastal ships from Seattle and San Francisco made regular calls at Mendocino. In the height of the logging boom residents numbered 3,500, and eight hotels went up along with 17 saloons and 15 or 20 bordellos. Today Mendocino is populated by about 1,000 people, some still employed in the lumber and fishing industries, many of them artists and artisans.

The entire town has been declared a historic monument, and although the brothels are, as far as I know, gone, and the saloons fewer, it still looks like a western movie set—much as it looked in an 1890 photo. Mendocino is one of the world's Shangri-las, a serene, romantic, away-from-it-all dream retreat. Don't miss it.

COUNTRY INNS AND RESTAURANTS: The accommodation of choice in Mendocino is **MacCallum House,** Albion Street, Mendocino, CA 95460 (tel. 707/937-0289), a 15-room historic Victorian gingerbread mansion constructed in 1882 by pioneer lumberman William H. Kelly as a wedding present to his daughter, Daisy, and her husband, Alexander MacCallum. Alexander died in 1908, but strong-willed Daisy lived to the ripe old age of 93 and became the town matriarch. She started the town's fire department, and, like the well-bred Victorian lady she was, kept busy teaching, studying botany and horticulture, traveling, enlarging her residence, and playing a leading role in community affairs. She died in 1953, but her son occupied the house until 1970, making so few changes that when Bill and Sue Norris bought the place in 1974 they said it looked as if she had gone out to walk the dog.

The Norrises, a young couple with know-how and reverence for authenticity, did a first-rate job with MacCallum House. I think Daisy would have approved. They were fortunate enough to purchase the mansion with all its invaluable original furnishings and contents. Every nook and cranny here reveals some delightful secret. Exploring the public areas, you might come across Daisy's books of pressed flowers, her scrapbooks full of Christmas cards and other mementoes, or her 4,000 books and countless magazines, the former still lining the dining room walls, the latter used to paper the attic. Here and there is an original Tiffany lamp or real Persian carpet.

Each guest room is unique, exquisitely papered and furnished, for the most part, with Daisy's old pieces. Your room might have a Franklin stove, handmade quilt, cushioned rocking chair, bed with high headboard, old sewing dummy, or child's cradle. Without a doubt these are the most charming rooms in town. Most have sinks and share common large baths, and there are no radios, TVs, or phones to disturb the tranquil atmosphere. Room rates range from $55 to $135 per night double occupancy; luxurious barn suites with stone fireplaces are at the top of that range, the latter big enough to accommodate six people. A generous continental breakfast is included in the price.

Not the least of MacCallum House's appealing features is the **MacCallum House Restaurant** (tel. 707/937-5763) and adjoining Grey Whale Bar & Parlor Café. Owner Rob Ferrero oversees a very professional staff. Superlatives are in order here for the exceptional food and for the decor—beautiful redwood and Douglas fir wainscoted walls lined with bookcases, and antique built-in sideboard with leaded-glass panels, shimmering rose-color draperies, huge old cobblestone fireplaces, and tables set with crisp white cloths, fresh flowers, and real oil lamps. Dinner entrees, priced at $12.95 to $18.95, might include confit of duck—succulent breast, leg and thigh, skin crisped to a golden brown and served with garlic-fried potatoes; or tender California lamb loin marinated in rosemary, garlic, and olive oil, roasted to order and served with a red wine sauce and fresh garden vegetables; or a superb grilled filet of salmon (in season) with basil butter. Desserts are all homemade and irresistible—a chocolate torte with espresso pastry cream and pistachios, or pear poached in champagne with Grand Marnier sabayon. Reservations are suggested. The establishment is open weekends mid-February to late March, and every night April through December. Weekdays, the Bar & Parlor Cafe are open for food from 4 p.m. to 10 p.m., from 11 a.m. on Saturday and Sunday. The Restaurant is open 6 to 10 p.m. nightly.

The Bar offers everything on the Restaurant dinner menu, plus assorted appetizers. *Note:* No credit cards.

Right on the town's Main Street is the **Mendocino Hotel,** Mendocino, CA 95460 (tel. 707/937-0511, or toll free 800/548-0513), a wood structure that dates from 1878 and is entered via beautiful beveled-glass doors. The lobby and public areas evoke the Victorian opulence of Gold Rush days, and furnishings in both the rooms and public areas utilize a harmonious combination of antiques and reproductions. The oak reception desk comes from a bank in Kansas. The 50 rooms all have hand-painted French porcelain sinks with floral designs, quaint wallpapers, and old-fashioned beds and armoires, cable TV, and phones; 38 have bathrooms.

About half of the 50 rooms are located just across the road in four small, handsome buildings, one of which is called the Heeser House, built in 1852 by one of Mendocino's pioneer families. Each room contains photographs and memorabilia reflecting the history of the town and its founders, and 22 out of the 25 rooms have fireplaces. A lovely English country garden surrounds the buildings. The hotel offers room service, and there is a nightly turndown accompanied by homemade chocolates. And there's a fine restaurant on the premises. Rooms range from $65 to $210 (for suites), single or double; lower rates are for those rooms without a private bath.

Making no attempt at quaintness, but relaxed, unpretentious, and homey nonetheless, the **Sea Gull,** on Lansing Street (at Ukiah), Mendocino, CA 95460 (tel. 707/937-2100), is a hub of Mendocino life day and night. On the premises is the Cellar Bar, ironically upstairs (it used to be in the cellar, but after a fire in 1976 it was moved), where residents gather nightly under a cathedral ceiling to drink, hang out, and listen to music; they always play good jazz, classical, rock, or whatever in the background, and often have live music. The comfy furnishings, woody decor, and very relaxed ambience make this the ideal spot to meet Mendocino's diverse and talented populace.

By day, the Sea Gull has to be the favorite breakfast spot in town, offering a complete breakfast menu with homemade breads from their new Bake Shoppe next door. Lunch features homemade soups and chili, along with gigantic sandwiches, fresh fish, and the very best cheeseburger in town. A hearty breakfast is about $3 to $8; lunch, $4 to $9.

Over the last couple of years, owners Jim and Rochelle Marquardt have created a veritable dining feast for the evening menu. The selection is excellent—fresh local seafood, chicken, and veal entrees, steaks, pasta—all at prices ranging from $7 to $16. Specialties of the house include their own Mendocino Seafood Gumbo, and an excellent traditional cioppino. There's a full bar plus an extensive wine list consisting of virtually all Mendocino County wines, many available by the glass.

The restaurant is open daily 8 a.m. to 9 p.m., the Cellar Bar from noon to midnight. *Note:* No credit cards are accepted.

Although Mendocino's hostelries all have fine dining rooms, there are also many restaurants in town worth checking out. None is more totally charming than the **Café Beaujolais,** 961 Ukiah St. (tel. 707/937-5614). Papered in Victorian reproduction wallpaper (the most beautiful pattern I've ever seen) this French country-style inn has oak floors, Victorian rose-colored carnival glass chandeliers suspended from a wood ceiling painted white, a wood-burning stove, spindle-back chairs, and substantial oak pedestal tables, each adorned with a posy of flowers. There's more seating on an outdoor deck overlooking the garden.

You couldn't find a more delightful place to begin the day, and here you can do so with homemade coffee cake and excellent coffee, or if the ocean air has given you a hearty appetite, with waffles in pure maple syrup or country sausage and three scrambled eggs, all for under $8. The lunch menu changes daily and might offer anything from a terrific burger served with country fries to an extraordinary black bean chili. Entrees are priced at $6 to $9. Dinner is served Thursday, Friday, Saturday, Sunday, evenings only, from 6:15 to 9:30 p.m. during the spring through fall only (about May through November). Once again, the menu is constantly changing; on different visits I've enjoyed the Beaujolais' chicken stuffed under the skin with eggplant and mushrooms, cheese, garlic, and fresh herbs, and roast filet of beef, for $12 to $20. Fresh salmon and roast leg of lamb are among the specialties of the house. "Decadent chocolate desserts" are worth the splurge.

MENDOCINO ART CENTER: Headquarters for much Mendocino cultural activity, as well as the coast's artistic renaissance, is the Mendocino Art Center at 45200 Little Lake Rd. (tel. 707/937-5818). The center offers classes and workshops covering a broad range of artistic disciplines, including a year-round ceramics program and a three-year certificate program in textiles. Founded in 1959, it was the creation of William Zacha, a painter, and his wife, Jenny, who had long dreamed of establishing a unique art school in an area of great beauty and creative energy.

In addition to classes, the Art Center offers a Sunday-afternoon concert series, an art library, and a gallery shop. And two art fairs (Thanksgiving and summer) yearly draw visitors from around the country and serve as a showcase for local and outside artists, musicians, and craftspeople.

They also publish a free monthly magazine called *Arts and Entertainment* that announces upcoming Mendocino and Art Center events and features interviews with local artists, short stories, poems, etc.

BOTANICAL GARDENS: Six miles north of Mendocino at 18220 North Hwy. 1, in Fort Bragg, you'll come to the **Mendocino Coast Botanical Gardens** (tel. 707/964-4352), a charming cliff-top park among the redwoods along the rugged coast. The gardens were fashioned by a retired landscape nurseryman who spent years reclaiming wilderness and nurturing rhododendrons, fuchsias, azaleas, and a multitude of flowering shrubs. The area contains trails for easy walking, rustic bridges, streams, canyons, dells, and picnic areas. From a cliff house overlooking the Pacific you can enjoy the play of the sea against the jagged rocks below. Open daily from 9 a.m. to 6 p.m. the gardens charge $5 admission for adults, $3 for ages 12 to 17, free for children under 12 accompanied by their parents.

MENDOCINO MISCELLANY: There's a tremendous amount to do on the Mendocino Coast—every kind of land and water sport, art galleries and antique shops to explore, rodeos, wine tasting, etc. For a rundown on what's available, stop in at the **Fort Bragg/Mendocino Coast Chamber of Commerce,** 332 N. Main St. (tel. 707/964-3153) in Fort Bragg, CA 95437 (about which more below) or send your request to the above at P.O. Box 1141, Fort Bragg, CA 95437.

Mendocino is also a great place to do nothing but gaze at the blue sea and white surf, stroll through hushed redwood forests, stroll along miles of deserted sandy beach strewn with driftwood, and enjoy the brilliant flowers blooming amid weathered barns and old picket fences. It's a place to replenish the spirit and bask in nature's bounty.

3. FORT BRAGG

Continuing along the Mendocino coast another ten miles, you'll come to Fort Bragg, the largest coastal city between San Francisco and Eureka. Its southern gateway is the harbor town of **Noyo,** sportfishing center of the county and locale of many gourmet seafood restaurants. Visit the **Noyo Store,** 32450 North Harbor (tel. 707/964-9138), to find out about fishing boats and to buy or rent tackle. It's in the heart of this small village. From Fort Bragg you can foray into the ageless redwood groves in nearby parks, many of which have camping facilities (for details on camping and anything else in Fort Bragg, visit Fort Bragg/ Mendocino Coast Chamber of Commerce, listed above.) If you're in Fort Bragg in March, be sure to see the annual Whale Festival.

You might consider staying overnight at the historic **Grey Whale Inn,** 615 N. Main St., Fort Bragg, CA (tel. 707/964-0640, or toll free 800/382-7244 in California), a handsome four-story redwood building that was a hospital from the early 1900s until 1971. It has no hospital feel now, however; it's spacious, elegant, and attractively furnished with some antiques and modern amenities such as a color TV with VCR in the Theater Room and a pool table in the recreation room. The Fireside Lounge is a great gathering place for guests. There are 14 guest rooms, all with private bath. Each room offers its own special features— some have an ocean view, or a fireplace, or a whirlpool tub; some have a private deck, or a shower with wheelchair access. Rates—which include a buffet breakfast of homemade bread or coffeecake, juice or fresh fruit, and a selection of hot beverages, cereals, and brunch casseroles—are $55 to $90 single and $65 to $135 double. Off-season rates, November through March, are half price for the second consecutive night on nonholidays. If you're in the area during whale-watching season, don't miss the opportunity to take one of the local boats and get a view of the gray whales. March sees Fort Bragg's annual Whale Festival.

One of the best ways to see the redwoods is to "ride the **Skunks"**— California Western Railroad's self-powered diesel trains. They were nicknamed "Skunks" for their original gas engines; people used to say, "You can smell'em before you can see 'em."

The trains, boarded at the foot of Laurel Avenue in Fort Bragg (two blocks from the Grey Whale Inn), travel along the Redwood Highway (U.S. 101) to **Willits,** 40 miles inland—a journey through the very heart of the towering redwood forest along a spectacular route inaccessible by auto. With windows front and side, they're wonderful for sightseeing.

The ride takes you across 31 bridges and trestles, and through two deep tunnels, its serpentine route encompassing changes of scenery from forest to sunlit fields of wildflowers, grazing cattle, and apple orchards.

The Skunks run all year, leaving Fort Bragg daily each morning. The round trip takes six to eight hours, which allows ample time for lunch in Willits before returning on the afternoon train. Half-day trips are offered only in summer from mid-June to early September, with daily Fort Bragg morning departures. The price of a round-trip ticket is $22, $18 one way. Children 5 to 11 pay half price. For further information and a time schedule phone 707/964-6371.

Another Fort Bragg attraction is the **Georgia-Pacific Corporation's Tree Nursery,** 275 N. Main St. at the junction of Hwy. 1 and Walnut Street (tel. 707/ 964-5651). You can stop in March to November weekdays 8:30 a.m. to 4:30 p.m., weekends 10 a.m. to 4 p.m. for a free look at some three million trees. There's a picnic area and self-guided nature trail, plus an interesting visitor center. They also operate a logging museum donated to the city of Fort Bragg on North Main Street near the Skunk depot; it's open Wednesday through Sunday from 8 a.m. to 4:30 p.m., and admission is free.

If it proves convenient, hit Fort Bragg on Labor Day Weekend, when crowds gather for **Paul Bunyan Days** activities: axe-throwing, pole-climbing, log-rolling, and the like.

More redwoods? Hop in the car again and head north to **Sylvandale,** six miles above Garberville on U.S. 101 (Rtes. 1 and 101 converge at Leggett). Soon you'll come to a sign directing you to one of the most spectacular routes in the West, the—

4. AVENUE OF THE GIANTS

Thirty-three miles long, this scenic avenue, roughly paralleling U.S. 101 (240 miles north of San Francisco), was left intact for sightseers when the freeway was built. Its giants are majestic coast redwoods—*Sequoia sempervirens*—some 43,000 acres of them making up the most outstanding display in the redwood belt. Their rough-bark columns climb 100 feet or more without a branch—some are higher than a football field is long and older than Christianity. The oldest dated coast redwood is over 2,200 years old.

Drive slowly, leaving your car occasionally for walks through the forest. En route you'll notice three public campgrounds: **Hidden Springs,** above Miranda; **Burlington,** two miles south of Weott; and **Albee Creek State Campground,** off to the left above Weott. You'll also come across picnic and swimming facilities, motels, resorts, restaurants, and numerous resting and parking areas.

You can have lunch a few miles past the end of the road in Scotia (there are picnic areas and a grocery), where you can also take a tour of the **Pacific Lumber Company,** one of the world's largest mills. If you're so inclined you can drive your car *through* a living redwood at **Myers Flat Midway,** along the Avenue of the Giants.

For more information, you can write to Avenue of the Giants, P.O. Box 1000, Miranda, CA 95553 (tel. 707/923-2555).

The village of **Ferndale,** 15 miles south of Eureka and in the northernmost part of the Avenue of the Giants, is a historic landmark. Ferndale is a fairytale spectacle of Victoriana—gables and gingerbread, Victorian homes, shops, a smithy, even a saddlery. For the contemporary, it has humor, a repertory company, artists, sculptors, dairy farms, hand-dipped chocolates, and the annual World Champion Kinetic Sculpture Race in May. What it does not have are some of the mean touches of uncivilization. There are no parking meters, no traffic lights, no mail deliveries. It's enchanted!

Part of Ferndale's enchantment is the **Gingerbread Mansion** (at 400 Berding St.), P.O. Box 40, Ferndale, CA 95536 (tel. 707/786-4000), a well-reviewed, frequently photographed peach-and-yellow gabled inn with elaborately elegant trim. The mansion is beautifully furnished with antiques, in keeping with its Victorian heritage. It is a masterpiece, proprietored by Wendy and Ken Torbert. You may never sleep in more comfortable beds or feel more pampered than you will at the Gingerbread Mansion. Attractive bathrobes are provided, extra-large thick towels, fresh flowers. One of the second-floor baths is 200 square feet, framed with mirrors and having a clawfoot tub on a pedestal. Hanging plants are all about and light filters through a lovely stained-glass window. If you must, there is a shower. Beds are turned down for the night, and you will find chocolates on the night stand. When you rise, there's morning coffee or tea outside your door, enough to sustain you until breakfast of fruit, cheese, muffins, and jam—all included in the rates, as is afternoon tea with cake.

The Torberts have yellow- and peach-colored bicycles available for use by the guests. Should it rain, they also have a supply of umbrellas and boots. There are nine large guest rooms, all with private baths and some with *two* old-fashioned clawfooted tubs for "his and her" bubble baths. Rates for two, including the breakfast and afternoon tea are $85 to $155 for two persons per room, $10 less for singles. For the comfort of others, smoking is permitted only on the verandas, and the inn does not accept children under age 10.

5. YOSEMITE NATIONAL PARK

You might call Yosemite National Park and Yosemite Valley breathtaking, spectacular, incredible, awesome, humbling—all of which adjectives are accurate and none of which even begin to describe the magnificence of this country and the many faces of its beauty. Yosemite Valley is a glacier-carved canyon with crashing waterfalls (come in May and June and see), dramatic domes, and sheer walls of granite extending thousands of feet upward from the valley's flat floor.

The evolution of Yosemite Valley began with glaciers moving through the canyon that the Merced River had carved with repeated geological rises of the Sierras. The ice worked its way through weak sections of granite, bypassing the solid portions—what you now see as El Capitan is a good example of such a rock mass—and substantially widening the canyon. When the glacier began to melt, the moraine (the accumulated earth and stones deposited by a glacier) dammed part of the Merced River to form Lake Yosemite in the new valley. Sediment ultimately filled in the lake, which accounts for the flat floor of Yosemite Valley. This same process, on a much smaller scale, is even now occurring with Mirror Lake at the base of Half Dome.

The Ahwahneechee had been living in the valley for several thousand years when their first contact was made with European people in the middle of the 19th century. Members of the Joseph Reddeford Walker party were probably the first non–Native Americans to see Yosemite Valley as they crossed over from the east side of the Sierra in 1833, though they did not come into contact with the Ahwahneechee. With the later encroachment of visitors and indiscriminate abuse of the environment and the threat of potential private exploitation (it was ever thus), President Lincoln granted Yosemite Valley and the Mariposa Grove of Giant Sequoias to California as a public trust. Federal legislation created Yosemite National Park in 1890. And by 1913 a different problem arose—the auto was permitted into Yosemite.

Still, with tender loving care, the valley has survived. It remains a sensual blend of open meadows, wildflowers (1,400 species), woodlands with Ponderosa pine, incense cedar, and Douglas fir. Wildlife from monarch butterflies and a world of birds (223 species) to mule deer and black bear flourish in the protected environment.

Today **Yosemite Valley** is a focal point of activities in one of America's most spectacular national parks, and the logical place to begin your visit. Though occupying only 7 of the 1,200 square miles that make up the park, the valley offers campgrounds, lodgings, shops, and restaurants. Visitors who are in the valley for the day only are encouraged to use the day-use parking at Curry Village. A free shuttle bus system travels on a continuous loop through the eastern portion of the valley and is quite convenient for visiting any of the above amenities.

Begin your explorations of Yosemite with a stop at the **Visitor Center** (tel. 209/372-0299) in the Village Mall to see audio-visual programs and other exhibits, and obtain maps and information. Here you'll find out about the many daily activities, ranger-guided walks, and demonstrations; those who are interested can learn about the geological sequence of Yosemite's development, from its beginnings eons ago with the formation of granite beneath the earth's surface, to the glacial action that carved the valleys and formed the lakes. You'll also want to know how to reach the museums, the sequoia groves, the inspiring granite summits, and the waterfall bases, and how to store food properly to avoid contact with wildlife. The Visitor Center is open daily from 9 a.m. to 5 p.m.

While the valley is the hub of everything that's happening, and contains many scenic features (Yosemite Falls, Bridal Veil Falls, Mirror Lake, Half Dome,

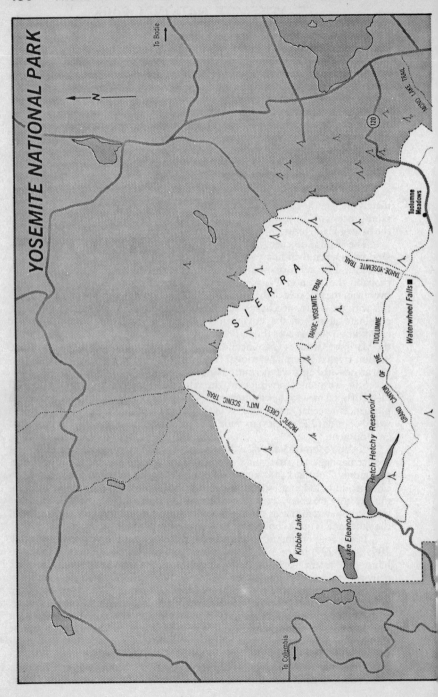

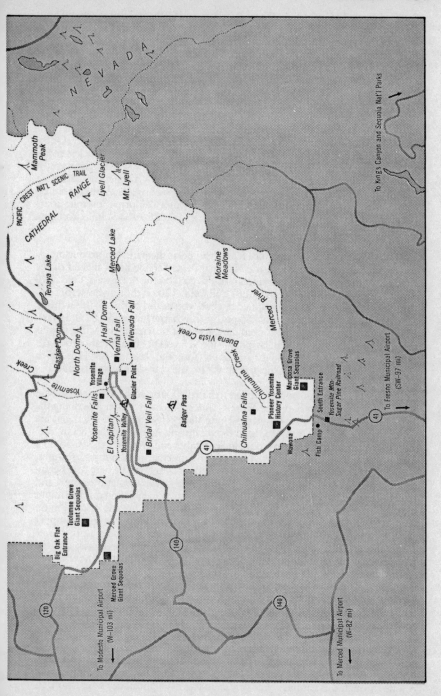

Sentinel Rock, El Capitan, the Three Brothers, and Cathedral Rocks), you'll want to leave the valley to explore the park's other natural bounties. There are 800 miles of trails you can cover, by horse, mule, or foot only, many leading up north in the mountain meadowlands, blanketed in wildflowers, which are known as the **High Country** and are snowed-in seven months of the year. There are 360 miles of road that you can traverse by car (rangers will recommend tours). And many bus tours are offered by the Yosemite Transportation System. Things to see and do are suggested below, but first—

GETTING THERE: From San Francisco by car, take Interstate 580, then Interstate 5 to the Gustine off-ramp, and finally Calif. 140 to Yosemite Valley. Of the westerly approaches, Hwy. 140 is less mountainous and tends to have less snowfall; 120 East (Tioga Pass) is open only in summer. In the winter, chains must always be kept in the car. You can also make the trip by air via American Eagle (tel. 209/722-1587) to Merced from San Francisco or Los Angeles. A direct connection in Merced with Amtrak trains is available through California Yosemite Tours (tel. 209/383-1563), and VIA Bus Lines (tel. 209/384-1315) links Yosemite with the Greyhound terminal in Merced.

ENTRANCE FEES: An entrance fee is charged at the park, but no one minds paying it after seeing how well the National Parks Service keeps its end of the bargain. At each of the four entrances—**Calif. 120** on the northwest, **Calif. 140** toward the west, **Calif. 41** on the south, and **Calif. 120** on the northeast (open in summer only)—rangers are stationed to check you in and out. As of this writing, the entrance permit still costs only $5 per car (no charge for seniors 62 and over). If you plan to stay longer than seven days, it might be worth your while to purchase an annual Golden Eagle Passport—for $25 you get free entrance to all national parks that charge fees—or an annual Yosemite Passport for $15, which allows you to leave and enter the park at will for the year your permit is valid.

THINGS TO SEE: As soon as you reach the valley, stop at the **Visitor Center** in Yosemite Village and pick up the *Yosemite Guide,* a free newsletter describing the week's activities, and a map for the Yosemite Valley free shuttle bus. Rangers are generally on duty here from 9 a.m. to 6 p.m. during April and May, 8 a.m. to 7 p.m. in the summer, 8 a.m. to 6 p.m. in September and October, and 9 a.m. to 5 p.m. in the winter. They will provide you with information about park features, services, activities, and regulations. Books and maps are on sale here too. Beginning each morning around 8:30 a.m. (sometimes earlier, sometimes later) and going till about 9 p.m., well over a dozen daily activities are offered. They might include lectures on photography, a 30-minute ranger-led fireside discussion on bears, a guided luncheon hike to a waterfall, a geological history tour, or a puppet show with an environmental theme. There are fewer activities off-season.

There are 216 miles of paved road which you can traverse by car, and the rangers can give you a recommended road tour. You'll also want to know how to reach the museums, the sequoia groves, the inspiring granite summits, and the waterfall bases, plus what to do if a begging deer or squirrel approaches you for a handout (absolutely nothing). Although some of Yosemite's deer seem tame, they are wild and unpredictable and capable of inflicting serious injury with their antlers or hoofs.

Not to be missed are the following highlights:

Tuolumne Meadows: Gateway to the High Country, at an elevation of 8,600 feet, this is the largest alpine meadow in the High Sierras. Closed in winter, it's 55 miles from the valley by way of highly scenic Big Oak Flat and Tioga roads. A walk through this natural alpine garden makes a delightful day's excursion. In

summer, the park operates a large campground and conducts a full-scale naturalist program here.

Happy Isles Nature Center: Another gateway to the High Country, Happy
Isles is also a trailhead for the John Muir Trail, and Vernal and Nevada Falls (the
Mist Trail). Accessible by shuttlebus, the center is manned by ranger naturalists
who provide information about traveling (or not) in the wildlands and **Mirror
Lake.**

The Mariposa Grove: One of three groves of giant sequoias, this is the largest, with hundreds of trees, over 200 of which measure ten feet or more in diameter; among them is the Grizzly Giant, largest and oldest tree in the park. (It takes
27 fifth-graders to reach around it, but only 18 to reach around a school bus.)
Private vehicles can drive to the entrance of the grove; beyond that you can hike
or board the free shuttlebus. There are stops where you can get off to hear nature
talks, stroll around, take photos, or just absorb the peaceful atmosphere of the
forest. The Mariposa Grove (not to be confused with the community of Mariposa) is 35 miles south of the valley; other redwood areas are Tuolumne and Merced
groves near Crane Flat.

Glacier Point: Offering a sweeping 180° panorama of the High Sierras, and
a breathtaking view from 3,200 feet above the valley, Glacier Point looks out over
Nevada and Vernal Falls, Merced River, and the snowclad Sierra peaks of
Yosemite's backcountry. The approach road from the Badger Pass intersection
(closed in winter) winds through verdant red-fir and pine forest and meadow.
Many fine trails lead back down to the valley floor.

Pioneer Yosemite History Center: Reached via a covered bridge constructed in 1858, the center, at Wawona, tells of man's history in the park. Exhibits include "living history" demonstrations, some of the early buildings and
horse-drawn vehicles. In a similar category is the—

El Portal Travel Museum: At El Portal (Hwy. 140), displays of old rail cars,
a train station from Bagby, etc.—tell the story of early-day rail and auto transportation in the Yosemite region.

Yosemite Indian Village: Behind the Visitor Center, during summer, you
can watch Native Americans demonstrating traditional techniques of basket
weaving, making arrowheads, and grinding acorns, among other things.

THINGS TO DO: A popular vacation destination in itself, Yosemite offers an
exceptionally wide variety of visitor activities, from bicycling, backpacking,
white-water trips, and mountaineering to the more rugged snow-related pur-
suits. Several are described in Chapter XIV—"Alternative and Special Interest
Travel."

Hiking and Backpacking

As I said before, over 800 miles of trails offer hiking possibilities to satisfy
the hardy and the frail alike, as well as everyone in between. You can take anything
from a leisurely stroll to a trip of a week or longer, on terrain ranging from plains
to jagged mountains. If you wish to penetrate the less-traveled back-country, a
free wilderness permit is required. (Permits limit the traffic here to help keep the
wilderness wild.) This can be obtained at any of the ranger stations or by writing
to Backcountry Office, P.O. Box 577, Yosemite, CA 95389. Fifty percent of the
permits are granted by reservation, by mail only; the other 50% are on a first-
come, first-served basis.

Horseback Riding

Yosemite has excellent stable facilities, fully staffed with expert horsepeople.
There are 30 miles of bridle paths in the valley, with all-day trips offered to the

valley's rim. Stables—in **Yosemite Valley** near Curry Village, **Wawona, White Wolf,** and **Tuolumne Meadows**—are open in summer season only. Two-hour guided horseback rides leave several times daily for tours of their areas. There are also half-day guided mule trips: from the Valley Stables, the ride goes to Clark's Point and Nevada Falls; from Wawona, to Alder Creek or to Chilualna Falls. Full-day guided mule trips leave from all stables to such places as the base of Half Dome via Vernal and Nevada Falls, Glacier Point, the top of Yosemite Falls, or Mariposa Grove.

Several days a week four-day and six-day guided saddle trips leave the valley and tour the High Sierra camps, stopping at a different one each night. About ten miles apart, each camp has dormitory tents equipped with mattresses, linens and blankets, hot showers, and a central dining tent.

Burros, especially popular with kids, are also rentable. You might let the younger tots ride a burro while you hike along one of the scenic trails.

For information about saddle trips, write to **Yosemite Park & Curry Co.,** High Sierra Desk, 5410 E. Home Ave., Fresno, CA 93727; or call 209/252-4848.

Swimming
Some accommodation facilities have swimming pools, but there are also the myriad sparkling streams, bracing rivers, and waterfalls to bathe in or under.

Bicycling
Why not see the sights on two wheels? Many trails are specially geared to cyclists, and you can rent a standard or multispeed bike from the Yosemite Lodge bike stand or the Curry Village bike stand.

Mountain Climbing
With vertical granite walls surrounding two-thirds of the valley, Yosemite is considered by experts to be one of the finest climbing areas in the Western world. And the **Yosemite Mountaineering School** at Curry Village has classes for beginning, intermediate, and advanced climbers. There are rock climbing, ice climbing, and natural history trips, not to mention beginning and advanced survival trips. Inquire at the Visitor Center.

Skiing and Other Winter Sports
The oldest ski resort in California, **Badger Pass** (a 23-mile drive from the valley) opened to skiers in 1935. Facilities include one triple-chair lift, three double-chair lifts, one T-bar, and a rope tow for beginners. Other facilities include a child-care center (for tots of 3 to 9 years) and fast-food area. It's open through Easter (weather permitting), and the terrain is geared to the intermediate level, with about 35% for beginners and 15% for experts. An expert staff of ski instructors offers introductory and refresher courses, as well as children's ski lessons.

There are 90 miles of trails marked for cross-country skiing, with lessons scheduled daily. And 22 miles of machine-groomed track are set several times weekly from Badger Pass to Glacier Point. Skiers can stay overnight at the **Glacier Point Ski Hut** or at **Ostrander Lake Ski Hut.**

Winter-sports enthusiasts can also use an outdoor ice rink at Curry Village, open daily (weather permitting). Rental skates are available. In addition you can rent cross-country ski equipment or snowshoes at Badger Pass. For nonskiers, Badger Pass offers a scenic "Snow Cat" ride to the top of the ski lifts.

For information on Yosemite ski facilities, write to Badger Pass, Yosemite National Park, CA 95389; or call 209/372-1330. For a daily update on ski, road, and weather conditions, dial the Badger Pass snow phone: 209/372-1338.

Fishing

Fishing licenses (required for anyone over 16) are easily obtainable at the Mountaineering School at Curry Village or at the Sports Shop in Yosemite Village. Beautiful High Country lakes, miles of rivers (the Merced and Tuolumne are especially popular), streams, and tributaries provide anglers with not only excellent fishing but unsurpassed views. Various kinds of trout are the main catch here.

WHERE TO STAY: From luxury hotel to woodland cabin to simple tent, Yosemite offers a wide choice of accommodations. I'll begin with facilities for—

Camping

Yosemite has over 300 campsites for year-round use, and 2,324 open in summer. They all charge a $5 entrance fee and a $10 daily camping fee. Campsites are scattered over 20 different campgrounds in three categories. Type A campgrounds are the most elaborate, with well-defined roads, parking, drinking water, flush toilets, and, generally, a fireplace, table/bench combination, and tent space. Type B areas may be accessible by road or trail, and conveniences are limited to basic sanitary facilities and a smattering of fireplaces and tables. Type C areas don't concern us, as they are limited to groups (like Boy Scout troops).

All campsites are on a first-come, first-served basis, and from June 1 to September 15 camping is limited to 7 days in the valley and 14 days in the rest of the park. The rest of the year the limit is 30 days throughout the park. Backcountry campers need a wilderness permit.

For more details on campgrounds, write to P.O. Box 577, Yosemite National Park, CA 95389; or call 209/372-0265, or 372-4845. Reservations can also be made through Ticketron; check your local phone book, or write to the Ticketron Reservation Office, P.O. Box 2715, San Francisco, CA 94126. Reservations can be made no more than eight weeks in advance.

Other Accommodations

Reservations are advised at all times and especially in summer for all hotels, lodges, and cabins in the park.

Within walking distance of the valley is **Yosemite Lodge,** with attractive deluxe units, hotel rooms with or without bath, and redwood cabins with or without bath. Rates are the same for one or two persons. Bathless hotel rooms are $38, bathless cabins are $34, cabins with bath run $45, standard hotel rooms cost $77. (In season, and during the holidays, reservations should be made one year in advance—it's that popular.) A coffeeshop, lounge, two restaurants, and a cafeteria are on the premises, as are several shops.

Rustic **Curry Village** also charges the same rates for singles and doubles. Hotel rooms with bath are $62, cabins with bath are $45, and cabins without bath run $33. Tent cabins (wood platform floors with canvas sides and roofs) are about $25 per night.

There's less roughing-it at the **Wawona Hotel,** near the southern end of Yosemite. It offers such gracious accoutrements as a swimming pool, tennis court, and nine-hole golf course, as well as a dining room and nearby stables. Single or double hotel rooms are $73 with bath; bathless rooms cost $60.

The luxurious, and very centrally located, **Ahwahnee Hotel** in Yosemite Village has lovely dining facilities, a lounge, and a gift shop. Rooms with bath are $160 single, $165 double.

At any of the above, a deposit covering one night's lodging is required to confirm reservations, refundable if cancellation is received seven days before your arrival date. In season, or during the holidays, make your reservations for any of the above one year in advance to avoid being disappointed. Write to the Reservation Department, Yosemite Park & Curry Co., 5410 E. Home Ave., Fresno, CA 93727 (tel. 209/252-4848).

Note: National Parks have toughened rules on drinking to cut down on drunk driving. New regulations outlaw open containers of alcoholic beverages in a car, specify a strict blood/alcohol level, and set penalties for anyone who refuses a breathalyzer test. The regulations are being enforced by the local police and by the park service's 2,800 rangers.

6. SOUTH LAKE TAHOE

"I ascended today the highest peak . . . from which we had a beautiful view of a mountain lake at our feet, about 15 miles in length, and so nearly surrounded by mountains that we could not discover an outlet." These are the words of John C. Frémont, the early California pioneer who discovered the "Lake of the Sky," set at 6,225 feet above sea level in the heavily timbered Sierra Nevada mountains on the Nevada-California border.

Said by many to be the most beautiful lake in the world, Lake Tahoe is famous for its 99.7% pure water—a dinner plate at a depth of 100 feet is clearly visible from the surface, and divers claim visibility at 200 feet under. The dimensions of the lake belie its immense capacity; the average depth is 989 feet, which is sufficient water to cover the entire state of California with 14½ inches of water! It is the third deepest lake in the world. More important to the visitor, though, the play of light during the day causes the color of the lake to change from dazzling emerald to blues and rich purples. And due to atmospheric conditions in the area, some of the most beautiful sunsets in the world are seen here.

The 72-mile circle around the lake is filled with recreational, historical, and scenic points of interest. In summer, you can enjoy the crystal waters of Lake Tahoe for swimming (if you're hearty enough for some pretty cold water), fishing, boating, and water sports. Lakeside beaches, picnic areas, and campgrounds are plentiful. In winter, Lake Tahoe becomes a popular ski resort. Year round, there's glittering Vegas-style gambling and big-name entertainment on the Nevada border. And that's not the half of it.

Lake Tahoe can be reached by American Airlines (tel. 800/433-7300) from San Francisco and Los Angeles. Most cities offer Greyhound bus connections. By car it's a fairly long drive—209 miles from San Francisco via Interstate 80 and Hwy. 50.

Make your first stop at the **South Lake Tahoe Chamber of Commerce,** 3066 Hwy. 50, three miles west of Stateline between Tallac and San Francisco Avenues (tel. 916/541-5255; mailing address: P.O. Box 15090, South Lake Tahoe, CA 95706), where a knowledgeable and friendly staff has oodles of printed information about local activities. For vacation information and reservations contact the **Lake Tahoe Visitors Authority,** P.O. Box 16299, South Lake Tahoe, CA 95731 (tel. 916/544-5050, or toll free 800/822-5922).

WHERE TO STAY: All the gambling action is just across Stateline (also known as the state line) in Nevada, and the closer you are to it, the more expensive are your accommodations. The four top choices are the big hotel/casino extravaganzas actually in Nevada, just a stone's throw from the California border. So popular is this multirecreational area that hotel rooms tend to get booked heavily in advance. Don't arrive without reservations or you may find yourself a reluctant camper.

Note: On weekends and holidays motel room rates tend to skyrocket in Tahoe; there seems to be a general philosophy of charging what the traffic will bear. If you're planning to come during one of these busy times, reserve especially far in advance, and try to get written confirmation of your room rate.

Harrah's, P.O. Box 8, Stateline, NV 89449 (tel. 702/588-6611, or toll free 800/648-3773). With 540 rooms, this 18-story facility is a 24-hour hub of Lake Tahoe activity. It's one of Mobil's four-star-rated hotels. Posh rooms all have color TV with bedside remote control that also works the lights and radio, a small bar and refrigerator (you can order a choice of 14 drinks via a pushbutton mechanism), TV and phone in each of the two baths, and ice water on tap. In addition to all these little luxuries, the rooms, each decorated to reflect one of the four seasons, happen to be gorgeous.

Of course, the principal attraction at Harrah's is the casino, a biggie with 65,000 square feet of gaming area offering everything from baccarat to Bingo.

In the South Shore Room there's big-name entertainment—headliners like Bill Cosby, the Oak Ridge Boys, Billy Crystal, Engelbert Humperdinck, John Denver, Liza Minnelli, Sammy Davis, Jr., Tony Orlando, Don Rickles, and Wayne Newton. Prices for dinner shows range from $25 to $40, $20 to $30 for the late (11:30 p.m.) show.

From 7 p.m. on you can also catch some pretty good acts at the Stateline Cabaret Lounge in the casino. No charge, just a two-drink minimum to see performers like Bill Medley and Tower of Power.

Harrah's chief dining facility is the very luxurious four-star and AAA four-diamond award Summit Restaurant, with glass walls allowing panoramic views of the lake and surrounding mountains. Open for dinner, the Summit features live music nightly except Sunday till 11:30 p.m. and continental gourmet specialties such as chateaubriand bouquetière for two, quail, and roast Long Island duckling, for $22 to $42 per person. Tableside flambé preparations add drama to a meal at the Summit. Other options include breakfast with a special Sunday brunch, lunch and dinner buffets in the Forest Restaurant, a 24-hour coffeeshop called the Sierra, and a steakhouse called Friday's Station; there are also six bars.

I'm not through yet. Harrah's has superb health-club facilities with massage, sauna, gym, and whirlpool for men and women (men get steam, too). Elaborately equipped right down to the dressing rooms with shampoo, deodorant, and cologne, there are even three-way mirrors and a scale to spur you on.

What does all this splendor cost? It depends on the season, but year-round the rates include free valet parking. During the summer standard singles and doubles are $125; deluxe rooms begin at $155. The rest of the year standard rooms are $105; deluxe rooms begin at $140. Suites begin at $500. An extra person pays $20 year round.

Another Stateline operation is the **High Sierra Hotel/Casino,** P.O. Box C, Stateline, NV 89449 (tel. 702/588-6211, or toll free 800/648-3395, 800/648-3322 in California). Rooms are luxurious and attractively modern, with full baths, direct-dial phones, and color TVs. It's been redecorated, in keeping with the hotel's western theme.

The main casino area is two city blocks in length and contains all the usual gaming action, including 1,000 slots.

The High Sierra's gourmet restaurant is Stetson's, a relaxed establishment with a classy western touch, complete with Stetson hat collection. The service is first class, and the continental cuisine excellent. Stetson's is open nightly from 5:30 to 11 p.m.

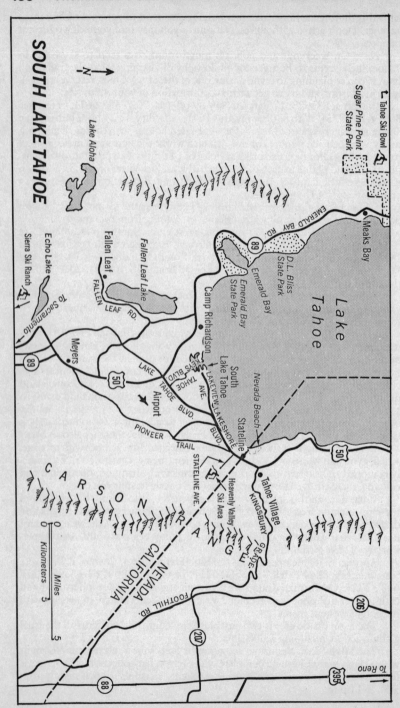

Other dining choices here: a 24-hour coffeeshop called the Four Seasons and the Chuckwagon for family dining.

The High Sierra has a big outdoor heated pool, hot tubs, barbershop and beauty salon, massage and sauna, shops and free valet parking for guests.

February through June and October through December, rates are $86 weekdays and $99 weekends; June through October, rooms cost $126. All rates are for single or double occupancy; an additional adult pays $10, and children stay free with their parents.

What began in the mid-1940s as a six-stool café with the only gas pump between Carson City, Nevada, and Placerville, California, has since become **Harvey's Resort Hotel/Casino,** P.O. Box 127, Stateline, NV 89449 (tel. 702/588-2411, or toll free 800/648-3361)—from humble beginnings to a Mobil four-star rated resort. Harvey's now towers 18 stories over the south shore of Lake Tahoe. The hotel/casino has 575 handsomely appointed French provincial rooms and suites, with spectacular lake and mountain views, and in-room amenities such as remote-control cable TV, two phones, an honor bar and refrigerator. There are six restaurants to satisfy most every taste, a new 275-seat enclosed entertainment cabaret, ten cocktail lounges, a skilled concierge staff, a 1,500-car parking garage, a new outdoor swimming pool and health spa, four tennis courts, and a gift shop. The hotel's original handful of slot machines has multiplied to over 2,000, and now there are 114 blackjack tables, as well as tables for baccarat, craps, poker, roulette, keno, Pai Gow, and Sic Bo. In 1988, a Race and Sports Book was added to round out the gaming attractions.

You can dine at the Top of the Wheel, enjoying stunning lake views 11 stories up in a South Seas setting of thatched roofing, rattan, and bamboo. The decor reflects the cuisine—entrees (costing $18 to $30) like shrimp curry Singapore and Polynesian honey duck served with wild rice and a plum sauce—although continental fare is also served. Intoxicating rum concoctions are also a specialty here. Entertainment and dancing nightly.

The Sage Room maintains its tradition of western elegance, specializing in steak and veal dishes, prepared tableside. Or for seafood in its many variations, the Seafood Grotto has a netful of fresh fish and shellfish beautifully prepared, plus an authentic Chinese menu featuring seafood and Szechuan entrees. The El Dorado Buffet and Brunch has an "all-you-can-eat" dinner for $8.95.

The ambience is rustic; it still has the original American Indian lighting fixtures, and framed western art prints adorn the rough-hewn walls. You can enjoy south-of-the-border cuisine in El Vaquero, a restaurant decorated in leather and wrought iron.

Rates for singles or doubles are $85 to $135, depending on type of accommodations and time of year. Suites are from $165.

The newest five-star resort at Lake Tahoe is the 15-story **Caesars Tahoe** at Stateline, P.O. Box 5800, Stateline, NV 89449 (tel. 702/588-3515, or toll free 800/648-3353). The resort hotel houses 446 large and luxurious guest rooms and suites. Rooms feature bathrooms with large sunken Roman tubs, suites have wide-screen TVs and wet bars. All accommodations are modern in decor and include amenities like two phones and two TVs (color in the bedroom, black-and-white in the bathroom).

The casino is one of the largest in the area, with blackjack, roulette, craps, pai gow, baccarat, keno, and poker. There are 1,000 slot machines, many with progressive slots, one of which paid the first $1-million jackpot, in 1981. The casino is also home to a large Race and Sports Book. Kids can try their luck in a video arcade stocked with all the latest games.

There are eight restaurants on the premises: Le Posh, a beauty with crystal, etched glass, plush booths, candlelight and gourmet dining; the Empress Court, for authentic Chinese food; the Broiler Room for steaks, seafood, and Cajun offerings; the Café Roma, a 24-hour restaurant offering breakfast, lunch, and dinner; the Evergreen buffet, serving all-you-can-eat lunches and dinners; the Primavera, specializing in Italian cuisine; the Post-Time Deli, for snacks or a quick bite; and the Sweet Suite with pies, pastries, ice cream, and yogurt.

Caesars has a major 1,700-seat showroom, the Cascade, featuring top-name entertainment: Julio Iglesias, Kenny Loggins, the Pointer Sisters, and Willie Nelson have all appeared here. The Crystal Cabaret is a 300-seat showcase for comedy, music, and revues.

And rounding out the facilities is the plush Caesars Spa. It features a lagoon-style pool with waterfalls; men's and women's spas, saunas, a massage room; a Nautilus weight and exercise room, two racquetball courts, four outdoor tennis courts, a pro shop, and sun decks for total relaxation. And because there are always those who would rather shop than gamble, there is a host of shops featuring gifts from throughout the world, located in the shopping galleria.

Rates for singles or doubles are $100 to $145. Suites begin at $275.

As you get farther from Stateline there are hundreds of motels, and generally rates decrease as you go west on Hwy. 50.

Of course, if you're willing to stay a little farther from Stateline, you can get both good rates and luxury accommodations. And all you really sacrifice is a few minutes' time getting back and forth to the casino area (even if you don't have a car), since there are shuttlebuses running along Hwy. 50 to and from the casinos throughout each day and into the night. One of the most elegant properties in town is the **Inn by the Lake,** 3300 Lake Tahoe Blvd., P.O. Box 849 (Hwy. 50, between Fremont and Rufus Allen), South Lake Tahoe, CA 95705 (tel. 916/542-0330, or toll free 800/822-5922), a Colony-managed resort, is just two miles from the casino action, and 1½ miles from Heavenly Valley. It's a quiet, elegant place, across the street from the lakeshore. The inn has 100 oversize rooms, all decorated in soothing neutral and pastel shades. Rooms at the front of the hotel have a breathtaking view of the lake, and are furnished with king-size beds, refrigerators, and wet bars. Queen-size rooms and double-queens at the back look out on the mountains. Furnishings are plush and comfortable; amenities include Touch-Tone direct-dial phones, cable color TVs, and sparkling modern tub/shower baths. There is a year-round heated pool, hot tub, Jacuzzi, and redwood sauna. Complimentary coffee, juice, and croissants are served daily by the fireplace in the lobby lounge.

Rooms at the Inn by the Lake cost $85 to $110, single or double; suites begin at $120. Seasonal rates apply.

Another pleasant property—this one directly on the lake—is the **Tahoe Marina Inn,** P.O. Box 871, on Bijou Street (off Lake Tahoe Boulevard) (tel. 916/541-2180). There are 77 units here, all with floor-to-ceiling glass doors.

The Tahoe Marina Inn has no restaurant, but there are several within walking distance. On the premises are a heated pool and a dry sauna; there's also a 500-foot-long beach.

Rooms at the Tahoe Marina Inn are $75 to $90, single or double, in summer (June through October), lower during the rest of the year. Kitchen apartments are $110 to $120.

Now, moving over to the California side of town, within easy walking distance of all casino action (a shuttlebus is available in any case) is the **Forest Inn,** 1101 Park Ave., P.O. Box 4300, South Lake Tahoe, CA 95729 (tel. 916/541-6655, or toll free 800/822-5950 in California). So close is this luxury resort to Stateline that it adjoins the side entrance of Harrah's casino. Set in 5 acres of garden and forest, it has 125 rooms housed in rustic buildings. There are three different types of accommodations. The first are regular motel units with all modern conveniences—color TV, dressing area, tub/shower bath, phone, alarm clock, air conditioning, and heating. Then there are one- and two-bedroom suites, which in addition to the above also have fully equipped modern kitchens with dishwashers, living rooms, and dining areas. All the accommodations are well appointed and spacious, with attractive modern furnishings.

Parking is included in the rates, and there are two large swimming pools with sunning areas, two whirlpools, and two sauna baths.

Motel units are $65 to $86, single or double; add $10 for an extra person. Kitchen units are $6 extra. Two-bedroom units are $105 and up, depending on the number of persons. Children under 16 are not accepted as guests.

You can make reservations for these and many other hostelries (including those listed below) through the **Lake Tahoe Visitors Authority,** P.O. Box 16299, South Lake Tahoe, CA 95731 (tel. 800/822-5922). Call from 8 a.m. to 6 p.m. weekdays (Pacific Time), or from 9 a.m. to 5 p.m. weekends.

Offering standard facilities and rates of about $55 to $75 double during the week, $65 to $85 double on weekends, are the **Lucky Lodge Motel,** across the street from Harvey's, at 952 Stateline Ave., P.O. Box 4385, South Lake Tahoe, CA 95729 (tel. 916/544-3369); the **Pacifica Lodge,** 931 Park Ave., P.O. Box 4298, South Lake Tahoe, CA 95729 (tel. 916/544-4131); and the **Riviera Inn,** 890 Stateline Ave., P.O. Box 4595, South Lake Tahoe, CA 95729 (tel. 916/544-3448).

Least expensive, and about two miles west of the California/Nevada border on Hwy. 50, is a **Motel 6,** 2375 Lake Tahoe Rd., P.O. Box 7756, South Lake Tahoe, CA 95731 (tel. 916/542-1400), with 140 units and a small pool. Singles are $25.95; $6 more for each additional adult. It's 3½ miles to the casinos. Need I tell you that you'll need reservations well in advance during the summer.

MORE CASINO ACTION: The biggest casinos are in the first four hotels described above, but Tahoe also has some independent casinos. They're all popular, since few gamblers are content to lose all their money in one place, under the theory that prosperity and a winning keno ticket are just around the corner. One of the biggest of these nonhotel casinos is **Bill's** (tel. 702/588-2455), just adjacent to Harrah's. It's open 24 hours a day the year round, believe it or not, there's a McDonald's in the casino, and most Tahoe motels give out Bill's coupons for free games and discounts. Coupons are also distributed for **John's Tahoe Nugget** (tel. 702/588-6288), with the same hours; it's about three-quarters of a mile east of Stateline on Hwy. 50.

The most important thing about Bill's and the Nugget is their year-round 24-hour free shuttlebus.

WHERE TO DINE: The most scenic choice is the **Top of the Tram** (tel. 916/544-6263), at the end of Keller Road in Heavenly Valley. The restaurant is open from Memorial Day, generally to the end of September, then Thanksgiving to April. Unless you're a hearty hiker, this restaurant can only be reached by car, which is left in the parking lot while you ascend 8,300 feet to the top of the mountain via cable car. The ride up is part of the fun, and the view from the restaurant is breathtaking. It's particularly exquisite in the early evening, when the magnificent Sierra sunset over the lake and mountains is yours to behold. There's an outdoor café area; inside there are windows on three sides.

The restaurant is open from 10 a.m. to 10 p.m. Monday through Saturday, on Sunday from 9 a.m. Light fare is served at lunch/brunch and averages $3 to $8 for sandwiches, salads, pasta, etc. Dinner is served from 5 p.m. and the single price for any complete dinner includes the tram ride to get to the restaurant

—$27 per person for prime rib, or filet mignon, rack of lamb, or a steak/seafood combination. A child's dinner is $13. Reservations suggested.

Should you choose to ride up simply for the incredible view, the tram trip costs $10 for adults, $6 for kids under 12.

One of the oldest and best-known restaurants in the area is the **Swiss Chalet**, on U.S. 50 four miles west of Stateline near Sierra Boulevard (tel. 916/544-3304). Cozy and candlelit, the Swiss Chalet is filled with beer steins, cuckoo clocks, paintings of the Alps, hanging copper pots, and large brass bells. It's really quite pretty, with more charm than kitsch, and the food is hearty and delicious. All entrees come with soup or salad, homemade rolls and butter. Those entrees, priced at $13 to $22, include German sauerbraten with noodles and red cabbage, cheese fondue for two, and beef Stroganoff. Be sure to leave room for the scrumptious dessert cakes or pastries. This is a good choice for family dining; complete children's dinners are about $5 to $8. Open nightly from 6 to 10:30 p.m. Closed Monday off-season. Reservations suggested.

As the name suggests, **The Greenhouse,** 4140 Cedar Ave., near Stateline (tel. 916/541-5800), abounds in hanging plants and has plush grass-green carpeting. It's quite a charming place, with Tudor-style beamed walls, a floor-to-ceiling brick fireplace, and many antique German and English stained-glass hangings. Tables are candlelit, with white linen cloths and white napkins elegantly wound in the glasses.

You might begin a meal here with escargots in fine herb butter; select an entree of roast prime rib au jus, chicken chasseur, sautéed scallops on rice, or veal marsala for $14 to $26; and finish up with an English trifle. All entrees come with fresh sautéed vegetables and rice pilaf or potatoes. A good wine list is available.

Just a short walk from casino action, The Greenhouse is open for dinner nightly from 6 to 10 p.m. Reservations essential. The Greenhouse bar, by the way, is a popular nighttime hangout.

A New England seafood restaurant serving fresh Maine lobster (you can select your own from a tank) is the last thing you'd expect to find in the Tahoe mountains. But here it is. **The Dory's Oar,** 1041 Fremont Ave., off Hwy. 50 (tel. 916/541-6603), looking ever so much like a quaint Nantucket eatery, and serving seafood flown in daily from the East Coast. The ambience is New England nautical, its pretty blue-and-white papered and barnwood-paneled walls hung with bronze-plated plaques describing ships, ship lights, and maps. There are white ruffled curtains on the windows; gaslight lamps, and dried flowers grace every table. Upstairs is a comfortable, pine-paneled, ski-lodge bar with a unique fireplace.

Dinners include bread, butter, salad-bar offerings, and fisherman's fries, rice pilaf, or a baked potato. House specialties include the above-mentioned lobster, baked stuffed baby salmon, and deep-fried softshell Maryland crab, for $12 to $30. For the steak lover, there is filet mignon, Porterhouse and New York steak. The Dory's Oar is open for dinner nightly from 5 to 10 p.m.

Chez Villaret, 900 Emerald Bay Rd. (Hwy. 89) (tel. 916/541-7868), is a cozy French country inn, its ambience enhanced at night by candlelight and taped classical music. Neat and pretty, it has tables covered in crisp white linen, curtained windows, and a few paintings and art prints on the walls. The menu features French nouvelle cuisine and changes daily according to what is available; there's a classic onion soup au gratin, and appetizers like steamed scallops or hearts of palm with raspberry vinaigrette. Entrees may include filet of veal with cream and wild mushrooms, filet of beef with three-peppercorn sauce, and dover sole with butter, lemon, and parsley, all for $16 to $26. Tableside preparation is a specialty here, as are flambé desserts like crêpes suzette ($8 for two). An impressive wine list comes bound in leather.

Chez Villaret is open daily from 6 to 11 p.m. Reservations are advised.

Friendly and casual, **Cantina Los Tres Hombres,** Hwy. 89, at 10th Street (tel. 916/544-1233), is a popular Tahoe hangout. It consists of several dining areas and a cozy cocktail lounge/bar, all filled with lots of live plants, rattan matting, pottery, and papier-mâché animals—a zebra, parrot, giraffe, peacock, and elephant. There's even a desert room with planters of cacti. Somehow it all combines to create an appropriately south-of-the-border ambience. There's usually a wait for tables at dinner (they don't take reservations), during which time you can sit in the lounge and sip margaritas and listen to music or watch major sporting events. One menu is offered throughout the day, with simple entrees, combination plates carnitas, fajitas, and specials of the day (Friday it's fresh fish), all in the $6 to $13 range.

Open daily from 11:30 a.m. to 10:30 p.m.

TAHOE SKIING: Sierra snow is unique. It falls quickly, often quite unexpectedly, and in great quantities (20 feet the average winter) about one day in four from late November to mid-May, and its crystalline structure retains a powdery perfection on the slopes. It's also unusually reflective, so skiers should beware of getting a bad sunburn.

Since the weather affects not only the slopes but also the roads to them, you'll want to call 916/577-3550 for driving conditions before setting out—and hope that conditions don't change on your way up. (Many roads require chains in the winter, and I've found that it's always wise to take them, even in late spring or early summer.)

About 25 ski resorts are clustered within 50 miles of the city. The largest and most famous are actually to the northwest of the lake near Tahoe City. Right in South Lake Tahoe, however, is one of America's largest ski areas—

Heavenly Valley

This vast two-state complex covers over 20 square miles of High Sierra ski terrain encompassing nine mountain peaks. About 25% of the slopes are geared to beginners, 50% to intermediates, and 25% to advanced and expert skiers, including the super-expert Mott Canyon. Ability levels and directions are carefully marked. An aerial tram and 25 other lifts convey 26,000 skiers an hour to the slope of their choice.

Both the Main Lodge on the California side and the two Nevada base facilities offer half- and full-day passes for adults for $22 and $38 respectively.

A full line of high-quality ski equipment can be rented at all three base facilities. Ditto ski lessons, using the ATM method and geared to various levels of ability, under the auspices of John Darby, who heads an expert staff of genial young American and European instructors, many of whom speak several languages. Private lessons are $42 an hour, $20 for each extra person. A full day of group instruction (morning and afternoon sessions) is $27, $20 for a half day. First-time beginners do not need a lift ticket (for obvious reasons). Heavenly Valley ski season is mid-November through mid-May. The Heavenly Valley Tram operates year round for sightseeing; fares are $10 for adults, $6 for children.

For further information about Heavenly Valley facilities, accommodations, package plans, etc., write to Heavenly Valley, P.O. Box 2180, Lake Tahoe, NV 89449 (tel. 916/541-1330 for information, 702/588-4584 for lodging and lift reservations).

Squaw Valley

Site of the 1960 Winter Olympics, Squaw Valley is located on Hwy. 89 between Truckee and Tahoe City. Once an old mining camp, it is now an alpine resort offering winter sports from November to May. The 27 major lifts carry 39,380 skiers per hour to slopes offering a wide range of challenges to skiers at all levels of proficiency. Facilities include a snow school center for children from ages 3 to 5 ($35 for 8:30 a.m. to 4:30 p.m., including lunch and equipment, plus lessons; $27 for a half day with lessons and snacks). Also at Squaw Valley: a ski school teaching the American Method, lodge accommodations, ski rentals, eating places, and après-ski bars.

All-day lift tickets are $33; a half day is $23. Children 12 and under, and seniors over 65, pay $5. The price goes down for tickets purchased for two to seven consecutive days.

The ski school offers a full day of instructions for $28. Private lessons are $41 an hour.

Squaw Valley also has day-care, exercise facilities for children 6 months to 3 years; a full day is $35, a half day is $25 with lunch and snacks.

Monday through Friday, during nonholiday periods, first-time beginners ski free; they receive a free lift ticket, free rentals, and a free lesson.

For further information about facilities, accommodations, ski clinics, and ski packages, write to Squaw Valley USA, P.O. Box 2007, Olympic Valley, CA 95730 (tel. 916/583-6985 for general information and 916/583-5585 for reservations, or toll free, 800/545-4350).

Information and Ski Packages

The above are the major ski resorts in the area. Also popular are **Kirkwood,** 30 miles southwest of South Lake Tahoe on Rte. 88 (P.O. Box 1, Kirkwood, CA 95646; tel. 209/258-6000), a rapidly expanding area with the highest base elevation (7,500 feet) in northern California, and offering complimentary shuttle from South Lake Tahoe; **Echo Summit,** Tahoe's newest family-oriented resort, only eight miles west of Hwy. 50 (P.O. Box 8955, South Lake Tahoe, CA 95731; tel. 916/659-7154); and **Sierra Ski Ranch,** 12 miles west of South Lake Tahoe on Hwy. 50 (P.O. Box 3501, Twin Bridges, CA 95735; tel. 916/659-7519), which also has free shuttlebus service from Stateline and South Lake Tahoe.

You can consult the individual resorts and your travel agent about ski packages. Packages can give you savings on air fare, ski schools, car rentals, tennis, golf, or casino shows—there are lots of different ones.

SUMMER RECREATION: Tahoe is more than just a little Las Vegas–cum–ski area. It's a year-round resort playground, probably offering more options to vacationers in one place than anywhere else in the world. There's enough to fill an entire book, but due to space limitations I can only skim the surface. In addition to what's been covered, there are countless historical sites around the lake and nearby. A tour around the lake, offered by major Stateline hotels, is a must—not to mention spectator sports, biking trips, sailing, waterskiing, antiquing, visits to ghost towns, backpacking, and even panning for gold. So to reiterate what was suggested earlier in this chapter—make your first stop the South Lake Tahoe Chamber of Commerce to discover the full range of activities available.

One such activity, very popular in this beautiful natural setting is—

Camping

Most of the campgrounds inside the Tahoe Basin are government operated (federal or state), and although a few operate sites on a first-come, first-served basis, reservations are highly recommended and often necessary in season. All California state campground reservations can be conveniently obtained through Ticketron. Privately owned campgrounds, however, usually provide more of the modern conveniences. I recommend the following:

Camp Richardson: A private campground two miles north of South Lake Tahoe on Hwy. 89 at Jameson Beach Rd., P.O. Box 9028, South Lake Tahoe, CA 95731 (tel. 916/541-1801), with 200 campsites for tent camping at $12 to $14 per day (forest or meadow), and 100 RV/trailer sites with full hookup at $16 per night. There are 30 RV/trailer sites with water and electricity only, at $14 per night. Included in all rates for all sites is the use of toilets, showers, and beach and recreation facilities. Campers pay $8 a day for two, $8 to $10 for the trailer park.

Campgrounds administered by the Forest Service include: **Nevada Beach** in Nevada, off Hwy. 50, one mile north of the state line ($9 per night); **Kaspian Walk-in Campground,** four miles south of Tahoe City ($3 per night); and **William Kent Campground,** two miles south of Tahoe City ($8 per night). For further information you can contact the U.S.D.A. Forest Service, P.O. Box 731002, South Lake Tahoe, CA 95731 (tel. 916/573-2600).

State park campgrounds include **Emerald Bay State Park** (tel. 916/525-7277), **D. L. Bliss State Park** (tel. 916/525-7277), and **Sugar Pine Point State Park** (tel. 916/525-7982), on Hwy. 89 on the California side; and **Tahoe State Recreation Area** in Tahoe City on Hwy. 28 (tel. 916/583-3074, summer only). Summer camping rates are $10 per night; day use is $3 per vehicle. Campsite reservations can be made through Mistix (tel. 800/446-7275). During the winter, all parks are closed with the exception of Sugar Pine Point State Park where camping is $10 per night; for cross-country skiing, parking is $3 per vehicle. You can get further information on the above parks from the Sierra District State Parks, P.O. Drawer D, Tahoma, CA 95733 (tel. 916/525-7232).

Golf and Tennis

Even the most dedicated craps-shooters might want to get out of the casinos once in a while to breathe the fresh mountain air and get a little more exercise than that involved in tossing dice. Gambler golfers needn't go far; one of the best courses in town is the **Edgewood Tahoe Golf Course,** at Lake Parkway and Hwy. 50 in Stateline, Nevada (tel. 702/588-3566), on the lake. Open May through November, this 18-hole championship course offers challenges to every golfer. *Golf Digest* rates it as one of the top 100 courses in the country. What's more, it's a public course! Greens fees, including cart (mandatory) and balls for the driving range are $80. The course has a fleet of 94 golf carts, a modern driving range, three practice greens, a fully equipped pro shop, and a lovely clubhouse with dining facilities. Clubs can be rented; tee-off reservations are required.

As to **tennis,** the area has yet to develop facilities commensurate with this sport's popularity. You can, however, use the four resurfaced and lighted courts at the South Tahoe Intermediate School at Hwy. 50 and Lyons Avenue or the six lighted courts at the South Tahoe High School, just off Lake Tahoe Boulevard, daily during the summer. The fee is $4 per hour for adults ($2 for those under 18 and seniors); reservations must be made in advance at the courts.

Hiking

A very big sport here, which is not surprising in a magnificent lake and woodland center. Both the South Lake Tahoe Chamber of Commerce and the **Visitor Center** (tel. 916/573-2674) operated by the U.S. Forest Service (off Hwy. 89 just past Camp Richardson) can suggest guided and self-guided nature walks and trails for hikers of varying heartiness. One interesting trek that begins at the Visitor Center is along the Rainbow Trail to the **Stream Profile Chamber,** for underground viewing of aquatic life beneath the surface of a flowing mountain stream.

Horseback Riding

Tahoe has many stables and miles of good riding trails. There's **Camp Richardson Corral** (tel. 916/541-3113), on Emerald Bay Road (Hwy. 89) in Camp Richardson, California (mailing address: P.O. Box 8335, South Lake Tahoe, CA 95731). Horses rent for $13.50 an hour for trail rides. Open from 8 a.m. to 5 p.m. May through October. In addition to trail rides, they feature steak rides, breakfast rides, overnight pack trips, and fishing trips.

Fishing

Within the Lake Tahoe Basin exists a great variety of opportunities for fishing enthusiasts. Should you need to obtain a fishing license while in California, the price is $19.50 for residents of California, $51 for nonresidents. A one-day license is $6.50 for both residents and nonresidents. Obviously if you come to fish just over the one weekend, it would be cheaper to buy two or three one-day licenses. If you already have a fishing license from California or Nevada, it is good for South Lake Tahoe. Headquarters for fishing information, equipment, and licenses is **The Outdoorsman** on Hwy. 50 at the Truckee River (tel. 916/541-1660); they also sell sports clothing and equipment for tennis, golf, jogging, etc.

Boat Cruises

If Lake Tahoe is too cold for swimming, non-Polar Bears can at least take a boat cruise on its waters. **Lake Tahoe Cruises,** P.O. Box 14292, South Lake Tahoe, CA 95702 (tel. 916/541-3364, or toll free 800/238-2463), is at Ski Run Boulevard, operating out of the Ski Run Marina (next to Heavenly Valley). It offers daily cruises year-round on a genuine 500-passenger Mississippi sternwheeler (don't ask how they got it up the mountain). There usually are four trips daily: at 11 a.m., 1:30 p.m., 3:55 p.m., and 7 p.m. (June to October). The schedule is subject to change depending on the number of passengers, so I suggest that you call ahead to confirm the time. The 7 p.m. trip is a dinner/dance voyage, with dinner optional. With the exception of the 7 p.m. trip, adults pay $14; children, $6. The dinner/dance trip is $18.50 for the cruise and dancing to the music of a live band; dinner is an additional $16.95 (usually including prime rib or halibut), and the romantic aura is free. The winter schedule (October through May) is usually a trip at noon and one at 6:30 p.m.—the dinner/dance.

CHAPTER VII

SOUTH ALONG THE SHORE

□ □ □

The tourist who skips from San Francisco to Los Angeles misses an awful lot. The stretch between Monterey and Santa Barbara, although not as celebrated as points north or south, is a delightful surprise. Throughout, the Pacific Coast scenery varies from picture-postcard-pretty to breathtaking (emphasis on the latter), with nary an eyesore along the way.

We'll begin in Steinbeck Country, Monterey; adjacent to it is the charmingly quaint village of Carmel, formerly starring Clint Eastwood as mayor. No one could be so jaded as not to find the rugged Big Sur coastline a thrill—and speaking of being jaded, there's Hearst Castle at San Simeon coming up. At the end of this stretch, you finally enter Southern California—although it seems more like a well-to-do Mexico—in the beautiful seaside resort of Santa Barbara. Santa Barbara's mission is the most idyllic of them all—set on a hillside, it looks like a little piece of heaven, though our basis for comparison has yet to come.

1. MONTEREY

Portuguese navigator Juan Rodriguez Cabrillo was the first to sight Monterey, while sailing to Spain in 1542. In 1602 Sebastian Vizcaino followed in search of a suitable harbor for Manila galleons sailing back from the Philippines. He named the area Monterey in honor of the Count of Monterey, Viceroy of Spain.

But many years passed before the area was colonized. It was well over 200 years after Cabrillo's discovery that the place Richard Henry Dana called "the pleasantest and most civilized place in California" was settled, when Father Serra established the second of his now-famous chain of missions there. His landing site is now a state historical monument, although the original mission has been moved to nearby Carmel.

Monterey was under Mexican rule from 1821 to 1846, and even today there are many architectural echoes—whitewashed adobe houses and pueblos—of this period. About a dozen such buildings have been preserved as historical monuments, among them the **Custom House,** across from the entrance to Fisherman's Wharf, where Commodore John Drake Sloat first officially raised the United States flag on July 7, 1846. It is the oldest government building in California and was built under the Mexican regime.

Monterey is also Steinbeck country. In the '40s Steinbeck wrote: "Cannery Row in Monterey . . . is a poem, a stink, a grating noise, a quality of light, a tone, a habit, a nostalgia, a dream." Returning in the '60s to the street he had given fame, he had this to say: "The beaches are clean where they once festered with fish guts and flies. The canneries which once put up a sickening stench are gone, their places filled with restaurants, antique shops, and the like. They fish for tourists, now, not pilchards, and that species they are not likely to wipe out."

It's true that Cannery Row is touristy. The entrepreneurs have moved in and upped the real estate value of the old waterside slum. They've planted sweet antique shoppes where Dora's girls once plied their profession, and laden the shaky wooden wharf with direct-import gifts. But there's no reason you have to go as a tourist. You can skulk down there, sans camera and in wrinkled jeans, scuff barefoot along the rocky shoreline, and give only one furtive glance toward Doc's house. Go down at dawn, at the "hour of the pearl," when the fishermen are just putting off from the docks, and you'll find that Cannery Row has not yet lost all its magic.

Monterey is easily reachable from points north or south (it's 330 miles north of Los Angeles, 130 miles south of San Francisco) via U.S. 101 and/or scenic Hwy. 1. By air, Wings West, West Air, Pacific Coast, and United Airlines serve the Monterey Peninsula.

WHAT'S DOING IN MONTEREY: There's so much to see and do in beautiful Monterey, and in the vicinity, that it's a good idea to make your first stop at the **Monterey Peninsula Chamber of Commerce** at 380 Alvarado St., between Franklin Street and Del Monte Avenue (tel. 408/649-1770). Here you can pick up maps and pamphlets, including several excellent free publications: *Monterey Peninsula Review, This Month on the Monterey Peninsula,* and guides to local restaurants and hotels, all chock-full of information about local attractions and facilities. Another free and comprehensive publication is *Key*—it's available at most hotels and shops.

In addition to exquisite natural beauty, the peninsula area offers a cornucopia of visitor attractions. Accommodations range from luxurious resorts to the charmingly quaint Carmel inns listed in a later section of this chapter.

The choice of fine restaurants is amazingly abundant—over 300 eateries serving Italian, Japanese, Mexican, German, Scandinavian, French, Filipino, Korean, Chinese, or whatever other cuisine your palate craves.

The sports-minded will find every kind of facility from golf and tennis to horseshoe throwing.

The Monterey Peninsula hosts the AT&T Pebble Beach National Pro-Am Golf Tournament in February, the Monterey Wine Festival in March, the Laguna Seca GT races in May, the Carmel Bach Festival in July, the oldest continuing Jazz Festival in September, and the Monterey Grand Prix Races in October.

And that's not to mention over a dozen movie theaters, parks, exciting annual events like rodeos, horse shows, golf tournaments, wine festivals, flea markets, fish fries, exhibitions by kilt-clad bagpipers, Sierra Club hikes, lectures, demonstrations, and dozens of art galleries. And then there are the major Monterey historical sights, detailed below.

PATH OF HISTORY: The Path of History is a delightful walking tour that takes in many historical landmarks. Depending on the intensity of your historical fervor, you might want to take in all of them, or do an abbreviated tour of those grouped in the area called **Monterey State Historic Park.** The park's offices are at 525 Polk St. (tel. 408/649-7118). An admission of $3.50 for adults, $2 for children 6 to 17; allows you entrance to all state buildings for one day. There is a single-building admission of $1 for adults, 50¢ for children 6 to 17. Highlights of the latter tour include:

Custom House (Custom House Plaza)

When the area of Monterey was under Mexican rule, custom duties collected here from foreign shipping formed the principal revenue source for the government. After inspection and payment of custom duties, a ship was permitted to trade on the California coast. The Custom House was the site where, on July 7, 1846, Commodore John Drake Sloat officially raised the United States flag. His action brought 600,000 square miles, including California, under the stewardship of the American government.

The north end of the Custom House, built about 1827, is the oldest part of the structure. In 1841 work was started to enlarge it, and by early 1846 it had been completed. The building was abandoned as a Custom House in about 1867 because, by then, San Francisco had become California's major port. Open from 10 a.m. to 5 p.m. March to October, till 4 p.m. the rest of the year.

Casa del Oro (corner of Scott and Olivier Streets)

This two-story adobe was built in the 1840s when it was used as a warehouse, barracks, and hospital quarters for American seamen left at the port under consular care. In 1849 the building was leased to Joseph Boston and Company, a general store. The reason it's called Casa del Oro (house of gold) is that miners stored their treasures in an iron safe here in Gold Rush days—or so rumor has it.

Today it is owned by the state and is preserved as a general store, stocked with burlap sacks full of coffee and beans, milk cans, ribbons, old tools, fabrics, dinnerware, and canisters of grains, noodles, etc. The building retains its original character and the merchandise is what could have been purchased in the mid-19th century. Open Wednesday to Saturday from 10 a.m. to 5 p.m., Sunday from noon to 5 p.m.

California's First Theater (corner of Scott and Pacific Streets)

California owes its first theater to Jack Swan, an English sailor of Scottish ancestry who settled in Monterey in 1843. Swan built the structure in 1846 as a boarding house and tavern. In 1847 the first stage performance was given by the soldiers of the New York Volunteer Regiment, using blankets as curtains, barrels and boards as benches.

The building was given to the State for preservation in 1906, and the original structure remains, looking much the same today as in earlier times. The tavern is still operating, and the theater is open for viewing Wednesday through Sunday from 11:30 a.m. to 5 p.m. (it's open daily during the summer). The Troupers of the Gold Coast put on authentic 19th-century melodramas every Friday and Saturday night year-round (except Christmas week), adding Wednesday

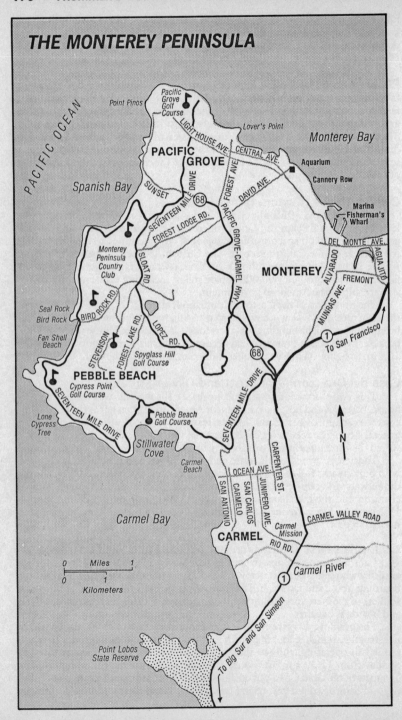

THE MONTEREY PENINSULA

PACIFIC OCEAN

Point Pinos

Pacific Grove Golf Course

LIGHTHOUSE AVE.

Lover's Point

Monterey Bay

PACIFIC GROVE

CENTRAL AVE.

Aquarium

Cannery Row

Spanish Bay

SUNSET

FOREST AVE.

DAVID AVE.

Marina
Fisherman's Wharf

SEVENTEEN MILE DRIVE

PACIFIC GROVE DRIVE

FOREST LODGE RD.

68

PACIFIC GROVE-CARMEL HWY.

DEL MONTE AVE.

AGUA JITO

MONTEREY

ALVARADO

FREMONT

Monterey Peninsula Country Club

SLOAT RD.

MUNRAS AVE.

Seal Rock
Bird Rock

BIRD ROCK RD.

FOREST LAKE RD.

LOPEZ RD.

1

To San Francisco

Fan Shell Beach

STEVENSON

Spyglass Hill Golf Course

68

PEBBLE BEACH

SEVENTEEN MILE DRIVE

Cypress Point Golf Course

SEVENTEEN MILE DRIVE

N

Lone Cypress Tree

Pebble Beach Golf Course

Stillwater Cove

CARPENTER ST.

Carmel Beach

OCEAN AVE.

CARMEL VALLEY ROAD

Carmel Bay

SAN ANTONIO

CARMELO

SAN CARLOS

JUNIPERO AVE.

Carmel Mission

RIO RD.

CARMEL

0   Miles   1

0   1

Kilometers

1

Carmel River

Point Lobos State Reserve

To Big Sur and San Simeon

and Thursday performances in July and August. The curtain goes up at 8 p.m. on all show nights.

The cost is $7 for adults, $6 for seniors (over 60), and $5 for teens and younger. It's a great night out (tel. 408/375-4916 after 1 p.m. Wednesday through Saturday).

Cooper-Molera Adobe (Corner of Polk and Munras Streets)

The Cooper-Molera adobe, a 2½-acre complex, was built in the 1830s by John Rogers Cooper. It was willed to the National Trust for Historic Preservation by Cooper's granddaughter, Frances Molera. Captain John Rogers Cooper was a dealer in hides, tallow, sea otter pelts, and general merchandise. He was the half-brother of Thomas Larkin. As Cooper became increasingly wealthy from his trading operations, he expanded his one-story home to a two-story structure, erected large barns, and enclosed the complex with a high shingle-capped adobe wall. More than any of the other historic sites, the Cooper-Molera adobe typifies life in early California, from the live-in kitchen to the barnyard animals. The adobe is open daily except Wednesday. March to October, tours are given on the hour (except 1 p.m.) from 10 a.m. to 5 p.m., to 4 p.m. the rest of the year.

Casa Sobranes (336 Pacific St.)

This adobe house was built in 1830 by Don José Rafael Estrada, the warden of the Custom House, for his bride, Concepción Malarín. It's a Mediterranean-style house, with a cantilevered balcony and tile roof. The house is completely furnished, and decorated with an extensive collection of art by local artists. It can be visited by tour only, except Thursday, offered on the hour from 10 a.m. to 4 p.m. (except 1 p.m.) in winter, till 5 p.m. March to October.

Larkin House (510 Calle Principal at Jefferson Street)

Built in 1834, this balconied two-story adobe was the home of Thomas Oliver Larkin, who served as U.S. consul to Mexico from 1843 to 1846. The house also served as the consular office. Furnished in the style of the period with many original pieces, Larkin House is a museum of architecture and Monterey life. Next door is the house used by William Tecumseh Sherman; it now contains a museum depicting the roles of the two men in California history. A 35-minute guided tour is offered throughout the day every hour on the hour (except noon) from 10 a.m. to 5 p.m. March to October, to 4 p.m. the rest of the year; closed Tuesday. The last tour begins one hour before closing.

Stevenson House (530 Houston St.)

The original portion of this two-story home dates to the late 1830s when it was the home of Don Rafael Gonzales, first administrator of Customs of Alta California. In 1856 a French pioneer, Juan Giradin, and his wife became the owners. They made some additions and rented spare bedrooms to roomers, one of whom was Robert Louis Stevenson (he occupied a second-floor room during the autumn of 1879). He had come from Scotland to persuade Fanny Osbourne to marry him (she did). While here he wrote *The Old Pacific Capital,* an account of Monterey in the 1870s. Poor, unknown, and in frail health, he was cared for by Jules Simoneau, in whose restaurant he had his one full meal of the day. The building has been restored to its period look, and several rooms are devoted to Stevenson memorabilia. In an upstairs children's bedroom, it has been said that a ghostly spirit is sometimes seen, which makes for an additional point of interest.

Open from 10 a.m. to 5 p.m. March to October, till 4 p.m. the rest of the year; tours are offered every hour on the hour (except noon). The last tour begins one hour before closing. Closed Wednesday.

The Pacific House (Custom House Plaza)

Built in 1847, Pacific House was first used for army offices and to store military supplies. Army horses were corralled behind the building, and this was a popular spot for Sunday bull and bear fights. Later it housed small stores, served as a public tavern, a courtroom, county clerk's office, newspaper office, law offices, a church—even a ballroom where a temperance society called the Dashaways held dances.

The Jacks family bought the property in 1880 and maintained the premises until 1954, when Miss Margaret Jacks made a gift of the historic building to the state. The first floor houses a museum of California history, the second floor an extensive collection of American Indian artifacts plus a few Mexican Indian and Eskimo pieces. Open from 10 a.m. to 5 p.m. March to October, till 4 p.m. the rest of the year.

Colton Hall (522 Pacific St.)

Named for the Rev. Walter Colton, U.S. Navy chaplain who impaneled California's first jury, co-founded the state's first newspaper, and built its first public building, Colton Hall was planned as the town hall and public school. It was the scene of California's constitutional congress in 1849, when the constitution was written and the great seal of the state designed. There's a museum upstairs, and Old Monterey Jail adjoins, its grim cell walls still marked with prisoner's scribblings. Open daily from 10 a.m. to 5 p.m.

Serra Landing Site (just south of Monterey Presidio on Pacific Street)

This is the site where Sebastian Vizcaino landed in 1602, and where, in 1770, Father Serra and Don Gaspar de Portola founded Monterey, future capital and port of entry of California.

From here you're in a good position to proceed to—

CANNERY ROW: Entering Cannery Row, you still drive under the covered conveyor belts that once carried tinned fish from cannery to warehouse. But the corrugated-steel warehouses, vacated by factories, have been renovated and now house restaurants, boutiques, art galleries, antique shops, and other browsables. There's even free tasting of wine from the **Bargetto Winery** at 702 Cannery Row (tel. 408/373-4053).

The best way to explore the Cannery is simply to start at one end and meander along. There are a few complexes of shops, etc. One such is the **Monterey Canning Company** at 700 Cannery Row, which contains the Bargetto Winery; stop in for free wine tasting. At no. 625 is **Cannery Row Square** (three restaurants and about 15 shops). The **Monterey Cannery** at no. 700 houses the **Historical Wax Museum** (tel. 408/375-3770), its exhibits including such California heroes as Thomas Oliver Larkin, John Charles Frémont, Juan Rodriguez Cabrillo, and Junipero Serra. Admission is $3.95 for adults, $2.95 for children over 12, (under 12, free with an adult); open daily from 9 a.m. to 8 p.m.

Whatever else you may want to see in Monterey, don't miss the **Monterey Bay Aquarium** at the west end of Cannery Row, 886 Cannery Row (tel. 408/375-3333). This is the largest exhibit aquarium in the nation. It is the $50-million creation financed by David Packard at the behest of four local marine biologists, including his daughter, brought up on the criteria of Ed (Doc) Ricketts, the marine biologist and prototype for "Doc" in Steinbeck's *Cannery Row*.

Statistics alone simply do not do justice to this spectacular living gallery of the sea. The building is on the site of the old Hovden sardine cannery and houses an astounding display of more than 5,000 sea creatures that literally surround you. You step into an enchanted new world at the bottom of a three-story kelp forest housed in an acrylic-windowed tank holding over 300,000 gallons of sea water with the seaweed waving gently as though moved by tidal surges. Sit down and quietly watch the hundreds of creatures slowly moving back and forth—the greenlings, sand sharks, jacksmelts, rockfish—and you feel like a scuba-diver in an underwater cathedral. And then there are the sea otters to see, the delightful clowns of the aquarium including the four orphans rescued by the staff. Feeding time for the otters is an acrobatic event you don't want to miss.

There are exhibits of coastal streams, tidal pools, a beach with sea birds that inhabit the salt marsh and sandy shore, and even a touching pool where you can stroke a living bat ray or a sea star.

The sea life you see here abounds in Monterey Bay and the Pacific. The aquarium borders on the Monterey Canyon, one of the largest submarine canyons in the world—wider and deeper than the Grand Canyon. It is this canyon which provides the nutrients to fuel the food chain in and around Monterey Bay and which you will see, in part, at the aquarium.

There's much to see, so allow two to three hours for your visit. The aquarium is designed as a self-guided tour, but there are guides to help you throughout. There is a café on the premises for lunch since you cannot bring in food or beverages.

The aquarium is open daily (except Christmas) from 10 a.m. to 6 p.m. Admission is $8 for adults, $6 for seniors over 65 and students, and $4 for children 3 to 12 years. Children under 3 are admitted free.

FISHERMAN'S WHARF: Like San Francisco, Monterey has not only a Cannery, but also a Fisherman's Wharf. This one, near the old Custom House, is lined with craft shops, boating and fishing operations, fish markets, and seafood restaurants.

If you want to do more than stroll, **Princess Monterey Cruises** (tel. 408/372-2628), at the end of the wharf, runs 30-minute bay pleasure cruises on fishing-party boats (no fishing on these trips). They depart from noon to 7 or 8 p.m. daily during summer. Everyone pays $2.50 (infants under 6 months pay $1.50 for insurance purposes). In winter, they also have 1½-hour whale-watching cruises (best times are December to February): $10 per person.

If, on the other hand, you'd like to do some fishing, **Sam's Fishing Fleet** has four fishing boats available, and they've been serving Monterey fisherfolk since 1914. Diesel-powered fishing boats, with deck lounges, depart at 7:30 a.m. weekdays, at 6:30 a.m. on weekends. Adults pay $22; children under 12, $14; weekends and holidays it's $24 and $15 respectively. Tackle can be rented and bait is free. Bring lunch and make reservations. And dress warmly. To reserve, call 408/372-0577.

There are quite a few shops selling candles, shells, and suchlike to browse in on the wharf.

Wharf Picnic

If you get hungry, the choice ranges from a paper cup of fresh shrimp to a full restaurant meal. To put together a picnic lunch (a bench on the wharf offers a great view), head for the **Little Gourmet Shop,** no. 20 (it's off to the right, a bit out of view), specializing in sandwiches to go, stuffed with imported meats and cheeses, on fresh sourdough bread or pita. You can also get salads and small bottles of wine here, as well as Greek pastries.

WHERE TO STAY: While the Monterey Bay Aquarium heads Cannery Row, a genteel gloved hand opens the door to the new and very grand **Monterey Plaza Hotel** at the opposite end of the Row, 400 Cannery Row, Monterey, CA 93940 (tel. 408/646-1700; or toll free 800/631-1339, 800/334-3999 in California). The hotel overlooks Monterey Bay and the Pacific and is just a short picturesque stroll to the Aquarium. This is a $60-million resort with 290 luxury-size rooms and suites that showcase the surrounding sea.

Anticipate the grand and you'll find it here. Beds are not king-size, but emperor-size. Rooms are furnished in natural wood tones, dark leathers, and designer fabrics in tones which vary from room to room. Armoires conceal the TV, desk, and drawers. As you might expect, bathrooms have telephones, his and hers bathrobes, extra-thick towels. Terraces overlook the bay and its spectacular sunsets.

The hotel provides a recreation director, as well as a concierge, and can arrange entry to several local golf clubs, tennis courts, sightseeing, and transportation as well as the usual services. Singles and doubles are $130 to $200; suites, $300 to $850; $25 for each extra person.

The hotel's restaurant, Delfino's, features northern Italian cuisine, of the Emilia-Romagna region. Delfino's conveys a feeling of old-world elegance: the wide polished ceiling beams, cloth-covered banquettes with dolphin prints, linen at lunch, wine-leather chairs with light walnut wood. The menu is à la carte and dinner entrees range from $13 to $26 for such delectables as homemade pastas to magnificent medallions of veal. With salad, and perhaps wine, dinner for two will probably be between $80 and $120. Let's just say that the food is as superior as the service, and all is graced by the sweeping view of the bay and its inhabitants. Delfino's is open daily from 7 a.m. to 11 for breakfast, noon to 2:30 p.m. for lunch, and 6 to 10 p.m. for dinner. On Friday and Saturday evening the restaurant is open to 10:30 p.m. On Sunday, Delfino's has a superb champagne buffet brunch from 10:30 a.m. to 2:30 p.m. for $18.50. Reservations are always advised for dinner.

Monterey Bay Inn, 242 Cannery Row, Monterey, CA 93940 (tel. 408/ 373-6242, or toll free 800/424-6242 California), is directly on Monterey Bay perched above the water, on the beach, at the park. And it provides special facilities for scuba-divers, if you're geared for it.

The inn has 47 spacious rooms surrounding an atrium. Each is elegantly decorated in coral, bone, and seafoam-green fabrics with light-toned woods. Photographs of the area decorate the walls to give the rooms a feeling of the sea and a bit of Monterey history. Apart from the usual amenities, each room also has a dry bar and refrigerator, handy full-length mirrors on the sliding closet doors, and luxurious terrycloth robes (for the asking). A hot tub is conveniently located at the atrium terrace on the 4th floor. There's a sauna in the workout room. The adjacent park affords access to the beach for scuba divers and beach loafers.

Single and double rooms range from $105 to $155, depending on the view; suites run $155 to $175. All rates include continental breakfast and use of the health club. Parking is conveniently located beneath the inn.

An alternative luxury accommodation in Monterey is the **Old Monterey Inn,** 500 Martin St. (off Pacific), Monterey, CA 93940 (tel. 408/375-8284). Ann and Gene Swett have turned their old family home into a country inn, and they've done a masterful job of it. The ten rooms have lyrical names like Dovecote, Madrigal, and Pinecrest. All have garden views, private baths, and beds with goose-down comforters and pillows. They're charmingly furnished, each in unique fashion, and special touches include fresh flowers, a sachet under your pillow, good soaps, books and magazines to read, and an information packet about local attractions. You can even get a picnic basket for a trip to Point Lobos or Big Sur. Seven of the rooms have wood-burning fireplaces, and one has a private patio. The baths are supplied with deodorants, toothpaste, shampoo, bath oil, etc.—even electric hair dryers and curlers.

At 5 p.m. daily guests can relax in the cozy living room before a blazing fireplace and partake of complimentary sherry, cheese, and crackers. Breakfast, included in the rates, is served in a delightful dining room wherein another fireplace, although you can also have it in your room or in the garden (weather permitting). It's quite a breakfast: fruit, juice, and fresh-baked breads—perhaps popovers, cheese rolls, croissants, banana or strawberry muffins, pumpkin bread, or danish pastries—with whipped sweet butter and homemade jams, and tea or coffee. On sunny days guests can loll about in hammocks in the garden and enjoy tea and cookies in the afternoon.

If you'd like to stay at the Old Monterey Inn, reserve far in advance. Rates are $140 to $210 for single or double occupancy. The secluded Garden Cottage is $220.

In a class by itself on 17-Mile Drive is the luxurious **Lodge at Pebble Beach,** Pebble Beach, CA 93953 (tel. 408/624-3811), of which the Pebble Beach Golf Links Spyglass Hill Golf Course is part. Though a long stay here could wreak havoc on your budget, you might want to spend a few nights at these posh digs while seeing the Carmel/Monterey area. In addition to the golf course, there's a beach, a heated swimming pool and sauna, fishing, 14 tennis courts, horseback-riding facilities, and 34 miles of bridle and hiking paths. Of course, the rooms are fitted out with every possible amenity; many even have wood-burning fireplaces. Single or double accommodations cost $215 to $280.

About the famous Pebble Beach Golf Links—if you're a guest at the lodge and want to play 18, you're given priority in booking tee time. The cost of a round is $115 for guests, $150 for others.

If you can't stay, you might at least want to dine at the lodge's posh French restaurant, Club XIX (tel. 408/625-8519). It's extremely elegant, with oak-paneled walls, burgundy and forest green carpeting and tablecloths, and fresh flowers in silver vases at every table. During the day you'll enjoy views of the golf course and bay; at night it's candlelit and romantic. A dinner at Club XIX might begin with an appetizer of foie gras with truffles or a Caesar salad for two, followed perhaps by a soup called veloute Bongo-Bongo—a creamy blend of oysters, spinach, herbs, and cognac. For an entree you might select stuffed quail in a potato nest with brandy sauce, or poached Monterey salmon, and finish off the feast with a soufflé Grand Marnier. If you're averse to spending $18 to $33 for an entree, come at lunch when lighter dishes are a more reasonable $8 to $14. Club XIX is open daily for lunch from 11:30 a.m. to 4:30 p.m., for dinner from 6:30 to 10 p.m. Reservations are advised.

Other dining choices at The Lodge include the exquisite Cypress Room, which overlooks the golf course, and the clubby Tap Room with a memorial wall dedicated to golfers and their game.

The Lodge has opened the **Inn at Spanish Bay.** The Inn is a deluxe 270-room full-facility resort alongside the Links at Spanish Bay designed by Tom Watson and Robert Trent Jones, Jr.

There is no question that bargains are few and far between in a popular haven for tourists, but one or two can be found in Monterey if you plan in advance and don't pick weekends such as that of the Grand Prix or the Monterey Jazz Festival.

Truly luxurious accommodations at a reasonable rate are what you'll find at the **Way Station,** 1200 Olmsted Rd., Monterey, CA 93940 (tel. 408/372-2945), just off Hwy. 68. This attractive redwood motel, set among beautifully landscaped pines and well-groomed grounds, is conveniently situated near the Monterey airport, but not a sound of air traffic interferes with your comfort. The guest rooms convey the feeling of a town house rather than a motel. Rooms are done in tones of brown or blue, and the carpeting is plush with an inset of beige. Handsome historical prints give a decorator touch. High ceilings add to the luxurious feeling of spaciousness. At one corner of the room there is a circular table and above, a conveniently placed chandelier. Comfortable leather chairs are on wheels. Several rooms have balconies with sliding doors and screens, comfortable for lounging; others have bay windows facing the beautiful landscaping. Rates are $75 for singles, $88 for doubles, $110 for the luxury suites. Each additional person pays $10.

Adjoining the Way Station is Papa's Restaurant. Entry is past the bar into a handsomely proportioned room with high, beamed ceilings, ceiling fans, huge potted plants, and carpeting to match the landscape. Booths are separated by frosted-glass panels with designs of the stagecoach of early California. Service is friendly and attentive. Touches like the thin slice of lemon in the glass of water reflect the thought given to the preparation and presentation of the food.

The quantity of the food is in keeping with the proportions of the room—very large and tastefully done. Breakfast is served all day and includes such toothsome dishes as carabaccia (poached eggs with vegetables) for $6 or pancakes covered with fresh fruit at $4.50. The salad bar has an exceptionally large number of choices and includes hot baguettes or sourdough bread, all for $5. But save yourself for dinner. Specialties of the house are veal and pasta. Seafood specials change daily. If you have a taste for Italian, try the chicken parmigiana-breast baked and topped with mozzarella at $12.95, or the tortellini with Alfredo sauce for $13.25. The daily pasta special is worth asking your server about. If the dinner hasn't yet left you breathless, top it off with the homemade cheesecake, a caloric joy, with blueberry or strawberry sauce. Papa's also has a fine selection of California and Italian wines, some by the glass. The restaurant is open daily from 7 a.m. to 11 p.m.

Need I remind you of **Motel 6,** 2124 Fremont St., Monterey, CA 93940 (tel. 408/646-8585), where rates are $29.95. Each additional adult is $6. TV is included, local calls are free. Reservations for summer months should be made at least six months in advance.

WHERE TO DINE: There are any number of places for dining in Monterey itself, not the least of which are **Delfino's** in the Monterey Plaza Hotel, **Club XIX** or the **Tap Room** at Pebble Beach, and **Papa's** at the Way Station (much more moderate in price). Each is described above.

On Cannery Row, a good dining choice is the **Whaling Station Inn,** 763 Wave St., between Prescott and Irving Avenue (tel. 408/373-3778). It's entered via a rustic, wicker-furnished cocktail area, with barnwood walls and potted ferns. The interior is in the same motif as the cocktail lounge, but an added elegance is achieved by white taper candles in wrought-iron holders, white linen tablecloths, and red napkins wound in the drinking glasses. The entire effect is warm and homey, complete with cluttery shelves of knickknacks.

All entrees include artichoke vinaigrette, soup, salad, and a fresh vegetable. Choices range from roast rack of lamb Dijon to medallions of beef to veal chop to a variety of fresh fish broiled over mesquite charcoal, for $17 to $33. Desserts prepared by the pastry chef are displayed in all their tempting splendor; try a homemade cannoli.

The Whaling Station is open daily from 5 to 10 p.m. Reservations advised.

GUIDED TOURS: One of the easiest and most enjoyable ways to see Monterey is to be taken around. **Steinbeck Country Tours** (tel. 408/625-5107) without a doubt provides one of the most popular tours of the area. The tour encompasses the entire Monterey Peninsula and takes three to four hours. You are picked up at your local hotel (in Monterey, Pebble Beach, Carmel, or Pacific Grove) and taken on an enjoyable, informative trip around the peninsula, including the original 17-Mile Drive, Cannery Row, Pacific Grove, and Carmel.

Steinbeck Country Tours also has regularly scheduled tours from the Monterey Peninsula to Hearst Castle. The castle tour via Big Sur is an all-day affair leaving at 8 a.m., returning at 6:30 p.m., and including a wine tasting at a local vineyard.

For reservations with Steinbeck Country Tours, call two to three days in advance or ask the guest representative at your hotel to make reservations. The cost of the Monterey Tour is $20, and well worth the price. The Hearst Castle Tour is $45 including the $10 entrance fee.

THE 17-MILE DRIVE: The whole Carmel–Pacific Grove–Monterey area, not to mention the breathtaking coast along Rte. 1, is so very scenic that the 17-Mile Drive may seem superfluous. But if you can't get enough of a good thing—and I can't—don't miss it. The 17-Mile Drive is situated in the Del Monte forest, and costs $7 per car. This private road, famous for magnificent landscapes and seascapes, can be entered from any of three gates. Most convenient from town is the Hwy. 1 Gate (take Munras Avenue to Hwy. 1). When you pay your toll, you'll be given a map that points out 26 highlights along the way, including several picnic areas, six golf courses, the famous **Lone Pine,** and **Seal and Bird Rocks,** where you can see countless gulls, cormorants, and other offshore birds, as well as offshore herds of seals and sea lions.

GOLF AROUND THE PENINSULA: Monterey is also the gateway to the excitingly beautiful Monterey Peninsula—Northern California's playland for golfers. In the area surrounding the city, there are sea views and scenic drives, ghostly cypress trees, and Seal Rocks. But most of all, there are golf courses. The famed **Pebble Beach Golf Links** is here, on which the AT&T National Pro-Amateur Golf Tourney is held every February.

Of the many golf courses on the Monterey Peninsula and nearby areas, four are open to the public: **Laguna Seca, Pacific Grove, Rancho Canada,** and **Del Monte.** Greens fees range from about $15 to $30 (plus cart) for 18 holes.

2. PACIFIC GROVE

The best-kept secret on the Monterey Peninsula is the little town of Pacific Grove. It occupies the northwest corner of the peninsula, between Monterey and Pebble Beach. The town got its start in the 1870s as a seaside resort for the Methodist Retreat Association of San Francisco. Tents would spring up in the summer, and church meetings would be held under the pines that gave the town its name. Before long, people started to settle in permanently; Pacific Grove has lots of houses that date from the late 19th century.

This quaint little town is nicknamed "Butterfly Town, U.S.A." The name comes from the **Monarch butterflies** that congregate by the thousands in groves of Monterey pines every winter. They come from as far away as Alaska to cling to the trees. One spot in town famous for its "butterfly trees"—is George Washington Park, at Pine Avenue and Alder Street. Pacific Grove's Butterfly Parade every October welcomes the Monarchs; the town even imposes a $500 fine on anyone caught "molesting butterflies."

Pacific Grove has other draws besides the butterflies. The oldest working lighthouse on the West Coast is here—**Point Pinos Lighthouse,** at the northwest point of the peninsula on Ocean View Boulevard. It dates from 1855, when Pacific Grove was little more than a pine forest.

Then there's **Marine Gardens Park,** a stretch of shoreline along Ocean View Boulevard on Monterey Bay and the Pacific. It's renowned not only for its gorgeous flowers but also for its tidepool seaweed beds.

Your first stop should be the **Pacific Grove Chamber of Commerce** at the corner of Forest and Central Avenues (tel. 408/373-3304). The friendly folks there can give you lots of information on Pacific Grove and its points of interest. (If you want to write in advance of your trip, write to P.O. Box 167, Pacific Grove, CA 93950.)

WHERE TO STAY: If you want to live, and not just see, the Victorian charm of Pacific Grove and the Monterey Peninsula, then don't miss the **Gosby House,** 643 Lighthouse Ave. (three blocks from Forest Avenue), Pacific Grove, CA 93950 (tel. 408/375-1287, or toll free 800/342-4888). It's one of the older houses in town, built by cobbler J. F. Gosby in the 1870s as a boarding house for Methodist ministers who came to town every summer for the Christian conferences.

It's a delightful place, with its dining room and parlor where a multitude of teddies reside and where guests congregate for breakfast in the morning and wine in the evening, getting a chance to relax and chat with strangers who rapidly become friends. The rooms—22 of them—are charmingly and individually decorated, with floral-print wallpapers, quilted beds, lacy pillows, and antique furnishings. Nine of the rooms have fireplaces; all but two have private bathrooms with tub or shower. There are no TVs here to break your peace and quiet, but you'll find that you don't miss them at all.

Breakfast every morning is included in the price of your room. There's always lots to choose from—fresh hot muffins and breads, egg dishes, cereals, yogurt, granola, fruits and juices, coffee and tea. Each evening you can join other guests for a glass of wine or sherry and a nibble or two before you go off to enjoy one of the Monterey Peninsula's fine restaurants. And for late-night snackers, there's milk and cookies before bedtime.

Rooms at the Gosby House cost $90 to $135, single or double. No smoking, please.

The Gosby House has a sister inn in Pacific Grove owned by the same chain—the **Green Gables Inn,** 104 Fifth Ave. (off Ocean Boulevard), Pacific Grove, CA 93950 (tel. 408/375-2095, or toll free 800/841-5252). Until a few years back it was the home of innkeepers/owners Roger and Sally Post, who opened their little gem to visitors in summer. Now it's a full-fledged inn, with eleven rooms. There are some rooms in the carriage houses out back, all with private baths. In the main house, a dainty Queen Anne, there's a suite with private bath; the other rooms share two immaculate bathrooms. Each of the rooms is individually decorated, and each is charming. The Green Gables' parlor is a delight; there's even an antique carousel horse on display. As at the Gosby House, there's a large breakfast spread every morning, and wine in the afternoon.

Rooms at the Green Gables cost $100 to $155, single or double, including breakfast, afternoon wine, tea, and hors d'oeuvres. The Green Gables requests that their guests not smoke in the house.

Among the architectural charms of Pacific Grove is a stately and beautifully renovated 1904 mansion, the **Pacific Grove Inn,** 581 Pine Ave. (at Forest), Pacific Grove, CA 93950 (tel. 408/375-2825). This handsome structure is just two blocks from historic Main Street and five blocks from the beach. The inn has ten elegant and charming rooms, all quite light and airy (with heavier Victorian touches), including two suites. Each has contemporary amenities including a private bath, TV, phone, and queen- or king-size beds. The proprietors are most helpful and gracious, and can supply you with a wealth of local architectural and historical data.

Room rates range from $50 to $80; suites are $90 and $100. A full, homemade buffet breakfast is $4.50.

WHERE TO DINE: What more can you ask of a restaurant than good food, a well-appointed bar, good service, moderate prices, daily hours, a handsome setting, and a delightful view. **The Tinnery** in Pacific Grove has them all at 631 Ocean View Blvd. (tel. 408/646-1040). The contemporary interior decor is sea gray with wood paneling, a perfect complement to the bay. Large black-and-white photographs of cannery operations are attractive reminders of one segment of Monterey's past. Indirect track and recessed lighting, banks of white mums dividing the dining rooms, ceiling fans, ficus trees, light-wood chairs, and a large fireplace all add to the welcome feeling of warmth in the Tinnery. A large expanse of window affords a broad view of Lovers Point Park and Monterey Bay. The roomy restaurant lounge, set apart from the main dining room, affords a comfortable spot for cocktails before dinner, and also has a limited menu for late dining until 1 a.m. There is live entertainment nightly until 1 a.m.

The Tinnery serves breakfast from 8 to 11 a.m. The crêpes Normandy—French pancakes with apples, cream, and brandy—while not your usual breakfast fare, are delicious.

Lunch is served from 11 a.m. to 5 p.m. and dinner from 5 to 11 p.m. Choices range from a delicious selection of sandwiches and burgers, salads and soups, at $4.50 to $8.95, to somewhat grander fare such as teriyaki beef kebab or Monterey Bay snapper for $10.95.

Dinner entrees are sufficiently varied to satisfy whatever your tastes may be. The Tinnery serves a superior prime rib for $15.95 and the Chinese chicken with snow peas and ginger sauce at $9.95 is a delicious change from the usual. All dinners are served with salad, vegetables, garnishes, and fresh baked bread. It's one of the best buys in town. And to add to the pleasure of your meal, there's a good selection of California wines. The Tinnery also has a children's menu for breakfast ($3.50), lunch ($4.50), and dinner ($4.50).

And when you leave the Tinnery after breakfast or lunch, turn left and walk down (or drive if you must) about 100 feet. Bring your camera. Directly below the narrow park bordering Ocean View Boulevard you'll see dozens of harbor seals perched on the rocks being viewed by you and by the black cormorants inhabiting the bayfront.

For another terrific dinner in Pacific Grove, try **Fandango,** 223 17th St., off Lighthouse Avenue (tel. 408/373-0588), just a short walk from the Gosby House. The restaurant is located in a long, thin building perpendicular to the street. Inside there are several rooms, all slightly different, all very pleasant, whether you choose to be seated in the dining room with fresh flowers and fireside dining, or in the terrace room with its delicate fragrances from the wood grill. The restaurant features a new menu with an excellent selection of provincial Mediterranean specialties. Appetizers can be ordered à la carte, beginning with a plate of assorted tapas for $3. Two very popular entrees you don't want to overlook include the seafood paella, long a specialty of the house, and the authentic North African couscous. The recipe for the couscous has been in the Bain family (the new and very gracious owners/operators) for 150 years, and they import the spices to maintain the authenticity of the dish. Among the other excellent Mediterranean dishes are the cassoulet maison, the canneloni niçoise, and the Greek-style lamb shank. There is also a good choice of pasta and fresh seafood dishes. Fandango has a very nice international wine list from which to choose, and their desserts are out of this world. The list begins with a lovely caramel custard or chocolate mousse and graduates in calorie count up to more spectacular choices including a Grand Marnier soufflé and profiteroles.

Dinner entrees range from $11.95 to $17.95. A prix-fixe dinner for $20.95 includes tapas, soup or green salad, and a choice of paella, couscous, cassoulet, or lamb shank, plus dessert. The Fandango also serves lunch (light entrees and sandwiches for $5 to $10) and Sunday brunch. The restaurant is open Monday through Saturday from 11 a.m. to 2 p.m. and 5 to 10 p.m., on Sunday from 9 a.m. to 2:30 p.m. There's plenty of free parking (a real plus). Reservations are advised.

3. CARMEL

The serene beauty of Carmel, a forest village encircled by mountains and rolling hills, makes it a must on every California visitor's itinerary. White beaches, gnarled cypress trees, magnificent landscapes and seascapes are the background for a sleepy village of narrow streets, quaint storybook houses, charming hostelries, and cozy restaurants. It's hard to imagine a more romantic setting.

Since the turn of the century the town has been a haven for artists and writers (galleries abound), and aesthetic considerations carry so much weight in the community that you might have difficulty identifying gas stations under their wooden eaves. Most of the houses don't even have street numbers, and according to local regulations large, gaudy, or illuminated retail signs in public places "shall not be suffered, permitted, allowed to be placed, erected or maintained." Nor can a tree be removed without specific permission from the city council, which is often not granted: a gladdening sight are the old trees smack in the middle of roads and in other unlikely places.

This is also a village of shops—more than 600 of them, mostly little boutiques dispensing such wares as basketry, pottery, imported goods, etc.

A yearly attraction is the annual **Bach Festival** in July, which brings lovers of baroque music from far and wide. For ticket information (you must purchase in advance), write to Carmel Bach Festival, P.O. Box 575, Carmel, CA 93921; or phone 408/624-1521.

For more information on this and other Carmel happenings, stop by the **Carmel Business Association,** on the second floor of Vandervort Court, on San Carlos between Ocean and 7th (tel. 408/624-2522); pick up maps, brochures, and the free publications mentioned in the Monterey section. It's open weekdays from 9:30 a.m. to 4 p.m. At any newsstand you can also get a copy of the *Carmel Pine Cone,* a weekly newsletter that has been keeping Carmel residents informed about local events for well over half a century.

There's also a **Tourist Information Center** at Mission Patio, Mission between 5th and 6th, P.O. Box 7430, Carmel, CA 93921 (tel. 408/624-1711) which can help you find accommodations. They're open from 9 a.m. to 4 p.m. Monday through Friday.

WHAT TO DO AND SEE: Carmel's principal village attractions (apart from its former mayor, Clint "Make my day" Eastwood) are along Ocean Avenue and its side streets between Junipero and San Antonio Avenues. Begin your explorations on Ocean at Junipero at the multilevel mall complex of gourmet and cheese shops, craft stores, restaurants, etc., called **Carmel Plaza,** and continue meandering along Ocean, stopping at some of the many galleries and shops. And speaking of shops, the most unique of shopping complexes is—

The Barnyard

Opened at the end of 1976, the Barnyard, on Hwy. 1, off Carmel Valley Road, is a cluster of 60 or so shops and restaurants housed in authentic early California barns in a landscaped setting. There's no major department store, but there is a windmill and a water tank; it's quaint Carmel's version of a shopping mall, an old-fashioned town where you can shop in fresh air rather than air-conditioned comfort.

Hub of the Barnyard is the **Thunderbird Bookshop** (tel. 408/624-1803), where you can browse through the 50,000 books for sale while you're eating—just be careful with the gravy. Lunch is $4 to $6; dinner, $7 to $14. Specialties are roast beef, fish, and great popovers. Lunch is served from 11 a.m. to 3:30 p.m., dinner from 5:30 to 8 p.m.

Biblical Garden

While you're in town, take a stroll through the Biblical Garden of the Church of the Wayfarer on Lincoln and Seventh Avenues. It's the second-oldest church in Carmel, dating back to 1904. The garden contains plants and trees mentioned in the Bible and indigenous to the Holy Land. Stepping stones lead to various flora, all of which are labeled as to biblical context, beginning with the apple tree—the tree of knowledge of good and evil forbidden to Adam and Eve. An interesting note from the Garden Committee brochure: some biblical authorities insist the forbidden fruit was actually the apricot!

Carmel Mission

Continuing on subjects spiritual, Carmel also houses the **Mission San Carlos Borromeo,** at Rio Road and Lasuen Drive. This mission is notable as the burial place of Father Junipero Serra, who founded it in 1770. The present stone church, with its gracefully curving walls, catenary arch, and Moorish bell tower, was begun in 1793. Its walls are covered with a lime plaster made of burnt seashells.

In the cemetery beside the church 3,000 Native Americans are buried, their graves decorated with seashells. Other interesting features include the old mission kitchen, the first library in California, the high altar, beautiful flower gardens, the sarcophagus depicting Father Serra recumbent in death, the cell where he died, and the silver altar service he used.

This is one of the largest and most interesting of the California missions. It's open to visitors daily from 9:30 a.m. to 4:30 p.m., on Sunday from 10:30 a.m.

WHERE TO STAY: Carmel boasts one of the highest rated resort hotels in the country, **Quail Lodge,** 8205 Valley Greens Dr. (off Carmel Valley Road), Carmel, CA 93923 (tel. 408/624-1581, or toll free 800/538-9516, 800/682-9303 in California). In a pastoral setting on 250 acres of sparkling lakes, woodlands, and meadows, Quail Lodge offers all the facilities of the prestigious Carmel Valley Golf and Country Club to its guests. In addition to the 18-hole golf course and clubhouse, amenities include four tennis courts, two swimming pools, bicycle rental, and a sauna for men, a redwood hot tub, as well as shops, and a beauty salon.

There are 100 rooms, suites, and cottages, of which I prefer the ones upstairs with cathedral ceilings. All have color TV and suchlike, dressing rooms, and balconies; some have fireplaces and wet bars. Furnishings are modern, with shag rugs, handsome hand-woven bedspreads, bamboo and rattan furnishings. There's complimentary fresh-ground coffee in every room, and afternoon tea from 3 to 5 p.m. Free newspapers are delivered daily.

The grounds are truly superb, with graceful bridges arching over duck-filled lakes and ponds; on occasion you'll see wild water birds or catch a glimpse of a deer.

The posh Covey Restaurant on the premises serves refined European cuisine nightly in warmly elegant surroundings (breakfast and lunch are served daily in the clubhouse). The interior is done in terracotta tones with teal and lilac accents. Tables are beautifully appointed in Belgian linen, set with Sienna china, adorned with fresh flowers, and lit by gaslamps. A delightful fireplace bar/lounge in Mexican motif adjoins.

You can begin your meal with an appetizer of a half dozen escargots. Entrees, served with potato and a fresh garden vegetable, include poulet à l'orange, fresh trout amandine, and a sizzling steak au poivre flambé in brandy, for $15 to $28. Specialties of the house are rack of lamb and fresh seafood. For dessert, I like the crêpes flambés au Grand Marnier. Jackets are required for men, and reservations are essential.

The cost of luxury living (February through November) at Quail Lodge is $185 to $260, single or double. Suites are $265 to $800. Third person in room, $25 extra.

The next three selections are all right in the heart of Carmel activity, and each has its own unique charm.

Normandy Inn, Ocean Avenue (between Monte Verde and Casanova Avenues), Carmel, CA 93921 (tel. 408/624-3825), is a delightful provincial hostelry housed in a shingled Tudor building. The terrace poolside patio (the pool is heated) is lined with trees, shrubbery, and potted plants.

Rooms are just lovely, although each is somewhat different: about a quarter of them have fireplaces and/or kitchen areas, all have color TV, and most baths have tub/shower combinations. All have switchboard phones and are charmingly decorated in country motif, with ruffled bedspreads, maple furnishings, shuttered windows, and old-fashioned print wallpapers.

Rates for single accommodations are $59 to $120, doubles run $81 to $120. Cottages for two to eight persons cost $120 to $219. Be sure to reserve far in advance, especially in summer, or it's unlikely you'll find a room at the inn.

More quaint rooms (these are Victorian in style) are found at the **Pine Inn,** Ocean Avenue (between Lincoln and Monte Verde), P.O. Box 250, Carmel, CA 93921 (tel. 408/624-3851). At the risk of being repetitious, I once again advise early reservations. The Pine Inn has an opulent lobby/lounge complete with red-flocked wallpaper, a blazing fireplace, plush furnishings, and a big grandfather clock. Each room is individually designed, but all are in turn-of-the-century motif—shuttered windows, lovely wallpapers, and antique furnishings, including brass beds in some rooms. Every room has a color TV, direct-dial phone, and tub/shower bath.

The Gazebo restaurant is on the premises, also a masterpiece of Victoriana, with large globe chandeliers, stained-glass panels, and the rest. Here, diners sit under a skylight dome that rolls back on sunny days and warm starlit nights. Both the Sunday champagne brunch and the Friday-night seafood buffet at the Pine

Inn are popular. Dinner features traditional American specialties like prime rib and fresh seafood—for $15 to $20. At lunch, lighter fare is served.

Rooms at the Pine Inn cost $75 to $155 a night, single or double.

Some of the loveliest rooms in town are at the **Carriage House Inn,** on Junipero, between 7th and 8th Aves., P.O. Box 1900, Carmel, CA 93921 (tel. 408/624-3851, or toll free 800/433-4732). This country-style inn, located in a quiet Carmel setting, has 13 rooms exquisitely decorated with Early American antiques. Amenities include king-size beds with down comforters, wood-burning fireplaces, small refrigerators, cable color TV with free Showtime movies, and direct-dial telephones. Most second-floor rooms have sunken baths and vaulted beam ceilings. You will be pampered with continental breakfast, brought to you each morning on blue willow china along with the morning paper, as well as with twice-daily maid service and fresh flowers in your room. It's a delight. Rates for one or two persons are $140 to $240.

The Village Inn, Ocean Avenue and Junipero Street, P.O. Box 5275, Carmel, CA 93921 (tel. 408/624-3864), is a pretty, well-run, well-located, and reasonably priced motor lodge, its rooms arranged around a courtyard/parking lot lined with potted geraniums. Rooms feature a tasteful homey decor with French country furniture. Complimentary continental breakfast is served to guests each morning. All of the 32 rooms are equipped with direct-dial phones, bath/shower, refrigerators, and cable color TVs. Singles and doubles pay $70 to $125, and rooms accommodating three to four people are $95 to $175. Children are welcome.

Finally, there's **San Antonio House,** on San Antonio between Ocean and Seventh Avenues (P.O. Box 3683), Carmel, CA 93921 (tel. 408/624-4334). Once again you have a garden setting with charming two- and three-room suites furnished with antiques and a private art collection. Karen and Dennis Levett unobtrusively see to the needs and comfort of their guests. All rooms have TVs, small refrigerators, fireplaces, private bathrooms, a patio or garden, and a private entrance. Guests are also pampered with cream sherry, fresh flowers, a morning newspaper, and a full European breakfast. Rates are $100 to $125, single or double; an additional person pays $20.

WHERE TO DINE: L'Escargot, Mission Street and Fourth Avenue (tel. 408/624-4914), has both superb French cuisine and a delightful interior. Housed in typical Carmel style in a shingle-roofed, beamed stucco building, it is warm and cozy within. Banquettes and chairs are upholstered in a quaint French fabric, and other provincial touches include hanging copperware, arrangements of dried and fresh flowers, leaded-glass windows, a beamed ceiling, and shelves of decorative plates. Desserts, wines, and a big pot of flowers are displayed on an oak centerpiece.

You might begin with an appetizer of escargots de Bourgogne, or the smoked salmon (cured and smoked by André). The choice is not an easy one—among the offerings are also braised fresh artichoke bottoms with herbs and a lovely puff pastry with wild mushrooms. As for the entrees, priced from $15 to $19.50, the house classic chicken with cream, foie gras, and truffles is still a vibrant memory. But anything you order will be superb. Other choices include a specialty of the chef, aiguillette de canard (breast of duck roasted with a special sauce); fresh scallops sautéed with orange-lemon butter; and, one of my favorites, sweetbreads with cream, madeira, and mushrooms. L'Escargot has an extensive list of French and California wines. And don't pass up the desserts, each a masterpiece—say, the exquisite chilled Grand Marnier soufflé, which has the consistency of a delicate light ice cream; the utterly delicious crème caramel; or the classic mousse au chocolat. Owner/chef André Françot takes infinite care in the preparation of every dish, and as his wine list is extensive and well chosen, it's not surprising that he is the winner of many a culinary award.

L'Escargot is open Monday to Saturday from 6 to 9:30 p.m. Reservations are advised.

Another award winner is **Raffaello,** on Mission between Ocean and Seventh Avenues (tel. 408/624-1541). The ambience here is hushed and rather formal (men are required to wear jackets), the decor elegant with dripping crystal chandeliers, tables clothed in white linen, low lighting, and walls adorned with antique Italian tapestries and mirrors. Bowls of fresh flowers grace every table. The cuisine is Italian, and entrees (costing $14 to $22) are served with soup, salad, and vegetables. Veal with fontina cheese and truffles, fettuccine romano, sweetbreads with cream and wine sauce, and filet of sole poached in white wine and herbs, stuffed with shrimp, are among the choices, as is homemade fettuccine al pesto. Although you might order assorted cheeses or a light strawberry mousse for dessert, you can always opt for the rich and creamy zabaglione.

Raffaello is open nightly except Tuesday from 6 to 10 p.m. Reservations are essential.

Belgian owners Gaston and Walter Georis designed **Casanova,** on Fifth Avenue between San Carlos and Mission (tel. 408/625-0501), to look like the European farmhouses of their childhood memories. Located in an old house (it used to belong to Charlie Chaplin's cook), Casanova is cozy and provincial with intimate dining areas under a low beamed ceiling. Heated by a wood-burning stove, it has checkered curtains and quaint lampshades from France, flower-bedecked tables with Mediterranean blue cloths, bentwood chairs, and antique ceramic tiles embedded into the walls. There's a heated area for outdoor dining with a little fountain. French and Italian music play in the background.

The menu changes seasonally. On my last visit luncheon choices ($7 to $10) included homemade linguine with prawns, scallops, mushrooms, and fresh tomatoes, basil, garlic, and white wine (served in the pot), with a salad; and fruit crêpes in Grand Marnier sauce. All dinners (which average $18 to $26) include an antipasto salad; a choice of soup, mushrooms in butter and herbs, or Gnocchi Verde alla Romana; and an entree like linguine with lobster, prawns, and shellfish, or rack of lamb. A list of over 650 French and Italian wines is available, and desserts are all homemade.

Open Monday to Saturday for breakfast from 8 to 11 a.m., lunch from 11:30 a.m. to 3 p.m. and for dinner daily from 5:30 to 10:30 p.m.; Sunday brunch is served from 10 a.m. to 3 p.m.

If you've been to the Fog City Diner in San Francisco, Mustards in Yountville, or the Tra Vigne in St. Helena, you'll recognize the sweet smell of success at the **Rio Grill,** at Calif. 1 and Rio Road in the Crossroads group of shops (tel. 408/625-5436)—brought to you by the same folks who put together the above-noted establishments (all recommended earlier in this book).

While you are waiting to be seated in the modern, southwestern-style dining room or in one of the cozy dining alcoves, you can watch the action in the Rio Grill's lively lounge or look at the cartoons above the bar of such famous locals as Bing Crosby and Clint Eastwood. The scene is fun, but you really come for the food, which is as impressive, attractive, and deliciously casual as the decor. You might start with one of the homemade soups that the Rio Grill offers daily, or choose the richer rabbit quesadilla with ancho chili and roasted tomatillo salsa. Then it's on to entree (or sandwich) heaven: a half slab of barbecued baby back ribs from the wood-burning oven perhaps, fresh fish from the grill, or maybe a skirt steak with sesame, soy, and ginger marinade. A different pasta is offered each day, as are hamburgers and cheeseburgers, but consider the joy of a grilled eggplant sandwich with roasted red peppers, Fontina cheese, and watercress. Leave room for dessert; I had trouble deciding between the caramel-apple bread pudding and the caramel custard with pistachios and cream.

Prices are moderate. Entrees go for $9 to $15, with most in the $10 area. Appetizers, soups, salads, and sandwiches are in the $3 to $8 range. The most expensive item on the menu is a delectable Rio Grill sweatshirt for $20.

Service is young, friendly, knowledgeable, and helpful. A good selection of wines covers a broad price range.

Rio Grill is open daily. Both the lounge and dining room are closed from 4 to 5 p.m., but otherwise the lounge serves food Monday through Saturday from 11:30 a.m. to 10 p.m. and on Sunday from 11 a.m. to 11 p.m.; and the dining room serves Sunday through Thursday from 11 a.m. to 10 p.m., on Friday and Saturday to 11 p.m.

Carmel has more than its fair share of charming village restaurants, but one of the most delightful is the **Tuck Box English Room,** on Dolores Street, near 7th Street (tel. 408/624-6365). In September of 1987, the Tuck Box was firebombed in the early hours of the morning. It's since been rebuilt to look exactly as it did before, with perhaps a few more tucks here and there, a new hardwood floor, and a light gray interior with charcoal trim. It's still just about everybody's favorite place for breakfast, locals and visitors alike.

In this small, shingle-roofed cottage, you can have breakfast, lunch, or a traditional afternoon tea (complete with hot buttered scones and homemade marmalade). The dining area is tiny, with a beamed ceiling, table bases that match the beams, a stone fireplace, and red-and-white-checked curtains in the front window. You can also dine outside at a few tables on the patio. At breakfast you can have fresh-squeezed orange juice for $1.50, and fresh fruit, bacon and eggs, with homemade muffins or scones, for $3.85. Lunchtime, the menu lists a choice of two or three entrees—for example, shepherd's pie, which is served with salad, vegetable, muffin or scone, at $4.40. For dessert there's homemade pie or cake with real whipped cream.

The Tuck Box is open from 8 a.m. to 4 p.m.; closed Monday and Tuesday.

The interior of **La Bohème,** Dolores and Seventh (tel. 408/624-7500), is cleverly designed to look like a provincial French street, complete with a painted blue sky and shingled houses. Tables are set with floral-print cloths in gay colors, blue-and-white hand-painted dinnerware and candleholders, and colorful posies of fresh flowers. Gleaming copper pots are hung from the wall.

Dinner is a three-course, prix-fixe affair consisting of a large salad, a tureen of soup, and an entree—perhaps duckling sauté with raspberry sauce, brochette de boeuf au poivre, Cornish game hen, or even paella. The price of dinner is around $18. Luscious homemade desserts are the perfect capper to a meal.

La Bohème is open daily for dinner from 5:30 to 10 p.m.

A charming little tea room, the **Pâtisserie Boissière,** in Carmel Plaza on Mission, between Ocean and Seventh Avenues (tel. 408/624-5008). Housed in a shingle-roofed stucco cottage, it boasts an entrance heralded by a real Parisian street sign reading Rue Boissière. The decor is cozily provincial, with white stucco walls and a low beamed ceiling, antique maple sideboard, tiled fireplace, and Louis XV–style chairs. You can also dine in a skylight café with garden furnishings. The food is exquisite, beginning with the homemade pâté. It's the perfect place for a light meal, at $3 to $6—perhaps a ham or camembert sandwich on French bread or a quiche Lorraine and salad with a glass of wine, topped off by a delicious homemade pâtisserie (like a chocolate eclair, or chocolate butter cream with crisp meringue) and coffee.

For a heartier meal, specialties include coquilles Saint-Jacques (scallops, shrimps, and fresh mushrooms, in a cream and sherry sauce), and a provincial chicken dish with white wine sauce, tomatoes, and olives, served with rice. Such entrees cost $9 to $13 at lunch, $13 to $16 at dinner.

The Pâtisserie Boissière is open from 9 a.m. to 10 p.m. every day. Reservations suggested.

Shabu-Shabu, in the Carmel Plaza Mall (tel. 408/625-2828), invites you to take off your shoes and refresh yourself with an oshibori (warm, moist towel). It's easy to relax over your sake in this lovely country-inn-style Japanese restaurant. You can sit the Japanese way on cushions at low tables, or Western style at highly polished redwood tables. Redwood-paneled walls are adorned with colorful Japanese kites and other folk-art items, a fireplace adds a cozy note, and Japanese music is played in the background.

The specialty is, of course, shabu-shabu for two; the name means "swish-swish," which is the procedure for cooking the meat. It consists of thin ribbons of beef, soybean cake, mushrooms, and fresh seasonal vegetables cooked at your table in a broth in an earthenware pot and served with dipping sauces. Yosenabe, made with fresh clams, scallops, shrimp, rock cod, and vegetables, is also available for two. Other items include prawn (enormous ones) and vegetable tempura; teriyaki steak, ten ounces of it; and teriyaki chicken. All dinners cost $14 to $24 and come with soup, spinach salad, tsukemono (Japanese pickle), an appetizer (perhaps sashimi or tempura), rice, and a pot of delicious genmai tea, which is steeped in toasted rice. Shabu-Shabu has a knockout dessert—the Japanese answer to the banana split and far superior: bananas deep-fried in tempura batter and topped with green tea ice cream.

A marvelous and very popular lunch is now served daily, except Sunday, from 11:30 a.m. to 2 p.m. Called obento, it features a Japanese-style lunchbox with several delicious courses ($5 to $7.50). The Miyako lunch includes tempura, chicken teriyaki, a California roll, rice, and soup; the Shogun lunchbox includes tempura, tuna sashimi, beef teriyaki wrapped around green onion, rice, and miso soup. Lunches are also prepared to go.

Shabu-Shabu is open daily for dinner from 5:30 to 10 p.m. Reservations are essential.

Almost everyone knows that Clint Eastwood owns a restaurant in Carmel, its name parodying the quaintness of its many competitors. The **Hog's Breath Inn,** San Carlos Street, between Fifth and Sixth Avenues (tel. 408/625-1044), is always mobbed, partly because it's a very comfortable hangout, and partly because you never know when Clint Eastwood, the former mayor of Carmel, is likely to drop in. Entered via a brick walkway, it has several dining and drinking areas. You can sit outdoors on a stone patio in director's chairs pulled up to tree-trunk tables, and there are two brick fireplaces to keep you warm. The main restaurant is dark and rustic with farm implements, dried flower arrangements, and celeb photos hanging on the walls. Another structure on the property is an equally rustic, very small pub, with a brick fireplace in the corner and two wild boars' heads mounted on the wall; a TV over the bar broadcasts sporting events.

Lunch at Hog's Breath, which costs $8 to $13, might consist of the fresh catch of the day, or a sirloin steak sandwich on whole-wheat toast, both of these served with the soup du jour. Dinner entrees—such as double cut of prime rib—come with soup or salad, baked potato or rice, and a vegetable for $14 to $20.

Open seven days, the Hog's Breath serves lunch Monday to Saturday from 11:30 a.m. to 3 p.m., Sunday brunch from 11 a.m. to 3 p.m.; dinner hours are 5 to 10 p.m. nightly, and the pub and patio stay open until 2 a.m. Reservations are taken for large parties only.

4. BIG SUR

Not a town, but rather a loose description of the famous 90-mile stretch of rugged coastline on Hwy. 1 between Carmel and San Simeon, the dramatic Big Sur region is probably the only place in the world described by its chamber of commerce as a place "to slow down . . . to meditate . . . to catch up with your soul." Flanked on one side by the majestic Santa Lucia Mountain Range, and on the other by the rocky Pacific coast, it is traveled via breathtakingly scenic Hwy. 1. Drive through slowly, making frequent stops at viewing turnouts, and taking in the sea and cliffs.

Although the area attracts many tourists, its highly individualistic residents make few concessions to them, and in no way is Big Sur touristy or in danger of becoming so. There are few recreational distractions—no town, no cute boutiques and art galleries, no tennis, golf, horseback riding, boating, or even movie theaters. Just the tranquility of unparalleled natural beauty where you can hike through redwood forests along miles of trails, picnic, go camping, fish, or enjoy the beach at several points along the coast: **Pfeiffer–Big Sur State Beach** (tel. 408/667-2315 for the park), **Kirk Creek, Plaskett Creek, Jade Beach,** and **Willow Creek Beach.** (The only beach accessible by car is Pfeiffer, via Sycamore Canyon Road.)

The River Inn, 29 miles south of Monterey on Hwy. 1, is generally considered the starting point of Big Sur, with most of the area's accommodations, restaurants, and other facilities between it and Deetjen's Big Sur Inn about six miles south. You can visit Big Sur on a day trip from Monterey or Carmel, perhaps stopping for lunch at Ventana or Nepenthe (details below). If you'd like to stay a while, the following is a pretty complete rundown on the accommodations situation.

Note: If you're planning a drive all the way south to **Morro Bay** (120 miles) on Hwy. 1, do it during periods of good and relatively dry weather. Not only is the view lovelier, but landslides have occurred during the rainy season. In any event, it requires time (allow a full day) and close attention to driving for the trip. If you have a fear of heights, avoid this route. Heavy fog can also make the trip trying rather than enjoyable, so check weather conditions before leaving.

WHERE TO STAY: Accommodations are many and varied, but few attempt the luxury-hotel trappings you'd find on any other major highway going through an area with such a high tourism rate—room service, even phones and TVs (the latter considered Philistine in these parts) are rare. Nevertheless, they all run at close to full occupancy, especially in summer, so reserve early. To write to any of the places below, just address inquiries to the name of the establishment, Big Sur, CA 93920. The same goes for the chamber of commerce.

Least typical of Big Sur hostelries is **Ventana Inn,** on Highway 1, 4.3 miles south of River Inn (tel. 408/667-2331, or toll free 800/628-6500), a luxurious wilderness resort on a 1,000-acre oceanfront ranch, high in the mountains overlooking the Pacific. Opened in 1975, it fulfills a long-standing need for accommodations worthy of the wild and magical Big Sur countryside. Among the notables who have flocked to pamper themselves at Ventana are Henry Winkler, Barbra Streisand and Jon Peters, Goldie Hawn, and Francis Ford Coppola, not to mention the prime minister of Finland. Debra Winger and Timothy Hutton were married here in 1986.

The resort's 59 guest rooms are housed in contemporary natural-wood buildings with slanted roofs that blend with the landscape. The interiors are exquisite, in blue or green color schemes, each with wall-to-wall carpeting color co-ordinated to patchwork-quilt bedspreads handmade in Nova Scotia. Walls are a combination of white stucco and cedar paneling, furnishings are wicker, and most have wood-burning fireplaces, others very high ceilings. All have dressing rooms, private terraces or balconies overlooking the ocean or forest (11 with their own hot tubs), Princess phones, color TVs, heating, air conditioning, and baths with tub and shower and goodies like bath oils, shampoos, and oversize towels.

There are two 90-foot heated outdoor swimming pools, each with its own bathhouse and Japanese hot bath, with multiple jets, where you can soak *au naturel*—one section for men, one for women, and one for the uninhibited mixed crowd.

Moving along now to culinary luxuries, complimentary breakfast (fresh-baked croissants, danish pastries, fresh-squeezed orange juice, homemade granola with yogurt and fresh fruit, and tea or coffee) is served in your room or in the guest lobby each morning. The restaurant on the premises is, like everything else, first-rate—it's had a Mobil 4-star rating for six straight years. The airy raw cedar interior, with heavy beams, two large stone fireplaces, and cedar tile floor, is furnished with redwood tables, cane and bentwood chairs, and rattan-shaded globe lamps overhead. Baskets of ferns, potted plants, and baskets of fruit are placed here and there.

You can dine on any one of three levels, with vista-revealing windows everywhere, or on a large outdoor patio terrace overlooking a dramatic expanse of ocean with the Big Sur coast in view for 50 miles.

Lunch fare ranges from $9 to $16 for entrees like smoked Big Sur trout or salad niçoise. For dinner you might order roast glazed duckling or roast rack of lamb, for $20 to $27. Desserts baked in their own French bakery are temptingly displayed and best chosen visually.

Ventana's restaurant is open weekdays from noon to 3 p.m. and 6 to 9:30 p.m., weekends from 11 a.m. to 3:45 p.m. Call for reservations. After you dine you can browse through the adjoining general store, which carries everything from imported buttons and bows to garden tools.

Rates for doubles begin at $155 and go up to $550 (the latter for a suite). If you can't afford to stay here, at least splurge at the restaurant, and take a look around. If you do want to stay here, be sure to make reservations in advance.

Traveling with the family? Best bet (unless you're camping, about which more shortly) is the **Big Sur Lodge,** located in Pfeiffer–Big Sur State Park, a little over two miles south of River Inn on Hwy. 1 (tel. 408/667-2171). The lodge has 61 units beautifully situated on over 800 parkland acres of towering redwoods, sycamores, big-leaf maples, and other sheltering trees. The cabins are quite large, with high peaked cedar and redwood beamed ceilings and walnut-paneled walls. The rooms are quite clean and most presentable. All are heated and equipped with private bath and parking spaces. Most of the cabins have either a fireplace or a kitchen, or both. All have a porch or deck with views of the redwoods or the Santa Lucia Mountains.

A great advantage in staying here is that you can use all the facilities of the park: fishing, hiking, barbecue pits, picnic facilities, plus the lodge's own large outdoor heated swimming pool with adjoining sauna, a gift shop filled with unique items, two grocery stores, and a laundromat.

The Big Sur Lodge dining room is open for breakfast and dinner from March through December. Full breakfasts are $3 to $6. Dinner entrees, at $7 to $13, are served with salad and baked potato or rice. The menu features fresh seafood, steaks, and pasta dishes. Be sure to try the homemade desserts made fresh daily.

The dining room is very pretty, by the way, with big windows all around providing glorious woodland views and an interior waterfall; if you want to be in the forest rather than looking at it through glass, there's lots of patio seating under umbrellaed tables overlooking the river.

The rate for cottages for one or two persons is $55, $65 for four, ascending to $95 for six (maximum occupancy). Fireplace units are $15 more, and those with kitchens are $10 over the base rates. Reservations are a necessity. For a summer weekend, call two months ahead for the best selection.

Camping

Once again, your best bet is the 40-acre campsite belonging to **Ventana,** off Hwy. 1 just before the resort (tel. 408/667-2331). The 98 campsites, in a gorgeous redwood setting, are spaced well apart for privacy. Each has a picnic table and fireplace, and bathrooms with hot showers are conveniently located. You can swim in the creek or at Pfeiffer–Big Sur State Beach, a mile away. Campsites are $16 for up to four people in a vehicle, $3 for each additional person, $2 per dog; and an electrical hookup is $3 extra.

Fernwood, about 2 miles south of River Inn (tel. 408/667-2422), has 63 sites on 23 beautiful woodland acres, each with electricity, water, and a fire pit. About half the sites overlook the river. Rates are $18 a night (with electricity), $16 without, for two people, $3 for each additional person. There's a restaurant on the premises open daily from 11:30 a.m. to midnight where they serve burgers, ribs, etc., and live music is presented on weekends; an attractive bar/cocktail lounge and a wine and cheese shop have been added. Also on the premises are a grocery store, where you can get wood, ice, and beer and wine; a gas station; and a motel with 12 units, all with shower and toilet. Singles pay $50 for motel accommodations; four people pay $68.

Another good choice for camping is the **Big Sur Campground and Cabins,** two-tenths of a mile below the River Inn (tel. 408/667-2322). Open year round, it has campsites, bathhouses with hot-water showers, laundry facilities, freshwater faucets within 25 feet of each site, a large river swimming area surrounded by towering redwoods, play area with swings, grocery store, etc., and a volleyball/basketball court. Each campsite has its own wood-burning fire pit and picnic table. Rates are $16 for two people in a car, $4 for each additional person. Electrical and water hookups are $3.

Three A-frame cabins on the premises, with fully equipped kitchens, fireplaces, private terraces, and shower baths, are $70 double, $10 for each additional person. They're very attractive, with high peaked raw-fir ceilings, throw rugs on glossy wood floors, and homey furnishings including a rocking chair. They sleep up to six. Two new modular units, with fireplace (and some wood supplied), but no kitchen, are $63 and suitable for two. Six additional modular units do have kitchens; these cost $73, $10 for each additional person. Tent cabins without a bath are $34.

More well-equipped camping facilities are in **Pfeiffer–Big Sur State Park**—with three areas of campsites open year round. There's a ten-day limit on stays; for information write to the Department of Parks and Recreation, P.O. Box 2390, Sacramento, CA 95811.

WHERE TO DINE: In addition to the many dining facilities at the above-mentioned accommodations, be sure to experience Big Sur's **Nepenthe,** five miles south of River Inn (tel. 408/667-2345). It stands on the site of the Log House, which was built in 1925, 808 feet above sea level. Housed in a redwood-and-stucco structure, the dining room is ski-lodgey, with a big wood-burning fireplace, director's chairs at heavy wood tables, redwood and pine ceilings, and lots of windows. But unless the weather is really bad, everyone sits outside on the ocean-view terrace enjoying one of the most awesomely magnificent vistas anywhere. It's a magical place to while away a lazy and delightful afternoon; stay long enough to catch the sunset. Usually there are a few musicians hanging out here, playing to a background of scores of gaily chirping birds, and, in general, it's a lively, unpredictable, idyllic, and fun place to be. Service is casual, in keeping with the casual style of the place, but no one really cares. A light lunch, with entrees averaging $7 to $11, might consist of a continental cheese board served with fresh fruit and bread and a liter of wine; follow up with a pot of English tea and dessert—perhaps homemade pumpkin spice cake. You can also get hamburgers, salads, and sandwiches at lunch. Dinner fare includes steak dishes, broiled chicken, and fresh fish of the day ($13 to $22). Open daily from 11:30 a.m. to midnight.

Just across the highway from the Glen Oaks Motel on Hwy. 1 is Marilee and Forrest Childs' **Glen Oaks Restaurant** (tel. 408/667-2623), a lovely place with a beamed ceiling, flower-filled windows, a wood-burning copper-chimneyed fireplace in the corner, and fresh flowers on every white-clothed table. Marilee's exquisite watercolors grace the walls; Forrest's masterpieces are culinary. The food is fresh and excellent, beginning with Sunday brunch, priced at $6 to $14. There is char-broiled steak and eggs with fresh blueberry muffin or an omelet with any of three ingredients—like ham, cheese, and mushrooms. Dinner costs $12 to $20 for entrees like gnocchi, cheese pillows in sage butter or fettuccine with scallops and lobster, eggplant parmigiana, and Chinese vegetables sautéed and served on a bed of wild rice. There's also fresh seafood charcoal broiled and served with a variety of sauces. Desserts are prepared daily on the premises, and a small collection of California wines is available. Taped classical music enhances the ambience. It's open daily from 6 to 9:45 p.m. and for Sunday brunch from 9 a.m. to noon. Reservations are recommended for brunch and dinner.

THE HENRY MILLER MEMORIAL LIBRARY: Henry Miller was probably Big Sur's most famous resident. He came here in 1944, and watched the area grow from a wilderness to a well-known artists' colony. In fact, his writings— works like *Big Sur and the Oranges of Hieronymus Bosch*—were instrumental in making Big Sur famous. Henry Miller fans will want to drop by the Henry Miller Memorial Library, about a mile south of the Ventana Inn. Miller's longtime close friend, artist Emil White (who moved to Big Sur just after Miller did), has turned his home and personal Miller collection into this tribute to his friend. It's a small, informal, cluttery place, often full of young researchers or browsers rummaging through Miller books and memorabilia, and White's paintings. The library's hours are informal; it's usually open daily from 11 a.m. to 7 p.m., unless the "closed" sign is posted outside. Call 408/667-2574 for information.

THE COAST GALLERY: This beautifully situated gallery (tel. 408/667-2301), eight miles south of River Inn, is Big Sur's original, and only, art gallery. Uniquely rebuilt from redwood watertanks after a flood in 1973, it shows works of over 200 local and California artists and craftspeople—pottery, woodcarving, macramé, paintings, sculpture, jewelry, etc. In addition, candles are made on the premises. The folks who run it are awfully nice, and it makes for good browsing. Open daily from 9 a.m. to 5 p.m.

5. SAN SIMEON

Ever wonder what you'd do if you had the really big bucks? Not just a million, but hundreds of millions?

In the verdant Santa Lucia Mountains of San Simeon, on a hill he called La Cuesta Encantada (The Enchanted Hill), William Randolph Hearst has left an astounding monument to wealth, a veritable shrine worthy of kings and maharajahs, the ego trip par excellence—**Hearst Castle.**

The history of Hearst Castle dates back to 1865 when 43-year-old George Hearst purchased a 40,000-acre Mexican land grant adjacent to San Simeon Bay. He built a comfortable ranch house on the property, ran large herds of cattle over its ranges and foothills, and also crossbred Arabian horses with Morgans on the premises. He often entertained at the ranch (it still stands today, incidentally), and his only son, William Randolph, developed a great liking for the informal life at "Camp Hill." As a young man, busy launching his newspaper career, W.R. would often steal off to the San Simeon property for a quiet retreat. In 1919, when George Hearst's widow, Phoebe Apperson Hearst, died and William Randolph came into possession of the ranch, the present castle was under way.

Located on Hwy. 1, about 94 miles south of Monterey, Hearst Castle was given to the state as a memorial to the late publisher in 1958.

The focal point of the estate is the incredible **Casa Grande,** with over 100 rooms all filled with priceless art treasures. There are Flemish tapestries, 15th-century Gothic fireplaces, 16th-century Spanish and intricately carved 18th-century Italian ceilings, a 16th-century Florentine bedstead, Renaissance paintings, and here and there are such items as a 3rd-century Etruscan jar, or an ancient Egyptian statue created over 3,000 years ago. That barely skims the surface. The Doge's Suite of the house was reserved for the most important guests, among them Winston Churchill and President Calvin Coolidge and his wife. In the library, 5,000 volumes (including some rare books) are housed, along with one of the world's greatest collections of Greek vases.

There are three opulent mini-castle guesthouses on the premises, also furnished with magnificent art treasures, which can be seen on the tour.

A lavish private theater was used to show first-run films twice nightly—once for employees and again for the guests and host. Guests could also play pool and billiards in a room that would make you feel as if you were shooting pool in the middle of the Louvre.

And there are two swimming pools—the Byzantine-inspired indoor pool with intricate mosaic work surrounded by the most famous statues of antiquity copied in Carrara marble (at night, light filtering through alabaster globes created the illusion of moonlight) and the Greco-Roman Neptune pool, flanked by Etruscan-style marble colonnades and surrounded by more Carrara statuary.

Which is not even to mention the magnificently landscaped grounds, where —in outlying areas—the world's largest private zoo once existed. Within a 2,000-acre enclosure, monkeys, cheetahs, giraffes, camels, elephants, bears, bison, llamas, zebras, deer, eagles, and other birds were kept. For riding, he had over 30 Arabian horses. Today only a few elk, Barbary sheep, Himalayan goats, deer, and zebras roam.

If you can fit San Simeon into your itinerary, it will make for a very interesting and enjoyable day's outing—a glimpse into a lifestyle that barely exists today, and that few, if any, of us have come near experiencing.

There are four tours that you can take of Hearst Castle and the grounds. Tour I is recommended for the first-time visitor (150 stair steps). It covers the gardens, a guesthouse, and the ground floor of the main house—including the movie theater, where you'll see Hearst "home movies." Tour II takes in the upper part of the main house, including Mr. Hearst's private suite, office, libraries, duplex guest room, kitchen, and pools (300 stair steps). Tour III visits the guest wing with its 36 bedrooms and sitting rooms, pools, and gardens, and deals with interior design changes over a 20-year period (300 stair steps). Tour IV (not offered in the winter) covers the grounds, offering an opportunity to see the conservation room, wine cellar, and lower floor of one of the guesthouses (300 stair steps).

The tours, each of which lasts 1¾ hours, are conducted daily, except Thanksgiving, Christmas, and New Year's, beginning at 8:20 a.m. Two to six tours leave every hour, depending on the season. Allow two hours between starting times if you plan to take more than one tour. Don't just arrive; make reservations for your tour by calling Mistix (tel. 619/452-1950, or toll free 800/444-7275 in California). Arrive without reservations and you're guaranteed a long wait; you may not get in at all. Tickets cost $10 for adults, $5 for children 6 to 12.

Visitors park their cars at the Visitors Center parking lot and are transported by bus to the castle. If you bring lunch, there are picnic tables; you'll also find a gift shop and snackbar at the parking lot. Wear comfortable shoes—you'll be walking about a half mile and climbing over 300 steps.

6. SAN LUIS OBISPO

What a pretty and delightful place is San Luis Obispo! Nestled in the Los Padres mountains midway between Los Angeles and San Francisco, it's an easygoing, postcard-picturesque little college town that grew up around an 18th-century mission. Among its tourist attractions are many historical landmarks, shops, restaurants, and sporting facilities. This is the beginning of Southern California beach country—the first point south where you don't have to be a member of the Polar Bear Club to dare stick your big toe in the water.

Other attractions? Concerts—an annual Mozart festival (first week in August), jazz and bands, etc.—often outdoors and under the stars, are frequent events, interspersed with dance performances, poetry readings, theater productions, and diverse activities ranging from wine-tasting dinners (many wineries within driving distance) to tug-o-war competitions. And San Luis Obispo has the largest farmer's market in California—every Thursday night from 6 to 9 p.m. It's *the* local event. There's entertainment, dancing, and all the stores are open till 9 p.m.

It's an easy town to walk around—most places of interest can be reached on foot—but the best thing about San Luis Obispo is the friendly townspeople, who always seem to have time to help a tourist, converse, and pass the time of day.

About 42 miles south of San Simeon on Highway 1, San Luis Obispo is a good base for visits to Hearst Castle.

Make your first stop in town the **San Luis Obispo Chamber of Commerce Visitors Center,** 1039 Chorro St. between Monterey and Higuera (tel. 805/543-1323). Open seven days a week, this is one of the best-run chambers of commerce I have ever come across—friendly, helpful, and extremely well informed. Drop in to ask questions and pick up maps, get a calendar of events, and all sorts of information on local sights.

THE PATH OF HISTORY: Like Monterey, San Luis Obispo has an easy-to-follow path, here linking about 20 historical landmarks. Get a map and follow the green line on the street. Highlights include—

Mission San Luis Obispo de Tolosa

The focal point of Mission Plaza, the old mission, P.O. Box 1483, San Luis Obispo, CA 93406 (tel. 805/543-6850), constructed of adobe bricks by the Chumash Indians in 1772, is one of the most beautiful and interesting of the

Franciscan chain. A 1793 statue of Saint Louis (San Luís) is above the altar, and the 14 Stations of the Cross in the main church date from 1812. The belfry houses three large bells that were cast in Peru in 1818.

Most interesting is the Mission Museum, which contains a wealth of mission artifacts, among them vestments, books, handmade knives, a wedding dress brought over from Spain in 1831, portraits and photos of mission workers, bisque dolls, samplers, a wine press, tallow-making pot, and corn sheller. Many Native American relics are also displayed here: flints, arrowheads, wampum beads, dolls, baskets, clothing, cooking pots, drums, grinding stones for making flour, and office furniture hand-carved by the Cherokees in 1880.

Particularly lovely is the mission's garden setting, with winding brick paths and benches by a creek, a small hill blanketed in morning glories as a backdrop. All is peaceful here.

The mission is open daily except for Christmas, New Year's Day, Easter Sunday, and Thanksgiving; hours are 9 a.m. to 4 p.m., till 5 p.m. in summer. A donation of $1 (or $2 per family) is requested.

San Luis Obispo County Historical Museum

A wonderful place to browse, this little museum, which is run by the San Luis Obispo County Historical Society, is housed in the early-20th-century Carnegie Library building at 696 Montgomery St. (tel. 805/543-0638). The emphasis here is—naturally enough—on San Luis Obispo County history. Special exhibits are displayed periodically. The museum houses an extensive research library, and owns hundreds of historical photographs. Permanent exhibits include artifacts of the Chumash Indians and early pioneers.

The museum is open Wednesday to Sunday from 10 a.m. to 4 p.m.; closed Christmas, New Year's Day, Easter Sunday, and Thanksgiving.

St. Stephen's Episcopal Church

Dating back to 1867, this pine-and-redwood structure is one of the first Episcopal churches in the state. The original pipe organ was donated by Phoebe Apperson Hearst (Patty's great-grandmother).

Romona Depot

An official depot of the Southern Pacific Railroad Company, built in 1889, it's the only vestige of the luxurious Romona Hotel, an elegant Victorian hostelry that once hosted President McKinley and Theodore Roosevelt.

The Ah Louis Store

Practically unchanged since it was opened in 1874, this century-old establishment at 800 Palm St. (tel. 805/543-4332) is still in the hands of the original Cantonese family. Ah Louis was lured to California by gold fever in 1856. Unsuccessful in this venture, he came to San Luis and took a job as a cook, but soon began a lucrative trade as a labor contractor, hiring and organizing Chinese crews to build the railroad. In addition to the store, he also started the first brickyard in the country, created county roads, had a vegetable and flower seed business, bred race horses, and was the overseer of eight farms.

Today you can chat with his son, Howard, who runs the store, while you browse about a clutter of Oriental merchandise. Hours are irregular, since Howard often just closes up and goes fishing; however, it's usually open daily, except Sunday.

Sinsheimer Bros. Store

Founded in 1876 by the pioneer brothers Bernard and Henry Sinsheimer, and built mainly of bricks from the Ah Louis brickyard, the building remains a living example of 19th-century mercantile architecture. The cast-iron colonnaded façade was cast in San Francisco and shipped here. Originally a general store catering to early ranchers, it was run until a few years ago as such by the Sinsheimer family. The building is currently unoccupied.

Bull and Bear Pit

This Court Street landmark is the site of a cruel sport indulged in by early Californians, when a bull and bear were pitted against each other in deadly combat.

MISSION PLAZA: In addition to the historical attractions, Mission Plaza houses several restaurants, shops, and boutiques that sell sandals, handcrafted gifts and jewelry, leather goods, pottery, and other such quaint-little-town-artsy-craftsy paraphernalia.

Also in Mission Plaza is the **Network,** 778 Higuera, a shopping complex.

THE CREAMERY: Californians just can't resist turning their old factories and whatnot into tourist attractions. The Creamery, located at 570 Higuera St., was originally the Golden State Creamery, built in 1906, and for the next 40-or-so years one of the most important milk-producing centers in the state. After that its importance began to decline, and in 1974 it was turned into a shopping and restaurant mall, centered around the old cooling tower. Old freezer doors, workhouse lights overhead, and milk-can lamps attest to the Creamery's original function. There's even an old Nickelodeon (costs a dime) showing scenes of devastation from the 1906 quake.

CALIFORNIA POLYTECHNIC STATE UNIVERSITY: It's not quite Berkeley, but it does have a beautiful 5,169-acre campus, much of it devoted to agricultural studies. Kids especially like to visit the feed mill, meat-processing plant, dairy operation, ornamental horticulture greenhouse, barns, and chicken coops. As well, there's some interesting experimental architecture to see (it's the largest architecture school in the country), and the student recreation center has everything from pinball to bowling.

Best time to visit is the last full weekend in April when a country fair called the Poly Royal takes place. There are rodeos, barbecues, soapbox races, and more.

Get a map outlining a self-conducted tour from the information desk in the administration building. A bus from City Hall goes right to the administration building.

BEACHES: The three main beaches in the area are **Avila Beach,** about a 10-minute drive south; **Pismo Beach,** about a 15-minute drive south; and **Morro Bay,** about 15 minutes away going north on Hwy. 1.

Avila Beach, a quaint seacoast village, offers chartered deep-sea fishing and scenic pleasure cruises from the Port St. Luis Marina. It's the best swimming beach in the area (the water is the warmest, although still not warm enough for me), and there are barbecue and picnic facilities.

Pismo offers a 23-mile stretch of beautiful sandy beach. Clam digging is a year-round favorite sport, as is exploring isolated dunes, cliff-sheltered tide pools, caves, and old pirate coves. There's fishing from the Pismo Beach Pier (other pier amusements include arcade games, bowling, billiards, etc.). It should be good, since the Spanish word *pismo* means "a place to fish." (On the other hand, this resort town may be named for the Chumash Indian word *pismu,* which means "the place where blobs of tar wash up on the beach.") You'll also find a wide variety of restaurants and shops in the area, and it's a good place for antique hunting.

Stop by the **Pismo Beach Chamber of Commerce,** 581 Dolliver St., Pismo Beach (tel. 805/773-4382), and pick up information about local attractions. (You can also get clamming instructions for the novice.) The office is open weekdays from 9:30 a.m. to 5 p.m., from 10 a.m. to 4 p.m. on Saturday.

Equally beautiful is **Morro Bay,** site of Morro Rock, the last of a chain of long-extinct volcanoes, and a winter and fall sanctuary for thousands of birds—cormorants, pelicans, sandpipers, even the rare peregrine falcon. It's wonderful to watch them from the beach or a window table at one of the bay-view restaurants.

The hub of the community is the **Embarcadero,** with its numerous seafood-with-a-view eateries; commercial fishing boats often unload their catch right at the restaurants. There are also seafood markets, boat and pier fishing facilities, shops, and art galleries to explore, as well as a nearby aquarium.

Morro Bay has many, many visitor attractions, including a state park, golf course, natural history museum, hiking trails, and of course, miles of beach. Atascadero State Beach, just north of Morro Rock, is popular with surfers and fishermen.

Once again, head for the **Morro Bay Chamber of Commerce,** 895 Napa St., Morro Bay, CA 93442 (tel. 805/772-4467), for information. They're open from 9 a.m. to 5 p.m. Monday through Saturday.

Warning: At any beaches north of Santa Barbara (where California begins to live up to its sunny rep) you might be happier in a sweatshirt than a bikini.

WHERE TO STAY: The **Madonna Inn,** at 100 Madonna Rd., San Luis Obispo, CA 93401 (tel. 805/543-3000), the unique, Disney-esque creation of Alex and Phyllis Madonna, is the most famous (or infamous) of the coast's hostelries. Nestled on 1,500 hillside acres, up a road lined with bubble-gum-pink streetlight posts, it's a fairyland castle with outdoor winding staircases, and a shingled roof topped with turrets and a weathervane. Each of the 109 rooms within is a uniquely eccentric thematic fantasy environment. The "Rock" or "Cave" rooms are among the most interesting, "Sir Walter Raleigh" the least. You can choose Spanish, Italian, Irish, Alps, Currier and Ives, super-romantic, American Indian, Swiss, or hunting decor. A "Canary Cottage" room is all yellow, with birdcage light fixtures; several are posh rock-walled caves; and there's even one for height-mismatched mates, with a bed five feet long on one side and six feet on the other.

When you enter the registration area, you can select the decor and theme of your room from a collection of hundreds of postcards. This doesn't mean you can just drop in and get a room—reserve as far in advance as possible; the place is always filled. Some favorite rooms—the results of careful perusal—are described below, and I suggest you ask for one that sounds appealing to you (maybe even give a few alternatives) when you make reservations. When you arrive, if something you prefer is vacant, you can always change.

One of the most romantic is "Love Nest," a honeymoon suite with a pink-carpeted winding stairway (all romantic-themed rooms lean very heavily to pink) leading to a cupola hideaway. In the same category is "Morning Star," a two-room suite with a high beamed cathedral ceiling, gold bed, gold tables, and gold-and-crystal chandelier. "Carin," named for a Swiss word of endearment, is also a honeymoon favorite, with gold cherub chandeliers over the bed, a peaked slanted ceiling, love birds adorning the bath, and lots of guess what color. A little less of said color—here only the carpet, drapes, bathroom walls, and phone are pink—in the delicate "Anniversary Room," with flowery rose light fixtures and floral-print wallpaper.

The rock rooms are plush stone-walled caves, many of which have working fireplaces and/or rock-walled waterfall showers. "Old World" is one that has both of these features, and a predominantly red decor. Fireplaces but no cascading showers are in "Yosemite Rock" and "Kona Rock," both furnished in lush green tones. On the other hand "Cave Man," with leopard-skin bedspread and upholstery, has the waterfall but not the fireplace. This room connects to make a suite, if you so desire, with "Daisy Mae," which has the most elaborate waterfall shower in the entire inn, and several stained-glass windows depicting Daisy Mae herself. Another favorite rock room is "Cabin Still" (there's a still in the bath).

Additional choices, these for fairytale prettiness, are: "Old Fashioned Honeymoon" (ornately Victorian) and "Victorian Gardens" (ditto); "Swiss Bell," "Wilhelm Tell," "Edelweiss," and "Matterhorn" (all with very charming Swiss decor); and finally the "Safari Room" (wild game theme) and "Buffalo Room," this latter of special significance to the Madonnas, since the buffalo head mounted on the wall was once attached to their very own buffalo, killed in an accident.

Each room has a color TV, direct-dial phone, and bath; you won't need a clock, since every hour is heralded by bells, Swiss yodels, and a musical passage on the Swiss alphorn.

Additional facilities in the main building include an enormous coffeeshop, a dining room (rather pricey), and two cocktail lounges, all as outlandishly ornate and plushly pink as the rest.

The rate schedule is as follows: singles are $77, doubles run $82 to $143, and suites with a fireplace are $135 to $180.

More conventional accommodations are available at any of three conveniently located, well-run little motels, all at the junction of U.S. 101 and Hwy. 1, within walking distance of each other and of town.

The **Apple Farm Inn**, 2015 Monterey St., at the end of the Monterey exit off U.S. 101 (tel. 805/544-2040, or toll free 800/255-2040 in California), sits sedately among the giant sycamores on the banks of San Luis Creek. Each of the 68 rooms in this handsome Victorian structure is a delightful blend of country charm and traditional elegance. All these pine-furnished rooms have gas-log fireplaces; some have four-poster or canopy beds, others brass beds. Some rooms have bay windows with window seats and a view of San Luis Creek. The rooms also have all the amenities of a well-thought-out contemporary inn—oversize tubs, color TV, and phones. An outdoor heated pool, with a Jacuzzi, is open year-round; two specialty rooms above the mill house have decks overlooking this vista. Adjacent to the inn is the Apple Farm Restaurant, described in delicious detail below.

Rates for single or double rooms are $55 to $95.

The **Coachman Inn**, 1001 Olive St., San Luis Obispo, CA 93401 (tel. 805/544-0400), is housed in a two-story shingle-roofed stucco building, with pots of geraniums enhancing the exterior. Rooms are large and comfortably furnished, with dressing areas, bath/shower combinations, direct-dial phones, and cable color TVs. Some rooms have refrigerators and some have king-size beds. There's a swimming pool on the premises, and a restaurant 100 feet away. The staff is most friendly and helpful.

Singles and doubles at the Coachman Inn cost $50 to $65; two-room suites are $60 to $86 for up to four, $5 per extra person. Lower rates from October to mid-May.

Just across the street at 1000 Olive St., San Luis Obispo, CA 93401 is the **Best Western Olive Tree** (tel. 805/544-2800), offering quality and pleasant accommodations. The Olive Tree has a restaurant on the premises, the Stuffed Olive, a reasonably priced coffeeshop. There's also a sauna here along with the pool; all rooms have color TVs, direct-dial phones, and clocks.

The most unique feature of the Olive Tree is its eight apartment suites, housed in an attractive shingled building, all with large terraces and big, fully equipped, modern kitchens. These cost $77 to $85 for four to six persons. Regular singles are $55; doubles and twins are $59. Once again, off-season rates are a few dollars less.

Completing this motel triangle is the **Homestead,** 920 Olive St., San Luis Obispo, CA 93401 (tel. 805/543-7700), with facilities—swimming pool, color TV, direct-dial phone, etc.—almost identical to those at the above-mentioned establishments. By way of differentiation, the Homestead has prettier rooms than the other two, with rather nice maple furnishings and quaint little paintings and prints on the walls. Singles pay $41 to $47; doubles, $51 to $65; a cottage with kitchen is $65 to $80. Off-season rates are slightly lower.

Another good choice is the friendly **Lamp Lighter Motel,** 1604 Monterey St. (at Grove), San Luis Obispo, CA 93401 (tel. 805/543-3709), with 40 neat and clean motel rooms. All have cable color TVs, with free HBO movies, complimentary continental breakfast, direct-dial phones, tub/shower baths; clocks and irons are available on request. Rates are $40 to $47, single or double.

Budget-minded travelers might want to stay at **Motel 6,** 1433 Calle Joaquin, San Luis Obispo, CA 93401 (tel. 805/549-9595), with 87 units and a swimming pool. Best if you have a car, since otherwise it's just a mite out of the way. As with all Motel 6 facilities, the units are simple, clean, and shower only— but it's hard to beat the price. Singles are $24.95, each additional adult is $6. Color TV is free; all rooms have phones and local calls are free.

Avila Beach

If you have a few days to relax in the San Luis area, why not put up at a hotel in one of the nearby beach resorts? Best of these is the luxurious 74-room **San Luis Bay Inn** in Avila Beach CA 93424 (tel. 805/595-2333). All of the rooms here offer sweeping coastal views of the ocean or mountains, and the beach is just across the street. But there's more to do here than laze about in the sun and sand. Facilities include a beautiful 18-hole golf course, four tennis courts, and a heated swimming pool. Sports fishing, horseback riding, and even hot tub mineral baths can be arranged, as can trips to Hearst Castle.

As for the rooms, they're just exquisite, newly renovated and decorated in pale shades of mauve, blues, and beiges. All have private balconies and extra-large bathrooms with sunken tubs. The especially attractive top floor rooms have sloped wood ceilings.

The inn's gourmet restaurant, The Cove, has windows all around providing great views. Luncheon fare features items like Templeton chicken breast, mesquite grilled with mushrooms, onions, bell peppers, and melted San Luis garlic cheese. Or make a choice from a selection of fresh salads and sandwiches ($8 to $18). The dinner menu changes daily to take advantage of the freshest, finest ingredients available that day. You might begin with wild mushroom crêpes or Oysters Rockefeller, perhaps followed by a Caesar salad. Entrees always include a wide range of choices such as fresh local abalone, venison, quail, filet mignon, or lamb. Prices range from $17 to $35. The restaurant offers an award-winning wine list, with selections to complement whatever you might order. A $17 prix-fixe Sunday brunch is also served here, and there's dancing in the adjoining lounge Thursday through Saturday nights. Mulligans Bar and Grill, with a wall of windows overlooking San Luis Creek, is another delightful dining option. It's a casual place where light fare is served.

To enjoy the leisurely country-club lifestyle at the San Luis Bay Inn in summer will cost $114 to $150, single or double, $10 for each extra person in the room. Suites with private hot tubs are also available for $190 to $300.

Camping

Facilities for camping abound in the San Luis area. For information about Pismo Beach and Morro Bay campsites, write to their respective chambers of commerce (addresses above). The San Luis chamber has a directory of about 40 local campgrounds included in their city map.

WHERE TO EAT: There are quite a few places in and around town, none of them dishing up unforgettable gourmet fare, but many offering good honest meals in very pleasant settings and hospitality you're not likely to forget. Such a one is **Linnaeas Café,** 1110 Garden St., between Marsh and Higuera Streets (tel. 805/541-5888).

Breakfast at Linnaeas is as relaxed and pleasant as it would be with longtime friends. What's more, the food at breakfast and lunch is delicious, creatively seasoned, and much of it ingeniously cooked right in front of you.

The café, with its wooden counter, simple stools, and small, circular table, also serves as an art gallery; all the pictures on the wall are for sale. On a lovely patio in the back, you can enjoy the morning or evening with comfortable company.

The breakfast event begins at 7:30 a.m. If you thought you've had eggs done in just about every conceivable way, order the egg burrito ($2.50) for a pleasant surprise: a flour tortilla lovingly enfolds fluffy scrambled eggs and a happy combination of chopped tomato, scallions, sliced black olives, and cheddar cheese, all topped off with a dollop of sour cream and guacamole. After breakfast I couldn't resist the café au lait—one of the 12 available varieties of hot coffee. The café also serves eight types of iced coffee.

If you're in a conservative mode, head for the granola table in the rear room, where you'll also find an overwhelming variety of yummies available to mix and match with your grains. Weekends, the café serves soufflés and other special Linnaeas delights.

If you thought breakfast couldn't be surpassed, just wait for the "SLO" rolls —you're in *San Luis Obispo,* remember—at lunch. An "SLO" roll is made of Armenian crackerbread and has various fillings, all with a cream cheese/mayo base. The Mexican variety is filled with cheese, tomatoes, chiles, and onions; the Italian version features zucchini, mushrooms, green olives, and jack cheese, with touches of parmesan and garlic. You buy the roll by the inch—$1.50 for each one-inch slice that looks much like a jelly-roll slice. In addition, choices of fresh-made soups and salads change daily: full-size salads are $4.50, smaller portions $2.75; soups are $2.25 per bowl, $1.50 per cup.

Linnaeas Cafe is not open for dinner, but wonderful things begin to happen about 6:30 p.m. Coffees from cappuccino to café au lait to Viennese are served with the desserts of the day—tortes, cranberry bread, carrot cake, Black Magic— all from $1.50 to $3.50 per portion. At about 8 p.m. the live music begins. During the Mozart Festival, the concerts are classical; other times, whatever suits the mood (when I was last there, singer/songwriter Nancy Vogl was scheduled to sing).

Breakfast is served to 11:30 a.m., lunch to 3 p.m., and coffee, dessert, and music go on until midnight. Bring your own conversation.

If you're fortunate enough to meet Linnaeas at the café—she's a joy—you'll begin to understand a lot more about the warmth and charm of San Luis Obispo.

Another fine eatery is **1865**, 1865 Monterey St., near Grand Avenue (tel. 805/544-1865), a ski-lodgey, redwood-paneled, candlelit restaurant with peaked 60-foot ceilings. Philodendrons 20 feet long hang from beams under the upstairs skylight, macramé hangings and color photographs adorn the walls, and one room has a corner fireplace with a large orange chimney. The bar is a comfortable hangout, and there's more seating outdoors, also around a fireplace. Tuesday to Saturday nights, jazz and other easy-listening music add to the friendly ambience. Steak and seafood entrees (like prime rib or fresh red snapper) are featured at dinner, all served with salad, rice pilaf or baked potato, and garlic bread. Prices range from $14 to $25. For dessert try the homemade chocolate mousse.

Open for lunch Tuesday through Friday (almost all entrees are under $12) from 11 a.m. to 2:30 p.m.; for dinner Monday through Thursday and Sunday from 5 to 10 p.m., Friday and Saturday to 11 p.m. Reservations suggested.

F. McLintocks Saloon, 686 Higuera St., between Broad and Nipomo (tel. 805/541-0686), is right out of the Old West, complete with cowboy-and-Indian theme paintings (but a large oil of a nude over the bar), historic photos of the West, an elk head trophy on one wall, turn-of-the-century lighting fixtures and bar. Cowboys and ranchers visiting town are naturally drawn to the place, further legitimizing the atmosphere. There's a patio with a few tables for outdoor dining. The menu lists typical fare like a large order of "genuine" western chili or an eight-ounce steak sandwich on garlic bread with ranch beans and salad, averaging $5 to $10. Deep-fried turkey nuts are a specialty appetizer.

F. McLintocks is open Monday through Saturday for breakfast, lunch, dinner, and late-night drinking and country and western music.

Down the road 12 miles is the larger **McLintocks Saloon and Dining House,** in Shell Beach at 750 Mattie Road (tel. 805/773-1892); take 101 and get off at the Shell Beach Road exit. Housed in what once was a real ranch house, the restaurant still retains its western spirit and style: swinging saloon doors, walls lined with hunting trophies and cowboy paraphernalia, lantern-lit checker-clothed tables, a blazing stone fireplace, and a craps table from speakeasy days. All this plus live music make the bar a cozy, popular local hangout.

Dinners include a salad of either fresh spinach or greens, ranch beans, salsa, garlic bread, tortillas, onion rings, ranch-fried potatoes, and after-dinner liqueur or sherbet. All this, with an entree like hickory-smoked barbecued spareribs in pineapple-honey sauce, a 14-ounce top sirloin, or fresh abalone with drawn butter, will run you from $15 to $22.

McLintocks Saloon and Dining House is open Monday to Friday from 11:30 a.m. to 3 p.m. for lunch and 3 to 10:30 p.m. for dinner; Saturday and Sunday dinner is served from 2 p.m. "Lite" dinners are served weekdays from 3 to 5 p.m., weekends from 2 to 4 p.m. BIG western breakfasts are served every weekend, Saturday from 8 to 11:30 a.m., Sunday from 9 to 11:30 a.m. Reservations are taken except for Friday and Saturday dinner.

The **Olde Port Inn** (tel. 805/595-2515) is superbly located at the end of the third pier on Avila Road right out on the boat-filled bay. Housed on two floors, it has windows everywhere providing wonderful views; inside there's lots of rustic nautical decor—columns made of pier pilings, oilcan bar stools, fishnet, weathered wood ceilings and beams, and walls lined with photos of local fisherfolk. Hanging lamps with red glass shades and candle lamps made from cut-tin clam juice cans create a cozy glow. The bar bounces; upstairs it's quieter.

The chef specializes in sautéing and charbroiling. Fish dinners simply do not come fresher; each day the chef goes down to the fishing boats and handpicks the catch for the evening. Similarly, the motto of the house is "use the freshest produce possible." These are clearly winning concepts: the restaurant has been under the same ownership for 17 years. Dinner entrees also include steak, pasta, and chicken, all served with chowder or spinach salad, a fresh vegetable, and new potatoes. Specialties of the house include prawns stuffed with jack cheese and wrapped with bacon, seafood pasta, a delicious cioppino, and a steamer special with crab claws, mussels, and clams in a butter and garlic sauce. Fresh fish entrees may include salmon, halibut, red snapper, petrale sole, mahi mahi, shark, and swordfish. Dinners cost $12 to $19.

The inn is open Saturday and Sunday for lunch (featuring slightly lower prices) from noon to 3 p.m.; dinner is served daily from 5:30 to 10 p.m. There's nightly entertainment—rock, '40s swing, and sometimes jazz—in the downstairs cocktail area. Reservations are essential.

Originally built as a residence circa 1917, **This Old House,** Foothill Boulevard toward Los Osos Valley Road (tel. 805/543-2690), was named for the '50s pop song. It was turned into a restaurant of sorts, serving beer, whisky, and fried chicken and potatoes on paper plates. It was a rowdy cowboy hangout complete with shooting contests and an occasional horse in the bar. In an attempt to give the place some class a model of Sputnik was put on the roof.

These days it's a real restaurant where shootouts are frowned on, but still very western in feel. Bare oak floors, rodeo photos, and cowboy paraphernalia adorn the walls; there's a fireplace, a beamed barn-like ceiling, simulated gaslight chandeliers, and antique furnishings from country farms and ranches.

All entrees cost $14 to $20 and are served with salad, relish tray, ranch beans, Texas toast, salsa, potato, and sherbet. Straight from the oak pit are barbecued beef or spareribs, half a barbecued chicken, steak, and ribs; there's also a catch of the day barbecued over oak. Kids' plates are available.

Open for dinner nightly from 5:30 to 9:30 p.m. Reservations essential.

Housed in the Network complex of restaurants and shops, the **Wine Street Inn,** 774 Higuera St., between Chorro and Broad (tel. 805/543-4488), is a low-ceilinged, long rectangular room, bordered by planters and dimly lit, even at lunch, by candles. Butcher-block and oak tables, some covered by red cloths, are arranged haphazardly on a brick floor. An old-fashioned bar spans one wall and wine and cheese shops adjoin. Lots of "atmosphere" here, to be sure.

At lunch, very good sandwiches are served on fresh-baked egg bread or dark bread, such as a Reuben, the Number One (cold beef, butter, bleu cheese, tomatoes, and chives), or guacamole and bacon. You can also partake of the salad bar. Swiss or cheddar cheese fondue, served with chunks of sourdough bread, is easily enough for two people. Lunch entrees cost $7 to $10.

Dinners are more elaborate. You might begin with an appetizer of pears and apples served with smoked cheese dip. The selection of fondues is increased to include beef bourguignon and shrimp fondue, served with rice or baked potato, salad, and sourdough bread. Other items served with same are teriyaki chicken and fresh baked red snapper. For dessert, I simply cannot resist the creamy chocolate fondue. Entrees cost $12 to $17.

As the name of the place suggests, the wine list is extensive. In addition, you can buy your own bottle at the adjoining wine shop and pay a corkage fee.

The Wine Street Inn is open for lunch from 11:30 a.m. to 2 p.m. Monday through Saturday, and for dinner nightly from 5:30 p.m.

The Apple Farm, 2015 Monterey St., at the end of the Monterey exit from U.S. 101 (tel. 805/544-6100), an attractive and charming Victorian structure, originally got its name because the owners set out to collect "apple art." But that's only the start of it. When you go to the Apple Farm restaurant, be sure to allow time for going through the grist mill, antique bakery, and gift shop.

The restaurant is a tribute to the best of American country fare because virtually everything (with obvious exceptions) is homemade and delicious—soups created from scratch, chili, apple pies, and incredible dumplings made from fresh apples. The Apple Farm is a place to enjoy simple but delicious home-style food, served with touches you don't usually find elsewhere, at a very modest price. Breakfast comes with hash brown potatoes or fresh fruit plus freshly baked muffins and biscuits. Lunch is accompanied by potato salad (homemade, of course) or fresh fruit, and there are three homemade soups daily to choose from. Dinner offers a simple but toothsome selection of chicken and dumplings, pork chops, baked half chicken, pan-fried trout, barbecued ribs, or prime rib, with baked or scalloped potatoes (when were you last offered scalloped potatoes?). Freshly baked corn bread (a specialty of the house) can be had with lunch or dinner. But save room for the famous hot apple dumplings, or one of the other luscious desserts. Breakfast or lunch will probably run $3.50 to $4.75; dinner, $7 to $12. All I can say is, *go!* If you must wait for a bit, wait; or call ahead and get on the waiting list before heading off to the restaurant. Open daily from 7 a.m. to 9 p.m.

At the Apple Farm Bakery you can watch apple dumplings and cinnamon rolls being made, and you can drool over a wide selection of pies, cookies, brownies, etc. Or visit the two-story gift shop, with a fascinating collection of decorative items. It got started when customers wanted to buy what they saw in the restaurant; now it offers models of California missions, wall hangings, books for all ages, toys, and cranberry glass, plus such goodies as apple butter and boysenberry spread. And you really should stop at the Old Mill House and watch the apple cider press and grist mill in operation. Apple Farm–brand flour, coffee, butter, and ice cream are produced there using the power of an authentic 19th-century water wheel. And, oh yes, there's a marvelous place to spend the night—the Apple Farm Inn, mentioned above in the "Where to Stay" section.

7. SOLVANG

If you're traveling south from San Luis Obispo, most of the spectacular California coast is behind you; if you're on your way north, it's yet to come. Now is a good time to head inland to the charming Santa Ynez Valley.

You can take Hwy. 246 into the valley from the north (it intersects with Rte. 1 at Lompoc, and U.S. 101 at Buellton), or Hwy. 154 from Hwy. 1/101 at the south, near Santa Barbara. Highways 246 and 154 intersect east of the town of Santa Ynez.

The Santa Ynez Valley has only five small towns: the aforementioned Buellton and Santa Ynez, as well as Los Olivos, Ballard (the oldest, founded in 1860), and Solvang, the main attraction in the valley. Founded in 1911 by a group of Danish-Americans, Solvang (which means "sunny valley" in Danish) was much like any other rural California mission town until the end of World War II. Word of the quaint town spread, and as its popularity grew, the townfolk worked all the harder to preserve their heritage.

Make your first stop the **Solvang Visitors Bureau,** 1623 Mission Dr., Solvang, CA 93463 (tel. 805/688-3317), for information. They're open daily from 9 a.m. to 5 p.m. Then set out to explore the town center, a cluster of little streets lined with quaint Scandinavian shops, inns, restaurants, and even windmills. You can wander about from shop to shop, or stop for a bite of Danish or Swedish food.

WHAT TO SEE AND DO: The oldest sight in Solvang is the **Mission Santa Ines,** 1760 Mission Dr. (Rte. 246). It was built in 1804, the 19th of Father Junipero Serra's series of 21 missions. Most of its buildings were destroyed by an earthquake in 1812 or ravaged by a fire in 1821, after which it was rebuilt. In the mid-19th century the mission was sold except for the church and living quarters. The rest deteriorated to ruins. It was restored to the Catholic church by Abraham Lincoln. Not until the early 20th century, however, did restoration work on the mission begin. In the winter of 1987, an extensive project restoring a large part of the convent and eight of the arches was begun; it was finally completed at the end of 1988.

Today Mission Santa Ines looks as it must have shortly after it was founded. It houses a museum of Indian and mission artifacts from the early days. The church, a chapel, the museum, and grounds are open daily for visitors: Monday to Saturday from 9 a.m. to 5 p.m. and on Sunday from noon to 5 p.m. in summer; the rest of the year, Monday to Saturday from 9:30 a.m. to 4:30 p.m. and on Sunday from noon to 4:30 p.m. The mission is closed Thanksgiving, Christmas, and New Year's Days. A donation of $1 is asked of adults.

The Santa Ynez Valley boasts a number of wineries that offer tastings. You can visit the **Firestone Vineyard,** Zaca Station Road in Los Olivos (tel. 805/688-3940); **Vega Vineyards,** at 9496 Santa Rosa Rd. in Buellton (tel. 805/688-2415); and the **Ballard Canyon Winery,** 1825 Ballard Canyon Rd. in Solvang (tel. 805/688-7585). See the Solvang Visitors Bureau for information on these and others, or call the wineries directly for tasting hours.

On your way out of Solvang going south on Rte. 154 you'll pass by one of the prettiest spots in the valley, the **Lake Cachuma Recreation Area** (tel. 805/688-4658). There are all sorts of activities year round: camping, boating, fishing, picnicking, and horseback riding, to name a few.

Passing from the Santa Ynez Valley to Santa Barbara, Rte. 154 goes through the San Marcos Pass and up onto a ridge that affords a spectacular view of the valley and then—on the far side—the Pacific and the Channel Islands in the distance.

WHERE TO STAY: If you decide to stay in the Santa Ynez Valley, you'll like the **Sheraton Royal Scandinavian Inn,** 400 Alisal Rd., Solvang, CA 93463 (tel. 805/688-8000, or toll free 800/325-3535). It features 135 luxurious, air-conditioned rooms with cable color TVs, direct-dial phones, heated pool and spa, restaurant, and cocktail lounge. Rates are $75 to $100, single or double.

There's also a **Motel 6** at 333 McMurray Rd., Buellton, CA 93427 (tel. 805/688-7797); it has 59 rooms and a pool. Rates are $23.95 for one person, $6 for each extra adult. All rooms now have phones and color TV; local calls are free.

8. SANTA BARBARA

The best thing that ever happened to Santa Barbara was an earthquake! On June 29, 1925, a quake with a Richter magnitude of 6.3 virtually destroyed the entire business district, leaving the uninspired architecture of the town in shambles. An Architectural Board of Review was formed soon after to guide the rebuilding of the city, and a brilliant decision was made that has been in effect ever since. All new buildings had to be in similar Mediterranean style—basically the California adobe characterized by light-colored, sparkling stucco walls, low sloping terracotta-tile roofs, a glimpse here and there of lacy wrought-iron grillwork, and above all, a comfortable human scale.

Although the buildings that sprang up here have many influences—Mediterranean, Spanish Colonial Revival, Mexican, Early California, Monterey, and even Moorish and Islamic—all are unified by the above standard, and all are in styles of architecture from areas with warm climates similar to Santa Barbara.

Already blessed with the Santa Ynez Mountains as a magnificent backdrop, and a mostly gorgeous coastline, Santa Barbara has, with careful planning, become one of California's most beautiful cities. It is also (at least part time) the residence of some notable personages—one president, and a bevy of show business personalities (Jane Russell, Karl Malden, Steve Martin, Robert Mitchum, Robert Preston, Jonathan Winters), and one remarkable chef, Julia Child.

The beauty of the Santa Barbara beach area cannot be disguised, even on an overcast day: then the ocean and mountains to either side have the same blue haze often seen in Japanese paintings. The only blight on the scene are the oil rigs out on the ocean—difficult to ignore whether the sun is shining or not.

As you drive along State Street (a plaza boulevard, and the town's main drag) from U.S. 101, you'll first pass through the old section of town, which is in a continual state of redevelopment. But once you get into the heart of the city, life changes. The sidewalks are wide and landscaped, enhanced by flowering trees and planting beds, store signs are limited in size, mailboxes and newsstands built into stucco walls, and at every pedestrian crossing is a living Christmas tree that serves as just a regular tree the rest of the year. Even billboards have been banned in this delightful city.

Just 92 miles north of Los Angeles and 332 south of San Francisco, Santa Barbara is reached by car via Hwy. 1 or U.S. 101. Several airlines link both major cities with Santa Barbara, as do Greyhound buses and Amtrak.

Once again, there's so much to do and see in this lovely beach resort city that I advise you to visit the new **Santa Barbara Visitor Information Center,** 1 Santa Barbara St., Santa Barbara, CA 93101 (tel. 805/965-3021) for maps, literature, and a calendar of the many and varied events taking place at all times. Among other things, they've planned out a scenic drive that takes in 15 major points of interest and a suggested walking tour of Santa Barbara's historical landmarks. It's especially important for you to have a map in Santa Barbara, particularly for evenings, when street signs are very difficult to see, much less read. Much of the city does not have street lights. The Center sells a map of the city for $1, which is extremely useful in finding your way around. The Information Center is open Monday through Friday 9 a.m. to 5 p.m., Saturday 9 a.m. to 4 p.m.; June to Labor Day it's open Sunday 9 a.m. to 4 p.m.

WHAT TO DO AND SEE: It would be a pleasure to while away an entire summer here, sunning oneself on the beach, taking long walks, visiting museums, dining in lovely restaurants, playing golf and tennis, horseback riding, bike riding, fishing, going to concerts, and luxuriating in the amazingly beautiful surroundings.

If you only have a few days, however, you might start with **State Street,** which has one of the most interesting and attractive collections of shops and cafés west of the Hudson River—perfect for strolling, spending money, noshing, watching the passing parade, whatever. Starting toward the north end at Victoria Street, you'll enjoy every block of a slow stroll down to Ortega Street—about half a mile. Along the way, for those who tire easily, there are wood and stone benches on every block. If you've run out of places to shop along the way, try **La Arcada** between Anapamu and Figueroa (on the east side of State), a gathering of elegant boutiques for children's clothing, leather, art, jewelry, apparel

(Pappagallo)—there's even a barber shop. The flowers, benches, and a fountain are there to help relax and refresh you. There's a cheese shop, too, and the Acapulco restaurant at the end of the arcade.

Some of the historic highlights of Santa Barbara that you can see along the way are:

El Paseo—The Street in Spain (814 State St.)

A picturesque shopping arcade with stone walkways, El Paseo is reminiscent of an old street in Spain. Built around the 1827 original adobe home of Spanish-born Presidio Commandante José de la Guerra, El Paseo is lined with charming shops and art galleries. This is the hub of the city. Across the street is the **Plaza de la Guerra,** where the first City Council met in 1850, and where the first City Hall was erected in 1875.

County Courthouse (1100 Anacapa St.)

Occupying a full city block on Anapamu Street, and set in a lush tropical garden, the County Courthouse (tel. 805/962-6464) is a supreme example of Santa Barbara nouveau-Spanish architecture—a tribute to bygone days when style and elegance outweighed more practical considerations. Few would guess that it was built as late as 1929. The architect, William Mooser, was aided by his son who, having spent 17 years in Spain, was well versed in Spanish-Moorish design.

Turrets and towers, graceful arches, unexpected windows, brilliant Tunisian tilework, winding staircases, intricately carved and stenciled ceilings, palacio tile floors, lacy iron grillwork, heavy carved-wood doors, and Spanish lanterns of hammered iron are among the impressive interior features. Magnificent historic murals by Dan Sayre Groesbeck, depicting memorable episodes in Santa Barbara history, are worth a visit in themselves. An elevator whisks visitors up to El Mirador—the 85-foot-high deck of the clock tower where there are sweeping views of the ocean, mountains, and terracotta-tile roofs of the city.

The courthouse is amazingly impressive and inspiring—don't miss it. It's open from 8 a.m. to 5 p.m. on weekdays, from 9 a.m. to 5 p.m. on weekends and holidays. You can take a free guided tour on Wednesday and Friday at 10:30 a.m.

Santa Barbara Mission (Laguna and Mission Streets)

Called the "Queen of the Missions" for its graceful beauty, this hilltop paradise overlooks the town—its gleaming white buildings surrounded by an expanse of lush green lawn, flowering trees and shrubs, a Moorish fountain under a pepper tree, and a misty backdrop of cloud-enshrouded mountains. It's the only California mission with twin bell towers and is regarded by many as the most beautiful.

Established in 1786, the present mission is still used today by the parish of Santa Barbara. On display within are a typical missionary bedroom, tools, crafts and artifacts of the Chumash people, 18th- and 19th-century mission furnishings, paintings and statues from Mexico, and period kitchen utensils—grinding stones, baskets, and copper kettles. You can take a self-guided tour any day from 9:30 a.m. to 5 p.m., on Sunday from 1 to 5 p.m. Adults are asked for a donation of $1; children under 16 go in free. For more information, call 805/682-4173 or 682-4175.

Museums

Three privately maintained Santa Barbara museums are open to the public and charge no admission.

The **Santa Barbara Museum of Natural History,** beyond Old Mission

Road, at 2559 Puesta de Sol Rd. (tel. 805/682-4711), is devoted to the display, study, and interpretation of Pacific coast natural history—flora, fauna, and pre-historic life. Museum architecture, in typical Santa Barbara style, reflects early Spanish and Mexican influence, with ivy-colored stucco walls, graceful arches, arcades, a central patio, and lovely grounds. Exhibits range from diagrams and photographs of the life cycle of worms, to Native American basketry, textiles, and a full-size replica of a Chumash canoe; from Native American art to fossil ferns to the complete skeleton of a blue whale.

In addition to halls dealing with Native Americans, birds, mammals, the Pa-leolithic age, minerals, and marine life, a planetarium offers shows on Saturday and Sunday.

Open from 9 a.m. to 5 p.m. Monday through Saturday, from 10 a.m. to 5 p.m. on Sunday and Christmas, New Year's, and Thanksgiving. Admission is $3 adults, $1 children.

The **Santa Barbara Museum of Art,** 1130 State St., at Anapamu (tel. 805/963-4364, or TTY 963-2240 for the hearing impaired), houses an extraordinary collection for a community its size. It includes Greek and Roman sculpture, painted vessels, and ancient glass; a European collection of impressionists like Monet, Pissarro, and Chagall, and early-20th-century European modernists like Hoffmann and Kandinsky; works of the Italian Renaissance and Flemish schools; a representative collection of American art by such artists as O'Keeffe, Eakins, Sargent, Hopper, and Grosz; Oriental sculpture, prints, ceramicware, scrolls, screens, and paintings; works on paper by such 15th- to 20th-century masters as Rembrandt, Canaletto, Fuseli, Ruskin, Degas, Picasso, and Miró; and a photog-raphy collection of over 1,500 images.

In 1985 the museum opened its expanded and renovated facility and cur-rently houses over 12,000 works, which are exhibited on a rotating basis in new climate- and light-controlled galleries.

Recent special shows at the museum included *Photographs by David Hockney*; *Orbis Pictus: The Prints of Oskar Kokoschka*; *Dressed in Splendor: Japanese Costumes from 1700 to 1926*; *Painters of Light: American Impressionism*; *Nancy Graves: A Sculpture Retrospective*; and *Robert Capa: A Retrospective*. In addition there are regular concerts, lectures, performance art events, and film series.

The museum is open Tuesday through Saturday from 11 a.m. to 5 p.m., Thursday till 9 p.m., Sunday from noon to 5 p.m. Admission is free. Docent-led tours, also free, are offered daily at 2 p.m.

The **Historical Society Museum,** 136 East De la Guerra St., at the corner of Santa Barbara Street (tel. 805/966-1601), deals with local lore. It's most inter-esting to take the free guided tour, given by a knowledgeable guide, on Wednes-day and Sunday at 1:30 p.m. Exhibits include paintings of California missions by Edwin Deakin done between 1875 and 1890; a 16th-century carved Spanish cof-fer from Majorca, home of Padre Serra; objects of the thriving Chinese communi-ty of Santa Barbara, including a magnificent carved shrine from the turn of the century; Peruvian silver stirrups and a Spanish cope, both of the 17th century; oil portraits and artifacts of the De la Guerra family and other early notables of Santa Barbara history; many interesting pieces of correspondence; antique dolls; lots of period clothing; and many other relics and memorabilia that make the area's his-tory come alive.

Open Tuesday through Friday from noon to 5 p.m., on Saturday and Sun-day from 1 to 5 p.m.

Santa Barbara Botanic Garden (1212 Mission Canyon Rd.)

About 1½ miles north of the mission, the Botanic Garden (tel. 805/682-4726), 65 acres of native trees, shrubs, cacti, and wildflowers, is also the site of a dam built by Native Americans in 1806. There are over five miles of nature trails to follow. Open daily from 8 a.m. to sunset, with free guided tours offered on Thursday at 10:30 a.m. and Sunday at 11 a.m. Free admission.

Moreton Bay Fig Tree (Chapala and Montecito Streets)

I'm not grasping for sightseeing attractions—this tree is really something! Native to Moreton Bay in eastern Australia, the *Figus macrophylla* is related to both the fig and rubber tree, although it produces neither figs nor rubber. The branch spread of this massive century-old (planted in 1877) example would cover half a football field, well over 10,000 persons could stand in its shade at noon, and over an acre of ground covers its woody roots, and is hands-down the largest in the world!

Once in danger of being leveled—for a proposed gas station, of all things— and later threatened by excavation for nearby U.S. 101, the revered tree has been fervently protected each time by its fans, who will no doubt go on protecting the fig tree's territorial rights for another century.

Santa Barbara Zoological Gardens (500 Ninos Dr., off Cabrillo Boulevard)

This is a good place to take the kids. Over 400 exotic animals are displayed in open, naturalistic settings. In addition, there are beautiful botanic displays, a farmyard, picnic areas with barbecue pits, a gift shop, a snackbar, a miniature train ride, and a small carousel. It's all open every day from 10 a.m. to 5 p.m. except Thanksgiving and Christmas (tel. 805/962-6310 for recorded information, or 962-5339). During the summer (mid-June through Labor day) the hours are 9 a.m. to 6 p.m. Admission is $4 for everyone over 12, $2 for seniors and those 2 to 12; under 2, it's free.

Andree Clark Bird Refuge (1400 E. Cabrillo Blvd.)

Adjoining the Zoological Gardens, the refuge is a lovely lagoon in a garden setting, where many varieties of freshwater fowl can be seen and fed. A foot and bike path skirt the lagoon, and it's so beautiful it doesn't even matter if you don't see birds. Serious birdwatchers can pick up a 50¢ eight-page pamphlet about local birds at the Museum of Natural History.

Antiquing, Gallery Browsing, and Shopping

There are close to 80 antique shops in Santa Barbara. **Brinkerhoff Avenue,** off Haley between Chapala and De La Vina Streets, is where you'll find the greatest concentration, selling Early American furnishings, quilts, antique china, jewelry, Orientalia, and memorabilia, not to mention bric-a-brac and interesting junk. The free *Santa Barbara Visitor Press* lists the most notable, along with the town's many art galleries, boutiques, leather and handicraft shops, etc. You can get it at the Visitor Center, along with a brochure that lists antique shops. In Santa Barbara you can buy everything from out-of-print books to mounted butterflies. Santa Barbara has 65 bookstores and 60 art galleries; and when you get hungry after shopping, there are over 300 restaurants to sustain your strength.

At 813 State St., a cluster of shops is located in an arcade called **Picadilly Square.** They range from an Native American art shop to a cheese store.

At the western end of State Street is **Stearns Wharf** (tel. 408/963-0611), Santa Barbara's answer to Fisherman's Wharf. Built on an 1872-vintage pier is a collection of shops, attractions, and restaurants, including the Harbor Restaurant (tel. 408/963-3311), a seafood eatery dating from 1941.

Boating and Fishing

Sea Landing, at the foot of Bath Street and Cabrillo Boulevard (tel. 805/ 963-3564), has four sport-fishing boats and two sport-diving boats. They offer a wide variety of fishing and diving trips, as well as daily twilight and half-day cruises ($19 for adults, $15 for children under 12), three-quarter-day cruises ($28 for adults, $20 for children), and full-day cruises ($39.50 for adults, $27 for children). All boats are totally equipped with stocked galley (food and drink served on board), rental rods and tackle available; rates include bait. Fishing licenses can be obtained at the office. Reservations recommended.

In the summer months they also offer three-hour dinner and cocktail cruises with dancing to live music ($30 for steak dinner, $20 for cocktails only); departures are at 7 p.m. And you can take whale-watching cruises from February to the end of April ($21 for adults, $15 for children).

Motorboats, sailboats, and rowboats are available for rent from **Santa Barbara Boat Rentals** (tel. 805/962-2826), at the Breakwater.

Bicycling

This scenic and relatively flat area is marvelous for biking: along the four-mile palm-lined coastal bikeway, through town, on miles of country roads, or to nearby Montecito. **Beach Rentals,** at 8 W. Cabrillo Blvd., right at the beach (tel. 805/963-2524), has carefully maintained one-speed, tandem, and ten-speed bikes and roller skates for rent, and they'll suggest bicycle tours too. Open seven days a week. Bring an ID (driver's license or passport) to expedite your rental.

Horseback Riding

Several stables in the area rent horses, and offer escorted trail rides along the many local trails. **San Ysidro Ranch Stables,** 900 San Ysidro Lane (tel. 805/ 969-5046), charges $20 for a one-hour guided trail ride; private lessons in western riding are $35 an hour, $20 per half hour. Reservations are essential.

Hiking

The **Sierra Club** (tel. 805/965-8709) is active in Santa Barbara. They can tell you about the many scenic trails in the Los Padres National Forest and other locations. The club does not have an office; any inquiries should be made by phone.

Golf

There are four public golf courses to choose from in the Santa Barbara vicinity. The 18-hole **Santa Barbara Community Course** is located at 3500 McCaw Ave., at Las Positas Rd. (tel. 805/687-7087). The course is 6,009 yards and has a pro shop and driving range. Weekday prices are $11; weekends you'll pay $12; for seniors, the charge is $7.50 weekdays, $10.50 on the weekend. Carts are $16, $13 for seniors.

The three remaining courses are located in nearby Goleta. The 18-hole, 6,600-yard **Sandpiper,** at 7925 Hollister Ave. (tel. 805/968-1541), has a pro shop and driving range. Weekday prices are $24, rising to $35 on the weekend. Carts are $20. The remaining two courses are both nine holes. **Ocean Meadows,** at 6925 Whittier Dr. (tel. 805/968-6814), is 3,033 yards. Prices are $8 during the week, $9 on the weekend. Carts cost $8 on weekdays, $9 on the weekend. The 1,450-yard **Twin Lakes,** at 6034 Hollister Ave. (tel. 805/964-1414), charges $5.50 during the week, $6 on weekends. Hand carts are $1.

Tennis

Public facilities include the night-lighted **Municipal Courts** near Salinas Street and U.S. 101 (access off Old Coast Highway); **Las Positas Courts,** 1002 Las Positas Rd.; and **Pershing Park** courts at Castillo Street and West Cabrillo Boulevard. In addition there are several private tennis clubs and country club courts, some of which allow guests. Check with the chamber of commerce.

You'll need a tennis permit to play on these public courts (all permits expire on April 30). It's available from the Recreation Department, 620 Laguna St. (tel. 805/963-0611, ext. 361). Adults pay $3 a day or $45 per year; children 17 or under play free.

Fiesta

The most exciting time to visit Santa Barbara is in early August during the **Old Spanish Days Fiesta,** since 1924 a yearly homage to the city's Spanish past, patterned after the community harvest festivals of Andalusia and Castile in Old Spain.

This is no piddling little festival—it's a big five-day bash (beginning the first Wednesday in August) with colorful costumes, an opening ceremony of pageantry and traditional blessings on the steps of the Old Mission, equestrian events, rodeo, famous flamenco guitarists and dancers, variety shows, barbecues, bigname entertainers, a Spanish marketplace, a dazzling parade down palm-lined Cabrillo Boulevard with dozens of fancy floats, art shows, carnivals, outdoor dancing on the beach, symphony concerts, folk dancing, and much, much more. Many events are free.

Plan to arrive a little before Fiesta (make reservations as far in advance as possible—the town gets booked up 100%), and to stay till it's over. Even if you could get a room, you mightn't be able to get to it during Fiesta; you'd have to lug your suitcases through the crowded streets, many of which are blocked to traffic. The same problem pertains to getting out. Another reason to arrive early is to have time to pore over the schedules of events, get tickets when required, and enjoy the quiet of the beach and town before all the excitement begins.

Nightlife

The **Lobero Theater,** 33 E. Canon Perdido St. (tel. 805/963-0761), dates back to 1872 when it was built by Giuseppi Lobero, an Italian who changed his name to José Lobero in deference to the Spanish traditions of Santa Barbara. When the theater went bankrupt in 1892, Lobero, faced with financial ruin and the failure of his dream, put a bullet through his head. By 1922 the building was closed and condemned.

The present Lobero Theater, built in 1924, stands on the same site, the locale of the original Opera House. Among those who have played here are Lionel Barrymore, Edward G. Robinson, Clark Gable, Robert Young, Boris Karloff, Betty Grable, and Anna May Wong (remember?) The Martha Graham troupe has also graced the stage, and concert luminaries have included Andrés Segovia, Artur Rubinstein, Igor Stravinsky, and Leopold Stokowski.

A wide variety of productions are offered throughout the year—concerts, dance programs, recitals, operas, plays, travel films, and lectures. Call the theater to find out what's on during your stay.

The **Arlington Center for the Performing Arts,** 1317 State St., between Victoria and Sola (tel. 805/966-9382), derived its name from a hotel that occupied the same site from 1872 to 1925. It opened in 1931 in grand style, at the birth of the talking-picture era, presenting movies, vaudeville, and stage shows.

The deluxe Arlington became Hollywood's testing ground for unreleased movies; big stars flocked to Santa Barbara to check audience reaction at Arlington sneak previews.

After World War II, when vaudeville had died, road shows began to book into the Arlington to supplement the movie fare. Mae West appeared here in *Diamond Lil*, and was panned!

In 1976 the old theater was given a total facelift: reupholstered seats, new furnishings, facilities, and even exterior landscaping. And although film festival classic movies are shown occasionally (and even first-run popular movies), the theater features primarily big-name entertainers like Lily Tomlin, Wayne Newton, and Ray Charles, world-famous symphony orchestras like the Los Angeles Philharmonic, and many of the jazz greats.

The Earl Warren Showgrounds

Banquets, antique shows, barbecues, rummage sales, famous flower shows, music festivals, horse shows, dances, cat shows, coin shows, the circus, a rodeo, or even a big-name entertainer is likely to be at the Earl Warren Showgrounds, Las Positas Road and U.S. 101 (tel. 805/687-0766). Check it out.

WHERE TO STAY: So popular is Santa Barbara in summer that you simply must book in advance.

A Deluxe Trio

Some of the most elegant digs in town happen to be at one of the most prestigious hotels in California—**Four Seasons Biltmore,** 1260 Channel Dr., Santa Barbara, CA 93108 (tel. 805/969-2261, or toll free 800/336-3442), located on 21 acres of beautiful gardens and private ocean beach in the exclusive Montecito community. It's a refined resort hotel of the old school. When it opened in 1927 a concert orchestra played twice daily in the dining room, and separate quarters were available for personal servants accompanying guests. Although few people travel with servants these days, the Biltmore is still heavy on service.

The award-winning Spanish architecture (what else in Santa Barbara?) was the work of Reginald Johnson. He utilized Portuguese, Basque, Iberian, and Moorish design elements in a graceful combination of arcades, winding staircases, ramadas, patios, and artistic walkways, with exquisite hand-painted Mexican tile and grillwork throughout. The beauty of the estate is further enhanced by imposing views of the Pacific, the Santa Ynez Mountains, and the hotel's own palm-studded formal gardens.

The 227 guest rooms are housed in terracotta-tile-roofed low stucco buildings and cottages. All have an ocean, mountain, or garden view, and all are extremely cheerful and lovely, decorated in sunny resort colors. There's an extra phone in every bath, a scale, and extra-thick towels; each room is also equipped with a refrigerator, remote-control color TV, a radio, an alarm clock, and a coffee maker. Cottages are lovely, and some have kitchens. About a quarter of the rooms also have fireplaces. Extra services include the maid's turning down your bed each evening.

The hotel has two heated pools, as well as a putting green, croquet, shuffleboard, badminton, and complimentary bicycles. Golf, tennis, and riding facilities are nearby.

Dinner is served in the elegant La Marina, with white stucco walls, carved oak doors, heavy wrought-iron chandeliers suspended from vaulted ceilings, and lovely panoramic views of the ocean. The cuisine is nouvelle and specialties are fresh seafood and veal. Dinner entrees range from $18 to $29. Sunday brunch is $25. Dinner is served from 6 to 10 p.m.; brunch, from 10 a.m. to 2 p.m. The Patio, for al fresco dining, adjoins. The restaurant's La Sala Bar features a pianist nightly and a band for dancing on Friday and Saturday nights. For casual dining at breakfast, lunch, and dinner, there's the airy Fountain Court overlooking the Pacific. And you can enjoy afternoon tea in the library lounge.

In summer, a room at the Biltmore is $210 to $250, single or double; suites run $390 to $600. Rates are a bit lower the rest of the year.

Meanwhile, back at the ranch . . . back at the **San Ysidro Ranch,** that is, 900 San Ysidro Lane (off U.S. 101), Santa Barbara, CA 93108 (tel. 805/969-5046), another famous Montecito hostelry nestles in the Santa Ynez Mountains. Originally part of a Spanish land grant on which the padres raised cattle, and later a citrus orchard (there are still orange groves on the property, the produce of which is used for fresh-squeezed juice each morning), San Ysidro opened as a guest ranch in 1893. Over the years Winston Churchill, Sinclair Lewis, Rex Harrison, Groucho Marx, and Sidney Poitier have signed the register, and Jack and Jacqueline Kennedy spent their honeymoon here.

A quiet, beautifully landscaped 540-acre retreat, San Ysidro offers its guests tennis, a swimming pool, riding stables, badminton, croquet, miles of hiking and riding trails, and nearby golf.

Gourmet French cuisine is served at the Plow and Angel dining room. The restaurant, housed in the old citrus-packing house, is a charming candlelit establishment with a beamed ceiling, shuttered windows, antique furnishings, and paintings of local landmarks adorning the white sandstone walls. A delightful and airy glass-enclosed café area adjoins, the view of the grounds enhanced by many hanging plants inside. I love to come here for a leisurely lunch—perhaps an omelet stuffed with mussels sautéed in garlic butter or a Greek salad, in the $10 to $14 range. Dinners are more elaborate—and expensive, at $22 to $32— for the likes of filet au poivre, steak sautéed in peppercorns and flamed in cognac, or medallions of veal with an artichoke mousse. Save room for a sumptuous dessert like crêpes filled with ice cream and topped with rum-laced bananas in a rich sauce.

Accommodations consist of 38 quaint cottages with exquisite country-inn antique furnishings. During the day a woodman makes the rounds with wood and kindling for your fireplace, and fresh flowers from the garden are left in your cottage. The cottages are all secluded in a random pattern among lush foliage and flowers, and most have a porch so you can sit outside and enjoy the view. All have direct-dial phones and modern baths, but no TV to interrupt the sounds of rustling leaves, gentle wind, and babbling brook. For diehards there is a TV in the lounge, where in also an honor-system bar. Ten cottages have Jacuzzis.

There are 12 doubles priced at $175 to $245; more luxurious cottage rooms, studios, and suites for two are $265 to $450. Additional persons in a room pay $15 each.

El Encanto Hotel and Garden Villas, 1900 Lasuen Rd., Santa Barbara, CA 93103 (tel. 805/687-5000), was originally built in 1915 and subsequently restored to its grace and elegance.

The property consists of 100 rooms, cottages, and villas nested on ten woodland acres overlooking the city and Channel Islands (it's not easy to find, so be sure to ask directions).

Exquisite landscaping has carefully tended gardens and brick walkways contrasting with areas of lush foliage, palm trees, and hibiscus. A lotus pond is surrounded by vine-covered old brick columns, and the music of thousands of birds permeates the atmosphere. Wandering the grounds is a delight.

The rooms and cottages are furnished in a combination of country French antique and tasteful modern. Most accommodations have patios, balconies, or verandas, about a third have kitchens, and half have wood-burning fireplaces. All are equipped with direct-dial phones, color TVs, and baths with tub or shower.

On-the-premises facilities include an outdoor heated swimming pool and sundeck, a tennis court, a delightful outdoor terrace (perfect for sunsets and brunches) and a very beautiful restaurant, both with views of the hills and the Pacific. With windows all around, the view alone would suffice to make the El Encanto's beam-ceilinged dining room magnificent, but it's equally impressive within. Furnished with Louis XVI–style chairs, the room is papered in a delicate pattern; there are a few antiques, like an oak sideboard used to display decorative plates, some hanging plants, and lovely flower arrangements on every table. The fare is as fine as the setting, from the fresh croissants available at breakfast to the French nouvelle cuisine entrees available for dinner. The adjoining wicker-furnished lobby bar offers a beautiful view of Santa Barbara and the ocean below. There's dancing to live music here Tuesday to Sunday nights.

Accommodations are priced from $110 to $140 for the "small and cozy"; $170 to $220 for "spacious and special"; and $220 to $330 for "magnifique." El Encanto lives up to its name—"The Enchantment."

At the Beach

The blue-roofed cottages and buildings of the **Miramar Hotel-Resort,** 1555 S. Jameson Lane (in Montecito), P.O. Box M, Santa Barbara, CA 93102 (take Hwy. 1 to the San Ysidro turnoff; tel. 805/969-2203), have long been a famous Santa Barbara landmark. The hotel dates to 1887, when the Doulton family began to augment the meager income from their farm by taking in paying guests. When the railroad was constructed right on the property Miramar became an important station, and affluent guests began arriving in their own private railroad cars. As the popularity of beach and ocean vacations grew, it became a very chic place to go. Old registers are signed by many famous people, even royalty.

Today there are about 200 units set on 14 garden acres overlooking the Pacific. Facilities comprise two swimming pools, four tennis courts, a tennis clubhouse, a paddle-tennis court, 500 feet of private sandy beach, saunas and exercise rooms for men and women, a Jacuzzi, bike rental, and table tennis. Golf and horseback riding can be arranged.

The Terrace Dining Room, filled with hundreds of lush tropical plants and overlooking the pool, is open for breakfast, lunch, and dinner. Steak and seafood entrees are featured. There's live music Thursday through Saturday nights in the adjoining cocktail lounge.

As for the accommodations, the furnishings are indifferent, but the rooms are nevertheless comfortable; Miramar itself is so appealing that room decor doesn't seem all-important. Most attractive are the homey cottages (some with fully equipped kitchens) and the second-floor rooms with peaked raw-wood ceilings in the hotel's poolside, lanai, and oceanfront sections. All rooms are equipped with switchboard phones, color TVs, and tub and/or shower baths.

Rates for singles or doubles are $75 to $115. One-, two-, and three-bedroom suites are $105 to $245.

Right in Santa Barbara is the pink stucco **Tropicana Motel,** 223 Castillo St. (between Montecito and Yanonali), Santa Barbara, CA 93101 (tel. 805/966-2219), a 29-unit accommodation just a short walk from the beach. Rooms are homey and attractive. All are equipped with color TV, AM/FM radio, phone, bath with tub and/or shower, and coffee maker.

There are also suites available—an excellent buy if you like to do your own cooking. These have large eat-in kitchens, fully equipped right down to eggbeaters and potholders, not to mention a good oven, stove, and toaster. The suites sleep up to four persons and must be rented for a minimum of three days.

Other facilities include a heated pool and Jacuzzi, both away from the street and very private, with lots of room for sunning.

Singles, which are hard to come by in summer, rent for $55 to $65, doubles and twins are $65 to $75, and three-room suites (bedroom, living room, and kitchen) are $85 to $120 for two persons; add $5 for each extra person.

Even closer to the beach is the **King's Inn**, 128 Castillo St. (between Yanonali and Mason), Santa Barbara, CA 93101 (tel. 805/963-4471), with 45 immaculate rooms in tip-top condition, a swimming pool with lots of sunning area, whirlpool, and sauna bath.

The rooms are pleasantly furnished, and all have cable color TVs, direct-dial phones, air conditioning, tub/shower baths, and dressing rooms with big mirrors, and they're all quite lovely. Some second- and third-floor rooms have balconies.

In summer, singles and doubles are $84 to $98. An additional person in your room is $6. Rates are slightly lower off-season (October to mid-May).

Budget visitors to Santa Barbara can seek refuge at **Motel 6**—there are two in Santa Barbara proper and one in nearby Carpinteria, about 10 minutes away by car.

The **Motel 6** at 443 Corona del Mar, Santa Barbara, CA 93103 (tel. 805/564-1392), is located right near the beach. It offers basic, clean accommodations; rates are $29.95 for a single, $6 extra for each additional adult. It features a small pool, and there's no charge for local calls or for TV. Be sure to reserve far in advance, as this motel gets booked up quickly.

A second **Motel 6** is at 3505 State St., between Las Positas and Hitchcock Way, Santa Barbara, CA 93105 (tel. 805/687-5400). Prices are the same; there is also a small pool and no charge for local calls or TV.

The **Motel 6** in Carpinteria is, as I mentioned, about a 10-minute drive from Santa Barbara, at 4200 Via Real, Carpinteria, CA 93103 (tel. 805/684-6921). Prices here are $23.95 for a single, plus $6 for each additional adult. Carpinteria also has a pool, and there's no charge for local calls or TV.

In Town

Most people prefer to stay at the beach, but if you have a car you might consider the **Best Western Encina Lodge**, 2220 Bath St. (at Los Olivos), Santa Barbara, CA 93105 (tel. 805/682-7277). Set in a quiet residential area, a short walk from the Mission and other attractions, it's a mere five-minute drive from the beach. All rooms are immaculate and tastefully decorated—furnishings, bedspreads, rugs, etc., all look spanking new. I especially like the rooms on the second floor of the oldest building, with beamed raw-pine ceilings. All rooms have color TVs, air conditioning, direct-dial phones, coffee makers, and clocks. Old-wing rooms have shower only; the rest have tub/shower combinations and dressing rooms. Apartments are also available.

Facilities include a pool, a whirlpool, sauna, lobby shop, beauty and barber shop, and a very fine restaurant (open from 7:30 a.m. to 9:30 p.m.) which you should try even if you don't stay here. An ever-changing lunch menu might feature sweet-and-sour chicken or barbecued ribs, both with soup or salad. I particularly recommend dinner here (5 to 9:30 p.m.), when you can try the award-winning crab Mornay, served with soup or salad, saffron rice or au gratin potatoes, rolls and butter; meals go for $14 to $20. Don't miss the homemade pastries for dessert. The ambience, by the way, is quite nice: candlelight, hanging plants, red-clothed tables, oak paneling, and beamed stucco ceiling. There's also a full bar now.

Single rates are $84 to $100; doubles cost $88 to $120.

The oldest hotel in Santa Barbara (est. 1871), the **Upham,** 1404 De la Vina St. (at Sola), Santa Barbara, CA 93101 (tel. 805/962-0058), is also one of the most charming. Built by Amasa Lyman Lincoln, a Boston banker, the hotel is designed to look like an old-fashioned New England boarding house. A two-story clapboard structure, it has wide eaves and is topped by a glassed-in cupola and a widow's walk for viewing the sea. The original hotel changed hands several times over the years, once to a Cyrus Upham, whose name has remained.

Fronted by two immense ivy-entwined palms, and entered via a large colonnaded porch, it is set in a well-tended garden with neat flower beds. The Upham was refurbished in 1983, and all 41 guest rooms now have antique armoires, brass or four-poster beds, and pillow shams; many have private porches and fireplaces. All of the rooms have modern amenities—Touch-Tone phone, color cable TV, and private bath. In the afternoon, wine, cheese, and crackers are served in the lobby and in the garden.

Louie's at the Upham is open for lunch, dinner, and Sunday brunch.

Rates are $85 to $160, $220 for a master suite with fireplace, Jacuzzi, private yard, and king-size bedroom. The Upham is located in the heart of Santa Barbara, two blocks from State Street.

The **Bath Street Inn,** 1720 Bath St. (between Valerio and Mission), Santa Barbara, CA 93101 (tel. 805/682-9680), is a handsome Queen Anne Victorian built over a hundred years ago. This historic residence has several unusual features—a semicircular "eyelid" balcony and a hipped roof, unique even for Santa Barbara. And the century-old trees, flower-filled patio with white wicker furniture, and brick courtyard add to the inn's charm, as does the graciousness of the innkeepers.

In the expansion and reconstruction of the inn, great care was taken to incorporate modern safety features, yet to preserve the 1800s atmosphere of the original home. The living room is comfortable and inviting. The fireplace, Chinese rug, period prints, sideboard with attractively displayed crystal, ivory-and-white wallpaper, and fresh flowers create a pleasant warmth. The dining area has a traditional blue-and-white floral-print paper that complements the finely crafted woodwork and furnishings.

There are seven guest rooms in the Bath Street Inn, all with private bath. Each of the rooms has its own charm and uniqueness: one with a king-size canopied bed; another under the eaves with a superb sunset view from a historic balcony; others with a mountain view or a window seat with a glimpse of the ocean.

Room rates, single or double, are $90 to $100 and include a substantial continental breakfast, evening refreshment, and the use of the inn's bicycles. Children and pets are not accepted.

WHERE TO DINE: A beautiful Santa Barbara restaurant is the **Epicurean Catering Co.,** 125 E. Carrillo St., between Santa Barbara and Anacapa (tel. 805/966-4789 or 962-6793). Fronted by a planter of lovely flowers (they change seasonally), it has an extremely pretty interior. An abundance of plants and flower arrangements complement French-reproduction floral-print wallpaper and cream-colored walls hung with framed botany prints. Carpeting is appropriately deep green. Decorative pewter and brass elk-shaped tureens adorn each candlelit table. There are three dining areas with skylights overhead, and a courtyard with latticework walls and a screened ceiling that rolls back in good weather for dining under the open sky. The whole effect is rather like a magic forest.

You might select an appetizer of bay shrimp, crab, and artichoke hearts, or a pâté of duck, veal, or pork with French bread. Soup comes with your entree—mushroom bisque with sherry or chilled borscht with sour cream—although you could opt for salad. As for the entrees, they range from $17 to $29, for steak and lobster, or filet of sole Epicurean, with mushrooms, toasted almonds, and hollandaise. Everything is perfectly delicious, and the ambience, enhanced by taped classical music, is delightful. An extensive wine list is available.

Epicurean Catering Co. is open for lunch weekdays, except Wednesday, from 11:30 a.m. to 2 p.m., Sundays from 10:30 a.m. to 2:30 p.m. It's open daily for dinner from 6 to 10 p.m. Reservations are suggested.

The elegant **Casa de Sevilla,** 428 Chapala St., between Haley and Gutierrez (tel. 805/966-4370), has been a local favorite for over half a century. It's divided into several dining areas; I particularly like the front room with its wood-burning fireplace and sloped beamed ceiling. The ambience is warm and intimate with shuttered windows, brass candle lamps on every table, and graceful chandeliers. Liberal use of sienna (drapes, walls, and carpeting) and antique bullfight posters provide a Spanish feel. In the evening, men are required to wear jackets.

The menu is the same at lunch (served from noon to 2 p.m.) and dinner (from 6 to 10 p.m.). You might begin with an appetizer of chili con queso, guacamole, or lobster cocktail. There are many barbecued entrees—salmon, filet mignon, and spareribs among them—for $14 to $23. A full Barcelona dinner, including Castilian soup (garbanzo purée), salad, relishes, chili con queso, rice or potato, dessert, and beverage, is priced according to entree at $16 to $28. The Kahlúa cheesecake is an excellent dessert. The restaurant is open Tuesday through Saturday.

Across the street from El Paseo is a restaurant that occupies a portion of Santa Barbara's old fortress, or presidio. It is the **Presidio Café,** 812 Anacapa St., between Canon Perdido and De La Guerra (tel. 805/966-2428). The café is a charming combination of the old and the new: a lovely outdoor area filled with lush plants and umbrella-covered tables surrounds a splashing fountain; one of the old presidio buildings—now with a glass wall—serves as a more elegant dining room (complete with white-clothed tables) overlooking the garden terrace; and the fortress's chapel (showing little trace of its original function) acts as a banquet room.

The service at the Presidio Café is as cheerful and friendly as its ambience. You can begin your day here with a hearty breakfast—perhaps an omelet or a croissant stuffed with fresh fruit or scrambled eggs, sausage, and cheese—for $5 to $8. Or you can enjoy a leisurely lunch of quiche, crêpes (such as crab and cheddar cheese with hollandaise), a generous salad, sandwiches, or the café's specialty, tortilla soup. Luncheon dishes cost $6 to $10. Portions here are quite healthy, but you may want to save room for the rich and sinfully delicious chocolate mousse pie.

The Presidio Café is open for breakfast and lunch daily from 8 a.m. to 5 p.m. Reservations suggested for lunch.

Needless to say, in Spanish-style Santa Barbara, **Mexican eateries** abound. Many Santa Barbarans maintain that the best Mexican eateries are the unpretentious Chicano haunts along State Street. They usually have a jukebox playing Spanish music, paintings on velvet of Mexican scenes, artificial flowers on the tables, and a warm, friendly, relaxed restaurant.

There are beautiful places to eat in Santa Barbara, elegant places, traditional places, some dripping with atmosphere, but there is one place where the food is head and shoulders above any of its kind between California and New York: **La Super-Rica Taqueria,** 622 N. Milpas St., between Cota and Ortega (tel.

805/963-4940). What makes it so? The cooking of the Gonzales family, and especially the incredible soft tacos. If you ever thought that a tortilla was a soft taco, oh were you wrong. La Super-Rica's soft tacos are as soft as a crêpe, about twice as thick (they have the texture of the blinis at the Russian Tea Room in Manhattan), and so delectable you could make a meal of these alone with the fresh salsa.

There's nothing grand about La Super-Rica except the food. The neighborhood once was a barrio, before gentrification, and the restaurant remains unadorned, though the clientele is now a mix of the very affluent and the somewhat less so. (It has been reported that even Julia Child comes for the frijoles—a joyous mix of pintos, sausage, chiles, bacon, and herbs.) The plates are paper, the cups Styrofoam, and the forks plastic, but the homemade soft corn tacos are thick enough to be leak-proof—just perfect for holding the delicious contents.

I had the Taco de Rajas—sautéed strips of chile pasilla with onions, melted cheese, and herbs on two soft tacos. Had I the appetite, I would also have ordered the Alambre de Pechuga, grilled chicken breast with bell pepper, onions, and mushrooms served on three corn tortillas. Those inclined to simpler fare might try the Taco de Costilla, tender strips of charbroiled top round served on two fresh homemade tortillas. Or if you're the type to go for it all, order the Super-Rica Especial, roasted chile pasilla stuffed with cheese and combined with charbroiled marinated pork, served with three soft tacos. For the vegetarian, the Cordita de Frijol fills thick corn tortillas with spicy ground beans. Prices range from $1.75 to $4.25.

And to accompany the food, the assortment of Mexican beers is first-rate. Be sure to try the Chihuahua.

La Super-Rica Taqueria is open Friday through Wednesday from 11 a.m. to 7 p.m., now and then to 8 or 9 p.m. If you're thinking of going late, call first to check.

All right, so you want something a bit tonier and could go for some delicious New Mexican food. Head straight for **The Zia Café,** 421 N. Milpas St., at Reddick (tel. 805/962-5391), the culinary child of Douglas and Jane Scott of Santa Fe.

Zia's New Mexican roots are immediately evident in the restaurant's sand-pink walls, light wood chairs, chiles drying in the windows, desert prints—all very inviting and relaxed.

Zia's offers a wide variety of enchiladas, burritos, and tamales, served with red or green chile. The names may be familiar, but there's nothing commonplace about any of these house specialties. The chiles relleños are prepared from two green-chile peppers stuffed with cheese and piñon nuts, dipped in batter, and deep fried. And the green-chile enchilada, layered chicken and sour cream served with blue corn tortillas, topped with sour cream and guacamole, is worthy of a three-page letter home. What's more, when you order a Zia specialty with chicken, you get a large portion of hot breast meat, enough to satisfy the appetite of the most voracious diner.

For breakfast, Zia's serves a flour tortilla with three scrambled eggs, covered with red or green chile, as well as huevos rancheros—blue corn tortillas topped with two fried eggs and, again, your choice of red or green chile. I always opt for the green chile myself—Zia Café serves the best kind, that found along the southern Rio Grande. The New Mexican favorites range from $4.75 to $7.25; combination plates are $7.95 to $8.25. Beer and wine are available by the glass or the pitcher and liter, respectively.

The service is as warm, friendly, and helpful as you would expect in a Santa Fe–style restaurant. The Zia Café is open for lunch Tuesday through Saturday 11 a.m. to 2:30 p.m., and for dinner 5:30 to 9:30 p.m., Sunday from 5 to 9 p.m.

Your Place, 22-A N. Milpas, near Mason (tel. 805/966-5151), has the look of a tourist restaurant, but a menu that belies its appearance.

Though the restaurant is relatively small, it holds carved screens, a serene Buddha, cloth butterflies, mirrored panels, and an impressive array of framed blow-ups of restaurant reviews. Two huge tanks of exotic fish divide the room in half.

Traditional Thai dishes, using distinctively fresh ingredients, are featured. The considerable menu includes appetizers, soups, salads, curries, vegetarian dishes, meat and poultry dishes, seafood entrees, noodle dishes, rice dishes—in fact, you may find the scope of the menu somewhat overwhelming (there are over 100 listings). If so, review the specialties of the house in the various categories.

You might begin with Golden Wing stuffed with ground chicken and bean thread, deep-fried and served with sweet plum sauce; or the Regal B.B.Q. spareribs marinated in a delicious "royal" sauce. Of the soup choices, I thoroughly enjoyed the Tom Kah Kai—hot and sour chicken soup with coconut milk and mushrooms. You can order soup by the bowl or by the hot pot, which offers more than enough for two; however, if you're dining with food-sharing friends, order by the bowl and do some sampling. Among the meat and poultry dishes, the Siamese duckling, prepared with sautéed vegetables, mushrooms, and a ginger sauce, is difficult to resist. However, above all, the seafood specialties are a great treat. An excellent sizzling seafood platter arrives on a hot stove. Other favorites are the yellow-curry crab claws or the sweet-and-sour fish, deep-fried and served with a sauce including onion, bell pepper, pineapple, and tomatoes. Several of the dishes on the menu are spicy and may be ordered mild, medium, hot, or very hot.

Prices are moderate; entrees range from $4.25 to $10.95. The restaurant serves wine, sake, beer—including Thai beer and ale—plus such nonalcoholic drinks as hot ginger tea. The restaurant is open Tuesday through Thursday from 11 a.m. to 10 p.m., Friday through Sunday to 11 p.m.

The Japanese cuisine offered at **Suishin,** 511 State St., between Haley and Cota (tel. 805/962-1495), is excellent and reasonably priced, and the surroundings are very pleasant indeed. I particularly like sitting in the intimate tatami rooms, separated from the main dining area by shoji screens, and decorated with murals of Japan, scrolls, and paintings. There are also booths and banquettes should you prefer dining at a table, and a sushi bar. Japanese music is played in the background, and kimono-clad waitresses provide deft and pleasant service.

All dinners here include soup, sunomono (salad), vegetable and shrimp tempura, tsukemono (Japanese pickles), rice, tea, and green tea ice cream, with entrees like sukiyaki, teriyaki, or sushi for $12 to $19. À la carte entrees cost $10 to $17.

Open daily from 5 to 11 p.m. Reservations suggested.

Joe's Café, 536 State St., at Cota (tel. 805/966-4638), a Santa Barbara institution since 1926 (in a new location since 1984), offers good home-cooking, and people mob the place every night to dig in. Inside, the decor is as downhome as the food: red-and-white-checkered tablecloths, captain's chairs, and mounted hunting trophies and photos of old Santa Barbara on the walls. Entrees, costing $7 to $15, and served with soup or salad, potato, pasta, or a vegetable, include rainbow mountain trout, home-style fried chicken, and a 12-ounce charbroiled sirloin steak. It's all prepared by chefs in big white hats working in an open kitchen. Sandwiches, pastas, and salads are also available (for $4 to $10), but there are no desserts. "We give them enough starch without it," explains the owner.

Joe's is open Monday through Thursday from 11 a.m. to 11:30 p.m., on

Friday and Saturday to 12:30 a.m., on Sunday from 4 to 11:30 p.m. Reservations are suggested (no reservations on Saturday).

In the same category, but even more authentic and traditional, is **Arnoldi's Café,** 600 Olive St., off Cota (tel. 805/962-5394). Italian immigrants Joe and Hilda Arnoldi built the place themselves over 40 years ago. There's a mural in the back room of the mountains surrounding Lake Como, the Arnoldis' village in northern Italy, and a photo of the founding couple (also in Lake Como) over the mahogany bar.

Candlelit tables are covered with red-and-white-checkered cloths. A TV over the bar is always tuned to sporting events at a low-decibel level; there are three enclosed mahogany booths up front for intimate dining, and a bocce ball court out back where oldtimers play on weekends. But most appealing is the wonderful jukebox of old Italian songs—Mario Lanza's "Be My Love," among other favorites.

And, of course, the food. All steaks are cut on the premises, all pasta and soups homemade, and portions are huge. A 1½-pound T-bone, top sirloin, or New York steak is served with soup, salad, spaghetti or potatoes, and coffee for $13 to $15. Spaghetti or ravioli dinners, served with soup, salad, and coffee, run $9 to $10. For dessert there's vanilla ice cream or spumoni.

Arnoldi's is open daily except Wednesday from 5 to 11 p.m.

9. OJAI VALLEY

It would be a shame to visit Santa Barbara and miss the nearby Ojai (pronounced O-high) Valley, just 32 miles southeast along one of California's most gorgeous roads, Hwy. 150. (It's also an easy day trip from Los Angeles.) The drive alone is scenic enough to justify the trip, but there's plenty to do in Ojai as well.

Traveling along 150 you'll pass **Lake Casitas,** a breathtakingly beautiful opalescent body of fresh water, with almost 100 miles of shoreline, that is a center for fishing (boats, bait, and such are available), boating, and camping (tel. 805/649-2233).

You can hike through the **Los Padres National Forest,** just north of town— over 500,000 acres of mountainous terrain, fields, valleys, and 140 miles of streams. There's hunting, camping, and picknicking throughout the forest.

There are more than 400 miles of riding and hiking trails in Ojai, not to mention an abundance of tennis and golf facilities. The **Ojai Valley Inn** riding stables, Hermosa Road (tel. 805/646-2837), charges $10 an hour for horse rental. You can play tennis free at **Soule Park,** off Boardman Road, and at **Libbey Park** in downtown Ojai across from the arcade. Golf is also offered at Soule Park's, 18-hole, par-72 championship course; greens fees are $15 on weekdays, $20 on weekends and holidays, carts are $18 (tel. 805/646-5633).

Just down the road a bit farther is **Bowman's** at Wheeler Hot Springs, 16825 Maricopa Hwy. (that's Hwy. 33; tel. 805/646-8131). It boasts not only the requisite mineral baths and massages expected at a spa (Thursday through Sunday from noon to 10 p.m.), but also has a terrific restaurant. After a tub and a rub, you can dig into a fine meal. The setting is rustic, with comfortable wood and wicker furniture and large fireplaces for the nippy days.

The emphasis all around is on health. The menu changes daily, but for dinner you might find a blue corn tamale pie with guacamole and sour cream; sole quenelles, and New York steak tacos—priced at $14 to $20. Wine and beer only are served. The restaurant is open from 5 to 10 p.m. Thursday through Sunday and from 11 a.m. to 3 p.m. for brunch on Saturday and Sunday. Be sure to reserve several days in advance for baths and meals.

Then there are antique shops, an art center, a historical museum, and many scenic drives, my favorite being to the spot where Ronald Colman viewed Shangri-la (it was Ojai Valley) in the movie *Lost Horizon* (go east on Ojai Avenue, then up the hill); a bench is provided, and there could be no more glorious spot for a picnic if you're so inclined.

On the other hand, you might just drive up for a meal. One of Ojai's most beloved restaurants is the **Ranch House,** 102 Besant Rd., at South Lomita (tel. 805/646-2360). It was started by Alan and Helen Hooker, who came to Ojai in 1949, interested in the philosopher Krishnamurti. They rented an old ranch house, which they then turned into a boarding house. Within a year they had opened the restaurant. It's no longer in that first rented building, but in a beautiful location surrounded by an orchard, a bamboo thicket, and herb and flower gardens. It's a serene and tranquil place.

You can begin a meal here with an appetizer like chicken liver pâté, dig into a soup of curried mushroom or Vietnamese chicken and crab, and then enjoy a prime rib, crab voisin, chicken champagne, or a nut loaf. All meals come with vegetables, salad, fresh-baked breads, potatoes or rice, and herb tea (the Ranch House grows its own herbs), coffee, or milk, and cost $18 to $22. Be sure to leave room for one of the delicious desserts—rum trifle, applesauce cake, lime cheesecake, or ice cream with a choice of special Ranch House toppings: fudge, green ginger, pomegranate, fresh coconut.

If you can't get enough of the Ranch House while you're there, you can pick up a loaf of fresh-baked bread at the bakery or a copy of Alan Hooker's cookbooks.

The Ranch House has dinner seatings Wednesday to Sunday at 6 and 8:30 p.m. Lunch is served Wednesday through Saturday from 11:30 a.m. to 1:30 p.m. Reservations requested.

Another charming eatery is **L'Auberge,** 314 El Paseo, at Rincon (tel. 805/646-2288). It occupies the ground floor of an old house; the dining room meanders through several small rooms and out to a delightful terrace with a lovely view. The decor is a pleasant lime and white. Owner Paul Franssen offers an array of crêpes (asparagus and mushroom, curried chicken) and omelets (cheese, mushroom, vegetable), along with salads and soups for brunch, all for under $10. Dinner can begin with an appetizer of snails in garlic butter, or smoked salmon. Entrees are varied, from filet of sole amandine to frogs' legs to sweet breads to a filet of beef with mushrooms, tomatoes, and madeira sauce. Entrees are all served with vegetables and bread, and cost $16 to $22. And for dessert there's white- or dark-chocolate mousse, cheesecake, or crème caramel. L'Auberge is open for lunch on weekends from 11 a.m. to 2:30 p.m., for dinner nightly except Tuesday from 5:30 to 9 p.m. Reservations are required for dinner.

You can also enjoy breakfast, lunch, or dinner daily at the **Ojai Valley Inn and Country Club** (tel. 805/646-5511), nestled in the lush, green rolling hills of the Sierra Madre mountains. The Café is open to the public by reservation. Lunch is served from 11 a.m. to 2:30 p.m. Complete dinners are $18 to $25, served from 6:30 to 9:30 p.m. It's absolutely lovely to dine here under umbrellaed tables overlooking the golf course.

You might also check out Ojai's shops. Most of the action is from Canada to Montgomery Streets within an area extending one block south and two blocks north of quaint Ojai Avenue. It includes the Arcade on Ojai Avenue and two shopping centers, the **El Paseo Mall** and **Arcade Plaza.**

The **Ojai Valley Chamber of Commerce** is at 338 E. Ojai Ave. (Rte. 150; tel. 805/646-8126). It's open weekdays from 9:30 a.m. to 4:30 p.m. Stop in for city maps, information, and a free copy of an informative booklet called *The Visitor's Guide to the Ojai Valley,* which lists scenic drives, galleries, and a calendar of events.

CHAPTER VIII

LOS ANGELES

□ □ □

How can one define the enigma that is Los Angeles? It's an unrelated string of suburbs in search of a city; a megalopolis sprawl connected by 1,500 or so miles of slowing freeway; a promised land of sea, sand, and year-round sunshine; decadent playground of the rich; stomping grounds of the stars; the most status-conscious city in the U.S.; a second home to New Yorkers who dismiss the rest of the country as "the flyovers"; headquarters for every kind of kook, cultist, and spiritual movement, a haven for the eccentric and yet a bastion of political conservatism. And finally, Los Angeles is about not caring what it's all about.

The variety of lifestyles, of activities and places to see and experience is mind-boggling. Don't waste time trying to understand this pleasure-oriented paradox. Forget your preconceptions, relax, enjoy. Let L.A. work its magic on you, and soon you'll be right at home in fantasyland.

There's so much to do, your only problems might be having time to do it all, where to start, and how to get there.

You'll want to tour the studios—thrill to the feigned attack of King Kong . . . see Johnny tape a "Tonight Show" . . . show off your new bikini (or perfect unclothed body) on the beach . . . go shopping in chic Beverly Hills . . . gape at the homes of the stars . . . bring the kids to or be a kid at Disneyland, Magic Mountain, etc., etc., etc. . . . eat homemade fudge, Belgian waffles, tacos, or shrimp Louie at the international stalls in Farmer's Market . . . have a drink and a celebrity gawk at the Polo Lounge . . . match your footprints with those of over 200 stars at Mann's Chinese Theatre . . . see hit shows at the Music Center, or big-name entertainment at the Hollywood Bowl.

That doesn't begin to skim the surface of visitor attractions that you'll be reading about in this chapter. They're seemingly endless, and they're scattered all over the place. First item on the agenda is to get a good map and orient yourself. Second is to get a copy of the Sunday edition of the *Los Angeles Times,* and take out the "Calendar" section to see what's going on that week. And third, plan out your sightseeing priorities.

GETTING YOUR BEARINGS: A glance at the map will show you that the center of Los Angeles lies east of the Pacific Ocean (about 12 miles), on a direct line with the coastal town of Santa Monica. This is the **downtown** business and shopping center of the city. Greater Los Angeles radiates out from the downtown area in an ever-increasing number of suburbs. A vast network of freeways links the separate districts to each other, and to downtown, and the city as a whole to the state.

Hollywood, which is on every tourist's itinerary, is just northwest of the downtown Civic Center via the Hollywood Freeway (U.S. 101). **Beverly Hills** adjoins Hollywood on the southwest. You can reach Beverly Hills by taking the Hollywood Freeway from the Civic Center and turning off on Santa Monica Boulevard.

Connecting the downtown area and Beverly Hills, then continuing on through **Westwood** en route to the **Santa Monica** shoreline beaches, is **Wilshire Boulevard,** L.A.'s main drag. As Wilshire enters Beverly Hills, it intersects **La Cienega Boulevard.** The portion of La Cienega that stretches north from Wilshire to Santa Monica Boulevard is known (for obvious reasons) as **Restaurant Row.**

The next boulevard to the north of Santa Monica is **Sunset Boulevard** in Hollywood. The next section on Sunset between Laurel Canyon Boulevard and La Brea Avenue is the famed **Sunset Strip** nightclub district. Above that is equally famous **Hollywood Boulevard.**

Farther north via the Hollywood Freeway is the **San Fernando Valley.** Here you'll find **Universal City;** a right turn on the Ventura Freeway takes you to Beautiful Downtown **Burbank.**

Venice, the yacht-filled harbors of **Marina del Rey,** and the **Los Angeles International Airport** are all south along the shore from Santa Monica.

1. GETTING AROUND

It's a theory of mine that one of the reasons behind the great interest in things spiritual and mystical in L.A. is that if residents could only achieve astral projection, they could finally get somewhere without a car. Los Angeles is car city. Where else can you find drive-in churches where the traditional response of "Amen," has been replaced by "honk, honk"?

Although there is bus service, everything is so spread out you usually have to make three transfers to get where you're going, and wait at least half an hour at each change. Whereas the elaborate network of freeways that connects this incredible urban sprawl will whisk you to your destination in a reasonable amount of time—unless, of course, it's rush hour when streams of traffic can sit around for hours with nothing to do. Do your homework with a good map, and you'll find getting around easy, if not always pleasant—the freeways are not what you'd call scenic routes. The most interesting things to look at are all the Rolls-Royces, Mercedeses, and Porsches driving along with you. If you haven't figured it out by now, always allow more time to get to your destination than you've been told it will take.

Car Rentals

The sights and restaurants are so far apart here, you'll probably do best to seek an unlimited-mileage arrangement, or at least one with sufficient free mileage to make your trip economical. On the freeways, those few "cents per mile" tend to mount rapidly into dollars. See the "Traveling Within California" section of Chapter I for some general advice about car rentals.

Car rentals of specific-size vehicles, including vans, are usually easier to ob-

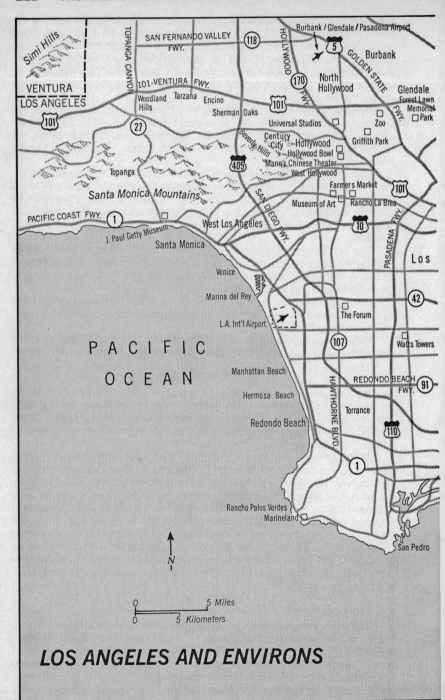

LOS ANGELES AND ENVIRONS

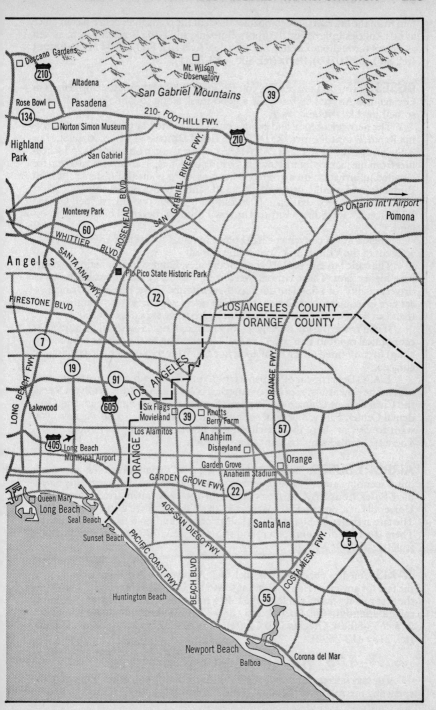

tain from the big rental-car companies. Each of the companies below has an office at Los Angeles International Airport, Burbank, and Long Beach Airports, as well as offices throughout Greater Los Angeles: **Avis** (tel. 800/331-1212), **Budget** (tel. 800/527-0700), **Hertz** (tel. 800/654-3131).

BUSES: If you don't have a car, you can reach most of the sightseeing centers in Greater Los Angeles by bus (take a good book along to while away ride time, something like *War and Peace*).

The network of local and express buses is operated by the Southern California Rapid Transit District (RTD). Their **Ticket Office** is at 419 S. Main St., Los Angeles, CA 90001 (tel. 213/626-4455), where you can obtain maps and schedules from the rack, or for instance, by writing or calling. You can also call them for detailed information on a given trip from point to point (for instance, "I'm in Burbank and I want to get to Wilshire and Santa Monica Boulevards").

The office provides a pamphlet outlining about two dozen "Self-Guided RTD Tours," including visits to Universal Studios, Beverly Hills, and Disneyland.

There's also a convenient RTD office in ARCO Towers, 515 S. Flower St., adjacent to the Visitors and Convention Bureau.

The basic bus fare is $1.10 for all local lines. Express lines utilizing freeways have higher fares. Those visitors over age 65 (Medicare card must be shown to driver) qualify for a 55¢ fare during off-peak hours. Drivers carry no change; exact fare is required. In addition, for those riders who travel into counties other than Los Angeles (for instance, to Disneyland) there are extra charges.

If you're staying in Los Angeles for a period of time you should consider the economical monthly passes: $42 to $102 (depending on the distance you're traveling) for unlimited riding on all local lines, $10 for the same privilege for senior citizens.

L.A.'s (Department of Transportation) minibuses run every five to ten minutes in the downtown area of Los Angeles, covering such areas as Olvera Street, the Civic Center, Chinatown, Pershing Square, the garment district, and Occidental Center. Fare is 30¢ (exact change, please). Hop on, get off whenever you want to visit or shop, then catch another bus later, paying only another 30¢. There are marked minibus stops along the route.

AIRPORT BUSES: Don't just hop in a cab at the airport unless you don't mind spending a small fortune getting to your hotel. **Airlink** has regularly scheduled buses from LAX to major hotels in the downtown area, Hollywood/Universal City, Beverly Hills, West L.A., the Wilshire district, and Century City. The fare averages $6.50 for adults, half price for children 5 to 11; under 5, free. There is a 10% discount for a round trip. Call 213/723-4636 for information (toll free 800/962-1976).

TAXIS: You don't hop cabs as blithely in L.A. as you do in other cities—it seems the fare for any given ride is always at least $10. L.A. cabs charge $1.90 drop (for the first two-tenths of a mile) and $1.40 a mile after that. Should you need one, call **Independent Cab Co.** (tel. 213/558-8294), **United Independent Taxi** (tel. 213/653-5050), **Checker Cab Co.** (tel. 213/624-2227), or the **Yellow Cab Co.** (tel. 213/413-7890).

2. THE ABC'S OF LOS ANGELES

For easy reference, here are some basic facts to help you orient yourself to the sprawling metropolis in the sun.

AIRLINES: Some 36 international carriers, and every major domestic carrier, serve the Los Angeles International Airport (LAX)—third largest in the world in terms of traffic. Domestic carriers include **Air Cal** (tel. 213/627-5401, or toll free 800/424-7225, 800/854-3511 in California), **Alaska Airlines** (tel. 213/628-2100, or toll free 800/426-0333), **American Airlines** (tel. 213/935-6045, or toll free 800/433-7300), **Delta Air Lines** (tel. 213/386-5510), **Eastern Airlines** (tel. 213/380-2070), **Northwest Airlines** (tel. 213/380-1511, or toll free 800/225-2525, 800/252-2168 in California), **Piedmont Airlines** (tel. 213/977-4937, or toll free 800/251-5720), **Southwest Airlines** (tel. 213/485-1221, or toll free 800/531-5601), **Trans World Airlines** (tel. 213/484-2244, or toll free 800/221-2000), **United Airlines** (tel. 213/772-2121), and **US Air** (tel. 213/410-1732, or toll free 800/428-4322).

AIRPORTS: The **Los Angeles International Airport** is situated at the far western end of the city. If you're driving, two main roads will get you there: Century Boulevard, which runs east–west, and Sepulveda Boulevard, running north–south. The San Diego Freeway (#5)—it's called that even in Los Angeles—and Hwy. 405 have exits to West Century Boulevard leading to the airport. Going north on Sepulveda Boulevard will take you directly to the airport; going south, you should turn right on 96th Street to get to the airport entrance. The city's RTD bus lines go to and from LAX; for the schedule and running times, call RTD airport information (tel. 213/646-8021). Free Blue, Green, and White shuttle buses ("Airline Connections") stop in front of each ticket building. Special handicapped-accessible minibuses are also available. If you need more information call (213) 646-8021.

Unless you plan to stay at one of the hotels near the airport, a taxi is *not* the preferred mode of transportation to your hotel or motel. Just about everything is miles away from the airport and the cost of taking a taxi can be more like a down payment on one. If you must take a taxi, confirm the price to your destination *before* getting in. Airport shuttles and commercial commuter vans provide direct airport service to most major hotels. Some smaller hotels also have private shuttles for their patrons; ask about transportation at the time you make your hotel or motel reservations.

Although LAX is the largest by far, in terms of size, service, and air traffic, Los Angeles is surrounded by airports. To the north is the **Burbank-Glendale-Pasadena Airport,** at 2627 North Hollywood Way, Burbank (tel. 818/840-8847); to the south are the **Long Beach Municipal Airport,** 4100 Donald Douglas Dr., Long Beach (tel. 213/421-8293), and the **John Wayne Airport,** 19051 Airport Way North, Anaheim (tel. 714/834-2400); and to the east, the **Ontario International Airport,** Terminal Way, Ontario (tel. 714/983-8282). Most of the smaller airports are for charters, commuter lines, or private planes.

AREA CODES: Unlike "all Gaul," Los Angeles has been divided into just two parts (by the telephone company). Area code **213** includes Los Angeles proper, while area code **818** encompasses Sherman Oaks, Van Nuys, Toluca Lake, Glendale, Pasadena, Burbank, and the San Fernando Valley. Therefore, if you are in the Valley and want to call Beverly Hills, you'll need to dial 1-213 and then your number. Conversely, if you're in Beverly Hills and want to call a number in the Valley, you'd dial 1-818 first. And because the phone company splits North Hollywood in half, some establishments have numbers with both area codes.

BABYSITTERS: If you're staying at one of the larger hotels, the concierge can usually recommend organizations to call. Be sure to check on the hourly cost

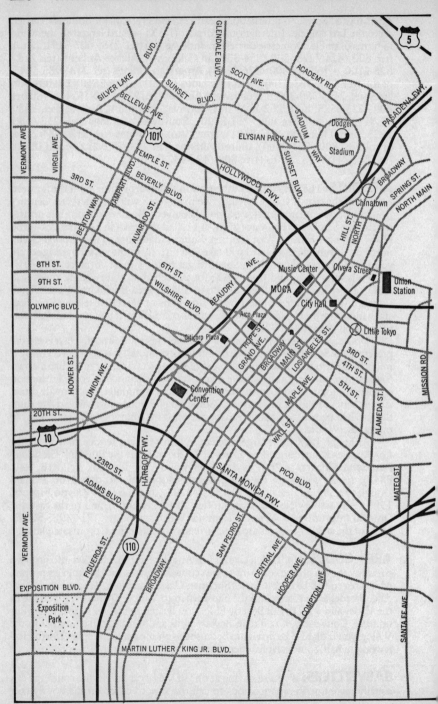

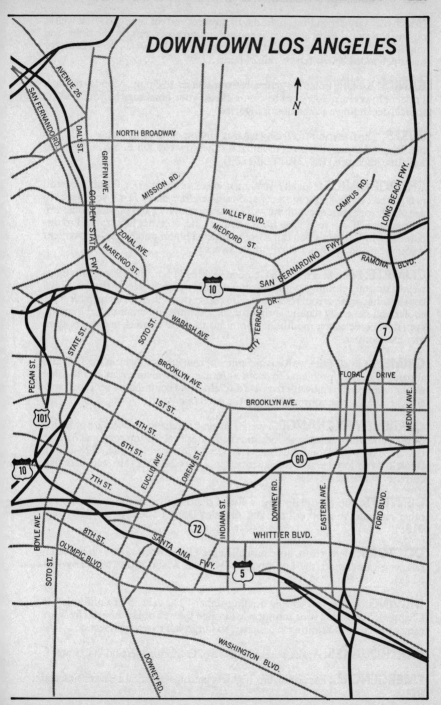

DOWNTOWN LOS ANGELES

(which may vary depending on the day of the week and the time of day), as well as on any additional expenses such as transportation and meals for the sitter. You might try the **Baby Sitters Guild**, 6362 Hollywood Blvd. (tel. 469-8246), for mature, bonded babysitters on call 24 hours.

BANKS: Banking hours are generally from 10 a.m. to 3 p.m., Monday through Friday. However, if you need to cash a check, your hotel may be your best resource, depending on the amount involved.

BUSES: The **Greyhound/Trailways Bus System** serves most cities in California. In Los Angeles, the main terminal is downtown at 208 E. 6th St. (6th and Los Angeles Streets) (tel. 213/620-1200).

CHARGE CARDS: Not all restaurants, stores, or shops in California accept all major credit cards, and some accept none. Therefore, check first if you expect to use plastic for a large expenditure—it can save annoyance and possibly some embarrassment. If you're visiting from another state, you may be surprised to discover that in California you can charge packaged liquor purchases—convenient if you're buying a case or two of vintage wines.

CLIMATE: From May through October, weather in Los Angeles warrants lightweight summer clothing, with a sweater or lightweight jacket for the occasional cool evening or supercool restaurant. November through April temperatures are cooler and generally require spring-weight clothing and a raincoat. However, even during the cooler months, it's not unusual to have a week or more of summer-like weather.

CRIME: As in all cities with a large influx of tourists from within the U.S. and abroad, crime is a problem. To avoid an unhappy incident or an end to what might have been an enjoyable trip, use discretion and common sense. Take traveler's checks and leave your valuables in the hotel safe.

CURRENCY EXCHANGE: Foreign currency exchange services are provided by the **Bank of America** at six locations in the Los Angeles International Airport (tel. 213/568-8064) and at its branch at 525 S. Flower St. (tel. 213/228-2721). **Deak International** at 677 S. Figueroa (tel. 213/624-4221) also offers foreign currency exchange services.

DENTISTS: Hotels usually have a list of dentists should you need one. For other referrals, you can call the **Los Angeles Dental Society** (tel. 213/481-2133).

DOCTORS: Here, again, hotels usually have a list of doctors on call. For referrals, you can contact the **Los Angeles Medical Association** (tel. 213/483-6122).

DRIVING: I refer you to this heading under "The ABC'S of California" in Chapter I. Navigating your automobile through the web of Los Angeles freeways can be a somewhat daunting experience, so I urge you to read this section.

EARTHQUAKES: Again, see the "ABC'S of California" section in Chapter I.

EMERGENCIES: For police, fire, highway patrol, or medical emergencies, dial 911.

EVENTS AND FESTIVALS: You can obtain a listing of special events in Los Angeles at the Visitors Information Center, weekdays 8 a.m. to 5 p.m., downtown at Arco Plaza, Level B, 6th and S. Flower Sts. (tel. 213/689-8822); or in Hollywood at the Janes House, Janes House Square, 6541 Hollywood Blvd. (tel. 213/461-4213), weekdays 9 a.m. to 5 p.m. The other option is to send a self-addressed, stamped, business-size envelope to *Datelines,* c/o GLAVCB, P.O. Box 71607, Los Angeles, CA 90071-9971, requesting a copy of this publication of the Visitors Information Center. For up-to-the-minute happenings, the Sunday edition of the *Los Angeles Times* has a "Calendar" section covering entertainment, the arts, studio gossip, museums, etc. (for Las Vegas as well as Los Angeles).

FOOD: There are lots of places to eat in L.A. for less than $5; the problem is that you can starve in the time it takes to get from one to the other. On the other hand, you can spend as much as $75 for a meal, per person, without wine or even valet parking. Los Angeles is a world with restaurants for everyone, more than you could believe would prosper—Chinese, Italian, Indian, American, Japanese, Moroccan, French, French-California, California-French, Japanese-French, elegant pizza, Greek, Czech, Jewish, Tuscan, vegetarian, Vietnamese, Lithuanian, Mexican, etc. And the food ranges from good to superb. I've tried to select some of the best in all price categories.

Not all restaurants are open daily. If you're planning an evening at one I haven't listed, call first and also ask if reservations are necessary. Check to see if they take plastic. Not all of the better restaurants do, and not all take every major credit card.

HAIR SALONS: If your hotel does not have a hair salon on the premises, they're usually glad to make a recommendation.

HOLIDAYS: Obvious holiday occasions and dates of major conventions are not the times to try for reservations on short notice. If you're not certain what events are in the offing, and you have specific vacation dates in mind, send for the annual list or call the Visitors Information Center—see "Events and Festivals" above.

HOSPITALS: To find a hospital near you, quickly, turn to the Community Access pages at the front of the Pacific Bell *Yellow Pages.* There you will find a list of hospitals, with their locations superimposed on a map of the city. This is an especially useful reference in Los Angeles because the city is quite spread out and you probably won't know locations by address.

INFORMATION: The **Los Angeles Visitors Information Centers** are located in downtown Los Angeles and Hollywood. Addresses and phone numbers are given above under "Events and Festivals." Beverly Hills has its own **Visitors and Convention Bureau** at 239 S. Beverly Dr. (tel. 213/271-8174).

LAUNDRY AND DRY CLEANING: Any one of the major hotels can take care of these services for you, but allow two days to do the job.

LIQUOR LAWS: Liquor and grocery stores can sell packaged alcoholic beverages between 6 a.m. and 2 a.m. Most restaurants, night clubs, and bars are licensed to serve alcoholic beverages during the same hours. The legal age for purchase and consumption is 21 and proof of age is required. As I mentioned under "Charge Cards" above, in California you can purchase packaged liquor with your credit card; however, most stores usually have a minimum dollar amount for charging.

NEWSPAPERS: The *Los Angeles Times* is widely distributed throughout the county. Its Sunday edition has a "Calendar" section which is an excellent and interesting guide to the entire world of entertainment in and around Los Angeles, the arts, what's doing, who's doing it, what's coming, and new restaurants, among other things.

RELIGIOUS SERVICES: Los Angeles has hundreds of churches and synagogues, and at least 100 denominations, formal and informal. Should you be seeking out a house of worship, your hotel desk person or bell captain can usually direct you to the nearest church of most any denomination. If not, the Pacific Bell *Yellow Pages* can usually provide the location and, frequently, the times of the services.

SPORTS (SPECTATOR): Los Angeles has two major-league baseball teams —the **Los Angeles Dodgers** (tel. 213/224-1400), and the **California Angels** (tel. 714/634-2000); two NFL football teams—the **L.A. Raiders** (tel. 213/322-5901) and the **L.A. Rams** (tel. 714/937-6767); two NBA basketball teams —the **L.A. Lakers** (tel. 213/673-1300) and the **L.A. Clippers** (tel. 213/748-8000). The Dodgers play at Dodger Stadium, located at 1000 Elysian Park, near Sunset Boulevard. The Angels and the Rams call Anaheim Stadium home at 2000 S. State College Blvd., near Katella Avenue in Anaheim. The Lakers hold court in The Forum at 3900 W. Manchester Blvd., at Prairie Avenue in Inglewood. And these days the Raiders do their dirty work in the L.A. Memorial Coliseum, 3911 S. Figueroa, with the Clippers nearby in the L.A. Sports Arena, at 3939 S. Figueroa.

And finally, there's the sport of kings. Lovely **Hollywood Park racetrack,** 1050 S. Prairie Ave. in Inglewood (tel. 213/419-1500), has thoroughbred racing from April through July. A computer-oriented screen offers a view of the back stretch and stop-action replays of photo finishes. There's also a children's play area with modern playground equipment and an electronic games area. Post times are 2 p.m. weekdays, 1:30 p.m. weekends and holidays. **Santa Anita racetrack,** 285 W. Huntington Dr. in Arcadia (tel. 818/574-7223), is one of the most beautiful tracks in the country and has thoroughbred racing from October through mid-November and December through late April. Weekdays, the public is invited to watch morning workouts from 7:30 to 9:30 a.m. Santa Anita also has a children's playground. Post time is 1 p.m. Finally, there's **Los Alamitos Race Course,** 4961 Katella Ave., in Los Alamitos (tel. 213/431-1361, or 714/995-1234), featuring quarterhorse racing from mid-November through January, and May through mid-August; harness racing is held from late February through April.

STORE HOURS: Stores are usually open from 10 a.m. to 6 p.m. Monday through Saturday, and closed on Sunday.

TAXES: California state sales tax is 6%.

TRAINS: **Amtrak** service south to San Diego and north to Oakland, Seattle, and points in-between, operates out of the station at 800 N. Alameda (tel. 213/624-0171).

USEFUL TELEPHONE NUMBERS: You can obtain **weather information** for Los Angeles at 213/554-1212, the **time** at 213/853-1212, and information on **local highway conditions** at 213/626-7231. For **nonemergency police matters,** phone 213/485-2121 or, in Beverly Hills, 213/550-4951. Dial 411 for **directory assistance** and 800/555-1212 to obtain telephone numbers of establishments that have **toll-free service.**

3. HOTELS

Generally, when you look for a hotel you try to choose one with a convenient location. In sprawling Los Angeles, however, a convenient location is a very limited concept. Nothing is convenient to everything, and wherever you stay you can count on doing a lot of driving to somewhere else.

The most elegant digs are, for the most part, in Beverly Hills and Bel Air. Hollywood is probably the most central place to stay; downtown is good for business people, and offers proximity to many cultural attractions; Santa Monica and Marina del Rey are right on the beach; and families with kids might want to head straight to Anaheim or Buena Park.

I've listed more deluxe and upper-bracket hostelries here than in other chapters—there are simply more of them in star-studded L.A. than in other cities.

Hotel listings are broken down by area, since L.A. communities are so far-flung, then further divided into the following categories: deluxe, upper bracket, moderately priced, and budget. All listings have been measured by the strict yardstick of value—the most for your money.

I'll lead off the hotel survey with glamorous—

BEVERLY HILLS—DELUXE: The **Beverly Hills Hotel,** 9641 Sunset Blvd., (at Beverly Drive), Beverly Hills, CA 90210 (tel. 213/276-2251), is the stomping grounds of millionaires and maharajas, jet-setters and movie stars. There are hundreds of anecdotes about this famous hotel and the world's most glamorous bar on its premises, the Polo Lounge.

For years, Howard Hughes maintained a complex of bungalows, suites, and rooms here, using some of the facilities for an elaborate electronic-communications security system, and keeping a food-taster housed in one room! Perhaps this is the only hotel in the world that would provide him with such services as 23 kadota figs (24 would be angrily returned) in the middle of the night.

Years ago Katharine Hepburn did a flawless dive into the pool—fully clad in her tennis outfit, shoes and all; Dean Martin and Frank Sinatra once got into a big fistfight with other Polo Lounge residents. And in 1969 John Lennon and Yoko Ono checked into the most secluded bungalow under assumed names, then stationed so many armed guards around their little hideaway that discovery was inevitable. So it goes. The stories are endless, and concern everyone from Chaplin to Madame Chiang Kai-shek.

What attracts them all? For one thing, each other. And of course you can't beat the service—not just the catering to such eccentricities as a preference for bear steak, but little things like being greeted by your name every time you pick up the phone.

And the Beverly Hills Hotel is a beauty, its green and pink stucco buildings set on 12 carefully landscaped and lushly planted acres. Paths lined with giant palm trees wind throughout, and the privacy of verandas and lanais is protected by flowering and leafy foliage. (It was the backdrop for Neil Simon's play, *California Suite.*)

Each of the 325 accommodations (which include 21 bungalows and garden suites) is custom-designed in the best Hollywood tradition, with tropical overtones—they're gorgeous. And of course you can count on every amenity in your room.

In addition to the world-famous Polo Lounge, rendezvous headquarters of international society for almost 40 years, the Beverly Hills also has the Loggia and Patio (which adjoin the Polo Lounge) for breakfast and luncheon in a delightful garden ambience.

Then there's The Coterie for gourmet dinners, done in coral and peach, with gold and copper accents and highly lacquered burnished sienna woodwork. Dinner here might begin with hors d'oeuvres ranging from pâté of duck liver to herring in sour cream. House specialties (costing $25 to $35) include veal sautéed with apples in Calvados, served with rice pilaf, and fresh California sand dabs sautéed in butter. For dessert there are fresh-baked French pastries, cakes, and pies, but I usually pass them up in favor of the sumptuous chocolate or Grand Marnier soufflé.

The Pool and Cabaña Club is centered around an Olympic-size turquoise pool, where hardly anyone ever swims, but from which it is imperative, if one is *anyone,* to be paged to the telephone. The club is surrounded by colorful tent-top cabañas, and also has two tennis courts. If you order lunch by the pool, it's not a hamburger on a paper plate—it's served up on fine china, and your little table is adorned with fresh-cut flowers.

An unusual facility is the Cinema Room, an intimate private screening room with the latest audio-visual equipment, and beverage service available.

Now for the rates, which are determined by the size and location of your room: singles and doubles range from $175 to $275; suites, from $375 to $1,300; and bungalows, from $475 to $1,300. If you can't afford to stay here for your entire L.A. trip, you might want to splurge for just a few nights to experience authentic Hollywood glamour at its best. If even that is out of the question, at least come by and have lunch or a drink in the Polo Lounge.

L'Ermitage, 9291 Burton Way (near Foothill Road), Beverly Hills, CA 90210 (tel. 213/278-3344, or toll free 800/424-4443), ranks with the finest hotels in the state. It has received the AAA's five diamonds.

Each of the 114 units is actually a small suite that includes a sunken living room, wet bar, dressing area, and powder room, as well as a fully equipped kitchen and balcony. These suites are furnished in residential motif, like rooms in a fine home, and all have fireplaces.

The rooms and hallways are hung with many paintings, but most impressive are those in the Café Russe, L'Ermitage's exceptional restaurant for the exclusive use of hotel guests. Here there's an original Van Gogh, Renoir, Braque, and de la Peña!

Guests at L'Ermitage enjoy a morning paper at no charge, and complimentary caviar each afternoon in the small bar on the top floor. Other services include shining shoes guests leave outside the door at night and a complimentary limo to whisk you off to Rodeo Drive shops. There's a rooftop spa with a heated pool and Jacuzzi.

All this luxury doesn't come cheap. One-bedroom executive suites are $235 to $285, one-bedroom town-house suites run $325 to $525, two-bedroom town-house suites are $425 to $535, and a three-bedroom town-house suite is $1,300.

BEVERLY HILLS—UPPER BRACKET: The **Beverly Hilton,** 9876 Wilshire Blvd. (at Santa Monica Boulevard), Beverly Hills, CA 90210 (tel. 213/274-7777), is one of the poshest of the Hilton chain. The decor is luxurious, with each room individually decorated; amenities include in-room first-run movies and refrigerators. Most of the 625 rooms have balconies, and overlook an Olympic-size pool and the surrounding hillsides.

A miniature city (like most Hiltons), this one has every kind of shop and service desk, not to mention two heated swimming pools, one Olympic size.

The Hilton's penthouse restaurant, L'Escoffier, combines gourmet cuisine with a panoramic view of the city. The plush decor utilizes such finery as lace tablecloths, gray velvet drapes, and Louis XVI–style chairs. There is a prix-fixe dinner for $61. À la carte entrees cost $25 to $35. Open for lunch weekdays and for dinner Monday to Saturday, L'Escoffier also has music for dancing and a delightful parlor lounge for cocktails.

The award-winning Trader Vic's offers exotic international cuisine in an atmosphere of Polynesian splendor. À la carte entrees are $14 to $30. A small red-lacquer bridge adds to the ambience. Celebrities can often be spotted here, dining on unique dishes and sampling exotic drinks.

Sunday champagne brunch ($25) and dinner buffets ($27), served nightly from 6 to 10:30 p.m., are most popular at Mr. H—another elegant Hilton eatery, this with rich, muted decor, crystal chandeliers, and Jacobean chairs. A $14 buffet lunch is also served here.

Room rates at the Hilton depend on size and location, with stiffer tabs for rooms overlooking the pool or on higher floors. Singles range from $160 to $215; doubles, from $180 to $230. A plus is that there is no charge for children (even teenagers) in the same room as their parents; a third adult in a room pays $20.

BEVERLY HILLS—MODERATE: Beverly Rodeo, 360 N. Rodeo Dr. (a

block north of Wilshire Boulevard), Beverly Hills, CA 90210 (tel. 213/273-0300, or toll free 800/421-0545, 800/441-5050 in California), has in the last few years been completely redecorated in French provincial style. Owner Max Baril has packed a lot of luxury into this intimate, 100-room, European-style hotel, beginning with the courteous attendant at the door.

Rooms are very pretty with matching floral-print spreads and draperies, and baths have marble-topped sinks and extra phones. All rooms have color TV, AM/FM radio, and air conditioning, and some have balconies and refrigerators.

The hotel's restaurant, the Café Rodeo (just great for people-watching along Rodeo Drive), is furnished in contemporary mode with natural woods and rattan. A charming outdoor courtyard—where breakfast and lunch are served—adjoins.

Rates for standard rooms at the Beverly Rodeo are $120 to $140; deluxe, from $127 to $147; and executive rooms, from $145 to $165; opulent suites cost $255 to $400. The one drawback here: no swimming pool.

The **Beverly Hillcrest,** Beverwill Dr. (at Pico Boulevard), Beverly Hills, CA 90212 (tel. 213/277-2800, or toll free 800/421-3212, 800/252-0174 in California), is a multi-million-dollar luxury hostelry at the southern edge of Beverly Hills. Rooms are notably spacious and elegantly appointed in restrained and tasteful French provincial decor, many with half-canopied beds. Each has a refrigerator (with ice), remote-control color TV and radio, genuine marble bath with an extra phone, and a balcony.

A gleaming steel-and-glass outdoor elevator whisks you up 12 floors to the Top of the Hillcrest, a rooftop restaurant offering views of Beverly Hills, Hollywood, and the Pacific Ocean. Its lavish interior is done up in gold-flocked draperies, gold-leather upholstered chairs, and glittering crystal chandeliers. Most luncheon entrees are in the $10 to $14 range; dinners including soup and salad range from $17 to $25 for the likes of coq au vin or steak and lobster.

Breakfast, lunch (except Sunday), and dinner are also served daily at

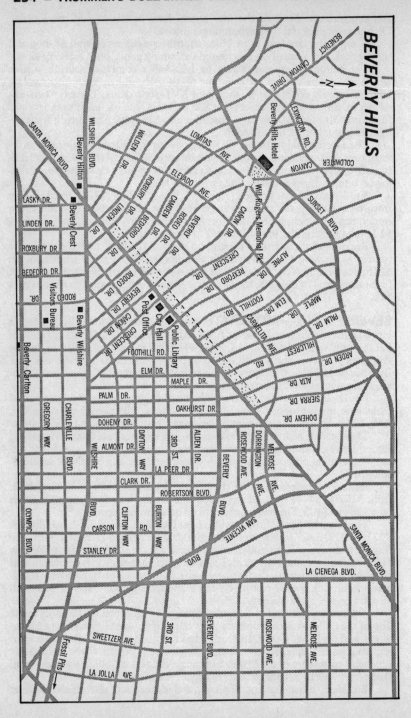

Portofino, a candlelit old-world Italian eatery with tufted red-leather booths, exposed brick and wood-paneled walls. Dinner entrees here include a salad, Italian bread, a cheese wedge, and a basket of fresh fruit. Scampi with rice, chicken cacciatore served with eggplant parmigiana, and fettuccine Alfredo are among the delicacies offered for $15 to $27. Cheesecake with warm cherries is a delicious dessert.

Other facilities: A swimming pool with a palm-fringed terrace for sunning and refreshments, and garage parking.

Single rooms at the Beverly Hillcrest are $120 to $125; doubles run $130 to $135; suites from $215 to $345. Special weekend rates are also available.

Not to be confused with the above is the 54-room **Beverly Crest Hotel,** 125 South Spalding Dr. (just south of Wilshire Boulevard), Beverly Hills, CA 90212 (tel. 213/274-6801). Many of the rooms overlook a courtyard wherein is a swimming pool surrounded by palm trees.

The guest rooms, which are on the small side, are done in pleasant shades of blue, peach, or orange and have a contemporary look with white or black lacquer furnishings. Rooms here have good closet space, full-length mirrors, direct-dial phones, color TVs, air conditioning/heating, and tub/shower baths.

Overlooking the pool is the Venetian Room Restaurant, serving breakfast, lunch, and dinner daily. And you can park your car in a spacious covered garage at no extra charge.

Single rooms are $78 to $95; doubles, $88 to $105.

HOLLYWOOD—UPPER BRACKET: The **Hyatt on Sunset,** 8401 Sunset Blvd. (two blocks east of La Cienega Boulevard), Hollywood, CA 90069 (tel. 213/656-4101, or toll free 800/228-9000), is popular with celebs (Gene Autry officially opened it and June Allyson cut the ribbon). It's a lively place, close to Restaurant Row on La Cienega Boulevard and Sunset Strip nightlife. The 300 spacious bedrooms, housed on 13 floors, overlook the Los Angeles skyline and the mountains. Rooms, decorated in subdued earth tones, have modern furnishings and dressing areas, plus all the conveniences: direct-dial phone, in-room movies on your color TV, and modern tub/shower bath. Most have a private balcony.

Facilities include the requisite shops, a rooftop swimming pool/sundeck and valet or complimentary self-parking.

The Hyatt's restaurant, the Silver Screen, pays homage to the old days of Hollywood. Large blowups of oldtime scenes create a nostalgic atmosphere that is augmented by actual cameras, lights, and a director's chair. It's open from 7 a.m. to midnight. The Sunset Lounge on the premises features live jazz Tuesday to Saturday.

Singles cost $80 to $110, doubles cost $95 to $115, and suites run $140 to $375. Special weekend rates are available.

There isn't enough space to list all of the famous people who have resided at the **Château Marmont,** 8221 Sunset Blvd. (at Marmont Lane), Hollywood, CA 90046 (tel. 213/656-1010), a château-style apartment hotel lodged on a cliff just above Sunset Strip. Humphrey Bogart, Jeanne Moreau, Boris Karloff, Al Pacino, James Taylor, Richard Gere, Bianca Jagger, John and Yoko, Sophia Loren, Sidney Poitier, and Whoopi Goldberg have all been guests. Carol Channing met her husband here; Greta Garbo used to check in under the name Harriet Brown, and even Howard Hughes once maintained a suite.

Guests often gather in the great baronial living room, furnished with grandiose Hollywood antiques. Otherwise you'll find them lounging around the oval swimming pool amid semitropical trees and shrubbery.

The entire place was remodeled a few years ago and nine cottages were added. All accommodations are furnished in tasteful English style, and all have color TV, direct-dial phone, and daily maid service. Room service is available daily from 6:30 a.m. to 12:30 a.m.

Regular rooms are $100, single or double. All the others have fully equipped kitchens and dens. Double rate in a studio with living room and bedroom is $130 a day; one-bedroom suites are $160 to $180 and two-bedroom suites run $215; a two-bedroom bungalow is $300, and penthouse suites are $250 to $450; cottages are $130 a night. Free valet parking is included in the rates.

HOLLYWOOD—MODERATE: Reliable standard accommodations can be found at the good old **Holiday Inn,** 1755 N. Highland Ave. (between Franklin and Hollywood Boulevard), Hollywood, CA 90028 (tel. 213/462-7181, or toll free 800/465-4329), a 22-story (they claim 23, but there's no 13th floor), 468-room hostelry in the heart of Old Hollywood. Rooms have been redecorated, and are pleasant and comfortable. Every room is equipped with a color TV, clock radio, air conditioning, direct-dial phone, and modern tub/shower bath. For your convenience there are three laundry rooms, and ice and soda machines on every floor.

A revolving circular rooftop restaurant, Windows on Hollywood, features dancing and dining with a panoramic Hollywood view. Down on the second floor guests can lounge around a swimming pool/sundeck. The Show Biz Café, the hotel's rather plush coffeeshop, serves breakfast, lunch, and dinner, and the Front Row Lounge, an intimate cocktail lounge, is open daily until 2 a.m. A garage on the premises offers free parking.

Single rooms are $83 to $95, and doubles cost $90 to $102; an extra person in the room is $10; children 18 and under stay free in their parents' room.

HOLLYWOOD—BUDGET: Convenient to many L.A. attractions, the **Saharan Motor Hotel,** 7212 Sunset Blvd. (two blocks west of La Brea), Hollywood, CA 90046 (tel. 213/874-6700), provides comfortable accommodations at economy prices. All rooms are centered around and overlook a flagstone courtyard that contains the swimming pool and sundeck.

Rooms are basic, satisfactory, contemporary, all with direct-dial phone, color TV, clock, a small refrigerator, and air conditioning. Extras include free parking and complimentary coffee all day. There's laundry and dry cleaning nearby.

Double- or twin-bedded rooms for one or two persons are $36 to $40, and double-doubles are $42 to $48 for up to four people; kitchenette suites are $55 to $70.

DOWNTOWN LOS ANGELES—DELUXE: California's most innovative hotel is the space-agey, 1,500-room **Westin Bonaventure,** 404 S. Figueroa St. (between 4th and 5th Streets), Los Angeles, CA 90071 (tel. 213/624-1000, or toll free 800/228-3000), its five gleaming gold cylindrical towers downtown's most distinctive landmark. It's the creation of world-famous architect John Portman (he also did San Francisco's innovative Hyatt Regency). The exquisite six-story skylight lobby (a Portman trademark) contains a one-acre lake, trees, and hanging gardens from upper floors; the sound of splashing fountains penetrates the area. Twelve glass-bubble elevators rise from the reflecting pools, whisking guests up to the 23 upper floors while providing spectacular views of Los Angeles. The entire effect of this strong architectural statement is thrillingly sci-fi; you feel as though you've wandered into the 21st century.

Above the lobby is the Shopping Gallery with five levels of diversified shops and boutiques—men's and women's clothing stores, a bookstore, French gourmet food shop, pre-Columbian art gallery, photography center, hairdressers for men and women, you name it. You can rest from shopping in one of the circular seating areas, seemingly suspended in space, overlooking the bustling lobby activity.

There's a large outdoor swimming pool and sundeck, with poolside dining; airline and car-rental desks; tennis and health club facilities for men and women located just across one of the pedestrian bridges at the Los Angeles Racquet Club; 24-hour room service; babysitting service; and round-the-clock valet parking.

Then there are the restaurants and cocktail areas. The Sidewalk Café and adjoining Lobby Court with tables under large fringed umbrellas is the scene of nightly entertainment; it varies from jazz combos to mariachi bands.

The all new Flower Street Bar, a rich mixture of marble, brass, and mahogany, is becoming the new downtown "hot spot" for cocktails. The rooftop Top of Five features gourmet continental fare in the $22 to $30 range—for example, filet mignon and lobster tail with béarnaise sauce—and panoramic views, with a revolving cocktail lounge (the Bona Vista) below it on the 34th floor; the latter is a favorite pretheater rendezvous. The elegant Beaudry's on the lobby floor, named for the famous 19th-century mayor, offers haute-cuisine fare in a stunning contemporary setting with 18 intimate dining areas sheltered by shimmering gold-mesh curtains. Beaudry's offers such tempting dinner entrees as lobster ragoût in a puff pastry graced with an excellent Nantua sauce. Entrees at lunch cost $13 to $18; at dinner they range from $19 to $27. Inagiku, a first-rate Japanese restaurant patterned after a Japanese village with winding walkways, is composed of a steakhouse for teppanyaki cooking and a dining room with sushi and tempura bars as well as regular tables and tatami rooms. There's also a lobby-level nightclub called Cabaret offering live music for dancing nightly.

As for the rooms, they're as modernistic and attractive as the rest of the hotel (no bedroom is more than six doors from an elevator); all are equipped with every luxury and have floor-to-ceiling windows. Done in subtle earth tones, with rattan furnishings adding an exotic note, the rooms are everything you'd expect from a first-class hotel—sophisticated and elegant with floor-to-ceiling views of the city.

In short, there's nothing wanting at this exciting hotel—if you don't stay here, come by for a look around.

Single rooms are $125 to $190, doubles run $150 to $220, and suites begin at $275.

Contrasting with the Bonaventure's futuristic appeal is the **Biltmore**, 506 S. Grand Ave. (between 5th and 6th Streets), Los Angeles, CA 90071 (tel. 213/624-1011, or toll free 800/421-8000, or 800/252-0175 in California), a gracious old grande dame (built in 1923) among Los Angeles's deluxe hotels. During the '30s and '40s the Academy Awards ceremonies were held here, including the year *Gone With the Wind* swept them all.

Always a beautiful hotel, the Biltmore today is looking better than ever following a $40-million facelift completed in 1987. The renovation enhanced the Biltmore's basic architectural structure while incorporating harmonious contemporary touches (such as the Jim Dine prints in the guest rooms) and updating to state-of-the-art its mechanical systems. The new entrance on Grand Avenue (formerly the back of the hotel) features a *porte-cochère* where valet parking is available.

The lavishly appointed rooms are spacious and attractively decorated in pastel tones. Traditional French furniture houses the desk and TV. The rooms are, of course, equipped with every modern amenity, and the Biltmore offers such luxurious extras as 24-hour maid service and room service, hand-delivered messages, and a multilingual concierge staff. The Biltmore Health Club, featuring an elegant Roman spa–like pool, steam room, sauna, Jacuzzi, Nautilus equipment, and weights, is open daily for hotel guests and members.

Once the lobby of the hotel, the spectacular Rendezvous Court now serves as a lovely lounge where you can enjoy afternoon tea or evening cocktails. Overhead an ornate cathedral-like vaulted ceiling was hand-painted by (who else?) an Italian artist, Giovanni Smeraldi.

The Biltmore's dining facilities include the prestigious Bernard's, a luxurious environment—fluted columns, hand-painted beamed ceilings—in which to enjoy a combination classic French and regional American cuisine. At dinner, you might begin with an appetizer of Westcott Bay oysters. Entrees, priced at $25 to $40, include specialties such as grilled medallions of veal served with artichoke fettuccine, or breast of chicken stuffed with chicken mousse. Lunch is a bit less costly, with entree prices from $19 to $28. The hotel's Court Cafe is open for breakfast, lunch, and dinner and features regional American cuisine in a warm Mediterranean atmosphere.

The Grand Avenue Bar offers a cold lunch buffet and in the evening showcases top-name jazz entertainment.

Rates for singles are $130 to $190; doubles $150 to $210; suites start at $355.

Returning once more to the dazzlingly ultramodern: the 487-room, 24-story **Hyatt Regency Los Angeles,** 711 S. Hope St. (at 7th Street), Los Angeles, CA 90017 (tel. 213/683-1234, or toll free 800/228-9000). It's part of Broadway Plaza, a 21st-century-style complex of shops, restaurants, offices, and galleries that includes a huge parking garage. The avant-garde tone is set by the two-story skylight-covered entrance lobby with a garden plaza, lounges, a sidewalk café, and boutiques. Wide escalators glide down to the lobby/reception area and gardens. Everything is a melange of rich browns, reds, rusts, and golds, adorned with super-graphics and warmly enhanced by exposed brick, potted plants, trees, old-fashioned gaslight street lamps, and overstuffed furniture.

Rooms at the Hyatt are innovative and attractive. Each has a full window wall offering surprisingly nice views for a downtown hotel, deep pile carpeting, oversize beds, dressing room, small sofa, color TV with in-room movies, etc. Strikingly futuristic in design and furnishings, they utilize the same bold textures and russet-gold color scheme prevalent throughout the building.

There's a revolving rooftop restaurant called Angel's Flight, offering a full-circle panoramic window tour of the city every hour and gourmet lunches and dinners. The opulent Pavan (open for lunch and dinner Monday through Saturday) is the Hyatt's premier gourmet restaurant, the Lobby Bar its most congenial spot for cocktails. Also on the premises is the Sun Porch, a sidewalk café-coffeeshop.

In addition, the Hyatt offers tennis and health club facilities in conjunction with the nearby Los Angeles Racquet Club, and guests can use the pool at the Wilshire Hyatt. A concierge and nighttime maid service are luxurious extras.

Rates are $120 to $165 single, $150 to $190 for doubles and twins, suites from $275.

The 900-room **Los Angeles Hilton and Towers,** 930 Wilshire Blvd. (at Figueroa), Los Angeles, CA 90017 (tel. 213/629-4321), is centrally located near downtown attractions and offers easy access to major freeway entrances. Many rooms overlook the oval swimming pool, set in a semitropical garden of palm and banana trees.

A $70-million project upgrading the decor and opening the premium-accommodation Towers was completed in 1987. The furnishings for this ultramodern building are contrastingly traditional—Queen Anne, Chippendale, and

Hepplewhite, for example. Every convenience and luxury is at hand, from 24-hour maid and room service to in-house movies, a writing desk, and double-panel glass windows to minimize outside noise. Nonsmoking rooms are available, as are those specially equipped for handicapped guests. And you can dine and drink by the hotel's outdoor swimming pool (usually closed in March and April when the weather is cool).

The premium Towers rooms (15th and 16th floors) have separate check-in facilities and a staff serving only Towers guests. The deluxe furnishings in these rooms include two-line telephones, morning newspaper delivery, and nightly turndown. The Towers lounge serves complimentary continental breakfast and provides the latest Dow Jones reports (assuming you really want to know), as well as two TV sets, reading material, and games; later a daily cocktail hour is held here, with complimentary hors d'oeuvres and beverages.

If you find it a matter of importance on your vacation (and some people do), the Hilton now has the only video teleconference room in a Southern California hotel, one of a national network of such two-way, interactive rooms put in place by Hilton and AT&T.

The hotel's four restaurants include the 24-hour Gazebo coffeeshop; City Grill with its California cuisine; and Minami of Tokyo, serving Japanese food nightly, as well as midday during the week. And the Lobby Bar serves cocktails and snacks, and provides musical entertainment. But above all, there is the ultracontemporary, ultra-elegant Cardini's for superb northern Italian cuisine. The emphasis is on light pastas, with a good selection of fish and veal dishes. But there are such first-course beauties as slices of eggplant gracefully encasing goat cheese, and such enticing entrees as black ravioli filled with shrimp and chives or the six-chop rack of lamb (forever a favorite of mine). At the end, pay attention to the pastry tray for just a few more gorgeous calories. Dinner for two, without wine, will be about $50 to $100. Lunch will run you somewhat less.

Room rates at the Hilton depend on placement and size. Singles are $125 to $160; double and twin-bedded rooms cost $145 to $180.

The **New Otani Hotel and Garden,** 120 S. Los Angeles St. (at 1st Street), Los Angeles, CA 90012 (tel. 213/629-1200, or toll free 800/421-8795, 800/252-0197 in California), is the city's only Japanese hotel, complete with a classical 16,000-square-foot Japanese garden for the exclusive use of guests. There's also a Japanese health club for men and women offering sauna, Japanese baths, and shiatsu massage in a garden setting.

The 446 rooms are housed in a 21-story triangular tower. Facilities include four underground parking levels, a shopping arcade of over 30 shops, car-rental desk, etc., airport limousine service, and a choice of restaurants. Golf and tennis are available in conjunction with a nearby country club.

The Canary Garden serves breakfast, lunch, and dinner (fresh-baked breads and pastries are a specialty). Pacific overtures and grilled specialties are the respective theme and fare at Commodore Perry's (most apt, since Perry is belatedly responsible for hotels like the New Otani in California). And A Thousand Cranes is the evocative name of the Otani's lovely Japanese restaurant, serving traditional breakfasts, lunches, and dinners (and a Japanese brunch on Sunday) in an authentic setting overlooking the waterfall and pond in the garden. It has sushi and tempura bars. Tatami rooms are available.

The luxurious rooms are mostly Western in style; each has a refrigerator, oversize beds, shower baths with extension phone and radio, button-selector radio with city and hotel information channels in Japanese and English, direct-dial phones with message-alert lights, alarm clocks, color TVs, smoke detectors, air conditioning, and heating.

A two-story shopping center adjoins the Otani.

Rates for single rooms are $120 to $140; doubles are $135 to $165. I particularly like the Japanese suites with tatami-mat bedrooms, deep whirlpool baths, and balconies overlooking the garden—beginning at $275 a night.

One of the newest in the downtown area is the **Sheraton Grande,** 333 S. Figueroa (between 3rd and 4th Streets), Los Angeles, CA 90012 (tel. 213/617-1133, or toll free 800/325-3535), a splendid smoky-mirrored-glass structure. It's gorgeous and luxurious, starting in the large, open lobby and lounge, decorated with skylights and plants. There's daily piano entertainment here, and tea served every afternoon.

The guest rooms—470 of them—are elegantly decorated in pastels with brilliant accents. Amenities include modern marble tub/shower baths, color TVs, direct-dial phones, butler service, and 24-hour room service.

The Sheraton Grande's restaurants include the Back Porch, an informal dining room overlooking the pool, serving three meals a day; and the gourmet room, Ravel, which serves California cuisine. There's also a nightclub, Tango, four movie theaters, a pool and sundeck, and a health club on the premises.

Rooms at the Sheraton Grande cost $155 to $190 single, $190 to $215 double, and $415 to $950 for suites.

EAST WILSHIRE—UPPER BRACKET: The **Hyatt Wilshire,** 3515 Wilshire Blvd. (at the corner of Normandie Avenue), Los Angeles, CA 90010 (tel. 213/381-7411, or toll free 800/228-9000), is a luxury hotel popular with business people for its pushbutton comfort and convenient location. Its 400 rooms are housed on 12 floors; each is furnished in attractive modern style with one all-glass wall and, of course, all amenities, including first-run movies on your color TV and clock radios. Facilities are those you would expect in a first-class establishment—boutiques, beauty and barbershops, car rental, etc., not to mention a heated outdoor swimming pool.

There's nightclub entertainment and dancing to a live combo Monday through Saturday at the Café Carnival, and a pianist entertains weekdays in the lobby bar from 5 to 9 p.m. Gourmet continental lunches and dinners are served at Hugo's; at dinner you might order two medallions of beef with béarnaise sauce on one and Madagascar peppercorns on the other ($22), the tab including salad bar, vegetable, hot Grecian-style bread, sherbet in between courses to refresh your palate, dessert, and a complimentary after-dinner drink.

Single rooms are in the $105 to $135 bracket; double and twin-bedded rooms are $120 to $160.

WEST WILSHIRE—DELUXE: Don't get confused about these Wilshire listings. The previous East Wilshire hotels are close to downtown. West Wilshire (it's a very long street) is slightly west of Beverly Hills, almost in Westwood.

Here we have a very special place, the **Beverly Hills Comstock,** 10300 Wilshire Blvd. (off Comstock Street), Los Angeles, CA 90024 (tel. 213/275-5575, or toll free 800/343-2184), that caters to the carriage trade, offering mostly luxury suites. Quiet and peaceful, it offers an intimacy and privacy not possible at larger hotels and has a considerable celebrity clientele.

Rooms are large and decorated in either traditional or California modern motif. Of course, all have color TV, direct-dial phone, tub/shower bath, etc.

All the suites surround the courtyard pool area, and have private balconies or patios.

A restaurant on the premises, Le Petit Café, serves breakfast, lunch, and dinner, and has a full-service bar. Rates, which include parking, are $140 to $210 for a one-bedroom kitchen suite, $265 to $320 for a two-bedroom kitchen suite. Monthly rates are available.

WESTWOOD—MODERATE: Wedged between Santa Monica and glamorous Beverly Hills, the student community of Westwood has over 400 shops, about 100 restaurants, and 15 first-run movie theaters. All of which combine to make it a convenient and pleasant place to stay.

The **Royal Palace Westwood Hotel,** 1052 Tiverton Ave., Los Angeles, CA 90024 (tel. 213/208-6677, or toll free 800/631-0100, 800/248-6955 in California), is just north of Wilshire, right in the heart of Westwood Village. At the hub of surrounding communities—Beverly Hills, Century City, Santa Monica, West Los Angeles, and Bel Air—it's convenient to Hollywood, the beach, the airport, and the San Diego Freeway. And should you be interested in nightlife, there's plenty of action within walking distance, including the Comedy Store.

Each room is nicely decorated and all of the bathrooms have marble vanities. All rooms have new Acme units with stove, refrigerator, and stainless counter tops. Some also have microwave ovens. You get color TV with three entertainment channels. Facilities include a game room, billiard room, and lounge.

Single rooms range from $59 to $84, doubles run $69 to $89, and suites are $100. Additional persons in a room pay $10 each.

An excellent choice is the **Century Wilshire Hotel,** 10776 Wilshire Blvd. (between Malcolm and Selby Avenues), Westwood, CA 90024 (tel. 213/474-4506, or toll free 800/421-7223). Housed in a white stucco building with blue shuttered windows, it has a homey appearance further enhanced by many strategically placed potted plants. In fact, it's one of the homiest hotels I've ever seen, right down to the charmingly furnished rooms that combine old-fashioned comfort with modern amenities like direct-dial phones and color TVs.

The swimming pool is adjacent to a delightful courtyard with a splashing fountain, garden furnishings, and lots of comfy chaises longues for sunning. Underground parking is free.

Single rooms are $70 to $80; doubles, $80 to $90. Terrific buys are the suites with fully equipped kitchen and dining room, for $130 to $160.

Another Westwood choice, for **Holiday Inn** fans, is a branch of said chain at 10740 Wilshire Blvd. (at Selby Avenue), Westwood, CA 90024 (tel. 213/475-8711, or toll free 800/472-8556, 800/235-7973 in California). This one offers 300 attractively furnished rooms—all twins with color TVs, direct-dial phones, tub/shower baths with marble sinks, mini-bars, and complimentary newspapers. Reflecting the English Tudor theme of the hotel's interior decor, there are hunting prints on the walls.

Facilities include a swimming pool, sundeck and Jacuzzi, and restaurant, the Café Le Dome, offering continental cuisine. The Café Le Dome Cocktail Lounge here is popular with local basketball and football teams, many of whom stay at the hotel.

Singles are $117 to $127; doubles, $127 to $137; and suites, $170 to $400. Since kids 18 or under can stay free in your double room, this is a good choice for families.

WEST LOS ANGELES—UPPER BRACKET: The **Bel-Air Summit Hotel** (formerly the Bel-Air Sands), 11461 Sunset Blvd. (at the San Diego Freeway), Los Angeles, CA 90049 (tel. 213/476-6571, or toll free 800/421-6649, 800/352-6680 in California), is just minutes away from Beverly Hills, Westwood Village and U.C.L.A., Century City, and ten miles from LAX.

The 162 large, air-conditioned rooms and suites all feature large balconies or lanais and are decorated in subtle colors and understated European decor. All rooms have remote-control color TVs, VCRs, hairdryers, refrigerators, electronic security keys, radios, and direct-dial phones. There are two heated pools and a tennis court on the premises.

The hotel's dining room is the Bel-Air Bar and Grill. Breakfast, lunch, dinner, and a fabulous Sunday brunch are served here, the last including champagne.

Rooms are $125 to $170 for singles, $145 to $225 for doubles; suites start at $265.

WEST LOS ANGELES—MODERATE: West Los Angeles, as a glance at your L.A. map will show you, is just slightly south of Westwood, and within easy access of Beverly Hills, Century City, and Santa Monica.

The **Los Angeles West Travel Lodge**, 10740 Santa Monica Blvd. (at Overland Avenue), Los Angeles, CA 90025 (tel. 213/474-4576, or toll free 800/255-3050), is a clean and friendly 53-room establishment offering quite good value in this area. The pleasant modern rooms are equipped with direct-dial phones, tub or shower baths, clocks, color TVs, in-room coffee makers, and refrigerators. There's an enclosed private swimming pool with a sundeck, plus plenty of free parking. Rates are reasonable, with single rooms at $55 to $65, and doubles at $60 to $80; $5 for an extra person.

CENTURY CITY—DELUXE: Built in 1966 on what was once the back lot of the Twentieth Century-Fox Corporation, the **Century Plaza**, Avenue of the Stars (off Santa Monica Boulevard), West Los Angeles, CA 90067 (tel. 213/277-2000, or toll free 800/228-3000), is a superstar in the galaxy of L.A. hotels. Designed by the celebrated Japanese architect Minoru Yamasaki, the 20-story hotel and 30-story tower occupy a commanding position adjoining Beverly Hills and right across the street from the ABC Entertainment Center, which houses an 1,850-seat Shubert legitimate theater and two ultramodern movie theaters. (The Century Plaza Tower is where President Reagan has stayed when in town.)

The hotel, together with its $85-million tower completed at the end of 1984, has a total of 1,072 rooms. The Tower's 30th floor is occupied by the 8,000-square-foot Plaza Suite. (Where else but in Los Angeles would you find one of the largest and most expensive suites in the world?) In total, the Century Plaza is enormous—it appears roughly the size of New York's Grand Central Station—with its vaulted cathedral ceilings, two-story windows, and sunken lounge areas. It has the feel of a bustling city of tomorrow.

The tower alone houses 322 rooms, but with only 14 (exceptionally spacious) per floor. All have private balconies. In addition to the usual amenities, each has a wet bar and refrigerator, three conveniently located phones, an all-marble bathroom with separate soak tub and shower, double vanity and washbasins, and a heat lamp. As you might expect, the TV is contained in an armoire. Writing desks have travertine marble tops, and there's a live tree (did you really expect plastic?) or lovely green plant in each room.

All tower rooms receive a complimentary newspaper each morning, soft drinks and ice each afternoon, deluxe bath amenities such as robes and oversize bath towels, twice-daily maid service, and 24-hour room service featuring items from La Chaumiere. There's also complimentary town-car service to and from Beverly Hills for shopping.

The 750 accommodations, apart from the tower, are furnished in garden motif with marble-topped oak furnishings and beautiful teal-blue or forest-green carpeting. Each has a balcony and is equipped with every imaginable amenity and luxury: color TVs discreetly hidden in oak armoires that double as desks; three phones (bedside, tableside, and bath); refrigerators; AM/FM radios; clocks; big closets; and tub/shower baths with marble sinks, oversize towels, and scales. Extras range from the ultramodern—an elevator kitchen to keep food warm on its way to your room—to the homey practice of leaving a mint and a goodnight note from the management on each guest's pillow when the beds are turned down for the night.

In addition to the Lobby Court (open from 11 a.m. to 2 a.m.), there are four major places to drink and dine. The newest restaurants are in the tower, La Chaumiere, which blends California and continental cuisine and presents it beautifully in a setting reminiscent of a fine European club and The Terrace for classic California dining. As with Yamato, there's more about this lovely restaurant in the dining section.

The lovely Garden Pavilion has floor-to-ceiling windows so that you can view the lush tropical gardens, reflecting pools, and fountains while you dine. It's open daily for breakfast, lunch, dinner, and dancing to live music Tuesday to Saturday, and is very popular with locals for Sunday brunch. The Café Plaza is a provincial-style coffeeshop, its walls hung with French travel posters; open from 6 a.m. to 1 a.m., it offers simple meals, sandwiches, and drinks. Yamato, a fine Japanese restaurant, is covered in the upcoming restaurant section.

Other Century Plaza facilities include two large outdoor heated pools, three Jacuzzis, a children's pool, and about ten shops, airline desks, car-rental offices, ticket agencies, sightseeing and tour desks, and of course a concierge service. Guests can use the tennis courts and a health club just across the street.

Rates at the Century Plaza are $165 to $180 single, $190 to $205 double; suites begin at $215. In the tower, singles are $215 to $230, doubles run $240 to $255, and suites begin at $950. The Plaza Suite is $3,500!

BEL-AIR—DELUXE: Neighborhoods just don't come more exclusive than Bel-Air, where every house is a mansion—and hotels don't exist that are more deluxe than the **Hotel Bel-Air,** 701 Stone Canyon Rd. (off Sunset Boulevard), Bel-Air, CA 90077 (tel. 213/472-1211). Set on exquisite tropical grounds, and surrounded by the Santa Monica hills and Southern California's most prestigious estates, the Bel-Air is entered via a long awninged pathway. It's actually an arched stone bridge over a swan- and duck-filled pond, with small waterfalls here and there. Everywhere you look you see flowering trees and plants, banana palms, bamboo, orange and lemon trees.

The architecture is Spanish, with arcades leading from one building to another. A large oval swimming pool is set amid the lush gardens and surrounded by a flagstone terrace. The public rooms are richly traditional, furnished in fine antiques, and a fire is kept burning in the entrance lounge.

There are 92 individually decorated rooms and garden suites, some with patios and a terrace, some with wood-burning fireplaces, all with picture windows, two phones (one in the bath), and radios, and all redecorated by five different decorators.

Whether you stay here or not, come by for a drink in the bougainvillea court or a meal in the traditional and lovely dining room. At dinner, such entrees as Muscovy duck with tangerine-essenced sauce and loin of lamb Wellington baked in phyllo range from $20 to $35. Come by at lunch for cold dishes like lobster sausage with basil oil, as well as sandwiches, egg dishes, and full entrees—most of them Italian or seafood selections.

Single or double rooms are priced at $210 to $420; suites are $500 to $1,400.

SANTA MONICA—UPPER BRACKET: Sun worshippers who prefer a beach location will do well to choose a Santa Monica hotel. Not only do these offer proximity to ocean beach, they also provide easy access to the airport, nearby Beverly Hills, and Westwood.

An elegant Santa Monica choice is the **Miramar-Sheraton Hotel,** 101 Wilshire Blvd. (between Ocean and 2nd), Santa Monica, CA 90401 (tel. 213/ 394-3731, or toll free 800/325-3535). Its name means "ocean view" and that's just what it's got—it sits on a cliff overlooking the Santa Monica beach. The hotel was built in the 1920s, and the slow elegance of that era is evident in the hotel's public areas. In the courtyard there's a century-old fig tree that casts its shadow over the garden. The lobby is decorated with comfortable, resort-like furniture, and the pool and surrounding garden beckon guests to swim and laze in the sun.

There are 305 guest rooms in the Miramar, in the older low buildings and the newer tower. All are comfortable and luxurious, with a king-size or two double beds, color TV, direct-dial phone, and digital clock radio. The bathrooms are equally plush, with an additional phone, honor bars, special soaps and shampoos, and oversize towels.

The hotel boasts several dining choices: the International Room, open for dinner; the Garden Room, overlooking the pool and garden, which serves breakfast and lunch; a coffeeshop; and for entertainment and dancing, the Stateroom Lounge.

Rooms at the Miramar-Sheraton are $120 to $165 for a single, $140 to $185 for a double, and $175 to $525 for a suite.

SANTA MONICA—MODERATE: The **Pacific Shore Hotel,** 1819 Ocean Ave. (at Pico Boulevard), Santa Monica, CA 90401 (tel. 213/451-8711, or toll free 800/241-3848), has 168 completely renovated air-conditioned rooms and suites with spectacular ocean or mountain views, color TVs, phones, AM/FM radios, and tub/shower baths. A large swimming pool, Jacuzzi, and saunas are surrounded by attractive tropical foliage. Other facilities include the Flamingo Lounge for cocktails, a gift shop, car rental, beauty salon, and guest laundry. Soft drinks and ice machines are on every floor. Parking is free.

Rates for singles are $85 to $120; doubles, $95 to $130; suites, $215 to $365.

The **Huntley,** 1111 2nd St. (at Wilshire Boulevard), Santa Monica, CA 90403 (tel. 213/394-5454, or toll free 800/556-4011, 800/556-4012 in California), offers 210 rooms and suites right near the beach. There's no swimming pool on the premises, but the ocean is a stone's throw away. The rooms are large and attractive (all have ocean or mountain views), and are equipped with color TV, AM/FM radio, direct-dial phone, and other modern amenities. Running up the front of the hotel is a glass elevator; the view on the way up (or down) is spectacular. Atop the hotel is a rooftop restaurant called Toppers, with terracotta tile floors, leather-upholstered chairs, hanging plants overhead, and magnificent views—be sure to see the sunset from here. Mexican cuisine is offered at lunch and dinner. In addition, there's a classy coffeeshop called the Garden Café on the premises; it has a patio for outdoor dining.

Single rooms at Huntley House cost $115 to $125, and doubles run $125 to $135; mini-suites rent for $155. Parking is free.

There are two Holiday Inns (tel. toll free 800/465-4329 for both) in Santa Monica. The **Holiday Inn Bay View Plaza,** 530 Pico Blvd. (at 6th Street, west of Lincoln), Santa Monica, CA 90405 (tel. 213/399-9344), has over 300 guest rooms, with color TVs, direct-dial phones, air conditioning, and private tub/ shower bathrooms, and nice views of the ocean or city. The Bay View Café serves three meals a day, and there's a pool and free garage parking for guests, and free airport service.

Rates are $95 to $115 single, $110 to $130 double, $180 and up for suites.
A few blocks away is another **Holiday Inn,** 120 Colorado Blvd. (at 5th Street), Santa Monica, CA 90401 (tel. 213/451-0676). It's the older of the two; rooms and facilities are similar, if less fancy. Its location is convenient, if less idyllic, pinned as it is between two freeways. Rooms here start at $88 single, $100 double.

MARINA DEL REY—DELUXE: Sandwiched between Santa Monica and
the Los Angeles International Airport, Marina del Rey is a very popular waterfront resort, just two minutes from major freeways that connect with most L.A. attractions. There are over 6,000 boats in the water—making it the world's largest small-craft harbor.

One of the most luxurious Marina del Rey hotels is the **Marina International,** 4200 Admiralty Way (at Palaway Way), Marina del Rey, CA 90292 (tel. 213/301-2000, or toll free 800/882-4000, 800/862-7462 in California), located directly across from an inland beach. There are 136 rooms and suites here, and very lovely rooms they are, recently redone in bright, light colors for a look of contemporary elegance. Of course, each room is fitted out with color TV, direct-dial phone, tub and/or shower bath, and the like.

Villas are individually decorated in such themes as Hollywood art deco, New Orleans French Quarter, Old Mexico, Japanese tea house, Tahitian lanai, King Tut's hut, and 2001 Space Age modern.

The hotel's Crystal Fountain restaurant offers continental cuisine in an indoor/outdoor garden setting. Other facilities include a swimming pool (the beach is right across the street) and free parking; golf and tennis can be arranged nearby.

A bonus is free limousine and bus service to and from the airport.

Rates vary according to room location. Singles are $125 to $160; doubles and twins run $140 to $170. Suites and villas are $190 to $290 single, $210 to $370 double.

Under the same ownership is the **Marina del Rey Hotel,** 13534 Bali Way (at Admiralty Way), Marina del Rey, CA 90292 (tel. 213/301-1000, or toll free 800/882-4000, 800/862-7462 in California). Particularly lovely here are the rooms with balconies looking out over the boat-filled harbor, a view that all guests can enjoy from the beautifully landscaped swimming pool and sundeck area. The hotel is on the marina's main channel and is surrounded by water. It's the only hotel on the waterfront.

Rooms are done in soothing blue and tan color schemes and fitted out with all modern conveniences, including color TVs, direct-dial phones, and AM/FM digital clock radios. Many have private balconies and patios so you can inspect the yachts moored nearby.

As at the International, tennis and golf can be arranged, the beach is a stone's throw away, and guests can utilize complimentary limousine airport service. Both hotels have a fleet of boats that guests can rent for harbor and party cruises.

The Dockside Café is the hotel's coffeeshop, and the Crystal Seahorse features continental fare at dinners. The latter overlooks the marina, and mirrored tables, walls, and ceilings reflect the view.

Single rooms cost $130 to $175, doubles run $150 to $195, and suites are $400 to $450.

MARINA DEL REY—UPPER BRACKET: The **Marriott Marina del Rey,**
13480 Maxella Ave. (near the Marina del Rey Freeway and Lincoln Boulevard), Marina del Rey, CA 90292 (tel. 213/822-8555, or toll free 800/228-9290), is a

delightful, resort-like place. It has 283 air-conditioned rooms, all with color TV (first-run movies available), direct-dial phone, AM/FM clock radio, and tub/shower bath. The hotel's Maxwell's Restaurant and Lounge serves American-continental fare in a cheery ambience. The Marriott is conveniently located next to the Villa Marina Center with 30 shops. There's a swimming pool, spa pool, and pool bar, all in a landscaped courtyard complete with a rock waterfall, pond, and a bridge over a stream. The tropical theme extends to rooms (many with lanais), which have splashy floral-design spreads and drapes and are equipped with all the modern amenities. Singles are $125 to $135; doubles and twins, $130 to $150; suites, $225 to $325. Airport transportation is complimentary.

UNIVERSAL CITY—UPPER BRACKET: Sheraton at Universal City (tel. toll free 800/325-3535) is a complex of two hotels—the **Sheraton Universal**, 333 Universal Terrace Pkwy., Los Angeles, CA 91608 (tel. 818/980-1212), and the **Sheraton Premiere**, 555 Universal Terrace Pkwy., Los Angeles, CA 91608 (tel. 818/506-2500). They sit on a hill on the edge of the Universal Studios property, overlooking the San Fernando Valley and parts of the studio lot.

The Universal is a 23-story white-and-glass building, with 500 pleasant and well-appointed guest rooms. Room tariffs are $90 to $160 single, $110 to $180 double, and $350 to $660 for poolside suites.

The Premiere is a smoked-glass tower with 24 floors. Three 40-foot-high pavilions, housing several of the public rooms, cluster at its base. There are 455 rooms here, and 26 suites that occupy the top five floors. Guest rooms are elegant and understated, and fully decked out with all luxury amenities. Singles rent for $130 to $185, doubles are $150 to $210, and suites cost $500 to $2,500.

Each hotel has an outdoor heated swimming pool and Jacuzzi. There's also a large parking garage for guests' use.

The Sheraton at Universal City has eight eating and drinking establishments. At the Universal are the Four Stages restaurant, where you can dine under klieg lights in any of four sets (a western saloon, Indian court, medieval castle hall, and clipper ship deck); the Café Universal, an outdoor café, and the Portuguese Lounge and Lobby Lounge, with live entertainment. At the Premiere are Oscars at the Premiere, serving a variety of "Americana" cuisine; Crystals, a Grand Café, for informal dining; Characters; and the Atrium Lounge for drinks.

Sheraton at Universal City has the advantage of being close to nearly everything. There's regular tram service to Universal Studios; the Universal Amphitheater is nearby, as are other restaurants, and Burbank and Hollywood are a short distance away. Since it's so close to everything, it's very popular with stars; you never know who you'll run into in a lobby or restaurant.

STUDIO CITY—MODERATE: A little farther west than the previous listing is the **Sportsmen's Lodge**, 12825 Ventura Blvd. (at Coldwater Canyon Avenue), Los Angeles, CA 91604 (tel. 818/769-4700, or toll free 800/821-8511, 800/821-1625 in California).

The hotel is nestled among redwood trees, with rustic wooden foot bridges crossing freshwater ponds (the hotel's name derives from the fact that guests used to fish for trout in these ponds; nowadays they're home to swans and ducks), waterfalls, rock gardens, and lush tropical greenery. There's an Olympic-size swimming pool with lots of sundeck area, a variety of shops and service desks, bowling and golf nearby, and airport limousine service.

A major asset is the next-door Sportsmen's Lodge Restaurant, 12833 Ventura Blvd. (tel. 818/984-0202). It's very attractive, the glass-enclosed main dining room overlooking a pond and small waterfall. You might begin a meal here with an order of baked clams topped with bacon bits and pimento, then order an entree of veal piccata or duckling à l'orange with wild rice priced at $15 to $28. An early-dinner menu (served from 5:30 to 6:30 p.m.) is cheaper. Cakes and rolls are fresh-baked daily. There's an extensive wine list, and an adjoining piano bar lounge serves late suppers from 10 p.m. Open nightly and for Sunday brunches. Reservations are a good idea.

There's also a coffeeshop on the premises serving breakfast, lunch, and dinner.

Rooms are large and comfortable and have been refurbished, but are not luxurious in any way; they do have color TVs, direct-dial phones, AM/FM radios, etc., and refrigerators are available. Many have balconies. The poolside executive studios ($141 single, $146 double) are the most attractive accommodations. Regular rooms are $85 to $95 single, $95 to $105 double.

PASADENA—UPPER BRACKET: The Huntington Hotel and Cottages, 1401 S. Oak Knoll (three-quarters of a mile north of Huntington Drive), Pasadena, CA 91109 (tel. 818/792-0266, or toll free 800/822-1777), is set on 23 exquisitely landscaped garden acres. It sits nestled in the shadows of the San Gabriel Mountains overlooking the San Gabriel Valley. The grounds are famous, particularly the Japanese garden with its little wooden foot bridge, and the wisteria-covered Picture Bridge adorned with Frank Moore's very charming paintings of early California scenes and accompanying verses of Don Blanding.

The main hotel is closed; however, the Huntington is now being operated as a quaint country inn, renting rooms in a small, central building and handsome cottages on or about the grounds. One- to three-bedroom accommodations range from $105 to $400. Weekly and monthly rates are available. A special $64 weekend rate is available year-round on a space-available basis.

The **Pasadena Hilton,** 150 S. Los Robles Ave. (at the corner of Cordova Street), Pasadena, CA 91101 (tel. 818/577-1000), is a 13-story hostelry crowned by a rooftop restaurant. Fifteen minutes from downtown Los Angeles, it's only a block and a half south of Colorado Boulevard, famed for its Rose Parade. Rooms have been redecorated in soft earth tones. Some have beds with elaborate high headboards; all have spacious baths, refrigerators, and color TVs with in-room movies.

Singles range in price from $98 to $129, and doubles run $113 to $144. The higher figures are for accommodations with king-size beds and balconies. One-bedroom suites cost $220 to $340. You can dine in Skylights, overlooking the entire San Gabriel Valley, or dance and enjoy live entertainment in the adjoining Slicks Night Club. Breakfast is served in the ground-level French-style Café Madagascar, and a lobby bar called Fanny's is a favorite rendezvous during Happy Hour. Other facilities include an outdoor swimming pool and parking; tennis and golf are nearby.

PASADENA—MODERATE: The Saga Motor Hotel, 1633 E. Colorado Blvd., between Allan and Sierra Bonita, Pasadena, CA 91106 (tel. 818/795-0431), is about a mile from the Huntington Library and reasonably close to Pasadena City College, Cal Tech, and the Jet Propulsion Lab. It's also well within striking distance of the Rose Bowl. But the bottom line is that the Saga has, by far, the most attractive rooms I've seen recently for the price, a fact suggested by the hotel's very inviting, sunlit, and spotlessly clean reception area.

The comfortable rooms are nicely decorated with beige carpeting, light walls, brass beds, blue-and-white checked spreads, and a blue-and-white tile bath with both shower and tub. Amenities include cable color TV and a phone. A number of the rooms are located in a single-story building surrounding a pool: the remainder, in a small three-story building, either overlook the pool or a quiet street at the rear of the building. The pool is heated year-round and is surrounded by a wide sundeck with comfortable chaises.

A large suite available on the third floor is comfortably furnished with a couch and oversize cocktail table, a small fridge, dining table for two, handsome upholstered club chairs, and a king-size brass bed. A small balcony holds enough furniture for relaxing and enjoying a midday or after-dinner libation.

Single rates are $50, doubles, $52; one or two persons with a king-size bed, $54, including a refrigerator; the suite, as described above, is $68. Complimentary coffee and doughnuts are included in the rates.

AIRPORT—UPPER BRACKET: The airport area has been developing in the last few years, and a recent addition is the 810-room **Sheraton Plaza La Reina,** 6101 W. Century Blvd. (near Sepulveda Boulevard), Los Angeles, CA 90045 (tel. 213/642-1111, or toll free 800/325-3535).

The rooms have a quintessentially California look with rattan chairs and live plants; color-coordinated drapes and bedspreads are dark green and burgundy. All rooms are equipped with direct-dial phones, digital alarm clocks, color TVs with free sports, news, and movie channels, AM/FM and radios, and have carpeted baths with tub/shower combinations. A complimentary daily newspaper is delivered daily to your door.

On-premises facilities include a heated outdoor pool, shops and boutiques, a unisex beauty salon, car-rental counter, laundry and valet cleaning services, and complimentary use of an exercise room outfitted with Universal equipment. Free airport shuttle service is available.

Restaurants include the Plaza Brasserie, an airy, contemporary café open from 6 a.m. to midnight; and Landry's, open for lunch and dinner, where the focus is on steak, chops, and seafood, including a sushi bar. Drinks can be enjoyed in Zeno's (and some great hors d'oeuvres) or in the Plaza Lounge in the lobby. Room service is available around the clock.

Singles at the Plaza La Reina are $85 to $150; and doubles go for $100 to $155; suites begin at $290.

The **Los Angeles Marriott,** Century and Airport Boulevards, Los Angeles, CA 90045 (tel. 213/641-5700, or toll free 800/228-9290), is another good airport hotel choice. It offers 1,020 cheerfully decorated bedrooms with all luxury extras, including bedside remote control of the color TV, AM/FM-stereo radios, alarm clocks, and even ironing boards, irons, and hair dryers if you like. There's also a guest laundry room—everything, in short, geared to the weary in-transit traveler.

There's a gigantic pool and garden sundeck, with a swim-up bar (the bar stools are actually in the pool), a whirlpool, and a cabaña for refreshments. It's just one of the many eating and drinking facilities here: the Fairfield Inn, a coffeeshop; The Lobby Bistro, serving buffet breakfasts, lunches, and dinners; and the Capriccio Room, for continental cuisine and Mediterranean ambience. Cocktails and entertainment are offered in a luxurious lounge called Gammon's; you can also have cocktails in the lobby lounge.

Courtesy limousine service to and from the airport is provided, and there's parking space for over 1,000 cars.

Singles go for $94 to $140; doubles, $100 to $150. Suites begin at $260.

4. RESTAURANTS

Los Angeles is one of the world's leading restaurant cities, almost as diverse in its range of ethnic eateries as New York. Its restaurants are exciting and utterly delightful, many of them taking advantage of the fine Southern California climate with outdoor seating, the rest creating unique and imaginative interiors (frequently with high noise levels) but with more aesthetic sophistication than gimmickry.

In the last decade or so Angelenos have become more knowledgeable about their food. They eat well and love to discuss restaurants and what appears to be a continually changing chef scene. Dining places are a major part of the star system and the status scene—you are where you eat, what you eat, and, more important, you are where you're seated. Almost every plush dining establishment has its "A" tables and its social-outcast sections. Unless you're rich and famous, you might as well decide you're above such snobbery; after all, no matter where you sit the food's the same. And no matter where you go, if it's good—from sleazy-but-great hamburger joints to bastions of haute cuisine—you're likely to see the stars. Part of the fun of L.A. dining is star-gazing—it adds glamour, and glamour is a big element in L.A.'s dynamic dining experience.

The first section of restaurant recommendations is devoted to the most glamorous, fashionable—and usually expensive—gathering places of the rich and famous. They're chosen, however, more for culinary excellence than chic popularity. The remainder are broken down into expensive, moderately priced, and budget categories, then further subdivided as to nationality or type of cuisine. This being L.A., many of the following are "in" places too. Many of the restaurants recommended in the hotel section above are equally good—be sure to consider them too. Reservations are advised at all Los Angeles restaurants, except Pink's Hot Dog Stand and suchlike. Reservations are imperative at—

THE TOP RESTAURANTS: The creation of the late Jean Bertranou, **L'Ermitage,** 730 N. La Cienega Blvd., just north of Melrose Place, West Hollywood (tel. 213/652-5840), is one of L.A.'s most highly acclaimed restaurants.

The new owner, Dora Fourcade, has enhanced L'Ermitage's reputation for fine cuisine and exquisite interior design. Since its inception, the restaurant has always maintained rigorous standards for the ingredients of its dishes. The wine list (all 12 pages) also reflects this pursuit of quality.

The delicate pastel-colored dining area is a masterpiece of understated elegance, reminiscent of private dining rooms in plush Paris homes. Tables are set with flowers, Christofle silver, and Villeroy and Boch china. Persian rugs on parquet floors and a wood-burning fireplace create a warm, sparkling atmosphere. A back patio with a fountain is enclosed by a domed glass skylight.

The menu changes seasonally. Since the incredibly light pastry at L'Ermitage is not to be believed, you would do well to begin with an hors d'oeuvre of puff pastry filled with a seasonal selection—perhaps tender stalks of young asparagus. The entrees on a recent visit included a sautéed veal chop with sweet pepper coulis; a paillard of salmon with fresh asparagus; and a timbale of lobster with linguine and morel mushrooms.

Whatever you order, pace yourself to leave room for an unforgettable dessert, like poached pear in red wine and blackcurrant sauce with homemade vanilla ice cream in a delicate pastry shell, or a wonderful apple tart, with a very thin and flaky crust.

Expect dinner to cost about $65 to $70 per person. L'Ermitage is open Monday through Saturday, for dinner only, from 6:30 to 10 p.m. Reservations are suggested.

The most talked-about restaurant in L.A. since its opening in April 1979 is Michael McCarty's **Michael's,** 1147 3rd St., just north of Wilshire Boulevard, Santa Monica (tel. 213/451-0843). The reason is simple: superb food, beautifully presented in a delightful setting. The interior is contemporary with forest-green, velvet-upholstered Breuer chairs and cream-colored walls hung with original works and prints of David Hockney, Jasper Johns, Richard Diebenkorn, and others. As at L'Ermitage tables are set with Villeroy and Boch china (here, 13½-inch plates provide a canvas for the artful presentation of your meal) and Christofle silver, although the effect is completely different. Large bouquets of flowers are exquisitely arranged. A favorite luncheon spot is the garden at Michael's, with tables under white Italian umbrellas.

Everything is light and delicious. The cuisine is unique—a sort of "modern American contemporary French"; the staff is American, but the menus are titled "Le Lunch" and "Le Diner," and the listings are in French. At Le Lunch you might opt for a salad of green beans, Maine lobster, duck liver, and mushroom vinaigrette. Le Diner begins with hors d'oeuvres like flaky pastry filled with seasonal fish and spinach in white wine butter sauce. There are intriguing salad offerings such as chicory, hot goat cheese, walnut vinaigrette; and entrees from a perfectly done steak frites to grilled quail with Maui onions. The excellent wine list is actually a computer printout of the cellar's daily inventory, so it's always up-to-date. As for the desserts, they're the stuff dreams are made of; don't pass them up. Dinner entrees average $30, lunch about $20. A service charge of 18% is added to all food and beverage items.

Michael's is open Monday to Friday from noon to 2 p.m. for lunch, Tuesday to Sunday from 6:30 to 9:45 p.m. for dinner. On Saturday and Sunday brunch is served from 10:30 a.m. to 2 p.m. Reservations essential.

L'Orangerie, 903 N. La Cienega Blvd., two blocks south of Santa Monica Boulevard, in West Hollywood (tel. 213/652-9770), is one of this city's most renowned French restaurants, and one of the most beautiful restaurants I've ever been in, and it features superb service. It reminds you of a French estate. It's light and airy thanks to multipaned arched floor-to-ceiling windows. Diners sit in Louis XVI–style chairs at tables elegantly set with Limoges china (made especially for the restaurant), Sheffield flatware, and long candles in elegant glass holders. The candlelight is gorgeous. Two murals depict L'Orangerie in the 17th century, and here and there throughout the restaurant are potted ferns and stunning floral displays. There's a stone-floored garden dining area under an awning complete with a fountain and vines climbing the latticework. The blue-and-white Portuguese-tile bar area is also inviting.

As you peruse the menu, you may want to sip L'Orangerie's special drink, a divine raspberry-champagne concoction. Appetizers include eggs scrambled with caviar, put back in the shells, and served in egg cups. The entrees are delectable (and expensive, at $60 to $80 table d'hôte—but worth every penny); you might try the veal medallions in a three-mustard sauce. Chicken-in-the-pot is hardly what you would expect to find listed on the menu at L'Orangerie, but there it is—one-half of a free-range beauty cooked in chicken stock and graced with simple herbs. The poached poulet, looking totally delectable, is surrounded by baby red potatoes and bits of carrots and turnips, eminently suitable for a centerfold spread and worth every bite of the $27.50. For dessert, don't miss the hot apple tarte or coussin au chocolat with vanilla sauce.

Dinner is served nightly from 6:30 to 10:45 p.m. Reservations are required, as are jackets for men.

Jimmy Murphy—for over a decade maître d' at the elite Bistro—struck out on his own several years ago with **Jimmy's,** 201 Moreno Dr., near Santa Monica Boulevard (tel. 213/879-2394), in Beverly Hills. Backed by none less than part owners Johnny Carson and Bob Newhart, Jimmy's was described as "a million-dollar-plus gamble that if you build a better VIP mousse trap, Los Angeles' top dining-out brigade will stand in line to be counted 'in'." Jimmy's is *the* place to be seen.

Such has proved to be the case, and with good reason. Jimmy has attracted personnel—waiters, bartenders, captains, etc.—from the best restaurants. He's also created one of the prettiest and most comfortable restaurants in town. The predominant color in the decor is the mossy gray-green of the lush carpeting and upholstery, set off by delicate blue-green accents. The walls are covered with exquisite wallpaper and fabric, and Baccarat crystal chandeliers are suspended from recessed ceilings painted to look like the sky. Tables are elegantly set with Limoges china, crystal glasses, and fresh flowers. One wall of windows overlooks the terrace, in which is a small garden, a fountain, shade trees, and tables under white canvas umbrellas. From the Chinoiserie statues at the entrance to the considered placement of mirrors, plants, and floral arrangements, Jimmy's is perfectly lovely in every detail, including the posh bar/lounge where a pianist entertains nightly.

You could begin lunch or dinner with an hors d'oeuvre of assorted shellfish or pheasant pâté with truffles. Dinner entrees, which cost $22 to $30, include filet mignon with foie gras and truffles wrapped in a fluffy pastry shell, salmon mousse with tomato and saffron sauce, and filet of sole with orange butter. The desserts—gloriously displayed—are superb.

At lunch you might opt for a very good seafood salad, cold salmon in aspic, white fish with limes, or glazed oysters cooked in champagne, for $15 to $22.

Jimmy's is open for lunch weekdays from 11:30 a.m. to 2:45 p.m., for dinner Monday to Saturday from 6 p.m. to midnight.

The movie set and other socially prominent citizens are oft seen at **The Bistro,** 246 N. Canon Dr., at Dayton Way, Beverly Hills (tel. 213/273-5633), a restaurant conceived about two decades ago by Billy Wilder and Kurt Niklas, previously maître d' at Romanoff's.

The charming decor here is authentically and elegantly Parisian belle époque, with mirrored walls, hand-painted panels of classical motif, tables clothed in white linen and set with gleaming silver, soft pink lighting, fresh roses on every table and beautifully arranged in baskets and pots here and there.

Both service and cuisine are top-notch. At lunch you'll find such excellent rich soups as superb lobster bisque and cream watercress, as well as an outstanding mussel soup. Two appetizer choices you don't want to overlook are the papillote of salmon and pheasant pâté. Cold entrees might include a duck or quail salad, or you may find the delicious shrimps and scallops atop angel hair pasta with caviar sauce on the menu. All the pasta is homemade and fresh. Dinner entrees might include eastern lobster on a bed of tagliatelle noodles, grilled salmon, or perhaps a rack of lamb. For dessert, a sumptuous chocolate soufflé is recommended. The gentle sounds of piano music accompany the fine cuisine at dinner.

Lunchtime entrees are generally in the range of $17 to $27; typical dinner offerings are about $24 to $32. Lunch is served from noon to 3 p.m. Monday through Friday; dinner, Monday through Saturday from 6 to 10:30 p.m. Reservations are essential, as are jackets for dinner.

The **Bistro Garden,** 176 N. Canon Dr., off Wilshire Boulevard (tel. 213/ 550-3900), is a lovely, comfortable part of the L.A. Very Important People restaurant scene, headquarters for the "movers and shakers," adorned by the "beautiful people." During the summer, you can dine under striped umbrellas amid trees and flowering plants in the lovely outside garden.

Lunch at the Bistro Garden features many cold dishes such as papaya filled with shrimp and a salad of cold lobster and vegetables; other choices are omelets, hamburgers, and broiled shrimps with mustard sauce. Entrees cost $13 to $17. Don't pass up those desserts on the piano. Variety is always the order of the day. Dinner might begin with an appetizer of pâté maison or marinated herring, and continue with an entree of linguine with clam sauce, paprika goulash, or roast rack of lamb for two, for $18 to $27 per person.

The Bistro Garden is open Monday through Saturday from 11:30 a.m. to

3:30 p.m. for lunch, from 6:30 to 11 p.m. for dinner. Dinner only is served on Sunday from 6:30 to 11 p.m. Reservations are always essential.

Jean Leon's La Scala, 9455 Santa Monica Blvd., between Rodeo and Beverly Drives, Beverly Hills (tel. 213/275-0579), is one of the liveliest and most glamorous celebrity-packed see-and-be-seen L.A. restaurants. Suzanne Pleshette, Warren Beatty, Candice Bergen, Robert Wagner, Jacqueline Bisset, and Michael Caine are just a few of those often seen at La Scala (and the adjoining Boutique).

Owner Jean Leon arrived here from Basque country in 1950, and began his American career bussing tables at the Café de Paris. By 1956 he had launched the now-renowned La Scala and was teaching President Kennedy how to distinguish superior from run-of-the-mill caviar!

Take your eyes off the glitterati for a minute or two and you'll see that the main dining room is a comfortable, cluttery, softly lit salon, with big bunches of flowers in brandy snifters and wine bottles everywhere. Leon is a connoisseur of fine wines who owns over 450 vineyard acres in northern Spain; his wine cellar is reputed to be one of the best in town. Seating is in striped velour booths.

At dinner, when entrees cost $19 to $32, the spaghetti carbonara is exquisite, made with minced bacon and raw egg; the cannelloni La Scala, a delicate crêpe stuffed with chunks of lobster, shrimp, and crab, smothered in white cream sauce with grapes, is also raveworthy. The calorie-conscious will do well to order a perfectly prepared filet mignon, but with dessert options like zabaglione or soufflé au Grand Marnier, who can remain virtuous?

Lunch also features many pasta items, along with a mushroom omelet, poached salmon, and grilled scampi with wine and herb seasoning, for $14 to $22.

La Scala is open for lunch weekdays from 11:30 a.m. to 2:30 p.m., for dinner Monday through Saturday from 5:30 p.m. to midnight.

The adjoining **La Scala Boutique** (tel. 213/550-8288), opened in 1962, also entices a perennial flow of celebs and notables who don't seem to mind standing on long lines until hostess Pierrette (by day) or maître d'Freddy (in the evening) can seat them at one of the few red-leather booths or handful of tables. Large windows look out on the Beverly Hills scene; inside there are shelves overflowing with gourmet fare—canned cassoulet, imported pâtés, etc.—wine racks, and a delicatessen showcase brimming with imported meats and cheeses. The walls are lined with Gerald Price caricatures of famous Hollywood faces, and Chianti bottles overhead add to the bistro ambience.

Overstuffed delicatessen sandwiches on rye or French roll—cold roast beef, deviled eggs, pâté de foie maison, etc.—served with potato salad and coleslaw are the most popular lunchtime fare, along with salads, cold plates, and pasta dishes, all in the $8 to $15 range. Dinners are more expensive, at $16 to $25.

You can dine here from 11:30 a.m. to 9 p.m.; closed Sunday.

Chasen's, 9039 Beverly Blvd., at Doheny Drive, Beverly Hills (tel. 213/271-2168), is a long-enduring favorite. The original Chasen's, a chili parlor, was financed by none other than *New Yorker* editor Harold Ross, and early patrons at this "Algonquin West" included Jimmy Durante and James Cagney. Once James Thurber spent hours drawing murals on the men's room wall—they were immediately removed by an unimpressed and overly industrious cleaning lady who was fired posthaste.

The main dining room is richly wood-paneled and softly lit, with beamed ceilings, brass reading lamps, and plush tufted red leather booths.

The menu has come a long way since chili (Elizabeth Taylor's favorite, she has it sent to her), but the continental fare retains an American simplicity that I'm sure Harold Ross would have approved. Specialties include the very special hobo steak (not listed on the menu), veal bone chop, or double lamb chops, in the $22 to $30 range. Everything is à la carte. You can top off your meal with the house special—banana or strawberry shortcake.

Chasen's is open for dinner only (by the way, they honor no credit cards) from 6 p.m. to 1 a.m.; closed Monday.

Housed in an Early California-style terracotta stucco building, **Le Restaurant,** 8475 Melrose Pl., off La Cienega Boulevard, West Hollywood (tel. 213/651-5553), has a star clientele and was actually once owned by singer Patti Page. It's truly beautiful, with an ambience as fresh as country air. The front room has pale mauve silk wall coverings, pink tablecloths, deep-green velvet booths, and a fireplace. There's lots of oak paneling throughout, and tables are separated by etched-glass dividers. Here and there are big floral displays. The treillage and patio rooms adjoin, both adorned with lots of latticework, the latter with a brick floor and a skylight roof from which many plants are suspended. A few intimate dining nooks are equally exquisite, and lovely watercolors by C. Terechkovitch further brighten the scene.

The menu is classically French. Dinner should begin with an appetizer, of which there is a wide selection ranging from a salad of endive and hearts of palm to foie gras de Strasbourg. Entrees like steak tartare, noisette of lamb served on fresh artichoke bottoms, and white fish stuffed with tarragon in a white wine sauce, are expertly prepared; they cost $20 to $34. For dessert, try the pâtisseries du chef.

Dinner is served daily from 5:45 to 10 p.m.

An appropriately impressive and posh haute-cuisine rendezvous is **Scandia,** 9040 Sunset Blvd., at Doheny Drive, West Hollywood (tel. 213/278-3555). It's divided into several dining areas. Very popular at lunch and brunch, when the sun streams in, is the Belle Terrasse, its garden ambience enhanced by hanging ferns, lots of white latticework, and fresh flowers on tables elegantly decked out in white cloths. The main dining room has taken on a new warmth and striking beauty rather different from its former Viking shield days (though a few remain). At center, a magnificent arrangement of fresh flowers opens the room toward the terrace. The comfortable new Art Deco–style chairs blend beautifully with the room's light and open feeling.

The shine has been restored to the copper-top bar and brass fittings of Scandia's cozy and club-like Bar and Skol Room. And of course there will always be the verdant, sparkling Belle Terrasse, sun pouring in during lunch, city lights at night.

Luncheons average $9 to $16 with entrees such as Biff Lindstrom—the Swedish chopped sirloin with beets, capers, and onions, served with a fried egg on top—or an open-face New York steak on garlic toast. The delicious assortment of salads includes poached Norwegian salmon with aspic and a Rosenberg salad, with lobster, crab, shrimp, and chicken breast.

You might begin dinner with Viking blinis, miniature pancakes flavored with akvavit and served with sour cream and Danish caviar, or, another favorite of mine, gravlaks with dill sauce. Dinner entrees ($14 to $24.50) include such Scandia specialties as Veal Oskar—a veal cutlet sautéed and garnished with asparagus, crab legs, and sauce béarnaise; lammesaddel (for two)—a young saddle of lamb roasted, carved, and served at your table with appropriate flourish; or Kalldolmar —tender leaves of white cabbage with a veal and pork stuffing. But the pièce de résistance is the Dover sole, poached in white wine and stuffed with coral-pink shrimp, in lobster sauce. You might ask the captain to introduce you to the prix-fixe dinner ($35, except for Sunday, when it's $30), offering a choice of appetizer, soup, entrees such as Veal Oskar, frikadeller, or veal sausage (on Sunday it might be roasted duck or whitefish), followed by a delicate dessert—perhaps Scandia's mouth-watering apple cake with vanilla sauce.

Lunch is served Tuesday to Saturday from 11:30 a.m. to 3 p.m., Sunday brunch from 11 a.m. Dinner is served Tuesday through Thursday from 6 to 11 p.m., Friday and Saturday to midnight, Sunday from 5 to 11 p.m.

One clue to the high quality of **The Windsor**, 3198 W. 7th St., at the corner of Catalina, East Wilshire (tel. 213/382-1261), is that the Los Angeles Gourmet Society throws its parties here. Another may be that it's had the same owner for over 35 years. Not only is the cuisine excellent, the ambience—very English clubby—provides a genuine feeling of well-being. The walls, paneled in rich mahogany or papered in flocked wall covering, are hung with coats-of-arms and $50,000 worth of original oil paintings. Lamp bases are statues of old English aristocrats, windows are leaded glass, seating is in substantial red-leather horseshoe banquettes, and fresh flowers adorn every table.

But it's not only the decor that's reassuring. The Windsor is the kind of place where a dedicated staff of 50 have been employed an average of 12 years.

When you sit down, you'll be presented with a lavish à la carte menu with loads of continental-style selections, a wine list to match.

Dinner is served Monday to Saturday from 4:30 to 11 p.m. You might begin with a smoked salmon hors d'oeuvre, a beautifully presented seafood platter, or marrow bordelaise. Specialties include steak Diane, veal chop Florentine en croûte, tournedos of beef, and a considerable list of pastas. Entrees range in price from $16 to $30. For dessert it's a hard choice between baked Alaska, soufflé Grand Marnier, or a variety of delectable pastries. In total, dinner for two averages about $80, without wine. However, a complete pretheater dinner is served from 5 to 7:30 p.m. for $25. And à la carte lunches, served weekdays from 11:30 a.m. to 3:30 p.m., are less expensive than dinner; a full meal can be had for $20. The de jour lunch is excellent at $16.50. Tuesday through Saturday evening, soft piano music adds to your dining pleasure. Reservations are a must.

EXPENSIVE RESTAURANTS: I must admit that there's a fine line differentiating the following restaurants from the preceding ones. The upcoming selections are an iota less celebrated and chic, possibly a trifle less expensive. And at lunch many are moderately priced. Reservations are, once again, advisable at these establishments.

American/Steaks/Ribs

Hy's, 10131 Constellation Blvd., across from the ABC Entertainment Center (tel. 213/553-6000), is among the most attractive restaurants in Los Angeles. Designed to impart the feeling of a European villa, the restaurant is entered via a massive *porte-cochère*. Inside, the foyer/lounge is dominated by a circular, stone-topped bar.

In the main dining area, natural light filters through skylights and sustains many lush plants. A woven-twig design gives texture to the high ceilings. Chairs are richly upholstered and the tables are handsomely set with white china and hand-blown crystal glassware.

If you've just about been nouvelle-cuisined to death, Hy's would be a good choice for your next meal. Hy's is a charcoal-broil specialty house. The restaurant features dry-aged beef (the aging, boning, and trimming are done on the premises), ribs, fresh seafood, salads, and live music. At lunch a good start would be the pâté maison or vichyssoise. Hot entrees afford a wide variety of choices, from shrimp and scallops en brochette to chicken sauté with Italian and bell peppers. The baby back ribs are delicious, as you would expect them to be. Lunch entrees range from $13 to $15.

Specialties of the house are steak, prime rib, chops, and Maine lobster. Hy's uses Hawaiian kiawe-wood charcoal to cook the beef with intense, even heat and keep in the very special flavor. A fine start to dinner would be a delightfully delicate vichyssoise or the terrine of scallops mousseline. You might then proceed to steak au poivre, chateaubriand, or rack of lamb—all presented tableside, with a flourish. This assumes, of course, that you can pass on the devilled prime rib bones. Beef, lamb, or veal entrees are served with a choice of potato (baked, twice baked, or shoestring) or pasta, plus hot cheese bread and garlic toast. Dinner entrees range from $20 to $32.

Hy's is open for lunch from 11:30 a.m. to 2:30 p.m. Monday through Friday, for dinner Monday through Thursday from 6 to 11 p.m., Friday to 1 a.m., Saturday 5:30 p.m. to 1 a.m. Reservations are necessary. So is a hearty appetite.

The **Musso & Frank Grill,** 6667 Hollywood Blvd., a few blocks west of Cahuenga (tel. 213/467-7788), bills itself as Hollywood's oldest restaurant (est. 1919). It's the kind of place people return to again and again for the comfortably substantial ambience, superb service, and consistently excellent food that they have been turning out for over half a century. It's where Faulkner and Hemingway hung out during their screenwriting days. Musso & Frank Grill is a favorite of Jonathan Winters, Merv Griffin, Raymond Burr, and Madonna and Sean Penn, among countless others.

The setting is richly traditional—beamed oak ceilings, red-leather booths and banquettes, mahogany room dividers (the kind with coathooks), and soft lighting emanating from wall sconces and chandeliers with tiny shades.

The menu is extensive, and everything—soups, salads, bread, vegetables, even sauces and dressings—is à la carte. Try the delicious seafood salads like the chiffonade or shrimp Louie, perhaps along with some camembert that comes with crusty bread and butter. Diners wishing heartier fare might consider the veal scalloppine marsala, roast spring lamb with mint jelly and baked potato, or broiled lobster. Entrees average $10 to $25. Sandwiches and omelets are also available. The back of the menu lists an extensive liquor and wine selection.

Open from 11 a.m. to 10:45 p.m. daily except Sunday.

A family enterprise started in 1938, **Lawry's The Prime Rib,** 55 N. La Cienega Blvd., just north of Wilshire Boulevard, Beverly Hills (tel. 213/652-2827), enjoys an excellent Restaurant Row location. It is the unique creation of Lawrence Frank, along with his brother-in-law, Walter Van de Kamp. Frank set out to offer "the greatest meal in America," serving one entree—the hearty prime rib he had enjoyed every Sunday for dinner as a boy (his father was in the meat business)—and serving it gloriously with flair and elegance. In order to showcase his famous beef, Frank originally purchased three gleaming silver carts (each cost as much as a Cadillac!) and hired experts to carve tableside. He also invented his now famous Seasoned Salt as the perfect seasoning for prime rib. When appreciative diners began swiping it off the tables, he turned an expensive trend into a very profitable operation; today Lawry's Seasoned Salt is marketed the world over.

The ambience at Lawry's is like an oversize English country estate or posh private club. You might start out in the homey cocktail lounge, where drinks are served from a pewter-topped wood-paneled bar. The dining room is richly decorated with valuable original oil paintings (including one of the Duke of Windsor at age seven), Persian-carpeted oak floors, plush burnt-orange-leather booths and high-backed chairs at tables decked out in orange-sherbet cloths, and graceful brass chandeliers overhead.

As noted before, there's only one entree—award-winning prime ribs of beef—a choice of four cuts, priced from $18 to $25. With it you get Yorkshire pudding, salad, mashed potatoes, and creamed horseradish. You can also get side dishes like creamed spinach or buttered peas, and a good wine list is available.

There are delicious desserts to end the "perfect meal." Always drawn by some mysterious force to the rich and creamy, I immediately gravitate to the chocolate pecan pie.

When you're in the mood for a traditional prime rib dinner, you just can't beat Lawry's. Open Monday to Thursday from 5 to 11 p.m., on Friday and Saturday to midnight, on Sunday from 3 to 10 p.m. Reservations suggested.

Lawry's also operates **Lawry's Westside Broiler,** 116 N. La Cienega Blvd., just north of Wilshire Boulevard (tel. 213/655-8686). Here the emphasis is on fresh seafood and steaks in a striking contemporary setting.

There is a small library bar to one side of the entrance, an inviting setting for before- or after-dinner cocktails. Steps lead down into the dining room which has booths and tables in front of the kitchen where diners can watch the chefs grilling meats over open fires of Mexican mesquite charcoal. The white walls, soft Chinese red lacquer accents, and sprays of fresh Thai orchids on each table provide a sophisticated backdrop for your meal.

Dinner might begin with mussels in garlic butter with pistachio nuts or fine rice-like pasta with a pesto sauce. Dinner entrees include a mesquite-broiled prime New York steak or a Delmonico steak, which is a specialty of the house. Seafood entrees include broiled Indonesian tiger shrimp and fresh Eastern bay scallops. There are also daily seafood specials. I enjoy the sautéed scampi served with white and green fettuccine. Dinner entrees range from $16 to $28. Desserts are a specialty, and many are made on the premises, including a heavenly coconut banana cream pie and a rich Belgian chocolate truffle.

An extensive list of California wines is available.

Dinner is served Monday through Saturday from 5 to 11 p.m.; Sunday, 3 to 10 p.m. Reservations are suggested.

R.J.'s The Rib Joint, 252 N. Beverly Dr., between Dayton Way and Wilshire Boulevard, Beverly Hills (tel. 213/274-7427), is fronted by a green-and-white awning. It's always mobbed, but it's no hardship to sit at the friendly bar for a little while until your table is ready. The floors are covered with sawdust here too, and the walls are hung with historic photos of Beverly Hills and oldtime actors and actresses. Lots of plants and overhead fans add to the atmosphere, but the room is dominated by what, at first glance, appears to be a massive produce display. Actually, it's the granddaddy of all salad bars. The "green grocery," as it is known, includes such offerings as spinach salad, big chunks of raw broccoli and cauliflower, fresh mushrooms, dates, guacamole, real roquefort dressing, herring in cream sauce, shrimp, beans, chick peas, sprouts, tomatoes, hearts of palm, and much more. All this is included with dinner entrees, but if salad bar fare is all you want it's about $10.

Sourdough rolls and butter are also served with the entrees, which cost $15 to $30 and include steaks, hickory-smoked chicken, crispy duck, or a bucket of clams. But the reason most people go to R.J.'s is for the beef and pork ribs that are grilled over oakwood and mesquite charcoal. Servings are huge, and for dessert a piece of R.J.'s chocolate cake is large enough for four; ditto the chocolate-chip cookie topped with vanilla ice cream, hot fudge, and real whipped cream. If you're like most customers here, you'll stagger out carrying leftovers wrapped in foil, creatively formed into various shapes—the swan is my favorite. Lunch is also served, for a less expensive $9 to $15.

In case you haven't gotten the message yet, the quality of the food served matches the amazing quantity. This also applies to R.J.'s well-stocked bar (over 500 brands). Only premium liquors and fresh-squeezed juices are used in drinks; they carry over 50 varieties of beer from all over the world.

R.J.'s is open Monday through Thursday from 11:30 a.m. to 10 p.m., Friday and Saturday to 11 p.m., Sunday from 10:30 a.m. to 10 p.m. Reservations are essential.

The **Pacific Dining Car,** 1310 W. 6th St., at Witmer Street (tel. 213/483-6000), is just a few short blocks from the center of downtown Los Angeles. The restaurant has been authentically decorated to evoke the golden age of rail travel. Walls are paneled in warm mahogany with brass luggage racks (complete with luggage) overhead. Old menus and prints from early railroading days line the walls, and brass wall lamps with parchment shades light some tables.

The atmosphere is warm and friendly, but the main reason for going to any restaurant is the food, and in this the Pacific Dining Car excels. Steaks are prime, aged on the premises, and cooked over a mesquite-charcoal fire. At dinner, top sirloin, a New York steak, fresh seafood, veal, and lamb are all served for $14 to $29. For starters the calamari is excellent, but weight-watchers might prefer the beefsteak tomato and onion salad.

Prices at lunch are less costly, at $12 to $24, and the menu items are basically the same. On a recent visit I enjoyed a perfectly char-broiled boneless breast of chicken, with choice of potato or tomato. There's an outstanding wine list. Desserts are simple fare such as apple pie. Breakfast here is one of the best bargains around. Two eggs with hash browns and sourdough toast is under $6.

There's a late-supper menu featuring egg dishes, salads, steaks—from 11 p.m. to 1 a.m. Prices are about $6 to $10.

Open 24 hours a day, seven days a week. Reservations are definitely advised for lunch and dinner. Great food!

Otto Rothschilds Bar and Grill (tel. 213/972-7322), on the ground floor of the Dorothy Chandler Pavilion, celebrates the unparalleled visual history of the motion picture industry and its stars. Photographs of stage and screen celebrities, taken by Otto Rothschild over a period of 40 years, adorn the walls of this handsome eatery. It's one of the most convenient and attractive downtown spots for breakfast, lunch, dinner, or an after-theater meal. The restaurant opens at 7 a.m. and offers the traditional egg-plus-whatever repasts, as well as some very exceptional omelets (including one with crab, avocado, and mushrooms); or you might consider such delights as the carameled apple pancake filled with sliced apples and dusted with a hint of cinnamon. Breakfast tabs range from $4.95 to $9.95. There's nothing commonplace about lunch, either, whether you opt for the grilled crab-and-cheddar sandwich on sourdough or Otto's shredded Oriental chicken salad. I tend to focus on the appetizers and light entrees such as the Szechuan grilled chicken tenderloins with two dipping sauces or the prime rib chili served with corn chips. Entrees such as the garden fettuccine with wild mushrooms, asparagus, sun-dried tomatoes, broccoli, and zucchini or the pan-seared chicken breast served over wild mushrooms appear regularly. Light entrees average $6.95, regular entrees about $8.95. The list of dinner entrees includes excellent choices of prime meats, seafood, and pastas. An herb-roasted prime rib is served with whipped horseradish sauce; the rack of lamb (I can rarely resist) comes crusted with Dijon herb crumbs; or, if you take your seafood spicy, try the Cajun broiled colossal shrimp. Dinner entrees range from $15.95 to $24.95. The after-theater menu ranges from such light entrees as the smoked ham and cheddar omelet, a Rothschild burger, or a salad to the more substantive pasta, fresh fish, or even the herb-roasted prime rib of beef—all from $9.95 to $16.95. The restaurant is open weekdays from 7 a.m. to midnight, weekends 11:30 a.m. to midnight. Reservations are essential.

A smashing addition to the restaurant scene is the **West Beach Café,** 60 N. Venice Blvd., one block from the beach in Venice (tel. 213/823-5396). It's a trendy eatery that specializes in California nouvelle cuisine. The decor is cool, modern, and minimalist, with white cinder-block walls, track lighting, and simple black chairs and white-clothed tables. The walls of the café serve as a gallery for an ever-changing variety of works by local artists.

Featured at lunch are hamburgers, Caesar salad, pasta, seafood, warm salad, and chicken, as well as many specials, which change weekly. Prices at midday average $9 to $18. Dinner entrees are more elaborate: among the favorites are grilled Spanish red shrimp in achiote oil with garlic and ancho chili with steamed potatoes tossed with cilantro and a side plate of steamed spinach. The menu changes weekly. Dinner prices range from $18 to $32. A special brunch is served on weekends, and includes eggs Benedict, Belgian waffles, huevos rancheros, and do-it-yourself tacos (you pick the ingredients), for $10 to $20. There's a fine wine list with selections to complement any meal.

The West Beach Café is open for breakfast ($6 to $10) weekdays from 8 to 11:30 a.m., lunch from 11:30 a.m. to 2:30 p.m., for dinner from 6 to 10:30 p.m., and for late-night pizzas (made with whatever's in the kitchen) from 11:30 p.m. to 1:30 a.m. ($13 to $17).

Chinese

One of the most "in" spots in Santa Monica is **Chinois on Main,** 2709 Main St. (tel. 213/392-9025), a high-fashion restaurant owned and operated by Wolfgang Puck and Barbara Lazaroff of Spago. It's a stunning extravaganza, decorated in green and pink with black touches. There are special details too: a pair of large cloisonné cranes, a Buddha over the bar, a large window full of blossoms, and exotic flowers all around.

But on to the fabulous food. Rather than the typical Chinese menu, Chinois on Main presents a delicious combination of Oriental, California, and French nouvelle cuisines. The à la carte menu is changed seasonally to take advantage of the freshest foods available. You might begin your meal with stir-fried garlic chicken with marinated spinach on radiccio leaves, or sautéed goose liver with warm ginger vinaigrette. First "flavors" (courses) range from $6 to $13. Entrees might include a whole sizzling catfish stuffed with ginger, phoenix and dragon (pigeon and lobster sliced on watercress with mushrooms and whole shallots, roasted in cabernet sauce), or charcoal-grilled Szechuan beef, thinly sliced, with hot chili oil and cilantro sauce. Entrees cost $15 to $28. And for dessert, you can partake of a rice tart flavored with lichee wine or assorted sherbets and fresh fruits, among other choices.

Chinois is open seven nights a week for dinner from 6 to 10:30 p.m., and Wednesday to Friday for lunch from 11:30 a.m. to 2 p.m. Reservations are essential and should be made as far in advance as possible. *Note:* The party atmosphere and acoustical design of the restaurant cause quite a din, so if you're looking for peace and quiet, Chinois may not be your dish. On the other hand, if you can't resist (and you really shouldn't), the only option is to dine early.

Continental/French

La Chaumiere, in the Century Plaza Hotel, Avenue of the Stars, off Santa Monica Boulevard in Century City (tel. 213/277-2000), is the new restaurant in the Tower of the hotel. The decor is elegant country French and the food is a blend of continental and California cuisines. As you enter, you'll first notice the fine wood paneling, brass fixtures, and large French tapestry. La Chaumiere thankfully has the peace and order of a private club; unlike a number of popular restaurants, your normal speaking tone can actually be heard by your dining companion.

For dinner, you might begin your meal with a marvelously creamy avocado soup with white wine and chunks of king crab at $7, or the coquille of shrimp, scallops, and morels with a brandy crayfish sauce for $9. Several excellent entree choices include an exceptional eggplant pirogue (it's rather like an eggplant boat) filled with shrimp, mussels, and crab, graced with a superb crayfish sausage, and topped with a Créole mustard sauce, for $24. Or you might be seduced by the delicate poached filet of sole with smoked salmon in a creamy watercress sauce, at $20. If you yearn for meat, last but far from least are the flavorful and incredibly tender tournedos of veal with morels and Calvados, for $26. And then there's dessert—the white-chocolate mousse quenelles with orange sauce at $6 is positively immoral.

If the above prices are too rich, go for lunch when entrees start at $10.

La Chaumiere is open for lunch Monday through Friday from 11:30 a.m. to 2:30 p.m., for dinner nightly from 6 to 11 p.m. Reservations are necessary.

Gourmet Organic/Natural Foods

The **Inn of the Seventh Ray,** 128 Old Topanga Canyon Rd., Topanga Canyon (tel. 213/455-1311), four miles from the Coast Highway, offers creekside dining under the shade of ancient trees in a tranquil canyon setting. The most orthodox, and the most beautiful, of L.A.'s natural-food restaurants, the inn was opened about 15 years ago by Ralph and Lucille Yaney as a place to practice and share their ideas about the relationship of food to energy. For this reason, entrees are listed in order of their "esoteric vibrational value"; the lightest and least dense (more purifying items) are listed first and are also less expensive. The back of the menu explains it all, as well as the quality of the food and drink and its preparation.

The good vibes you get from lovingly prepared food are further enhanced by the natural setting (about half of the seating is outdoors) and carefully selected music. Tables overlook the creek and much untamed foliage. Trees provide shade and there are fresh flowers on every table.

There's indoor seating too, in a slope-roofed shingled and stucco building with one glass wall overlooking the verdant mountain scene. The interior reminds me of a country church, with a peaked raw-wood ceiling from which many flourishing plants are suspended, stained-glass windows, simple wood furnishings, a central fireplace, Persian carpeting, flickering candles, and fresh flowers on every table.

All foods and baked goods are prepared on the premises, all soups are homemade, and the greatest care is taken to see that everything is fresh and natural, without chemicals or preservatives. Even the fish is caught in deep water far offshore and served the same day. And everything is as delectable as it is healthy. The dinner menu contains ten entrees, priced from $12 to $22, all served with soup or salad, complimentary hors d'oeuvres, steamed vegetables, baked potato or herbed brown rice, and stone-ground homemade bread. The lightest item is called Five Secret Rays: lightly steamed vegetables served with lemon-tahini and caraway cheese sauces; the densest, vibrationally speaking, is a ten-ounce New York steak cut from beef fed on natural grasses, char-broiled and served with two steak sauces. A glass of delicious fruit wine is suggested as an apéritif, and delicious desserts are also available.

At lunch options expand to include sandwiches like avocado, cheese, and sprouts, a cheese and fruit board, and additional salads. Omelets, quiche, and waffles are offered at Sunday brunch. Lunch and brunch entrees are mostly priced from $4 to $9.

Open weekdays for lunch from 11:30 a.m. to 3 p.m., on Saturday from 10:30 a.m., and on Sunday for brunch from 9:30 a.m. Dinner is nightly from 6 to 9:30 p.m. Whether you're into natural foods or not, all the dishes are excellent and you will enjoy the setting. Reservations are essential for dinner.

Indian

Good Indian cuisine is as hard to find in California as a Big Mac in New Delhi. So **Gitanjali of India,** 414 N. La Cienega Blvd., between Oakwood and Rosewood Avenues, half a block north of the Beverly Shopping Center (tel. 213/657-2117), which could hold its own in New York or London, is all the more valuable a find here in Los Angeles. The setting is charming and exotic. Minaret-shaped wall panels frame 16th-century Mogul-style paintings, candlelit tables are elegantly set with brass plates and napkins wound high in drinking glasses, Indian music plays softly, and the turbaned waiters are dressed in the manner of the sons of Punjab maharajas.

The menu is sufficiently varied to satisfy any taste. Don't pass up the scrumptious appetizers: sweet-and-spicy shrimp served with puffed Indian bread, chicken cooked in mild spices and served cold, artichoke with spiced creamy dressing, etc. Tandoori specialties are featured among the entrees, which cost $12 to $20. An order of tandoori chicken is served with soup or salad, buttered saffron rice, dal, and homemade yogurt, as is a combination of tandoori dishes—chicken, lamb, shrimp, and lobster. For dessert, try the fruit salad with honey, cream, saffron, nuts, and rosewater. A good wine list is available, a rarity in Indian restaurants.

It's open for dinner weekdays from 6 to 10:30 p.m., Saturday and Sunday to 11:30 p.m. Reservations suggested.

Irish

Tom Bergin's Tavern, 840 S. Fairfax Ave., just south of Wilshire Boulevard at Barrows Drive (tel. 213/936-7151), is headquarters for L.A.'s Irish community and, like many an Irish bar, a famous gathering place for sports writers, athletes, and rabid fans. The tavern celebrated its 50th anniversary in 1986—remarkable for any Los Angeles restaurant.

This was the first L.A. restaurant to charter buses to pro football games— they still do, and hold 230 seats to the games reserved five years in advance. I always thought this kind of place existed only in New York and Dublin, but Bergin's has been going strong since 1936. Actors Bing Crosby and Pat O'Brien were early friends of the house.

The dimly lit pub ambience consists of photos and paintings of Bergin's friends plastered all over richly wood-paneled walls, not to mention some 1,000 cardboard shamrocks attached to the beamed ceiling above the bar. Jack Ohlsen, general manager emeritus, dreamed up the idea of hanging shamrocks to please Saint Patrick—each one bears the name of a favorite customer.

Irish coffee is a house specialty. But you can also sit down to a hearty dinner in a rather charming candlelit dining room where curtained windows, green-clothed tables, and a fireplace create a homey warmth. At dinner a mesquite-charcoal-broiled New York steak with onion rings, garlic cheese toast, salad, and potato is served. More traditional Irish fare, served with soup or salad and garlic cheese toast, is Dublin-style corned beef and cabbage with a steamed potato or chicken Erin, simmered in cream and cider sauce, with bacon, leeks, mushrooms, and rice pilaf. Entrees cost $11 to $19. Burgers and salads are also listed, and for dessert you can sample the pieman's wares—fresh fruit pies—or imbibe the Bailey's Irish Cream cheesecake.

Lunch or "pub grub" (served at the bar, from $6 to $8) is less expensive, with entrees like Irish pot roast served with soup or salad, potato, and garden vegetables ($9).

For the record, Bergin sold the tavern in 1973 to two trusted regulars, Mike Mandekic and T. K. Vodrey, both of whom he knew would stick to traditions.

Bergin's serves lunch from 11 a.m. to 4 p.m. weekdays, dinner from 4 to 11 p.m. daily. The bar is open till 2 a.m.

Italian

Emilio's, 6602 Melrose Ave., at Highland, in Hollywood (tel. 213/935-4922), is an award-winning restaurant that attracts a celebrity clientele with its true Italian cooking. The downstairs dining room centers around the "Fountain de Trevi," bathed in colored lights. The decor is unrestrainedly ornate, with marble columns from floor to lofty ceiling, brick archways, stained-glass windows, lots of gilt-framed oil paintings, and fresh flowers on every table. You can also dine in the wine room, but my favorite spot for tender evenings is the cedar-paneled balcony, intimate and softly lit.

As for the regional Italian cuisine, forget your budget and your diet; plan to order lavishly and savor every bite. You might begin with the clams oregano or mussels al vino. The brodetto Adriadico (it's like cioppino) is heartily recommended, as are any of the nine veal entrees. You can also order a complete dinner —priced at $16 to $32—which includes soup or salad and tea or coffee, and features entrees like manicotti, spaghetti with oil and garlic, and calamari della casa.

The other desserts here are probably wonderful, but I've never been able to resist the creamy-rich zabaglione. And *do not miss* Emilio's cappuccino—it's incredible.

Emilio's is open nightly from 5 to midnight.

Chianti Cucina, 7383 Melrose Ave., at Martel, in Hollywood (tel. 213/653-8333), was opened in 1936 by the famous New York restaurateur Romeo Salta. This charming northern Italian ristorante has a long history in Hollywood, going back to the days when the cast party for *Gone With the Wind* was held here. And the young Mario Lanza was discovered while singing at Chianti. It's still the prestigious winner of many awards (even the wine list has garnered awards), and it's certainly one of the most popular restaurants in town. The decor successfully combines turn-of-the-century and art nouveau elements with traditional Italiana: walls adorned with patinaed murals of Italy and gilt-framed oil paintings, romantic Italian background music, candlelight, and fresh flowers on every table.

The fare is the authentic *alta cucina* of northern Italy. An antipasto makes a good beginning and gives you a sampling of everything; or start with the roasted mushrooms and peppers. From there you might proceed to pasta (all home-made), preferably the fettuccine Alfredo (one order is enough for two people if this isn't the main course). Veal dishes are the specialty, and I suggest you choose one for your entree—maybe scaloppine al marsala, or with lemon and butter. Also excellent—and unique—is scampi alla gradese—prawns with prosciutto, wine, garlic, parsley, and croutons. All entrees—priced at $17 to $24—are served with fresh vegetables. And to accompany your entrees, there's a fine wine from their choice list. For dessert, why not linger over assorted fruits and cheeses, or perhaps cannoli, with a pot of espresso?

Chianti is open for dinner nightly from 5:30 to 11:30 p.m. Reservations are essential.

Harry's Bar & Grill, 2020 Ave. of the Stars, on the Plaza Level of the ABC Entertainment Center, Century City (tel. 213/277-2333), is almost a mirror image of its namesake in Florence. The bar is very European, with its high walnut counter and tall wooden stools. The intimate dining areas have the wonderful pink light characteristic of Florence. Owners Larry Mindel and Jerry Magnin (they also own Chianti) hand-picked the paintings, tapestries, and furnishings on trips to Florence. They even made a mold of the oak wainscoting so that it could be duplicated in L.A., commissioned artist Lazero Donati (who created an oil painting for the Florence Harry's) to do a similar painting for their establishment. The *original* Harry's, by the way, is in Venice, not Florence; it was a hangout of the late Ernest Hemingway, who wrote about Harry's in his novel *Across the River and Into the Trees.*

As much attention has been paid to cuisine and service as to lore and decor. At dinner the food is authentic northern Italy, with such superb Venetian and Florentine specialties as homemade duck prosciutto, beef pasta with Gorgonzola and pine nuts, and veal scaloppini with balsamic vinegar and mustard. As you might guess when you taste it, all pasta is homemade. And seafood lovers: look out for the special catch of the day. Entrees average $17 to $25. At lunch you might opt for a pasta salad, hamburger, steak sandwich, or even grilled double lamb chops for $10 to $24.

Harry's is open for lunch Monday to Saturday from 11:30 a.m. to 3 p.m., nightly from 5:30 to 10:30 p.m., and for late supper after 10:30 p.m. Reservations are essential.

Another "in" L.A. restaurant is **Spago,** 8795 Sunset Blvd., with its entrance at 1114 Horn (tel. 213/652-4025), in West Hollywood. It's another of Wolfgang Puck's places, decorated by his wife, Barbara Lazaroff. It's simple and elegant, in white, pink, mauve, and peach with lots of flowers. The restaurant has a huge picture window, so diners can gaze out at the expanse of the city below it. Out back is an enclosed garden patio. The kitchen staff works in an open kitchen along one side of the dining room.

Pizza is a specialty here, though it looks nothing like the product of a neighborhood parlor. Wood-burning ovens cook your meal in the dining room. The pizza here comes with exotic ingredients like duck sausage, shiitake mushrooms, leeks, or artichokes, or even with lox and cream cheese! If you prefer pasta, there's black fettuccine with smoked scallops and sweet peppers, or angel-hair spaghetti with goat cheese and broccoli, or ravioli filled with lobster. And there are more substantial dishes still, including roast Sonoma lamb with braised shallots and herb butter or grilled chicken with garlic and parsley. Entrees range in price from $18 to $23. To finish off, you can select one of the 36 pastry varieties made daily by the pastry chef and displayed on the kitchen counter.

The food is superb, the place is noisy, the celebrities are many, and you'll enjoy every minute of it. Spago is open nightly from 6 to 11:30 p.m. Reservations are required, and should be made *three to four weeks in advance.*

Japanese

I've already made mention of **Yamato,** in the Century Plaza Hotel, Century City (tel. 213/277-1840), in the hotel listings, but it merits a second placement here. It's one of L.A.'s most beautiful Japanese restaurants, adorned with valuable antiques from Japan. Two massive Buddhist temple dogs—at least four centuries old—stand as guardians against evil in the foyer. The elaborately carved overhead beams, 350 years old, are from Kyoto, and the fusumas—made into decorative panels—are 250 years old.

You can dine Occidental style at tables with bamboo chairs, but I much prefer the privacy of the shoji-screened tatami rooms, where you sit on cushions. These latter rooms are simply adorned with a flower arrangement and a Japanese painting or scroll. Shoes are checked, and your meal is served by a waitress in classic kimono. There's no problem sitting, as there's a well under the table—actually you can change positions with much more freedom than at a regular table. And it's lovely lingering over relaxed conversation and sake in your own private dining compartment. If you want a tatami room, it's a good idea to so specify when making a reservation.

Downstairs, a sushi bar is at the center of things. Another room has eight teppanyaki tables, and there are 12 tatami rooms as well as regular seating. Upstairs, tables and tatami rooms are in a Japanese garden setting.

The fare is authentic and artfully prepared, and where concessions are made to the Western palate they're so innovative that they enhance rather than diminish the traditional cuisine. A five-course gourmet dinner "planned with the emperor in mind" might include such dishes as shrimp tempura and beef teriyaki. A combination multicourse family-style dinner for two can also be ordered. From the hibachi, you can savor such delights as charcoal-grilled, basted sirloin teriyaki, or poached salmon with cucumber. Entrees are served with soup, rice, vegetables, and green tea. Desserts include mandarin orange sherbet and a lovely green tea ice cream. Dinners range from $12 to $28.

Catering to the ABC Entertainment Center crowds from across the street, Yamato also offers very reasonable pretheater specials. Meals are also moderately priced at lunch, served weekdays only from 11:30 a.m. to 2:30 p.m. Dinners are served Monday to Saturday from 5 to 11 p.m., on Sunday from 4:30 to 10 p.m.

Among the most popular Japanese restaurants in L.A. is **Tokyo Kaikan,** 225 S. San Pedro St., between 2nd and 3rd, downtown in Little Tokyo (tel. 213/489-1333). It's designed to look like a traditional Japanese country inn with colored globe lights overhead, barnwood, bamboo- and rattan-covered walls adorned with straw baskets and other provincial artifacts. In addition to the regular seating, there are three food bars—tempura, shabu-shabu, and sushi.

À la carte dinner entrees, priced at $10 to $17, served with soup and rice, include beef sukiyaki, shrimp and vegetable tempura, and chicken and beef teriyaki. Full dinners average $16 to $22. The lunch menu offers a combination plate among its selections, which costs $9. Either meal, green tea or ginger ice cream is the perfect dessert.

Tokyo Kaikan is open for lunch weekdays from 11:30 a.m. to 2 p.m., for dinner Monday to Saturday from 6 to 10 p.m.

An excellent choice for Japanese fare is **Horikawa,** 111 S. San Pedro, off 1st Street, downtown (tel. 213/680-9355). At the entrance of this tranquil restaurant is a small fountain such as is found in traditional Japanese gardens. There's a separate Teppan Grill Room, its beamed white walls hung with reproductions of works by Japanese artist Shiko Munakata; their perusal alone makes a visit here worthwhile. The sushi bar is adorned with wooden signs naming famous wholesale fish markets in Tokyo. As for the main dining room, its walls are covered with brown-and-white photomurals of famous Kyoto gardens. More traditional in appearance is the cocktail bar, with decor featuring murals of plum trees in the Ogata Korin style. Recently added is a complete new section, Ryotei Horikawa, built in authentic Sukiya style, with haute cuisine prepared by noted chefs from Japan.

You can begin your dinner at Horikawa with a sushi sampler or a seafood teriyaki. Complete dinners, priced at $35 to $70, might include shrimp tempura, Japanese salad, uo-suki (a sort of Japanese bouillabaisse), New York steak, rice, tea, and ice cream or sherbet. You can also order à la carte. In the Teppan Room you might opt for filet mignon and lobster tail served with fresh vegetables, in the $15 to $30 range. Most luncheon entrees in either room are in the $9 to $12 range.

What really sets this restaurant apart are the kaiseki dinners—an extraordinary ten-course dining experience (five-course for lunch) dinners require two days' notice. The courses vary and are best discussed in advance once you know the number in your group; ask to reserve one of the lovely tea-house rooms.

Horikawa is open for lunch weekdays only from 11:30 a.m. to 2 p.m., for dinner Monday to Thursday from 5:30 to 10:30 p.m., on Friday from 5:30 to 11 p.m., on Saturday from 5 to 11 p.m., and on Sunday from 5 to 10 p.m. Reservations advised at dinner.

Moroccan

Pass through the immense and magnificent carved brass doors and you're in another world, the exotic Arab world of **Dar Maghreb,** 7651 Sunset Blvd., at Stanley Avenue, Hollywood (tel. 213/876-7651); the entrance is on Stanley Avenue. You enter into a Koranic patio, at the center of which is an exquisite fountain under an open skylight. The floor is marble, and the carved wood and plaster walls are decorated with handmade tiles in geometric designs. A kaftaned hostess greets you and leads you to either the Rabat or Berber Room. The former, named for the palatial decor typical of wealthy Rabat homes, features high ceilings intricately hand-painted in geometric patterns. There are rich Rabat carpets on the floor, marquetry tables, silk cushions with spun-gold-thread designs, and velvet-covered straw bread baskets from Fez strewn about. The Berber Room is more rustic, reflecting the homes of the cold mountain country of the High Atlas. Warm earth tones—orange, brown, and gold—are used, the rugs are from the mountain areas, brass tables and trays from Marrakech replace the marquetry ones, and the wood-beamed ceilings are painted in a traditional design.

In both rooms diners sit on low sofas against the wall and on goatskin poufs (cushions). Berber and Andalusian music is played in the background and there is belly dancing nightly.

The meal is a multicourse feast, including a choice of chicken, lamb, rabbit, squab, quail, and a new addition, shrimp, eaten with your hands and hunks of bread, and shared, from the same dish, with other members of your party. It begins when a waiter in traditional costume comes around and washes everyone's hands in rose-scented water. There are six possible dinners, priced at $16 to $27 per person. The Fassi Feast (from Fez) begins with three Moroccan salads of cold raw and cooked vegetables, including tomatoes, green peppers with cucumbers, eggplant, and carrots. You scoop it up with hunks of fresh-baked bread. Eat sparingly and slowly—there's a lot more to come. Next is b'stilla, an appetizer of shredded chicken, eggs, almonds, and spices wrapped in a flaky pastry shell and topped with powdered sugar and cinnamon.

Now comes a tajine of chicken cooked with pickled lemons, onions, and fresh coriander. By this time you're well into enjoying eating with your hands, and, hopefully, you've ordered some wine to drink each course down with. The next course is couscous with lamb and vegetables—squash, carrots, tomatoes, garbanzo beans, turnips, onions, eggplant, and raisins. All of the feasts include another entree of lamb and honey.

Dessert is a basket of fresh and dried fruits and nuts, and Moroccan cookies. Now it's time for another hand-washing, with hot towels perfumed with rose water, followed by the tea-pouring ceremony—a veritable performance, the mint tea poured with expertise from a height of several feet.

The emphasis is on relaxed and leisurely dining; you'll enjoy it most if you eat just a little of everything, and eat very slowly. Don't miss Dar Maghreb; it's a memorable experience. Dinner is served nightly from 6 p.m. Reservations are recommended.

Polynesian

What once was the glory of Polynesian restaurants has since turned from island to sea. **Trader Vic's,** 9876 Wilshire Blvd., at Santa Monica Boulevard (tel. 213/274-7777), has created an interesting nautical look in the Beverly Hilton Hotel with ship's models and tropical shells. The Captain's Cabin has been expanded to accommodate merchant seamen, and the dark bar is now a somewhat more sophisticated lounge. But don't despair; all has not been abandoned at sea. The pleasant rum drinks with the cute little umbrellas remain, and some interesting additions have been made to the list of edibles.

The pupus (otherwise known as hors d'oeuvres) include an absolutely delicious crisp calamari. The padang prawns saté are also worthy of serious consideration—gently sauteed, skewered, brushed with a saté-chili butter, then finished via a short trip to the broiler. Or you might begin your meal with an order of barbecued spareribs from the Chinese oven or a salad of mixed Chinese vegetables with black mushrooms.

Newer Trader Vic entrees include two delicious veal dishes—a T-bone–size veal steak and the barbecued veal kidney. On the other hand, if matured beef is your passion, the restaurant offers a chateaubriand for two.

For dessert, there's mud pie or the Aloha ice cream—vanilla in mango sauce topped with banana chips.

Entrees are about $15 to $30, appetizers about $5 to $8, and desserts in the neighborhood of $5. Trader Vic's is open daily from 5 p.m. to midnight.

The ambience and views at most Marina del Rey harborside restaurants are generally better than the food. Nonetheless, everyone occasionally likes to go there to eat, especially for "islands" food. **The Warehouse,** 4499 Admiralty Way, near Lincoln and Bali Way (tel. 213/823-5451), is the creation of photographer Burt Hixson, who traveled 23,000 miles, ostensibly in a quest to find the perfect decor for his dream restaurant. Remembering the exotic wharves he had seen, he erected a two-level dockside structure, where one now dines on casks and barrels, or inside wooden packing crates. Burlap coffee bags line the walls; netting, rope, and peacock chairs further enhance the setting. The place is entered via a tropical walkway of bamboo and palm that extends over a large fish pond. Hixson's photos line the walls in this unusual restaurant, which is not only colorful but surprisingly unfunky and elegant. Most of the tables have a view of the marina, and many are outside right on the water.

Lunches range from $9 to $16. Dinner is à la carte for $16 to $28, with entrees from the world over: Tahitian chicken cooked over hickory wood, Malaysian shrimp, steak teriyaki. Drink it down with beer from whatever nation you wish, or with an exotic rum concoction. Throughout the afternoon and evening there's the oyster bar for snacks like garlic bread, nachos, or quesadillas, and lots of seafood selections (shrimp, oysters, clams, chowder). Is the Warehouse touristy? Certainly, but with good food and all that atmosphere, who cares?

Open for lunch Monday to Friday from 11:30 a.m. to 2:30 p.m., for brunch Saturday and Sunday from 10 a.m. to 2:30 p.m. Dinner is served daily from 5 to 10 p.m. No reservations, except for groups of ten or more.

Seafood

Gladstone's 4 Fish, 17300 Pacific Coast Hwy., at Sunset Boulevard, Pacific Palisades (tel. 213/GL-4-FISH), is right on the ocean, with an incredible view.

There's sawdust on the floor here along with stained-glass hangings, hanging plants, and big tanks filled with live Maine lobsters and other future seafood entrees. The ambience—including the bar with its stained-glass windows—is casual, fun, funky, and comfortable.

The day at Gladstone's starts at 7 a.m. with breakfast. In addition to the usual fare, there are seafood omelets, crab Benedict (poached egg, lots of crab, hollandaise), and even a "hangtown fry"—eggs, onions, bacon, capers, and fresh oysters all scrambled together. And then there's lox Benedict on a bagel! Most dishes are available for under $8. All during the day there are sandwiches of tuna, crab, or shrimp salad, or a variety of fried seafood, and all sorts of seafood salads for $10 to $16.

Only the freshest fish and seafood are served and mesquite charbroiled specialties are featured. The menu is eclectic, including such varied items as the daily specials, sashimi, cioppino, fried scallops, clams, and shrimp. Entrees ($14 to $25) are served with salad or chowder, coleslaw, sourdough bread, plus a choice of rice, potatoes, or fresh vegetable. Of course Maine lobster is also available (priced subject to market). For the confirmed non-seafood-eater there's a dinner offering of New York steak. And for dessert you can dig into the biggest piece of cake you've ever seen, which is enough for four people, or a hot fudge sundae that defies description.

To sum it all up, the food is good, the portions are gigantic, and you could spend your visit to L.A. just eating your way through the menu. The restaurant has a fine wine list to choose from, and if you truly enjoy martinis, ask about their Farkletini. Only premium liquors and fresh-squeezed juices are used in their drinks—it's bar policy.

Gladstone's is open daily from 7 a.m. to 10:30 p.m. Sunday through Thursday, and until 11:30 p.m. on Friday and Saturday. The regular menu is served at all times, but a breakfast menu is also served from 7 a.m.

Jack's at the Beach, 2700 Wilshire Blvd., at Princeton Street, Santa Monica (tel. 213/829-2846), has been going strong since 1917. Granted it has moved from oceanside since then, but it remains a good, reliable fish house with somewhat gussied-up decor. The front wall at the entrance is lined with photos of celeb clientele at their tables. The decor consists of plush leather booths, many mirrors, and white-clothed tables handsomely set with crystal candleholders and fresh flowers. A comfortable bar/lounge area is done mostly in forest green.

You might make a complete dinner of the King Neptune's salad—mixed greens with lobster, crab, and shrimp. But this is really the kind of place to linger over a full dinner, beginning perhaps with a cold half lobster or a Caesar salad. A large selection of seafood entrees includes poached salmon in hollandaise sauce, imported lobster tails in drawn butter, shrimp curry with rice pilaf, and filet of sand dabs amandine. If you've never had sand dabs, try them when they're available—they're delicate, light, and quite probably the best fish I have ever eaten. Charbroiled filet mignon is another option. Dinner entrees at Jack's cost $15 to $30. Desserts from the pastry cart taste as good as they look, and the wine list offers many varied selections.

Jack's is considerably easier on the budget weekdays at lunchtime, when cold poached salmon with cucumber salad, sautéed scallops, and shrimp Louie are among the entrees, costing $10 to $18.

Open weekdays from 11 a.m. to midnight, Saturday and Sunday from 4 p.m. to midnight.

MODERATELY PRICED RESTAURANTS:

The following kinder-to-your-wallet selections are in the price range most of us choose when dining out if there's no special occasion. But take note that many of the aforementioned expensive places are very affordable at lunch.

American

There's fancy seaside dining galore, and then there's the great and simple food at **Aunt Kizzy's Back Porch,** 4325 Glencove Ave., in the Villa Marina Shopping Center (tel. 213/578-1005), which lends credence to the notion that "all-American food is still *in*." It's southern home-cooked food prepared from time-honed recipes (collected from relatives and friends) that will keep your soul, body, and pocketbook intact. The cook is from Cleveland, Mississippi, and she has prepared southern-style and Creole food for 38 years or more.

Nothing is easy to find in the Shopping Center, but you'll locate Aunt

Kizzy's Back Porch if you face Von's (on foot), turn right, cross the small drive-way, and walk straight on toward a discreet red neon sign bearing the restaurant's name.

Aunt Kizzy's has moved to larger quarters since I first told you about the place, but fear not: they still offer the same great food, if now in somewhat snazzier surroundings. Wood-paneled walls, parquet floors, red-and-white checked tablecloths, and lace café curtains have been added, but the walls are still covered with pictures of entertainers (you can't miss Whoopi Goldberg in the collage of black performing greats on display where you enter). As always, the restaurant is busy.

And what food! For lunch any day of the week you can have fried chicken, plus two vegetables, rice and gravy (or cornbread dressing and gravy) and corn-bread muffins—all for $5.95. Depending on the day, that same $5.95 buys a choice of smothered steak, chicken and dumplings, some of the best smothered pork chops you've ever tasted, turkey wings and drumsticks with dressing, chicken pot pie, meatloaf, smothered liver and onions, or the fish of the day (Friday only).

Specialties of the house (served Sunday only) are baked chicken with corn-bread dressing and pungent barbecued beef ribs. The daily dinner menu includes most of the lunch entrees plus (are you ready?) chicken Creole; chicken and sausage jambalaya; catfish with heavenly hush puppies (fried to order); Uncle Wade's baked beef short ribs—truly lean, meaty, and falling off the bone; red beans and rice and hot links; and, for the nonmeat eaters, an all-vegetable plate. All are $9.95, except the delicious catfish ($10.95), the meat loaf ($8.95), the beans, rice, and hot links ($6.95), and the vegetable plate ($5.95). Dinner entrees include the same extras as lunch entrees. Old-Time Country Desserts are extra, but $2 will buy a soul-satisfying portion of Grandmother Zady's peach cobbler, Miss Flossie's floating sweet potato pie, or "Sock-it-to-me cake" filled with walnuts, cinnamon, and served warm.

There's a down-home Sunday brunch for $10.95, served buffet style, that defies the capacity of most humans. How about some scrambled eggs with a choice of bacon, sausage, grits, or grilled potatoes, followed by smothered pork chops or fried chicken (to name just two options) and a choice of five vegetables, topped off by peach cobbler or Sock-it-to-me cake. All this comes with fruit juice, tea, coffee, or milk. *Note:* No toting privileges.

Aunt Kizzy's doesn't offer beer or wine, but the ice-cold lemonade served in a Mason jar is just about the best possible complement for the down-home cooking. Aunt Kizzy's is open for lunch from 11 a.m. to 4 p.m. Monday through Saturday, to 3 p.m. Sunday; dinner from 4 to 10 p.m. Sunday through Thursday, to 11 p.m. Friday and Saturday.

Chinese

Twin Dragon, 8597 W. Pico Blvd., at Holt Avenue, just south of Beverly Hills (tel. 213/657-7355), is the domain of owner/chef Mr. Yu-Fan Sun, a master of Shanghai culinary arts, and his brother, manager James Sun. Twin Dragon is a large and comfortable restaurant with Chinese instruments and shell paintings decorating the walls, colorful antique tasseled lamps overhead, a medallion of a dragon complete with red electric eyes, and a gorgeous saltwater fishtank over the bar.

The menu is extensive, in good Chinese-restaurant tradition. Highly recommended are the spicy diced chicken with peanuts, braised shrimp spiced with chili peppers, and the fresh asparagus with prawns. Entrees cost $9 to $17. Peking Duck is $24 and requires one-day advance notice. It's a good idea to put yourself in the hands of the chef, who will prepare specialties not on the menu.

Open daily from 11:30 a.m. to 10 p.m. (till 11 p.m. on Friday and Saturday nights). They take reservations for large parties only, and often there's a wait at dinner.

Shanghai Winter Garden, 5651 Wilshire Blvd., corner of Hauser Boulevard (tel. 213/934-0505), is one of my favorite Los Angeles Chinese restaurants. Tables are clothed in cheerful pink; an archway depicting a phoenix and dragon, set in an intricately carved teak wall, separates the dining areas; Chinese paintings and woodcarvings adorn the walls; and overhead are large tasseled Chinese lamps. It all combines to create a very elegant effect, and the ambience is enhanced by taped Chinese music.

The menu offers a wide selection—over 150 entrees to choose from. Among the specialties are diced fried chicken sautéed with spinach, shrimp with bamboo shoots and green peas in a delicious sauce with crisp sizzling rice, crispy duckling made with five spicy ingredients and served with Chinese bread, and crushed white meat of chicken sautéed with diced ham, pine nuts, and green peas. Entrees are priced at $9 to $25. As you can see, this is a place for culinary adventures. For dessert, fried banana or apple serves four. Shanghai Winter Garden also offers daily lunch specials—eggroll, fried rice, and entree—for about $10.

Shanghai Winter Garden is open Monday to Friday for lunch from 10:30 a.m. to 3 p.m., Saturday from 11:30 a.m., for dinner nightly from 4 to 10:30 p.m. Reservations accepted.

Grand Star, 943 Sun Mun Way, off North Broadway between College and Bernard Streets (tel. 213/626-2285), is owned by Frank and Wally Quon and their mother, Yiu Hai Quon. There are four complete meals priced at $10 to $16 per person. The latter is the gourmet selection, including spiced tender beef, rumaki, barbecued ribs, golden-fried shrimp, wonton soup, lichee chicken delight, Mongolian beef, lobster Cantonese, snow peas with barbecued pork, fried rice, tea, and dessert. If there are four or five in the party Mama Quon's chicken salad is added. You can also order à la carte items ranging from dumplings flamed in rum to lobster sautéed in ginger and green onion for $8 to $14. Steamed fish, priced according to size, is a specialty, as are the cashew chicken, Mongolian beef, and Chinese string beans.

On the street level the Grand Star looks more Italian than Chinese; it's dimly lit with black-leather booths and big bunches of dried flowers here and there. I prefer to sit upstairs where tables are covered with red cloths and the family's exquisite collection of Chinese embroideries adorns the walls. Entertainment, usually a female vocalist, with piano accompaniment, is featured at cocktail time and on most evenings.

Open daily for lunch and dinner from 11:45 a.m. to 11 p.m.

Desserts

If your sweet tooth is acting up, head over to the **Beverly Hills Cheesecake Factory,** 364 N. Beverly Dr., off Brighton Way (tel. 213/278-7270), or the **Cheesecake Factory of Marina Del Rey,** at 4142 Via Marina (tel. 213/306-3344). They offer relief in the form of a profusion of delicious baked goods—every conceivable variation of cheesecake (over 40 concoctions, including the incredible white-chocolate/raspberry truffle, fresh strawberry, coffee/brownie chunk, and Kahlúa almond fudge). There are also chocolate mousse pie, carrot cake, and much, much more. Prices average $3.75 to $8 for a portion of sheer bliss.

The Cheesecake Factory is also a reasonably priced, casual, and friendly restaurant with a substantial list of delicious dishes, including mouth-watering barbecue-style chicken and ribs and such spicy specialties as cashew chicken and shrimp, Louisiana blackened fish, and blackened steak. You can also get a whole breast of chicken served in several styles—teriyaki, garlic-basil, Dijon, and California (with avocado, mushrooms, tomato, green onion, and melted Jack cheese). There are also more than 10 varieties of fresh pasta, wonderful hot sandwiches, great omelets, and burgers. Entrees range from $5 to $15.

The desserts are all on display up front, so you can fantasize while waiting for a table. No reservations are taken, but your patience will be rewarded, I assure you. The Cheesecake Factory also has a good selection of wines and beers.

The Beverly Hills Cheesecake Factory is open daily, on Monday through Thursday from 11:30 a.m. to 11:30 p.m., on Friday and Saturday to 12:30 a.m., on Sunday from 11 a.m. to 10 p.m. The Marina del Rey branch is open the same days and hours with the exception of Sunday, when it's open from 10 a.m. to 11 p.m.

Italian

Little Joe's, 900 N. Broadway, at College Street (tel. 213/489-4900), is a vestige of a once-Italian neighborhood in now-touristy New Chinatown. Opened as a grocery in 1927, it has grown steadily over the years; it now has several bars and six dining rooms. It's a wonderfully cozy restaurant with sawdust on the floors, hand-painted oil murals of Rome and Venice, soft lighting, and seating in roomy leather booths.

A meal at Little Joe's ought to begin with a plate of the special hot hors d'oeuvres—fried cheese, zucchini, and homemade ravioli. A complete six-course meal including soup, antipasto, salad, pasta, vegetable or potato, bread and butter, and dessert, is priced according to entree: $10 to $19 for the likes of veal parmigiana, scallops, or butterflied halibut. Full pasta dinners are even less, and you can also order à la carte, for $7 to $16. At lunch, entrees are less expensive, at $5 to $9 for dishes like eggplant parmigiana, sausage and peppers, rigatoni, or a sausage sandwich. Little Joe's is the best occidental restaurant in Chinatown.

It's open Monday to Saturday from 11:30 a.m. to 9 p.m. Reservations are taken.

Sarno's Caffè Dell 'Opera, 1714 N. Vermont, in Hollywood (tel. 213/662-3403), is a delightful place that combines two naturals—Italian food and opera. Owner Alberto Sarno is a former opera student himself, so he combined the family business with his love of singing. The restaurant is dim and cluttered, with lots of small tables, heavy antique chandeliers, bronze statuary, and hanging grape clusters.

The food is good and hearty. You can dine on fresh river trout in white sauce, chicken cacciatore, veal parmesan, or one of many pasta dishes, or—if you have a real appetite—a complete dinner including fresh vegetables, soup, salad, bread, pasta, an entree, dessert, and coffee, tea, or milk. Pasta dishes cost $7 to $10, full dinners range from $13 to $17, and à la carte meat dishes (which are served with salad, roll, and beverage) cost $10 to $12. And if you want a light meal, there are salads and sandwiches to choose from, at $6 to $9. Pizza is $10 to $12, depending on the toppings.

The fun at Sarno's begins at 8:30 p.m. At that time Alberto, and members of the staff and customers, take turns regaling the restaurant with their renditions of opera arias, show tunes, and old Italian favorites. It's fun for everyone, and a great place for people with a yen to sing for a crowd.

Sarno's is open Sunday to Thursday from 11 a.m. to 1 a.m., on Friday and Saturday till 2 a.m.

Pizza in Beverly Hills? Yes, but a very special kind of pizza—at **Prego,** 362 N. Camden Dr., at Brighton Way, in Beverly Hills (tel. 213/277-7346). When Prego arrived on the restaurant scene, it was an instant success with its combination of elegance and simplicity. It's a lovely place, all brick, white, and wood, with unusual modern art on the walls and sprays of seasonal flowers to add a touch of cheer. Music from Italy plays softly in the background.

Prego is basically a trattoria. The food is prepared in an open kitchen by expert chefs. There are lots of antipasti to choose from, like focaccia al formaggio (layers of thin Italian bread and stracchino cheese) and insalata Prego (romaine lettuce, carrots, celery, bell pepper, mushrooms, and vinaigrette). For an entree you have a choice of homemade pasta, like ziti with fresh tomato and basil or green tagliatelle with mushrooms and cream, or grilled dishes like fresh fish, lamb with sage, rosemary, and butter, or Italian sausage with spinach. And then there are the pizzas—gourmet creations like the Puttanesca (my favorite), with tomatoes, black olives, capers, mozzarella, artichokes, and oregano; or Dell'Adriatico, with prawns, tomatoes, mozzarella, garlic, and basil. Entrees range in price from $11 to $20. For dessert there's assorted fruits and cheeses, pastry, and a variety of ice cream dishes like semifreddo al caffè—white-chocolate ice cream with espresso and whipped cream.

Prego is open Monday to Saturday from 11:30 a.m. to midnight, and on Sunday from 5 p.m. to midnight.

Japanese

I like **Fuji Gardens,** 424 Wilshire Blvd., between 4th and 5th Streets, Santa Monica (tel. 213/393-2118), a pretty little place with comfortable leather booths, bamboo-pattern wallpaper, blue flags hanging from a roof-like structure over one wall of tables, and tablecloths of the same Japanese-restaurant blue.

Combination dinners here are an excellent value, like the beef teriyaki and lobster tail combo, which comes with salad, chilled noodles, sashimi or tempura, an appetizer, tsukemono, soup, rice, and green tea. Most of these dinners are in the $10 to $15 range; you can also order à la carte items like salmon teriyaki with vegetable salad and noodles.

Lunches are also a terrific buy. A Makunochi lunchbox with entree, soup, tsukemono, rice, and tea costs $8 to $11; pork cutlet with tongkatsu sauce comes with the same accompaniments. The food here is as excellent, by the way, as it is reasonably priced. For dessert at either meal, try the green tea or ginger ice cream.

Fuji Gardens is open for lunch weekdays from 11:20 a.m. to 2:30 p.m., for dinner from 5 to 10 p.m., on Saturday from 5 to 11 p.m., Sunday 5 to 10 p.m.

Miyako, 139 S. Los Robles Ave., between Green and Cordova Streets in Pasadena, in the basement of the Livingston Hotel (tel. 818/795-7005), offers fine Japanese cuisine in an attractive setting. It gives you a choice of both tatami room and table service, and fresh flower arrangements are placed about discreetly. From the tatami room, you can enjoy a view of a small Japanese garden, while attended by waitresses traditionally attired in kimonos. Subtle understatement is the order of the day.

I like to begin with a sashimi appetizer of tuna slices. A full Imperial dinner offers a combination of shrimp tempura, chicken teriyaki, and sukiyaki. Dinners and à la carte entrees cost $7.50 to $19. Lunches are priced around $6 to $13. The Miyako is on the same street as the Hilton.

Miyako is open for lunch weekdays from 11:30 a.m. to 2 p.m., for dinner Monday through Thursday from 5:30 to 9:30 p.m., Friday and Saturday to 10 p.m., on Sunday from 4 to 9 p.m.

Jewish Deli

So where do you get a good pastrami on rye in this town? **Nate & Al's,** 414 N. Beverly Dr., off Brighton Way, Beverly Hills (tel. 213/274-0101), has been slapping pastrami on fresh-baked rye since 1945, not to mention chopped liver and schmaltz, kosher franks, and hot corned beef. Seating is in comfortable booths, and lighting is pleasantly low. A big counter up front handles take-out orders (everything from halvah to brie) and there's always a line waiting to get in (no reservations), and probably half are New Yorkers.

Rather than strictly kosher, it is kosher style, which means that the incredibly extensive menu can range around both meat and dairy items. There are pastrami and corned beef sandwiches (all sandwiches are one size—huge), chopped liver, and other traditional favorites like cream cheese and Nova Scotia salmon on a bagel and the famous Reuben. An appetizer of gefilte fish with horseradish or chicken soup with matzoh ball or kreplach is a good beginning for any meal. And then there are potato pancakes, and cheese, cherry, or blueberry blintzes with sour cream and apple sauce, and roast turkey with potatoes, cranberry sauce, and vegetables. All these goodies cost $7 to $13. Leave room for a homemade dessert, perhaps apple strudel or chocolate cream pie. Wine and beer are available. Open daily from 7:30 a.m. to 8:45 p.m., on Saturday till 9:30 p.m.

A year after Nate & Al's came on the scene, **Zucky's** appeared on the boardwalk in Santa Monica, then moved to 431 Wilshire Blvd., at 5th Street (tel. 213/393-0551). It has typical modernistic Jewish-deli decor with orange-and-gold leather booths, Formica tables, and glass cases filled with Jewish delicacies.

It's not a kosher deli; you can even get a seafood platter of shrimps, scallops, and sole or an omelet of crab, bay shrimp, and whitefish for lunch. But it does offer all the traditional favorites like cheese blintzes with sour cream, a chopped liver on rye, and chicken in a pot with matzoh balls, kreplach, vegetables, soup, and noodles, at $8.90 for two. The menu offers something for everyone. Sandwiches, omelets, salads, and hamburgers are a reasonable $5 to $7, and full hot meals cost $6 to $8. There's a wide choice of desserts from apple strudel to chocolate mousse, and drinks range from Dr. Brown's cream soda or an egg cream to beer and wine.

Zucky's is open 24 hours a day. Reservations are accepted.

A year later—1947—yet another Jewish deli appeared in a different part of town: **Langer's,** 704 S. Alvarado, at 7th Street, downtown (tel. 213/483-8050), where the walls are lined with portraits of the Langer family and grandchildren. It's a big, roomy place with counter seating and brown tufted-leather booths. A corner location (two windowed walls) makes it light and airy.

Once more the fare is kosher style rather than kosher, which means you can order the likes of pastrami and Swiss cheese on rye. An order of stuffed kishka with soup or salad, vegetable, and potatoes, or meat blintzes with gravy, and an interesting sandwich combination of cream cheese and cashews are among the available entrees, for $6 to $14. Langer's is open daily from 6:30 a.m. to 1 a.m.

Mexican

There's "gringo food"—fiery, lots of cheese, sour cream, beans, tamales— and then there's the subtle, delicate, delicious Mexican cooking of **Antonio's,** 7472 Melrose, West Hollywood, CA 90046 (tel. 213/655-0480). Antonio's is the picture of the sedate and proper Mexican restaurant—no bright reds, yellows, and greens here, but rather the quiet tans and browns suggestive of an aristocratic Spanish heritage. The warmth comes from the very gracious welcome and attention you'll receive and from the guidance you'll be offered if you've never had authentic Mexico City–style cuisine. The health- and weight-conscious should note that, unlike its "gringo-style" counterpart, the true cuisine of Mexico City is delicious and perfectly seasoned while being high in protein, low in cholesterol, and lean on the calories (which may account for the number of celebrities and dignitaries who dine here). A variety of fresh seafood and meats with exotic vegetables are featured and the majority of entrees are steamed, rather than fried.

Dinner entrees ($13 to $17) are light and unusual, such as Costillas de Puerco en Chiptole—flavorful spare ribs served in a chile and herb sauce—or Antonio's Chayote Relleno, featuring the tasty chayote squash filled with lean ground beef, ricotta cheese, and spices in a light tomato sauce.

The menu changes daily, but fresh fish is available at all times. When I was there, the catch of the day was delicious, steamed with a colorful bouquet of beautifully seasoned vegetables: if you've never truly enjoyed fish, Antonio's can completely change your attitude. Chicken is served for a variety of tastes—Guadalajara-style in tamales stuffed with assorted fresh vegetables or stewed in a delicate green sauce of tomatillos, green peppers, and exotic spices. The cabbage leaves stuffed with a mixture of ground beef, chorizo, and herbs graced with chipotle sauce might interest meat lovers. Half orders of evening specials are available for the undecided. All entrees are accompanied by green-corn tortillas. If you're really counting calories, note that most dishes have fewer than a hamburger.

All this is not to say that if you crave cheese enchiladas, a hamburger, tacos, or enchiladas with guacamole, you won't find them here, but the true beauty of dining at Antonio's rests with the restaurant's simple seafood, meat, and chicken dishes.

A cozy wine room, lined with vintage bottles, is available for a small dinner party.

Antonio's serves lunch Tuesday through Friday from noon to 3 p.m., dinner from 5 to 11 p.m.; Saturday and Sunday from 2 to 11 p.m.

A second Antonio's is opening on Santa Monica's "restaurant row" at 1323 Montana Avenue at 14th Street.

Natural Foods

The Source, 8301 W. Sunset Blvd., at Sweetzer Avenue, West Hollywood (tel. 213/656-6388), is where Woody Allen met Diane Keaton for a typical L.A. lunch in *Annie Hall*—part of his New York–oriented statement about Southern California. Bean sprouts poke out of almost every dish here, and there's a special chef on hand just to make juices.

Inside it's cozy, with curtained windows, tables set with fresh flowers, and a plant-filled stone fireplace in one corner. Those who want fresh air with their health food shouldn't be in L.A., but they can gasp for what's available while dining outside at one of the umbrellaed tables.

A typical dinner (which costs $8 to $10) is the cheese walnut loaf, served with soup or salad, and a basket of whole-wheat rolls and butter. Homemade soups, salads, and sandwiches are also available. Most of the fare is vegetarian; chicken and fish are served, but on separate dishes. Portions are huge. Lighter fare—crêpes, sandwiches, salads, etc.—costs $5 to $9. For dessert there's a so-good-it's-hard-to-believe-it's-healthy homemade date-nut cheesecake. Drinks range from yogurt shakes to the "Hi-Potency Drink" (orange juice, banana, wheat germ, and honey; or with milk and molasses). Of course there's always beer or wine.

Open Monday through Friday 8 a.m. to midnight, on Saturday and Sunday from 9 a.m. to midnight. For breakfast, how about hot cereal made from ground oats and wheat, topped with sunflower seeds, raisins, bananas, apples, and nuts?

Diagonally across from the Farmer's Market is the **Golden Temple,** 7910 W. 3rd St., near Fairfax Avenue, Hollywood (tel. 213/655-1891), its large windows overlooking the busy intersection. Hanging plants and stained-glass panels add color to the interior, but you might prefer to dine on the small patio with a colorful landscape mural on one wall.

The chef prepares a special soup and entree each day. On a recent visit there was a delicious lentil-vegetable soup with chunks of fresh vegetables followed by homemade lasagne with spinach noodles and a perfectly blended fresh tomato sauce with herbs. Regular menu items include light fare at $6 to $9, like Santa Fe enchiladas—two corn tortillas layered with natural cheese, onion, and a mild chili salsa; it's topped with guacamole and sour cream, and served with refried beans. Other dishes include a vegetarian burger topped with sautéed mushrooms and scallion sauce, served with a baked potato and sour cream, and a steamed vegetable plate with rice and sesame sauce. Servings are large, and dinner— priced at $10 to $15—includes soup or salad and homemade bread. If you're not too hungry, you could make a meal of a bowl of soup and a guacamole salad or Chinese spring rolls with sweet-and-sour sauce. A selection of fresh juices includes carrot, pippin apple, watermelon, and pink grapefruit. Homemade desserts are prepared daily and can be purchased to go.

The lunch menu is similar, but prices are lower.

The Golden Temple is open weekdays from 11:30 a.m. to 3:45 p.m. and 5:30 to 9:45 p.m., on Saturday from 5:30 to 9:45 p.m.

Omelets

The Egg and the Eye, 5814 Wilshire Blvd., right across from the La Brea Tar Pits between Stanley and Curson Avenues (tel. 213/933-5596), is one of the most popular restaurants in town. As the name implies, the Egg stands for about 37 varieties of omelets featured upstairs in a pleasant and airy restaurant; the Eye symbolizes the visual arts and crafts found in the galleries on the first and third floors—works ranging from Moroccan handmade rugs to painted eggs to art deco jewelry to posters. You can enjoy the exhibits before or after dining, and perhaps make a purchase (everything's for sale). If there's a long line (a more than likely occurrence), give your name to the maître d' and you can browse around until your table is ready.

The reason for the lines is that the omelets are excellent, artfully prepared the French way and filled with all kinds of good things: caviar and sour cream; potatoes, sour cream, and chives; pâté de foie gras, truffles, and asparagus spears; etc. If dining with a friend, you might want to share an omelet (they're big) and a salade niçoise. Omelets range in price from $5.50 to $11. A basket of black raisin bread and butter comes with all meals, and although there are dessert omelets (shaved chocolate, powdered sugar with rum flambé), I prefer a more traditional homemade cheesecake with strawberry sauce.

Open Tuesday through Saturday from 11 a.m. to 2:30 p.m., Sunday from 10:30 a.m. to 1 p.m.; closed Monday. Reservations essential.

BUDGET RESTAURANTS: With all the struggling young actors and actresses in this town, you'd better believe there are quite a few places where you can eat cheaply. The surprising thing is that some of the places below are actually quite chic, and you'll see the famous lining up to get in with the would-be famous.

American

Good old-fashioned value and quality is what **Philippe The Original,** 1001 N. Alameda St., at the corner of Ord Street (tel. 213/628-3781), is all about—as well as the best French-dip sandwiches (beef, pork, and lamb) on the lightest, crunchiest French rolls you'll ever sink your teeth into (about $3). Philippe's has been around since 1912, and there's nothing stylish about the place. It's democracy in action: you stand in line while your French-dip sandwich is being assembled with whatever goodies you want on the side, and you carry it to one of several long wooden tables where there are movable stools. Everything Philippe offers is delicious, all the way through to the doughnuts and coffee. The only changes I've noticed in the 40 years since I first discovered the restaurant's gastronomic joys are a little less sawdust on the floor and shorter hours. But coffee is still a dime!

Philippe's is open daily for breakfast, lunch, and dinner from 6 a.m. to 10 p.m. Beer and wine are available. Cash only. There's parking in the rear and a lot across the street.

Proximity to CBS Studios alone would probably guarantee **Roscoe's House of Chicken 'n' Waffles**, 1514 N. Gower St., off Sunset Boulevard (tel. 213/466-7453), a celebrity clientele. Its devotees have included Jane Fonda, Stevie Wonder, Flip Wilson, Eddie Murphy, Alex Haley, and the Eagles. The setting is very simpático, with slanted cedar and white stucco walls, changing art exhibits, track lighting overhead, lots of plants, and good music in the background.

Only chicken and waffle dishes are served, for $2.75 to $7.50, though that includes eggs and chicken livers. A chicken-and-cheese omelet with french fries accompanied by an order of homemade biscuits makes for a unique and delicious breakfast at $5.75. A specialty is a quarter chicken smothered with gravy and onions, served with waffles or grits and biscuits. You can also get chicken salad and chicken sandwiches. Homemade cornbread, sweet potato pie, homemade potato salad, greens, and corn on the cob are all available as side orders, and there's wine or beer to have with your meal.

Roscoe's is open Sunday through Thursday from 9 a.m. to 11 p.m., Friday and Saturday till 3 a.m. Cash only. There's another Roscoe's in Los Angeles (mid-city), 4907 W. Washington Blvd., at La Brea (tel. 213/936-3730).

The Original Pantry Café, 877 S. Figueroa, at 9th Street, downtown (tel. 213/972-9279), has been open 24 hours a day for over 60 years. Never closed, they don't even have a key to the front door. Its well-worn decor consists of shiny cream-colored walls graced with old patinaed oil paintings and hanging globe lamps overhead; big stainless-steel water pitchers and bowls of celery, carrots, and radishes are placed on every Formica table. In addition to that bowl of raw veggies, you also get a whopping big portion of homemade creamy coleslaw and all the homemade sourdough bread and butter you want—a meal in itself before you've even ordered. When you do order, you'll be amazed at the bountiful portions of delicious food set before you by waiters in long flowing aprons.

A Pantry breakfast might consist of a huge stack of hotcakes, big slabs of sweet cured ham, home-fries, and cup after cup of freshly made coffee, for under $5. A huge T-bone steak, home-fried pork chops, baked chicken, and macaroni and cheese are served later in the day for $5 to $10.

The Pantry is an original—don't miss it.

The oldest restaurant (est. 1930) in downtown Los Angeles is **Vickman's**, 1228 E. 8th St., off Central Avenue in the produce market (tel. 213/622-3852), open at 3 a.m. During Depression days Vickman's sold a beef tip sandwich for 10¢, less than today's tax on the same item. Nowadays, prices are of course considerably higher, though still low by current standards. Practically unchanged, however, is the decor (or lack thereof): creamy walls, linoleum tile floors, fluorescent lighting, big Formica tables, and wooden booths ranging the walls. For some reason there's a huge scale in one corner. Mr. and Mrs. Vickman (he's the son of the original owner) are always on the scene making sure the service and food are up to snuff. It is, and their clientele is so loyal it amounts to a cult.

They come for hearty breakfasts, perhaps a Spanish omelet, fresh-baked danish pastries, or the market omelet with fresh mushrooms and shallots for $6 to $7. Fresh-squeezed orange juice is also available. At lunch there are blackboard specials like cold poached salmon with caper sauce, stuffed pork chops, and boiled chicken. On the other hand, you could order a bagel with cream cheese and lox, a chopped liver sandwich, or a bowl of chili and beans. Leave room for a big hunk of home-baked fresh-fruit (strawberry, peach, etc.) pie with gobs of real whipped cream. It's all cafeteria style with no table service.

Vickman's is open weekdays from 3 a.m. to 3 p.m., on Saturday from 3 a.m. to 1 p.m.; closed Sunday. No dinner. No credit cards. No reservations.

Clifton's Brookdale Cafeteria, 648 S. Broadway, at 7th St. (tel. 213/627-1673), is one of a chain of economy cafeterias that has kept the less prosperous of Los Angeles nourished for five decades. Clifford Clinton—not Clifton—founded the business on what, today, would seem to be a very unique principle: "We pray our humble service be measured not by gold, but by the Golden Rule." During the Depression he kept thousands from starving by honoring an extraordinary policy: "No guest need go hungry. Pay what you wish, dine free unless delighted."

Those shopping or sightseeing downtown can enjoy a huge, economical meal that might consist of split-pea soup (75¢), hand-carved roast turkey with dressing ($4), baked squash with brown sugar (99¢), and Bavarian cream pie ($1.30)—not a bad meal for under $7.50. Entrees cost $3 to $6, vegetable side dishes and soup are under $1, and salad platters and sandwiches run $2.50 to $4. There are over 100 à la carte items at modest prices. However, since there is a charge for everything, including bread and butter, you must limit your choices to make your meal economical. It's all fresh, delicious, and homemade, too; even the baking is done on the premises. Fresh bakery items are sold at the front counter.

Clifton's Brookdale is open every day of the week from 6 a.m. until 9 p.m. There is another Clifton's, downtown at 515 W. 7th St. at Olive (tel. 213/485-1726), open weekdays from 7 a.m. to 3 p.m.

Chinese

Grandview Gardens, 944 N. Hill Street, between College and Bernard Streets (tel. 213/624-6048), is especially famous for dim sum. You can order drinks in the cocktail lounge which is guarded by a huge gold Buddha at the door. The long dining room has a peaked beamed ceiling and burnt-orange walls lined with Chinese paintings. Especially on weekends, its Formica tables are crowded with Chinese families partaking of dim sum delicacies. Generally there are three items to a plate, and each plate is priced at about $1.50 to $2. Pastries filled with barbecued pork, curried beef turnovers, ribs in black-bean sauce, lotus-bean pastry, stuffed duck feet, fried dumplings, and steamed noodle rolls are among the many offerings. In addition to dim sum there are about 100 à la carte listings ranging from sweet-and-sour pork to slow-cooked chicken with coconut for $6 to $10. Low-priced family dinners are also served.

Grandview Gardens is open daily from 10 a.m. to 10 p.m.; dim sum is served from 10 a.m. to 3 p.m.

Hot Dogs and Hamburgers

Everybody lines up for **Pink's Hot Dogs,** on the northeast corner of La Brea and Melrose Avenues (tel. 818/931-4223), near the heart of old Hollywood. The walls are lined with photos of famous hot dog fans, all signed affectionately to Paul Pink. The big treat is the chili dog, loaded with chili and onions and served with infinite skill by the "Great Johnny" for three decades. It costs about $2.25. Some 4,000 of these delicious beef dogs are sold daily between the hours of 7 a.m. and 2:30 a.m. Outdoor tables are placed at the corner, but most people eat standing up.

If you want a gourmet hot dog (where else but in L.A.?), try **The Wurst,** 10874 Kinross Ave., in Westwood (tel. 213/824-9597). Sausages and hot dogs are the order of the day here, for under $3. All are specially prepared—steamed, then grilled over mesquite charcoal, and served in fresh French baguette rolls. A variety of gourmet condiments is offered, including wine kraut, three types of mustard, the Wurst relish, and grilled onions; and fresh-cut french fries cooked in peanut oil are a perfect accompaniment. There's a bar-style counter with seating, as well as a stand-up counter that accommodates about 20. Unusual for a restaurant of this type is the background music—classical.

The Wurst is open Sunday to Thursday from 11:30 a.m. to 10:30 p.m., on Friday and Saturday till 11 p.m.

The search for the perfect hamburger has ended. Just head on over to **Cassell's Patio Hamburgers,** 3300 W. 6th St., at Berendo, East Wilshire (tel. 213/460-8668), where Alvin Cassel dedicated his life for 30 years to perfecting a gastronomic triumph—the compleat burger. The place changed hands a few years back, but the current owners haven't changed a thing.

They begin each exquisite creation with over a third of a pound of freshly ground USDA prime Colorado beef, grinding it personally each day after trimming off every bit of suet. Your burger is cooked to exact specification on a uniquely slanted range that griddles the bottom and broils the top. Then it's served on a five-inch bun—the most natural kind obtainable and always fresh. You can top it with what amounts almost to a buffet of all-you-can-eat fixin's: lettuce, homemade mayonnaise, homemade roquefort dressing, freshly sliced tomatoes, onions, pickles. You can also have all the peaches, pineapple slices, cottage cheese, and homemade potato salad you want. Even the produce is all carefully selected. These divine burgers (plus a variety of sandwiches) and all the trimmings cost about $5. The perfect drink with your perfect burger is homemade lemonade. There are tables inside (no ambience whatsoever; the place looks like a dive) and on the umbrella-shaped terrace.

Open Monday through Saturday from 10:30 a.m. to 4 p.m.

5. SIGHTS

There's more to do in L.A. than just laze around sun-drenched beaches. Hollywood's movie studios long ago opened their doors to visitors, revealing their fascinating "special effects" to one and all. Needless to say, these people can put on quite a show—it's their business. And in Hollywood-influenced L.A., even non-showbiz attractions take on a dramatic quality. The natural history of the La Brea Tar Pits takes on the aura of a sci-fi horror movie with life-size replicas of ancient beasts struggling for their lives in a bubbling death pit right in the center of town. Even death is more dramatic here, as you'll see at Forest Lawn, where funerals are "staged."

All of which makes sightseeing in Los Angeles very special fun. I'll begin in—

DOWNTOWN LOS ANGELES: This ever-expanding sprawl of a city did have a germination point, in and around the Old Plaza and Olvera Street. Later growth pushed the heart of the city about seven blocks west to **Pershing Square.** Opening onto the square (now tunneled with parking garages), the deluxe **Biltmore Hotel** was constructed, and elegant residences lined **Bunker Hill** in the late 19th century, the mansions on the hill connected to the flatlands by a cable car poetically named Angels' Flight.

Then came the earthquake scare, and buildings over 150 feet tall were prohibited by city-planning authorities. This limitation drove many companies out to Wilshire Boulevard and the outlying areas, and Los Angeles proper fell into relative disrepair, with beautiful town houses giving way to slums.

It wasn't until 1957 that the ban on tall structures was removed (ostensibly because new building techniques have lessened earthquake disaster potential). At any rate, the removal of the ban marked the beginning of a renaissance in the downtown area. The **Civic Center,** which had been expanding since the mid-'20s, culminated in the 28-story **City Hall.**

The shimmering, $35-million **Music Center** went up in the '60s, making downtown a cultural center. New office and exhibition buildings were erected in great numbers; the **Los Angeles Convention & Exhibition Center,** occupying a 38-acre site at 1201 S. Figueroa St., was erected, and, more recently, the **Seventh Market Place** at 725 S. Figueroa Street. New hotels have sprung up and old ones have been given a facelift. While you're downtown, take a look at the architecturally innovative **Westin Bonaventure Hotel** (see listing in hotel section).

And now, in downtown Los Angeles, at the heart of California Plaza on Bunker Hill, you will find the magnificent **Museum of Contemporary Art (MOCA),** designed by Japanese architect Arata Isozaki. For details, see the separate section on this exciting museum, below.

Although much of downtown is still rundown and undeveloped, that state of affairs is rapidly changing. There's much here to draw the visitor.

A Walking Tour of Old Los Angeles

This is one of the few areas of L.A. that you can see without your wheels. It's the district around **El Pueblo de Los Angeles,** the birthplace of the city in 1781, now restored along with 42 surrounding acres as a state historical park. Organized walking tours are conducted from the Docent Office, 130 Paseo de la Plaza, next to the Old Plaza Firehouse at 501 N. Los Angeles (tel. 213/628-1274); there's no charge, and they leave Tuesday through Saturday at 10 and 11 a.m., noon, and 1 p.m.

The tour begins at **Old Plaza,** near the site where Spanish governor Felipe de Neve purportedly founded the pueblo. The founding was part of Spain's plan to colonize California by establishing presidios, missions, and pueblos. Planting lands were given to the first 11 families who settled here, and five years later each settler received title to his house and lot. Nowadays concerts and religious festivities take place here.

Opening directly on the plaza is the **Plaza Church,** on which construction was started in 1818 and continued till 1822. Although much of the original structure is gone or restored, it is filled with paintings and ecclesiastical relics, and open daily to visitors.

Many of the area's attractions are along colorful **Olvera Street,** one of the oldest streets in Los Angeles. It was originally called Vine Street because of the vineyards growing along it. In 1930 it was established as a typical Mexican marketplace, paved with bricks and Spanish tile. It contains over 85 shops and stalls, open from about 10 a.m. to 8 p.m. daily, to 10 p.m. in summer, selling pottery, jewelry, leather goods, piñatas, and simple Mexican food. There's even a blacksmith.

Also on Olvera Street is the **Avila Adobe,** the oldest existing residence in the city, dating from 1818; it was damaged by an earthquake in 1971. It has been restored and is open free of charge to visitors daily except Monday from 10 a.m. to 3 p.m. weekdays, to 4:30 p.m. weekends.

Across the street is **Pelanconi House,** the finest of the early Los Angeles brick structures built in mid-19th century. It first served as living quarters and wine cellar for the original owner; Pelanconi did not purchase the place until

1865. Subsequently it became a warehouse for Chinese merchants, and today it houses a Mexican restaurant, Casa La Golondrina. The Victorian **Sepulveda House** is also of interest.

The **Pio Pico House,** completed in 1870 and the first three-story building in Los Angeles, was designed to be the finest hotel in the city at a then-astronomical cost of $82,000. Lighted with gas, and housing several bathtubs, it was considered the last word in luxury.

Just south of Pio Pico House is the first wooden-frame building erected in Los Angeles—the **Merced Theater,** undergoing restoration. It opened in 1870, with seating for about 400, and performances were advertised in Spanish. In later years it was used as a saloon, a Methodist church, and an armory.

The Museum of Contemporary Art

Thousands upon thousands of words have appeared in publications from New York to Los Angeles and from San Francisco to San Diego—some flattering, some not so—about the city's new Museum of Contemporary Art (MOCA). Among all the verbiage, the most important message might well be: "Don't miss visiting this museum." The only Los Angeles institution devoted exclusively to exhibiting art from 1940 through the present, MOCA, in the downtown L.A. business district, at the heart of California Plaza on Bunker Hill, 250 S. Grand Ave. (tel. 213/626-6222 or 621-2766), formally opened in December 1986. No matter what's on exhibit at the time you're in Los Angeles or how much you like contemporary art, a visit to this magnificent jewel in its handsome setting of skyscrapers is worth your time.

MOCA is the first United States creation of Tokyo architect Arata Isozaki. The birth of this unique edifice involved the efforts of an incredible mix of financial, political, and creative personalities (with some overtones of *The Fountainhead*). MOCA is ultimately a tribute to the brilliance of its architect and the planning push of Los Angeles. The physical constraints of the new museum were considerable—MOCA had to be built above a parking garage, yet the height of the museum was not allowed to compete or interfere with adjoining structures to be developed by the partnership underwriting its cost. Because MOCA would eventually be dwarfed by the surrounding buildings, Isozaki needed to attract attention with its materials and shapes.

The building's warm red sandstone blocks were quarried by hand in India and refined in Japan. There is a great deal to marvel at—the copper roofs, dark-green alumimun panels cross-hatched with bright-pink joints, the pyramid skylights, and the magnificent outdoor spaces. Two long rectangular reflecting ponds flanked by benches and trees are a perfect focus for quiet meditation after visiting the museum.

Seven gallery spaces comprise the heart of the museum. Gallery A rises 58 feet to the top of a pyramidal skylight; the remaining gallery spaces are 15- to 20-feet high. Stark white walls, unencumbered by moldings or baseboard, offer a pristine surface for the art.

MOCA's Ahmanson Auditorium is the site for the intimately scaled live performances offered throughout the year, as well as for film and video programs intended to further development in these forms—a mark of MOCA's commitment to contemporary art. For information and tickets, call the MOCA Box Office (tel. 213/626-6828).

A courtyard to the right of the museum ticket booth is the setting for the "Il Panino" café (after the popular Italian *paninoteca,* or sandwich bar). The café serves a marvelous selection of sandwiches, soups, desserts, and beverages, soft and harder (beer and wine). As might be expected in this artistic milieu, the sandwiches are creative, from the Capri—smoked salmon and Mascarpone cheese, garnished with salmon roe, capers, and chives—to the Milano—sliced turkey breast, goat cheese, avocado, sun-dried tomato, and arugula, served on Italian Ciabatta bread.

The museum is open from 11 a.m. to 6 p.m. on Tuesday, Wednesday, Saturday, and Sunday; to 8 p.m. on Thursday and Friday. Regular admission is $4; students and seniors pay $2; children under 12 go in for free. The museum store, featuring changing displays of artist-designed objects, exhibition posters, catalogues, art books, and contemporary jewelry, is open during regular museum hours.

The Music Center of Los Angeles County

This $35-million gleaming glass complex of buildings, located at 135 N. Grand Ave., at 1st Street (tel. 213/972-7211), houses three theaters: the 3,000-seat **Dorothy Chandler Pavilion,** for opera, recitals, musicals, and dance performances (home of the Los Angeles Philharmonic; on the fifth floor is the Pavilion Restaurant); the **Mark Taper Forum,** seating 750, for intimate drama and forums; and the 2,100-seat **Ahmanson Theater,** for plays and musical dramas. The Center's five resident companies—the Los Angeles Philharmonic, Center Theatre Group, Los Angeles Music Center Opera, the Joffrey Ballet LA/NY, and the Los Angeles Master Chorale—perform year-round.

In another part of the Pavilion building are Otto Rothschilds Bar and Grill and the Backstage Café.

Free tours of all three theaters are conducted year round on Monday, Tuesday, Thursday, and Friday from 10 a.m. to 1:30 p.m., and on Saturday from 10 a.m. to 12:30 p.m. For reservations, call 213/972-7483. For parking in the garage during weekdays, you pay a $9 deposit on entry. The cost is $1.50 for 20 minutes with a $9 maximum until 5 p.m. If you enter after 5 p.m., or any time on weekends or holidays, it's $4 maximum. On matinee days after 11 a.m. the cost is $1.50 for 20 minutes, $4 maximum. The garage is open until 11:45 p.m.

New Chinatown / Little Tokyo

Neither is as big a deal as its San Francisco counterpart, but both are enjoyable clusterings of ethnic shops and restaurants. **New Chinatown** is bounded by North Broadway, North Hill Street, Bernard Street, and Sunset Boulevard. Mandarin Plaza, 970 N. Broadway, is the center of the action.

Little Tokyo is between Alameda and Los Angeles Streets and 1st and 3rd Streets, close to City Hall; its central mall is Japanese Village Plaza.

To explore either of these areas an hour or two is sufficient.

Wells Fargo History Museum

This museum chronicles the history of the American West, focusing on Southern California and Wells Fargo. It's located in the Wells Fargo Center, at 333 S. Grand Ave., near 4th Street (tel. 213/683-7166). Among over 1,000 objects on display in this well-lit, pleasantly laid-out museum is a stagecoach under construction, along with the tools used to build it. There's also an authentic 19th-century Concord stagecoach, designed to carry nine people for long distances. You can sit inside it and listen to a narrative read from the diary of a young Englishman who made the long, arduous coach trip to Los Angeles. Other items on exhibit include mining artifacts, Wells Fargo memorabilia, and a two-pound gold nugget (76% pure) discovered in 1975!

The Wells Fargo Museum is open weekdays from 9 a.m. to 5 p.m.; it's closed on bank holidays. Admission is free.

Los Angeles Children's Museum

This delightful museum at 310 N. Main St. (tel. 213/687-8800) is a place where children learn by doing. Everyday experiences are demystified in an interactive, play-like atmosphere; children are encouraged to imagine, invent, create, pretend, and work together. In the Workshop Plaza they can make everything from Mylar rockets to finger puppets. There's a City Street where they can sit on a policeman's motorcycle, play at driving a bus, or being firemen. Kids can become "stars" in the recording or TV studio; learn about health in a doctor's and dentist's office, and about X-rays in an emergency room; see their shadows frozen on walls in the Shadow Box; and play with giant foam-filled Velcro-edged building blocks in Sticky City.

In addition to the regular exhibits, there are all kinds of special activities and workshops, from cultural celebrations to T-shirt decorating and musical-instrument making. There is a 99-seat theater for children where live performances or special productions are scheduled every weekend. Call the museum for upcoming events.

The museum is open on Saturday and Sunday from 10 a.m. to 5 p.m., on Wednesday and Thursday from 2 to 4 p.m. Summer hours are 11:30 a.m. to 5 p.m. Monday through Friday, and from 10 a.m. on Saturday and Sunday. Admission is $4.50; children under 2 years are admitted free.

Natural History Museum

Located in **Exposition Park,** this exciting museum, the largest of its kind in the West, houses seemingly endless exhibits of fossils, minerals, birds, mammals, and suchlike.

Exhibits and displays chronicle the history of human beings and their environment going back some 300 million years before we appeared on the scene and up to present day. They range from the dinosaur age to Maya, Aztec, Inca, and pre-Inca arts and crafts from the period 2500 B.C. to A.D. 1500. Animals are shown in their natural habitats; there are halls detailing American history from 1660 to 1914, mineral halls, bird halls—even a few dinosaurs on hand. In the Cenozoic Hall you can see mammal fossils from 65 million years ago; also shown here is the complete evolution of the horse from a fox-terrier-size animal to today. Other permanent displays include the world's rarest shark, Megamouth; a walk-through vault containing priceless gems; and an extraordinary collection of Los Angeles–built automobiles. There's much more, all of it fascinating.

The Natural History Museum, 900 Exposition Blvd. (tel. 213/744-3411), is open Tuesday to Sunday from 10 a.m. to 5 p.m. Admission is $4 for adults; $2 for children 12 to 17, seniors, and students with ID; $1 for kids 5 to 12; under 5, free. The first Tuesday of every month admission is free.

HOLLYWOOD: The legendary city where actresses once pranced with leashed leopards, and Louella Parsons daily chronicled everyone's most intimate doings, is certainly on everyone's must-see list. Unfortunately the glamour—what's left of it—is tarnished, and Hollywood Boulevard has been labeled "the Times Square of the West."

But Hollywood seems unaware of its own demise. For one thing, the **HOL-LYWOOD sign** is still on the hill and its price keeps going up. According to the *Los Angeles Times Magazine,* the cost of the original in 1922 was $21,000; the cost of building a new one in 1978 was $250,000. And for another, salaries in the never-aging movie industry are forever on the rise—in 1984, they totaled about $4 billion.

And still, if you look down, you'll be thrilled to see the bronze medallions

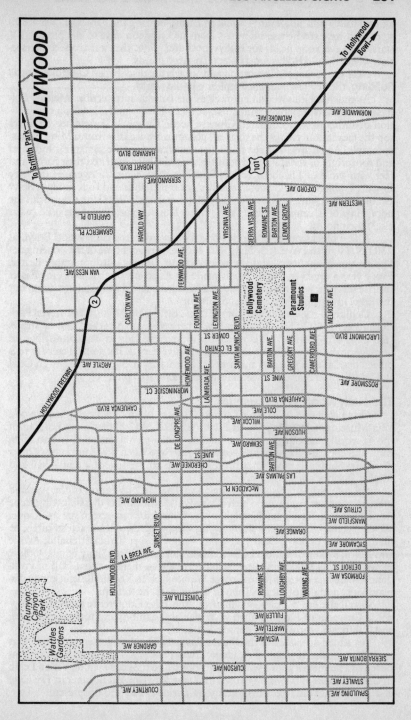

along Hollywood Boulevard's **Walk of Fame,** bearing the names of over 1,800 stars who have trod these sidewalks from nickelodeon days to the present TV stars. And everyone heads for **Hollywood and Vine,** that star-crossed intersection where the old **Hollywood Palace Theater** stands.

Near the corner of Hollywood and Vine is the disc-shaped **Capitol Records Building,** the first circular office building in the world.

As much a Hollywood landmark as the famous intersection, **Mann's Chinese Theatre** (formerly Grauman's), at 6925 Hollywood Blvd., is a combination of authentic and simulated Chinese decor. Original Chinese heaven doves top the facade, and two of the theater's columns are actually from a Ming Dynasty temple. An enclosure in the forecourt was created for the signatures and hand and footprints of the stars, and countless visitors have matched their hands and feet with those of Elizabeth Taylor, Paul Newman, Ginger Rogers, Humphrey Bogart, Frank Sinatra, etc., etc., etc. It's not only hands and feet, though; Betty Grable made an impression, as always, with her shapely leg, Gene Autry with the hoofprints of Champ, his horse, and Jimmy Durante and Bob Hope used (what else?) their noses.

A few blocks north of Hollywood Boulevard is the **Hollywood Bowl,** at 2301 N. Highland Ave. (tel. 213/850-2060), summer home of the Los Angeles Philharmonic Orchestra and the world's most famous outdoor amphitheater. Every year a predawn pilgrimage is made by Angelenos to the Bowl for Easter sunrise services, which are televised and broadcast across the nation (more about the Bowl in the nightlife section, coming up).

Dedicated movie buffs might want to visit the **Hollywood Memorial Park Cemetery,** at 6000 Santa Monica Blvd., between Van Ness and Gower Streets (tel. 213/469-1181). This is where the mysterious lady in black annually paid homage at the crypt of Valentino on the anniversary of his death. Peter Lorre is buried here, as are Douglas Fairbanks Sr., Norma Talmadge, Tyrone Power, Cecil B. DeMille, and Marion Davies. Hours are 8 a.m. to 5 p.m.

The Hollywood Wax Museum

One block east of Mann's Chinese Theatre is Spoony Singh's Hollywood Wax Museum, 6767 Hollywood Blvd. (tel. 213/462-8860), a last holdout of movie-world glamour. Singh, a bona-fide turbaned and bearded Indian Sikh, took over the barn-like museum some 25 years ago when it was in a state of utter disrepair; Shirley Temple's head had shrunken to the size of a tennis ball and Mickey Rooney's arms had dropped off.

Spoony built up his wax collection to 185 famous figures of the past and present, the most famous of which is Marilyn Monroe in her dress-blowing scene from *The Seven Year Itch.* Although most of the figures are screen stars—Raquel Welch (whose bras, under a shimmering silver midriff, were stolen so often, he finally left her braless), Danny Thomas, Bing Crosby, Barbra Streisand, Archie and Edith, Sylvester Stallone, Chris Reeve, Steve McQueen, Jane Fonda, Goldie Hawn, Michael Jackson, Bruce Springsteen, etc.—there is also a Hall of Presidents where first citizens from George Washington to Ronald Reagan are on display. Most popular of these is John F. Kennedy at the lectern.

You'll also see tableaux ranging from the Yalta Conference to the Last Supper, a Chamber of Horrors filled with maniacal demons and torture machines, and California's early history depicted in wax.

An added attraction is the **Movie Awards Theater,** presenting a film that spans more than 40 years of Academy Award history. The sound track is composed of a medley of award-winning hit songs, and the clips include Vivian Leigh in *Gone With the Wind,* Bing Crosby in *Going My Way,* Yul Brynner in *The King and I,* and other old favorites right up to *Chariots of Fire* and the present.

The museum is open daily from 10 a.m. to midnight (on Friday and Saturday till 2 a.m.). Adult admission is $7; juniors (ages 6 to 12), and senior citizens pay $5 (under 6, free).

GRIFFITH PARK: To the northeast of Hollywood lies lovely, verdant Griffith Park, at 4,253 acres the largest park within the boundaries of any American city, and the second-largest city-owned park in the world (the largest is in West Berlin). Home of the Los Angeles Zoo and the Observatory, it offers wide-ranging facilities, including golf courses, a large wilderness area, a bird sanctuary, tennis courts, a huge swimming pool, picnic areas, and even an old-fashioned merry-go-round. Other attractions are the **Greek Theater** (see nightlife section) and **Travel Town Transportation Museum** (tel. 213/662-9678), where the kids can explore and climb all over retired rail cars and airplanes. Admission is free, and it's open from 10 a.m. to 4 p.m. weekdays, to 5 p.m. weekends and holidays, from November 1 to April 30; to 5 p.m. and 6 p.m. respectively the balance of the year. There's a miniature train ride on weekdays from 10 a.m. to 4 p.m., to 5 p.m. on weekends (adults pay $2; children 2 to 13, $1.50; those under 2 go in for free).

Major park entrances are at the northern tip of Western Boulevard (at the prettiest part of the park, **Ferndell,** where New Zealand horticulturists have created a lush setting of planting ferns from around the world); at the northern extremity of Vermont Avenue (leading into the part of the park containing the Greek Theater, the Observatory, bird sanctuary, and Mount Hollywood); and at the junction of Los Feliz Boulevard and Riverside Drive (leading to the municipal golf course, miniature trains, and Children's Zoo). At the junction of the Ventura and Golden State Freeways is yet another entrance to the Zoo and Travel Town.

The Los Angeles Zoo
Only in Southern California would a zoo bill its offerings as a "cast of thousands." Here you'll see over 2,000 mammals, birds, and reptiles on a 113-acre "stage" divided into continental habitat areas: North America, South America, Africa, Eurasia, and Australia. Active in wildlife conservation, the zoo houses about 50 vanishing species. There's also an aviary with a walk-in flight cage, a reptile house, aquatic section, and a children's zoo.

Admission to the zoo is $5 for adults, $4 for seniors, $2.50 for ages 2 to 12, and free for under-2s. The zoo is open from 10 a.m. to 5 p.m. (to 6 p.m. in summer) every day except Christmas.

Griffith Observatory and Planetarium
Atop the hill, closer to the heavens, is the Griffith Observatory and Planetarium, where the "great Zeiss projector" flashes five different shows a year across a 75-foot dome. Excursions into interplanetary space might range from a search for extraterrestrial life to a search of vital interest to locals—for the causes of earthquakes, moonquakes, and starquakes. One-hour shows are given daily except Monday (seven days in summer); for show times, telephone 213/664-1191 (for a human, call 213/664-1181). Admission is $3 for adults, $2 for children 5 to 15. Those under 5 are not admitted except to the children's programs at 1:30 p.m. on Saturday.

At night the Planetarium is the setting for cosmic light-show/concerts under the stars. Powerful lasers produce dramatic effects covering the entire sky. Shows are presented Tuesday through Sunday; call 818/997-3624 for show times. Tickets cost $6 for adults, $5 for children 5 to 16.

Also here is the **Hall of Science,** with many fascinating exhibits on galaxies, meteorites, and other cosmic subjects. And the public can gaze through the Observatory telescope on any clear night (except Monday) until 10 p.m., nightly during the summer.

BEVERLY HILLS: A cartoon which once appeared in *Playboy* showed a bunch of glamorous-looking people boarding a bus, with a local explaining to a perplexed passerby, "Here in Beverly Hills, we've got more celebrities than we actually need. We felt the decent thing would be to bus a few of them to the more deprived areas of Los Angeles." Ain't it the truth?

Beverly Hills is, as everybody knows, the adopted hometown of many a motion-picture and TV star—Lucille Ball, George Burns, Michael Caine, Warren Beatty, James Stewart, Kirk Douglas, Linda Evans, Harrison Ford, Ann-Margret, Dean Martin, and Jack Nicholson, just to name a few. Its first mayor was homespun philosopher/comedian/star Will Rogers.

It's a fantastic city, and if you hurry up, you may just make it in time for the big bash: Beverly Hill is celebrating its Diamond Jubilee through to September 1989. Every six weeks the city will salute different countries with special events. The joyous celebration will conclude on Labor Day with the world's largest fashion show, to be held down Rodeo Drive. For a special tour of one of the world's most glamorous spots, contact the city's docents (tel. 800/345-2210); they are available for tours of the star's homes and walk/shop tours of the city's "golden triangle."

Within Beverly Hills are some of Southern California's most prestigious hotels, restaurants, high-fashion boutiques, and department stores—all used to catering to the whims of decades of TV and film personalities, and the very wealthy. It is the gathering place for a remarkable assemblage of European-based stores, many along Rodeo Drive. A shopping guide is available from the **Beverly Hills Chamber of Commerce & Visitors Bureau,** 239 S. Beverly Dr., between Charleville Boulevard and Gregory Way (tel. 213/271-8126 or, 271-8174). It's open weekdays from 9 a.m. to 5 p.m.

Douglas Fairbanks and Mary Pickford led the migration of stars to the area when they built their famous home "Pickfair" crowning the ridge at 1143 Summit Drive; today a drive through the glens, canyons, and hillsides of Beverly Hills will reveal one palatial home after another. And where else is there a city which would refurbish and redecorate a "convenience station" at a bus stop where household employees wait.

It was once a big tourist trend to visit stars' homes, with bus tours and local visitors bureaus pointing the way. This activity is discouraged these days, celebs demanding privacy—at least in their own homes—from gaping and often inconsiderate crowds. You will see youngsters on the drive going into Beverly Hills hawking "Maps of Stars' Homes," but I don't vouch for their accuracy—many of the occupants pinpointed have not only moved, but have moved to Forest Lawn!

Beverly Hills is a part of town to drive around in, oohing and aahing and probably fantasizing that you too live here. Stop in at the Polo Lounge in the Beverly Hills Hotel for a drink, lunch at La Scala Boutique, dine at one of its posh eateries like the Bistro or buy a little something at Giorgio, and absorb the glamour.

TOURING THE STUDIOS: Want to see what goes on behind the scenes at movie and TV studios? Universal Studios and NBC-TV have both arranged entertaining and informative tours, during which you might even get to see some of your favorite performers. If you only have time for one tour, Universal's is the more elaborate.

Universal City Studios

The largest and busiest movie studio in the world, Universal began offering tours to the public in 1964. Since then, it has been attracting some two million visitors a year to the world of make-believe to see the where, why, and how of the studio that produced movies from *My Little Chickadee,* to *E.T., Jaws,* and *Conan the Barbarian,* and popular TV series from "Dragnet" to "Incredible Hulk." Universal also produces MCA records, handling such big names as Olivia Newton-John, Loretta Lynn, Elton John, and Merle Haggard.

The guided tour of the studio's 420 acres aboard a tram takes about 2½ hours, after which you can stay for exciting live shows at the **Entertainment Center.** You'll pass stars' dressing rooms and countless departments involved in film production. And at Stage 32 you'll learn about special effects. You'll also see backlot sets like Six Point, Texas, the western town that has been used since the days of Tom Mix; that's not to mention the typical New York street (although it was devastated for *Earthquake*). The reason you don't recognize these streets from movie to movie is that they are constantly undergoing alterations in landscaping and exteriors to prevent audiences from becoming too familiar with them.

The tram encounters countless disasters along the way: an attack by the deadly 24-foot *Jaws* shark, a runaway train, a laser battle with Cyclon robots, an Alpine avalanche, the complete collapse of a rickety wooden bridge you happen to be crossing, a flash flood, and more. And now there's a once-is-enough encounter with a 30-foot-tall King Kong. You're carried into a dark sound stage and suddenly you're on an elevated train in New York, you listen to newscasters warning about King Kong, then sirens, screams, and finally King Kong—raging, tearing, just three feet away. Universal Studios estimates that 3.5 million people saw Kong the first year.

At the conclusion of this terrifying journey (or before it) visitors can wander around the Entertainment Center, where several times each day skilled stuntmen fall off buildings, dodge knife blows, and disappear into quicksand pits. In addition, you can perform as a "guest star" at Screen Test Comedy Theater in scenes that are filmed and intercut with actual footage from classic comedies with such greats as the Keystone Kops and Harold Lloyd.

One of the newest features on the studio tour is the *Miami Vice* action spectacular. More than 50 stunts and special effects are packed into a 15-minute show —something never done before.

There is a complete restaurant on the premises, Victoria Station, plus a Famous Amos.

Universal Studios is located in Universal City, just off the Hollywood Freeway at the Lankershim Boulevard exit (tel. 818/508-9600). Tours are given daily, except Thanksgiving and Christmas, from 9 a.m. to 5 p.m. in summer, and on holidays year round (from 10 a.m. to 3:30 p.m. the rest of the year; 9:30 a.m. to 3:30 p.m. on weekends). Those over 12 pay $18.95; seniors, $13.95; children 3 to 11, $12.95; under 3, free.

You can see a television show being taped at Universal too. Call 818/506-0067 for information and schedules, or write in advance to Universal Studios, 100 Universal City Plaza, Universal City, CA 91608.

NBC Television Studios

The largest color studios in the U.S., NBC-TV's Burbank facilities are home for the "Tonight Show," Bob Hope specials, and many others. "Wheel of Fortune," "Super Password," and "Sale of the Century" are taped here. A behind-the-camera glimpse at this complex will take you to the sets of the above shows;

it's not guaranteed that you'll actually meet a star, but it's not impossible either —maybe Johnny Carson or one of his many guests or substitute hosts.

Aside from the glamour aspect, the tour is most interesting, including an inside look at scenery in production, wardrobe, props, special effects (where you can see yourself fly like Superman), the sound effects center, and rehearsal halls.

The NBC Studios in Burbank are located at 3000 W. Alameda Ave., Burbank, CA 91523 (tel. 818/840-3537), easily accessible via the Hollywood or Ventura Freeway or by bus. No reservations are necessary for the one-hour tours, which run from 8:30 a.m. to 4 p.m. weekdays, 10 a.m. to 4 p.m. on Saturday, to 2 p.m. on Sunday. The charge is $6.50 for adults, $5.50 for seniors, $4.25 for children 5 to 14, and free for children under 5. There's lots of free parking for tours and shows.

For tickets to any of the shows taped at NBC Studios (including the "Tonight Show"), you may write to the address above. You'll receive a "guest letter" in response to your request, which can be exchanged for tickets on your arrival in Los Angeles. The ticket office is open from 8 a.m. to 5 p.m. weekdays, 9:30 a.m. to 4 p.m. weekends. (*Note:* Tickets for the "Tonight Show" are available only on the day of the show; tickets for other shows may be picked up in advance. Minimum age limits vary from 8 to 18; it's 16 for the "Tonight Show.")

HOLLYWOOD **ON LOCATION**:
This great service, at 8644 Wilshire Blvd., four blocks west of La Cienega Boulevard, between Carson and Willaman, in Beverly Hills (tel. 213/659-9165), tells you exactly where and when to find the TV and movie stars filming that day and night around the streets of Los Angeles. Each weekday at 9:30 a.m. they publish a new location list with the title and stars of each TV series, movie, and movie video being filmed that day and through the night until the following dawn. They also give the exact addresses and the starting and ending times for the location site. The list also describes whether the filming is outside or inside, plus the stunts and special effects if any. On a typical day there's more filming than you can possibly cover, with about 35 locations listed—almost always within ten miles of the office.

Jack Weinberg, who started this unique service in 1982, makes it easy for you to find the stars and shows you want to see. He contends (with a smile) that armed with his large-scale, detailed maps, pinpointing all the location sites, and the *Rand McNally Los Angeles Street Atlas* which they give you, none of their customers has ever driven off the edge of Los Angeles.

You can start out anytime since, most days, filming goes on till dawn. It's a good idea, though, to start as early as possible so that all your choices are ahead and you can find the stars wherever you're going.

The $29 fee for the package includes the location list and maps; it covers everyone going in your car. The package is available between 9:30 a.m. and 4:30 p.m. each weekday at the office of Hollywood **On Location** only. Sales are limited, so reservations are suggested but not required.

Will you really get to see the stars? When you go to pick up the packet, you can check out everything on that day's list (except the actual addresses) before you decide to buy. Take a look at the "Wall of Fame" displaying hundreds of snapshots that customers have taken and sent back, showing the stars they've seen and posed with—Robert Redford, Sylvester Stallone, Kirk Cameron, Robert Wagner, Elizabeth Taylor, and Michael Landon, as well as the "Dynasty" folks, the teams from "Cagney & Lacey," "Moonlighting," and "L.A. Law"—right down to "what's his name."

Back home, when they ask, "See any stars in L.A.?" be gracious when you show them your snapshots.

THE BURBANK STUDIOS: Home of Warner Bros. and Columbia Pictures, the Burbank Studios, 4000 Warner Blvd. (tel. 818/954-1744), offer the most comprehensive and least Disney-esque of studio tours. They call it the VIP tour, because it's created not for mass audiences but for small groups—no more than 12 persons. It was, in fact, originally designed to introduce visiting VIPs to the workings of the studio and was later made available to film buffs.

The tours are very flexible, taking in whatever is being filmed at the time. Perhaps an orchestra is scoring a film or TV program—you'll get to see how it's done. Whenever possible, guests visit working sets to watch actors filming actual productions such as "Head of the Class," "Designing Women," "Houston Knights," "Growing Pains," and "Night Court." You'll also tour set environments from jungles to Arctic tundra, from the Wild West to slum tenements. The wardrobe department and the mills where sets are made are also possible stops. It all depends what's going on the day of your tour.

Because you're seeing people at work, who musn't be disturbed, there are only two tours a day (more during summer), weekdays at 10 a.m. and 2 p.m., and children under 10 are not admitted. Admission is $22 per person, and you must make reservations at least one week in advance.

BURBANK HISTORICAL SOCIETY: Burbank has been the butt of numerous jokes of late (thanks to Johnny Carson, who works there), but in fact it's a pleasant little town that's rapidly growing into a bustling city. It's headquarters to movie studios, TV stations, and record companies.

Burbank is proud of its heritage too. In 1871 Dr. David Burbank, a New England dentist, purchased the Rancho La Providencia Scott Tract and raised sheep. The Providencia Land Water and Development Company built the Burbank Villa Hotel in 1887 and so began the enterprising city of Burbank. The Burbank Historical Society has put together the **Gordon R. Howard Museum Complex,** 1015 W. Olive Ave. (tel. 818/841-6333), which details the city's 100-year history, with dioramas of life in the early days, and some of its most famous residents—Lockheed, Moreland Bus, Disney Studios, and NBC. Gordon Howard displays a number of his antique motor vehicles at the museum, including a 1922 fire engine, a 1937 Mercedes, a 1937 Rolls-Royce, a 1939 Daimler, and the 1922 Moreland bus that Marilyn Monroe, Jack Lemmon, and Tony Curtis rode in the movie *Some Like It Hot.* Also on the grounds is one of the original houses built around the turn of the century to lure people to this new town in the valley. The Historical Society has done a good job of restoring and furnishing it.

The Gordon R. Howard Museum is open only on Sunday, from 1 to 4 p.m. While there is no charge for admission, the museum appreciates a donation—usually $1.

FOREST LAWN: There aren't many cities where a cemetery is on every tourist's sightseeing agenda, but then, there aren't many cemeteries like Forest Lawn. (Actually there are five Forest Lawns in L.A., but the most famous one is at 1712 S. Glendale Ave. at Los Feliz Road, Glendale; tel 213/254-3131). Pick up a map at the Information Booth when you arrive. It lists the major points of interest. When you go to see the displays which have timed showings, be sure to arrive ten minutes early. Gates close promptly.

Comic Lenny Bruce called it "Disneyland for the dead," and Evelyn Waugh wrote a satire, *The Loved One,* about it. But to founder Dr. Hubert Eaton, Forest Lawn was the cemetery of his dreams that would symbolize the joys of eternal life—"a great park, devoid of . . . customary signs of earthly death, but filled with towering trees, sweeping lawns, splashing fountains, singing birds, beautiful statuary, cheerful flowers . . . a place where lovers new and old shall love to stroll and watch the sunset's glow."

Highlights for the living include: Rosa Caselli Moretti's stained-glass recreation of da Vinci's *The Last Supper* displayed in the Memorial Court of Honor of the Great Mausoleum. Moretti is the last member of a Perugia, Italy, family known for its secret process of making stained glass. Thousands of Southern Californians are entombed in the Great Mausoleum, among them Jean Harlow, Clark Gable, and W.C. Fields. The art terraces and the corridors are lined with reproductions of great works of Michelangelo and Donatello. In the Court of Honor are crypts that money cannot buy—they're reserved as final resting places for men and women whose service to humanity has been outstanding.

The big draw on the hill—next to the Forest Lawn Museum—is a special theater used for the presentation of two paintings, the *Crucifixion,* conceived by Paderewski and painted by Jan Styka, dramatically depicting the moment before Christ is placed on the cross (Pope John Paul II hailed it as "deeply inspiring"); and *The Resurrection,* by Robert Clark, which was conceived by Dr. Eaton. The paintings are shown every hour from 10 a.m. to 4 p.m. daily.

Other attractions include reproductions of Ghiberti's *Paradise Doors* and Michelangelo's *Sotterraneo;* the Court of David, housing a reproduction of Michelangelo's famous masterpiece; churches like Wee Kirk o' the Heather, modeled after the 14th-century Scottish church where Annie Laurie worshipped; and the Church of the Recessional, a memorial to the sentiments expressed by Rudyard Kipling.

Forest Lawn isn't just for the dear departed. The churches have also been the setting for numerous christenings, services, ordinations, and some 60,000 or so weddings. It can be visited admission free from 9 a.m. to 5 p.m. daily.

WILSHIRE BOULEVARD: L.A.'s main street—it might be called the city's Champs-Élysées (and then again, it might not)—but would that famed Parisian street ever have a section called the **Miracle Mile?** No, that's strictly Americana, and it refers to the portion of Wilshire between Highland and Fairfax. The boulevard passes through **MacArthur Park,** with its own lake, as well as **Lafayette Park.** Near the eastern edge of Miracle Mile, in **Hancock Park,** are the **La Brea Tar Pits.**

Los Angeles County Museum of Art

A complex of four modern buildings around a spacious central plaza, the Los Angeles County Museum of Art at 5905 Wilshire Blvd. (tel. 213/857-6000) in Hancock Park is considered by many to be one of the finest and largest art museums west of the Mississippi.

The **Ahmanson Building,** built around a central atrium, shelters the permanent collection, which encompasses prehistoric to conceptual art. The museum's holdings include Far Eastern and pre-Columbian art; American and European paintings, sculpture, and decorative arts; a unique glass collection from Roman times to the 19th century; selections from Dr. Armand Hammer's European master paintings collection; the renowned Gilbert collection of mosaics and monumental silver; one of the nation's largest holdings of costumes and textiles; and an Indian and Islamic art collection considered to be one of the most important in the world.

Major special exhibitions, as well as galleries for prints, drawings, and photographs, are in the Frances and Armand Hammer Building.

The **Robert O. Anderson Gallery** features 20th-century painting and sculpture, as well as special exhibits. The Leo S. Bing Center has a 600-seat theater, where lectures, films, and concerts are held, and the indoor/outdoor Plaza Cafe.

The **Pavilion for Japanese Art,** scheduled for completion in early 1989, will display the internationally renowned Shin'enkan collection of Japanese paintings, rivaled only by the holdings of the emperor of Japan. It will also exhibit the museum's collection of Japanese sculpture, ceramics, lacquerware and paintings.

The museum offers a continuing program of outstanding special exhibitions, a film series, lectures, concerts, guided tours, and a variety of educational events. Admission is $5.50 for adults; $4.50 for students Tuesday through Sunday, seniors Tuesday through Friday; $3 for children. The admission fee includes entrance to special exhibits. Free tours covering the highlights of the permanent collections are given daily. The museum is open from 10 a.m. to 5 p.m. Tuesday through Friday, till 6 p.m. on Saturday and Sunday. The second Tuesday of each month is free for all. The museum is closed every Monday, Thanksgiving, Christmas, and New Year's Day.

Rancho La Brea Tar Pits/George C. Page Museum

Even today a bubbling murky swamp of congealed oil, the tar pits are a primal sci-fi attraction right on the Miracle Mile. Part of Hancock Park, at 5801 Wilshire Blvd., the pits are the richest fossil site inherited from the Ice Age. They date back to prehistoric times (some 40,000 years back), when they formed a deceptively attractive drinking area for mammals, birds, amphibians, and even insects (many of which are now extinct), which crawled in to slake a thirst and stayed forever. Other animals, seeing them trapped, thought the victims easy prey and jumped into the mire to devour them. Although the existence of the pits was known as early as the 18th century, it wasn't until 1906 that scientists began a systematic removal and classification of the fossils. In subsequent years specimens brought up included ground sloths, huge vultures, mastodons (early elephants), camels, and prehistoric relatives of many of today's rodents, bears, lizards, and birds, as well as plants and freshwater shells. In one pit, the skeleton of a Native American—dating, it is thought, from 9,000 years ago—was unearthed.

Over 100 pits, or excavations, have been made and over 3 million specimens removed in Hancock Park since the turn of the century. Currently there are six pits (places where asphalt seeps to the surface to form sticky pools) scattered throughout Hancock Park, including the Observation Pit and the Active Dig.

More than two dozen of the specimens have been mounted and placed for exhibition in the **Hancock Park George C. Page La Brea Discoveries Museum** at the east end of Hancock Park (tel. 213/936-2230). And replicas of the original trapped birds and animals stand fully life-size in their original setting, to spur your imagination.

At the museum you can see a 15-minute documentary film and slides about the La Brea tar pits and test the adhesive quality of the death-trap asphalt for yourself. Over 30 exhibits include reconstructed skeletons of Ice Age animals.

The museum is open Tuesday through Sunday from 10 a.m. to 5 p.m. The Paleontology Laboratory, where scientists can be viewed cleaning, identifying, and cataloging fossils, is open Wednesday through Sunday. Museum tours are given Tuesday through Sunday (call for times). Admission is $4 for adults, $2 for seniors 62 and over and students, $1 for children ages 5 to 12; those 4 and under get in for free. Admission is free the second Tuesday of every month.

The Observation Pit, at the west end of Hancock Park behind the L.A. County Museum of Art, is open weekends only from 10 a.m. to 5 p.m. Tours of the tar pits start from the Observation Pit and are conducted at 1 p.m. on Saturday and Sunday.

The Pit 91 Viewing Station is open occasionally for visitors to peer down into the "active" excavation where scientists continue to unearth and remove fossils.

WATTS TOWERS: A little-known American saga is the story of Simon Rodia, an Italian immigrant who came from one of the poorest districts in Rome, grew up in Watts, and worked as a tile setter. At the age of 40, he was impressed with the need to create something, to leave something behind in his adopted country. The result of this desire—after 33 years of work with no encouragement, no help, and no equipment other than his tile-setting tools—is Watts Towers.

Ignoring the jeers and scorn of his neighbors, Rodia scavenged the city for bits and pieces of iron and tin, steel rods, seashells, broken tiles, old bottles (especially green ones), chips of flowered dishes, etc. With no blueprints, he turned this junkyard of items into the Watts Towers, two of which soar ten stories high (nearly 100 feet), the others averaging 40 feet. Outline designs have been made in the walls with hammers, horseshoes, and cookie cutters.

His task completed in 1954, Mr. Rodia suddenly and mysteriously left Watts. He was no longer there to guard his life's achievement, and in the years following, the towers fell into disrepair, attacked for sport by vandals. As it turned out, the greatest danger to the towers was not from vandals, but from the municipal building department, which ordered the towers to be leveled as "hazardous to the general public."

The issue became a nationwide cause célèbre. Art lovers from all over the world—including New York's Museum of Modern Art, which called them "works of great beauty and imagination"—protested vigorously. And a private Committee for Simon Rodia's Towers in Watts was formed for their protection, demanding that the towers be given a fair test. In front of national television cameras and newspaper reporters, the crucial experiment was performed—the towers were subjected to 10,000 pounds of pull by a derrick. Only one seashell toppled, and the city deemed them safe enough to stand. In 1963 the towers were designated a cultural monument by the City Cultural Heritage Board.

As for Rodia, he never returned to his towers. He was tracked down in 1959 in Martinez, California, but he seemed not to care about his amazing creation anymore. Some speculated that an artist has no further interest in his work after it is completed, others said he was broken by the criticism his work had engendered. Whatever the reason, he died with the secret in 1965, and a memorial service was held for him at the towers.

The towers are at 1765 E. 107th St., Watts, but they're still closed for renovation. You can see the towers from the outside, however, and there's an adjoining art center, open weekdays from 9 a.m. to 5 p.m., on Saturday from 10 a.m. to 2 p.m. (tel. 213/569-8181). To reach them, take the Harbor Freeway toward San Pedro, getting off and turning left at Century Boulevard. Go right on Central, left on 108th Street, then left onto Willowbrook to 107th Street.

HIGHLAND PARK: When you take the Pasadena Freeway to Avenue 43, you'll find yourself in the great Southwest, that is, at—

The Southwest Museum
Crowning a steep hill overlooking Arroyo Seco, the Southwest Museum is Los Angeles' oldest art treasury. The museum was founded in 1907 by amateur historian and Native American expert Charles F. Lummis, utilizing private funds. It contains one of the finest collections of Native American art and artifacts in the United States. Located at 234 Museum Dr., at Marmion

Way (tel. 213/221-2163, recording; or 221-2164), it can be approached either via a winding drive up the hill or else through a tunnel at its foot, which opens onto an elevator that will carry you to the top.

Inside the two-story structure, the whole world of the original Americas opens onto a panoramic exhibition, complete with a Cheyenne summer tepee, rare paintings, weapons, moccasins, and other artifacts of Plains peoples' life. A two-level hall presents the culture of the native people of southeast Alaska, Canada's west coast, and the northern United States. A major exhibition interprets 10,000 years of history of the people of the Southwest, featuring art and artifacts of the native peoples of Arizona, New Mexico, Colorado, and Utah.

A new study-storage area in the Caroline Boeing Poole Memorial Wing offers a changing display of more than 400 examples of native North American basketry from the museum's 11,000 plus collection.

The museum has an exceptionally interesting changing calendar of events and exhibitions throughout the year, such as the Native American Film Festival of documentaries and short subjects; lectures on the sacred art of the Huichols; Mexican song, dance, and costumes; and Mexican masks; to name just a few.

The Southwest Museum has undergone significant changes over the past six years, and if you've never visited before or haven't been there recently, you'll find it fascinating and well worth your time. The museum is open Tuesday through Sunday from 11 a.m. to 5 p.m. Adults pay $3; seniors and students, $1.50; young people 7 to 18, $1; for those under 7, it's free.

And you can also visit the home of founder Charles F. Lummis, **El Alisal,** nearby at 200 E. Ave. 43 (tel. 213/222-0546). Lummis built this two-story, 13-room "castle" himself, using rocks from a nearby arroyo and telephone poles from along the Santa Fe Railroad. His home was a cultural center for many famous personages in the literary, theatrical, political, and art worlds. It's open free to the public Wednesday to Sunday from 1 to 4 p.m.

One of the very interesting aspects of El Alisal is the new and most attractive water-conserving garden. The primary plants are those which thrive in a Mediterranean climate. The experimental section, the yarrow meadow, is a substitute for a water-consuming lawn.

Yet a third attraction in the area is the **Casa de Adobe,** 4605 N. Figueroa St. (tel. 213/225-8653), a re-creation of an early 19th century Mexican-Californian rancho. Latino art and artifacts are on exhibit from the Southwest Museum permanent collection, along with Spanish Colonial period furnishings. It's open Tuesday to Saturday from 11 a.m. to 5 p.m., on Sunday from 1 p.m. Admission is free (donations are accepted).

SIX FLAGS MAGIC MOUNTAIN: The thrill you've always wanted just might be Free Fall, a roller coaster–like ride that ascends to a height of about 100 feet, then plummets rapidly to earth in a free-fall drop. Or Colossus, billed as "the world's largest double-track wooden roller coaster." Or Shock Wave, the first stand-up roller coaster in the West, expected to be the premier "white knuckle" ride. Or Roaring Rapids, a whitewater rafting adventure complete with stair-step rapids and waterfalls (you will get wet). Those are just a few of about 100 rides and attractions—among them another thriller, the Great American Revolution—a huge roller coaster with a 360°, 90-foot-high vertical loop (that's right, you turn completely upside down). Aha! But wait until you try Ninja, the black belt of roller coasters. It's the first and only suspended coaster on the West Coast which propels passengers from an overhead track through trees and along hills at angles of up to 110° and speeds of 50 mph.

All of these, and more, are at Magic Mountain, a beautifully landscaped,

260-acre amusement park in the green rolling hills of Valencia, 25 miles northwest of Hollywood. In addition to the above-mentioned roller coasters, the most popular rides (some of which cost as much as $6 million to construct) include the Buccaneer, a pendulum-shaped giant pirate ship that swings to and fro in a 70° arc; the Log Jammer, a log flume ride culminating in a 47-foot plunge into Whitewater Lake; the Gold Rusher, trapped in a runaway mine train, you careen crazily, roller-coaster–style, across hill and dale; and the Jet Stream, the closest you're ever likely to come to crossing Niagara Falls in a barrel. There's also a beautiful turn-of-the-century carousel.

Attractions geared to tots are Bugs Bunny World, with rides and creative play equipment specially designed for them. Bugs personally greets his tiny guests, and the Animal Farm is right next door. And over at Spillikin Handcrafters Junction—an authentic 1800s crafts village—they can watch craftspeople (woodcarvers, weavers, etc.) at work.

In the Aquatic Stunt Arena daily entertainment includes dolphin shows, high divers, and more.

In summer, the TDK Theater features big-name entertainers. And year round, extravaganza variety shows, marching bands, magic acts, and local rock groups round out the bill.

You can pack a picnic lunch if you like, but there are many eateries in all price ranges offering everything from chili to chicken yakitori. Not to mention countless stands selling pizza, hot dogs, burgers, tacos, corn on the cob, hot buttered popcorn, and other amusement park staples.

A one-price ticket admits visitors to all rides, amusements, and special attractions, including the big-name entertainment. Adults pay $19.95; seniors, $10; children under 48 inches, $10 (those under 2, free). The park is open in summer from 10 a.m. to midnight daily. Off-season hours (weekends and some holidays only) vary, so it's best to call ahead (tel. 805/255-4100 or 818/992-0884) for information.

Magic Mountain is reached from Hwy. 101 in Ventura by taking Calif. 126 through Fillmore to Castaic Junction, then turning south for about one mile at the junction of 126 and Interstate 5. From either direction, the park is two minutes west of the Golden State Freeway (Interstate 5) at the Magic Mountain Parkway exit.

THE SPANISH MISSIONS: Throughout this book I've mentioned as sightseeing attractions many of the 21 missions created by Franciscan padre Junipero Serra (soon to be canonized). Built between 1769 and 1824, they reach from San Diego to Sonoma. In the Los Angeles area is one of the most visited of all the missions—

San Juan Capistrano

About 56 miles south of L.A., the little island town of San Juan Capistrano is known for the swallows that return there every year (though they're getting fewer in number) on March 19, Saint Joseph's Day. On October 23, the Day of San Juan, the swallows punctually leave for their home to the south, probably somewhere in South America. It's called the "miracle of the swallows," although, in fact, all swallows come and go at regular dates. The mission here dates from 1775. The grounds contain the remains of what is considered the oldest building in California, and the altar, from Catalonia, dates from the 17th century.

The mission may be visited from 7:30 a.m. to 5 p.m., and the admission charge is $2 for adults, $1 for youngsters under 12 if accompanied by their parents. For information, call 714/493-1111.

Mission San Fernando

Closer by, at 15151 Mission Blvd. (at the junction of the Golden State and San Diego Freeways in San Fernando), the Mission San Fernando (tel. 213/361-0186) has seven acres of beautiful grounds as well as a convent. Dedicated in 1822, with an arcade of 21 classic arches and adobe walls four feet thick, it was a familiar stop for wayfarers along El Camino Real. The museum and the adjoining cemetery (where half a dozen padres and hundreds of Shoshone Indians are buried) are also of interest. Open from 9 a.m. to 4:30 p.m.; $1 admission for adults, 50¢ for children 7 to 15.

Mission San Gabriel Arcangel

Nine miles northeast of downtown L.A., at 537 W. Mission Dr., San Gabriel (tel. 818/282-5191), this formerly was one of the best preserved of the missions, tracing its origins to 1771.

Due to the earthquake of October 1st and 4th, 1987, it has been necessary to close the church, museum, and winery. Just when the Mission will be able to open depends on how long it will take to raise the $3 million needed to repair and restore the buildings. The remainder of the grounds are still open to visitors.

In the church (with walls five feet thick to withstand the ravages of time) is an oval-faced, sad-eyed "Our Lady of Sorrows"—said to have converted the native peoples with its serenity. The museum houses "aboriginal" American paintings on sail cloth depicting the 14 Stations of the Cross.

HUNTINGTON LIBRARY, ART COLLECTIONS, AND BOTANICAL GARDENS:

At 1151 Oxford Rd. in San Marino (tel. 818/405-2100), the 207-acre former estate of rail tycoon Henry E. Huntington has been converted into an educational and cultural center housing rare books (including a copy of the Gutenberg Bible printed in 15th-century Mainz), original manuscripts, and great works of art.

His home is now one art gallery, where paintings, tapestries, furnishings, and other decorative arts are exhibited—chiefly English and French 18th-century works. The most celebrated is Gainsborough's *The Blue Boy,* but the art gallery also contains Rembrandt's *Lady with the Plume,* Sir Joshua Reynolds's *Sarah Siddons as the Tragic Muse,* and a collection of Beauvais and Gobelins tapestries.

The Scott Gallery for American art was opened in 1984. Paintings range over a 200-year span from the 1730s to the 1930s. Some of the better known are Gilbert Stuart's portrait of *George Washington,* John Singleton Copley's *Sarah Jackson,* George Caleb Bingham's *In a Quandary,* and Mary Cassatt's *Breakfast in Bed.*

The library's remarkable collection of English and American first editions, letters, and manuscripts includes the original manuscript of Thoreau's *Walden,* a 1410 copy of Chaucer's *Canterbury Tales,* and Benjamin Franklin's *Autobiography* in his own writing. All told, there are over two million manuscripts and 300,000 rare books ranging from the 11th century to the present.

If all that culture sets your mind aboggle, take a stroll in the magnificent Botanical Gardens: there's a Desert Garden filled with many varieties of cactus; a Camellia Garden with 1,500 varieties; an Australian Garden; a Japanese Garden, complete with an authentically furnished 16th-century samurai's house; a Zen Garden and bonsai court; a Rose Garden; and a Shakespeare Garden of flowers and shrubs mentioned in plays by the Bard. Self-guided tour pamphlets of the gardens and the art gallery cost a quarter at the bookstore.

The museum and grounds are open Tuesday through Sunday from 1 to 4:30 p.m. (closed on major holidays). A donation of $2 per adult is suggested. *Note:* Sunday visitors must have advance reservations.

THE NORTON SIMON MUSEUM OF ART: Formerly the Pasadena Art Museum, this important collection at Colorado Boulevard and Orange Grove, Pasadena (tel. 818/449-6840), sits among broad plazas, sculpture gardens, semitropical plantings, and a reflection pool.

Important areas covered here are old masters from the Italian, Dutch, Spanish, Flemish, and French Schools, impressionist paintings, Franco-Flemish tapestries, and 20th-century painting and sculpture. Some highlights of the collections are works by Raphael, Rubens, Rembrandt, Rousseau, Courbet, Matisse, Picasso, Corot, Monet, and Van Gogh. A superb collection of Southeast Asian and Indian sculpture is also featured.

The museum is open Thursday through Sunday from noon to 6 p.m. Admission for adults is $3; students and senior citizens over 62 pay $1.50; under-12s are free when accompanied by an adult. There is a $4 admission for everyone on Sunday. The bookshop closes at 5:30 p.m.

DESCANSO GARDENS: E. Manchester Boddy began planting camellias in 1941 as a hobby. Today the Rancho del Descanso (Ranch of Rest) that he started contains thousands of camellias with over 600 varieties and over 100,000 plants —making it the world's largest camellia gardens. The County of Los Angeles purchased the gardens when Mr. Boddy retired in 1953, and over the years they have become an attraction that has delighted countless visitors.

In addition to the camellias, there is also a four-acre rose garden, which includes some varieties dating from the time of Christ. A stream and many paths wind through a towering oak forest, and a chaparral nature trail is provided for those who wish to observe native vegetation. Each season different plants in the garden are featured: daffodils, azaleas, and lilacs in the spring; chrysanthemums in the fall; and so on. Within the gardens monthly art exhibitions are held at the Hospitality House, and in the camellia forest (because the camellia originated in the Orient), the Teahouse. The latter, for which the landscaping money was donated by the Japanese-American community, features pools, waterfalls, and a rock garden, as well as a gift shop built in the style of a Japanese farmhouse. The Teahouse serves tea and cookies Tuesday through Sunday from 11 a.m. to 4 p.m. Other features include lunches served daily at the Cafe Court; docent-guided walking tours on Sunday at 1 p.m.; a gift shop; guided tram tours Tuesday through Friday at 1, 2, and 3 p.m., and at 11 a.m. on Saturday and Sunday.

Located at 1418 Descanso Dr. (at the junction of the Glendale and Foothill Freeways), La Canada (tel. 213/790-5571), the gardens are open daily from 9 a.m. to 4:30 p.m. Admission is $4 for adults, $2 for seniors and $1 for children ages 5 to 12; persons under 13 must be accompanied by adults. Picnicking is allowed in specified areas. Parking is free.

ORGANIZED TOURS: If you're pressed for time and want to see a lot, or if you just feel like being lazy and leaving the driving to others, organized sightseeing may be for you. The largest selection of tours is available from **Gray Line Tours Company,** 1207 W. 3rd St., Los Angeles (tel. 213/481-2121). In air-conditioned coaches, with commentaries by guides, the individual tours include such attractions as Disneyland, Sunset Strip, the movie studios, Farmers Market, Hollywood, homes of the stars, San Diego, Catalina Island, Tijuana, the *Queen*

Mary and *Spruce Goose,* Magic Mountain, Beverly Hills, Universal Studios, and Movieland Wax Museum. All fares include admission to any attractions visited.

6. AFTER DARK

The days when Los Angeles nightlife was one glamorous whirl under the scrutiny of gossip columnists is long gone, if indeed it ever really existed outside movie mags and columns. Basically, Los Angeles residents are suburban types, whose idea of a good way to spend an evening is to have friends in for drinks, poolside barbecues, and hot-tubbing. When they do go out on the town, it's usually for dinner at some posh restaurant.

But that doesn't mean there's nothing to do. It's just that Angelenos, like New Yorkers, take their abundant nightlife for granted and only bother with it when they have out-of-town guests—then they have a great time and vow to "do this more often."

The entertainment business—film, TV, records, theater—is still the most important industry in Los Angeles. In and around L.A. there are over 150 active theaters, large and small, with plays, revues, concerts. There are over 60 jazz clubs. And in addition to all this, the Pacific Amphitheater and the Universal Amphitheater feature name performers, as do the Greek Theatre, the Hollywood Bowl (mostly classical), The Forum in Inglewood, and the Meadows Amphitheatre in Irvine.

If you'd like an idea of what's going on any given week (the schedule of events can change weekly), buy the Sunday *Los Angeles Times.* The "Calendar" section is what you want to save. "Outtakes" updates the lowdown; "Movies" hypes the new faces in films and new films in production. There's a parental film guide and a handy list of family attractions, a description of new movie openings and special programs (offbeat films) showing that week, plus all the museums, lectures, and exhibits you'd ever want to see. And if you have it in mind to make a side trip to Las Vegas, Laughlin, Reno, or Lake Tahoe, there are ads for many of the hotels, the headliners, and what's being offered that week in special rates. The "Calendar" also lists theaters, club acts, and what's opening or closing, including restaurants.

LIVE MUSIC: Gazzarri's on the Strip, 9039 Sunset Blvd., near Doheny Drive (tel. 213/273-6606), used to call itself "Hollywood's oldest disco." They've now changed to a live-music format, offering rock 'n' roll bands for dancing nightly from 8 p.m. to 2 a.m. Thursday through Saturday. Admission is about $8 to $14, depending on the performers. The age group is early 20s; dress is casual. No credit cards. There's no drink minimum, and you must be at least 18 to get in.

The Lighthouse, 30 Pier Ave., Hermosa Beach (tel. 213/872-6911), makes a sensible and needed contribution to the nighttime scene in this beachfront town. The music varies from night to night, but it's among the oldest jazz establishments in L.A. You might hear reggae, rock, or rhythm and blues any Saturday night. The stage is in the middle of the room surrounded by tables filled with people eating and drinking. The decor definitely is not fancy. Show times vary and there is seldom a cover charge. Special attractions, once a month, have a cover, depending on the artist appearing. Most drinks are $3; those under 21 are not admitted without a parent or guardian. There's a $5 minimum. The Lighthouse is open Monday to Friday from 4 p.m. to 1:30 a.m., on Saturday and Sunday from 10 a.m.

Donte's, 4269 Lankershim Blvd., between Moorpark and Ventura Boulevards, North Hollywood (tel. 818/769-1566 or 213/877-8347), is a contender for the best jazz supper club in the Greater Los Angeles area. Open Monday through Saturday, it often features big-name acts. In the past such stars as Count

Basie, Buddy Rich, Chuck Mangione, Maynard Ferguson, and Freddie Hubbard have put in an appearance here. Drinks start at $3.50. In the food department, you can order steaks, seafood, or Italian fare with entrees in the $8.95 to $16 range. "Jazz dinners" are served from 6:30 to 11:30 p.m. Dinners are in addition to the cover ($6 to $12, depending on the performer), but you avoid the two-drink minimum if you dine. There are two or three shows nightly, depending upon the performer.

FOR COMEDY: The **Comedy Store,** 8433 Sunset Blvd., one block east of La Cienega Boulevard, West Hollywood (tel. 213/656-6225), is the most important showcase for rising comedians in Los Angeles and probably in the entire United States. Owner Mitzi Shore has created a setting in which new comics can develop and established performers can work out the kinks in new material. It's always vastly entertaining.

There are three major parts to it. The **Mainroom,** which seats about 500, features an "open mike" (anyone can do three minutes of comedy) from 8:30 to 10 p.m. on Monday, followed by professional stand-ups from 10 p.m. to 1 a.m. Admission is free, but there is a two-drink minimum. Other nights there's a continuous show of comedians, each doing about 15-minute stints. The talent here is always first rate, ranging from people you've seen, or may see, on the "Tonight Show" and suchlike to really big names. Admission is $9 Tuesday to Thursday and $14 for the 9 p.m. and 11:30 p.m. shows on Friday and Saturday, with a two-drink minimum.

The original **Comedy Store,** open nightly with two shows on Saturday at 8:30 p.m. and 10:30 p.m., charges $7 for the early show, $9 for the late show, $7 on all other nights, and has a two-drink minimum. About 15 to 20 comedians perform. Monday night is amateur night when anyone with enough guts can take the stage for three to five minutes; there's no cover, but there is a two-drink minimum.

Finally, there's the **Belly Room,** with Thursday nights reserved for comediennes starting at 9 p.m.; there's a $3 cover and a one-drink minimum. Other nights you can enjoy music at the piano bar. There's no cover, but there is a one-drink minimum. Drinks are $3.50 to $7.

Improvisation, 8162 Melrose Ave., at Crescent Heights Boulevard, West Hollywood (tel. 213/651-2583), offers something different each night. Sometimes comedy segments of TV shows and cable TV shows are filmed here.

The club's own television show, "Evening at the Improv," is filmed here for national distribution. Although there used to be a fairly active music schedule the Improv is mostly doing what it does best—showcasing comedy. Major stars often appear here—people like Jay Leno, Billy Crystal, and Robin Williams.

There is continuous comedy Tuesday through Saturday from 8:30 p.m. to 2 a.m. Comedy auditions are held on Sunday from 7 to 9 p.m., and a comedy group called Off the Wall performs each Monday at 9 p.m. Admission is $8 Monday through Thursday; on Friday it's $9 at the 7:30 p.m. show, $12 at the 9:45 p.m. show, and $9 at the 11:45 p.m. show; on Saturday it's $10 at the 7:30 p.m. show, $12 at the 9:45 p.m. show, and $10 at the 11:45 p.m. show. There is a two-drink minimum.

DISCOS: Chippendales, 3739 Overland Ave., one block north of Venice Boulevard, West Los Angeles (tel. 213/202-8850), is the brainstorm of Bombay bachelor Steve Banerjee, who pioneered several disco trends. Wednesday and Thursday nights from 8:45 p.m., a cast of macho male dancers and strippers puts on a one-hour, ostensibly titillating show for an all-female audience, while handsome, bare-chested hosts serve the drinks. Friday and Saturday shows are at 7 and

9:30 p.m. The dancers receive celebrity billing. It's not a show for the prudish, but can be a ball if you're not.

The interior of Chippendales is quite nice, with lots of plants hanging from latticework overhead. There are comfortable conversation areas away from the dance floor, including seating around a wood-burning fireplace and a backgammon room. The place is something of a celebrity haunt.

Chippendales is open to 2 a.m., on Friday and Saturday till 4 a.m. Admission is $20 with a two-drink minimum. Drinks average $4.50. Reservations are required. Men, admitted after 10 p.m. only, pay less.

CONCERTS—CLASSICAL, POP, ROCK, ETC.: The **Hollywood Bowl**, 2301 North Highland Ave., at Odin Street (tel. 213/850-2000), is an outdoor amphitheater with perfect natural acoustics. It's the summer home of the Los Angeles Philharmonic Orchestra. The season begins in early June and ends around mid-September.

Nowadays, internationally known conductors and soloists join the Los Angeles Philharmonic in classical programs on Tuesday and Thursday night. The Philharmonic's Friday and Saturday concerts are more pop oriented. The season also includes a jazz series, a Virtuoso series, and a Sunday Sunset series. Several weekend concerts throughout the season feature fireworks, including the traditional July 4th Family Fireworks picnic concert.

Part of the Bowl ritual is to order a picnic basket from the Bowl caterers (call 213/851-3588 the day before the concert to order) or bring your own.

Seats for classical concerts start at $2 and ascend to $18 for bench seats, $30 to $70 for box seats. The box office opens in May, Monday through Saturday from 10 a.m. to 6 p.m.; from July 4 and for the rest of the summer, it's open to 9 p.m. and from noon to 6 p.m. on Sunday. Parking space can be reserved for $9 (subject to availability), although at lots adjacent to the Bowl entrance, you can park for $6 and then take a shuttle. For evening performances be sure to bring a sweater or jacket—it gets chilly in those hills.

The **Greek Theater,** 2700 N. Vermont Ave., Griffith Park (tel. 213/665-5857), is a place where the entertainment ranges from performances by the Dance Theatre of Harlem to artists like Barry Manilow, Ben Vereen, Joan Baez, Manhattan Transfer, Natalie Cole, Neil Diamond, and Tom Jones. The theater is patterned after the classic outdoor theaters of ancient Greece. Dance groups and national theater societies also perform here. The season runs from late May to early October. Tickets range in price from about $20 to $50. The ticket office is open weekdays only from 10 a.m. to 6 p.m.

The **Universal Amphitheater,** 100 Universal City Plaza, just off the Hollywood Freeway, Lankershim Boulevard exit (tel. 818/980-9421 for a helpful human), is a 6,251-seat enclosed theater adjacent to the Visitors Entertainment Center at Universal Studios. It's well designed—no seat is more than 140 feet from the stage—and only top names perform here, usually for three to five days. Tickets are often sold out well before the concert dates, so haunt the box office in advance (hours vary; call the above numbers for information). Who might you see here? Elton John, the Temptations, Bob Hope, Frank Sinatra, Gladys Knight and the Pips, Paul Simon, Linda Ronstadt, Herb Alpert, George Carlin, Robin Williams, George Burns, etc., etc., etc. Tickets are priced from about $20 to $50, depending on the performer.

THEATER: The **Music Center,** 135 N. Grand Ave., at 1st Street, downtown, is L.A.'s most prestigious performing arts facility. It consists of three theaters:

The **Dorothy Chandler Pavilion** (tel. 213/972-7211), home of the Los Angeles Philharmonic, is a 3,250-seat hall where concerts, recitals, opera, and dance performances are presented. Every year the L.A. Civic Light Opera has its summer season here. The American premiere of the London hit musical, *Me and My Girl,* was presented here.

The **Ahmanson Theater,** a 2,100-seat legitimate playhouse, is (along with the Mark Taper Forum) home base of the Center Theater Group, who perform four plays here from mid-October to early May. Recent offerings include Christopher Reeve in *Summer and Smoke,* Daniel J. Travanti in *I Never Sang for My Father,* and the West Coast premiere of Neil Simon's *Broadway Bound.* A variety of international dance companies and concert attractions round out the season.

Prices generally range from $12 to $40, but there are reductions available for students and senior citizens for specified performances. Phone the Music Center at 213/972-7211 for ticket information.

The **Mark Taper Forum** is a more intimate, circular theater with 750 seats. The emphasis here is on new and contemporary works, although you might catch something like Shakespeare's *The Tempest* as well. Recent productions included *Green Card, Rat in the Skull, The Immigrant,* and *Ghetto.*

Needless to say, with all this diversity, I can't begin to quote prices. There are reductions available to many performances for students and senior citizens. Phone 213/972-7373 for all ticket information.

The **James A. Doolittle Theater** (formerly the Huntington Hartford Theater), 1615 N. Vine St., near Hollywood Boulevard (tel. 213/462-6666), offers a wide spectrum of productions. For instance, they've had Kate Mulgrew in *Hedda Gabler,* and Michael Gross and Linda Purl in *The Real Thing.* Evening shows are at 8:30 p.m. Tuesday through Saturday night, at 7:30 p.m. on Sunday. Ticket prices generally range from $15 to $30.

The **Wilshire Theater,** 8440 Wilshire Blvd., near La Cienega, Beverly Hills, opened in 1980 with *The Oldest Living Graduate* starring Henry Fonda. Recent productions have ranged from musicals like *A Chorus Line* to *Aren't We All?* with Rex Harrison and Claudette Colbert. "In concert" offerings have included Shirley MacLaine, Charles Aznavour, the Spandau Ballet, and Eurythmics. Tickets are in the $15 to $40 range. There's parking for 1,200 cars.

The **Pantages Theater,** 6233 Hollywood Blvd., near Vine Street (tel. 213/410-1062), is a Hollywood landmark dating from 1930. Built at a cost of $1.25 million (the equivalent of $10 million today), it was incredibly luxurious. For ten years it was the setting for the presentation of the Academy Awards, including the first televised Oscar ceremony. It's been through several incarnations, including one as a fine movie house. In 1977 it began a new life as a leading legitimate theater with a production of *Bubbling Brown Sugar.* Recent productions have included *Tango Argentino,* Bob Fosse's *Dancin', Joseph and the Amazing Technicolor Dreamcoat,* and *Lena Horne: A Lady and Her Music.* Ticket prices range from $23 to $45.

SOUTH-OF-THE-BORDER: I'm not talking about flying down to Tijuana; there's festive Mexican entertainment offered at **Casa La Golondrina,** W-17 Olvera St., downtown (tel. 213/628-4349). Located on the city's oldest street, it's housed in the historic Pelanconi House (circa 1850). The café itself dates from 1924. You can sit by the fireplace, dine on Mexican fare, or just sip a margarita while enjoying strolling mariachi troubadours, flamenco guitarists, and the like. "Fiesta" night entertainment is featured every Friday and Saturday night. There's no cover charge or minimum. Drinks and Mexican beer cost less than $3; a margarita, about $4.50. For dinner you can have a complete meal with two entrees (perhaps arroz con pollo and chile relleno), salad, Spanish rice, beans, coffee, and dessert, for under $8.

The café is open Thursday through Tuesday from 10 a.m. to 10 p.m.

MIXED BAGS: The **ABC Entertainment Center,** Century City, directly across from the Century Plaza Hotel, offers a variety of nightlife options. For openers, there's the **Shubert Theatre** (tel. 213/553-9000), presenting big-time musicals—like *Cats* and *Les Miserables.* Evening prices range from about $25 to $55.

There are four plush first-run movie theaters in the complex (tel. 213/553-5307 to find out what's playing).

Then there's **Harry's Bar & Grill** (tel. 213/277-2333), which looks just like its namesake in Florence, for drinks and northern Italian dinners (see the restaurant section for details).

The **Hollywood Palladium,** 6215 Sunset Blvd., near Vine Street (tel. 213/466-4311), provides a wide spectrum of entertainment. Traditionally it was the place for big bands, and they still play here on occasion—Ray Anthony, Tex Benecke, etc.—and Lawrence Welk used to do his famous New Year's Eve from the Palladium. The Palladium more recently has offered rock groups like The Ramones. Latin music is also popular. Prices and hours vary with the attraction.

CHAPTER IX

DISNEYLAND AND ENVIRONS

□ □ □

1. ANAHEIM
2. BUENA PARK
3. IRVINE

Although physically Anaheim, Buena Park, and Irvine are among the most unprepossessing towns in California, they are also the ones that attract the most visitors. For if the natural surroundings are uninspiring and the streets lack any vestige of charm, the man-made attractions off the streets are enchanting—transformed by the magic wand of Walt Disney into a wonderful world of make-believe. And Disneyland is just one of the spectacular attractions in the area. There's also Knott's Berry Farm, the Movieland Wax Museum, and more. So take the kids—and if you don't have any kids, be a kid.

1. ANAHEIM

Just 27 miles southeast of downtown Los Angeles, reached via the Santa Ana Freeway, Anaheim is Disneyland. Once a sleepy little town in the Valencia orange-grove belt, it offers excellent hotels and motels to handle the masses of visitors who come to visit the world-famed attraction. Disneyland is on everyone's must-see list.

If you're going by car, just get on the freeway heading south, and you'll be in Anaheim in about an hour. If you go by bus, take no. 460 from the RTD/Greyhound terminal downtown at 6th and Los Angeles Streets. Fare is $2.50 each way.

DISNEYLAND: This world of charm and magic is at 1313 Harbor Blvd. (tel. 714/999-4565), off the Santa Ana Freeway. Opened in 1955, the $307-million, 76-acre entertainment complex is "the happiest place on earth." Can you believe that in 1988 Mickey Mouse had his 60th birthday? Disneyland is split into seven themed lands, each with its own rides and attractions. You might start at the entrance and work clockwise, but the best plan of attack is to arrive at opening time and do all the most popular rides first—Space Mountain, Big Thunder Mountain Railroad, Pirates of the Caribbean, etc. The themed lands are as follows:

Main Street U.S.A., the main drag of a small turn-of-the-century American town, is at the entrance to the park. This is a good area to save for the end of the day—particularly the Main Street Cinema where you can rest your weary feet while enjoying silent film classics and cartoons. If you want to tour the entire park, trains (all 1890 or earlier vintage) of the Disneyland Railroad depart regularly from the Main Street Depot and completely encircle the park, with stops at Frontierland and Tomorrowland.

After sunset, there's a Main Street Electrical Parade spectacular—fabulous whirling lights followed by Fantasy in the Sky fireworks.

Adventureland is inspired by exotic regions of Asia, Africa, and the South Pacific. Here electronically animated tropical birds, flowers, and tiki gods present a musical comedy in the Enchanted Tiki Room. Within a spear's throw, a jungle cruise is threatened by wild animals and hostile natives.

New Orleans Square re-creates the atmosphere of that city around the mid-1800s. Of course, you take a trip through the Haunted Mansion inhabited by 999 ghosts, always (heh! heh! heh!) in search of "Occupant 1,000." Pirates of the Caribbean takes you down a plunging waterfall through pirate caves, ending in a dynamite explosion set off by a "band of befuddled buccaneers."

Bear Country is inspired by the great outdoors. What better way to see this rugged country than in Davy Crockett Explorer Canoes? Best of all, between the Haunted Mansion and Country Bear Playhouse, you'll find Splash Mountain, the largest towering log-flume attraction in the world, the most elaborate and exciting ever created. Each log vehicle sends eight guests speeding through twisting waterways and scenic chutes. There's a chase through swamps, caves, and beehives of backwoods bayous, before a rise that leads to a 52-foot plunge into a briar-patch pond. Splash Mountain is a fantastic extravaganza, combining music, water, sudden falls, snapping alligators, harmonizing vultures, and angry bees; it also brings to life the escapades of Brer Rabbit, Brer Bear, and Brer Fox. You'll want to sing along when you hear "Zip-A-Dee-Doo-Dah" in the finale, an animal chorus celebrating Brer Rabbit's return to the briar patch.

Frontierland, with a log-walled stockade entrance, is America in the early 1800s—a land of dense forests and broad rivers inhabited by hearty pioneers. You can ride a raft to Tom Sawyer's Island, visit Big Thunder Ranch, and Big Thunder Mountain Railroad takes you in old ore cars through a deserted 1870s mine; during the trip the train is menaced by swarming bats, a waterfall rushing the tracks, an earthquake, falling rocks, etc.

Fantasyland has a storybook theme and rides—you can attend the Mad Hatter's wild Tea Party or fly over London to Never Never Land with Peter Pan and Tinker Bell. One of the park's most popular rides is in Fantasyland, the Matterhorn Bobsleds, a roller coaster kind of ride past waterfalls and culminating in a big splash into glacier lakes at the bottom of the mountain. Bobsledders experience sudden drops in temperature as they race through chilling caverns, penetrate drifting fog banks, and encounter the Abominable Snowman.

Tomorrowland explores the world of the future. It has some of the most terrific Disneyland attractions, including Space Mountain, where you become an astronaut and experience a voyage through the cosmos. Other Tomorrowland attractions are the 3-D motion picture *Captain Eo,* a musical space adventure starring Michael Jackson performing his original score, and a cast of merry, mythical space characters. The super-realism of the 3-D makes it seem as though the Superstar were dancing off the screen and into the theater, and as though lasers were firing overhead at hovering spaceships. Add to that the new *Star Tours,* which puts you aboard a StarSpeeder as it takes off for the Moon of Endor, only to encounter a spaceload of misadventures. As you enter the Tomorrowland Spaceport, C-3PO and R2-D2 (the endearing and dynamic duo from *Star Wars*) are on hand to greet you. You board your own 40-passenger StarSpeeder, fasten your seat belts, and you are off on a remarkably real intergalactic adventure, with visual sensations and actual motion combining to create a thrill not to be believed until you've tried it. The Mission to Mars and the Submarine Voyage are two additional treats at Tomorrowland.

And don't forget to visit the **Wonders of China,** a marvelous tour of all the remarkably beautiful and historical wonders of that extraordinary land.

That, of course, is not the half of it. There are costumed Disney characters, penny arcades, restaurants and snackbars galore, fireworks (summer only), mariachi bands, ragtime pianists, parades, shops, marching bands, etc.

General admission to Disneyland is $21.50 for adults, $17.25 for seniors, and $16.50 for children ages 3 to 11. Admission includes unlimited rides and all entertainment.

During the fall, winter, and spring seasons (mid-September through May), Disneyland is open Monday through Friday from 10 a.m. to 6 p.m., and from 9 a.m. to midnight on weekends. In the summer season and on the Thanksgiving, Christmas, and Easter holidays, it's open every day from 9 a.m. to midnight. The parking lot ($4 charge) may be entered from Harbor Boulevard.

THE ANAHEIM CONVENTION CENTER: Yes, Virginia, there is something else in Anaheim. The Anaheim Convention Center, 800 W. Katella Ave. (tel. 714/999-8900), is a $60-million, 40-acre exhibit facility—the largest such complex on the West Coast—located directly opposite Disneyland. A variety of events are always going on here—they might include a Helen Reddy concert, boxing, an ice revue, antique fair, recreational-vehicles show, or even the circus. Check it out.

THE CRYSTAL CATHEDRAL: It's worth a visit to see the church from which the Rev. Robert Schuller broadcasts every Sunday on TV; it's at 12141 Lewis St., Garden Grove (tel. 714/971-4000). The structure was designed by Philip Johnson, the world-famous architect, for the Garden Grove Community Church. The cathedral is an all-glass, star-shaped building towering 125 feet heavenward. The organ in the cathedral is magnificent and has over 13,000 pipes to generate an incredible richness of sound.

WHERE TO STAY IN ANAHEIM: Families and Disney freaks might want to make Anaheim their Southern California base while taking in Disneyland and all the other nearby attractions.

Disneyland Hotel, 1150 W. Cerritos Ave., Anaheim, CA 92802 (tel. 714/778-6600, or toll free 800/854-6165), is just adjacent to the park, and Disneyland's Monorail stops right on the premises. Located on 60 attractively landscaped acres, it offers 1,174 guest rooms, six restaurants, five cocktail lounges, 35 shops and boutiques, every kind of service desk imaginable, an international artisans bazaar, a walk-under waterfall, two swimming pools, ten nightlit tennis courts, and a babysitting service. And what other hotel has a panoramic rooftop cocktail lounge that looks out over the Magic Kingdom?

All rooms are attractively furnished and equipped with every modern amenity. Rates for singles are $103 to $186 a night; doubles and twins cost $103 to $207, and suites begin at $210.

The **Sheraton-Anaheim Hotel,** 1015 W. Ball Rd., Anaheim, CA 92802 (tel. 714/778-1700, or toll free 800/325-3535), features a unique English Tudor castle architecture. Public facilities include an award-winning dining room, a nightclub, a lounge, a heated outdoor swimming pool, and shuttle service to and from Disneyland and the airport.

The hotel's 500 rooms are irreproachably modern, some with refrigerators; all have color TV, radio, direct-dial phone, dressing room, tub/shower bath, and the like. Singles range from $75 to $105, doubles run $85 to $115, and there's no charge for children 17 and under occupying the same room as their parents.

Very nice accommodations too at the **Anaheim Aloha TraveLodge,** 505 Katella Ave. (one block from Disneyland), Anaheim, CA 92805 (tel. 714/774-8710, or toll free 800/255-3050). The 50 rooms are attractive standard motel units, all with color TV and free cable movies, direct-dial phone, modern bath, and in-room coffee makers. There's a heated swimming pool with a slide.

Rates are seasonal but always include a continental breakfast. From May 15 to September 15 singles are $54; doubles and twins, $65. Off-season rates are lower. Children under 17 stay free in their parents' room the year round. In peak season, two-bedroom units that can accommodate six to eight persons are $98.

Last and least (least expensive, that is), there's a **Motel 6** at 921 S. Beach Blvd. (near Ball Road), Anaheim, CA 92804 (tel. 714/220-2866). There are 54 air-conditioned units, color TV is available, and there's a swimming pool on the premises. It's easy on the budget, clean, efficient, and comfortable. Singles are $29.95, plus $6 for each extra adult. Motel 6 now has in-room phones and levies no charge for local calls. Color TV is also included in the rates.

WHERE TO DINE: Anaheim is not exactly one of the world's gourmet capitals. If you're just in town for the day, you'll probably eat at Disneyland, and if not, the Disneyland Hotel has a restaurant to suit every taste; most other hotels also have reasonable dining facilities.

If you should feel like a night out, however, try **Mr. Stox,** 1105 E. Katella Ave., between the Santa Ana Freeway and State College Boulevard (tel. 714/634-2994), offering hearty steak and fresh seafood dinners in an Early California setting. Hot entree specialties costing $12 to $19 include roast prime rib of beef au jus or mesquite-broiled fish, veal, and lamb; sandwiches and salads are also available, for $6 to $13. Homemade desserts like the chocolate mousse cake are excellent. Mr. Stox has an enormous wine cellar, as well. At night there's entertainment while you dine.

Open for lunch weekdays from 11 a.m. to 3 p.m. (the menu is lower priced) and for dinner nightly from 6:30 to 10 p.m. Reservations suggested.

2. BUENA PARK

Just five miles from Anaheim is Buena Park, with three major attractions: Knott's Berry Farm, the Movieland Wax Museum, and the tournament/banquet Medieval Times. Don't even think of doing them all in one day, much less combining them with Disneyland. If you want to see every attraction, it's advisable to stay in the area.

KNOTT'S BERRY FARM: In 1920 Walter and Cordelia Knott arrived in Buena Park in their old Model T and leased ten acres of land. When times got hard during the Depression, Cordelia set up a roadside stand selling pies and preserves. As traffic increased, she added home-cooked chicken dinners to her offerings. The first day she sold eight, by the end of the year she was selling about 90 a day, and today the world-famous **Chicken Dinner Restaurant** serves up over a million chicken meals a year! But even the first few years, lines were so long that Walter decided to create an Old West Ghost Town as a diversion for waiting customers. That's how it all began. The Knott family is still running the farm, and it has become the nation's third-best-attended family entertainment complex (the two Disney parks are before it). It's at 8039 Beach Blvd., Buena Park, (tel. 714/220-5200), just south of the Santa Ana and Riverside/Artesia Freeways. It's divided into five "Old Time Adventures" areas. They are:

Old West Ghost Town, the original attraction, a collection of authentic buildings, refurbished and relocated from actual deserted western ghost towns. Guests can immerse themselves in rip-roarin' Wild West lore—pan for gold, climb aboard the stagecoach, ride rickety train cars through the Calico Mine, get held up aboard the Denver and Rio Grande Calico Railroad, or hiss the villain at a melodrama in the Birdcage Theater.

Fiesta Village is a south-of-the-border environment of open markets, strolling mariachis, wild rides like the Tampico Tumbler, and, in summer, nightly fireworks. In addition, there's Montezooma's Revenge—a loop roller coaster that not only turns you upside down but goes backward.

The $1-million Pacific Pavilion, with 1,200 seats, features *Splashdance,* with Dudley the sea lion and co-starring two dolphins.

Roaring '20s Amusement Area contains the thrilling Sky Tower, a parachute jump that drops riders 20 stories (over 200 feet) at free-fall speeds. In addition to the 12 chutes, there's an observation car called the Sky Cabin, which revolves 360° while traveling up and down the tower. Thrill-seekers will also want to try the "Corkscrew" roller coaster with two 360° loops (this was the world's first upside-down double-looped roller coaster). A Knott's restaurant is in this section too—Captain Kelly's, a replica of a 1920s airplane hangar, where buffet meals are served. The Cloud Nine Ballroom, with musical revues, is also in this section, as is Knott's new $7 million "Kingdom of the Dinosaurs" ride.

And don't miss "Wild Water Wilderness," the newest theme area, opened in May 1988. It's a $10 million, 3½-acre, turn-of-the-century California wilderness park with an exciting white-water rapids ride.

Camp Snoopy is Knott's themed area of the picturesque California High Sierra. It is a home for Charles Schulz's beloved beagle, Snoopy, and his pals, Charlie Brown and Lucy, who greet guests and pose for pictures. With 30 rides, shows, and attractions, it's six rustic acres of fun for the young of all ages.

In addition to the themed areas, there's the 2,100-seat **Toyota Good Time Theater,** presenting a top show daily throughout the summer.

Knott's is open year round except December 25. In summer, Sunday to Thursday it's open from 10 a.m. to 11 p.m., on Friday to midnight, on Saturday to 1 a.m.; the rest of the year hours are 10 a.m. to 6 p.m. (till 10 p.m. on Saturday night and till 7 p.m. on Sunday).

Visiting Knott's costs adults $19.95 for admission and unlimited access to all rides, shows, and attractions. Children (ages 3 to 11) pay $15.95; those under 3 are admitted free.

MOVIELAND WAX MUSEUM: Movieland features over 240 celebrity images of Hollywood's biggest movie and TV stars in over 100 authentic movie sets, including the latest additions: Elvira as the *Mistress of the Dark* and Sylvester Stallone as *Rocky.* Experience the thrill of stepping into supersets like the capsized ship in *The Poseidon Adventure,* snowbanks in the *Dr. Zhivago* set, and the bridge of the Starship *Enterprise.* And there are 15 sets and wax figures that re-create the special effects that made movies like *The Exorcist* and *Psycho* famous. The newest wax figures are of Roger Moore (as James Bond Agent 007), Mel Gibson, Jonathan Winters, Arnold Schwarzenegger, and Toshiro Mifune.

Unique gifts and movie memorabilia are available in gift shops, and there is a large collection of mutoscopes and biographs, the first movie machines.

The museum is open every day, rain or shine. Winter hours are from 10 a.m. to 9 p.m., summer hours from 9 a.m. to 10 p.m. Admission is $10.95 for adults, $8.95 for seniors, $6.95 for children 4 to 11 years; under 4, no charge. Parking is free. Movieland is located one block north of Knott's Berry Farm in Buena Park, Orange County. Take the Beach Boulevard exit South from the Santa Ana Freeway (Hwy. 5) and the Riverside Freeway (Hwy. 91).

MEDIEVAL TIMES: Great fun at 7662 Beach Blvd., right near the Movieland Wax Museum in Buena Park (tel. 714/521-4740, or toll free 800/826-5358, 800/438-9911 in California). If you haven't already collapsed from the excitement of the rides, the walking, and gawking, Medieval Times offers entertainment straight out of the 11th century (or thereabouts) in a castle setting. Here you can applaud tournaments, sword fights, jousts, and feats of skill performed by colorfully costumed knights on horseback—all this while being served dinner by serfs and costumed wenches.

Shows are Monday through Thursday at 7:30 p.m.; Friday and Saturday at 6 and 9 p.m.; Sunday at 1, 4:45 and 7:30 p.m. The price for adults is $28; for children 12 and under, it's $19. Medieval Times is an extremely popular year-round attraction so I suggest that if you plan to attend and cheer on your favorite knight, you make reservations at least two months in advance. A good time will be had by all.

WHERE TO STAY: If you're thinking of staying in Buena Park, you'll find that the **Farm de Ville,** 7800 and 7878 Crescent Ave. (at Hwy. 39), Buena Park, CA 90620 (tel. 714/527-2201), has a lot to offer. It's located at the south entrance to Knott's Berry Farm, it's convenient to all nearby attractions, and buses to Disneyland (ten minutes away) stop right at the door. The 130 rooms are spacious, immaculate, and stylishly furnished; each has a color TV, radio, air conditioning, direct-dial phone, tub/shower bath, dressing area, and individually controlled heat and air conditioning. Facilities include two swimming pools with slides and diving boards, two wading pools for the little folk, two saunas, and a coin-op laundry; a Baker's Square restaurant, open from 6:30 a.m. to midnight, is on the premises.

Summer rates are $42 single, $44 double, with a charge of $4 for each additional person. Family units, accommodating four to six persons, cost $71. The rest of the year, rates are about $2 less.

3. IRVINE

Wild Rivers, a new family attraction, is off the San Diego Freeway (Hwy. 405) at 8800 Irvine Center Dr. (tel. 714/768-9453). It's a 20-minute drive from Disneyland.

Wild Rivers is 20 acres of more than 40 water rides in a tropical setting. There's Wild Rivers Mountain, nearly five stories high, with 18 water rides. You can innertube it down or take a dark, turning, and splashing ride into the mountain, and go for a downhill slide that's about the length of a football field.

Or you can relax at Explorers Island with its three pools, including a paddling pool for small kiddies, and hot springs. There's even a sunshine terrace with lounges and tables (dressing rooms and lockers are available). Picnic areas have also been set aside.

Wild Rivers charges $15.75 for those over 12, $10.75 for seniors over 55, $12.75 for children 3 to 11, and free for under-3. Parking is $2 per vehicle. The park is open mid-June through Labor Day, daily from 10 a.m. to 9 p.m.; weekends only through October 12, to 6 p.m.

CHAPTER X

PALM SPRINGS

□ □ □

1. WHERE TO STAY
2. WHERE TO DINE

Golf, tennis, and swimming pool capital of the world, Palm Springs has been the playground supreme of the rich—home to the Gabor sisters, Kirk Douglas, Liberace, and Dean Martin, among many others. The honorary mayor, by the way, is Bob Hope, whereas the elected one is now Sonny Bono (formerly of Sonny and Cher).

The sun shines 350 days a year in Palm Springs (well, almost). Any number of golf tournaments are held in the area annually, including the Bob Hope Desert Classic and the Nabisco Dinah Shore Invitational. There are more than 300 tennis courts in the area, 42 golf courses (but only seven 18-hole courses are public, with average green fees of $45), and as for those swimming pools, they number over 7,000—one for every five residents!

Getting to Palm Springs is easy. It's 104 miles southeast of Los Angeles, about a two-hour drive via the San Bernadino Freeway (Interstate 10). You'll recognize it by the 1,336 windmills (a bit tall for Don Quixote, but enough to keep him busy). By plane (Delta, US Air, Continental, United, and American Airlines, among others) the trip takes 36 minutes from Los Angeles.

Once you're in Palm Springs, it's easy to get around via minibuses. Typical of the luxurious lifestyle here, they're carpeted, air-conditioned, and equipped with stereophonic music. It's 50¢ to board and another 25¢ for each town you enter. The buses run from 7 a.m. to 7 p.m.

To gain a bird's-eye perspective, take a ride on the **Palm Springs Aerial Tramway,** which travels a distance of 2½ miles up the slopes of Mount San Jacinto. It takes you from the desert floor to cool alpine heights in less than 20 minutes; in winter the change is dramatic, from warm desert to deep snowdrifts. At the end of the ride is a restaurant, cocktail lounge, gift shop, game room, and picnic area, and also the starting point of 54 miles of hiking trails dotted with campgrounds. The tramway is located at Tramway Drive-Chino Canyon, off Hwy. 111 north. Parking is free. It's open daily from 10 a.m. weekdays and from 8 a.m. weekends. The last tram up is at 8 p.m. May 1 to Labor Day, and the last comes down at 9:45 p.m. The rest of the year the last cars are one hour earlier. Round-trip fare for adults is $13.95, and children 3 through 11 pay $8.95. You can also get a ride-'n'-dine combination for a sunset dinner at the Alpine Restaurant at the top. You can only buy the combination ticket at the bottom after 2:30 p.m.; it's $17.95 for adults, $11.50 for children—a great bargain. For further information, call 619/325-1391.

A not-to-be-missed Palm Springs attraction are the ancient Indian **Palm, Andreas,** and **Murray Canyons,** a beautiful area of hiking trails, palm groves, even a waterfall with picnic tables nearby.

As elsewhere, make a stop at the **Greater Palm Springs Convention and Visitors Bureau,** conveniently located at Airport Park Plaza, Suite 315, 255 N. El Cielo Rd. (tel. 619/327-8411). They can answer all your questions and provide you with informative brochures and maps. It's open weekdays only, from 8:30 a.m. to 5 p.m.

1. WHERE TO STAY

Some of the most exquisite rooms in town are at **Ingleside Inn,** a charming hideaway estate at 200 W. Ramon Rd. (at Belardo), Palm Springs, CA 92262 (tel. 619/325-0046). Each of the 29 rooms and villas is uniquely decorated with antiques—perhaps a commode used by Mary Tudor, a canopied bed, or a 15th-century vestment chest will grace your room. Many rooms have wood-burning fireplaces; all have in-room whirlpool and steambaths, refrigerators stocked with complimentary light snacks and beverages, and whatever other luxuries you might crave, including a complimentary continental breakfast. Once you pass the imposing wrought-iron gates (most of the traffic passing through them is Rolls-Royces, Mercedeses and the like), you leave the bustling world of the 20th century behind and enter an old-world era of luxurious relaxation and fine, remarkably friendly service. Facilities include croquet, shuffleboard, and a large swimming pool and Jacuzzi; golf, tennis, and horseback riding can be arranged.

Melvyn's, one of Palm Springs' most prestigious "in" spots, is on the premises. It was here that Frank and Barbara Sinatra hosted an "intimate" dinner for 66 close friends on the eve of their wedding. The food is excellent, the celebrity-watching first rate, and the decor lovely—an 1895 carved oak-and-mahogany bar with beveled mirrors, pale-beige and chocolate color scheme, lots of potted ferns, wicker and tapestry-upholstered furnishings, and white lace curtains. If you don't stay at the Ingleside Inn, at least come by for a meal at Melvyn's. At dinner you might begin with a pâté de foie gras and follow with an entree of veal sautéed with avocado and fettuccine. Your entree, ranging from $18 to $32, is served with soup or salad and vegetable. The wine list is distinguished. For dessert the chocolate mousse pie is excellent. If that meal sounds a bit disastrous for your budget, come at lunch when you can have a cheeseburger with french fries and other hot entrees and cold plates for $8 to $15. It's also popular for Sunday champagne brunch at $20.

If you do decide to stay here, you'll join the ranks of Elizabeth Taylor, Howard Hughes, Mervyn Leroy, Ava Gardner, John Wayne, Bette Davis, Clare Booth Luce, Salvador Dali, Andre Kostelanetz, Gary Cooper, John Travolta, and Penny Marshall, all of whom have enjoyed the luxurious facilities at one time or another. Singles or doubles from October 1 to June 1 range from $125 to $600; rates are reduced considerably in summer.

The **Palm Springs Plaza Resort & Racquet Club,** 400 E. Tahquitz Way (just two blocks west of Palm Canyon Drive), Palm Springs, CA 92262 (tel. 619/320-6868), is one of Palm Springs' most glittering resorts. The 263 rooms are built around a central garden and swimming pool. The three-story building blends into the natural environment and reflects the sand colors of the desert.

The lobby, rooms, and restaurants are filled with original works of art, mostly contemporary serigraphs by David Weidman and sculptures by local artists. The atmosphere here is more like a country club than a hotel.

The rooms, done in soft earth tones, are large and residential in feel, with sitting areas and large wooden shutters on the windows. All rooms have patios or balconies, large baths with thermostatically regulated showers and brass fixtures, color TVs, direct-dial phones, and individual temperature controls.

Recreational facilities, in addition to a swimming pool that is among the largest in the area, include two Jacuzzis, six tennis courts with a pro shop, exercise room, and children's game room. Golf can be arranged at nearby courses, and many resort shops are within easy walking distance.

The gourmet restaurant, The Tapestry, is located off the lobby and features continental cuisine Tuesday to Saturday from 6 to 10:30 p.m. The Tapestry closes during the summer (June 1 to October 1). It is small and intimate, with Venetian crystal chandeliers and burl tables. The Terrace, also off the lobby, overlooks the swimming pool/garden area and is open daily for breakfast, lunch, and dinner. It offers coffeeshop fare, including low-fat, low-cholesterol dishes. There's also a poolside dining facility for snacks, and Harvey's, a piano bar/lounge.

Rates in season (December to May) are $180 to $260 single or double; suites range from $300 to $600; rates are lower the rest of the year. Children under 17 stay free in a room with their parents.

There's an elegant, old-world charm about the **Villa Royale,** 1620 Indian Trail, Palm Springs, CA 92262 (tel. 619/327-2314), a true international beauty with the atmosphere of a European-style country inn.

This extraordinary, 3½-acre bed-and-breakfast resort is made up of a series of interior courtyards replete with statuesque pillars and antiques, shade trees and bougainvillea; in a fountain courtyard you can quietly listen to classical music. An attractive outdoor living room with a fireplace (really) and comfortable Italian wicker chairs affords luxurious relaxation to the pleasant sounds of a water garden.

Each of the 31 units reflects the character, colors, texture, and beauty of a particular country—Portugal, France, Italy, or England are just a few examples. The owners spent six years buying in Europe and sending their treasures back to Palm Springs; you'll find them in every room—carvings, sculptures, woven hangings, even custom-designed quilts and ruffled pillows. But there are some strictly American features as well: several rooms have their own Jacuzzis on private patios, all rooms have color TV and private phones, and room service is available for all meals. Two large swimming pools offer a modern complement to the more rustic pleasures of the Villa Royale.

As you might guess, dining facilities are attractive and the food is excellent. There is a poolside breakfast room as well as a full-service dining room (the Europa room) for gourmet lunches and dinners. To enhance your dining enjoyment, the Villa Royale has put together—and is still accumulating—a collection of fine California and European wines and champagnes. Imported and domestic beers are also served. You can arrange (in advance) for a romantic, candlelit private dinner in your room or in the water-garden gazebo. Upon request, the kitchen will also pack a picnic lunch for you (with knapsack) to take on your excursions. A complimentary continental breakfast is served daily at the Terrace Room, and a wine and cheese party around the outside fireplace is held for guests every Saturday evening.

Other pleasant touches—the *Los Angeles Times* is delivered to your door each morning; bicycles are available for your use at no charge; golf and tennis reservations can be made at nearby courts and courses. If you wish to have outside guests for dinner at the Villa Royale, this can be arranged in advance; however, outside guests cannot use other facilities, such as the pools.

Standard guest rooms, single or double occupancy, are $70 to $215, with a Jacuzzi $165 to $195; one-bedroom suites are $140; one-bedroom villas $150 to $225, with Jacuzzi, $245; two-bedroom villas (four persons) $195 to $300. All rooms are on ground level. Extra-person occupancy is $25 per person. The Villa Royale does not accept children under 18 or pets.

One of the more unique choices in Palm Springs is the **Spa Hotel & Mineral Springs,** 100 N. Indian Ave. (at Tahquitz Way), Palm Springs, CA 92262 (tel. 619/325-1461, or toll free 800/854-1279, 800/472-4371 in California). It is the only full-service "spa" resort in Palm Springs. Formerly the site was a shrine for the Cahuilla Indians, who claimed the springs had magical powers to cure illness. Today vacationers come here to "take the waters" and otherwise pamper body and soul. There are three pools on the premises, one of which is a conventional outdoor swimming pool with sundeck; the other two are filled from underground natural springs brimming with revitalizing minerals. In addition to the outdoor pools, there are 30 indoor sunken Roman swirlpools, also fed from the springs. And that's not all. There's massage, complete gymnasium facilities, a eucalyptus vapor-inhalation room, and a rock steam room, where natural mineral waters are turned to three beneficial heat levels of steam. Guests can further enhance their healthy new appearances with facials, manicures, pedicures, and other beauty treatments. Facilities also include three night-lit tennis courts; golf is available to guests at a nearby country club.

The rooms are luxurious and elegantly appointed; all have refrigerators, direct-dial phones, color TVs, and baths with Travertine marble sinks. And the French cuisine served in the lavish Rennicks' Dining Room is excellent— California cuisine with a dash of French influence.

Rates for single or double rooms from mid-September to mid-December and May to June are $75 to $140, $25 for an additional person. From mid-December to late April, they are $105 to $180. During the summer, rates are much lower ($50 to $80).

In the style and tradition of a French Mediterranean auberge, **Le Petit Chateau,** 1491 Via Soledad, at Palmera, Palm Springs, CA 92264 (tel. 619/325-2686) is, as far as I know, the only clothes-optional B & B inn in the country. Le Petit Chateau is located in a very quiet, residential part of Palm Springs, about one mile from the downtown center. It's a charming separate environment, a "cocoon," as its owners Don and Mary Robidoux describe it, surrounded by bougainvillea-covered walls and hedges. Access is only for guests, so privacy and security are assured. The very pleasant aura of Le Petit Chateau is derived partly from the peace and solitude it affords; partly from the charm of its owners; partly from the tasteful country-French style of each of the comfortable rooms, most with delightful brick patios; and partly from the option to enjoy the sun the way nature intended—"au naturel" poolside (or with clothing if you prefer). To enhance your tan, Le Petit Chateau also has a unique Mist Tanning System to keep you cool and your skin moist and soft. Don't worry about your age or your shape; guests range from their early 20s to late 60s, and most are world travelers with a love for an all-over tan.

Don and Mary Robidoux run Le Petit Chateau lovingly and casually. Breakfasts are an inviting combination of goodies to suit almost any appetite; Mary prepares a complete European-style repast with eggs, sausages, ham, muffins, sweet rolls, fresh-ground coffee, fresh fruit, and on and on. In the late afternoon, there's a buffet table with wines and a variety of fruits and cheeses.

There are only ten rooms, so don't expect to call at the last minute and find accommodations (besides, the front gate is locked). But it's this very petit size that generates the comfortable social atmosphere. You can choose to be alone, but the great warmth and friendliness tends to draw one into the group. All rooms have TV, and there are three phones for common use by guests.

Rates are $100 for larger rooms with a kitchen, Friday and Saturday; $89, Sunday through Thursday. For the smaller rooms without a kitchen, the cost is

$93 Friday and Saturday; $82, Sunday through Thursday. Prices are the same year-round. All rates include double occupancy, European breakfast, and afternoon hors d'oeuvres. Remember, prior reservations are necessary.

The **Palm Springs Riviera Hotel,** 1600 N. Indian Ave. (at Vista Chino Drive), Palm Springs, CA 92262 (tel. 619/327-8311, or toll free 800/367-3296 in California), is a 17-acre luxury resort boasting the largest swimming pool in Palm Springs (augmented by a second pool complex) and tennis courts (most with night lights; there's a small fee for court use).

Continental cuisine is served in the Café Riviera, overlooking the pool.

The 468 guest rooms have a definite resort feel, most with color-coordinated, fern-motif draperies, bedspread, and vinyl wall coverings, orange or garden-green color schemes, and white bamboo. Others are done in desert color schemes with contemporary furnishings. All rooms have color TVs, direct-dial phones, refrigerators, and outside patios.

Rates from December 26 to June 1 are $95 to $150, single or double; June 2 to Labor Day they're $70 to $80, single or double; the rest of the year it's $80 to $130, single or double. All year there's no charge for children under 12 in a room with their parents.

Among the more reasonable establishments in Palm Springs is the **Estrella Inn,** 415 S. Belardo, Palm Springs, CA 92262 (tel. 619/340-4117), located just a block from the center of town, but on a quiet, secluded street that seems to be miles from everywhere. The rooms here vary widely in size—from very small quarters, to suites with lanai decks, wet bars, full kitchens, and fireplaces, to multiroom cottages. All rooms have air conditioning, direct-dial phones, and cable color TV.

On the premises are two adult swimming pools, one children's pool, two spa pools, two Jacuzzis, and a lawn and court games area. There's no restaurant, but the inn serves complimentary coffee and danish every morning in the lobby lounge.

Rates at the Estrella Inn are $90 for a very small room, $110 for a room with two queen-size beds, and cottages are $160 to $220. Off-season rates are about 30% lower; weekly and monthly rates are also available off-season, monthly rates in-season. All prices are for single or double occupancy.

And forever there will be a Motel 6. In Palm Springs, however, it's **Hotel 6** (there is no "motel" classification here), at 595 E. Palm Canyon Dr., Palm Springs, CA 92262 (tel. 619/325-6129). Advance planning is the key if you hope to stay here during the season—reservations should be made 12 months in advance. Singles are $30.95, plus $6 for each additional adult. It's clean, efficient, and convenient, and has a pool. All local calls are free, as is the TV. Need more be said?

If Hotel 6 in Palm Springs can't accommodate you, try **Motel 6** at 78100 Varner Rd., Bermuda Dunes, CA 92201 (tel. 619/256-0653). It's about 15 driving-minutes east of Palm Springs and has a smaller pool, but is just as clean and efficient, and costs a bit less per night. Singles are $25.95, plus $6 for each additional adult; no charge for color TV or local calls.

RANCHO MIRAGE: This rapidly developing southward expansion of Palm Springs is just 12 miles south via Hwy. 111. It already has a restaurant row and many famous residents, among them Gerald and Betty Ford. It also contains one of the area's most luxurious accommodations, the Mobil five-star **Marriott's Rancho Las Palmas Resort,** 41000 Bob Hope Dr. (off Hwy. 111), Rancho Mirage, CA 92270 (tel. 619/568-2727, or toll free 800/228-9290), set on 26½ beautifully tended garden acres. Opened in February 1979, the Marriott has 456 spacious rooms housed in two-story terracotta-roofed stucco buildings. Decorated in bright resort colors, the rooms are equipped with every luxury—oversized beds, color TVs with in-room movies, etc. As for the hotel's facilities, they include three restaurants decorated in Early California hacienda motif plus a lounge and disco; two large outdoor swimming pools and Jacuzzis; and the requisite shops, hospitality, tour, and car-rental desks. Guests become automatic members of the Rancho Las Palmas Country Club down the road; it has 25 tennis courts, a 27-hole championship golf course, pro shops for both sports, a driving range and putting green, a swimming pool, and a restaurant and snackbar. And anything not on the premises—from ballooning to horseback riding—can probably be arranged.

Rates for single or double occupancy are $240 to $255 from late December to early May, $90 to $180 from May to mid-September, and $170 to $190 from mid-September to mid-December. Extra adults pay $10 year round; there's no charge for children under 18 occupying the same room as their parents.

A more economical choice in Rancho Mirage is the **Allstar Inn,** 69–570 Hwy. 111 (between Date Palm Drive and Frank Sinatra Drive), Rancho Mirage, CA 92270 (tel. 619/324-8475). As with all the Allstar Inns, the guest rooms are nicely furnished and spotlessly clean, plus they have a full tub and shower and free color TV. At Rancho Mirage, there is a small pool and Jacuzzi. Singles are $31.95, doubles, $34.95; summer rates are $7 lower. Reservations for the winter season (October through May) should be made well in advance.

2. WHERE TO DINE

Some of the best restaurants in town are at the hotels already mentioned—**Melvyn's** at Ingleside Inn, **Rennicks'** at the Spa Hotel, etc. There are, however, other choices.

When you're in Palm Springs and in the mood for a seafood dinner, the place to go is **Sorrentino's,** 1032 N. Palm Canyon Dr. (tel. 619/325-2944), undoubtedly the best seafood restaurant in town. As you may have guessed by the name, its origins are Italian-American, a fact reflected in the decor: green banquettes rest against red walls decked with oil paintings; diners sit on red vinyl straight-backed chairs, and the room is lit by wrought-iron–encased fixtures. All in all, the restaurant has a warm, familiar feeling that makes dining a very pleasant experience.

Virtually all the fish is fresh, and when it's "fresh frozen," Sorrentino's tells you so. Some of the great choices on the extensive menu include a hearty seafood-and-chicken gumbo with andouille sausage and steamed rice; sautéed sand dabs (a particular favorite of mine); king crab legs; swordfish steak; shrimp scampi-style; jet-fresh Maine lobster; abalone steak; and, of course, cioppino. While Sorrentino's is primarily a seafood house, the quality of the meat here is excellent. Some of the fine meat dishes include veal osso buco Genovese; Steak Sinatra, with peppers and mushrooms; filet mignon; and a tender, moist, delectable roast rack of lamb. Sorrentino's also has a children's dinner (under 12) for $7.50 to $11.50, which offers a choice of four entrees. Entrees and specials for grown-ups range from $11.95 to $26.95. Sorrentino's has desserts one might expect in an Italian seafood restaurant—with one notable and surprising exception, English trifle.

Whether you're a party of one or eight, service is very attentive without being overbearing. The wine list, domestic and imported, is limited but good.

Sorrentino's has a huge bar adjacent to the main dining room, so if you have to wait for a few minutes, you'll be comfortable. Open nightly from 5:30 to 10:30 p.m. Reservations are necessary.

The exterior of **Alfredo's,** 292 E. Palm Canyon Dr., at Via Entrada (tel. 619/320-1020), has always attracted me. It's simple, uncluttered, and inviting with a forthright "Alfredo's" sign in neon script. The restaurant is just as handsome inside—dusty-rose and cream walls, with complementary maroon-and-cream furnishings, scenic lithographs, smoked mirrors, and frosted-glass art-deco lamps overhead. It has a friendly feeling, pleasant, quiet, and a menu that's perfectly suited to almost any taste—including the most demanding of quality.

Appetizer prices start from $3.50 for Mama's fava beans or a Sicilian-style artichoke and go on up to $7.95 for the antipasto Alfredo. In the middle, at $5.95, is a favorite of mine, mozzarella marinara—deep-fried cheese cooked with the chef's special sauce. An interesting selection of salads range from the house's dandelion salad at $3.95 to a cold seafood and linguine combination for $11.50.

Entrees to satisfy all appetites range from veal marsala or filet mignon "Alfredo style" to pizza. And the spicy chicken wings have to be the best this side of Buffalo, N.Y. (Alfredo's home town). They come in hot, medium, or mild. ("Medium" was just right for me—hot, but not enough to create an unredeemable scorch.) Served in true Buffalo style—with celery sticks and blue-cheese dip—the wings were absolutely delicious ($5 for 10 pieces, $11.50 for 30 pieces).

If you thought that spaghetti and meatballs was hardly an inspired choice for dinner, at Alfredo's the toothsome flavor and rich texture of the homemade meatballs will prove you wrong. Not to be ignored either is a magnificent veal "Alfredo"—veal cutlets and eggplant in light batter, sautéed, separated with prosciutto, topped with mozzarella, then baked and finished with Alfredo's special sauce. As you might expect, Alfredo's has veal in its many Italian forms. For poultry lovers, the chicken à la Nardizzi offers a delectable combination of chicken breast sautéed with seasonings, mushrooms, and marsala wine, served with the pasta of the day.

And when was the last time you had steak and dandelions? Try it here for a light dinner: choice tenderloin broiled to order and smothered in Alfredo's house specialty—sautéed dandelions served on an Italian roll. The somewhat reluctant dandelion gourmet might go for an appetizer-size order or the fresh dandelion salad. Seafood entrees, including calamari, are served with Alfredo's pasta and artichoke sauce. Pasta specialties come with salad or soup.

Dinner entrees are $14 to $19 and include salad or soup, pasta, chef's vegetable, and fresh Italian bread. All recipes are cooked to order. There's a good selection of wines to accompany your meal.

Alfredo's is open nightly from 5 to 11 p.m. A small parking lot is located right behind the restaurant, off Via Entrada.

Lyon's English Grill, 233 E. Palm Canyon Dr., at Via Entrada (tel. 619/327-1551), has an almost theatrical woody English-pub ambience composed of stained-glass windows, old pub signs and maps, Tudor beamed walls, and heraldic banners suspended from the ceilings—not to mention waitresses in serving-wench costume. Even the menus were made in England, originally for a restaurant in Hampton Court. The most traditional thing to order is a prime rib dinner. Less expensive entrees are—in descending price order—roast duckling with wild rice, baked sea bass, and roast chicken. All entrees are priced from $12 to $18, and are served with soup or salad, a baked potato, and hot popovers. Open daily from 5 to 11 p.m.

For hearty home-cooking, a great selection, huge portions, and small-town ambience, head for **Billy Reed's,** 1800 N. Palm Canyon Dr., near Vista Chino (tel. 619/325-1946). Billy Reed's entry has the characteristic Palm Springs hacienda look—small fountain, foliage, and cool patio—but the Spanish resemblance ends there. Wicker furniture graces the outer lobby, and the interior is American/Victorian, with lace curtains and Tiffany stained-glass lamp shades.

Somehow it all works. And though the place is huge, the low ceilings, break-fronts, and overhead pot-and-mug collections afford a feeling of warmth.

You can start your day here with a breakfast (priced under $7) such as sausage and eggs served with hash browns, toast, and butter. At lunch, you might order the shrimp or crab Louis, served with garlic toast or cornbread, a delicious chicken pot pie, or a bowl of chili with cubed sirloin and beans (from $5 to $14). Dinner entrees (for $10 to $19) include soup or salad, a fresh vegetable, and a baked potato or rice pilaf. Among the options are scampi, top sirloin, fried chicken, prime rib, or broiled scallops en brochette with bacon, mushroom caps, and onions. Seafood is really fresh, as evidenced by the orange roughy I ordered. Everything is truly delicious and, as I said before, portions are very large. Furthermore, instead of rolls, warm miniature loaves of bread are served. Service is also first-rate.

Billy Reed's only takes reservations for very large parties, so you may have to wait a bit for a table, but the estimated time for seating is remarkably accurate and the food is really worth a bit of patience.

Drink strengths are as generous as food portions. Wine choices are limited, but good.

The entire menu is served all day, every day (except major holidays), from 7 a.m. to 10:45 p.m. Weekdays an early-bird dinner is served from 3 to 6 p.m. for $8 to $10.

For Italian fare, another place to go is **Perrina's,** 340 N. Palm Canyon Dr., between Amado and Alejo Roads (tel. 619/325-6544). It's small, unpretentious, and the hangout of the sports crowd. Larry Perrina's wife and daughter carry on the service. Larry used to play baseball in the minor leagues, and one wall of the restaurant is lined with photos of sports figures who were friends of his. The specialty is veal—piccata, scaloppine, marsala, etc.—served with soup or salad and fresh vegetables, but there's lotsa pasta on the menu too: fettuccine Alfredo, manicotti, and linguine with garlic, olive oil, and anchovies—and the food is as good as ever. Meat dishes average $13 to $18; pasta runs $8 to $12. A side order of pasta with a regular entree is $2.

Perrina's is open daily for dinner from 5 to 11 p.m.

One of the really enjoyable eating experiences in Palm Springs is **Nate's Delicatessen and Restaurant** (also known as Mister Corned Beef of Palm Springs), 100 S. Indian Ave., at the corner of Tahquitz Way (tel. 619/325-3506). Unlike its New York, Los Angeles, or San Francisco deli counterparts, Nate's looks like a well-bred restaurant, but not to worry—it has all the great aromas of a super deli. Seating arrangements are very comfortable, and the modern, subdued decor is easy on the eyes. For entertainment, study the cartoons of character types on the walls—the maven, shiksa, feinshmacher; you're certain to find a few you know. The dining room is quiet even when crowded, and service is efficient, knowledgeable, and pleasant.

If you're a deli-lover, you'll want to eat your way through the entire menu. For breakfast, there are omelets in every conceivable combination: with salami, pastrami, corned beef, chopped liver, etc.; and then there are eggs with onions, with lox, whitefish—even grilled knackwurst. If you insist, there's always ham or bacon or sausage with eggs (no, this is not a kosher deli), french toast, or pancakes.

For lunch, there are sandwiches piled high with meats of your choice and served on Nate's hot rye bread (or whatever bread or roll you prefer), and a relish tray of kosher pickles and old-world sauerkraut. Corned beef, pastrami, chopped liver, tongue, salami, pepper beef, on down the list, are served in various combinations: a "1½ sandwich" includes one half each of chopped liver, pastrami, and corned beef, for example, and the "Fresser Sandwich" offers any combination of up to three items on three deckers. You want a salad? They have eight varieties. You have a taste for blintzes, a cold gefilte fish plate, potato pancakes, a knish? Nate's has those, too.

Save room for dinner. Nate's has a nine-course meal for $10.95 including the aforementioned relish tray and sauerkraut; an appetizer of juice or homemade chopped liver; soup or salad; entrees ranging from baked or fried chicken to corned beef, brisket or seafood catch of the day; a vegetable; potato; hot rye bread; dessert; and coffee. Or you might simply indulge a taste for boiled chicken "in the pot," with matzo ball, noodles, rice, and carrots accompanied by salad or appetizer and beverage. Nate's also serves a daily dinner special for $7.95 from 4 to 8:30 p.m.

Breakfast prices range from $3.50 to about $8.50, though some of the more baroque special combinations—say, a plate of lox *and* whitefish *and* cod *plus* two eggs with bagel and cream cheese—will raise the rate to $17.50. Luncheon sandwiches are in the range of $6 to $8; salads cost about $8. Dinner is a bargain at $8 to $11. Beer and wine are available.

Nate's is open daily from 8 a.m. to 8:30 p.m.

A real fixture on the Palm Springs eating scene is **Louise's Pantry,** 124 S. Palm Canyon Dr. (tel. 619/325-5124). It's a small place—just 52 seats—but it packs 'em in every day and night. It's easy to spot—just look for the long line out front that's always there.

Home-cooking is the order of the day. Louise's squeezes fresh orange juice daily, grinds their own beef, and bakes the sweet rolls, cornbread, pies, and cakes on the premises. Entrees include lamb shanks, chicken pot pie, roast turkey, baked ham, fried chicken, and leg of lamb. Stuffed bell peppers, chicken and dumplings, beefsteak pie, and roast beef are served daily. At lunch your special comes with soup or salad, and costs $3.75 to $4.75. At dinner you can eat your fill of soup, salad, roll, entree, and dessert for $7.50 to $9.50. Louise's Pantry may simply be described as providing good food that most everyone likes, all at moderate prices, plus very good service. Louise is no longer around to oversee the cooking and baking, but the current owner and staff still maintain the same exacting standards.

Louise's Pantry is open daily from 7 a.m. to 9:45 p.m.; it's closed every year from mid-June to the end of September.

Another pleasant restaurant in town is **Las Casuelas Terraza,** 222 S. Palm Canyon Dr. (tel. 619/325-2794). It's a charming Mexican place with white walls, archways, plants, and birds—some papier-mâché parrots and two real macaws. The waitresses wear Mexican peasant dresses, and a band plays in the bar. There are a number of separate dining areas, including two patios that look out on the action of Palm Canyon Drive. One even has a gently splashing fountain.

The food is as pleasant as the ambience. You can nibble on guacamole or nachos and sip a margarita while you decide on your meal. There are lots of entrees to choose from, including a chimichanga; chicken with avocado, melted cheese, and ranchero sauce; white fish filet with butter and toasted almonds; and a wide variety of combination platters served with rice and beans. They range in price from $10 to $19. Lunch is less expensive at $6 to $10. To finish off your meal there's an empañada apple pie, flan, and a variety of liqueur-laced coffees to choose from.

Las Casuelas Terraza is open daily from 11 a.m. to 10 p.m. for dinner (to midnight for drinks on Friday and Saturday). Reservations are advised.

There are two other Las Casuelas in the Palm Springs area: the original, at 368 N. Palm Canyon Dr. (tel. 619/325-3213), and the more formal Las Casuelas Nuevas at 70050 Hwy. 111, in Rancho Mirage (tel. 619/328-8844).

The last is larger than either of the other locations with a lovely 200-seat formal Spanish garden.

PALM SPRINGS NIGHTLIFE: The major star-studded disco in town is **Cecil's,** 1775 E. Palm Canyon Dr., corner of Sunrise Way (tel. 619/320-4202), complete with a posh supper club and backgammon room.

There's also the **Comedy Haven,** 123 N. Palm Canyon Dr. (tel. 619/322-6500, or 320-7855), located at Delmonico's Fish Market in the Desert Fashion Plaza. This comedy/improvisation supper club serves Italian cuisine as well as steaks, prime rib, and a variety of fish specialties. The food is excellent. Dinner is served from 7 p.m. If you're eating, the cover charge for the show is $6; without dinner, it's $8 plus a two-drink minimum. The show is from 9 to 10:30 p.m., with dancing afterwards. Off season (June through November), shows are on Friday and Saturday night; December through May, performances run Wednesday through Sunday.

FROM MALIBU TO NEWPORT BEACH

□ □ □

A visit to Southern California ideally includes a few days' retreat at one of the many beach resorts dotting the shore from Los Angeles to San Diego. But if you haven't the time for a relaxing seaside vacation, day trips to many of the areas listed below make for very pleasant excursions. You might want to explore the *Queen Mary* or *Spruce Goose,* both now permanently docked in Long Beach, browse through the shops at San Pedro's quaint Ports O'Call Village, take a cruise to cove-fringed Catalina Island and see the marine forest from a glass-bottom boat, or just laze in the sunshine at any of the sandy coastal beaches described below.

1. MALIBU

Just 25 miles from Los Angeles Civic Center, Malibu is the stretch of shore-line beginning at Topanga Canyon and extending westward along the Pacific Ocean (West Pacific Coast Highway 101-A) to the Ventura County line. Once a privately owned rancho (purchased for 10¢ an acre), Malibu is now a popular resort city and acreage has become infinitely more expensive. During the '20s the emerging movie colony flocked here, and Malibu was famous for wild parties and extravagant *Great Gatsby* lifestyles. There are still many famous residents, but they tend to keep a low profile.

ACTIVITIES: Malibu's beaches delight thousands of visitors every year who engage in every activity from nude sunbathing to grunion hunting. Boating is also a popular activity.

WHERE TO STAY: For such a wealthy community, Malibu is singularly lacking in glamorous accommodations. The reason is simple: the residents are comfortably ensconced in their own gorgeous houses, and they don't want their quiet retreat turned into a bustling tourist resort. Local ordinances are designed to work against such a contingency.

Best bet is the **Casa Malibu,** 22752 Pacific Coast Hwy., Malibu, CA 90265 (tel. 213/456-2219), a hacienda-style accommodation built around a palm-studded inner courtyard with cuppa d'oro vines growing up the balcony and well-tended flower beds. The 21 rooms are cheerful and attractively furnished—all with private balconies. Each is equipped with a shower bath, phone, oversize beds, and color TV. Singles or doubles cost $100 to $115 overlooking the water, $85 to $95 if fronting the patio or coastal highway. Each extra person in a room pays $10 (over two); rooms with kitchens can be rented for an extra $10 per day (five-day minimum rental).

What once was the **Tonga Lei Motel** and Don The Beachcomber is scheduled to be replaced in early 1989 by the new **Malibu Beach Inn,** at 22878 Pacific Coast Hwy., Malibu CA 90265 (tel. 213/456-6444), on the beach next to Malibu Pier. By the time you read this, Malibu's first all-new beachfront motel in some 37 years should be renting its all-oceanfront rooms with private balconies, color TV, VCR, phone, etc., for about $125 to $150 for singles and doubles, continental breakfast included. Suites will be available.

WHERE TO DINE: Repeat visitors to Malibu take note: **Alice's** has moved to Pacific Palisades, at the corner of Pacific Coast Hwy. (known locally as "PCH") and Sunset Blvd. (tel. 213/456-6646) in the Pacific Sunset Building. (For those of you unfamiliar with the area, Pacific Palisades is between Malibu and Santa Monica.) Alice's is a bit larger but continues to look pretty much as it always has—somewhat aged decor with touches of the fresh and new, including a patio. The very fine chef remains and the menu is still mostly seafood—as always, beautifully fresh.

Some of the great entrees are the shrimp scampi with fresh broccoli, the kettle of steamed clams, or the simple Malibu burger with potatoes. You might opt too for calamari dipped in cracker crumbs and a Creole rémoulade spiced with horseradish, tabasco, and Dijon mustard. And there's a superb tuna steak topped with an extraordinary cactus ratatouille. The best of the pastas usually include seafood—for example the linguine with scallops and smoked roe. For the light approach, an avocado filled with crab salad is an option. Omelets, burgers, and sandwiches cost $6 to $9; salads run $10 to $15; hot entrees, $15 to $30. The lunch menu is similar, though prices are slightly lower. Carrot cake makes a delicious dessert, but my personal favorite remains the caramel custard.

Alice's is open weekdays from 11:30 a.m. to 9 p.m., Saturday 11 a.m. to 10 p.m., and Sunday 10:30 a.m. to 10 p.m. Reservations are advised.

Carlos and Pepe's, 22706 Pacific Coast Hwy. (tel. 213/456-3105), is a delightful weathered-wood seacoast structure. Inside you'll find a few touches from south of the border, including papier-mâché banana trees at the bar, complete with tropical birds. The interior is designed so that each table has an ocean view. An immense aquarium filled with tropical fish separates the bar and dining areas. Best place to sit is on the plant-filled, glass-enclosed deck directly overlooking the ocean.

The menu features Mexican entrees, fresh seafood, and steak. A choice of fresh fish daily specials, including blackened swordfish and blackened Mahi Mahi, are $16 to $21; Alaskan King Crab legs go for $26. Such enjoyable dishes as chowder, steamed shrimp, or fried calamari with homemade coleslaw and sourdough bread are in the $3 to $9 range. A wide variety of Mexican dishes, including crab enchiladas, chimichangas (a burrito fried crisp), and "Carlos' Wild Tostada," cost $4 to $11. But the most popular here are fajitas, either steak or chicken, arriving hot from a skillet containing peppers, onions, and tomatoes, served with flour tortillas, guacamole, salsa cruda, lettuce, and beans. And there are also "Gringo Specials"—hamburgers, omelets, and steaks, for $7 to $15. For dessert, you might try delicious mud pie (chocolate), the deep-fried ice cream, or one of the great (uncooked) ice-cream flavors. A wide selection of wines and imported beers is available, and there's a well-stocked liquor bar. But above all, Carlos and Pepe's is famous for their delicious 16-ounce margaritas, made with fresh-squeezed juices.

Open daily from 11:30 a.m. to 2 a.m., they serve appetizers until 1:30 a.m. Meals are served till 11 p.m. Sunday to Thursday, till midnight on Friday and Saturday. No reservations.

La Scala Malibu, in the Malibu Country Mart, 3835 Cross Creek Rd., off Pacific Coast Hwy. (tel. 213/456-1979), is the venture of Jean Leon, whose ultra-chic Beverly Hills restaurants are hangouts for Jacqueline Bisset, Robert Wagner, and Suzanne Pleshette, among others. It looks very much like its Beverly Hills counterparts, with the same tufted red-leather booths, clutter of wine bottles, walls lined with gilt-framed oil paintings and Gerald Price caricatures, and displays of cheeses, desserts, hanging sausages, and gourmet fare. Curtained windows create a country feel. You can dine al fresco at La Scala Malibu under the shade of umbrella tables and a huge bougainvillea-covered eucalyptus tree.

Lunch at La Scala might begin with gazpacho, followed by fresh turkey salad with sliced tomato and hard-boiled egg, a cold plate of broiled chicken, smoked salmon with onions and capers, or a hot entree such as eggplant parmigiana or rigatoni Malibu, for $12 to $14. For dessert, try the homemade ice cream with fresh raspberries. Dinner begins with antipasti like steamed mussels and ratatouille niçoise, and continues with entrees such as spaghetti carbonara and veal piccata. Entrees cost $16 to $28.

La Scala Malibu is open for lunch Tuesday to Friday from 11:30 a.m. to 2:30 p.m., for dinner Tuesday through Thursday from 5:30 to 10:30 p.m., on Friday and Saturday from 5:30 to 11 p.m., Sunday to 10 p.m.

For leisurely breakfasts or lunches there's the **Sand Castle,** just off the pier at 28128 W. Pacific Coast Hwy. (tel. 213/457-2503). Housed in a gray shingled building, complete with weather vane and widow's walk, it's right on the beach and has a wall of windows overlooking the ocean. The interior is rustic with many nautical touches (ship-light chandeliers, rigging, etc.), and a big fireplace (ablaze at night) connects the restaurant and lounge. (The latter sees a lot of action on weekend nights).

Breakfast can be a big order of steak and eggs with hash browns or home-fries and hot buttered toast; an avocado, bacon, and jack cheese omelet; or butter-milk pancakes with bacon—each $6 to $10. Champagne brunch, served from 9 a.m. to 4 p.m. daily (till 2:30 p.m. on Sunday), comes with a glass of champagne and a choice of entrees—perhaps a seafood crêpe in Mornay sauce served with a fresh fruit cup. Lunch fare runs the gamut from a Monte Cristo sandwich to scallops sautéed in white wine, for $8 to $15. An excellent buy are the sunset dinners, served from 5 to 7 p.m. (4 to 7 p.m. on Sunday). For about $12 these include soup or salad and a choice of entrees—London broil au jus with whipped potatoes, chicken Ballottine with apple stuffing, beef Stroganoff, etc.

The Sand Castle is open daily for breakfast from 6 to noon, for lunch from 11 a.m. to 4 p.m., and for dinner from 5 to 10 p.m. (till 11 p.m. on Friday and Saturday). Reservations advised at dinner.

J. PAUL GETTY MUSEUM: The J. Paul Getty Museum, 17985 Pacific Coast Hwy. (tel. 213/458-2003), is a spectacular reconstruction of the Roman Villa dei Papiri, which was buried in volcanic mud when Mount Vesuvius erupted in A.D. 79, destroying Pompeii and Herculaneum. Set on ten acres, it houses the magnificent J. Paul Getty collection, which fittingly is strong on Greek and Roman antiquities. However, new collections include Medieval and Renaissance illuminated manuscripts, sculpture, and drawings (15th century to the end of the 19th), and 19th- and 20th-century European and American photographs. The museum is heralded by a colonnaded peristyle garden with a graceful reflecting pool and replicas of bronze statues found at the site of the original villa. Reproductions of ancient frescoes adorn the garden walls, and over 40 different types of marble were used in the halls and colonnades. In addition to the Greco-Roman pieces, the collection is also rich in Renaissance and baroque paintings from Europe and 18th-century decorative arts from France. Notable works include a 4th-century B.C. Greek sculpture, *The Victorious Athlete* (known as the Getty Bronze), possibly done by Lysippus, court sculptor to Alexander the Great; and an archaic Greek kouros (male nude youth), dating from 530 B.C.

The museum's decorative arts collection features 18th-century French furniture and tapestries. The painting galleries contain an extensive Italian Renaissance collection (including the only documented painting in the country by Masaccio) and a Flemish baroque collection, as well as several important French paintings by such artists as Georges de la Tour, Nicolas Poussin, Jacques-Louis David, Jean-Francois Millet, and Francois Boucher.

The Getty Museum is open Tuesday through Sunday from 10 a.m. to 5 p.m. (the gate closes at 4:30 p.m.), and there is no admission charge. Docent orientation lectures are given at the ocean end of the main peristyle garden every 15 minutes between 9:30 a.m. and 3:15 p.m.

Note: Because there are limited parking facilities, if you plan to come by car and park, *without exception* you must make a parking reservation 7 to 10 days in advance (by mail or by telephone). Visitors who do not have a car or who are unable to make parking reservations may enter the museum grounds by bicycle (racks are available), motorcycle, taxi, RTD bus #434 (please request a museum pass from the driver), or by being dropped at the gatehouse by car. No walk-in traffic is permitted with the exception of RTD bus passengers.

2. REDONDO BEACH

In the 1880s Redondo Beach was the largest shipping port between San Diego and San Francisco. With the decline of commercial shipping, it became—and still is—a modest beach resort, just a few minutes south of the Los Angeles International Airport.

The **Fisherman's Wharf** pier is a maze of architecturally attractive restaurants, over 50 shops, galleries, penny arcades, and fishing equipment outlets. Although the restaurants concentrate on seafood, there is also Japanese, Polynesian, and Mexican cuisine available.

For a complete rundown on Redondo Beach facilities, boating, sailing, and fishing trips, maps, brochures, etc., stop in at the **Redondo Beach Chamber of Commerce,** 1215 North Catalina Ave. (tel. 213/376-6911).

WHERE TO STAY: Every room at the **Portofino Inn,** 260 Portofino Way, Redondo Beach, CA 90277 (tel. 213/379-8481, or toll free 800/338-2993, 800/468-4292 in California), has a balcony overlooking the yacht harbor or ocean. And very nice rooms they are, most with grasspaper wall covering, about half with fully equipped kitchenettes, and some with nautical touches like headboards constructed of oars. All have color TV, radio, direct-dial phone, and tub/shower bath. Drinking and dining facilities include the Sea Bucket Restaurant, specializing in barbecued ribs and seafood, and the Oar Room Coffee Shop. An open-air heated swimming pool overlooks the ocean.

Rooms range from $95 to $130, single or double; $185 to $375, suites.

The Portofino Inn is within walking distance of some famous beaches, the historic Redondo Pier, and over 25 major restaurants. Guests have the benefit of free bicycle rentals as well as the facilities of a nearby Sports Center.

WHERE TO DINE: The Red Onion, 655 N. Harbor Dr. (tel. 213/376-8813), with its elaborate decor, is billed as a "Mexican Restaurant and Social Club." The ceiling is bamboo, an eclectic selection of chairs leans heavily to bamboo and rattan, ceiling fans whir slowly overhead, and photos of Mexico adorn the walls. Most tables afford a view of the harbor; there's an open brick-and-tile fireplace, attractive Persian carpeting, and ubiquitous foliage. A terrific bargain here is the Happy Hour, 4 to 8 p.m. on weekdays. Order a drink, and you can partake of an immense Mexican buffet—easily a full meal. However, if you should decide to dine at other hours, you'll find menu prices most reasonable, with hearty and delicious combination plates ranging from $9 to $13, and many, many à la carte items.

Open seven days from 11 a.m. to 2 a.m. Food is served until 11 p.m. on Friday and Saturday, till 10 p.m. all other nights.

3. SAN PEDRO

Farther down the beach, picturesque San Pedro, the bustling port of Los Angeles, handles an estimated two million tons of cargo every month. It definitely merits a day's visit, to see a little village-within-a-town created simply for tourists, which is nevertheless charming and fun.

PORTS O' CALL VILLAGE AND THE WHALER'S WHARF: Combining the atmosphere of old California with a 19th-century New Bedford whaling port, the wharf and village have over 80 international specialty shops and restaurants along winding cobblestone streets. Part of the fun is watching the steady stream of yachts, luxury liners, tankers, freighters, schooners, and sailboats cruise past.

The village itself achieves an Early California motif with Spanish colonial-style architecture, archways, wrought-iron enclosed balconies, and an abundance of bougainvillea vines and banana palms. Across a graceful bridge the elm-shaded brick lanes of the wharf evoke New England with shingle-roofed buildings, lantern lights, multipaned windows, and tavern signs. Throughout, there are strolling entertainers and musicians (occasional band concerts in summer), and the very browsable shops provide a dazzling display of imported international merchandise ranging from Philippine jewelry to Japanese gun-powder tea.

Buccaneer-Mardi Gras Cruises (tel. 213/548-1085) harbor tours leave daily at frequent intervals year round, and offer brunch, dinner, and afternoon cocktail cruises; from January to April **Ports O' Call Sportfishing** (tel. 213/547-9916) offers special whale-watching cruises as well. In addition, helicopter rides leave Whalers Wharf every few minutes for an aerial tour of the inner harbor area and Ports O'Call.

For meals, you can stop off at the **Ports O' Call Restaurant** at Berth 76 (tel. 213/833-3553); it's easy to spot because a red Chinese junk is moored in a pond near the footbridge to the entrance. The interior is nautical/Polynesian in motif. The menu features South Seas specialties like Java seafood curry and steak teriyaki, along with steak and seafood "mainland fare." Dinner entrees are priced at $14 to $22. Luncheon entrees are in the $9 to $14 range. The restaurant is open daily. Lunch, Monday through Saturday, is from 11 a.m. to 3 p.m.; dinner, Monday through Thursday from 4 to 11 p.m., Friday and Saturday to midnight; Sunday brunch is from 10 to 2:30 p.m., dinner from 4:30 to 10 p.m.

If, on the other hand, you're in a New England mood, head for the **Yankee**

Whaler Inn at Berth 75 (tel. 213/831-0181). Designed to look like a 19th-century waterside whaling inn, it has a weathered clapboard and shingle façade, and a quaint interior with several working fireplaces, curtained windows, and oil lamps on every table. Diners can sit indoors (most tables overlook the water) or outdoors on a brick terrace. Dinner offerings ($14 to $25) include a great New England clam bake for two with Maine lobster, shrimp, mussels, clams, red-skin potatoes, and corn on the cob.

Lunch is served Monday through Saturday from 11 a.m. to 3 p.m., on Sunday from 10 a.m. to 3 p.m.; dinner is from 4 to 10 p.m. weekdays, to 11 p.m. weekends.

To reach Ports O' Call, take the Harbor Freeway to the Harbor Boulevard off-ramp and turn right. The admission-free village and wharf (at Berth 77) are open daily from 11 a.m. to 9 p.m. in summer, till 7 p.m. the rest of the year (tel. 213/831-0287).

Near Ports O' Call is the **S.S. Princess Louise Restaurant,** Berth 94 under the Vincent Thomas Bridge in San Pedro (tel. 213/831-2351). Launched in 1921, the S.S. *Princess Louise* was called "The Queen of the Northern Seas," and traversed a route from Vancouver, British Columbia, to Skagway, Alaska. She was converted into a restaurant in 1966.

Lunches, at about $6 to $9, are available at the oyster and sandwich bar from 11 a.m. to 3 p.m. Dinners, in the $11 to $25 range, include soup or salad, an entree, and hot sourdough bread with whipped butter. Specialties include rack of lamb and fresh seafood. While dining, guests enjoy views of the busy harbor.

The *Princess Louise* is open for dinner from 5 to 10 p.m. Sunday through Thursday, to 11 p.m. on Friday and Saturday. Lunch is served daily.

To get to the S.S. *Princess Louise,* take the Harbor Freeway (Hwy. 11) south, get off at Harbor Boulevard, and follow the signs for Catalina.

4. LONG BEACH

Continuing south along the shore we come to Long Beach, the sixth-largest city in California, which does, in fact, offer a "long beach"—5½ miles of beckoning sand. It's also well equipped with tennis, golf, sailing, fishing, and boating facilities (departures from Pierpoint sport fishing landing and Belmont Pier), plus the picturesque **Seaport Village** shopping complex at the southeastern edge of the city.

But the principal attraction of this resort town is the **Queen Mary** (tel. 213/435-3511), docked at the terminus of Pier J (at the southern end of the Long Beach Freeway, Hwy. 710) since the completion of her final 14,500-mile journey around South America in 1967.

An imposing sight, her black hull and white superstructure a fifth of a mile long, and her three vermilion stacks jutting 150 feet into the air, the former Cunard liner has been inspected by more than ten million persons since the first paying customers trooped aboard. Tourists can explore the ship's engine rooms, boilers, turbines, and machinery; the aft steering station (an emergency facility); the elegant three-deck-high Grand Salon; re-creations of all classes of accommodations, and the contrasting GI quarters used when the *Queen Mary* transported 800,000 troops in World War II.

Next to the *Queen Mary,* under an aluminum geodesic dome, is Howard Hughes' famous World War II all-wood 200-ton seaplane, the **Spruce Goose.** It's the largest plane ever built—it had room for 750 troops—but flew only once. It's quite a big bird, with a wing-span (320 feet) that's longer than a football field.

A tour of the *Spruce Goose* affords you a look into the plane's cockpit and hold. You can also see a video of the plane's test flight. A special platform built adjacent to the *Goose* allows guests to see the cockpit, cargo area, and flight deck up close. Surrounding the mammoth plane are a variety of unique displays, and audio-visual presentations detailing the plane's construction, its one-and-only flight, and Howard Hughes' aviation career.

Tickets for the *Queen Mary* and the *Spruce Goose* combined cost $16.50 for adults, $10.50 for children 5 to 11 (under 5, free); seniors, $15. The sights are open from 9 a.m. to 9 p.m. daily from July 4 to Labor Day; otherwise from 10 a.m. to 6 p.m.; the ticket booth closes at 4 p.m.

Special exhibits include the ship's sound-and-light show in the Engine Room, re-enacting a near-collision at sea; in the wheelhouse, ship's officers relate the history of on-board communications—undoubtedly very important when it comes to "near-collisions." There's also an extensive World War II display depicting the *Queen*'s active role as a troop ship. And if you're at all interested in model-ship building, you'll find a fine exhibit in the Hall of Maritime Heritage.

While you're in Long Beach you can dine at one of the three restaurants on board the *Queen Mary*—all with views of the city's skyline and small-boat harbor—serving both lunch and dinner (tel. 213/435-5671 for reservations). The Promenade Café serves breakfast, lunch, and dinner, with a variety of entrees including English specialties such as prime rib and steak-and-mushroom pie. The Chelsea is open daily for lunch and dinner, and specializes in fish and seafood. The Sir Winston, a beautifully appointed room filled with Churchill memorabilia and offering a panoramic harbor view, serves continental cuisine (jackets and ties required for men). And as in former days, there are about 25 specialty shops on board and a chapel for "at sea" weddings.

Want to spend the night? The ship has been turned into the 390-room **Queen Mary Hotel** (tel. 213/435-3511, or toll free 800/421-3732). Many of the luxurious original furnishings remain, although modern conveniences— phones, air conditioning, color TV, etc.—have been added. Singles are $74 to $104; doubles, $90 to $130; suites, $175 to $650. Parking is $4.

5. CATALINA ISLAND

Relatively few tourists have seen this quaint, cove-fringed island just 22 miles off the Long Beach shoreline, yet Catalina offers scores of resort attractions. Crystal-clear water makes for excellent boating, fishing, swimming, scuba-diving, and snorkeling. There are miles of hiking and biking trails. The beautiful **Wrigley Memorial and Botanical Garden** is here. Camping, golf, tennis, and horseback-riding facilities abound. Big-band concerts in summer at the Catalina Casino, fabulous undersea gardens, and, finally, the picturesque town of Avalon (the island's only city), named for a passage in Tennyson's *Idylls of the King*, round out the Catalina scene.

So different is Catalina from Los Angeles in every way that it seems almost like a different country, remote and unspoiled. Separated from the mainland over half a million years ago, it evolved to meet its environmental challenges, and even today there is unique plantlife. Archeology has revealed that at one time in history a race of giants lived here, and as late as the 1600s Spanish explorers found a Stone Age culture on the island. After Sebastian Vizcaino visited the island in 1602 (searching for a pirate-free port for his treasure galleons), the islands were left in peace for about 150 years. But the sea otter, which was to play a large part in California history (see Chapter IV), was also to be the agent of the Catalina Indians' downfall when they were discovered in abundance in the area. In the early 1800s the island's native people and the sea otters were both wiped out by Russian fur hunters. It was, however, soon repopulated by pirates using its coves to store booty, plus cattle- and sheep-herders, and deported Orientals who hid here until they could be smuggled back to the mainland. Then in the 1860s a mining boom hit the island and lasted until Union troops put an end to the "gold rush" during the Civil War.

After that Catalina changed hands several times, finally beginning to take its present shape in 1892 when the Banning brothers bought it to develop as a fashionable pleasure resort. A fire wiped out the Bannings, however, and in 1915 they sold to William Wrigley, Jr., of chewing gum fame. During the '20s Wrigley brought the Chicago Cubs (he owned the team) to Catalina for spring training, and sportswriters helped publicize the island's romantic mystique. It became a favorite vacation spot of the wealthy and famous, with big-name bands playing in the Casino Ballroom (they still do) and yachts filling Avalon's harbor. This tourist boom was interrupted by World War II, when Catalina was an important military base.

Today Catalina is well enough known for all of its hotels to be fully booked months in advance (reserve early), but it is untouristy, a genuinely tranquil and charming island retreat. Ownership of 86% of the island by the Santa Catalina Island Conservancy has helped to preserve the island's natural resources.

The **Catalina Express** (tel. 213/519-1212, or toll free 800/257-2227 in California) operates regular service between San Pedro and Catalina year round. They make 13 daily round trips in summer, 7 in the fall, and 6 in the winter. Fares are $14 one way, $28 round trip, for adults; seniors pay $12 and $24; children pay $9 and $18; and babies under 2 cost $1. You can make your reservations by phone, and pick up your tickets at least 45 minutes before your departure. The *Catalina Express* leaves Berth 95 in San Pedro, next to the *Princess Louise* Restaurant. To get there from Los Angeles, take the Harbor Freeway (Hwy. 110) south to the Harbor Boulevard exit in San Pedro. Follow the Catalina signs across Harbor Boulevard into a large parking lot; the Catalina building is almost directly under the Vincent Thomas Bridge behind the parking lot.

Service from Redondo Beach should be starting up quite soon; call Catalina Express for information on schedules and fares.

Note: There are very specific baggage restrictions on the Catalina Express. Luggage is limited to 50 pounds per person. If you plan to camp, a camping permit can be obtained from L.A. County (tel. 213/510-0688) or Catalina Cover & Camp (tel. 213/510-0303). Reservations are necessary for bicycles, surfboards, dive tanks, etc. The U.S. Coast Guard prohibits carrying certain commodities on passenger vessels; if you have any questions about what you can take, call in advance. There are also restrictions on transporting domestic pets—again, ask.

Service to Catalina is also offered by **Catalina Cruises** (tel. 213/775-6111) in Long Beach and San Pedro at Berth 95, the **Catalina Passenger Service** in Newport Beach at the Balboa Pavilion (tel. 714/673-5245), **California Cruisin'** from San Diego (tel. 619/235-8600), and the **Helitrans Helicopter Service** in San Pedro at Berth 95 (tel. 213/548-1314).

When your boat arrives in Avalon, as soon as you've finished oohing and aahing over the breathtaking view, head for the **Catalina Chamber of Commerce** on the Green Pleasure Pier for maps, brochures, and information on island activities. You can also call them (tel. 213/510-1520) for information and direct lines to airlines, hotels, boat transport, or to find out about camping, hiking, fishing, boating, tennis, diving, golf, or horseback-riding facilities, or even inquire about the weather. For an extremely useful 48-page brochure, including a calendar of events, send $1 (for postage and handling) to the Catalina Chamber of Commerce, P.O. Box 217, Avalon, CA 90704.

SIGHTSEEING: The **Visitors' Information and Services Center,** on Crescent Avenue across from the Green Pleasure Pier (tel. 213/510-2000, or toll free

800/428-2566 in California), offers numerous island tours. (Ticket and information booths are also located at Island Plaza between Catalina and Sumner, and at the Green Pleasure Pier.) They include the **Skyline Drive** (one hour and 45 minutes) costing $9.25 for adults, $8 for seniors, $4 for children 5 to 11; and the **Avalon Scenic Tour** (50 minutes), priced at $4.25 for adults, $3.25 for seniors, and $2.75 for children. The three-hour **Inland Motor Tour** is one of the most interesting, much of it penetrating the 66 square miles of preserve owned by the Santa Catalina Island Conservancy. You'll see El Rancho Escondido where purebred Arabian horses are raised, and likely view buffalo, deer, goats, and boars. Price: $17 for adults, $13.50 for children. A 45-minute **Casino Tour** ($4.25 for adults, $3.75 for seniors, $3 for children) explores Catalina's most famous landmark.

Not-to-be-missed are: the 40-minute **Glass-Bottom Boat** trip to view Catalina's exquisite undersea gardens and colorful fish ($4 for adults, $3 for children); the 45-minute **Coastal Cruise** to Seal Rocks, where you'll see seals, and possibly sea lions, at play in their natural habitat ($3.75 for adults, $3 for children); and the one-hour **Flying Fish Boat Trip** ($5.25 for adults, $3 for children), during which an occasional flying fish even lands right on the boat!

There also are two lovely dining cruises. The **Sunset Buffet Cruise** (May through September) takes you aboard a historic paddle-wheeler along Catalina's coastline. Cocktails are served plus a scrumptious buffet. The **Twilight Dining at Two Harbors Cruise** (June through September) packages some of the nicest things about Catalina into one evening. The cruise makes its way along Catalina's coastline to dinner at the Harbor Reef, with a complimentary cocktail, music, and dancing, and a flying fish trip on the way home. The Sunset Buffet Cruise is on Wednesday, and Friday through Sunday; the Twilight Dining at Two Harbors Cruise is on Tuesday only. Both cruises are the same price: $29.50 for adults, $27 for seniors, and $15.50 for children.

And finally, should you wish to explore on your own, you can rent a U-Drive (like a cross between a Jeep and a golf cart) or bicycle (the former for licensed drivers only, the latter for those with good leg muscles) at any of a number of rental agencies on the Crescent and throughout Avalon. You cannot, however, penetrate the island's interior with either of these vehicles.

FOOD AND LODGING: In keeping with Catalina's untouristy image, the 30 or so hotels on the island, while all beautifully situated, maintain an almost pretentious unpretentiousness. Not only are there no big Hyatt, Hilton, Sheraton-type hotels—a factor I fully approve of—the existing hostelries seem, regrettably, to go out of their way not to be quaint or charming. However, to carp about decor is petty, since there's nary an eyesore on the entire island, and perhaps the refusal to cater to tourism is the reason. Charming or not, as I said before, the hotels tend to be fully booked in season, so reserve early.

The little **Hotel MacRae,** 409 Crescent, Avalon, CA 90704 (tel. 213/510-0246), is a pleasant, two-story hostelry right across from the beach. It's decorated in bright, cheerful colors—parrot green, orange, yellow, red, and white. There are 23 rooms here, with a wide range of accommodations. Each room has a private bathroom, black-and-white or color TV, and heater for chilly nights. A complimentary continental breakfast is offered every morning, and wine, cheese, and crackers are served in the evening. In the center of the hotel is a large, open courtyard, perfect for lounging or sunning.

Rates are $90 for a standard single or double room, $90 to $200 for suites. Kitchen units are available.

At the **Island Inn,** 125 Metropole (just half a block from Crescent), Avalon, CA 90704 (tel. 213/510-1623), innkeepers Martin and Bernadine Curtin have created the most attractive accommodations in town. The hotel's rooms are freshly painted pale blue-gray accented in peach set off by blue carpeting and blue and peach bedspreads. Shuttered windows, antique furnishings, and stained-glass lighting fixtures add further charm. All rooms have color TV and private baths (some with tubs all with showers); most also have AM/FM radio. The front desk will take phone messages, transportation is provided from the boat, complimentary coffee, juice, and a specialty bread are offered each morning, and there are ice and soda machines in the hall.

Rates for single or double occupancy are $85 to $145, $175 for a suite, all May to September. October to May, rooms are $30 less, excluding holidays.

Also on the beach, **Hotel Villa Portofino,** 111 Crescent, Avalon, CA 90704 (tel. 213/510-0555), has 34 rooms all newly redecorated. They are all equipped with dressing areas, private baths (stall showers), and color TVs; none has a phone. The adjoining Ristorante Villa Portofino has been remodeled and features northern Italian cuisine. A buffet Sunday brunch is featured during the summer.

Accommodations at the Villa Portofino $69 to $165 (higher rates on weekends), single or double; lower off-season.

The most superb views on the island are from the lofty **Zane Grey Pueblo Hotel,** P.O. Box 216 off Chimes Tower Road, Avalon, CA 90704 (tel. 213/510-0966). This Shangri-la mountain retreat is the former home of novelist Zane Grey, who spent his last 20 years in Avalon enjoying the isolation, the ocean view and harbor. He wrote many books here, including *Tales of Swordfish and Tuna,* which tells of his fishing adventures off Catalina Island. (The hotel has teak beams that the novelist brought from Tahiti on one of his fishing trips.) In another work, *What the Open Means to Me,* Grey described his ecstatic feelings about the island: "It is an environment that means enchantment to me. Sea and Mountain! Breeze and roar of Surf! Music of Birds! Solitude and Tranquility! A place for rest, dream, peace, sleep. I could write here and be at peace. . . ."

The hotel has a swimming pool/sundeck nestled in the mountains with chairs overlooking Avalon and the ocean, and most of the rooms also have large windows and ocean or mountain views. There's also a patio with "the view," and a fireplace lounge wherein is a TV and piano. All the rooms are being renovated with new furniture, new carpeting, ceiling fans, and other touches to make life more pleasurable. All rooms have private baths (mostly with showers) and no phones or TVs. Coffee is served all day, and there's a courtesy bus to town.

In summer rooms cost $75 to $105 for one or two people, including continental breakfast. Off-season rates are lower.

The **Catalina Canyon Hotel** (formerly the Paradise Island Inn), 888 Country Club Dr., Avalon, CA 90704 (tel. 213/510-0325, toll free 800/253-9361), is set on beautifully landscaped grounds in the foothills of Avalon. There are 80 guest rooms, tastefully decorated and comfortably furnished. All include a tub/shower bath, color TV, AM/FM radio, phone, and balcony overlooking the outdoor pool and Jacuzzi. The Canyon Restaurant is on the premises for breakfast and lunch, and offers a continental dinner menu. Room service is available. Cocktails may be enjoyed in the lounge or on the outdoor terrace overlooking the pool. The hotel is adjacent to a golf course and tennis courts. The hotel courtesy van meets guests at the air and sea terminals.

Rooms are $140 to $170, single or double, based on location and season, $10 for each additional person.

El Galleon, 411 Crescent (tel. 213/510-1188), is a large, warm, and woody nautical affair, complete with portholes, rigging, anchors, big wrought-iron chandeliers, oversize tufted-leather booths, and tables with red-leather-upholstered captain's chairs. There's additional balcony seating and outdoor café tables overlooking the ocean harbor. In summer, the luncheon menu offers fresh seafood, salads, and sandwiches. The dinner menu features many seafood items, like cioppino, fresh swordfish steak, and broiled Catalina lobster tails in drawn butter. There are also a number of nonseafood entrees, ranging from country fried chicken and beef Stroganoff to broiled rack of lamb with mint jelly. Dinner prices range from $12 to $24.

Open for lunch and dinner.

The Busy Bee, 306 Crescent, at the end of Metropole (tel. 213/510-1983), has been an Avalon institution for many years—since 1923, to be exact. In all those years it's undergone numerous changes, as witnessed by photos of its various incarnations on the wall of one dining area. The Busy Bee sits on the beach directly over the water. You can eat in several locations, including a lovely wraparound patio (perfect for summer lunches) with an indoor room furnished with ceiling fans, plants, and tables. Even from here you have a terrific view of the bay through picture windows.

The fare is light—deli style. Breakfast, lunch, and dinner are served all day. The day starts with omelets and other breakfast dishes for under $6. Throughout the day there are over 100 items to choose from; hot and cold sandwiches, salads, Mexican specialties, pasta, burgers, etc. Some of the more popular items are the Chinese chicken salad, Buffalo burger, and a one-pound hamburger that almost defies consumption. The Busy Bee grinds its own beef daily and cuts its own potatoes for french fries; salad dressings are also made on the premises. The tab for these tasty dishes ranges from $5 to $17.50. All this, plus the irrefutable fact that the Busy Bee is Avalon's only waterfront bar with a harbor view.

The Busy Bee is open daily from 8 a.m. to 10 p.m. in summer, to 11 p.m. on weekends; winter hours are 8 a.m. to 9 p.m. daily.

The Sand Trap, on Avalon Canyon Rd. (tel. 213/510-1349), on the way to Wrigley Botanical Gardens, is a local favorite and a great place to escape from Front Street crowds. They serve breakfast, lunch, and snacks from 7:30 a.m. to 3 p.m. The specialty is omelets, to be enjoyed while looking out over the golf courses.

6. NEWPORT BEACH

Newport Beach is a world-famous recreational resort—kind of an American Riviera. Once cattle-ranch land above an uncharted estuary, Newport is now a busy harbor town that embraces the delightful peninsula/island town of **Balboa.** The phenomenal growth of hotel and restaurant facilities in the last few years indicates that Newport Beach is fast becoming the most popular of Southern California's coastal towns between L.A. and San Diego. Many tourists now use it as a vacation base from which to visit Anaheim, Buena Park, and other Orange County attractions. Convenient bus tours are available—check at your hotel or the **Newport Beach Chamber of Commerce,** 1470 Jamboree Rd., at Santa Barbara Drive, Newport Beach, CA 92660 (tel. 714/644-8211); they're very helpful and some of the nicest people around.

ACTIVITIES: A major focus of activity in the area for nearly a century is a California historic landmark, the cupola-topped **Balboa Pavilion,** 400 Main St., which originally served as a bathhouse. Home of the **Tale of the Whale** seafood restaurant, the oldtime **Spouter Saloon,** and a country store, it is also the Newport departure point for boat service to Catalina, narrated cruises of Newport Harbor, whale-watching cruises, skiff rentals, and a large fleet of modern sport fishing boats. For cruise and charter information, call 714/673-5245; for sport fishing information, call 714/673-1434. At the pavilion you can take a ferry to

Balboa Island, the ride costing 85¢ for cars, 35¢ for adult passengers, and 25¢ for children ages 5 to 11.

The best way to see the bay is to buy a ticket for a narrated harbor cruise. In summer, the Catalina Passenger Service (tel. 714/673-5245) offers several trips daily leaving from the **Fun Zone Boat Co.** (tel. 714/673-0240) near the ferry landing. A 45-minute cruise costs $6 for adults, $5 for seniors, $1.50 for children under 12; under-5s, free.

You can also rent roller skates and bicycles here, right in front of the Balboa Inn.

Newport Beach, in California tradition, also has a waterfront complex of 40 restaurants and shops. Called **Lido Marina Village,** it's located at Via Lido, just south of Pacific Coast Hwy. off Newport Boulevard. A unique feature of this complex: about 8 of the establishments here sell yachts!

The **Newport Harbor Art Museum,** 850 San Clemente Rd., adjacent to Fashion Island and Newport Center, off Santa Barbara Drive (tel. 714/759-1122), merits a visit. The museum presents a varied schedule of exhibitions featuring 20th-century art from its collection of over 1,000 works, consisting predominantly of California paintings, sculpture, objets d'art, and photographs. The museum is open Tuesday through Friday from 10 a.m. to 5 p.m., Saturday to 6 p.m., Sunday from noon to 6 p.m.; closed Mondays. Admission is $4 for adults, $2 for children.

WHERE TO STAY: Located on 26 hilltop acres, **The Newporter Resort,** 1107 Jamboree Rd. (near Backbay Drive), Newport Beach, CA 92660 (tel. 714/644-1700 or toll free 800/341-1474, 800/422-4240 in California), is a resort complex par excellence, and an important hub of activity in this beach town. It's looking especially spiffy following a $25-million renovation. The John Wayne Tennis Club is on the premises, and guests can use its facilities for a reasonable fee; they include 16 championship courts (all lit for night play), spa equipment, steam/sauna, and a clubhouse. In addition, the hotel boasts three heated Olympic-size swimming pools, three whirlpools, and a children's pool. Guests can also use the facilities at the Newport Beach Country Club across the street, which include an 18-hole championship golf course. Three meals a day are offered in the Jamboree Café.

The 410 rooms are decorated in pastel tones with contemporary furnishings. All have balconies or lanai terraces with a view, plus air conditioning, direct-dial phone, color TV (with in-house movies), radio, and tub/shower bath.

Singles are $135 to $155; doubles, $155 to $175.

The 400-room **Newport Beach Marriott Hotel and Tennis Club,** 900 Newport Center Dr., Newport Beach, CA 92660 (tel. 714/640-4000, or toll free 800/228-9290), which opened its doors in April 1975, is my favorite Newport Beach accommodation. Built around a nine-story atrium—of which a 19th-century Italian Renaissance-style fountain is the focal point—the hotel was designed so that over 85% of the guest rooms would offer ocean views. The rooms are strikingly decorated with cheerful drapes and bedspreads. Most have balconies overlooking the fountain courtyard hung with ivy and bougainvillea. All are equipped with bedside remote-control color TV, radio, direct-dial phone, climate control, tub/shower bath, and a convenient amenity—an ironing board (irons on request). Two swimming and hydrotherapy pools are surrounded by a palm-lined sundeck. Ten tennis courts (eight of them night-lit) are on the premises (along with a pro shop and snackbar), as well as a health club, and there's golf at the adjoining Newport Beach Country Club's 18-hole course.

The Marriott has two restaurants: Nicole's Grill, serving continental and nouvelle cuisine in an elegant French provincial setting, and the cheerful indoor/outdoor Mediterranean-style Capriccio Café, serving crêpes and sandwiches.

Rates for single rooms are $165 to $175; twins and doubles are $180 to $190.

A month previous to the opening of the Marriott, a **Sheraton Newport** opened its doors at 4545 MacArthur Blvd. (at Birch Street), Newport Beach, CA 92660 (tel. 714/833-0570, or toll free 800/325-3535). The 342 rooms and five beautifully appointed suites are also centered around an atrium lobby, with ivy-draped balconies reaching upward to a skylight roof. Facilities include two night-lit tennis courts (no charge for courts), a heated swimming pool and Jacuzzi, and plenty of free parking. There are three restaurants: the Palm Garden, offering a steak-and-seafood menu at lunch and dinner; the Boardwalk Cafe, a garden-ambience eatery serving breakfast, lunch, and dinner; and the Palm Court, open for lunch only. The Reefwalker features live music for dancing Monday through Saturday nights.

Rooms are attractively color-coordinated in three different schemes—mauve, teal, and lavender. Furnishings are oak, with two leather armchairs in each room and every modern amenity.

The Sheraton charges $110 to $145 single, $120 to $155 double, including full buffet breakfast daily and an evening cocktail party. Packages are also available.

WHERE TO EAT: Best bets are branches of two favorite L.A. restaurants: **R.J.'s The Rib Joint**, at 4880 Campus Dr., off MacArthur (tel. 714/979-7427); and **Gladstone's 4 FISH**, at 900 Bayside Dr. (tel. 714/645-3474). See Chapter VIII for details.

For family dining (kids love it) consider the **Reuben E. Lee**, 151 E. Pacific Coast Hwy., near Bayside Drive (tel. 714/675-5790), a free-floating genuine replica of a famous 19th-century Mississippi riverboat, the *Robert E. Lee*. It's entered via canopied gangplanks, and the promenade decks are elegantly turn-of-the-century.

The restaurant specializes in fresh fish, shell fish, steaks, and chops, all prepared to perfection. A featured entree is the New Orleans bouillabaisse (a tasty concoction made with whole shrimps, lobsters, scallops, clams, fresh fish filet, and crabs' legs, all skillfully blended with tomato sauce and laced with wine). Other specials are the Captain's Platter for two with whole Maine lobster, beer-batter shrimp and fried oysters, a bouillabaisse with all sorts of seafood, and six combination platters. Steaks and chops come in all sizes and for all tastes. Dinner entrees cost $16 to $28. At lunch, sandwiches, salads, and hot entrees are in the $8 to $14 range. On Sunday the champagne brunch is not to be believed. There is a spectacular buffet: whatever you enjoy or have ever wanted for brunch is probably there, plus all the champagne you'd like, and a glass of Schnapps to boot. The spread is $17.95 for adults, $9.95 for children, and worth every penny.

The Sea Food Deck is open Monday to Thursday from 11 a.m. to 10 p.m., on Friday and Saturday to 11 p.m., on Sunday from 10 a.m. to 2:30 p.m. for brunch, to 10:15 p.m. for dinner. Reservations are advised.

The Cannery, 3010 Lafayette Ave., at Lido Park Drive (tel. 714/675-5777), is housed in a remodeled 1934 fish cannery which used to turn out 5,000 cases of swordfish and mackerel a day. Now it's a historical landmark. The two-story restaurant is a favorite spot for locals and tourists alike—for good food, a colorful atmosphere, and friendly service. In the upper lounge, tables surround a corner platform where there's live entertainment every night from 8:30 p.m. and on Sunday afternoon.

Fresh fish and local abalone are specialties here. At dinner there's always a super-fresh chef's special catch of the day. Other good choices are eastern beef, chicken teriyaki, and rack of lamb. Dinner entrees cost $14 to $28. At lunch you might ask for the house special of the day, shrimp and fries, or sandwiches and salads for $6 to $11. Sunday champagne brunch is popular at $13 to $16, depending on the entree you select. The restaurant also serves a champagne buffet brunch while you cruise Newport Harbor aboard the Cannery's *Isla Mujeres;* the cost is $27. There's a Sunday champagne supper cruise, also for $27.

Open Monday to Saturday for lunch from 11:30 a.m. to 3 p.m., on Sunday for brunch from 10 a.m. to 2:30 p.m., and for dinner nightly from 5 to 10 p.m. The seafood bar offers a limited menu until 1 a.m. Reservations are advised.

Chanteclair, 18912 MacArthur Blvd., opposite the Airport Terminal between Campus Drive and Douglas (tel. 714/752-8001), is designed like a provincial French inn. A rambling stucco structure with a mansard roof, built around a central garden court, it houses several dining and drinking areas: a grand and petit salon, a boudoir, a *bibliothèque,* a garden area with a skylight roof, and a hunting-lodge-like lounge. Furnished in antiques, it has five fireplaces.

The cuisine is continental. At lunch you might order double-ribbed lamb chops, creamed chicken in pastry, or steak tartare, for $10 to $12.

Dinner is an experience in fine dining—a worthwhile splurge, with entrees costing $19 to $30. You might begin with the house pâté de Strasbourg, or perhaps an order of beluga caviar with blinis and garniture (if you have to ask, you can't afford it). I'm also partial to the salads—a spinach salad flambé or hearts of palm. For an entree I recommend the rack of lamb served with a bouquetière of fresh vegetables and potatoes Dauphine. There's a considerable listing of domestic and imported wines to complement your meal; if you don't know what to select, the captain will be happy to help you choose. A soufflé Grand-Marnier is the perfect dessert, which should be ordered ahead.

Chanteclair is open for lunch weekdays from 11:30 a.m. to 2:30 p.m., for dinner nightly from 6 to 10 p.m. Reservations are essential.

Marrakesh, 1100 W. Coast Hwy., near Dover Drive (tel. 714/645-8384), is a variation on the theme of Dar Maghreb, a Moroccan restaurant previously described. The decor is exotic, with dining areas divided into intimate tents furnished with Persian carpets and authentic Moroccan pieces. Moroccan music enhances the exotic ambience. Seating is on low cushioned sofas, and the entire meal is eaten without silverware—you use your hands, and it's a remarkably sensual experience! It's something of a ritual feast, which begins, appropriately enough, when a server comes around to wash your hands. Everyone in your party shares the same meal—an eight- or nine-course feast priced at $18 to $25 per person. It consists of Moroccan soup, a tangy salad that is scooped up with hunks of fresh bread, b'stila (a chicken-filled pastry topped with cinnamon), or kotban (a lamb shish kebab marinated in olive oil, coriander, cumin, and garlic), a choice of four entrees (baked squab with rice and almonds, baked chicken with lemon and olives, baked fish in a piquant sauce, or rabbit in garlic sauce), lamb and vegetables with couscous, fresh fruits, tea, and Moroccan pastries.

Open for dinner from 6 to 10 p.m. Monday to Thursday, from 5:30 to 11 p.m. Friday to Sunday. Reservations suggested.

THE BOTTOM LINE: SAN DIEGO

□ □ □

California history began in San Diego with the arrival of Juan Cabrillo at Point Loma in 1542; later Father Junipero Serra established the first historic mission of El Camino Real here. The city's Spanish heritage is preserved in Old Town, a reconstruction of the first settlement, and the mission has been beautifully restored. Proximity to Mexico further enhances the Spanish flavor. But the most striking note in this coastal city is not its early California overtones. The predominant impression is water—seemingly endless vistas of the blue Pacific, of boat-filled harbors, quiet coves, and sparkling bays fringed with 70 miles of sandy shoreline beaches.

A couple of years ago San Diego was the third-largest city on the West Coast. But the numbers who came to look and decided to stay kept increasing, and today it's second in population. Now San Diegans (excluding the land developers) are beginning to wonder about the virtues of beauty.

San Diego is probably the best all-around vacation spot in the country, and blessed with the best climate. It's now the eighth-largest city in the U.S., though if you stood at its busiest corner you'd never know it. San Diego's secret is sunshine (most of the time), mild weather, soft winds, one of the most famous natural harbors in the world, and a very informal lifestyle. This adds up to sailing on Mission Bay or the Pacific; fishing, snorkeling, scuba-diving, and surfing (what else do you do with 70 miles of county waterfront); lots of golf (there are over 60 courses) and tennis, biking, jogging, sunbathing, even hang-gliding. Or you can just go fly a kite any day.

Mission Bay Park alone has 4,600 acres for boating and beachcombing. However, to save San Diego from being totally overrun by visitors, the Lord, in His infinite wisdom, gave the city an ocean cooled to a chilly average of 62°—

not exactly bathtub temperature for swimming, but not bad for surfers who wear wet suits (and who cares if you're fishing).

Then there's the surrounding territory. Within reasonable driving time you can be in the desert, the mountains, or even another country.

About 6,000 pleasure boats are moored in the San Diego Harbor and that's where the U.S. Navy berths the Pacific submarine fleet, along with an impressive collection of over 100 warships.

Many of San Diego's most popular attractions are discussed below; however, listings of entertainment happenings are best found in the Sunday edition of the *San Diego Union*, in the *La Jolla Light*, a weekly newspaper, and the *Reader*, a weekly tabloid appearing every Thursday with more about San Diego and what's happening than you'll ever need to know.

Every sport and activity connected with water is popular. Sport fishing in the ocean is among the finest on the Pacific coast. **H & M Landing**, 2803 Emerson St., Point Loma (tel. 619/222-1144), offers the largest variety of fishing and whale-watching excursions. Charter fishing boats also leave from **Islandia Sportfishing**, 1551 W. Mission Bay Dr. (tel. 619/222-1164), in Mission Bay. You can also fish (for no charge and with no license) off the **Ocean Beach Pier** (tel. 619/224-3359) at the foot of Niagara Street in Ocean Beach, and from the many city lakes (a daily recreation permit is required). For information on lake fishing, contact the **Lakes Recreation Section** of the San Diego Water Utilities Department (tel. 619/465-FISH). Sailing, scuba-diving, surfing, swimming, and waterskiing are equally popular, as are nonwater sports from tennis (about 100 public courts, not to mention those at hotels and country clubs) and golf (there's a choice of 68 excellent courses) to sky-diving. Less sportive types can opt for harbor cruises aboard **San Diego Harbor Excursions** sightseeing boats. One-and/or two-hour cruises depart daily from the foot of Broadway at Harbor Drive. For information call 619/234-4111.

Facilities are so abundant that I can't begin to list them here; see the "Information" entry in the "ABCs" section for some guidance on what to see and do.

1. GETTING AROUND

Finding your way around San Diego requires only that you have some sort of a map; almost any will do. Everything connects with everything else in a most sensible fashion. Then all that's required is a vehicle to transport you.

Forget about the bus system. You'll use up at least 50% of your time getting from point A to point B. Public transportation in San Diego is somewhat comparable to the public transportation in Los Angeles—only it runs less frequently. If you have no other way of getting around, pick up a map of the complete bus system downtown at the **Transit Store**, 449 Broadway (corner of Fifth Avenue). Maps for individual bus lines, indicating express and local stops, are also available there. The Transit Store is open from 8:30 a.m. to 5:30 p.m. Monday through Saturday, noon to 5:30 p.m. on Sunday. Express bus fare is $1.25, local fare is $1. If you need detailed information and can't make the trip downtown, call **San Diego Transit** at 619/233-3004.

There is the taxi alternative, but distances can be considerable and thus so can fares. If, for example, you want to go from La Jolla to the San Diego Zoo, the tab would be about $18 plus tip.

And so we come to the last option.

Car Rentals

Sights are so far apart in San Diego, you'll probably do best to find an unlimited-mileage arrangement, or at least one with sufficient free mileage to make your trip economical. On the freeways, those few "cents per mile" tend to mount rapidly into dollars.

As I pointed out in this discussion in Chapter I, my first words of advice are *plan ahead.*

See the "Traveling Within California" section for other precautions to take.

Car rentals of specific-size vehicles, including vans, are usually easier to obtain from the big rental-car companies. Each of the companies below has an office at Lindbergh Field, as well as offices throughout Greater San Diego: **Avis** (tel. 800/331-1212); **Budget** (tel. 800/527-0700); and **Hertz** (tel. 800/654-3131).

2. THE ABC'S OF SAN DIEGO

Although the city is by no means as difficult to negotiate as Los Angeles, San Diego presents its own set of confusions for the first-time—and repeat—visitor. These alphabetically arranged entries are designed to help resolve some basic information needs.

AIRLINES: Most of the major domestic carriers serve San Diego International Airport: **Alaska Airlines** (tel. 619/696-0101, or toll free 800/426-0333); **American** (tel. 619/232-4051, or toll free 800/433-7300); **Delta** (tel. 619/235-4344); **Eastern** (tel. 619/233-3047); **Northwest** (tel. 619/239-0488, or toll free 800/447-4747); **Piedmont** (tel. 800/251-5720); **Southwest** (tel. 619/232-1221, or toll free 800/531-5601); **Trans World Airlines** (tel. 619/295-7009, or toll free 800/221-2000); **United** (tel. 619/234-7171); and **USAir** (tel. 800/428-4322).

AIRPORTS: San Diego has one airport for commercial passenger service: **Lindbergh Field** (otherwise known as **San Diego International Airport**), just west of the San Diego Freeway (#5) at 3665 N. Harbor Dr. (tel. 619/231-7361). The airport is very convenient if you are staying west of #5 (for example, the Pacific Beach area, or La Jolla), if you're in the downtown area or if you're situated not too far east of #5—near Hotel Circle, say. The taxi fare from somewhere as far as La Jolla is not unreasonable. To get to the airport going south on #5, exit at Sassafras, continue south to Laurel, turn west on Laurel to Harbor Drive (stay in the right lane approaching Harbor Drive), and then turn north on Harbor Drive to the airport signs. To get to the airport going north on #5, exit at Brant (Hawthorn), go north on Brant to Laurel, and west on Laurel as above. A number of the larger hotels have shuttle service to the airport.

AREA CODES: The area code for San Diego is **619,** as it also is for Palm Springs.

BABYSITTERS: If you're staying at one of the larger hotels, the concierge can usually recommend organizations to call. Be sure to check on the hourly cost (which may vary depending on the day of the week and time of day), as well as on any additional expenses such as transportation and meals for the sitter.

BANKS: Banks are generally open from 10 a.m. to 3 p.m., often to 4 p.m., Monday through Friday. However, if you need to cash a check, your hotel may be your best resource, depending on the amount involved.

BUSES: The **Greyhound/Trailways Bus System** serves most cities in California. In San Diego, the main terminal is at 120 W. Broadway (tel. 619/239-9171).

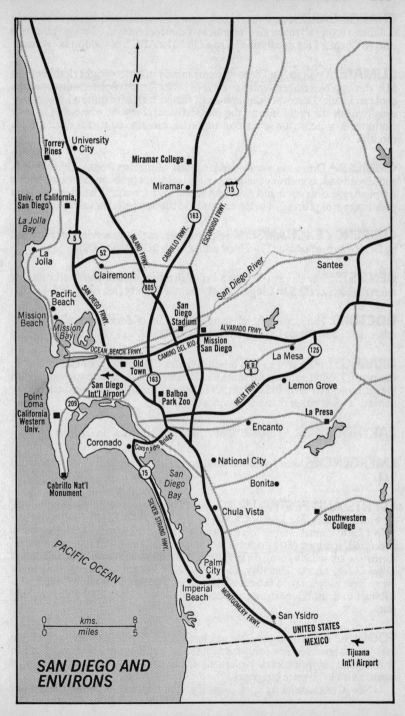

SAN DIEGO AND
ENVIRONS

CHARGE CARDS: As I've said before, not all restaurants, stores, or shops in California accept all major credit cards, and some accept none. I suggest that you turn to Chapter I for details on this topic in "The ABC'S of California" section.

CLIMATE: A visit to San Diego warrants mostly summer-weight clothing from May through November, with a sweater or jacket for the cool evenings or super-cool restaurant. December through April temperatures are quite a bit cooler— usually from the mid-fifties to the mid-sixties, and require somewhat warmer clothing. A raincoat, or at least an umbrella, can also be useful during these months.

CRIME: San Diego has a considerable influx of tourists from within the U.S. and abroad and, as with any such city, crime is always a problem. My best advice is simply to use discretion and common sense. Take traveler's checks, don't leave your luggage in plain sight in the car, and use the hotel safe for valuables.

CURRENCY EXCHANGE: Foreign currency exchange services are provided by **Deak International** at 177 Horton Plaza (tel. 619/235-0900).

DENTISTS: Hotels usually have a list of dentists, should you need one. For referrals, contact the **San Diego County Dental Society** (tel. 619/484-4795).

DOCTORS: Here, again, hotels usually have a list of doctors on call. For referrals, call the **San Diego County Medical Society** (tel. 619/565-8161).

DRIVING: I refer you to this heading under "The ABC'S of California" in Chapter I. I might add that for some inexplicable reason, the freeway signs in San Diego, more often than in Los Angeles or San Francisco, indicate direction by the name of a town rather than the compass direction.

EARTHQUAKES: Again, see "The ABC'S of California" in Chapter I.

EMERGENCIES: For police, fire, highway patrol, or medical emergencies, dial 911.

EVENTS AND FESTIVALS: The San Diego International Visitors Bureau, 11 Horton Plaza, San Diego, CA 92101 (tel. 619/236-1212), can supply you with a list of annual events. You can stop by or send the request, enclosing a self-addressed, stamped (50¢ postage) business-size envelope. An alternative for information on what's going on in a given week is the Sunday edition of the *San Diego Union,* or, on Thursday, the free weekly *Reader* which covers virtually everything happening in the county, in detail. The *Reader* is rather spottily distributed to delis, liquor stores, and convenience stores, but it's worth searching out.

FOOD: San Diego has a good, though limited, selection of restaurants; with rare exceptions, however, few compare with the best of those in Los Angeles or San Francisco at any price level. Nevertheless, I've tried to select some places well worth a visit in all price categories.

Not all restaurants are open daily. If you're planning an evening at one not listed here, call first and ask if reservations are necessary. Check to see if they take plastic. Not all of the restaurants do, and not all take every major credit card.

HOLIDAYS: Superbowl dates or the week of the America's Cup races are definitely not the times to try for reservations on short notice. If you have specific vacation dates in mind, send for the annual list of events in town at that time or call the Visitors Information Center—see the "Events and Festivals" entry, above.

HOSPITALS: To quickly locate a hospital near you turn to the "Community Access" pages at the front of the Pacific Bell *Yellow Pages*. You'll find a listing with locations superimposed on a map of the city. This is a very useful reference since San Diego is quite spread out and you probably won't know locations by address.

INFORMATION: The excellent **San Diego Convention and Visitors Bureau and International Visitors Information Center,** 11 Horton Plaza, at 1st Avenue and F Street (tel. 619/236-1212), is open daily from 8:30 a.m. to 5:30 p.m. It offers visitors to San Diego a one-stop service center (staffed by multilingual attendants) for information on hotels, entertainment and sightseeing, fishing licenses, and boating permits, as well as information about excursions to Mexico. For a recorded message about local events, call 619/239-9696.

A similar helpful service is offered by the **Visitor Information Center** at 2688 E. Mission Bay Dr. (tel. 619/276-8200), off Interstate 5 at the end of the Claremont-East Mission Bay Drive off-ramp. They're open from 9 a.m. to 6 p.m. (sometimes 5:30 p.m.) Monday through Saturday, to 4:30 p.m. on Sunday.

LIQUOR LAWS: Liquor and grocery stores can sell packaged alcoholic beverages between 6 a.m. and 2 a.m. Most restaurants, night clubs, and bars are licensed to serve alcoholic beverages during the same hours. The legal age for purchase and consumption is 21 and proof of age is required. In California some liquor stores accept credit cards for the purchase of package liquor; however, most have a minimum dollar amount for charging.

NEWSPAPERS: The *San Diego Union* (the morning paper) and the *San Diego Tribune* both have countywide distribution; however, the free weekly *Reader,* distributed each Thursday, gives comprehensive coverage on all special events (and some less than special) in greater detail. As noted in the "Events and Festivals" entry, distribution of the *Reader* is rather erratic; the paper is found primarily in delis, stationery stores, liquor stores, and convenience stores. It's definitely worth seeking out.

RELIGIOUS SERVICES: Places of worship are never in short supply in California, whatever the denomination. Should you be seeking out a house of worship, your hotel desk person, or bell captain, can usually direct you to the nearest church of most any denomination. If not, the Pacific Bell *Yellow Pages* can usually provide the location and, frequently, the times of the services.

SPORTS (SPECTATOR): San Diego has a major league baseball team—the **San Diego Padres** (tel. 619/283-4494); an NFL football team—the **San Diego Chargers** (tel. 619/563-8281, or 280-2111); and a professional soccer team— the **San Diego Sockers** (tel. 619/226-8212). The Padres and the Chargers play at Jack Murphy Stadium, 9449 Friars Rd., off Hwy. 805; the Sockers play at the Sports Arena, 3500 Sports Arena Blvd., west of #5.

For watching the sport of kings, there's the **Del Mar Race Track** (tel. 619/755-1141), at the Del Mar Fairgrounds west of #5. The Del Mar Racing season is for 60 days during the months of August and September.

STORE HOURS: Stores are usually open from 10 a.m. to 6 p.m. Monday through Saturday, often to 9 p.m. on Thursday; they're generally closed on Sundays.

TAXES: California state sales tax is 6%.

TRAINS: Amtrak has service north to Los Angeles, and from Los Angeles on to Oakland, Seattle, and points in-between. Amtrak also has daily service to Las Vegas. The station in San Diego is at 1050 Kettner Blvd. (tel. 800/872-7245), at the corner of Broadway.

USEFUL TELEPHONE NUMBERS: You can obtain **weather information** for San Diego at 289-1212, the **time** at 853-1212, and information on **local highway conditions** at 293-3484. For **nonemergency police service,** call 531-2000. Dial 411 for **directory assistance** and 800/555-1212 to obtain telephone numbers of establishments that have **toll-free numbers.**

3. THINGS TO DO AND SEE

In addition to the beach, a wealth of tourist attractions await the visitor to San Diego. We'll begin at the edge of downtown, at 1,400-acre—

BALBOA PARK: One of the nation's largest municipal parks, this one houses the San Diego Zoo and eight museums, including the Reuben H. Fleet Space Theater (about which more below). Inside the **California Building,** with its 100-bell carillon tower, is the **Museum of Man,** 1350 El Prado (tel. 619/239-2001), tracing the natural and cultural history of man; emphasis is on the native cultures of the Americas. Admission is $4 for adults, $1 for those 13 to 18, 25¢ for ages 6 to 12. It's open daily from 10 a.m. to 4:30 p.m.

The **International Aerospace Hall of Fame and San Diego Aerospace Museum,** 2001 Pan American Plaza (tel. 619/234-8291), is the home of the history of the great achievers of aviation and aerospace, and of a superb collection of historical aircraft and aviation and aerospace artifacts including art, models, military accoutrements, dioramas, and filmstrip displays. Heroes honored range from the early experimenters to the astronauts, and the planes, from the early gliders to spacecraft. Admission is $4.50 for adults and $1 for children under 17. Open daily from 10 a.m. to 4:30 p.m.

The **Natural History Museum,** on the east end of El Prado (tel. 619/232-3821), has a large number of exhibits of plants, animals, birds, fish, insects, fossils, and minerals of the Southwest. Admission is $4 for adults, $1 for students 6 through 17. Open daily from 10 a.m. to 4:30 p.m.

Along the north side of El Prado is the **Timken Gallery** (tel. 619/239-5548), which houses works of many old masters, such as Boucher, Rembrandt, and Brueghel. The gallery also exhibits a rare collection of Russian icons and 19th-century American paintings. Admission is free. Hours are Tuesday through Saturday from 10 a.m. to 4:30 p.m., on Sunday from 1:30 to 4:30 p.m. The gallery is closed during September.

The **San Diego Museum of Art,** 1450 El Prado (tel. 619/232-7931) contains an impressive collection of painting and sculpture, as well as old masters; it also offers noteworthy traveling exhibits. Admission is $4 for adults, $3 for those over 65, $2 for children 13 to 18; ages 6 to 12 pay $1. Admission is free the first

Tuesday of each month. It's open Tuesday to Sunday from 10 a.m. to 4:30 p.m. Outside the gallery is a café and a small but beautifully designed sculpture garden including, among others, works by Henry Moore and Jacques Lipchitz.

The **Hall of Champions,** 1649 El Prado in the Casa de Balboa (tel. 619/234-4542), honors San Diego's athletes who have achieved national or world recognition in sports, among them Bill Walton and Maureen "Little Mo" Connolly. The theater runs sports films throughout the day. Admission is $3 for adults; $1 for seniors, students, and military with ID; 50¢ for children 6 to 17; under 6, free. Hours are 10 a.m. to 4:30 p.m. Monday to Saturday, and noon to 5 p.m. on Sunday.

THE REUBEN H. FLEET SPACE THEATER AND SCIENCE CENTER:

The largest theater/planetarium in the United States, and the first in the world to have a tilted hemisphere screen, the Reuben H. Fleet Space Theater uses the most modern techniques, sophisticated effects and equipment to give simulated journeys an incredible feeling of reality. In addition to space-tripping, the giant dome is the setting for thrilling travelogues and voyages under the sea and inside a volcano.

Several other such films have included the story of *Niagara, Water and Man,* and, at the Laserium, *Moon Rock,* and *Laser Rockets.* (Children under 5 are not permitted in the laser shows.) One historic film shown here was *Hail Columbia!,* which traced the trip of the space shuttle *Columbia* from hangar to launch, through space, and back to earth at Edwards Air Force Base in California. It includes shots of earth from space and of astronauts working in zero gravity. The launch coverage is spectacular, as the camera is able to follow the craft farther into space than the human eye can see.

Adjoining the theater is the 8,000-square-foot Science Center, with more than 30 visitor-participation exhibits that beep, blink, float, whisper, and reveal, to make science come alive for visitors of all ages. This is no "hands-off" museum. Here you can match wits with a computerized teaching machine, compete in electronic tic-tac-toe, create designs with sand pendulums, or examine the iris and pupil of your own eye.

The Space Theater is located in Balboa Park two blocks from the Zoo and just across from the Natural History Museum.

Admission to the Science Center is $2 for adults, $1 for juniors ages 5 to 15. Admission to the Space Theater/Laserium varies according to show, from $5.50 to $6 for adults and $3 to $4 for juniors. And, again, children under 5 are not admitted to the laser shows. The building is open daily from 9:30 a.m. to 9:30 p.m. For recorded information on shows and times, call 238-1168; otherwise 238-1233.

San Diego Zoo

One of the most exotic collections of wild animals in the world—over 3,200 of them—lives at the San Diego Zoo in Balboa Park. Set in a lavishly planted 100-acre tropical garden, the zoo is famous for its rare and exotic species: cuddly koalas, long-billed kiwis, wild Przewalski's horses from Mongolia, pygmy chimps, and Galápagos tortoises. Of course, the usual lions, elephants, giraffes, and tigers are present too, not to mention a great number of tropical birds. Most of the animals are housed in barless moated enclosures that resemble their natural habitats. A recent addition to the zoo is the simulated rain forest home of the Sumatran tigers.

A 40-minute guided bus tour provides an overview ($3 for adults, $2.50 for kids 3 to 15). Alternatively, you can get an aerial perspective via the **Skyfari Tramway** ($2 for adults, $1.50 for kids under 16).

The **Children's Zoo** is scaled to a youngster's viewpoint. There's a nursery with baby animals and a petting area where kids can cuddle up to sheep, goats, etc. Admission is 50¢; kids under 3, free.

Admission to the zoo is $10.50 for adults; children 3 to 15 pay $2.50. From July to Labor Day the hours are 9 a.m. to 5 p.m. Between Labor Day and the end of June the zoo closes at 4 p.m. For further information, call 619/234-3153 or 231-1515.

WILD ANIMAL PARK: A sister institution of the San Diego Zoo, Wild Animal Park, 30 miles north of downtown San Diego via Interstate 15 and Rancho Parkway, is an 1,800-acre wildlife preserve dedicated to the preservation of endangered species. Some 2,500 animals from Asia, Latin America, Australia, and Africa roam freely in natural habitats, and about 2,000 birds are housed in an immense aviary and other areas of the park. You can lead your own safari along the 1¼-mile **Kilimanjaro Hiking Trail,** which offers many good spots for photographing animals; or explore a jungle biome (a natural habitat complete with tropical plants) in **Tropical Asia.** Both of these attractions are in **Nairobi Village,** a 17-acre complex of native huts, with a Gorilla Grotto, waterfowl lagoon, petting area, gift shop, and animal shows. In addition, there's the five-mile **Wgasa Bush Line Monorail Tour,** a "train" safari through sweeping savannas and veldts, with ample stops for viewing. There are also four amphitheaters where you can see animal shows, plus several restaurants, gift shops, and exotic botanical displays.

The Wild Animal Park is open daily from 9 a.m. to 6 p.m. Monday through Thursday, to 8 p.m. Friday through Sunday in summer, closing at various earlier hours (4 or 5 p.m.) the rest of the year. An adult ticket package costs $14.95 and includes admission, shows, and the monorail tour; those ages 3 to 15 pay $8.95. Parking is $2. Call 619/747-8702 for further information.

SEA WORLD: Mission Bay Park, just north of downtown San Diego on Rte. 5, is a multimillion-dollar aquatic playground with 4,600 acres of land and water area and facilities for every kind of water sport—sailing, boating, waterskiing, fishing, swimming, etc. But its main attraction is Sea World, a 135-acre marine zoological park and family entertainment center where the performers are dolphins, killer whales, otters, sea lions, even a performing walrus, and seals.

Seven shows are presented continuously throughout the day—Shamu, the 7,000-pound killer whale, does high jumps and back flips in the 6-million gallon aquarium at Shamu Stadium; sea lions explore a "Spooky Kooky Castle"; high-flying dolphins and two species of small whales perform in "New Friends"; world-class skateboarders and BMX bike riders do their thing in "City Streets"; and thrilling high-diving and comedy are part of "Muscle Beach."

Cap'n Kids World, a nautically themed playground, is (you guessed it) for kids. Other exhibits range from a whale and dolphin petting pool (adults can participate) to one of the largest collections of waterfowl in the world. Rounding out the bill are shops, band performances, costumed characters (most are part of the Sea World show), rides, and a wide choice of eateries.

One price ($19.95 for adults, $13.95 for seniors, $12.95 for children 3 to 11, free for under-3s) admits you to all shows and exhibits. Sea World is open daily from 9 a.m. to dusk, with extended hours during summer and holiday periods when there may be special entertainment, musical groups, or even a spectacu lar fireworks display. Allow a full day (about 8 hours) to see all the shows and exhibits; you'll enjoy it. Parking is free.

CABRILLO NATIONAL MONUMENT: Commemorating the discovery of the west coast of the United States by European man in 1542 are a statue of Juan Rodrigues Cabrillo, an exhibit room, and audio-visual programs that tell his story, located in a park at the southern tip of Point Loma (take Hwy. 209). Nearby is the restored **Old Point Loma Lighthouse.** From the tower, visitors have a sweeping vista of the ocean, bays, islands, mountains, valleys, and plains that comprise the area, and from mid-December to February it's a terrific vantage point for watching the migration of the gray whales (a tape-recorded message and audio-visual programs discuss the migrations). Also, stop at the visitor center (tel. 619/557-5450) on the premises to learn about Cabrillo whales, tidepools, and other aspects of the park. It's open daily from 9 a.m. to 5:15 p.m. (to sunset in summer). Admission is $3 per private vehicle, or $1 per person in commercial vehicles.

MISSION SAN DIEGO DE ALCALA: While you're experiencing early California history, a visit to the first of Father Serra's missions, at 10818 San Diego Mission Rd. (tel. 619/281-8449), takes you back to 1769 with a museum of liturgical robes, books, and other relics. Open daily from 9 a.m. to 5 p.m. A $1 donation is requested. Continue your historic explorations at—

OLD TOWN: The spirit of the founding of California is captured in the six-block area northwest of downtown San Diego called Old Town. Although the Old Town was abandoned over a century ago for a more convenient business center near the bay, it has regained interest—this time as a State Historic Park. The park is bounded by Congress, Twiggs, Juan, and Wallace Streets. Many of its buildings have been fully restored and are open to the public. In addition, there are shops, restaurants, art galleries, antique and curio shops, and handcraft centers, including a complex called **Bazaar del Mundo,** on Juan Street, a modern version of a Mexican street market.

Among the historic buildings which have been reconstructed are the magnificent **Casa de Estudillo,** the **Machado/Stewart Adobe,** the **San Diego Union newspaper office,** the old one-room **Mason Street schoolhouse,** and the stables from which Alfred Seeley ran his San Diego–Los Angeles stagecoach line.

Just outside the boundary of the park are the "haunted" two-story **Whaley House,** once the focal point of high society, and **La Casa de Juan Francisco Lopez,** 3890 Twiggs St., which now houses a candle shop.

There are three large parking areas at the entrance to the park, right next to the **Visitors Information Center** at 2654 San Diego Ave. (tel. 237-6770), open 9 a.m. to 5 p.m. Here you can get maps and tour information. The Historical Society offers free one-hour guided walking tours daily at 2 p.m.

Old Town is reached from Interstates 8 or 5. Take the Old Town Avenue exit off I-5 or the Taylor Street exit from I-8.

Adjacent to Old Town is **Heritage Park,** where old Victorian buildings built between 1850 and 1865 have been moved, restored, and preserved.

THE MARITIME MUSEUM: Located at 1306 N. Harbor Dr. (tel. 619/234-9153), this is a nautical museum that consists of three restored historic vessels docked at the Embarcadero, downtown. They are the *Berkeley,* the first successful propeller-driven ferry on the Pacific coast, launched in 1898 (she participated in the evacuation of San Francisco following the great earthquake and fire of 1906); the *Medea,* a steam yacht built in Scotland in 1904 (she fought in both world wars); and the *Star of India,* the oldest square-rigged merchant vessel still afloat, launched in 1863.

You can purchase a boarding pass good for all three ships: $6 for adults, $5 for ages 13 to 17 and seniors, $1.50 for children under 12. Open daily from 9 a.m. to 8 p.m. including a museum gift shop.

SEAPORT VILLAGE: One of San Diego's centers for shopping and dining is Seaport Village, 849 W. Harbor Dr., at Pacific Hwy. (tel. 619/235-4013). It is easily reached by following Harbor Drive south from the Maritime Museum.

The 22-acre complex is beautifully landscaped and has more than 70 shops including galleries and boutiques selling handcrafted gifts, collectibles, and many imported items. Two of my favorite shops are **Hug-A-Bear** (tel. 619/230-1362), with a selection of plush bears and woodland animals; and the **Seaport Kite Shop** (tel. 619/232-2268), with kites from around the world. I also enjoy the **Upstart Crow & Co.** (tel. 619/232-4855), a delightful combination bookstore and coffeehouse.

The restaurants in and near Seaport Village run the gamut from take-out stands to a Mexican bakery and more conventional facilities. The **Harbor House,** at 831 W. Harbor Dr. (tel. 619/232-1141), offers good seafood with a pleasant view.

Adding to the charm of the area are the three plazas that re-create an eastern seaport village, Victorian San Francisco, and a traditional Mexican village.

4. WHERE TO STAY

The hotel setup in San Diego subdivides into several areas where hotels are clustered. They are as follows:

DOWNTOWN: The **Westgate,** 1055 Second Ave. (between Broadway and C Street), San Diego, CA 92101 (tel. 619/238-1818, or toll free 800/221-3802), is a luxury hostelry of the first order. The tone is set as soon as you set foot in the posh lobby, hung with Aubusson and Beauvais tapestries and furnished in priceless antiques. The pattern of the parquet floors is copied from that at Fontainebleu, and the carpets on it are Kermin Oriental. Among the works of art, *The Prodigal Son* by Velásquez is valued at half a million dollars.

Each of the 225 spacious guest rooms is uniquely furnished, although the basic decor combines elements of Louis XV, Louis XVI, Georgian, and English Regency periods. All rooms have a phone and a scale in the bath; the color TV is discreetly hidden in an elegant cabinet.

Le Fontainebleu, the Westgate's award-winning restaurant, has been called "the most elegant dining room built in this century." It should come as no surprise that the cuisine is continental; the Westgate Dining Room (off the lobby), on the other hand, serves traditional American fare. The Fontainebleau is open weekdays for lunch from 11:45 a.m. to 2 p.m.; dinner from 6:30 to 10 p.m., except Friday and Saturday when dinner is served from 6 p.m. (dinner entrees run about $22 to $35). The Westgate Dining Room is open nightly for dinner from 6 to 11 p.m. Across from the Westgate Dining Room, the intimate Plaza Lounge is also open daily; it's a local gathering spot for many of San Diego's most talented performers.

Rates are $120 to $140 for singles, $130 to $150 for doubles or twins. Suites begin at $290.

HOTEL CIRCLE: Mission Valley is the most centrally located resort area in San Diego. Around its Hotel Circle are many restaurants, motels, hotels, and the largest shopping complex in the country, Fashion Valley Center. Recommended in Hotel Circle are:

Fabulous Inn, 2485 Hotel Circle Pl., San Diego, CA 92108 (tel. 619/291-7700, or toll free 800/824-0950, 800/647-1903 in California), is a moderately priced, modern four-story, 178-room complex at the extreme western end of the Circle. All rooms are large and attractively furnished; they have balconies, king- or queen-size beds, color TV, air conditioning, bath with phone, dressing area, direct-dial phones, and some with refrigerators. A heated outdoor swimming pool and Jacuzzi are on the premises, and a restaurant adjoins. There are good tennis facilities just across the street, as well as an 11-hole golf course (that's what I said, 11 holes), and another restaurant.

The Fabulous Inn is almost at the intersection of two major freeways—#8 and #5—so you can reach almost any area of San Diego within a reasonable amount of time.

Singles are $55 to $72, doubles $72 to $82; rooms with double-doubles or king-size beds, $75 to $85. Suites are $185 to $260.

Town & Country, 500 W. Hotel Circle North, San Diego, CA 92108 (tel. 619/291-7131, or toll free 800/854-2608, 800/542-6082 in California), with over 1,000 rooms one of the largest hotels in San Diego, is a "city within a city" with seemingly every facility you could want or imagine—even a gas station. There are shops, car-rental, airline, and tour information desks, shuttle service to the airport and shopping, four swimming pools (one Olympic size), a therapy pool, sauna, four restaurants, two coffeeshops, a disco, and two nightclubs. In addition, guests can use the Atlas Health Club across the street for a nominal fee. Club facilities include racquetball and tennis courts, weight and aerobics rooms, massage therapists, an outdoor lap pool, and an indoor whirlpool spa.

When it comes to good food and drink, the Town & Country offers a world of variety with its four restaurants plus the Lanai Coffee Shop and Sunshine Deli. The Gourmet Room, featuring mouth-watering prime rib; Bonacci's, offering zesty Italian dishes; Kelly's Steak House serving guess what; and Cafe Potpourri all make dining a pleasure at Town & Country.

Entertainment ranges from the unbounded energy of Crystal T's Live to the simplicity of the piano bar at Kelly's and the live bands and good-hearted imbibing in the Abilene Country Saloon and Le Pavillon Lounge.

Needless to say, the rooms are pleasantly decorated and have every amenity as well, including color TV and weekday newspaper delivery.

Singles are $77 to $120, doubles and twins are $97 to $145, and parlour suites go for $195 to $385.

Under the same ownership is the 426-room **Hanalei Hotel,** 2270 Hotel Circle, San Diego, CA 92108 (tel. 619/297-1101, or toll free 800/854-2608). The hotel has an eight-story open atrium with waterfalls and ponds; glass elevators give you a splendid view on the way up to the 450 rooms. Appointments and facilities are similar to those at Town & Country. There's dining in the Polynesian Islands Dining Room, the Peacock, and the Oyster Bar. You can work out in the pool, relax in the Jacuzzi, or play golf or tennis. Guests can also use the Atlas Health Club for a nominal fee.

Single rooms are $70 to $85; doubles and twins, $80 to $97.

There's a convenient **Motel 6** at 2424 Hotel Circle North, San Diego, CA

92108 (tel. 619/296-1612). As with all Motel 6 locations, rooms are efficient, clean, and comfortable, and there's a small pool on the premises. Rooms have free television, air conditioning, and now phones—no charge for local calls. The room rate is $29.95 for one person, $6 for each additional adult.

MISSION BAY: The **Bahia Resort Hotel,** 998 W. Mission Bay Dr., San Diego, CA 92109 (tel. 619/488-0551, or toll free 800/821-3619, 800/542-6010 in California), has a lovely situation on the peninsula of Mission Bay, with marine views in every direction. Sailboats and paddle boats are rentable at the Bahia dock, and there's an Olympic-size swimming pool, a therapy bath, and two tennis courts.

The rooms are pleasant and airy, furnished in modern motif. Each has a picture window (most with water views), color TV, direct-dial phone, and tub/shower bath with dressing area. About half the rooms have kitchens and balconies or patios.

Off the cozy fireplace lobby is a coffeeshop serving breakfast, lunch, and dinner. The world's oldest Mercedes, built in 1902, sets the theme in the continental dining room and cocktail lounge. Virtually a Mercedes museum, the restaurant features Mercedes-logo carpeting, plus Mercedes posters and drawings of antique models on the walls. Adjacent is the Mercedes lounge, which offers live entertainment nightly.

One other unique offering of the Bahia is a pond containing four resident seals.

Rates for one or two persons during the summer are $104 to $195, single or double. They're less the rest of the year.

The **Catamaran,** 3999 Mission Blvd., San Diego, CA 92109 (tel. 619/488-1081), is beautifully situated on Mission Bay, just a scenic, few-minute walk from the ocean. The hotel has 275 rooms, a new Atoll Restaurant, the Cannibal Lounge with live entertainment, and Moray's—a small piano bar. Rates are $100 to $170, single or double.

The San Diego Princess, a Princess Cruises resort (formerly Vacation Village), 1404 West Vacation Rd., San Diego, CA 92109 (tel. 619/274-4630, or toll free 800/542-6275), offers 449 modern rooms situated on 43 lushly landscaped tropical acres, with freshwater lagoons spanned by graceful bridges. Each of the modern rooms is equipped with every up-to-date amenity as well as a patio or lanai, dressing area, in-room coffee maker, and refrigerator.

Facilities include five swimming pools, eight tennis courts, a sailboat marina, a bicycle rental outlet, three restaurants—the Dockside Broiler (very good for steaks and seafood), the Polynesian Princess, and the Village Cafe (coffee shop)—a cocktail lounge, and a mile of white sand beach.

Rates are $130 to $150, single or double occupancy.

A sternwheeler called the *Bahia Belle* cruises the bay, running hourly in summer (less often in winter) and stopping at the Bahia, the Catamaran, and The San Diego Princess. At night there's dancing to live music and cocktails aboard the *Belle;* fare is $7 per adult, $5 for children under 12.

HARBOR ISLAND AND SHELTER ISLAND: These two man-made peninsulas—just minutes from the airport and downtown—are a hub of San Diego hotel, nightlife, and restaurant activity.

The former contains the **Sheraton on Harbor Island** (tel. toll free 800/325-3535), actually a complex of two hotels, the **Sheraton Harbor Island East,** 1380 Harbor Island Dr., San Diego, CA 92113 (tel. 619/291-2900), and **Sheraton Grand on Harbor Island (West),** 1590 Harbor Island Dr., San Diego, CA 92101 (tel. 619/291-6400). The properties boast a total of 1,100 handsomely furnished rooms, complete with color TVs, direct-dial phones, individual air conditioning, and king-size or double-double beds. All rooms have balconies and most have marine views.

The facilities at the Sheraton on Harbor Island are extensive: health club, five pools (two for kids), saunas, whirlpools, four night-lit tennis courts, jogging course, boat and bike rental, shops, and laundromat. There are a variety of dining choices too: Sheppard's (at the East), a gourmet restaurant; Spencers (at the West), specializing in Black Angus beef; and the Café del Sol (in the East), a coffeeshop. There's also Reflections (in the East), an elegant entertainment lounge.

Rooms at the Sheraton Grand on Harbor Island cost $128 to $160 single, $143 to $175 double. At the Sheraton Harbor Island East, singles are $120 to $155; doubles, $135 to $170.

A favorite accommodation, not just on Shelter Island but in all of San Diego, is **Humphrey's Half Moon Inn,** 2303 Shelter Island Dr., San Diego, CA 92106 (tel. 619/224-3411, or toll free 800/542-7401, 800/542-7400 in California). It offers 141 rooms, all with water views and set amid lush tropical plantings. Not only are the views lovely, but the interior of each room is very attractive, with beamed pine ceilings (especially nice on upper floors where ceilings are sloped), bamboo and rattan furnishings, and blue seashell-motif bedspreads. Amenities include double sinks and makeup lights in the bath, direct-dial phones, color TVs, etc. There's also free in-room coffee, 24-hour switchboard, complimentary movie channel, and free transportation to the airport or the Amtrak station.

The adjacent restaurant, Humphrey's, has a very delightful garden decor and large windows providing views of the boat-filled marina. You can dine outdoors under white umbrellaed tables or inside where there's an abundance of plants and potted palms. Seafood is the specialty here. Humphrey's is also the setting for nightly entertainment, and a pianist plays during Happy Hour.

From April to October, the hotel helps sponsor great jazz concerts with top-name performers in the park by the bay.

Facilities include heated pools for adults and children, a Jacuzzi, table tennis, bicycles, and a nine-hole putting green.

Rates are $89 to $109, single or double. Suites are $135 and up. Children under 16 in a room with their parents are free.

CORONADO: The grande dame of San Diego's resort hotels, the **Hotel del Coronado,** 1500 Orange Ave., San Diego, CA 92118 (tel. 619/522-8000), opened its doors in 1888, and was designated a national historical landmark in 1977. The last of the extravagantly conceived seaside hotels, it is a monument to Victorian grandeur with its tall cupolas, turrets, and gingerbread trim. The register over the years has listed thousands of celebrity guests—11 U.S. presidents, and movie stars like Tony Curtis, Jack Lemmon, Robert Wagner, and Stephanie Powers are just a few. Former Secretary of the Interior Stewart Udall was moved to write a poem about the beauty of the early morning in Coronado during his visit, and rumor has it that Edward, Prince of Wales, met Wally Simpson here.

The hotel's facilities include two swimming pools, six lighted championship tennis courts, a white sand beach, and a health spa for men and women. The hotel overlooks a beautiful sand beach, and a championship 18-hole golf course and boat rental are nearby. There are four areas for dining and cocktails, including the majestic Crown/Coronet Rooms, magnificently unchanged since the turn of the century; the Prince of Wales, for gourmet dining; the Del Deli; and the Ocean Terrace Lounge.

And accommodations are fittingly exquisite, with custom-made furnishings and all conveniences. Rates range from $135 for street-side standard rooms (single or double) and go up to between $275 to $300 for a deluxe lanai double with oceanfront or bay view (many options in between). Suites are $320 to $500. To stay here is a unique and memorable pleasure; if it's not in your budget, at least come by for a meal and stroll around the grounds.

5. WHERE TO DINE

For what is probably the best restaurant in all of San Diego (and possibly one of the most expensive), see my review of Gustaf Anders in the La Jolla section.

Lubach's, 2101 N. Harbor Dr., corner of Hawthorn Street (tel. 619/232-5129), located on the Embarcadero, is an award-winning restaurant with a comfortably traditional decor. The wood-paneled walls are adorned with ship models, wagon-wheel chandeliers are suspended from the ceilings, the tablecloths create a sea of white linen, seating is in shiny red-leather banquettes, and a vase containing one or two rosebuds graces every table. A blazing fire in a brick fireplace adds a homey touch. The food is delicious—a combination of culinary art and the use of fresh fish and produce. A specialty is poached salmon in hollandaise sauce. Nonseafood entrees include boneless squab with wild rice and beef Stroganoff with noodles. Dinner entrees cost $15 to $25. There's a selection of imported and California wines to complement your meal. For dessert you might sample one of the French pastries from the cart (baked fresh each morning). Luncheon salads and sandwiches are $8 to $14.

Open for lunch weekdays from 11:30 a.m. to 4 p.m., for dinner Monday through Saturday from 4 p.m. to midnight. Jackets are required for men at dinner. There is free valet parking. Reservations are essential.

Another Embarcadero seafood eatery of renown is the Ghio and Weber families' **Anthony's Star of the Sea Room,** 1360 Harbor Dr., at Ash Street (tel. 619/232-7408), next to the three-masted *Star of India.* Dramatically set overlooking the San Diego harbor. Anthony's interior is newly decorated, elegant, and comfortable. Specialties include the cioppino à la Catherine (Catherine is Anthony Ghio's mother) and oven-baked sole stuffed with lobster, shrimp, and crab. Dinner entrees cost $15 to $27.

It's open daily for dinner from 5:30 to 10:30 p.m. Reservations essential.

Adjoining is **Anthony's Fish Grotto** (tel. 619/232-5103), also run by the Ghio and Weber families. The decor is a shade less elegant, although you still have the panoramic harbor view, and prices are lower. Featured here are as many fish delicacies as the Oyster Bar in New York City offers. Reservations are not accepted—you just arrive. To continue the analogy, it's a bit like waiting for a train during rush hour in the home of The Oyster Bar, Grand Central Station, but don't let that discourage you; things move right along here.

One of several house specialties is shellfish casserole à la Catherine (made with lobster meat, crab legs, shrimp, and scallops). But I suggest that if sand dabs are on the menu that day, order them; I've never tasted a more delectable, light, toothsome, elegant fish. Most entrees are priced from $8 to $14 and the portions are large. Hours are 11:30 a.m. to 8:30 p.m.

Across the street is **Anthony's Harborside** (tel. 619/232-6358). It also features seafood, and at night puts out a terrific salad bar. It's open weekdays for lunch from 11:30 a.m. to 4:30 p.m., and for dinner nightly from 4:30 to 10:30 p.m. Reservations are essential.

Tom Ham's Lighthouse, 2150 Harbor Island Dr., Harbor Island (tel. 619/291-9110), is built at the tip of Harbor Island beneath a lighthouse (the official Coast Guard No. 9 beacon). You get not only good meals here, but can enjoy a museum as well. A collection of marine artifacts was gathered from around the world, forming a nostalgic reminder of San Diego in the early 1800s. Featured on the menu are many New England and early California specialties. The seafood chowder, included in the price of your dinner entree, is based on an early California recipe; or you can choose a tossed green salad or vinaigrette salad with shrimp. The house specialty is carne asada (cuts of marinated beef tenderloin pan-broiled and served with a special Mexican sauce). Dinner entrees cost $13 to $25. Lunch fare is sandwiches, salads, and hot specialties for $6 to $12. Desserts include apple pie.

Open for lunch weekdays from 11:15 a.m. to 3:30 p.m., for Sunday brunch (an $8.95 buffet) from 10 a.m. to 2 p.m. Dinner is served Monday to Thursday from 5 to 10:30 p.m., on Friday and Saturday to 11 p.m., and on Sunday from 4 to 10:30 p.m.

Cafe Del Rey Moro is at 1549 El Prado in Balboa Park (tel. 619/234-8511). It would be a shame if you got lost, so let me point out that El Prado is the attractive extension of Laurel Street once it passes east of Sixth Avenue and enters Balboa Park. (Drive slowly and enjoy the sights.)

A San Diego landmark since 1914, when it was the Foreign Arts Building during the Panama California Exposition, Cafe Del Rey Moro is located in the historic House of Hospitality near the San Diego Museum of Art and close to the Old Globe Theatre. Set off from a central courtyard with all the trappings of a Spanish hacienda—central fountain, much greenery, small palms, wrought-iron benches—it's a perfect place to sit and relax on a warm summer day.

The café rests serenely among gardens surrounded by high-flying eucalyptus and palm trees. You can dine outside on a brick terrace, with its white pillars, vine-covered trellises, and yellow-and-white striped awnings, overlooking a lower patio with a small fountain and lush gardens. Inside, the red tile floors, the wall of glass doors, and the greenery hanging from a latticework ceiling give one of the sense of still being outside on the terrace.

The fare is generally light—fresh fish and seafood simply prepared with a variety of local vegetables, herbs, delicate sauces, and a touch of Mexico's spices. The zarzuela, however, is a meal in itself—a hearty bouillabaisse with fresh fish, king crab, shrimp, and clams simmered in a lovely fish stock. The brandy scallops are superb, served with oven-fresh sourdough bread for dipping. Among the meat dishes, one of my favorites is the loin of pork adobo—tender filets of pork loin marinated in a sauce of tomatoes, onion, garlic, and spices, then slowly braised. Dinners include salad, vegetable du jour, and sourdough bread.

For lunch, if you've never had it, order the tortilla soup. Another meal in itself, it's absolutely delicious—chicken stock simmered with tomatoes, avocados, onion, tortillas, and Monterey jack cheese. The selection of luncheon entrees is wide-ranging and sufficient to satisfy any appetite. There are great sandwiches, salads, omelets, soups mother never knew how to make, munchies, enchiladas, burritos, fajitas, etc. Dinners range from $8.75 to $13.95, lunches from $4.75 to $6.95.

Margaritas are always available, as is Sangria; Cafe Del Rey Moro has a well-stocked bar. They also offer a remarkably good selection of nonalcoholic beverages.

Topping the menu is a luscious list of desserts and exotic coffees. Try the irresistible raspberry macaroon torte, or, if you feel stuffed or righteous, polish off your meal with one of the restaurant's good coffees.

Luncheon is served daily from 11 a.m. to 4 p.m., dinner Tuesday through Sunday from 5 to 8 p.m. Sunday champagne brunch is 10 a.m. to 3 p.m.

In Old Town, at 2836 Juan St. (tel. 619/297-1631), **La Piñata** is a cozy, friendly restaurant with a happy collection of the brightly colored Mexican toys which give it its name (donkeys, parrots, toros, rocket ships, elephants) hanging from the reed ceiling. It's just a bit out of the main stream of people traffic, which makes it a pleasant alternative to the larger, somewhat noisy, tourist emporiums. And it has a small outdoor patio (with heaters, yet) where you can dine even on a coolish day and share your cheese quesadilla with the sparrows.

La Piñata is understandably popular among locals: it's attractive, the food is always good, prices are moderate, and service is pleasant and prompt. The restaurant prepares familiar dishes tastefully, be it fajitas, enchiladas, burritos, tacos, tostados, or any combinations thereof. Caldo de Albondigas con arroz y tortillas is a great, hearty homemade soup, cooked to order, and any one of the salads is a substantial accompaniment to an entree. For those who prefer very late breakfasts (after 11 a.m.), La Piñata has huevos rancheros, huevos with chorizo, or huevos with asada (charbroiled strips of sirloin).

Lunch or dinner at La Piñata costs about $2.50 to $10. A compliments-of-the-house cheese quesadilla always precedes your order. Don't overlook the delicious margaritas, offered in small, medium, or large (the large is about the size of a small bird bath). There's also a good selection of beer. If you decide to nosh on some of the marinated vegetables at your table, be forewarned—they're tonsil scorchers, especially those innocent-looking carrot slices.

La Piñata is open weekdays from 11 a.m. to 9 p.m., weekends to 9:30 or 10 p.m. *Note:* You can buy a piñata should you take a fancy to one.

The **Cotton Patch,** at 2720 Midway Dr., near Rosecrans (tel. 223-7179), is my kind of place—a great down-to-earth restaurant that serves great down-to-earth food at reasonable prices. It's a bit out of the usual tourist route (a short distance east of #5), but well worth the minor side trip. Under the family guidance of Fred and Lorraine Halleman, the Cotton Patch has been doing a land-office business with locals for over 40 years, so you know they must be doing something right.

Walk through an outdoor patio with a fireplace, and you'll see a rustic restaurant with a log cabin–type interior: post-and-beam construction, and deer heads competing for wall space with oil paintings and antique cooking and farming tools.

But to get down to basics: everything comes in generous portions at the Cotton Patch—the drinks, the food, the quality, and the hospitality. When you sit down for dinner, you're promptly brought a pot of deliciously marinated red kidney beans (you could make a meal of these alone). As you peruse the menu, you're bound to notice that the specialty of the house is "meat." The house specialty is a generous portion of prime rib of beef au jus, done to perfection and served with a creamy horseradish sauce that can bring tears to your eyes. But there are also the rack of lamb, 20-ounce porterhouse steak, New York steak, barbecued spare ribs, plantation-style southern fried chicken, plus veal and shrimp done in several delectable ways—in other words, something to satisfy every appetite. Dinner entrees are served with soup or salad, your choice of potatoes (I challenge you to eat your way through the huge portion of fries), and some absolutely delicious hot corn bread. If after all this you still have room for dessert, the Cotton Patch features pecan pie, cheesecake, and an ultrarich Mississippi mud pie.

The luncheon menu changes daily and is more limited, but still offers steaks reasonably priced. Prime rib is not served midday.

Dinner entrees range from $7.95 to $18.95. The top of the line is steak and Alaskan king crab; lobster is priced according to the market. Lunch costs from $5.25 to $8.50.

If the parking lot in front is jammed when you arrive, don't despair; there's space in back—enter via the lane between the Cotton Patch and the adjacent fire-engine-red Boll Weevil.

The Cotton Patch is open weekdays for lunch from 11 a.m. to 1 p.m. and nightly for dinner from 4 p.m. to midnight.

Sandtrap Restaurant and Lounge, 2702 N. Mission Bay Dr. (tel. 619/ 274-3314), at Mission Bay Golf Course, south of Grand Street (turn right, and right again, just before the freeway entrance south). When you think you've exhausted all possibilities for having a really great breakfast at 7 a.m. without resorting to fast food, head for one of San Diego's best kept secrets, the Sandtrap. It's a happy restaurant: it has a small counter, and a large pub-like dining room that overlooks a duck pond with its waterfall and the course's putting green.

The prices are right, the food's terrific, and the service is cheerful— especially hard to find at 7 a.m. The omelets are delicious in whatever form you choose. For a real heart-warmer, there's a memorable jalapeño-and-cheese omelet you'll probably write home about. And that's just the beginning. There's always a big breakfast special, usually accompanied by fries or fresh fruit, for a modest $4.

For breakfast, lunch, or dinner, the quantities served require a hearty appetite—even the salads are a full meal. For lunch, try one of the delicious daily specials, or the sea legs suprême salad ($5 to $6). Two of the most popular lunchtime sandwiches at the Sandtrap are the six-ounce sirloin steak at $5.75 and the half-pound hamburger, done exactly as ordered, for $4.25, both with fries or fruit. Homemade soups are a specialty of the house and a bargain at $2. Dinners range from $6 to $13 (the highest price is for the peppersteak or prime rib). There's also fresh fish daily for lunch and dinner. With your entree there's a choice of soup or salad. You can't beat the quality, price, and the service. There's a full bar, and color TV to boot, dancing and entertainment in the evening.

The restaurant is open from 7 a.m. to 9 p.m. Sunday to Thursday, to 10 p.m. on Friday and Saturday. If you want to try the Mission Bay 18-hole Executive Golf Course after breakfast or lunch, bring your clubs (or you can rent them in the pro shop).

6. LA JOLLA

"La Hoya" (that's how it's pronounced) is an oceanside residential portion of the coast, at the northern and western edge of San Diego. It successfully retains its "old-money" image, although adventurous young people are moving in on the coterie of millionaires, navy families, and retired citizens. For half a century the wealthy have been building beautiful retirement estates here, having selected the site for its lushness and rugged coastline, its beaches and cultural facilities. Along Prospect Avenue, running parallel to the coast, are about five blocks of boutiques, shops, restaurants, cafés, and art galleries. A tasteful, restful, interesting place to visit.

The Scripps Aquarium Museum, 8602 La Jolla Shores Dr. (tel. 619/534-6933 for a recorded message with general information, or 534-3474), at the Scripps Institution of Oceanography, is world renowned for the research it does in the oceans. It invites visitors to view its aquarium of marine life and outdoor tidepool exhibit, with many of the specimens captured on scientific expeditions. The aquarium bookshop (tel. 619/534-4085) specializes in ocean-related books for students and scholars of all ages—preschool to postgraduate to "just interested." The aquarium is open daily from 9 a.m. to 5 p.m., and no admission is charged. Donations are accepted but not requested. Nearby are excellent beach and picnic areas.

WHERE TO STAY: La Valencia, 1132 Prospect St. (corner of Herschel Avenue), La Jolla, CA 92037 (tel. 619/454-0771), is a gracious old Mediterranean-style resort that delights the senses at every turn. Dramatically situated on the ocean, it was designed in archetypical Early California Spanish style by architect Reginald Johnson back in 1926. From the Mediterranean-style colonnaded entrance to the lush gardens that surround the large swimming pool, to the exquisite mosaic tilework within, it's a beauty.

The hotel's entrance is in the center of the village, though its rear faces the ocean. You enter via a tiled loggia with a vine-covered trellis. On your left is a dining patio in a small garden with a fountain and flowering subtropical shrubbery. It's old Spain revisited. La Valencia has been beautifully kept up. Its rooms (for the most part, with ocean views) have been refurnished in European antique reproductions and fitted out with every modern amenity. At the back, garden terraces open toward the ocean. Here, a free-form swimming pool is edged with lawn, flowering trees, shrubs, and a flagstone sunning deck. Other facilities include sauna, whirlpool, and three delightful restaurants: the rooftop Sky Room, where superb prix-fixe meals are offered; the Mediterranean Room, with its adjoining patio for al fresco dining; and the Whaling Bar and Grill, where the ambience is New England nautical.

Singles are $108 to $130; doubles, $118 to $140.

Another elegant Old California accommodation is **Sea Lodge,** 8110 Camino del Oro (at the foot of Avenida de la Playa), La Jolla, CA 92037 (tel. 619/459-8271), overlooking the Pacific on a mile-long beach. Its 101 rooms are housed in a long and low stucco building with terracotta-tile roof, highlighted by fountains, beautiful landscaping and flower beds, open-air walkways, ceramic tilework, graceful arches, and Mexican antiques like the 200-year-old cathedral doors leading into the main dining room.

An immense swimming pool gleams jewel-like in the courtyard, where umbrellaed tables are set up for outdoor dining. Other facilities include three championship tennis courts (no charge for use), a sauna, and a nine-hole pitch-and-putt golf course next door at the La Jolla Beach and Tennis Club. The Shores Restaurant (that's the above-mentioned main dining room) serves three meals a day, seven days a week, under a peaked beamed ceiling. The decor is richly Spanish and arched windows provide a view of the beach.

As for the rooms, they're large and lovely, all with one barnwood wall (third-floor rooms—my favorites—have high sloped barnwood ceilings as well), and almost all have an ocean view. There is no air conditioning. All are equipped with carved wooden beds, walls adorned with Mexican bark paintings, large dressing rooms, refrigerators, and handsome ceramic-tile baths, as well as balconies or lanais and all the modern amenities. Some have kitchenettes.

Rates are seasonal: July through mid-September singles cost $125 to $265; doubles, $140 to $280, suites, $310 to $330. Rates are lower the balance of the year.

WHERE TO DINE: The unpretentious exterior of **Gustaf Anders,** located in La Jolla Shores, 2182 Avenida de la Playa, off La Jolla Shores Drive (tel. 619/459-4499), disguises an award-winning restaurant deemed to be one of the best —if not *the* best—in the entire San Diego area. One thing is certain: the continental cuisine of Gustaf Anders offers a dining experience par excellence.

The understated elegant decor is a good indication of the quality of the cuisine. All is white, gray, black, mirrored, with immense groupings of fresh flowers. As you enter, to your left is the handsomely decorated black granite bar with its beautifully arranged caviar offerings. Passing through the bar, you enter into a group of four intimate dining areas, each of which is as complementary a setting for the excellent cuisine as the gleaming white napery and sparkling glasses. Flower arrangements in mirrored alcoves and their miniatures add a lovely touch of color on each table.

An additional dining area is a patio complete with an unintrusive fountain and a lovely shade tree. It's pleasantly quiet despite being just off the street.

A separate bar menu including dessert is served in the bar until midnight. Highlights are the caviars—keluga from the Amur and the more familiar beluga, to the American Golden caviar from whitefish—all served with small blinis. Prices per ounce are $9 for the domestic caviar to $42 for the keluga. Other cold appetizers range from gravlax to a rich and delectable duck foie gras.

The entree menu changes weekly and affords a selection of specialties to please every taste: filet of beef with mustard sauce, loin of veal lightly touched with tarragon, sea scallops baked in a herb tomato sauce are a few. And if you've never had a parsley salad, this is the place to order it. You're in for an extraordinary taste treat guaranteed to change your entire attitude toward parsley.

Every touch is fresh and flattering to the whole dining experience, from the tiny parsley flowerette on the butter serving to the freshly cut lemon peel in the Kir. The maître d' and waiters are polite, friendly and helpful. Service is excellent. Adequate time is given between courses, yet you never feel abandoned.

The menu is à la carte. Dinner entrees are priced at $20 to $27; lunch, at $13 to $17. With an appetizer and a choice from an excellent domestic wine list, expect a tally of at least $80 for dinner for two. And should you be tempted by one of an exceptional selection of madeiras and eau de vies, or a sumptuous dessert, dinner for two enters the range of $100 or more, but the dining experience will be deliciously memorable. Is it worth the price? Absolutely! An alternative? Go for lunch at about half the cost—same elegance, same thoughtful service, same quality.

7. AN EXCURSION TO TIJUANA

While you're this far south, you may as well go the extra 20 miles (via Interstate 5 or 805) and cross the border to Tijuana, gateway to Mexico. Here you can see thoroughbred-racing at **Agua Caliente** every Saturday and Sunday at noon in winter, at 1:15 p.m.; the rest of the year greyhound racing is scheduled Wednesday through Monday nights.

Mexico's top matadors perform in two different rings every Sunday at 4 p.m. between May and September.

And then there are jai alai games, often called the fastest sport in the world, played nightly except Thursday starting at 8 p.m. at the **Fronton Palacio,** Avenida Revolución at Calle 7. For information, call 619/282-3636.

You can also visit the **Tijuana Cultural Center,** located less than a mile from the border and across from the Plaza Rio Shopping Center. It was designed to celebrate Mexico's heritage, and contains an Omnimax Space Theatre, an anthropological museum, a bookstore, arts and crafts center, and a performing arts center. Finally, you'll want to do some shopping at the duty-free stores along Tijuana's main street, Avenida Revolución.

One of the easiest ways to get to the border is the **Tijuana (San Diego) Trolley** (tel. 619/233-3004. Big red trolleys (actual electric streetcards imported from Germany) depart from the corner of Kettner Boulevard and C Street, just across the street from the Amtrak station, every 15 minutes from 5 a.m. to 7 p.m., and every 30 minutes thereafter, with the last trolley returning from the border at 1 a.m. The one-way trip to or from the border takes 45 minutes and costs $1.50 per person one way from Kettner Boulevard; have exact change in coins. There are 18 stops on the line, since it doubles as commuter transportation, but it's a comfortable, interesting, and inexpensive way to reach the border. Once at the border you'll need a taxi to get into town.

If you're driving into Mexico, you might prefer to park on the U.S. side and walk or take a bus or taxi into town (three-quarters of a mile). There are about half a dozen parking lots on either side of I-5, and by leaving your car on the U.S. side you avoid long waits when return traffic jams up at the border.

One way to avoid car problems is to take the **Mexicoach** (tel. 619/232-5049). Daily round-trip scheduled express buses go to downtown Tijuana, the Tijuana airport, the jai alai games, and bullfights ($11 round trip, $5.75 one way). Buses depart from the Amtrak terminal, 1050 Kettner Blvd., at Broadway in San Diego, at 9 a.m. and 11 a.m., then at 2, 4, and 6 p.m. The trip takes about 35 minutes going, 45 minutes to one hour returning (to pass through Immigration). The last bus returns at 6:45 p.m. weekdays, 9 p.m. weekends.

And of course, **Gray Line Tours,** 1670 Kettner Blvd. (tel. 619/231-9922), has a full range of Tijuana Tours.

If you'd like to do it yourself, stop by the **San Diego Convention & Visitors Bureau International Visitor Information Center** at 11 Horton Plaza, downtown (tel. 236-1212); they have information about Tijuana attractions. There is also a tourist information center at the border crossing.

Note: If you do drive in, be aware that *no U.S. insurance is valid in Mexico.* If you should be involved in an accident across the border, this can be troublesome at best. But you can buy special coverage near the border for a few dollars a day, or from AAA if you're a member. Whatever, *don't* go into Mexico without it. By the way, American citizens don't need a passport within 75 miles of the border for visits of less than 72 hours (foreigners should carry theirs) to go to Tijuana, and you can shop with American dollars. However, it's wise to have identification (like a driver's license) with you.

DINING IN TIJUANA: You won't find the perfectly charming little south-of-the-border restaurant of your dreams here. Best bet is **La Costa,** Calle 7A #150, off Revolución (tel. 706/685-8494), a dimly lit, wood-paneled restaurant with big black tufted-leather booths that looks no more Mexican than many places in New Jersey.

What it lacks in ambience, however, it makes up for in excellent fresh fish and seafood meals so good they're worth the trip to Tijuana alone. A recent meal priced at about $11 consisted of two fish hors d'oeuvres, tomato salad, seafood soup, fresh-baked rolls and butter, broiled shrimp wrapped in bacon with rice, dessert, and coffee. La Costa is open daily from 10 a.m. to midnight.

Just around the corner is **Pedrin's,** 1115 Avenida Revolución (tel. 706/685-4052). It's fancier than La Costa—all wood and white, with plants. On the bar there's an attractive seafood and wine display. On the second floor there's a terrace overlooking the street. The fare is seafood here too. For $5 to $11 you get the house hors d'ouevres, a homemade soup, piping-hot bread, rice, an entree—fish, lobster, king crab, abalone, shrimp, oyster, almost anything you can think of—and dessert and coffee. It's a delightful place, a perfect spot to rest your feet after a long shopping spree.

Pedrin's hours are 11 a.m. to midnight daily.

LAS VEGAS

□ □ □

Las Vegas—Disneyland for the 21-and-over set . . . playground of the rich, the would-be-rich, the tourist from Albuquerque, the sophisticate from New York City. There's something here for everyone, and more often than not, everyone leaves a little something here. That's the rule of the game, and games are what Las Vegas is all about. Emotion runs high as money runs low, but there's always someplace to go to work off those lost-green blues.

Where else could you play tennis or work out at a health club 24 hours a day, seven days a week? Get to see Sinatra, Dolly, and Liza all in one week? Dine while watching a three-ring circus?

The funny thing about Las Vegas is that it's never really been any different. From the start, the lure of Nevada was all glitter and gold. During the California Gold Rush it became a lucrative stopping-off place for prospectors. Gold, silver, and other precious metals were mined into the early 1900s, when the rich ore veins were finally picked clean.

The next boom came in on the tail of the Gold Rush, around 1905, when the Union Pacific Railroad built a depot in what immediately and henceforth became known as Las Vegas. As the iron horse flourished, so did Nevada property values. And always there was gambling—finally made legal in 1931—and big-time gamblers, who helped to make Las Vegas a legendary town, while becoming legends themselves. Perhaps the most notorious of these was Nick the Greek, King of Gamblers from 1928 to 1949. In his time it's been said he won and lost more than $50 million—and managed to die broke.

Whether or not you aspire to the big time, Las Vegas will welcome you with open casinos, and enough excitement and entertainment to keep you coming back again and again.

1. GETTING AROUND

Not only does Las Vegas have the distinction of being the oasis in an otherwise desert state mostly owned by the government (ours), it is also Nevada's largest city. The sections that will interest you most as a tourist, however, are contained in a fairly compact area.

The **Strip,** more formally known as **Las Vegas Boulevard South,** and the **downtown Casino Center,** provide the major entertainment and casino activity. The Strip runs from the Sahara Hotel south to the Hacienda Hotel, while the downtown Casino Center is concentrated on Fremont Street and the adjoining area.

Strip **buses** ply the route from the Hacienda to Fremont Street, stopping at all major hotels on the Strip. To return to the Strip from downtown, go to the corner of 3rd and Fremont Streets. Bus fare is $1, and you'll need exact change. If you plan on using the bus several times, buy a ten-ride commuter card from the driver for $6.65. For transit information, call 702/384-3540. **Taxis** cost $1.70 for the first sixth of a mile, $1.40 for each mile after that. The **airport limo** from the airport to the Strip hotels costs $3 per person, $4.50 to downtown Las Vegas.

Car Rentals

I've covered this topic under San Francisco, Los Angeles, and San Diego, but it still bears repeating because of its importance to all travelers, especially those who do not write it off as a business expense.

If you intend to do much traveling, let's say down to Laughlin and back, or to Boulder Dam, or covering much of the desert landscape, you might do best to find an unlimited-mileage arrangement, or at least one with sufficient free mileage to make your trip economical. On the highways, those few "cents per mile" tend to mount rapidly into dollars.

Whatever your destination, my advice is *plan ahead*. The general information given in the "Traveling Within California" section of Chapter I applies here too; you might want to refer to it.

Car rentals of specific-size vehicles, including vans, are usually easier to obtain from the big rental-car companies. Each of the companies below has an office at McCarran International Airport, as well as offices throughout Las Vegas: **Avis** (tel. 800/331-1212), **Brooks** (tel. 702/735-3344), **Budget** (tel. 800/527-0700), and **Hertz** (tel. 800/654-3131).

Brooks Rent-a-Car, 3039 Las Vegas Boulevard South, at Convention Center Drive, tries to maintain the lowest rates in Las Vegas. They also have a free shuttle service which takes customers to or from their office and any Las Vegas hotel or McCarran airport, available from 6 a.m. through 11 p.m. daily.

2. THE ABC'S OF LAS VEGAS

As with the "ABC's" for all the major California cities, this section organizes, in alphabetical order, some basic information (and some not so basic) intended to help make your trip as enjoyable and hassle-free as possible.

AIRLINES: Nonstop flights connect Las Vegas with a number of cities in California: **Bakersfield** (Delta), **Burbank** (America West, US Air), **Fresno** (Delta), **Long Beach** (America West), **Los Angeles** (American, America West, Delta, Eastern, US Air), **Ontario** (America West, Sunworld International), **Orange County** (America West, Southwest Airlines, US Air), **San Francisco** (America West, United, US Air), **San Jose** (America West, Delta, US Air), **Santa Barbara** (Delta), **Santa Maria** (American).

Nonstop service to the **New York City area** is available from America West and Continental, both leaving from Newark Airport.

AIRPORT: Las Vegas has one main airport—**McCarran International Airport.** The $7.50 surcharge on your ticket to Las Vegas pays for this ultramodern airport, where you can begin gambling at the slots as soon as you disembark.

It takes about 15 minutes and $7 to $9 to get to the middle of the Strip by taxi. In addition to the base fare of $1.70 for the first ½ mile and 20¢ for each additional ½ mile, there is also a 20¢ tax per load for pickups at the airport and a

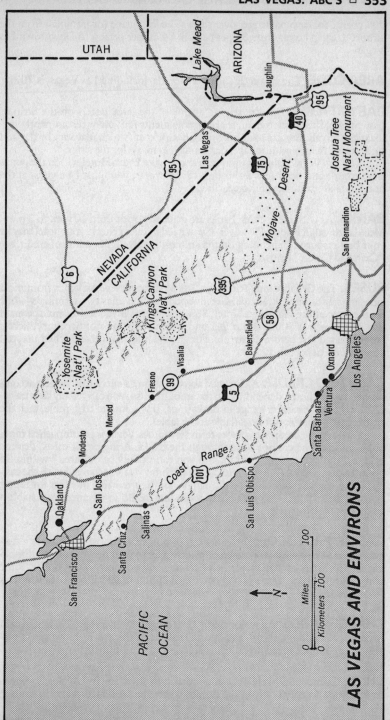

LAS VEGAS AND ENVIRONS

20¢ charge for each passenger over three. The limousine (or minibus) from the airport to Strip hotels costs $3 per person, $4.50 per person to Downtown Las Vegas.

AREA CODE: The area code for all of Nevada, including Las Vegas, is **702**.

BABYSITTERS: If you're staying at one of the large hotels on the Strip or Downtown, the concierge can make arrangements for you or recommend organizations to call. Be sure to check on the hourly cost (which may vary by day and time) as well as any additional expenses such as meals for the sitter.

The Las Vegas Hilton is unique in that it has a Youth Hotel within the premises for girls and boys ages 3 through 18. However, you must be a guest at the hotel to take advantage of these facilities.

BANKS: As with most cities, banks are generally open from 10 a.m. to 3 p.m., Monday through Friday. However, if you need to cash a check, your hotel may be your best resource, depending on the amount involved. For a line of credit, see "Cash and Credit" below.

BUSES: The **Greyhound/Trailways Bus System** serves Las Vegas from most cities in California and Nevada. Greyhound/Trailways has two terminals—one on the Strip at the Flamingo Hotel, 3555 Las Vegas Blvd. South, and the main one downtown at 200 S. Main. Advance reservations are not necessary; tickets are purchased just before departure. For general information and schedules, call your nearest ticket office.

CASH AND CREDIT: As I've said above, cashing a check may be best accomplished at your hotel, depending on the amount. Also, you can readily cash traveler's checks at the cashier's cage in the casinos. If you intend to gamble, cash the checks first—they're not negotiable at the tables.

Establishing credit for a short-term stay in Las Vegas is accomplished more often through the casinos than through the banks. Bring credit cards, driver's licenses, and other identification, and you can usually be "cleared" within 24 hours to cash personal checks, etc., up to the limit you've arranged with the casino. Once you've established credit with a casino, it remains in effect for repeat visits to the city. It's also possible to write to a casino in advance and establish credit before you arrive.

CASINO PROTOCOL: You can wear, or not wear, almost anything at a casino. And at a craps table you can whoop and holler to your heart's content. Smoking is permitted at the majority of tables, but you may now notice some nonsmoking tables. There is one strict prohibition in all casinos—no cameras are allowed.

CHARGE CARDS: All major credit cards are generally accepted in lieu of cash at hotels, restaurants, shops, and sports facilities in this town. However, it's always wise to check ahead if you're considering an exceptionally large purchase.

CHIPS: Casino chips were once as good as cash anywhere in Las Vegas. Nowadays they are accepted only in the casinos where they're issued—and in church;

some people still drop them into collection boxes, an old Las Vegas tradition. Reason for the change in use as currency: a rash of counterfeit chips began to show up. So cash in your chips before you leave any casino, unless you're planning to return there.

CLIMATE: It can be cold December through March, with evening temperatures dropping to the mid-30s to 40s; daytime highs are around the 50s or low 60s, if that. So bring warm clothing if you plan to leave your hotel at any time. April through October is summerwear time, but women might bring a lightweight sweater or stole. Many's the restaurant that has winter temperatures (especially those requiring jackets for men).

CRIME: In any city where as much money changes hands as in Las Vegas, you will also find crime. To avoid an unhappy incident, use discretion and common sense. If you're carrying a handbag, don't, for example, put it on the ledge just beneath the craps table where players rest their drinks. It's out of view and a tempting target. Always keep your handbag close to you and in plain sight.

DENTISTS AND DOCTORS: Hotels usually have a list of dentists and doctors, should you need one; in addition, they are listed in the Centel *Yellow Pages*. For dentist referrals, call the **Clark County Dental Society** (tel. 435-7767); for a doctor, call the **Clark County Medical Society** (tel. 702/739-9989).

DRIVING: Any trip to Las Vegas from California involves desert driving. Take basic precautions at all times, but especially during the summer. Before leaving, check your tires, water, and oil. Take about five gallons of water in a clean container so that it can be used for drinking or for the radiator. Pay attention to those road signs suggesting when to turn off your car's air conditioner. Slow but continuous climbs through the mountains can cause overheating before you notice it on your gauge. And don't push your luck with gas. It may be 35 miles or more between gas stations, so fill up before you begin to run low.

If your car overheats, *do not* remove the radiator cap until the engine has cooled, and then only very slowly. Add water to within an inch of the top of the radiator while the engine is running.

FESTIVALS AND EVENTS: The best and most comprehensive source for this information is the **Las Vegas Chamber of Commerce,** 2301 E. Sahara Ave., Las Vegas NV 89104 (tel. 457-4664). The Chamber is open weekdays from 8 a.m. to 5 p.m.. You can send a request for a list of the annual events, enclosing a stamped, self-addressed envelope.

You'll also find weekly information in the Friday edition of the *Las Vegas Review-Journal* and in *Today in Las Vegas;* see the "Information" entry below.

While every day is "party day" in Las Vegas, the obvious holiday and special-event occasions are not the times to try for reservations on short notice; you might write ahead to the Chamber of Commerce for a list of the less-obvious big events. (Be advised that it's unwise to come without reservations since you may not get a room, much less a seat at a $2 blackjack table.)

FOOD: Prices range from 89¢ to $70, with lots of choice in-between. The bargain meals are usually breakfast and lunch; dinner tends to run higher. One of the city's main draws has always been its good food at moderate prices, calculated to bring in the gambling customers. Not only the downtown hotels but most of the Strip establishments have all kinds of gimmicks such as 89¢ breakfasts and eat-all-you-want buffet tables (which, for the most part, are no bargain). Scattered around town there are plenty of nationally known franchise restaurants—pancake houses, taco stops, fish and chips, pizza parlors, and the so-called steak houses.

At the dinner shows at the larger hotels, the quality of the food is reasonable, and dinner plus a top-notch show for around $40 to $50 per person is not a bad buy—or at least it doesn't seem so in a city where visitors tend to let money flow like water.

Unlike casinos, not all restaurants are open daily. If you have your heart set on a special place for dinner, be sure to check when it's open.

HAIR SALONS: First, ask at the hotel if there's a hair salon on the premises. If the hotel does not have one, ask for a recommendation. As a last measure, ask a blackjack dealer with a desirable hair style for a referral (need I suggest that you ask when she's not busy?).

INFORMATION: For brochures, maps, information on accommodations, etc., stop at the Las Vegas Chamber of Commerce, a very helpful center for visitors. Their address, phone number, and hours are given above in the "Festivals and Events" entry. For Nevada tourism information, including that for Las Vegas, call 800/638-2328 (a 24-hour line). For Las Vegas reservations and show information, call 800/423-4745.

One of the best sources of information on what's doing in Las Vegas is *Today in Las Vegas*—a free weekly publication you'll find at almost any bell desk in a large hotel, as well as at the airport. It includes up-to-the-minute reviews and listings of all shows and events, as well as the performance times.

LIQUOR LAWS: There are no restrictions on the hours when liquor can be sold or served, but you must be 21 to buy or imbibe legally.

NEWSPAPERS: The *Las Vegas Sun* is the town's morning paper. The Friday edition of the afternoon paper, the *Las Vegas Review-Journal,* offers a rundown of the shows in town, as well as an overview of most other forms of entertainment, restaurants, and happenings in nearby resorts.

PETS: As in California, hotels and motels generally will not accept pets; ask before making the reservations. Motel 6 does accept a pet (within reason), but will not permit the animal to be left unattended.

If you travel via RV, motor home, or with trailer or van, and take pets with you, an ideal location next to the Strip is the Circusland RV Park, adjacent to the Circus Circus Hotel. Circusland has family and pet sections with dog runs.

POLICE: For **emergency** help, dial 911. The **nonemergency** Police Department number is 385-1111; that for the **Nevada Highway Patrol** is 385-0311.

RELIGIOUS SERVICES: The Las Vegas area has hundreds of churches and synagogues (at last count about 380) representing virtually every denomination. It's been said that on a per capita basis there are more houses of worship in Las Vegas than in any other metropolitan area in the nation, and we all know what everyone's praying for. The breakdown: 49% Protestant, 24% Roman Catholic, 23% Mormon, 3% Jewish.

The houses of worship listed below are located along the Strip and downtown (for other denominations and locations, consult the Centel *Yellow Pages*): **First Baptist,** 300 S. Ninth St., at Bridger Ave., downtown (tel. 702/382-6177). **First Southern Baptist,** 700 E. St. Louis Ave., on the Strip (tel.

702/732-3100). **Guardian Angel Cathedral** (Roman Catholic), 302 E. Desert Inn Rd., on the Strip (tel. 702/735-5241). **Joan of Arc** (Roman Catholic), 315 S. Casino Center Blvd., downtown (tel. 702/382-9909). **Reformation Lutheran,** 1580 E. St. Louis Ave., near the Strip (tel. 702/732-2052). **First United Methodist,** 231 S. Third St., downtown (tel. 702/382-9939). **Temple Beth Sholom,** 1600 E. Oakey Blvd., near the Strip (tel. 702/384-5070).

STORE HOURS: Stores are usually open from 10 a.m. to 9 p.m. Monday through Friday, to 6 p.m. Saturday, 11 a.m. to 5 p.m. Sunday.

TAXES: Sales tax in Las Vegas is 6%.

TIPPING: Those over 21 undoubtedly already know about tipping the usual 15% in restaurants. However, when you're at a table in a casino, be it craps, black-jack, roulette, baccarat, or whatever, a cocktail waitress will be around to ask if you want anything to drink. There is no charge for the drink, hard or soft, but it is appropriate for you to tip (or "toke") the waitress—$1 (or a comparable chip) is about right, more if you wish.

At the gaming tables, it's perfectly acceptable to tip the dealer or croupier in proportion to the service you've been getting and the size of your winnings.

When checking into a hotel with several bags, a tip of $5 is par for the course.

Valet parking is a great convenience at any of the Las Vegas hotels. A tip of $1 is appropriate, and it's not much to pay for the service.

When you leave the hotel, a tip of $1 per day for the period of your stay, left with the maid or in the room, is a most reasonable amount and will be appreciated.

If you want a better-than-average seat at any one of the shows, tip the maître d'. The usual donation is $5, but if it's a "big name" show, you might up the ante to $20 for the seating *you* want, though the top of the range is optional.

TRAINS: The **Amtrak** station is on One North Main St., at Union Plaza (tel. 386-6896, or toll free 800/872-7245).

USEFUL TELEPHONE NUMBERS: You can obtain **weather information** for Las Vegas at 736-6404, **information on highway conditions** at 385-0181, **the time of day** at 118 (a three-digit number, similar to **directory information,** 411).

3. FOOD, FUN, AND SHELTER IN THE CASINO/HOTELS

In previous chapters of this book, the questions of where to eat, where to stay, and what to do were separate categories, handled for the most part independently of one another. In Las Vegas, many of the top restaurants are right in the big hotels, ditto the casinos and the nightclubs. So I've organized things differently here, exploring the abundance of eating and entertainment facilities at each super-hotel at the same time I'm discussing accommodations. As per usual, I've begun with the most lavish Strip hotels and worked downward on the price scale (the last two casino/hotels, the Golden Nugget and the Union Plaza, are downtown). At the end of this chapter is a selection of good independent restaurants (not in a hotel) you won't want to pass up. There, too, I've begun with the most expensive and worked downward in price.

ABOUT THE HOTELS: There are three major locations for big-hotel action in Vegas: along **The Strip,** in the **downtown** area on Fremont Street, and in a kind of P.S. to the Strip, along **Convention Center Drive,** which meets the Strip between the Riviera Hotel and the Desert Inn. In this chapter, these last are lumped in with the Strip hotels.

No matter how many hotels are contained in those areas, however (last count showed over 50,000 hotel and motel rooms for let—and I'm talking about doubles), a busy weekend still turns up one "No Vacancy" sign after another. Come weekends, convention time, any feeble excuse for a holiday or celebration, it's all full up. So *do not* come without a reservation.

As this book goes to press, construction of the **Golden Nugget on The Strip** has not yet been completed. This spectacular hotel is being built on 88 acres of county property, adjacent to Caesars Palace.

Whether you plan to stay there or not, it's got to be the place to see and an extraordinary place to dine. Steve Wynn's remarkably successful touch with the Golden Nugget downtown will undoubtedly make this new Strip hotel a winner.

The Golden Nugget on The Strip will have 3,000 to 3,600 rooms, a showroom, and seven restaurants—one Japanese, done like a teahouse, set on a mountain top; one Chinese, very exotic, much like Shanghai in the 30s; one continental; one steakhouse; and, the crowning glory, a seafood restaurant with Hawaiian decor, rather like an old whaling village of the type once found on Maui. There will also be two 24-hour coffeeshops for late-night snackers.

The hotel will be in a Y configuration on top of the casino so that you can enter the arena at various points.

There will be a unique swimming area, designed to provide fun as well as exercise. You can swim among islands, grottos, even in and out of lagoons. For tennis buffs, several courts will be equipped for night play.

For the exact date of the opening of the hotel, I suggest that you contact your local travel agent.

BALLY'S—LAS VEGAS: 3645 Las Vegas Blvd. South, Las Vegas, NV 89109 (tel. 702/739-4111, or toll free 800/634-3434, 800/634-6363 in Arizona, California, Idaho, Oregon, and Utah).

Totally rebuilt since the 1980 fire, Bally's is more than a complete resort. It is, rather, like a self-contained suburb, or an entire town—and not a small one either. Tourists detour just to see it, and a guest could spend an entire vacation without venturing out. Everything is right here: a shopping arcade, a huge gaming casino, a movie theater, two nightclub theaters for big shows, six restaurants, four cocktail lounges, two swimming pools (one Olympic-size), a therapy pool

---

KEY TO NUMBERED REFERENCES ON OUR MAP OF THE LAS VEGAS STRIP. 1—Vegas World; 2—Sahara; 3—Algiers; 4—Main Post Office; 5—Circus Circus; 6—Riviera; 7—Westward Ho; 8—La Concha; 9—El Morocco; 10—Stardust; 11—Villa Roma; 12—Landmark; 13—Las Vegas Hilton; 14—Convention Center; 15—Fashion Show Mall; 16—Convention Center Lodge; 17—Frontier; 18—Desert Inn; 19—Brooks Rent-a-Car; 20—Future home of Golden Nugget on the Strip; 21—Imperial 400; 22—Tam O'Shanter; 23—Sands; 24—Holiday Inn Center Strip; 25—Imperial Palace; 26—Caesars Palace; 27—Flamingo Hilton; 28—Barbary Coast; 29—Maxim; 30—Dunes; 31—Bally's Grand; 32—Mini-Price (Koval Lane); 33—Ambassador Inn; 34—Holiday Inn South; 35—Aladdin; 36—Hacienda; 37—Tropicana; 38—Motel 6.

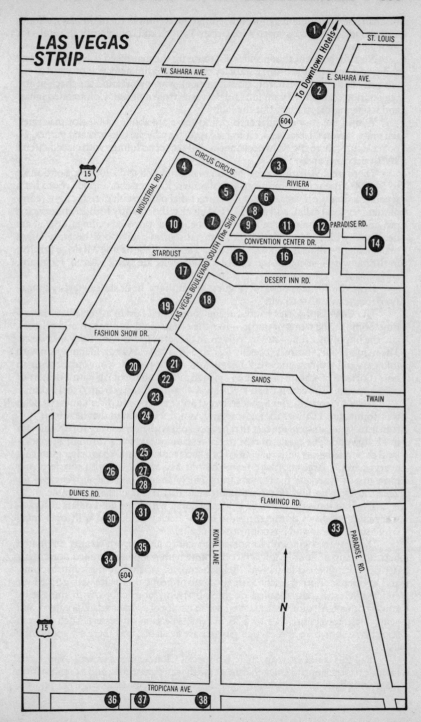

that can seat 50 people at a time, ten tennis courts (four lit for night play), a Youth Center (adjacent to a Swensen's Ice Cream Parlor), and complete health clubs for men and women.

Now for some of the specifics. Coming up the marqueed driveway, the first thing you notice is the bronze statuary grouping. From here, you proceed to the entrance floor ("lobby" hardly does it justice), where you'll find the check-in and registration counters to your left and the casino to your right. Colonnaded pillars and white marble statuary dot the lobby.

Within the rosy chandeliered casino there are about 1,000 slot machines, ten craps tables, 61 blackjack tables, six roulette wheels, two baccarat games, 16 poker setups, three Big Six wheels, and a 200-seat keno lounge with closed-circuit TV to the other areas.

There are 2,900 guest rooms that range from $85 to $120, single or double to $1,000 a night for sumptuous Royal Suites. Each air-conditioned room has a separate living-room area, a color TV, direct-dial phone with message light (complimentary local calls), and an AM/FM clock radio; nightly turndown service is provided. Some rooms even have round beds and mirrored ceilings, and all are decorated with a jazzy flair. There's a metal star on every door, because Bally's management still feels that every guest is a star. And bona fide MGM greats live in the hallways—hanging there in black and white are Gable, Garbo, Hepburn, and others.

If the comfortably ensconced guest gets hungry, he or she can satisfy a variety of food cravings—to wit:

The **Café Gigi** serves haute-cuisine continental fare in a Versailles-like setting. Some of the items of decor—like the ornate gold wall panels and mirrors, and the imposing door—are actually from the set of the movie *Marie Antoinette*. The menu proffers entrees (costing $27 to $40) like veal Oscar, filet mignon with foie gras and truffles, and steak Diane. You might precede your entree with an hors d'oeuvre of scampi or a wilted-spinach salad, and top it off with a dessert of crêpes suzette. The café is open Wednesday through Sunday from 6 to 11 p.m.

Tracy's is named after Spencer Tracy (don't tell me you didn't guess it), who was nominated 11 times for an Academy Award. He insisted that he was an "unromantic type" despite the fact that he appeared with nearly every top female star in Hollywood. The escalator ride to the restaurant takes you through a wonderland of beveled glass with reflections of a spectacular crystal chandelier glittering everywhere. A large montage from the old MGM studios with movie poster blow-ups of Tracy and his co-stars from *Thirty Seconds Over Tokyo*, *Woman of the Year*, *Pat & Mike*, and *Boys Town* assures you that you're in the right place.

The interior is done in soft shades of coral, with large gold pillars and two-story-high windows dominating the room. Each round table is lit by a small white-shaded lamp and has comfortable chairs.

Dinner can begin with imported prosciutto and melon, creamy marinated herring, a cup of double chicken consommé with noodles or chilled borscht, or perhaps Tracy's salad bowl with Belgian endive, artichokes, fresh mushrooms, and watercress. Entrees include mignonette of prime beef sauté with goose liver and truffle sauce, and broiled double-rib spring lamb chops with mint jelly, among others. All dinners are served with a choice of soup or salad, potatoes, and vegetables, entrees are $14 to $25. A large selection of desserts such as fresh strawberry shortcake and French pastries are available, and there's a good wine list.

If all this is not enough, there is a special Chinese menu as well. Appetizers include paper-wrapped chicken, rumaki with water chestnuts, and a combination plate with barbecued spareribs, eggroll, paper-wrapped chicken, fried prawns, and fried wonton. Soups range from egg flower to chicken broth with noodles and pork. There's a spicy Szechuan chicken with sautéed Chinese vegetables, Mongolian beef, and fresh shrimps with sautéed vegetables. Other selections include lemon chicken and lobster Cantonese. All entrees are served with steamed rice, Chinese tea, and fortune cookies. Desserts include fresh pineapple, Chinese kumquats and lichee nuts, and homemade almond cookies.

Entrees range in price from $13 to $20. Dinner at Tracy's is served Friday to Tuesday from 5 to 11 p.m.

At **Caruso's,** Italian specialties are served in an atmosphere of Venetian elegance. Cobblestone-motif carpeted floors, antique iron ovens, and classical statuary grace the room, and menus list pasta dishes (served with garlic bread, and a dessert of tortoni or spumoni), and lots of other entrees (served with pasta and garlic bread) including eggplant parmigiana, mountain brook trout sauté amandine, veal scaloppine, and chicken cacciatore, all for $15 to $25. For dessert there's a delicious Italian rum cake. Caruso's is open from 6 to 11 p.m. Friday through Tuesday.

At **Barrymore's,** copper and carved oak accents create a warmly intimate ambience. Seafood is the specialty, with entrees like tempura shrimp island style. You can also get a prime-rib dinner served with Yorkshire pudding. Entrees range from $18 to $50. Barrymore's is open nightly from 6 to 11 p.m.

The **Deli** is a New York–style eatery, its walls lined with caricatures of MGM stars. Its immense menu offers an astounding number of choices. Combination sandwiches include salami, Swiss cheese, turkey breast, coleslaw, and Russian dressing. And among the traditional favorites are cream cheese and Nova Scotia salmon on a bagel, pastrami on rye, a Reuben with corned beef, Swiss cheese, and sauerkraut grilled on rye, matzoh ball soup, brisket on rye, herring in cream sauce, and cheese blintzes, all for $5 to $12. For dessert try the deep-dish fruit pies with vanilla ice cream. The Deli is open daily from 8 a.m. to 1 a.m.

The **Orleans Coffee House** is open around the clock and features a French Quarter decor. Most of the above-mentioned Deli fare is available here too, but you can also get hot entrees such as fried prawns with a choice of soup or salad, fresh vegetable, potato du jour, and rolls and butter.

The **Celebrity Room** features mega-stars—the likes of Frank Sinatra et al. Dinner shows are about $30 to $50, midnight shows $25 to $40 (including three drinks), depending on the performer.

The **Ziegfeld Room** offers the musical super-spectacular *Jubilee*. Cocktails and show in the Ziegfeld Room cost $25.

The **Cub Bar,** off the lobby and close to casino action, also offers live entertainment nightly. And **Bally's Theater** screens old movie greats.

CAESARS PALACE: 3570 Las Vegas Blvd. South, Las Vegas, NV 89109 (tel. 702/731-7110, or toll free 800/634-6001, 800/634-6661 for reservations).

Arriving at Caesars Palace is supposed to be like a giant step back in time to ancient Rome, and, more specifically, to Caesar's palace. Caesar should have had it so good! Outrageous overwhelming opulence is what this resort complex is all about.

Lining the entranceway are double rows of cypress trees interspersed with magnificent fountains. Marble statues are scattered thither and yon. And you can't miss the People Mover, an automatic sidewalk originating from a Temple of Diana—or the newer People Mover leading to a geodesic dome that houses Omnimax. Omnimax is a tilted-dome theater with a wrap-around screen. It's film productions are thrilling with sensational audio-visual effects. Be sure to catch a show here. At night, the hotel bathes itself in a blue-green light that glows and reflects over the entire couple of blocks that make up its facade. And the exterior of the Omnimax Theater is used for a light show. The main floor is also dotted with marble statues, the most imposing being the 18-foot-high replica of Michelangelo's *David*.

On the premises are six restaurants, a giant 24-hour gambling casino, a nightclub featuring top entertainers, shops and service desks, eight tennis courts, golf nearby, two Olympic-size pools, and a fully equipped health club for men and women.

In June 1988, Caesars Palace broke ground for what will become **The Forum** at Caesars—an enclosed, air-conditioned 150-store shopping complex. If you don't part with your entire bankroll at the gaming tables, the Forum is intended to help you dispense with the rest of it. Ultimately, the grand design will encompass 875,000 square feet; the first phase (expansion to 575,000 square feet) is scheduled for completion in 1990.

The private rooms are every bit as luxurious as the public ones. Rates go from $110 to $160, single or double; add $15 for a third person in the room. Suites range from $230 to $900. The decor is last-days-of-Rome-ornate, with mirrored walls, deep carpeting, and fancy arched dividers separating living area from sleeping area. Some of the rooms even have beds on raised platforms, with steps leading up. Even the drinking glasses are wrapped in gold foil. Of course, all the modern amenities are present and accounted for.

As for restaurants, the **Bacchanal** continues in the style to which you quickly become accustomed at Caesars Palace. Done up in lavish Roman decor, complete with girls in harem outfits to pour your wine, it is open for dinner only and is "prix-fixed" at about $60 per person for a banquet with appropriate wines included. Your evening repast will include tidbits, served with your apéritif, followed by more serious hors d'oeuvres, a variety of soups, fish, "a parade of gastronomical surprises," vegetables, desserts, cheeses, fruits, and coffee. The Bacchanal is open Tuesday through Sunday. There are two seatings, 6 to 6:30 p.m. and 9 to 9:30 p.m.

Equally super-posh is the **Palace Court,** serving classic French cuisine in a mini-museum setting. It's reached via a round elevator with a crystal-and-bronze car. Works on display here include paintings of the 12 Caesars by the Bolognese 17th-century artist Camillo Procaccini. A weeping fig tree surrounded by chrysanthemums under a domed stained-glass skylight is the centerpiece. This is a place to go when you're willing to spend freely—it's easy to work up $70-per-person tabs. Dinner is served nightly, and specialties include fresh braised salmon Véronique, which you might precede with an appetizer of pike mousse. Entrees cost $25 to $55. A knowledgeable staff of sommeliers is on hand to help you select the proper wine. Lunch is also served, with entrees from $9 to $17. Dinner hours are 6:30 to 9:30 p.m. nightly. Lunch is served Thursday through Sunday from 11:30 a.m. to 2:30 p.m.

Primavera, overlooking the Garden of the Gods swimming pool and spa, offers gourmet Italian cuisine with specialties from the North and South of Italy. For a first course, the antipasti cart presents an outstanding array of cold appetizers. Or you might defer to a house specialty such as the fried mozzarella or the elegant consommé garnished with egg flakes, spinach, and grated cheese.

The entree list begins with pasta, all homemade, including the chef's specialty of ravioli lightly filled with spinach and essence of veal, served with your choice of bolognese, marinara, or butter sauce. Several of the pasta entrees are also available as side dishes.

The many veal entrees range from the veal marsala to a simple veal with prosciutto and fresh sage. One of the unusual poultry choices features thin slices of sautéed breast of chicken with kiwi fruit and lemon butter, finished with rich sherry wine. Prime sirloin steak is served sautéed and topped with a tomato sauce, or panfried with a touch of garlic. Maine lobster is served in a spicy marinara sauce. And look for the chef's specialty each evening.

Primavera offers a pastry cart of Italian specialties, as well as cheese with fresh fruit in season. Ice-cream desserts are meals in themselves—say, the Cassata Caligula with layers of pistachio, zabaglione, and chocolate ice cream.

Meat or seafood entrees cost $24 to $45, pasta dishes are $10 to $15, and appetizers $7 to $17. To help sustain your appetite, Primavera offers a good selection of still and sparkling Italian wines.

Primavera is open daily for breakfast at 7:30 to 11 a.m., for luncheon at 11:30 a.m. to 2:30 p.m., and for dinner at 6 to 11:30 p.m.

Other dining options include the **Ah-So Steak House,** serving table d'hôte Japanese teppanyaki dinners (about $45 per person) in an Oriental garden setting (open from 6 to 11:30 p.m. nightly); **Spanish Steps,** combining Moorish design with modernistic gleaming copper and brass decor and offering entrees ranging in price from $17 to $45 for arroz con pollo to steak and lobster (open from 6 to 11:30 p.m. nightly); the **Palatium** for buffet-style meals; and the **Café Roma,** a 24-hour coffeeshop.

For entertainment (in addition to the above-mentioned Omnimax) there's **Circus Maximus,** featuring acts like Tom Jones, the Pointer Sisters, Cher, Diana Ross, Frank Sinatra, and Sammy Davis, Jr. There are cocktail shows only—at 8:30 p.m. and 11:30 p.m.—priced at $25 to $50, depending on the performer and not including drinks. Closed Tuesday.

And rounding out the bill is **Cleopatra's Barge,** a replica of Cleopatra's trysting ship, complete with hydraulic mechanism to keep it in constant motion afloat on the "Nile." Open from 9:30 p.m. to 4:30 a.m., with a live band for dancing.

THE LAS VEGAS HILTON: 3000 Paradise Rd. (adjacent to the Las Vegas Convention Center), Las Vegas, NV 89109 (tel. 702/732-5111, or toll free 800/732-7117).

Calling itself a vacation spa, the Las Vegas Hilton is the largest resort hotel in the world, with 3,174 rooms. It contains a corps of international restaurants, a grand casino, about 20 shops, and a landscaped ten-acre recreation deck on the third-floor roof with six night-lit tennis courts, an 18-hole putting course, shuffleboard, and what must be the largest swimming pool in Nevada! There's more. An 18-hole golf course is a mere step away, there are pagoda-style huts for card-playing and snacking . . . well, you get the picture.

The extravagant lobby is hung with tier upon tier of glistening imported crystal chandeliers and boasts a 100-foot reception desk. Extravagance doesn't stop in the lobby. If anything, it is accentuated in the rooms, executed in a continental decor with one floor decorated in Spanish style, another in Oriental, another in French, and so on. The prevailing theme, whatever the floor, is luxury. Singles or doubles go for $70 to $130; suites, $325 to $950.

One particularly enticing feature for families is the "Youth Hotel." Supervised 24 hours a day, it even contains a supervised dorm for kids ages 3 through 18. Every conceivable kind of craft, sport, and activity is available to entertain the young while mom and dad are out on the town. Rates are about $4.50 an hour for each child. During the summer and on weekends and holidays throughout the year, kids can stay overnight for $25 (calculated from midnight to 8 a.m.). Should you be coming without the kids, however, the ultimate bargain is the three-day/two-night package plan called the "Winners Holiday." Arrive Sunday through Thursday and the cost is $42.50 per person, Friday or Saturday, $54.50 per person, double occupancy including admission to the show in the main showroom with two cocktails, or dinner for two in any restaurant designated by the hotel.

Now, how about a meal? There are offerings from the delicate delights of Japan, the light pastas and veal dishes of Italy, the subtle and elegant cuisine of France, as well as the finest beef fare selected for Hilton steaks and prime ribs.

Le Montrachet, the pride of the Las Vegas Hilton, features continental cuisine and a wine cellar with over 400 wines from around the world.

Le Montrachet was created to achieve the utmost in elegant dining. The dark walls, plush banquettes, and flattering light create a rich, relaxed atmosphere, conducive to appreciation of the chef's superb creations.

Dinner at Le Montrachet was one of the finest I have had at any restaurant from New York to California. Ordering from the six-course, prix-fixe menu, I began my meal with chilled foie gras of duck on a checkerboard of miniature green beans. Then came poached oysters on the half-shell, topped with orange butter glaze, followed by a delicate sweet basil sorbet. Choice of entrees was between roast rack of lamb marinated with sweet basil, fresh dill, mint, shallots, and tarragon; or medallions of veal and morel mushrooms with Noilly cream sauce. (Are your salivary glands coming to life?) A salad of lamb lettuce, endive, and watercress—tossed with walnuts, Dijon mustard, and lemon juice—was next, and all of the above was capped by a hot apple tart topped with caramel ice cream. The prix-fixe dinner is $60—about $25 less than if each course is ordered individually.

Should you decide to order à la carte, I suggest that you try something a bit different, and then wait for a very pleasant surprise. You might choose the raviolis of fresh crabmeat and morel mushrooms, or the mousse of lobster wrapped in a flaky strudel. A first or second course might be the chilled avocado soup topped with fresh beluga caviar.

Entrees include seafood choices from Maine lobster to Dover sole either grilled or boned and filled with mousse of lobster and served with truffle slices. And consider the medallions of venison or the sautéed breast of pheasant stuffed with duck liver. The broiled veal chop stuffed with wild mushrooms and served with Madeira sauce and truffles is excellent too, as is the broiled filet mignon served with a puff pastry shell of wild mushrooms and a pinot noir and Sandeman port wine sauce.

Then by all means review the pastry cart. If by some quirk nothing catches your eye, scan the dessert list and consider the Swiss chocolate soufflé, crème anglaise with Cointreau, or the Painter's Palette with sorbets and fresh fruits of the season.

Hors d'oeuvres range from $10 to $23, soup or salad from $7 to $9. Entrees are about $23 to $38, desserts $7 to $11.

Most dramatic of the restaurants is **Benihana Village,** a complex of three Japanese restaurants for robata (barbecue), hibachi, and tempura specialties, and four cocktail lounges set in a life-size Japanese village complete with lush gardens, running streams, and an Imperial Palace. Guests are treated to periodic thunder and lightning storms and pouring rain (not on diners), electric fireworks displays, and dancing waters. Full dinners with appetizer, soup, salad, rice, vegetables, tea, and dessert cost $15 to $40. Dinner is served nightly from 6 to 11 p.m.

The **Hilton Steak House,** serves immense Texas-style meals in a western setting. Entrees cost $17 to $30—served nightly from 6 to 11:30 p.m. The **Barronshire Prime Rib Room,** sporting a bibliothèque decor, offers full prime rib dinners for $20 to $25.

For light Italian fare, the new, lovely **Andiamo** features an open kitchen where guests can watch the chefs busily turning out delicious meals.

The à la carte lunch and dinner menus both offer a remarkable selection. Lunch at Andiamo might begin with hot or cold antipasti, including such delectables as fresh asparagus with sweet pepper sauce, and crisply fried squid with fresh tomato sauce. Pizzas are decidedly not those found at your local parlor —the Porcini e Salsiccia, for example, is composed of porcini mushrooms, Italian sausage, and tomato sauce with mozzarella, fontina, and provolone. Pasta? Try the Ravioli Neri all' Aragosta with lobster, tarragon, and lobster sauce. An impressive list of entrees includes selections such as salmon, swordfish, a sirloin minute steak, and osso buco Andiamo. Your tab for lunch, without antipasti, wine, dessert, or coffee, will be about $9 to $16.

Andiamo's dinner menu is expansive, and the antipasti include one of my favorites, Carpaccio di Manzo—wafer-thin slices of tenderloin of beef blessed with parmesan, olive oil, and lemon juice. Among the pasta entrees, you might choose the Fettuccine Verdi al Pomodoro e Melanzane—spinach egg noodles with eggplant, tomatoes, and sweet basil. Other entrees are exceptional too—a whole baby salmon sautéed in butter, a veal chop with morel mushrooms and marsala sauce, or a charcoal-broiled filet mignon with Barolo Riserva red wine sauce. Pasta entrees run $10 to $16; seafood and meat courses will set you back $14 to $17. Should you still have space for dessert, and the patience to wait 30 minutes, the soufflés at $5.50 are heavenly—there's a choice of Amaretto, Galliano, or lemon. Or you might consider the Venetian Dream of white espresso ice cream in a chocolate gondola.

Andiamo is open daily for lunch from 11:30 a.m. to 2:30 p.m. and for dinner from 6 to 11 p.m. Reservations are suggested.

And finally there's **Mamchen's Deli,** western in decor with Mamchen's lettered in Hebrew-style characters. The menu is typical New York deli. Sandwiches, chicken soup with kreplach, chopped liver, etc. range from $7 to $10. Open daily from 11:30 a.m. to 10 p.m.

The 2,000-seat **Hilton Showroom** (Barbra Streisand was the first act when it opened) is currently featuring a succession of superstars—Bill Cosby, Wayne Newton, Dionne Warwick, etc. The 8 p.m. show costs about $25 to $40; the midnight show is $20 to $25 including two drinks. Closed Monday.

The **Casino Lounge** turns into a disco at night, offering live and taped music from 8 p.m. to 3 a.m. No cover or minimum.

DESERT INN HOTEL: 3145 Las Vegas Blvd. South (directly opposite the Frontier Hotel), Las Vegas, NV 89109 (tel. 702/733-4444, or toll free 800/634-6906).

The handsomest facade of any hotel/casino on the Strip belongs to the Desert Inn, a 200-acre resort currently completing a multimillion dollar redecoration and general improvement program. The beautifully landscaped grounds contain a lake, pond, and waterfall, as well as an Olympic-size swimming pool, large sundecks, ten outdoor Jacuzzis, an 18-hole PGA-class championship golf course (greens fee for guests is $65, for nonguests $110), ten tournament-class tennis courts, and two shuffleboard courts. Other facilities include a gorgeous casino, five restaurants, four bars, a lounge, showroom, shopping arcade, and beauty and barber shops.

There is also a luxurious health spa which is second to none as a relaxation and fitness facility; it includes a gym, Jacuzzis, saunas, massage, skin care, and a nutrition program that flies in the face of all that you've probably been eating and drinking in Las Vegas.

The Desert Inn's 821 rooms, including 95 suites, are situated in several buildings. Approximately half of the rooms were completely redecorated in 1987, the remainder in 1988. Guests now have a variety of room options to choose from including private patios, hydrowhirl tubs, wet bars, refrigerators, bathroom phones, and more. Each room offers a spectacular view of either the Strip or the pool and the golf course, plus color TV with a movie channel, climate control, and touchtone phones.

As for dining, guests have a choice of the very posh balcony-level **Portofino's** (it overlooks the casino) for northern Italian gourmet fare, where tableside cooking is a specialty and entrees are $20 to $32; the **Monte Carlo Room,** with burgundy carpeting, plush velvet furnishings, and French haute cuisine at $19 to $35; the elegant **Ho Wan,** for northern and southern Chinese cuisine, at $14 to $38; the country club's sporty **Grill Room,** overlooking the golf course, for steaks, salads, sandwiches, and omelets; and the **La Promenade,** an elegant 24-hour coffeeshop with white-umbrellaed tables and an abundance of flowers and plants.

The showplace of the Desert Inn is the **Crystal Room,** featuring big-name entertainment like Rich Little, Crystal Gayle, Louie Anderson, Suzanne Somers, and Andy Williams. Shows usually cost $25 to $30, depending on the performer. There are no dinner shows, only cocktail shows, Tuesday through Sunday at 8 and 11 p.m., 9 p.m. on Thursday and Sunday.

The **Raffles Bar,** a luxurious British colonial–style casino lounge, also offers continuous top-talent musical presentations from 4 p.m. to 3 a.m. daily.

Rooms at the Desert Inn are $90 to $175, single or double; one-bedroom suites are $200 to $560; one- to four-bedroom suites run from $500 to $2,000. Prices vary with amenities and location.

THE TROPICANA RAMADA RESORT & CASINO: 3801 Las Vegas Blvd. South, Las Vegas, NV 89109 (tel. 702/739-2222, or toll free 800/634-4000).

Located at the least flashy extremity of the Strip, the Tropicana replaces the glitter and razzle-dazzle that is the norm in Vegas with subtle (for this town) elegance. A major renovation a few years ago added a $25-million, 600-room tower, a spectacular *porte cochère* entranceway; and a tri-level atrium with marble fountains, Aubusson carpets, and shop façades designed to look like the Champs-Élysées. Its art nouveau casino, under a stained-glass skylight ceiling, is exquisite. A second reconstruction completed in 1986 added another 22-story tower with 806 rooms (bringing the room count to 1,913), and a spectacular five-acre water park and "island" with its own lagoons. The hotel also expanded the casino and redecorated several public rooms.

The hotel is set on lush tropical grounds, which make a nice background for what seems like the largest indoor/outdoor swimming pool in the world! Across from the hotel is an 18-hole, par-70 golf course with a clubhouse, pro shop, and locker rooms. The Tropicana Racquet Club offers 24-hour play on its four outdoor courts.

Rooms are done in light, airy, tropical decor and fitted out with all the modern amenities. Standard accommodations are priced at $70 to $110 a night.

El Gaucho is the Tropicana's steak-and-chop house, done in an Argentinian motif: beamed ceilings, hides on the walls, bits, branding irons, halters, cinches, stirrups, woven shawls. Beef is the specialty of the house—steaks, ribs, and combination plates. Entrees range from $15 to $27.50; the top end of the range is a steak-and-seafood platter. El Gaucho is open only for dinner from 6 to 11 p.m.

The **Rhapsody** offers an excellent selection of entrees for all tastes. Whether you're moved toward Long Island duckling, veal piccata, filet mignon, rack of spring lamb, scampi, rainbow trout, Columbia River salmon, cioppino (San Francisco), or broiled Australian lobster tails, the Rhapsody will delight your appetite. And the desserts are not to be ignored: there's peach Melba, baked Alaska, French pastries, chocolate mousse—many of those wonderful things you never seem to have enough room for.

Most entrees on the à la carte menu cost $16.50 to $27.50 per person, but some of the dishes are priced for two—for example, the Chateaubriand for $39.50. The Rhapsody is open Tuesday through Saturday from 6 to 10:30 p.m.

The Tropics is just that—a Polynesian aura with beaded curtains, colorful banners, tiki figures, lighting glowing from large shells, and its own waterfall running through the center of the restaurant. The view to the outside is lovely. The restaurant has three tiers, glassed in, which overlook an "island" and all the activities and shows. The Tropics serves breakfast, lunch, and dinner from 7 a.m. to 10 p.m. Polynesian delights are the specialty of the house. Breakfast will cost $5 to $7.50; lunch, $7 to $13; and dinner, $12 to $19.

And there's a 24-hour coffeeshop, the **Java Java Coffee Room,** as well as **Antonio's Pizzeria,** the **Mizuno's Teppan Dining,** and the **Island Buffet.**

Finally, there's the **Tiffany Theater,** which is only incidentally a restaurant. It's primarily the setting for the lavish *Folies Bergère,* a dazzling musical extravaganza that has been delighting audiences since 1959. It's racy and funny and spectacular, with French cancan acts, live chimps, a horse, acrobats, comedians, magicians, and hundreds of semi-clad and/or elaborately costumed lovelies. The 8 p.m. dinner show is about $27.50 to $40, depending on your choice of entree; the 11 p.m. show is $22.50 including two drinks. There is no performance on Thursday.

THE RIVIERA HOTEL: 2901 Las Vegas Blvd. South, Las Vegas, NV 89109 (tel. 702/734-5110, or toll free 800/634-6753).

Another of the handful of Vegas hotels that projects a refined image, the Riviera attempts to cater "to the carriage trade." The lobby is tastefully arranged, with slot machines discreetly off to one side. Off the lobby is the hotel's promenade, lined with fashionable boutiques, shops, and airline offices. In addition to an immense and very popular casino, facilities include an Olympic-size pool surrounded by manicured lawns, and a palm-lined sundeck with piped-in music.

The addition of the Lanai Tower brought the Riviera's room capacity to 1,250. A third tower, under construction, will raise the room count to 3,975. Completion is scheduled for the end of 1989, at which time there will also be a total of nine showrooms.

The Lanai Tower is tastefully furnished, with bedroom and bath separated by a walk-through closet. Rooms cost $55 to $94 a night for double or single occupancy; suites run $120 to $575. All rooms have double or king-size beds.

The award-winning gourmet restaurant here is **Delmonico,** after the famous eatery once in the Wall Street district of New York City. It has just been redecorated—rich pearl gray walls are a backdrop for tables set with exquisite china, gleaming silver, and sparkling crystal; soft lighting from magnificent cut-crystal chandeliers; and dark wood chairs with gray cushioning. A well-stocked wine cellar is on the premises. A meal at Delmonico might begin with an appetizer of a fresh pâté (created daily). Sumptuous entrees include sautéed medallions of veal with fresh melon and port wine. Entrees cost $17 to $35.

The **Ristorante Italiano** offers a romantic Venetian setting under a ceiling of twinkling stars. Entrees are priced from $16 to $32, include osso buco, veal shank sautéed in olive oil with tomatoes, onions, celery, green pepper, and herbs; an accompanying order of broccoli in oil and garlic is a good idea.

The **Rik'Shaw,** the Riviera's new Chinese restaurant—all done in bamboo and Chinese red, with temple paintings, dragons, and rickshaws—is a pleasant warm place for reasonably priced dining.

Entrees cover the range of beef, pork, seafood, and poultry favorites such as roast pork with bok choy, lobster Cantonese, and sweet and sour chicken. Chef's specialties include a delicious lemon chicken and a pineapple duck. Prices range from $8.95 to $13.95. Combination dinners, which include appetizer, soup, and entree, cost $11.95 to $14.95. One very pleasant note: I found the service at Rik'Shaw to be superior to that of other restaurants where entrees were twice the price. Open nightly from 5 to 11 p.m.

Of course, in this 24-hour town there's a 24-hour coffeeshop, **Katy's Brasserie.**

Don't mention it to a soul, but for the best snack bargain in town, go to the Riviera's **Mardi Gras Plaza** snackbar (near the Burger King). They've got a super-delicious seafood cocktail for 99¢. The place is hard to find, but it's worth the effort.

Currently running in the **Versailles Theater** is *Splash,* an aquacade spectacular. It's a great family show, with diving and swimming stars, mermaids, dancers, and showgirls. The 8 p.m. dinner show and the 11 p.m. cocktail show are priced at $24.50 and $19.50 respectively. The dinner show is a buffet with two drinks. The theater is closed Wednesday.

At the Mardi Gras Plaza is a brilliant and long-running revue, *An Evening at La Cage,* starring a bevy of female impersonators—the best in town. It's clever, hilarious, and thoroughly enjoyable. The production is spectacular with its beautiful costuming and dance numbers. Shows are at 7, 9, and 11 p.m.; admission is $15, which includes a buffet or two drinks. Closed Tuesday.

THE FLAMINGO HILTON: 3555 Las Vegas Blvd. South, Las Vegas, NV 89109 (tel. 702/733-3111, or toll free 800/732-2111).

From its façade frieze of prismatic neon pink and orange flamingos to its tropical-resort-look palm-studded pool area, the Flamingo Hilton is one of my favorite Las Vegas hotels. A renovation a few years back added: a 28-story, 500-room tower; a keno lounge; a modernistic casino with the familiar Hilton neon rainbow motif; several new restaurants; and an underground parking garage.

Rooms here are especially attractive. Those in the older building, which are convenient to the pool, are pretty and quaint, with homey furnishings and old-fashioned lamps and quilts. Accommodations in another new 800-room tower (total room count is 2,920) offer spectacular views of the Strip or garden and are done in one of four color schemes (rust, green, beige/yellow, or peach) with cordinated wallpaper and drapes. They're large, attractive, and equipped with every luxury, including closed-circuit gaming instructions on the color TV. The tower has a health club, indoor/outdoor pool, tennis courts for day and night play, and a new gourmet restaurant, the Flamingo Room.

The **Flamingo Room** is a pleasant place to relax over breakfast, lunch, or dinner. The room is done in pastels, light woods, with soft recessed lighting and a large expanse of windows overlooking the pool. The salad bar for lunch has an appetizing array (one of the largest in town) of beautifully fresh choices, even including large shrimp. Dinner entrees offer a good selection of fresh fish, steaks, and rack of lamb for $15 to $26, though an average is about $18. Among the specialties of the house are a delicious mixed grill, and the Flamingo barbecue. The Flamingo Room is open daily from 7 a.m. to 11 a.m. for breakfast, 11:30 a.m. to 2 p.m. for lunch, and 5 to 11 p.m. for dinner.

The innovative **Food Fantasy Restaurant** is a 24-hour "buffeteria" with a sumptuous display of food; the Old West-motif **Beef Barron** features (you guessed it) beef dinners, ribs, black-bean soup, and corn on the cob (a five-course steak dinner with wine is $46 for two); the **Peking Market** is designed to suggest a bustling Chinese marketplace and serves Cantonese fare; **Lindy's** is patterned after the famous New York deli; and the **Crown Room Buffet** serves breakfast and dinner buffets at very low prices.

The Flamingo's showroom presents *City Lites,* a lavish ice spectacular, complete with gorgeous costumes, stunning sets, and all the rest. Dinner shows (at 7:45 p.m. nightly) begin at $22.95; the 11 p.m. show is $17.95, including two drinks.

There's also continuous entertainment almost around the clock in the Casino Lounge—singers and combos alternating with disco dancing.

Rates at the Flamingo Hilton are $70 to $118 a night, single or double.

ALADDIN HOTEL & CASINO: 3667 Las Vegas Blvd. South, Las Vegas, NV 89109 (tel. 702/736-0111, or toll free 800/634-3424).

With all the bidders for the once-defunct Aladdin Hotel, including such heavy hitters as Wayne Newton and Johnny Carson, when the hands were finally played out, the winner for the hotel was a Korean-born resident of Japan with a very large wallet. The Japanese seem convinced of Las Vegas's success in the high-stakes contest for top billing as the gambling, entertainment, and convention center of the country. After all, Las Vegas is just a short jump from the La Costa Resort in Carlsbad—purchased by the Japanese in 1987 for $250 million. And La Costa, or any one of several Japanese-owned hotels in San Francisco, is little more than a five-hour hop from Japanese holdings in Hawaii.

In January 1986, Ginji Yasuda bought the Aladdin Hotel & Casino (then in bankruptcy) for over $54 million. Mr. Yasuda became the first non–U.S. citizen to own a casino on the Strip, and the first to be licensed to operate a casino in the U.S.

The hotel has 1,100 modern, spacious rooms, totally redecorated and refurnished. The beige and gold furnishings convey a luxury theme, whether you choose to stay in one of the remodeled rooms or in a newly created duplex suite. Room rates are $70 to $100 per night, single or double occupancy. One- and two-bedroom suites are $400 to $700, and the duplex, super-suite extravaganza is $2,500.

To keep you fit, comfortable, and relaxed, the Aladdin sports a rooftop recreation center with a pool, lighted tennis courts for night play, and a snackbar for the lounge lizards.

The Aladdin has three entertainment venues: the 700-seat **Bagdad Showroom,** the 100-seat **Sinbad Lounge,** and, topping all the hotels in Las Vegas, the 7,000-seat **Aladdin Theatre for the Performing Arts**—the largest theatre in Las Vegas (apart from that at the University) and undoubtedly the one with the best acoustics. The theater has featured a remarkable range of performers from Rudolf Nureyev to Anita Baker, Fleetwood Mac, Tina Turner, and in an historic charity reunion, the Doobie Brothers.

And what would a Las Vegas hotel be without its own version of a perpetual-motion machine—the nonstop, 24-hour casino. Among the usual games, the Aladdin also features a new poker room and a high-limit race and sports book.

The Aladdin has three excellent restaurants, a deli, and the usual 24-hour coffeeshop so necessary to survival in Las Vegas. Most prestigious of the eateries is **The Florentine,** which offers French, Italian, and continental cuisine prepared tableside. This elegant restaurant, as its name suggests, is graced with Florentine frosted-glass panels, as well as floral murals and crystal chandeliers. House specialties are veal marsala and sumptuous braised sweetbreads. Entrees on the à la carte menu are priced from $22 to $48. Wines from cellars all over the world are available here. Open Wednesday through Sunday from 6 to 12 p.m.; reservations are suggested.

Another handsomely designed restaurant is **Wellington's,** an American version of an English pub—very masculine, with dark woods, brick floors, wrought-iron chandeliers, hunting prints, and, in the center of it all, a brass rotisserie. This beef house features certified black Angus aged beef, as well as first-rate steaks and barbecued selections. Wellington's prepares excellent salads tableside and offers an extensive wine list. Entrees range from $18 to $25. Open Friday through Tuesday from 6 to 12 p.m.; reservations suggested.

Fisherman's Port has been a hit with diners from the day it opened. The restaurant features fresh seafood flown in from the East Coast. Despite the Cajun character of much of its cuisine, Fisherman's Port looks more New England than New Orleans, with its board floors, stanchions, captain's chairs, netting, and seascapes. The menu features soups, bisques, and bouillabaisse, and entrees range from orange roughy to Alaskan king crab, crawfish étouffé, and blackened red fish, all accompanied by hush puppies and black-eyed peas; the popular Cajun dishes are served spicy or mild, to suit your taste. Entree prices range from $15 to $23. There is a special wine list to complement the unique cuisine. The Fisherman's Port is open Wednesday through Sunday from 6 to 12 p.m.

The Delicatessen looks like an oldtime deli—dark wood chairs with red cushions, red-and-black carpeting, and a counter that looks like an old-fashioned bar. You can watch the specialties of the house being prepared in an open kitchen —everything from scrambled eggs with lox and onions to cheese blintzes with sour cream or blueberries. Combination sandwiches, in an incredible variety, are served on three slices of thin corn rye and accompanied by potato salad, relish bowl, and garnish. For dinner, you can order the likes of boiled chicken in the pot, pot roast, or linguine and clams or shrimp. Should you feel you have room for dessert, everything from cheesecake (five varieties) to a banana split can be enjoyed while watching the keno board. Prices for luncheon or dinner range from $4 to $10, for breakfast from $2 to $5. The Delicatessen is open daily from 10 a.m. to midnight.

And **The Oasis,** the Aladdin's 24-hour coffeeshop, is ready whenever you are with sandwiches, salads, main dishes, desserts, and fountain selections. Prices go up to $10.

THE SANDS HOTEL & CASINO: 3355 Las Vegas Blvd. South, Las Vegas, NV 89109 (tel. 702/733-5000, or toll free 800/634-6901).

A Las Vegas landmark since 1952, the Sand's balconied white circular tower (bathed in green light after dark) climbs 18 stories skyward. In total, the hotel offers 750 rooms, some of which are housed in smaller units named after famous racetracks; these are grouped around palm-fringed gardens and a putting green.

Facilities comprise two large swimming pools, six night-lit tennis courts, boutiques, beauty salon and barbershop, car-rental desk, and the rest. And, of course, there's the ever-present casino, large and plush.

The spacious rooms are softly color coordinated in lovely hues. Fully equipped with all amenities, they're quite spacious. Rates, single or double, run from $65 to $180, depending on location.

The Sands boasts a prestigious restaurant: the opulent **Regency Room,** which serves French/continental cuisine like prime rib with Yorkshire pudding or roast duckling, for $19 to $45.

What would a Las Vegas hotel be without a restaurant serving Italian specialties? The **Mediterranean** offers an enticing selection of antipasti, hot and cold, from the shrimp sautéed in garlic with cream and basil sauce, to the antipasto Freddi with marinated vegetables, calamari salad, roasted peppers, and mushrooms. Entrees include chicken breast prepared several ways, any one of which is bound to please you—chicken Angelo is simmered with artichoke hearts, mushrooms, and grapes in a white wine sauce; Romano is sautéed and finished with a cream sauce and strips of red and green peppers; and Sicilian is sautéed with zucchini, summer squash, and eggplant, touched with a hint of garlic, and flamed with white wine. The Mediterranean also prepares delectable standards such as veal marsala and veal milanese. Seafood focuses on shrimp or scampi prepared fra diavolo or on pescattore with garlic, basil, and white wine.

The à la carte dinner entrees are $9.50 to $14. The Mediterranean is open daily from 5 p.m. to 1 a.m.

The **Garden Terrace** offers 24-hour dining—you guessed it—on the terrace, with a wide range of breakfast, lunch, and dinner choices.

Breakfast, served around the clock, offers a variety of omelets, scrambled eggs with nova and onions, eggs "your way," blintzes, griddle cakes, danish, and the usual assortment of beverages, juices, and fruit. For midday hunger pangs, there is a good selection of sandwiches, including "create your own" hamburgers and a few good waist-watchers such as lemon baked chicken and a delicious vegetable plate. Dinner entrees range from tenderloin of pork or prime rib to stuffed red snapper. For the incurable steak-lover, the Garden Terrace has sirloin or filet mignon.

In addition to all of the above, the Garden Terrace has a Chinese menu during dinner hours. The Chinese Kitchen lists everything you expect, and a lot you do not, from shredded pork in brown sauce (the most famous Peking-style dish) to Peking duck (on 24-hour advance notice).

The occidental menu ranges from $6 to $19. The Chinese Kitchen entrees are $11 to $27.50, the average being about $14; top of the line is the Peking duck.

The Garden Terrace is open daily and serves breakfast around the clock, lunch from 11 a.m. to 3 p.m., and dinner from 5 to 11 p.m. The Chinese Kitchen serves from 5 p.m. to 2 a.m.

Nightly entertainment is in the **Copa Room** (made famous by Sinatra), where stars like David Brenner, Wayland Flowers and Madame, Dionne Warwick, and Doc Severinsen have all appeared. Cocktail shows at 7 p.m. and 10 p.m. vary from $11 to $25, depending on who's appearing or the particular revue. There's also live entertainment in the **Winner's Circle Lounge,** off the casino, from 5 p.m. to the wee hours.

DUNES HOTEL AND COUNTRY CLUB: 3650 Las Vegas Blvd. South, Las Vegas, NV 89109 (tel. 702/737-4110, or toll free 800/634-6971).

The Dunes is another large Vegas hotel, with 1,285 rooms in two towers and a cluster of smaller buildings. Facilities include an 18-hole championship golf course and country club, health club for men and women, restaurants and bars, two immense pools (both Olympic size), many shops, and an opulent casino.

The Dunes is one of the many Las Vegas hotels recently acquired by Japanese investors. It was purchased in August 1987 for the tidy sum of $157.7 million, and it has been announced that the owners intend to spend $300 million more to double the hotel's capacity.

The private guest rooms are spacious and color coordinated. Each has running ice water, a separate theatrically lighted makeup area, and a table for in-room dining. Prices for singles or doubles range from $60 to $90 per night.

The Dunes also has a year-round "Drive-In" package for three days/two nights. Weekdays the total package price is $110, double or single occupancy:

weekends the cost is $140. The package includes accommodations, one buffet breakfast, the Oasis Lounge show with two drinks, the main show (*Comedy Store*) with two drinks, a free keno ticket, a $100-value fun book, and all taxes and gratuities.

One of the major dining rooms is the exotic, palatial **Sultan's Table.** The motif comes from Kismet, a pleasure palace of the Far East. This one features lots of stained glass, a waterfall, and a tented entrance. The gourmet continental menu features entrees (priced from $20 to $27.50) like breast of capon Kiev with wild rice.

The **Dome of the Sea** is a seashell-shaped seafood restaurant with flying fish projected on the walls and a blond mermaid playing the harp from a floating gondola. The basic color scheme is blue and green, with varicolored lights pouring through the domed ceiling. Among the specialties of the Dome are lobster thermidor in casserole, shrimp curry with rice pilaf, and bouillabaisse, for $25 to $35.

Other choices include the **Chinese Kitchen** and a 24-hour coffeeshop called the **Savoy.**

Currently the **Casino Theatre** features *The Comedy Store,* a riotously funny revue from its L.A. namesake. There are two cocktail shows nightly ($14.50, including two drinks) at 9 and 11:30 p.m., on Saturday at 8, 10, and midnight. Closed Monday.

FRONTIER HOTEL: 3120 Las Vegas Blvd. South, Las Vegas, NV 89109 (tel. 702/734-0110, or toll free 800/634-6966).

The horseshoe-shaped Frontier is heralded by a 200-foot-high sign. The hotel itself is surrounded by beautiful grounds, manicured lawns, fountains, and little rustic bridges over a reflecting pool. Within is an enormous and lavish casino, along with 600 guest rooms plus shops and services. A broad range of recreational facilities are on the premises: an Olympic-size swimming pool, three tennis courts (all lit for night play), and a putting green; golf is available nearby at the Desert Inn.

Rooms are decorated in bright mauves, teals, and blues. Rates are $60 to $110, single or double.

The Frontier's **Branding Iron Steak House** has a rustic/formal western theme; specialties include a variety of steaks and seafood dishes, like Florida stone crab on ice, for $14 to $29.50.

At **Diamond Jim's** you'll find a down-home mix of Gay Nineties and Southern atmosphere. In contrast to the ambience, the menu is decidedly upscale. Appetizers include oysters Rockefeller, clams casino, and snails Escoffier. For a simpler approach, there are Blue Point oysters or cherrystone clams on the halfshell. The Florida stone crab featured in the Branding Iron restaurant is also on the appetizer list here.

Diamond Jim's list of specialties has something for everyone—roast prime rib served with Yorkshire pudding, Long Island duckling à l'orange roasted and basted in Grand Marnier, or, for seafood-lovers, bouillabaisse with garlic bread, a whole Dover sole, or shrimp "inferno" (spicy hot jumbo shrimp said to have been created for Diamond Jim himself). All veal dishes, from veal oscar to veal française, are served with linguine tossed in oil and butter, or with fettuccine Alfredo.

Entrees are $19 to $26 à la carte. A daily "special" full-course dinner is always available; the price varies with the entree.

Diamond Jim's tempting dessert list includes your turn-of-the-century peach Melba and, if you're going all out, an impressive list of flambé specialties for two, including baked Alaska flambéed at your table, cherries jubilee, and crêpes Suzette.

Diamond Jim's is open Wednesday through Sunday from 6 p.m. to midnight.

There's also daily breakfast, lunch, and dinner fare at the **Longhorn Café.**

The **Wild Horse Lounge,** off the casino, offers live entertainment into the early-morning hours. No cover, two-drink minimum.

SAHARA HOTEL AND CASINO: Las Vegas Boulevard South and Sahara Avenue, Las Vegas, NV 89109 (tel. 702/737-2111, or toll free 800/634-6666 or, 800/323-3466).

Situated at the north end of the Strip, the Sahara's 24-story skyscraper and 14-story tower buildings are set on a 20-acre complex that contains 932 rooms, four restaurants, a showroom, two swimming pools, shops, and services. And, of course, there's an enormous casino with the usual accoutrements.

The rooms are spacious and bright, with neat, modern decor and all the modern amenities. All have individual dressing rooms. Singles and doubles rent for $60 to $110 per night.

Restaurant options range from the South Seas to the "veddy English." In the latter category is the classic gourmet **House of Windsor,** done in regal red tones, with beamed ceilings and pewter and stained-glass fixtures. Specialties of the house are more continental than English, however, running the gamut from chicken Kiev with Oriental rice to frogs' legs meunière, for $18 to $35. The South Seas fare is at a **Don the Beachcomber** restaurant on the premises, featuring the usual exotic Polynesian decor and live music for dancing nightly. Full Polynesian dinners (with entrees like boned Mandarin duck, and lobster in rice wine sauce) and American-style steak and seafood are served for $14 to $26. There's also a 24-hour coffeeshop, the **Caravan Room,** which turns out, among other things, huge, heavenly banana splits. For those who prefer buffet dining, the **Garden Room** offers a table piled high at every meal.

The **Congo Theatre** presents two cocktail shows nightly at 8 and 11 p.m. Prices vary depending on the entertainer or show. Appearances have been made by George Carlin and Don Rickles.

STARDUST HOTEL: 3000 Las Vegas Blvd. South, Las Vegas, NV 89109 (tel. 702/732-6111, or toll free 800/634-6757).

The Stardust is centrally located (right in the center of the Strip), and its immense casino is one of the liveliest in town. The hotel has 1,400 rooms located in six buildings and a tower. Facilities include an Olympic-size swimming pool, four restaurants, and a shopping arcade; there's even a huge campsite.

Accommodations run the gamut from camper parking to penthouse, with camperland sites (with hookups) for $10 a day; attractive poolside units are priced at $89 to $112. Poolside mini-suites or tower suites begin at $140. All rooms have every modern amenity. Inquire about package plans, which include show tickets, etc.

Among the restaurants on the premises is **Tony Roma's** for ribs ($6 to $13). **Ralph's Diner** is the Stardust's contribution to memories of places where some of us ate in the '50s and early '60s. There are a black-and-white checkerboard tile floor, stainless-steel everything, an old juke box, tiered booths, and a snackbar/soda fountain. About the only items missing are pictures of James Dean, Marilyn, and Elvis.

Can you guess what, besides nostalgia, is served in Ralph's Diner? Hamburgers, fries, steaks, and those fountain drinks that somehow don't taste quite the same now. Meals cost $3.75 to $10.95. The diner is open daily from 6:30 a.m. to 2 a.m.

William B's is a toned-down version of a Texas steakhouse—dark, masculine, and woody. The prime attraction here is steak and more steak, with seafood running a strong second. Steaks range from the usual New York steak, filet, and rib eye to prime rib, all of which are offered at $12.95 to $25.

William B's is open from 5 to 11 p.m. Sunday through Thursday, till midnight Friday and Saturday.

There's also the **Buffet Room** serving low-priced all-you-can-eat meals, and the **Temporary Coffeeshop,** a garden-motif 24-hour coffeeshop.

The big show takes place in the **Café Continental**—it's the lavish *Lido de Paris* revue, a Las Vegas tradition since 1958. Like the others of its ilk, it's great fun, with incredible sets and costumes, acrobats, and Bobby Berosini and his orangutans. There are two cocktail shows at 7 and 11 p.m., priced at $25, including two drinks. Closed Tuesdays.

THE CIRCUS CIRCUS HOTEL: 2880 Las Vegas Blvd. South, Las Vegas, NV 89109 (tel. 702/734-0410, or toll free 800/634-3450, 800/634-6833 in Arizona, California, Idaho, and Utah).

The most unusual hotel on the Strip, Circus Circus has a building shaped like an enormous big-top tent, and its immense sign is clown-shaped. That's because inside there are world-famous circus acts going on every day (free) from 11 a.m. to midnight. The entire show—trapeze artists, acrobats, tightrope walkers, etc.—takes place in the world's largest permanent circus, on the mezzanine level, surrounded by an exciting arcade of midway games where kids (and adults) can play and watch the circus acts.

Other guest amenities include a shopping promenade, five restaurants, three snack bars, casinos, race and sports book, and (can you believe it?) a wedding chapel.

The pleasantly decorated rooms (of which there are about 2,793, with 1,188 in the new Circus Skyrise across the street), are priced from $22 to $45, single or double. Or you can park your camper in the Circusland RV Park for $10 a night, with all utility hookups.

For dining, you have your choice of the 24-hour **Pink Pony** coffeeshop; the 24-hour **Skyrise Dining Room** (entrees about $6.95); **The Steak House,** a casual place for prime ribs, seafood, etc. ($15 to $28); the **Circus Circus Buffet,** for an all-you-can-eat buffet breakfast ($2.50) with over 40 items of all kinds, lunch ($2.75), and dinner ($3.95); the **Snack Train,** for fast-food service; and the **Circus Pizzeria,** featuring—you guessed it—pizza (and pasta) at $7 to $14; and two snack bars.

For liquid refreshment you can visit the **Gilded Cage Lounge,** the **Skyrise Lounge,** or the revolving **Horse-A-Round Bar** with a view of the circus acts.

Fun things galore are tucked into the Circus Circus cornucopia of goodies. This is a sensational hotel-casino-circus that truly must be seen to be believed.

EL MOROCCO: 2975 Las Vegas Blvd. South, Las Vegas, NV 89109 (tel. 702/735-7145).

Contemporary in motif, but Moorish in ambience, the El Morocco shares its facilities with its next-door neighbor, La Concha. These include a nice-size pool, sundeck, beauty parlor, and gift shop. On its own, El Morocco has Las Vegas–style plush rooms, with flocked red and gold curtains painted behind the beds. Priced at $39 to $48, single or double (the less expensive ones are on the outside, not facing the pool), the rooms are spacious and contain two double or two queen-size or one king-size bed. Each is equipped with color TV, radio, clock, direct-dial phone, and tub/shower bath.

On the premises is a good restaurant called the **Carving Cart,** for steak, seafood, and prime-rib dinners.

LA CONCHA MOTEL: 2955 Las Vegas Blvd. South, Las Vegas, NV 89109 (tel. 702/735-1255).

This hotel, just a dice throw from the El Morocco, has no casino and no dining facilities. It offers, instead, the use of all the amenities at El Morocco, which is under the same ownership.

The 100 rooms here contain either two double or one king-size bed. Once again the only-in-Vegas decor features flocked striped wallpaper, pineapple lamps, and gold sparkles on the ceilings. There are dressing areas in each room. Singles and doubles are available at $37 to $45 per night.

MINI-PRICE MOTOR INN: 4155 Koval Lane, Las Vegas, NV 89109 (tel. 702/731-2111, or toll free 800/634-6541).

The budget traveler should consider this pleasant hostelry right behind Bally's Grand. It has a swimming pool and sundeck, a Jacuzzi, a gift shop, and a small casino. There's also a coffeeshop and bar near the registration desk. Rooms have color TVs, direct-dial phones, and air conditioning.

Rates are $32 to $40, single or double. An extra adult adds $5. There's ample free parking.

MOTEL 6: 195 E. Tropicana Ave. (at Koval Lane), Las Vegas, NV 89109 (tel. 702/798-0728).

Just two blocks off the Strip, this branch of the amazingly low-priced and well-located Motel 6 chain has 877 units and is growing by the minute. All rooms have air conditioning and shower bath, as well as free color TV, and phones in all rooms (no charge for local calls). There's even a swimming pool and a therapy pool.

Room rates are $22.95 for one person, $28.95 for two. Ask about the Family Plan if there are three or more of you. Be sure to reserve early and you'll not only enjoy very adequate accommodations, but save lots of money that will come in handy for shows and casinos.

ALLSTAR INN: 5085 S. Industrial Rd. (just south of Tropicana Avenue), Las Vegas, NV 89118 (tel. 702/739-6747).

This branch of Allstar Inns is one block west of the Strip. It's low priced, has handsome, modern furnishings, and is very comfortable and meticulously clean. All rooms have a full tub and shower, and air conditioning. It's a very attractive bargain. There's a swimming pool and, surprisingly enough, a putting green. TV is free, and so are the local phone calls. Room rates are $22.95 to $28.95 single, $27.95 to $33.95 double.

There's another Allstar Inn at 4125 Boulder Hwy. (between Desert Inn Road and Sahara Avenue), Las Vegas, NV 89121 (tel. 702/457-8051). Rates and accommodations are the same as above. There's a pool, but (alas) no putting green.

GOLDEN NUGGET HOTEL AND CASINO: 129 E. Fremont St. (at the corner of Casino Center Boulevard), Las Vegas, NV 89101 (tel. 702/385-7111, or toll free 800/634-3454).

When you consider accommodations in Las Vegas, among the best and most luxurious is the all-new Golden Nugget Hotel and Casino. Gone is the fantasy of the Wild West that once characterized the hotel. Today this extraordinary downtown establishment commands top rating among all hotel-casinos. A hint of its interior elegance is presented by a new façade of pure-white Grecian marble, cut, hand-carved, and polished by old-world artisans, by the white canopies, Tivoli lights, and beveled mirrors, and by a white-on-white motif subtly accented with brass. Hundreds of palm trees in planter beds surround the entire property.

As you enter the driveway, you arrive under a gleaming white portico. Oval etched-glass panels flank the doors which lead directly to the hotel registration and lobby areas—you don't have to work your way through a casino to arrive at the front desk. Inside, the decor is opulent, from the Verdi marble-inlaid floors inset with custom-woven wool carpet to the antique furnishings and stained-glass panels.

Oversize guest rooms have been decorated in soothing pastels, soft creams, and desert shades. All rooms are equipped with every modern amenity: direct-dial phones, AM/FM radios, color TV, tub/shower baths, oversize terry towels, toilette articles, and more. Of course the hotel affords the services of a concierge, 24-hour room service in addition to that of the coffeeshop, same-day laundry and dry-cleaning service, car rental, valet parking, and other comfortable touches. The Golden Nugget prides itself on attention to detail, whether in the hotel's elegant appointments or in the extra effort extended by the staff to make a guest's stay enjoyable.

Set among beds of flowers and palm trees is an outdoor pool (open May through October) with a whirlpool spa, a snackbar, and a poolside lounge area. If relaxing in the desert sun is too much of a good thing, there's always the spa, a health emporium geared for body building, exercise, and aerobics. There are separate men's and women's facilities for massages, steamrooms, sauna, and whirlpool spas. A full-service beauty salon provides services for men and women.

The 30,000-square-foot casino is handsomely styled and designed, and well equipped for the total comfort of its customers. There are 42 blackjack tables, eight craps layouts, three roulette wheels, 13 poker tables, a Big Six wheel, three baccarat tables, and a luxurious keno lounge. A full assortment of more than 700 video and traditional slot machines, all brass clad, add the finishing touch to the casino area.

In addition to fine restaurants, the Nugget offers two notably beautiful drinking establishments. The **Canopy Bar,** just off the casino, features, a gleaming brass bar top and richly colored stained glass depicting 19th-century saloon scenes; and the exquisite **Victoria Bar** contains overstuffed furnishings, marble-topped tables, a magnificent wood-and-mirrored bar, a 24-carat gold-plated espresso/cappuccino machine, and a bar rail made of onyx.

Rates for the hotel's rooms are $65 to $95, single or double; suites start at $230 and go up to $800. Children under 12 stay free in a room with their parents; extra adults pay $10 a night.

Top-of-the-line restaurant at the Golden Nugget is **Elaine's.** It's located on the second level of the Spa Suite Tower. As you approach the ebony-black entry, you won't expect the classic French decor inside. The dining room is elegant, and the effect is rich. Your eye is caught by a superb Venetian crystal chandelier and the impressionist-style paintings. There's a feeling of privacy you rarely find in a dining room, undoubtedly effected by the curtained booths and well-spaced tables. The menu is à la carte. Among Elaine's excellent specialties are rack of lamb, chicken with wild mushrooms, bouillabaisse, and a fabulous quail with a mousse of veal. Entrees range from $25 to $35. The wine list is of the same fine quality as the food. Jackets are required for men and reservations are suggested. Elaine's is open nightly from 6 to 11 p.m.

Stefano's is the northern Italian restaurant in the Golden Nugget. As you

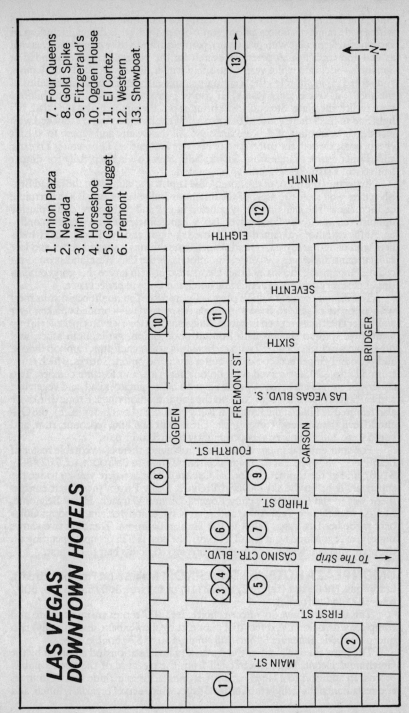

LAS VEGAS
DOWNTOWN HOTELS

1. Union Plaza
2. Nevada
3. Mint
4. Horseshoe
5. Golden Nugget
6. Fremont
7. Four Queens
8. Gold Spike
9. Fitzgerald's
10. Ogden House
11. El Cortez
12. Western
13. Showboat

enter, the feeling is that you're in an Italian garden. Stefano's has a varied menu with a wide range of choices among some dozen fresh pasta dishes, including an exceptional fettuccine with prosciutto, parmesan, and a silky cream sauce, as well as veal and fresh fish. A perennial search for the perfect veal piccata ended at Stefano's—delicate white veal, exquisitely tender, lightly touched with lemon, and served piping hot. It's the seemingly simple dishes that display the genius of the chef (this one is from Rome). If you've ever wanted to indulge a childlike urge to lick the plate, Stefano's will bring it on. Be sure to order the salad. It's light and so fresh there's sure to be a garden by the kitchen. And it's touched with just the right amount of delicate dressing. All this beauty and superb food isn't cheap, but it's worth the price. And the service is attentive. The menu is à la carte and dinner entrees range from $17 to $35. Stefano's is open daily for dinner from 6 to 11 p.m. Reservations are suggested.

Reflecting the decor of the hotel, **Lillie Langtry's,** named for the famed British actress who stole the heart of the infamous Judge Roy Bean, is a masterpiece of Victoriana. The walls are richly paneled in oak and mahogany, chairs plushly upholstered in a lovely floral velvet, tables handsomely set with wheat-color linen. At the entrance is a stained-glass domed skylight, and overhead globe chandeliers with dangling crystal; potted palms, brass railings, swagged velvet and lace café curtains, flickering gaslamps, fine murals of the Old West, and pressed-tin ceilings are among the many other elements that help create this gorgeous setting. Like every other part of this fine hotel, it is done in perfect taste.

The dinner menu at Lillie's place is Cantonese. You might begin your meal with an order of golden-fried shrimp or crispy rumaki—broiled chicken liver and water chestnut wrapped in bacon. Suggested entrees: lemon chicken; shrimp Cantonese (jumbo shrimp with minced pork, onion, garlic, bean sauce, and other spices); chicken sautéed with cashew nuts, water chestnuts, bamboo shoots, and peas; and ginger beef cooked in oyster sauce and onion. Entrees, which range from $12 to $20, are served with oolong tea, rice, and fortune cookies. Two American entrees are listed—prime rib with baked potato, salad, and vegetable, and barbecued spareribs with corn on the cob and onion rings. Exotic drinks are also featured at Lillie's: the Rangoon Ruby (vodka and cranberry juice), the Oriental Devil (banana and rum), or the Great Wall of China (coconut, rum, and vodka), etc. Lillie Langtry's is open nightly from 5 to 11 p.m.

For your entertainment at the Golden Nugget there is a veritable roster of headliners (who appear at the magnificent new **Theatre Ballroom,** tel. 702/386-8100), and at the intimate, informal **Cabaret.** This is where you go to see the superstars light up the sky—David Brenner, Dolly Parton (her debut engagement was in the Cabaret), Kenny Rogers, Dionne Warwick, Harry Belafonte, Melissa Manchester, Paul Anka, and Alan King, among others. Whoopi Goldberg made her Las Vegas debut in the Theatre Ballroom. There are two shows nightly, except Monday, at 8 and 11 p.m. The cost is $25 on up, depending on the performer and whether or not dinner is served, so it's best to call first.

UNION PLAZA HOTEL AND CASINO: 1 Main St. (at Fremont Street), Las Vegas, NV 89101 (tel. 702/386-2110, or toll free 800/634-6575, 800/634-6821 in California).

This is another nice downtown choice. Its 1,037 rooms are immaculate, and complete with color TV, direct-dial phone, tub/shower bath, and (usually) two queen-size beds. Rates are $45 to $65 single, $50 to $70 double.

The hotel is connected to the Amtrak railroad station and adjoined by the Greyhound Depot, but you can't tell from the elegance of the hotel's public rooms. In addition to a large, modern casino, facilities include several lounges and restaurants: the delightful **Center Stage,** which serves breakfast, lunch, and an elegant dinner from a unique vantage point overlooking the lights of Fremont Street; **Kung Fu Plaza,** which serves Chinese-Thai food; and the 24-hour **Plaza Diner and Snack Bar.**

The **Sports Deck** features a heated pool, lighted tennis courts, and a quarter-mile jogging track.

The 650-seat **Plaza Theater Restaurant,** in which Broadway-style musicals are featured, has in the past been the home of *South Pacific, Gypsy,* and *The Odd Couple.*

There are two shows nightly (except Monday) at 8 and 11:30 p.m. The 8 p.m. show costs $14 to $22 and includes dinner; the 11:30 p.m. show is $9.50, with two cocktails.

The Union Plaza also offers entertainment from 3 p.m. to 3 a.m. in the **Omaha Lounge,** off the casino. On Monday at 8 p.m. there's a talent showcase. No cover or minimum.

4. MORE RESTAURANTS

As I pointed out earlier, not all of the best restaurants are in the hotels. Here are some excellent choices, depending on your tastes and pocketbook. I've started with the most expensive and worked downward in price.

One last note: if you've never been to Las Vegas before, or have eaten only within the hotels, you may find the seafood to be adequate but not exceptional. It's certainly not up to the standards of the Oyster Bar in Grand Central Station in New York City, for example. All this may change with the advent of the Golden Nugget On The Strip. It's the intention of the hotel to have the finest seafood restaurant in the country, and what the Golden Nugget wants, the Golden Nugget usually gets. In the meantime, there are a number of good places to eat outside of the hotels.

Whatever the length of your visit to Las Vegas, make the **Golden Steer,** 308 W. Sahara Ave., just west of the Strip (tel. 702/384-4470 or 387-9236) one of your required stops for dinner. (I wouldn't want you to miss the Golden Steer as I almost did: directly after heading west on Sahara turn into the lot after the Texaco sign on your right.)

The bar on your left as you enter has an Old West look and feel—red leather, a forest-green ceiling, steer horns, antique guns, western paintings, framed silver dollars, and red velvet curtains. To one side there's a beautiful old glass-encased slot machine that's never had the opportunity to gobble up a single coin.

Among the excellent entrees offered, there are a number you would expect to find (and some you would not) in a restaurant called the Golden Steer. Choices range from half a broiled spring chicken at $12 to the prime rib (called a Diamond Lil or Diamond Jim) at $19.50 or $24. But then you may prefer either the moist and delicious rack of lamb or the chateaubriand for two at $24 per person.

You can also enjoy a somewhat more unusual and sumptuous meal of Bob White quail—a pair for $24 per person. A Beef and Bird entree offers some of the best of both worlds, with quail and a petit filet mignon accompanied by wild rice for $21.

There is nothing commonplace about the veal or chicken specialties, though you may have seen them listed on other restaurant menus. The quality is exceptional, whether you choose the veal française—dipped in egg batter and sautéed with mushrooms and lemon; or the Chicken of the Angels—a boneless breast sautéed with mushrooms and hearts of artichokes. Chicken and veal specialties, served with spaghetti or toasted ravioli, go for $16.50 to $17.50.

As for the seafood, the highlight of the menu is an extra-large imported Dover sole for $22, served à la carte with a baked potato. Other specialties from the sea include Australian lobster tail and Alaskan king crab legs priced according to market.

One of the pleasant surprises here: without a doubt, the Golden Steer has the best baked potato I've ever eaten in any restaurant at any time; it's indicative of the quality you may expect, whatever you order. I also hear from a good source that the restaurant has the best Caesar salad, bar none. I simply did not have room to try it.

The house offers a good selection of imported and domestic wines at reasonable prices. The Golden Steer menu identifies what it pours when you order your booze by its generic name—the quality, as you might expect, matches that of the food.

If you have room for dessert, there are several varieties of delicious cheese cake, or if you're a chocolate freak, the chocolate bomba ice cream may be just what it takes to hit the spot. Desserts range in price from $3 to $3.85.

You don't want to join the crowd at the Golden Steer if you plan to eat and run back to the baccarat table. Service here is appropriately paced for dining, not gulping. Open daily from 5 p.m. to midnight, closed on Thanksgiving and Christmas. Reservations are suggested.

Step inside **Pamplemousse,** 400 East Sahara Ave., one block east of the Strip (tel. 702/733-2066), and you're no longer in Vegas but on the Côte d'Azur. Pamplemousse is an intimate and elegant restaurant decorated in subtle shades of pink and wine, with candles and flowers and ceiling fans. Classical music or light jazz plays softly in the background. There's a wood-burning fireplace that's used on cool evenings, and an outdoor garden area under a bit of tenting. For small private parties, there's a dining area secluded from the main dining room. It's all extremely charming and un-Vegasy.

The restaurant's name, by the way, which means grapefruit, was suggested by the late singer Bobby Darin; it just appealed to him for some reason. Darin was one of French owner Georges La Forge's numerous celebrity friends and patrons.

Pamplemousse has no fixed menu. The restaurant's talented chef prepares four entrees every evening from the freshest ingredients available. The house specialty is duck, served with one of four sauces—kiwi, orange, cherry, or banana rum. There are also fresh fish selections, and a beef or veal dish. But if there's something you're particularly craving, Pamplemousse will prepare a meal to order with 24 hours' notice. The $20 to $24 price of your entree includes fresh breads, fresh boiled eggs, and a basket of fresh raw vegetables served with a dip. And to accompany your meal, you can select from perhaps the most extensive wine list in Las Vegas, chosen personally by Georges La Forge with great care. Beer is available, but no hard liquor is served. And you can round out your meal with a delectable dessert—perhaps a tarte, a mousse, a crème caramel, homemade ice cream, or a flambé.

Pamplemousse is open Tuesday through Sunday from 6 to 11 p.m. Reservations are essential.

The theme of **Freddie G's,** 355 Convention Center Dr., near Paradise Rd. (tel. 702/735-3653) is "feed them well," and so they do, from appetizer to dessert.

Freddie G's, opened in January 1987, has a New England look, though it serves up food from many regions of the country. The characteristic brick, stone, vaulted ceilings, exposed beams, and seascapes are contrasted and complemented by warm rose-brown banquettes and tables. Soft-pink track lighting gives the room a feeling of intimacy. Delicate china, attractive stemware, Evian water served with a slim slice of lemon—all foretell a similar attention to detail in the food.

Hot sourdough bread (and it truly is hot) is served with your order. The presentation of the crab Louie that I ordered indicated a chef who took great pride in his work, and the tomatoes in the salad tasted wonderfully bush-ripened. Salads aren't your favorite for lunch? The broiled boneless breast of capon with sautéed mushrooms is thoroughly soul-satisfying. Or if you seek beef, there are huge San Francisco half-pound sourdough burgers, plain or with various combinations of American or mozzarella cheese, prosciutto, onions and peppers, bacon and green chilis, or avocado and bacon. Lunch will be about $5.50 to $8.75 for salads, $7.75 to $9.75 for entrees (the capon is $8), and $5.75 to $6.75 for the sourdough burgers.

But the exceptional dining experience at Freddie G's is the evening meal. A good selection of Cajun specialties (running from $16 to $22) includes chicken Dijon baked in bread crumbs with a distinctive mustard flavor, blackened redfish, and Freddie G's jambalaya, all served with salad, red beans and rice, and Cajun vegetables. Other entrees include "the ultimate Porterhouse," Piero's roast kosher chicken, Maine lobster, and Chicago-style calf's liver, at a range of $17 to $26 (the lobster priced according to market). Non-Cajun entrees are served with the house salad, baked potato, and a garden-fresh vegetable.

Desserts are excellent, and one of my favorites has always been the simple rice pudding, unadorned but certainly not pedestrian at Freddie G's. Fresh cinnamon, a raisin or two, cream, and the rice cooked to absolute perfection—it's scrumptious.

Freddie G's has a remarkable selection of wines, both domestic and imported.

And one of the fine touches to an enjoyable lunch or dinner: the service is very attentive and well informed without being intrusive.

Freddie G's is open for lunch weekdays from 11:30 a.m. to 2:30 p.m. Dinner is served nightly from 5 p.m. to midnight. Reservations are suggested for dinner.

Keller and Fox Ltd., 850 S. Rancho Dr., near Charleston (tel. 877-2711) is as lacking in flamboyance as a Las Vegas restaurant can possibly be. A few minutes west of the Strip, the restaurant is well worth the detour for the food and the environment in which it's served. You'll find here the understated elegance of a beautiful English country home, a far cry from the decor of most Las Vegas eateries.

Luncheon specials at Keller and Fox change daily and generally include choices of pasta, crêpes, English pies, eggs, fish, fowl, or meat. Among the crêpes you might find one filled with beef Stroganoff, or one filled with chicken and duck curry. The savory English pies do not include the overworked standard of beef and kidney, but, rather, a more interesting choice of spinach, chicken, or vegetable. The roast game hen with fresh plum sauce tempted me, but I chose the salmon with lime and ginger, and it surpassed my best expectations.

Among the standard light-lunch selections are cold pasta primavera, salade niçoise, and a Windsor salad with poached breast of chicken in champagne sauce. Diehard beef-eaters are also accommodated here, though: the day of my lunch, a top sirloin au poivre was on the menu. Luncheon specials range from $4.75 to $8.50, standard entrees from $7.75 to $14.50.

Dinner is a delight. Keller and Fox serves superb roast duckling—among the best I've ever had. The duckling is offered three ways: with garlic, herbs, duck stock, and cream; with raspberry sauce; or with fresh pineapple, sautéed bananas, and Jamaican rum. It isn't an easy choice. Nor does the rest of the menu make deciding any simpler. Lamb chops en croûte, individually wrapped in puff pastry with a veal and truffle filling, competed for my attention, as did the poached salmon with caviar mousseline, and the tournedos Valoise—two tenderloins of beef sautéed and garnished with artichoke hearts and mushrooms and served in a veal stock and burgundy-hollandaise sauce. Entrees range from $16.50 to $22.50.

Desserts, or "confections" as they're dubbed here, are all made on the premises and vary daily; the price for each is $3.75.

The restaurant takes special care of its patrons and will prepare low-cholesterol and/or low-sodium meals on request in advance. Keller and Fox's quality is also reflected in the very attentive and helpful service of the immaculately attired waiters.

Open for lunch Monday through Friday from 11:30 a.m. to 2:30 p.m., for dinner Monday through Saturday from 6:30 to 10:30 p.m. Reservations advised.

As you pass through a simple granite courtyard, the small Japanese-style bridge on your left spans a pond that requires only a few koi (goldfish) to complete the tranquil introduction to **Oh No Tokyo,** 4455 W. Flamingo Rd., near Arville Street (tel. 876-4455). The entry prepares you for the lovely California/Japanese interior, vertical black blinds, shoji screens, and hanging half-curtains that divide the serving areas from the main rooms. You can choose to dine at a table or in one of several tatami rooms (assuming that everyone in your party has socks of whole cloth—remember, shoes are removed before you enter).

The last time I had Japanese food of comparable quality and diversity to that served at Oh No Tokyo was in New York City. The à la carte sushi menu is quite broad; it includes seaweed rolls and specialty rolls, among which is a superb Emperor's roll with shrimp tempura, scallops, green onion, and masago (smelt eggs). Prices are $3 to $4 for a two-piece order; quail eggs are 50¢ each. Plates of assorted sushi range from $5.95 to $10.95 and are served with soup. Other Japanese dinners, priced from $6.95 to $10.95, include such standards as shrimp and vegetable tempura, beef and chicken teriyaki, sukiyaki, and grilled mackerel, salmon, or the catch-of-the-day. Special combination plates (teisuoku) offer a choice of one appetizer and two entrees, with soup, rice, tea, and ice cream, for the reasonable sum of $14.95. The lunch menu also offers a choice of delectable and light udon dishes (steaming noodle soup), with egg, chicken, or beef, at $4.25 to $5.95.

For more occidental tastes, Oh No Tokyo adds charcoal-grilled dinners to the menu "in the tradition of Japanese boatmen." Entrees range from breast of chicken to steak and lobster, all served with soup, salad, vegetable kebab, and steamed rice. Prices begin at $7.95 and top at $19.95 for the steak and lobster.

Soft drinks are available, as are domestic and Japanese beers, Japanese draft beer, house wine by the glass or bottle, and plum wine by the glass.

Lunch is served weekdays from 11 a.m. to 2:30 p.m., dinner daily from 5 p.m. to 10:45 p.m., when the last order is taken.

Should you call the **Café Santa Fe,** 1213 Las Vegas Blvd. South, near Charleston (tel. 384-4444), you will first reach the adjacent Thunderbird Hotel. As a matter of fact, you can dine, nap, get married, and drink in the café's all-night bar (though not necessarily in that order) within the same enclave, since the hotel has a wedding chapel.

The Café Santa Fe is just a bit away from the main action on the Strip, but it's well worth the visit. The Karamanos family has tried, by way of its southwestern menu and handsome restaurant design, to capture the feeling of the true Southwest. The pink stucco walls, wooden pillars, beamed ceiling, Native American rugs, straight-backed Spanish chairs, cacti, and tiled floors all reflect the unique combination of Native American, Spanish, Mexican, and southwestern traditions found in the restaurant's cuisine.

If you arrive for breakfast, there are the usual gringo offerings as well as those with a southwestern flair. Among the "Omelettes Grandes" are the Santa Fe Joe, with ground beef, panfried onions, mushrooms, spinach, and Swiss cheese; and the South of the Border, with shredded beef chili, onions, and Monterey Jack cheese. The caballero with a hearty appetite might also order three fresh eggs served with medallions of beef tenderloin, chili relleño, and casera potatoes. All egg orders come with casera potatoes, buttermilk biscuits, and preserves. Breakfast ranges from $2.95 to $4.75; the eggs with beef tenderloin is $7.95.

Highlights of the luncheon menu are two freshly made beef patties with chili and cheese, the BBQ sliced pork in a zesty sauce, or the Santa Fe filet sandwich broiled and served open-faced with onion rings. The choices range from $4.75 to $5.75. Salads "from the pantry" include one with freshly cut greens topped with chili con carne, shredded cheese, diced tomato, sour cream, and guacamole; served with salsa and tostados. Salads, served with bread and butter, are $5.95 and $6.95.

Ah, but dinner's my favorite, and I simply could not resist the barbecued baby back ribs—absolutely delicious and served with frijoles covered with cheese and chunky french fries. What I could not finish I took home and it was just as good the next day. Conservative types might choose the boneless breast of plump chicken Mexicaine, marinated and topped with mushrooms, green chili salsa, diced tomato, and glazed Monterey Jack cheese.

Vegetarian customers will enjoy the café's beautifully fresh vegetables, steamed and served with cheddar cheese. Guayamas jumbo shrimps, Veracruz filet of sole, and broiled halibut steak amandine comprise the seafood offerings. For beef-lovers, the tournedos Taos—cooked the Zuni way, with broiled tomato, banana fritters, and horseradish sauce—is a dish large enough to satisfy any appetite and then some, as are the "Texas Cut" T-bone steak, the broiled New York–cut sirloin with mushrooms and fried onions, and the steak Tampico—a skirt steak marinated, broiled, and served with Spanish rice, frijoles de la olla, salsa, and flour tortilla. Entrees, served with salad or soup, potato or pasta, vegetable, and bread, range from $6.95 to $15.75.

The Santa Fe's late-night menu combines a number of the specialties from breakfast and lunch with its South of the Border pot of chili. Prices range from $2.95 to $7.95.

Sweet Santa Fe desserts expand from deep-dish apple pie for $2.45 to rich chocolate cake with fudge frosting (big enough for two) for $4.95.

And all this is served with warmth, thoughtfulness, and attention to detail.

The Café Santa Fe is open daily from 7 a.m. to 11 p.m. The bar is open all night. The café offers a good selection of beers and wines with dinner, as well as the usual alcoholic beverages.

Battista's Hole in the Wall Italian Restaurant, 4041 Audrie St., at Flamingo Road, just east of the Strip (tel. 702/732-1424), is a popular Italian restaurant worth considering. A favorite of many celebrities, including Merv Griffin, Sergio Franchi, Dean Martin, Bill Cosby, Robert Goulet, and Tony Bennett, Battista's is famous for its full-bodied home-cooking and warm, inviting atmosphere. It's a festive place, the food is fresh, homemade, and terrific, and no one goes away hungry.

There are seven intimate dining rooms, all decorated in unrestrainedly Italian rococo. "Mooosolini" the moose hangs over the bar. The walls are plastered with celebrity photos, and clam buckets, fishnet, chianti bottles, strings of garlic and peppers; a revolving barber's pole, and an arbor of plastic grapes are among the many adornments. A collection of 2,800 miniature liqueur bottles is displayed in the bar, whence you'll also find a few slot machines.

Dinners are priced at $13 to $24, and they all include the following abundant courses: an Italian salad with cheese and salami (sort of a mini-antipasto), all the homemade garlic bread you can eat, a homemade minestrone soup, your choice of about 30 entrees, and a pasta side dish (as much as you want of it). You also get all the wine you can drink to wash down these tasty victuals (they go through about 500 gallons a week!), and all the cappuccino you want—at no extra cost.

To enhance the very Italian ambience, Battista plays Italian music, grand opera, etc., in the background; he also sings for guests and sometimes gives away his own records. As a devoted fan I could eat here every night just on the chance that he might perform.

Battista's is open for dinner from 5 to 11 p.m., seven nights a week. Reservations are essential. It's a not-to-be-missed experience.

The Vineyard, 3630 S. Maryland Pkwy., off Twain Avenue, in the Boulevard Mall (tel. 702/731-1606), is quite a production—a bustling indoor Italian street café with exposed brick and patinaed walls, terracotta-tile floors, street lamps, and shelves cluttered with wine barrels, crates of plastic grapes, etc. One wall is hung with shellacked-over Italian movie posters and ads for Cinzano, Alitalia, etc. Completing the festive ambience are high-backed rattan chairs at tables with checkered cloths and a huge salad bar, called the "Groceria," under a green-and-white-striped awning. There's more seating and similar decor upstairs. The whole thing is quite charming, and the fare delicious. Fresh fruits and vegetables, homemade pasta, and fresh baked breads are served.

For openers, you can toddle up to the salad bar and help yourself to all you want of its abundant offerings. They're included in the price of your dinner entree. You can also opt for the salad bar as your entire meal: about $8 at dinner, $5 at lunch. When this fabulous smörgåsbord was last seen, it included meatballs, baked spaghetti, greens, a wide choice of fresh fruits, many salads, brussel sprouts, marinated mushrooms, big chunks of provolone cheese, pepperoni, artichoke hearts, real roquefort, hard-boiled eggs, sausages, chick peas, bean sprouts, fresh-baked breads, and more—all of it delicious.

Should you want an entree as well, dinner fare ranges from $8 to $16 for pasta dishes like manicotti, cannelloni, and lasagne, or steak or shrimp scampi; sandwiches and pizza are also available. Lunch fare is mostly under $6. Prices on some items are reduced for children under 10. On Sunday there's a Family Feast —all you can eat for $7.

The Vineyard is open daily from 11 a.m. to 11 p.m., on Friday and Saturday till midnight.

Ricardo's, 2380 Tropicana Ave., at the corner of Tropicana and Eastern (tel. 702/798-4515), is a handsome brown ranch-like building you might easily mistake for a new mission. The interior is every bit as attractive as the outside. As you enter, ahead is what appears to be a small Mexican plaza—pillars, tall cacti, a lovely fountain with a small balcony above, decorative tiles above and around the fountain, Corrida de Toros posters, and a beamed ceiling so high it's not readily noticed. This is the main dining room. A skylight adds to the feeling of being outside. Booths and tables are well spaced. The fabric covering the cushions on the bentwood chairs and booth seats is a pleasing rust, beige, brown, and blue Mexican design.

On your right is the Cantina, a large bar room with wooden booths, tables —mobbed, friendly. Two other dining rooms, La Sala and Hotel Aristos, carry through the Mexican decor with wrought-metal chandeliers, upright leather-covered chairs, dark-brown wood tables—more austerely Spanish than Mexican in feeling.

Ricardo's serves what I've found to be the best Mexican food in Las Vegas. It's delicious and the portions are huge—bring a big appetite. The corn chips, alone, are a quarter the size of a corn tortilla, served with deliciously hot salsa.

Ricardo's has both meat and seafood dishes, and dinners range from $9.25 to $12. The carne Ortega is a generous portion of broiled top sirloin, thinly sliced, and smothered with steaming mild Ortega chiles and melted cheese. Those who enjoy seafood, a Ricardo's specialty, the likes of which you won't find anywhere this side of the border, should try their enchilada a la Puerto Vallarta—a seafood enchilada consisting of a flour tortilla filled with shrimp, crab, and whitefish sautéed with onions, mild chiles, wine, and spices. The enchilada is covered with Ricardo's ranchero sauce and garnished with guacamole and sour cream. Or there's the arroz con pollo, prepared from boned chicken breast over Mexican rice, topped with Ricardo's special sauce and melted cheese, and garnished with mild chiles and pimientos. Specialties of the house are served with cheese salad or soup, Mexican rice, and refried beans. The tostados entrees are truly an unforgettable experience—they're massive, delicious, and inexpensive, at $5.75 to $6.50. You can have all beef, or chicken, seafood, or diced pork. Whatever your choice, it's heaped on a crisp corn tortilla spread with refried beans, and covered with shredded lettuce, tangy sauce, guacamole, two kinds of grated cheese, sour cream, and olives.

After several meals at Ricardo's (and I never reached the flan or deep-fried ice cream) I decided it's all delicious, and you'll never leave feeling as though you could eat more. To wash all this down, Ricardo's has a good selection of beers, wines, margaritas (small, medium, large, and by the pitcher), fruit margaritas, sangría, and piña coladas.

Service is attentive and prompt. Two strolling guitarists look, sing, and play as though Mexico was their home—not Tante Elvira's flamenco, but gentle music to dine by.

Reservations are essential for dinner as the restaurant is usually full by 6:30 p.m., especially on weekends. Ricardo's is open Monday through Thursday from 11 a.m. to 11 p.m., on Friday and Saturday to midnight, and on Sunday from noon to 10 p.m.

Marie Callender's, 600 E. Sahara Ave., at Sixth Street (tel. 702/734-6572). The Callender family began making pies in 1948 when they sold their car for $700 and used the proceeds to start a small pie bakery. At first Marie baked about 10 pies a day, but after two years she was baking 200 a day. When the orders reached into the thousands the family opened their first pie shop in Orange, California. Today there are some 150 Marie Callender restaurants in the West, three of them in Las Vegas. They serve not only pies, but wholesome, home-style food.

The restaurant is now open for breakfast with a heart-warming array of all-American favorites—ham and eggs, french toast, pancakes, as well as Belgian waffles with fruit and a delicious quiche Lorraine. Breakfast is served until 11 a.m. weekdays, to 1 p.m. on weekends.

Different soups—potato cheese, clam chowder, etc.—are featured each day by the bowl or tureen; they're accompanied by croissants or home-baked cornbread. Also available are selections from the salad bar, a Frisco burger (served on toasted sourdough bread and sprinkled with parmesan cheese), a tuna stack sandwich piled high with white albacore tuna salad, or an avocado and alfalfa sprout creation sprinkled with walnuts. All these delights fall in the $6 to $8 price range.

The menu is in effect all day. Dinner (or lunch) favorites range from shrimp linguine (served with salad and bread), to chicken au gratin pot pie, to a hamburger steak with a trip to the salad bar, or chicken topped with a cream and cheese sauce. The restaurant grinds its own meat and makes its own pasta. Prices range from $6 to $8.

Leave room for some pie. Apple, rhubarb, cream cheese, lemon, peanut butter, coconut, custard, banana, black bottom, etc., are all baked fresh daily, and all can be ordered with ice cream, whipped cream, or heavy cream.

Marie Callender's is open daily from 7 a.m. to midnight.

Popular with Vegas show people, the **Savoy French Restaurant and Bake-**

ry and Sidewalk Café, 4149 S. Maryland Pkwy., at Flamingo Road in Tiffany Square (tel. 702/732-7373 or 733-9505), is a bright and sunny little café done in brick and redwood with a Mexican tile floor. There are café curtains in the windows, and a few tables are placed outside for al fresco dining. As you enter, you'll pass a glass case filled with croissants, gâteaux, and pâtisseries. Since all baking is done on the premises, this is an ideal place to come for your morning croissants and coffee, not to mention your afternoon cappuccino and cheesecake. Everything (I tried to eat it all) is great! The country breakfasts are huge. Throughout the day you can order five-egg omelets, the largest in Las Vegas, with mix-and-match delights like ham and cheese, asparagus, corned beef hash, or shrimp, olives, and Créole sauce. If restraint is more in your nature, try the eggs Benedict or a variation thereof—a made-on-the-premises croissant à la Benedict with fluffy scrambled eggs, bacon, and hollandaise.

For lunch, French onion soup, sandwiches, and quiches are all in the $3 to $7 range. And the Savoy serves a half-pound hamburger that is among the juiciest and tenderest in town. If your palate follows the esoteric, go for the homemade croissant stuffed with crabmeat. The Savoy also offers salads—like the Neptune, a seafood delight—as well as homemade soups. All in all, everything is delicious and prepared to order. Wine and beer are both available, as are soft drinks and juices.

The Savoy has been run by the Seraccia family (just ask Joe) for over 12 years and was voted the #1 bakery-café in Las Vegas for two consecutive years; it's evident in the quality, quantity, and price.

A lively little place at all hours, the Savoy is open Monday through Saturday from 7 a.m. to 6 p.m., Sunday till 3 p.m.

Don't leave Las Vegas without going to **Flakey Jake's,** 2870 S. Maryland Pkwy. near Vegas Valley (tel. 702/794-0900), for a huge half-pound "build it yourself" hamburger on a sesame-seed bun that's been baked right there. But that's just for openers. If a hamburger bun could ever be called a work of art (you can see them being baked), this is it—they're also the tallest I've ever seen.

Entering Flakey Jake's is much like going into a spotlessly clean produce market with a bakery and meat store to one side. Boxed tomatoes, purple onions, bags of hamburger bun mix, and vegetables are neatly stacked on pallets around the inside of Jake's. If you weren't hungry before, the fragrance of freshly baked bread and cookies will surely send your salivary glands into ecstatic anticipation. To your left is an island of carts containing every conceivable addition for a sandwich. Meat for the hamburgers is ground in a glass-enclosed room that's on your right.

Go up a couple of steps—on your left are tables with blue-and-white-checked cloths; behind the tables is the cookie and baked goods counter. The floor is brown tile, the ceiling a beamed warehouse-type structure with fans and industrial lamps. As you might expect from a produce center, the interior color is brown/white and yellow/white, quite spacious with many tall ficus trees and hanging plants as well as latticework separating the three dining areas. Old movie posters decorate the walls. To the rear of the restaurant is an open kitchen.

You can get a half-pound ("Big Jake") or a third-of-a-pound ("Butcher's Choice") hamburger and stack it yourself from the condiment carts. You can order any of seven "enhancers"—grilled onions, onion rings, chili, guacamole, and on. There's also a good selection of other sandwiches and "features." The char-broiled chicken sandwich is delicious, either with the lemon-pepper or teriyaki marinade. Flakey Jake's serves the ultimate hot dog—a one-third-pounder, charcoal broiled and served open-faced on a sesame-seed bun. However, my demise is the taco salad—a four-ounce portion of spicy taco meat on a bed of lettuce in a crisp, deep-fried flour tortilla. Or you can order one of Jake's Platters, like the top sirloin, cooked the way you like it, to order, served with a baked potato or fries, side salad, and a dinner roll. It's a great buy for $7.95. Sandwiches, hamburgers, or one of the tacos will cost $3.50 to $5.

Flakey Jake's has a Sweet Shoppe designed to test the will-power of the most determined calorie counter. There's a brownie à la mode with two scoops of vanilla ice cream topped with hot fudge, whipped cream, nuts, and a maraschino cherry—all on top of a deliciously fattening brownie.

Flakey Jake's serves draft beer by the mug or pitcher, a good assortment of bottled beers, wine, and the usual beverages.

You can buy cookies, pies, and hamburger or hot dog buns to go. Flakey Jake's is open daily from 11 a.m. to midnight.

The **Garden Eatery/Omelet House,** 2150 W. Charleston, near Rancho Drive (tel. 702/384-6868), has to be one of the best breakfast/lunch establishments in Las Vegas in terms of quality, quantity, and price. As you walk up to the restaurant, you may feel that you're about to enter the local betting parlor—no windows. The interior is very rustic, the bare ranch-house feeling: simple unpolished wooden booths and tables, wall lights, simple hanging lamps. But let's get down to the basics. You can just have eggs with the usual accompaniments, or you can have them with Vienna/Polish sausage. But why? There are 32 omelets and quiches to choose from ($2.75 to $5.50), including a real barn-burner, the Rio Grande Surfer, with chorizo sausage, onion, and cheddar cheese, plus 16 extras available to add on. Look for the "Flatlanders Special."

You're a traditionalist? Try the old-fashioned buttermilk pancakes. You can even have them with apples, bananas, or blueberries and whipped cream (so much for tradition). For the super-hearty eater, there's a "flap special" with two pieces of bacon or sausage, pancakes, and two eggs—all for $3.25.

On the other hand, if you arrive just in time for lunch, there's an assortment of absolutely delicious hamburgers served on fresh onion rolls (with spuds or a side of salad, pickle, and fruit garnish), salads, homemade soups, with pumpkin-nut bread or one of your choice, chicken fingers, or homemade chili. The "chile size" contains a third of a pound of lean ground chuck sprinkled with mixed cheeses and onions for $3.95, or there's a cup for $1.35. The Italian beef sandwich is a winner. Like everything else, it's big—tender roast beef chunks simmered in Italian sauce (gravy, to you purists) and served on Italian bread, then sprinkled with jack cheese, for $3.95. The top price on the menu is $5.50. All drinks are of the "soft" variety, but for a great refresher, have their Freshen-Up, a delectable combination of orange juice, Fresca, and "special secret ingredients."

The Garden Eatery/Omelet House is open daily (except Thanksgiving and Christmas) from 7 a.m. to 3 p.m.

CHAPTER XIV

ALTERNATIVE AND SPECIAL-INTEREST TRAVEL

□ □ □

1. ADVENTURE/WILDERNESS TRAVEL
2. HEALTH AND FITNESS VACATIONS
3. PEOPLE-TO-PEOPLE VACATIONS
4. FOR THE OVER-60 SET

More and more, the world of travel is being segmented into small packages, labeled not so much with destinations as with the activities (or inactivities) a-waiting us when we arrive. That's what special-interest travel is all about; it encompasses everything from adventure/wilderness vacations to educational and study travel, health and fitness travel, political travel, and vacations for seniors.

The size of California is such that it affords many opportunities for adventure and wilderness travel. And on a per capita basis, California seems to offer more in the way of health and fitness vacations (mental and physical) via spas, yoga retreats, macrobiotic centers and whatever, than any other state—or, in fact, than most other countries. (Meditate on the significance of that, if you will.) And the many older Americans who retire to or visit California are often afforded the opportunity here to do things outside of the usual.

Below I've covered a variety of special interest vacations and activities offered throughout California, as well as a few in the Las Vegas area.

When it comes to considering alternative and special interest travel, don't limit your vision. There's a great deal to do, to learn, many new interests to discover, whatever age you may be. One of the most interesting, useful, thought-provoking books about travel it's ever been my joy to read is *The New World of Travel 1988,* by Arthur Frommer (published by Prentice Hall). Read it—you'll see what I mean.

1. ADVENTURE/WILDERNESS TRAVEL

If running up and down Kilimanjaro or cross-country skiing 600 miles to the South Pole is your idea of a thrilling vacation, California may not be your cup of herbal tea. However, it can come close in terms of low- to medium-anxiety adventure, and can offer a lot of fun and excitement (even apart from that derived from driving the freeways).

SADDLE TRIPS: In the southeastern part of Yosemite National Park, high on the Sierra Nevadas' west side, the **Minarets Pack Station** serves the Ansel Adams Wilderness area in the Sierra National Forest. From the awesome heights of Banner Peak and Mount Ritter down to the roaring San Joaquin River, Minarets Pack Station can outfit you for an extraordinary vacation in the area of your choice. Whether you simply want to absorb the exceptional beauty of the Ansel Adams Wilderness or fish and hunt, Minarets supplies the surefooted animals and competent staff for your excursion.

For a Spot Trip, the Pack Station will pack you and your gear off to a campsite and pick you up for the return on a specified date—or, if you wish, the packer and stock will remain with you; you provide the provisions and choose the itinerary.

Minarets can also plan and prepare a Deluxe Trip, providing you with camping gear, food, cook, packers, and stock for your entire wilderness stay. If you're the hardy type, on the other hand, you may prefer to backpack it—be packed up and sent out to ride or walk. In addition, Minarets Pack Station has a five-day hands-on, professionally taught packing course, with all meals and two-day pack trip included. Finally, special deluxe outfitted and guided hunts can be arranged.

Minarets Pack Station, in Miller Meadow, 95 miles northeast of Fresno, is open from June through October. Prices vary according to the area you'd like to visit, the number of persons in the group, and the type of trip that appeals to your outdoor instincts. Write for details; you'll receive a very informative folder with a map of the areas covered by the Pack Station, plus rates, dates, etc. Before June 1, send your request to Larry Lovelace, Manager, 39249 Road 800, Raymond, CA 93653 (tel. 209/966-3082); after June 1, address Minarets Pack Station, 23620 Robertson Blvd., Chowchilla, CA 93610 (tel. 209/665-3964, or 209/665-1959).

In July and August, **Yosemite Stables** have saddle trips to the High Sierra camps. Because mules are used as opposed to horses, the rides are quite easy. The camps, about eight miles apart, are equipped with tents containing beds with sheets, blankets, and mattresses; there's usually (though not always) at least one hot shower. Hot meals are provided for breakfast and dinner; midday there's a sack lunch. A four-day saddle trip (three nights and four days, each night at a different camp) costs about $400 per person, and a six-day trip (five nights and six days, each night at a different camp) runs each person about $600. These trips are quite popular so it's a good idea to make your reservation early (the preceding December would be about right). For information, call the **High Sierra Reservations Desk** (tel. 209/454-2002) or write, detailing your interests, to **Yosemite Reservations**, 5410 E. Home Ave., Fresno, CA 93727.

If you're accustomed to being on horseback for prolonged periods of time, **Rock Creek Pack Station,** P.O. Box 248, Bishop, CA 93514 (summer tel. 619/935-4493, winter tel. 619/872-8331), has a truly extraordinary vacation for you. This outfit schedules four-day mustang-tracking trips in the rarely visited Pizona area of the Inyo National Forest—the natural habitat of wild mustangs. You'll be accompanied by experienced tracker-guides who will share their knowledge of the social behavior of the horses and their environment. Rock Creek supplies everything except your bed roll, setting up tents at a new location each afternoon and serving meals chuck-wagon fashion. The cost is about $400 per person, all inclusive; write to the address above for details.

Rock Creek also has seven-day cattle drives on which you help gather and drive them dogies (remember "Rawhide"?) from Nevada to the Pizon Range into California. You can really participate in the western feel of the working ranch. Once again, it's not a trip for first-time riders. Cattle drives are scheduled according to the needs of the ranchers.

Rock Creek Pack Station does have an ideal five-day trail ride into the John Muir Wilderness for beginning riders, offering an opportunity to explore the lakes and streams of the Mono Creek area. On layovers, participants can swim, fish, hike—or just relax and do nothing. The trip begins and ends at Rock Creek (cost is about $425).

All of the Rock Creek trips are educational to some degree if you've never before been in the spectacular John Muir or Ansel Adams Wilderness. However, Rock Creek also has several trips specifically designed to expand your vision and insight into the wonders of this country. An eight-day horseback natural history expedition into the John Muir Wilderness (including the remarkable Mono Creek, Bear Creek, and French Canyon areas) is accompanied by a naturalist who shares his experience and knowledge of the wildlife, flora, glaciers, and history of the country. It's a great opportunity to fish for Golden trout and to photograph nature (cost is about $700).

The 14-day Evolution Valley trail ride explores the majestic central section of the John Muir Trail, heading over Mono, Selden, Muir, and Bishop Passes with time to enjoy Bear Creek, Evolution Valley, and LeConte Canyon. There's enough layover time to explore many remote parts of the High Sierras. The trip is limited to 10 guests (cost for the 14 days is about $1,300).

If you'd rather put together your own private trail ride (minimum of 12 people), the cost per person will be about $90 per day.

BACKPACKING, TREKKING, AND CAMPING: Backpack along what has been called "the finest mountain walk in western America" into the dramatic high country of Yosemite National Park, with its wildflowers, beautiful Budd Lake, and snowfields. Hikers' camps in the Yosemite back country provide shelter and meals for wilderness travelers. It's a great way for beginners to decide if back-country hiking is their bag before investing in expensive wilderness-tripping accoutrements. Each of the five camps has a dining room for family-style meals and washrooms with hot showers (most of the time). You'll sleep in canvas tent-cabins, men separated from women. Camps are open late June through Labor Day, depending on the weather. Seven-day hikes with a naturalist cost about $450 per person. Backpackers who want to avoid the hassle of lugging food can arrange for breakfast and dinner at $25. For information, contact **High Sierra Reservations,** Yosemite Park and Curry Co., 5410 E. Home Ave., Fresno, CA 93727 (tel. 209/252-3013).

Another great group of backpacking trips is offered by **California Adventures,** the outdoor recreation program of the University of California at Berkeley. For eight years, California Adventures has provided a wide variety of fascinating outdoor trips. Though most are for three or four days, California Adventures also has backpacking trips for one or two weeks. You might hike around the lonely canyons, alluvial fans, and rugged hills of Death Valley, both on and off trail, on the way home enjoying a good long soak in a natural hot spring. Or you might head up to a hiking adventure in Kings Canyon-Sequoia National Park; Kings Canyon is the deepest chasm on earth, with a descent of over 7,000 feet from the rim of the canyon to the south fork of Kings River at the bottom. Prices for nonstudents of all ages and levels of experience range from $125 to $300 for most of the trips. The price of each trip includes van transportation, group equipment, and experienced leadership, but not food. For more information on the wide variety of activities offered, write to California Adventures, University of California, 2301 Bancroft, Berkeley, CA 94720 (tel. 415/642-4000).

Cooperative camping tours are becoming increasingly popular, and they certainly are among the least expensive modes of travel. Up to 14 people share a van, cruising by day and camping at night. The vehicle comes with camping equipment and the services of a professional tour escort. All you need to bring is a sleeping bag, a sense of adventure (though physical challenges are rarely involved), and some extra spending money for the occasional hotel stays or meals out included in the itinerary.

You decide on the type of tour, the departure date, and the tour length. The first day of the trip, a "food bank" is established (usually about $30 per person, per week). All members of the group take turns shopping for food along the way, and preparing meals at the camping ground. You are responsible for pitching your pop-up tent at night and packing it away in the morning. The driver's chore is driving.

One of the largest and most successful cooperative camping organizations is **Trek America,** P.O. Box 1388, Gardena, CA 90249 (tel. 213/321-0734). Among its many tours, Trek America has several leaving from Los Angeles, traveling up and around the west coast for two to three weeks, and stopping at several scenic wonders. Prices range from $550 to $875, depending on distance and duration. Note, however: all Trek America tours are for those 18 to 35 years only. For an extensive catalog, write or call Trek America.

Without a doubt, one of the most unique approaches to touring is that of the **Green Tortoise** line, described as a "hostel on wheels." Take one large motorcoach, remove all the seats, replace same with a foam rubber platform and there you have it—room for a group of about 35 hardy souls to stretch out, recline, or sleep, as required. As per the Green Tortoise coach itself, each trip is a new adventure, with a flexible schedule, which allows all aboard the opportunity to explore, camp out, hike, whatever. Food costs are about $6 per day for breakfast and dinner; everyone helps in the preparation of meals—basically vegetarian —and with the cleaning up. Green Tortoise trips go everywhere (well, almost) and each varies in its destination and stops; in fact, the only guarantee you have is that you'll begin and end at a designated spot. For California, most trips begin at San Francisco and go north to Napa Valley; they may then go on to Lassen Volcanic National Park, Shasta National Forest, Trinity Alps, Redwoods National Park, and Fern Canyon, then back to San Francisco. The price of such a six-day northern California loop is $160, plus the noted $6 per day for group cookouts; add to that the cost of a couple of restaurant meals. For detailed information, write to Green Tortoise, P.O. Box 24459, San Francisco, CA 94124 (tel. 415/ 821-0803, toll free 800/227-4766 outside California).

ROCK CLIMBING: If you've ever harbored fantasies of joining the mountaineering set, you should know that Yosemite is world-renowned as a rock-climbing area. The **Yosemite Mountaineering School,** Yosemite, CA 95389 (tel. 209/ 372-1335), has a reputation for excellence in rock-climbing instruction. Multiday, multiskill classes are available (weather permitting) for all levels of expertise. Reservations and information are available at the Yosemite Mountaineering School at Tuolumne Meadows from June through late-September, then at Curry Village in Yosemite Valley (tel. 209/372-1244).

For a rock-climbing comprehensive, **California Adventures,** University of California at Berkeley, 2301 Bancroft, Berkeley, CA 94720 (tel. 415/642-4000) offers introductory climbing trips to various locales, including selected sites in the Sierra. While all the rock-climbing trips are relatively short (at the most three days), you'll be packing a lot of fun and adventure into those days among some of the most magnificent landscapes in the West. Transportation is by car pool, and all group camping and climbing equipment is provided. The price to nonstudents is $140.

Female staff members of California Adventures also offer the same course for an all-women's group at Yosemite. Women of all skill levels are encouraged to join.

California Adventures has private rock-climbing instruction for individuals or groups of up to three people, customized to personal abilities and goals. Whether your interest lies in advanced multipitch ascents or simply in working with and improving the skills you've acquired on your own, California Adventures will design a trip for you.

RAFTING: Also at Yosemite, you'll find one of the most popular rafting rivers, the Tuolumne, where miners once panned for gold. The river pours out of the national park and rushes down a thrilling and relentless series of rapids through a breathtakingly beautiful canyon. If you're game, the **American River Touring Association (ARTA),** a nonprofit organization, offers a three-day raft trip, departing in July and August, for $375. For information, contact ARTA, Star Route 73, Groveland, CA 95321 (tel. 209/962-7873 or toll free 800/323-2782).

Another organization offering white-water rafting down the Tuolumne River is **Sierra Mac River Trips,** which has conducted excursions for thousands of people from 5 to 75 years of age. (When food celebrity Craig Claiborne went on one, he took along a good supply of California wines.) An excursion following the rapids of the main Tuolumne River lasts three days and two nights. The price, $525, covers the cost of guides (one for every four or five passengers), meals, equipment, and wet suits; sleeping gear can be rented for $20. Sierra Mac also offers non–white water three-day trips down the main Tuolumne for $375. For further information, write to Sierra Mac River Trips, P.O. Box 366, Sonora, CA 95370 (tel. 209/532-1327).

Among the many river trips available, all-women excursions, conducted by feminist tour operators, afford women wonderful opportunities to gain confidence and self-esteem, and to discover physical and inner strengths while trying something new, challenging—and fun. **Mariah Wilderness Expeditions** offers a two-day, one-night all-woman trip down the Merced, a free-flowing river during most of May. The trip begins at the western entrance to Yosemite, where the current is swift and the rapids mostly continuous. Wildflowers blanket large portions of the green hills in the area. The campsite, located deep in the canyon, is quite private. Limited to 25 women, the trip costs $210 per person. To go on this journey, one should either have white-water experience or the capacity for adventure. Mariah also offers a two-day, one-night trip on the Tuolumne River at Yosemite for $275 per person, limited to 20 women. For details on these and other enticing tours (via sea kayak or cross-country skiis, for example) write or call Mariah Wilderness Expeditions, P.O. Box 248, Point Richmond, CA 94807 (tel. 415/233-2303).

For all the fun and excitement to be found in Las Vegas, there's not much that can beat a five-day Colorado River trip with **O.A.R.S. (Outdoor Adventure River Specialists).** You fly from Las Vegas, arriving at the Bar 10 Ranch in time for lunch and an afternoon of such dude ranch specialties as a minirodeo, trail rides, hiking, horseshoes—whatever you choose—followed by a first-class dinner. After breakfast the next morning, you'll be flown by helicopter into the Grand Canyon. Your four days of rafting begin at Mile 188, Whitmore Wash, and cover 90 miles to Pierce Ferry, just past the point where the Colorado River joins Lake Mead. This spectacular stretch of the river offers broad views of the Grand

Canyon, and the modest rapids here give you the opportunity to decide if you'd like to try a little more white water some other time. You spend the nights ashore in tents supplied by O.A.R.S. If you don't bring your own sleeping bag, you can rent one from O.A.R.S. for about $35.

There are a limited number of dates for the five-day trips out of Las Vegas— six in all from mid-April through the end of August—so it's wise to call for reservations at least a month in advance. The $750 price includes transportation to and from Las Vegas, meals, use of the tents, and the overnight stay at Bar 10. For detailed and helpful information, call or write O.A.R.S, Inc., P.O. Box 67, Angels Camp, CA 95222 (tel. 209/736-4677).

BICYCLING: **Backroads Bicycle Touring,** P.O. Box 1626, San Leandro, CA 94577 (tel. 415/895-1783), offers a number of five-day luxury tours in California through some of the state's most spectacular natural attractions—wine country (including sampling), the Redwood empire, the Mendocino coast, and Death Valley. The tours are leisurely, offering participants a choice of daily distances to match their cycling abilities, as well as a choice of bed and breakfast or camping accommodations. Each of the tours is accompanied by two professional tour leaders; a support van and trailer carry all gear, baggage, and provisions. You can bring your own bicycle or rent one of Backroads' custom-built bicycles. Groups are for all ages; if seniors find some trips a bit wearing, they can ride in the support van for part of the day. Most tours average $155 to $170 per day, with the camping tour a bit lower (about $120 per day). For further information and a copy of a free 50-page catalog, write or call Backroads Bicycle Touring, P.O. Box 1626-PR2, San Leandro, CA 94577 (tel. 415/895-1783).

Arrow to the Sun Bicycle Touring Company, P.O. Box 115, Taylorsville, CA 95983 (tel. 916/284-6263), has a great selection of tours ranging from 7 to 24 days, primarily in Northern California. The itinerary includes some of the most beautiful spots in the state—the Marble Mountains east of Eureka and west of Yreka, set aside as wilderness for generations, and the Sierra rim, including Lake Tahoe and Feather River country. There are a number of interesting "theme" tours: a hot springs and wine tour; a coastline bed-and-breakfast tour; a California Goldtrails tour; and a forest tour through the lush Indian Valley; to name a few. Tours through Baja California are also on the agenda. Groups, accompanied by a support van, usually consist of 15 or fewer. The tours accommodate varying levels of ability, from beginner or energetic beginner to intermediate to advanced; 30 to 50 miles are common distances traveled daily. The tours average $90 to $100 per day (a bit less in Mexico); prices include lodging, meals, and road snacks. Write or phone for further information or a copy of a detailed descriptive booklet.

If you're the adventurous type, and don't need the luxury of a fine hotel or a superior B & B inn, consider the itineraries offered by the **American Youth Hostels.** You don't have to be under eighteen; some trips are designed to include people of all ages, while others are planned for specific age groups. Travelers stay primarily in hostels; every group is accompanied by a trained trip leader. One of the great advantages of American Youth Hostel adventure trips is cost. The organization has a 22-day California coast cycling trip, from San Francisco to San Diego. You may stay overnight in a genuine lighthouse hostel at Montara; tour Hearst Castle; visit Disneyland; and dig your toes into the sand at the beaches along the way—all for about $750, which includes lodging (tents, cooking utensils, and stoves when camping), group-prepared meals, a group activities budget, and the leadership costs. But American Youth Hostel trips are not limited to cycling. The group also offers hiking trips, motor trips, and other adventure trips. You can get a catalog of current offerings by writing or calling American Youth

Hostels, Central California Council, P.O. Box 28148, San Jose, CA 95159 (tel. 408/298-0670).

HOUSEBOATING: For a special do-it-yourself vacation that includes fishing, sunbathing, swimming, hiking, sightseeing, and exploring, it's hard to beat a week or two on a houseboat. Houseboats give you the option of being with a congenial group or being alone, and afford you the choice of more activities than you ever thought you could squeeze into your trip. And they're easy to operate, even if you've never been at the helm before. Nearly everything you need to create your own fun is provided for you: fully equipped kitchen, a bathroom with shower, hot water, air conditioning, heating units, built-in beds, deck chairs, ice chests, and barbecue are usually standard. All you need to bring is food, your personal gear, and fishing tackle (and, in some cases, bed linen).

Houseboats are relatively economical on a per person basis. (When comparing costs among houseboat rentals, always check on the number of *adults* the houseboat will sleep, the supplies offered, and both the boarding and return times.) Houseboats that will sleep four adults generally range from $675 to $1,200 per week, depending on the season; those sleeping six adults cost about $725 to $1,370, again depending on the season. Larger boats, accommodating as many as ten, are also available. One of the largest of the houseboat rental companies is **Seven Crown Resorts,** which has vacation packages on Nevada's Lake Mead, the man-made wonder created by Hoover Dam, about 35 miles east of Las Vegas; and Lake Mohave, south of Lake Mead and just north of Laughlin, Nevada. The outfit also rents houseboats at Lake Shasta at Redding, California—about a three-hour drive north of San Francisco—and at the Sacramento River Delta, an endless and fascinating network of rivers and channels near Stockton, California. For information, call or write Seven Crown Resorts, P.O. Box 1409, Boulder City, NV 89005 (tel. toll free 800/752-9669).

WHALE WATCHING: Few annual events attract as much attention and interest in California as the migration of the whales. Among the naturalists in this field and other guides offering trips to observe the migration and calving, **Biological Journeys,** 1876F Ocean Dr., McKinleyville, CA 95521 (tel. 707/839-0178, or toll free 800/548-7555), is the largest. Using its own small cruise ships departing from San Diego, the organization takes amateur naturalists on its scientific journeys (January to about the first week of March) along the coast of Baja California to the San Ignacio Lagoon (with daily hikes ashore). Trips take ten days to two weeks and accommodate 10, 20, or 32 passengers. The cost is $1,300 per person.

Other full-fledged naturalist-led whale-watching expeditions are conducted by **Special Expeditions,** 720 Fifth Ave., New York, NY 10019 (tel. toll free 800/762-0003), whose prices include one-way air fare from Los Angeles to La Paz or Cabo San Lucas. Special Expeditions offers 11-day voyages which start at San Diego and end up at La Paz, sailing the Pacific coast and the Sea of Cortez, and 15-day trips with more calls, including the Sea of Cortez's northern islands. Fares range from $2,500 to $4,250. Special Expeditions generally runs its trips from a relatively luxurious 238-foot ocean-sailing vessel that accommodates 80 passengers, but is limited in its approaches to the shore because of size.

The **San Diego Natural History Museum,** P.O. Box 1390, San Diego, CA 92112 (tel. 619/232-3821), offers a nine-day excursion for 28 people at the beginning of March; it includes three days in San Ignacio lagoon observing the birth of gray whales and the fare is about $1,200.

H & M Landing, 2803 Emerson St., San Diego, CA 92106 (tel. 619/

222-1144), has 7- to 11-day trips from San Diego. The 11-day voyages, aboard an 88-foot vessel, include 30 passengers, one naturalist, and an assistant. Because it has smaller boats, H & M has permission to enter the wildlife sanctuaries. Trips cost from $950 to $1750.

2. HEALTH AND FITNESS VACATIONS

A great many California time-off approaches to health and fitness, physical and mental, fall under this aegis, from the ultrachic to the simple yoga retreat.

SPAS: And so we start with the pampered, health- and fitness-inducing vacation. And where better to begin than at the totally renovated, 1,000-acre **La Costa Hotel and Spa,** Costa del Mar Rd., Carlsbad, CA 92009 (tel. 619/438-9111, or toll free 800/854-6564), a Southern California hotel and spa with 172 new luxury guest units. Tennis courts, pools, golf courses, customized diets—there's much for everyone, including celebrity guests. But there's a price, of course: at the lower end of the scale, double rooms are $215 to $235; for double rooms on the golf course, the tab is $265; suites cost $325. The Introduction to the Spa Plan (three days, two nights including sports and five treatments) is $215 per person per night, double; $315, single. The Original Spa Plan, including spa meals, a variety of health and beauty treatments, all sports, and much personal attention, is $340 per person, per night, double; $470, single.

You may have already guessed that La Costa is not for the relaxed, washed-jeans and beat-up-sneakers set; it is, rather, a "designer" spa, attracting sleek, well-coiffed guests who don fancy resort wear in the evening. It may be that the new Japanese owners, Sports Shinko, intend La Costa to be their first posh resort link to Hawaii. La Costa is about 1½ hours south of Los Angeles, just off Hwy. 5, between Carlsbad and Del Mar; and about a half hour north of San Diego.

A most attractive and beautifully groomed environment for fun and fitness, **Murrieta Hot Springs Resort & Health Spa,** 39405 Murrieta Hot Springs Rd., Murrieta, CA 92362 (tel. 714/677-7451, or toll free 800/322-4542, 800/458-4393 in California), is devoted somewhat more to your well-being than your coiffure. About an hour-and-a-half drive southeast of Los Angeles, or about an hour-and-a-quarter drive north of San Diego, the hot mineral springs are on the site of what once was a Temecula village and were valued for their therapeutic properties.

Murrieta Hot Springs is spread over 47 acres of rolling hills. Three outdoor natural mineral pools of varying temperatures and sizes, from an Olympic pool to a bubbling Jacuzzi, are there to relax you. For the more energetic, there are 14 tennis courts, pathways for strolling or jogging, and a golf course at the adjacent Rancho California Country Club. As to the health part of the resort, you can soak away whatever may be making you stressful in a soothing hot mineral bath (with essential oils), followed by a body wrap; and the spa's mud bath is truly a balm for the body and spirit. An incredible variety of massages, European facials, and Finnish saunas will help refurbish the exterior. Mineral-bath prices, with various additions, range from $15 to $31; mud "experiences," massages, and facials begin at $30 and proceed up to $73 for the deluxe European facial.

As to the cuisine, all meals are vegetarian and delicious. What's more, your nutritional and respiratory environment could not be much healthier, since it is alcohol- and smoke-free.

Singles are $50 to $60, doubles $55 to $65 for lodging only. Lodging with three meals is $72 to $82 for singles, $99 to $109 for doubles. Should you prefer to stay for a week, singles are about $990, doubles $840, including meals, classes, Energy Balancing massage, spa mineral baths with bodywrap, exercise program, mud bath, and use of the hot springs pools and sauna. You may never be healthier.

TOWARD PERSONAL GROWTH: At the other end of the spectrum, in terms of distance and direction (literal and otherwise), is the **Esalen Institute,** at Big Sur, CA 93920 (tel. 408/667-3000). Esalen was created in 1962, at the beginning of the upheaval years, as a center for encounter therapy. It has since evolved into a personal-growth center to explore a range of psychological subjects.

The Esalen catalog is the simplest way to find out what the institute offers, from a visit to the hot springs, on up to a residency program. Call or write away for one.

Esalen seminars or workshops may be held over a weekend ($295) or a period of five days ($580); costs include room, board, and studies. For those new to Esalen, *Experiencing Esalen* is an orientation workshop which offers a great variety of subjects from which to choose.

Studies are among some of the most relaxed surroundings imaginable: lush gardens, magnificent views, and natural hot springs, where you can soak as you watch the sun set into the ocean below. Should you prefer swimming, you can use the large pool, with or without swimsuit. Dress is casual for breakfast, lunch, dinner, and all hours in between (although not as casual as for swimming). The shared rooms are comfortable and simple, but lack telephones, TV sets, or radios —it is a retreat, after all. Some rooms have patios and ocean views, but you can hear the sound of the surf from any room. Meals are served buffet style in a friendly lodge dining room, and the food is absolutely delicious. It may also be some of the most wholesome you've had in years. At dinner time there is a beer-and-wine bar.

Workshops and bed spaces fill up early during the summer, so it's important to plan in advance for Esalen. During the winter, when the 100 guest beds may not be fully booked, it is possible to stay at Esalen without enrolling in a seminar or workshop; you may simply want to meditate, write, or quietly relax. The cost would be in the range of $60 to $85 for a night and a day including dinner, breakfast, and lunch. For a complete weekend, without workshops or seminars, you can stay at Esalen for about $160, meals included, as space is available.

However much time you spend at Esalen, don't miss out on its famous massage—$60 for an hour of sheer bliss. Your body will reimburse you.

Esalen is located about 300 miles north of Los Angeles and 175 miles south of San Francisco, just south of Monterey and overlooking the spectacular surf.

Yoga Retreats

About 50 miles northeast of Sacramento off Hwy. 80 (about 1½ hours driving) and up some dirt roads, you'll find the **Yoga Farm** at Grass Valley. (Come to think of it, it might be the place for a contemplative stop when returning from Reno.) This is undoubtedly the cheapest of the residential ashrams ($30 a night, $160 per week, $600 per month, including meals) and among the smallest, with space for only 30 guests. Life at the ashram is rustic, simple, and quiet, consisting of a changeless routine of meditation and exercises. During your free time you can hike to a nearby hill and view the timeless beauty of the magnificent Sierras. For a very special vacation, write or phone **Sivananda Ashrama Vrindavan Yoga Farm,** 14651 Ballantree Lane, Grass Valley, CA 95949 (tel. 916/272-9322).

Also near Grass Valley is the **Expanding Light,** close to Nevada City. This yoga ashram is located on the grounds of a Christian community—the Ananda World Brotherhood Village. At the Brotherhood Inn, up to 125 visitors can engage in a retreat which includes classic yoga routines. There are morning and afternoon asanas (gentle stretching exercises), meditations, and classes on both

Christian and Eastern themes. A week's stay is $50 in a dorm, $60 in a shared room, and $140 in a private room, including three vegetarian meals and classes. Ananda is 12 miles from Nevada City and about 60 miles northeast of Sacramento. Write or call **The Expanding Light,** c/o Ananda World Brotherhood Village, 14618 Tyler Foote, Nevada City, CA 95959 (tel. 916/292-3494).

About 70 miles due north of Sacramento, just off Rte. 70, the **Vega Study Center** of Oroville, California, resides in a town of old Victorian homes and shops dating back to the early 1900s. The Vega Study Center is the teaching base for Cornelia and Herman Aihara and their macrobiotic hands-on cooking classes, which run for one to three weeks. The cost, including full board, is $500 for one week, $900 for two weeks. Guests share rooms and sleep on pine beds with marvelous futon mattresses. Rising time is 7 a.m. for meditation, Eastern-style exercises, and tea. Lectures are by Herman Aihara, and classic macrobiotic meals are often prepared by Cornelia. For a catalog or other information, write or call **Vega Study Center,** 1511 Robinson St., Oroville, CA 95965 (tel. 916/533-7702).

In the mountains of Santa Cruz, looking down toward Monterey Bay, the **Mount Madonna Center** at Watsonville is a yoga-oriented conference and retreat facility used for discussions of some of the hottest (and coolest) psychological issues of the day. Over a long weekend or on a weeklong vacation, you might choose to focus on such broad issues as *Creativity and Success, Dying— Opportunity of a Lifetime,* or, perhaps, *Self-Hypnosis.* (Somehow, the fresh air and walks through the redwood forests always help to clarify the issues.)

A room and two vegetarian meals daily, plus snacks, ranges from $35 (dorms), to $40 (semiprivate rooms), to $55 (private rooms); add about $80 for the courses and seminars you'll doubtless select. Watsonville is about equidistant between Monterey and Santa Cruz (somewhat inland), and about 30 miles from San Jose.

For detailed literature, contact Mount Madonna Center, 445 Summit Rd., Watsonville, CA 95076 (tel. 408/722-7175, or 408/847-0406).

3. PEOPLE-TO-PEOPLE VACATIONS

A small but growing trend in vacations has been toward those that satisfy a desire for selfless involvement in other lives and in other modes of living.

POLITICAL: Habitat for Humanity asks for just such selfless involvement. Hundreds of Habitat volunteers spend retirement time (as did Jimmy and Rosalynn Carter) or vacation time at Habitat locations helping to build sturdy, low-cost houses side-by-side with the people in need. Volunteers pay for their own transportation and food, sometimes receiving only the most basic accommodations at the construction site. No prior construction experience is required, and almost anyone can be taught a useful skill.

Habitat for Humanity wants to make shelter a matter of conscience so that one day shacks will be gone, collapsing tenement houses will be no more, and there will be no homeless people sleeping on city streets.

For information on how you can devote your vacation to Habitat for Humanity and share in an experience that can change your life, contact Habitat for Humanity, Habitat and Church Streets, Americus, GA 31709 (tel. 912/924-6935). Within California, there are Habitat for Humanity offices in San Jose, Santa Rosa, Pittsburg, Ventura, Stockton, Fresno, Sacramento, and San Diego; all need volunteer help.

PERSONAL: When it comes to the basic, people-to-people vacations, few get down to the rudiments quite like a country holiday spent on a farm or ranch. Some accommodate only a few guests in bunkhouses, with activities such as hiking, trail rides, campouts, fishing, and cattle drives for would-be cowboys. Other ranches, somewhat more citified, offer square dancing, steak fries, swimming in a heated pool, dinner theater, and private cabins. Invariably, they all offer good, wholesome food—all you can eat—and much of it home-grown.

Far and away, the best source of ranch and farm information nationwide, grouped by state, is a 224-page guidebook written by Patricia Dickerman of New York and sold through the mails. The book has nine detailed descriptions of ranches in various locations throughout California. For a copy of the book, send $12 to **Farm/Ranch & Country Vacations,** 36 E. 57th St., New York, NY 10022 (tel. 212/355-6334).

4. FOR THE OVER-60 SET

There are some programs designed expressly for those over 60, one of which is described below. This is not to say that being over 60 precludes an interest in backpacking, white-water rafting, bicycling, fitness vacations, etc.; if you fall into that category and any of the previously described special vacations interests you, contact the source. Many are designed to include several age groups.

PACK AND LEARN: One of the most successful and lowest-cost vacation plans for persons aged 60 and older is that of **Elderhostel.** Short-term study tours—usually one- to three-week courses at colleges and universities in the U.S. and around the world—are the focus of the Elderhostel program. Elderhostel charges one fee, giving no guarantee of single or double rooms; housing is usually in university residence halls, sometimes dormitories, segregated by sex. At the low end of the scale, for $215 a week (plus air fare) you receive room, board, and tuition including classroom instruction each day. If you're concerned about being the only single woman in the group—no need to fret. Singles constitute about one-third of Elderhostel's volume, and two-thirds of these are women. For a catalog of current trips and study groups, call or write to Elderhostel, 80 Boylston St., Boston, MA 02116 (tel. 617/426-7788). A $10 annual donation to the organization's Independence Fund will keep U.S. and foreign studies information flowing to you.

Index

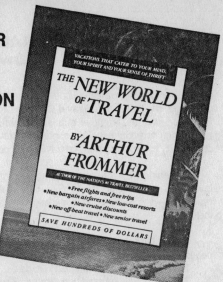

NOW, SAVE MONEY ON ALL YOUR TRAVELS!
Join Frommer's™ Dollarwise® Travel Club

Saving money while traveling is never a simple matter, which is why, over 27 years ago, the **Dollarwise Travel Club** was formed. Actually, the idea came from readers of the Frommer publications who felt that such an organization could bring financial benefits, continuing travel information, and a sense of community to economy-minded travelers all over the world.

In keeping with the money-saving concept, the annual membership fee is low—$18 (U.S. residents) or $20 U.S. (Canadian, Mexican, and foreign residents)—and is immediately exceeded by the value of your benefits which include:

1. The latest edition of any TWO of the books listed on the following pages.
2. A copy of any Frommer City Guide.
3. An annual subscription to an 8-page quarterly newspaper *The Dollarwise Traveler* which keeps you up-to-date on fastbreaking developments in good-value travel in all parts of the world—bringing you the kind of information you'd have to pay over $35 a year to obtain elsewhere. This consumer-conscious publication also includes the following columns:
   Hospitality Exchange—members all over the world who are willing to provide hospitality to other members as they pass through their home cities.
   Share-a-Trip—requests from members for travel companions who can share costs and help avoid the burdensome single supplement.
   Readers Ask . . . Readers Reply—travel questions from members to which other members reply with authentic firsthand information.
4. Your personal membership card which entitles you to purchase through the club all Frommer publications for a third to a half off their regular retail prices during the term of your membership.

So why not join this hardy band of international Dollarwise travelers now and participate in its exchange of information and hospitality? Simply send $18 (U.S. residents) or $20 U.S. (Canadian, Mexican, and other foreign residents) along with your name and address to: Frommer's Dollarwise Travel Club, Inc., Gulf + Western Building, One Gulf + Western Plaza, New York, NY 10023. Remember to specify which *two* of the books in section (1) and which *one* in section (2) above you wish to receive in your initial package of member's benefits. Or tear out the next page, check off your choices, and send the page to us with your membership fee.

FROMMER BOOKS
PRENTICE HALL PRESS
ONE GULF + WESTERN PLAZA
NEW YORK, NY 10023

Date_____

Friends:
Please send me the books checked below:

FROMMER'S™ $-A-DAY® GUIDES
(In-depth guides to sightseeing and low-cost tourist accommodations and facilities.)

☐ Europe on $30 a Day $14.95	☐ New Zealand on $40 a Day $12.95
☐ Australia on $30 a Day $12.95	☐ New York on $50 a Day. $12.95
☐ Eastern Europe on $25 a Day $12.95	☐ Scandinavia on $50 a Day $12.95
☐ England on $40 a Day. $12.95	☐ Scotland and Wales on $40 a Day. . . .$12.95
☐ Greece on $30 a Day $12.95	☐ South America on $30 a Day $12.95
☐ Hawaii on $50 a Day $13.95	☐ Spain and Morocco (plus the Canary Is.)
☐ India on $25 a Day. $12.95	on $40 a Day. $13.95
☐ Ireland on $30 a Day $12.95	☐ Turkey on $25 a Day. $12.95
☐ Israel on $30 & $35 a Day $12.95	☐ Washington, D.C., & Historic Va. on
☐ Mexico (plus Belize & Guatemala)	$40 a Day. $12.95
on $25 a Day. $13.95	

FROMMER'S™ DOLLARWISE® GUIDES
(Guides to sightseeing and tourist accommodations and facilities from budget to deluxe, with emphasis on the medium-priced.)

☐ Alaska $13.95	☐ Cruises (incl. Alask, Carib, Mex, Hawaii,
☐ Austria & Hungary $14.95	Panama, Canada, & US) $14.95
☐ Belgium, Holland, Luxembourg $13.95	☐ California & Las Vegas $14.95
☐ Brazil. $14.95	☐ Florida. $13.95
☐ Egypt. $13.95	☐ Mid-Atlantic States $13.95
☐ France $14.95	☐ New England $13.95
☐ England & Scotland $14.95	☐ New York State $13.95
☐ Germany $13.95	☐ Northwest $13.95
☐ Italy. $14.95	☐ Skiing in Europe. $14.95
☐ Japan & Hong Kong $13.95	☐ Skiing USA—East $13.95
☐ Portugal, Madeira, & the Azores $13.95	☐ Skiing USA—West. $13.95
☐ South Pacific. $13.95	☐ Southeast & New Orleans $13.95
☐ Switzerland & Liechtenstein $13.95	☐ Southwest $14.95
☐ Bermuda & The Bahamas $13.95	☐ Texas $13.95
☐ Canada $13.95	☐ USA (avail. Feb. 1989). $15.95
☐ Caribbean $13.95	

FROMMER'S™ TOURING GUIDES
(Color illustrated guides that include walking tours, cultural & historic sites, and other vital travel information.)

☐ Australia $9.95	☐ Paris $8.95
☐ Egypt. $8.95	☐ Thailand. $9.95
☐ Florence. $8.95	☐ Venice $8.95
☐ London $8.95	

TURN PAGE FOR ADDITIONAL BOOKS AND ORDER FORM.

FROMMER'S™ CITY GUIDES

(Pocket-size guides to sightseeing and tourist accommodations and facilities in all price ranges.)

☐ Amsterdam/Holland $5.95	☐ Montreal/Quebec City. $5.95
☐ Athens. $5.95	☐ New Orleans. $5.95
☐ Atlantic City/Cape May $5.95	☐ New York $5.95
☐ Boston. $5.95	☐ Orlando/Disney World/EPCOT $5.95
☐ Cancún/Cozumel/Yucatán. $5.95	☐ Paris $5.95
☐ Dublin/Ireland $5.95	☐ Philadelphia $5.95
☐ Hawaii. $5.95	☐ Rio $5.95
☐ Las Vegas. $5.95	☐ Rome. $5.95
☐ Lisbon/Madrid/Costa del Sol $5.95	☐ San Francisco $5.95
☐ London $5.95	☐ Santa Fe/Taos (avail. May 1989) $5.95
☐ Los Angeles $5.95	☐ Sydney (avail. Feb. 1989) $5.95
☐ Mexico City/Acapulco. $5.95	☐ Washington, D.C. $5.95
☐ Minneapolis/St. Paul $5.95	

SPECIAL EDITIONS

☐ A Shopper's Guide to the Caribbean. .$12.95	☐ Motorist's Phrase Book (Fr/Ger/Sp) . . .$4.95
☐ Beat the High Cost of Travel $6.95	☐ Paris Rendez-Vous $10.95
☐ Bed & Breakfast—N. America $8.95	☐ Swap and Go (Home Exchanging). . . .$10.95
☐ Guide to Honeymoon Destinations	☐ The Candy Apple (NY for Kids). $11.95
(US, Canada, Mexico, & Carib) $12.95	☐ Travel Diary and Record Book $5.95
☐ Manhattan's Outdoor Sculpture $15.95	☐ Where to Stay USA (Lodging from $3
	to $30 a night) $10.95

☐ Marilyn Wood's Wonderful Weekends (NY, Conn, Mass, RI, Vt, NH, NJ, Del, Pa) $11.95
☐ The New World of Travel (Annual sourcebook by Arthur Frommer previewing: new travel trends, new modes of travel, and the latest cost-cutting strategies for savvy travelers). $12.95

SERIOUS SHOPPER'S GUIDES

(Illustrated guides listing hundreds of stores, conveniently organized alphabetically by category)

☐ Italy. $15.95	☐ Los Angeles $14.95
☐ London. $15.95	☐ Paris $15.95

GAULT MILLAU

(The only guides that distinguish the truly superlative from the merely overrated.)

☐ The Best of Chicago (avail. April 1989)$15.95	☐ The Best of New England (avail. April
☐ The Best of France (avail. July 1989) . .$15.95	1989) $15.95
☐ The Best of Italy (avail. July 1989). . . .$15.95	☐ The Best of New York. $15.95
☐ The Best of Los Angeles $15.95	☐ The Best of San Francisco $15.95
	☐ The Best of Washington, D.C. $15.95

ORDER NOW!

In U.S. include $1.50 shipping UPS for 1st book; 50¢ ea. add'l book. Outside U.S. $2 and 50¢, respectively. Allow four to six weeks for delivery in U.S., longer outside U.S.

Enclosed is my check or money order for $_____

NAME _____

ADDRESS _____

CITY _____ STATE _____ ZIP _____